Christian Imaginations of the Religious Other

Christian Imaginations of the Religious Other

A History of Religionization

MARIANNE MOYAERT

WILEY Blackwell

This edition was first published 2024
© 2024 John Wiley & Sons Ltd

All rights reserved. No part of this publication may be reproduced, stored in a retrieval system, or transmitted, in any form or by any means, electronic, mechanical, photocopying, recording or otherwise, except as permitted by law. Advice on how to obtain permission to reuse material from this title is available at http://www.wiley.com/go/permissions.

The right of Marianne Moyaert to be identified as the author of this work has been asserted in accordance with law.

Registered Office(s)
John Wiley & Sons, Inc., 111 River Street, Hoboken, NJ 07030, USA
John Wiley & Sons Ltd, The Atrium, Southern Gate, Chichester, West Sussex, PO19 8SQ, UK

For details of our global editorial offices, customer services, and more information about Wiley products visit us at www.wiley.com.

Wiley also publishes its books in a variety of electronic formats and by print-on-demand. Some content that appears in standard print versions of this book may not be available in other formats.

Trademarks: Wiley and the Wiley logo are trademarks or registered trademarks of John Wiley & Sons, Inc. and/or its affiliates in the United States and other countries and may not be used without written permission. All other trademarks are the property of their respective owners. John Wiley & Sons, Inc. is not associated with any product or vendor mentioned in this book.

Limit of Liability/Disclaimer of Warranty
While the publisher and authors have used their best efforts in preparing this work, they make no representations or warranties with respect to the accuracy or completeness of the contents of this work and specifically disclaim all warranties, including without limitation any implied warranties of merchantability or fitness for a particular purpose. No warranty may be created or extended by sales representatives, written sales materials or promotional statements for this work. This work is sold with the understanding that the publisher is not engaged in rendering professional services. The advice and strategies contained herein may not be suitable for your situation. You should consult with a specialist where appropriate. The fact that an organization, website, or product is referred to in this work as a citation and/or potential source of further information does not mean that the publisher and authors endorse the information or services the organization, website, or product may provide or recommendations it may make. Further, readers should be aware that websites listed in this work may have changed or disappeared between when this work was written and when it is read. Neither the publisher nor authors shall be liable for any loss of profit or any other commercial damages, including but not limited to special, incidental, consequential, or other damages.

Library of Congress Cataloging-in-Publication Data applied for:
Paperback ISBN: 9781119545507

Cover image: © Kostbarkeiten aus alter und neuer Zeit/Wikimedia Commons
Cover design by Wiley

Set in 10/12pt STIXTwoText by Straive, Pondicherry, India

SKY10065386_011924

I dedicate this book to my husband Michael, and to our children, Lucas, Norah, Nathan, and Simon, who fill our lives with laughter and love

Contents

LIST OF TEXT BOXES   xiv

Introduction   1
1 On the Notion of Religionization   2
2 Mechanisms of Religionization   4
  Naming/Renaming   4
  Categorization and Classification   5
  Essentialization   5
  Governance   6
3 The Particular Contribution of This Book   6
4 The Risk of Systematization and How I Seek to Avoid It   7
5 The Use of the Text Boxes   9
6 A Word of Gratitude   10
Notes   11
References   11

Part 1   Religionization in Early Christianity: Christians, Heretics, Jews, and Pagans   13

1   The Creation of Key Religionized Categories in Early Christianity   15
  1 *Religio* and Its Counterpart *Superstitio*   16
    Religio in Antique Times   17
    Antiquity and Ethnicity of *Religio*   17
    Pax Romana, Pax Deorum   18
    Superstitio and *Religio*   19
  2 Christians as Targets of Religionization   21
    Christian Apologists and Ethnoreligious Reasoning   23
    Crafting a Sense of Christian Ethnicity   23
    Crafting Christian *Religio* as the Most Ancient   26
  3 Christians against the Nations: The Distinction between *Religio Vera* and *Falsa*   27
    Religio as True Worship of the True God   27
  4 Crafting the Jew as Un-Christian   30
    Jews, Christ-following Jews, and Christians from Gentiles   31
    Adversus Iudaeos   32
    Anti-Jewish Typologies   33
    The Supersessionist Logic   35
    The Deicide Charge   36
  5 Making the Figure of the Heretic   38
    The Notion of Heresy   39
    Adversus Haereses   40
  6 Conclusion   43
  Note   43
  References   43

viii Contents

2 The Coercive Turn: Institutionalizing Religionized Categories 46
  1 On Heresiology: Epiphanius' *Panarion* 48
    The Microscopical 'Ethnographic' Work of Epiphanius 48
    Epiphanius' Universal Account of History 50
  2 When Heresiology Intersects with Imperial Law 51
  3 The *Codex Theodosianus* and the Criminalization of Heresy 52
    The *Codex Theodosianus*: *De Haereticis* 54
    Augustine and the Persecution of Heretics 56
  4 The Constantinian Turn and the Destruction of Paganism? 56
    The Pagan as a Hermeneutical Figure 57
    The *Codex Theodosianus*: *De Paganis* 59
  5 Anti-Jewish Rhetoric and the Establishment of Jewish Tradition as *Religio Licita* 61
    Anti-Jewish Rhetorics: Chrysostom as a Case in Point 62
    Augustine's Doctrine of Jewish Witness: A Different Sound 64
    The *Codex Theodosianus* and the Jews 66
  6 Islam Enters the Scene 67
    Early Christian Interpretations of Islam 67
    Jews and Ishmaelites and Their Place in Christian Imagination 70
    Christian Saracen Law 71
  7 Conclusion 72
  Notes 73
  References 73

Part 2 Body Politics in the Aftermath of the Gregorian Reform 77

  An Ongoing Spiritual Drama 78
  References 79

3 Unification, Purification, and Dehumanization 81
  1 The Time of the Crusades and Dehumanizing Saracens 82
    The Emergence of Crusading Ideology 82
    The Saracen as Pagan 84
    Defiled, Monstrous Black Bodies 86
    The Danger of Blurring Religious Boundaries 87
    The Conflation of Jew and Muslim 89
  2 The Deteriorating Fate of the Jews 91
    Flashback: The Jews and the Legacy of Antiquity 92
    The Jews under the Frankish Merovingians and the Carolingians 92
    The Jew: From Unwilling Witness to Enemy, Child Murderer, and Usurer 93
      Crusading Ideology and the Jew as Christianity's Internal Enemy 94
      Jews and Usury 94
      Blood Libels 95
    Blackness, Disfiguration, and Bodily Afflictions 96
  3 The Return of the Problem of Heresy 98
    Flashback on Heresiology 98
    The Disappearance and Return of the Problem of Heresy 98

The Cathars and Waldensians **99**
Polemical Depictions of Heresy **100**
  Heretics as Foxes **100**
  Heretics as Morally and Sexually Perverse Creatures in the Service of Satan **102**
The War on Heresy **104**
  Preaching **104**
  Crusading **104**
  The Inquisition **105**
4 The Fourth Lateran Council **106**
5 Conclusion **109**
Notes **109**
References **109**

4 The Spanish Catholic Monarchy and Religio-racialization 113
1 The *Reconquista* and the Re-Christianization of the Iberian Peninsula **114**
  Reclaiming Space: Converting and Cleansing Mosques **116**
  Law Making **117**
  On the Jews (*De los judíos*) **118**
  On the Moors (*De los moros*) **119**
2 The Long Road towards Blood Purity Laws **120**
  Crusading Ideology and the Ideal of Christian Visigothic Descent **120**
  Increasing Anti-Judaism **122**
    The Conversionist Programme of the Mendicant Orders **122**
    Conspiracy Theories: Treason, Ritual Murder, and Poisoning **123**
  Economic Motives **123**
  Political Instability **124**
3 Forced Mass Conversions **125**
  Questions about Authenticity **125**
  Conversos Destabilize Boundaries **126**
4 Law Making: *Limpieza de Sangre* **128**
5 The Catholic Monarchs and the Purgation of the Spanish Monarchy **130**
6 The Religio-racial Project of the Spanish Catholic Monarchy:
    An Exceptional Case? **133**
7 Columbus, New Worlds, and the Question of Religion **134**
  First Encounters **135**
  No Religion **136**
8 Conclusion: Blurring Boundaries between Racialization and Religionization **139**
Notes **141**
References **142**

Part 3 The Long Reformation 145

5 The Turn Inwards 149
1 Mediation, Fear of Death, Excess, and Corruption **151**
  The Church and the Mediation of Salvation **151**
  Death, Purgatory, and Intercession **153**
  Corruption, Abuse, and the Practice of Indulgences **153**
  Catholic Piety under Critique **154**

x Contents

2 The Modern Devotion **155**
  Geert Grote: The Fountain of Modern Devotion **156**
  The Brethren of the Common Life and the Reinterpretation of *Religio* **157**
3 Christian Humanism **159**
  In Praise of Folly **159**
  Scripture as the Cornerstone of Christian Life **161**
  Erasmus on Judaism **162**
4 Martin Luther **164**
  A Reformed and Purified Christian Norm **165**
5 Erasmus and Luther: Profound Disagreements **166**
  Reforming Christian Faith and Projecting False Religion onto the Enemies
    of God **168**
6 The Colonial Project and the Question of True Religion **171**
  Context **171**
  Juan Ginés de Sepúlveda **172**
  Bartolomé de las Casas **173**
  José de Acosta **174**
7 Protestantism and the Rejection of the Principle of Mediation **175**
8 Conclusion **177**
Notes **178**
References **178**

6 The Fragmentation of Religion and the Re-creation of Society **181**
1 Polemics and the Dehumanization of Religious Others **182**
  Sexual Slander **183**
  Corrupted Souls and Diseased Bodies **184**
2 Protecting the Socio-political Order: Expulsion, Confiscation, Torture **187**
  Rituals of Purgation **189**
    Iconoclasm **189**
    Humiliating, Killing, and Exhuming Heretical Bodies **190**
3 The Legal Establishment of the Fragmentation of Religion **190**
  Peace Treaties and the Redefinition of the Binary of Orthodoxy/Heresy **191**
    The Peace of Augsburg **192**
4 Religionization as Confessionalization **195**
  Confessionalization and the Making of Bounded Communities **197**
  The Propagation of True Christianness **197**
    Ritual **199**
    Space **201**
    Education **202**
    Censorship **203**
    Discipline **204**
5 The Parting of the Ways and Confessional Identity Markers **204**
6 Conclusion **205**
Notes **206**
References **207**

7 Reconfiguring True Religion in Terms of Toleration **211**
1 Sebastian Castellio: Beyond Coercion **213**
  Context **214**

Contents **xi**

    Preface Dedicated to Count William of Hesse **215**
    Dedication to Duke Christoph of Württemberg **218**
2 John Locke on Toleration **220**
    Toleration as a Characteristic of Being a True Christian **221**
    True and False Religion **222**
    The Magistrate **223**
      What Is a Church? **224**
    The Scope of Tolerance: Jews, Muslims, and Pagans **226**
      Extending Toleration to the Pagans **227**
      The Limits of Toleration **227**
      Crafting Judaism, Islam, and Paganism as 'Religions': Legal and Political
        Consequences in Europe and Beyond **228**
3 Voltaire and the Problem of Fanaticism **229**
    Context **230**
    The Case of Jean Calas **230**
    The Fanatic as a Rhetorical Figure **231**
    Refuting Theological Religion **233**
      Christianity **234**
      Judaism **235**
      Islam **237**
    Deism/Theism **238**
    Deism, Orientalism, and the Construction of the Religion of India **240**
    Comparing Religions in Voltaire's Work: Decentring
      and Recentring Christianness **242**
4 Conclusion **243**
Notes **244**
References **245**

Part 4 The World Religions Paradigm and the Turn to Dialogue **249**

1 What Is the World Religions Paradigm? **249**
2 Old Patterns of Religionization Function as Building Blocks **250**
    Interiorization **251**
    Confessionalization **251**
    Religio-secularization **252**
3 Gathering Data in a Context of Colonization **253**
4 The World Religions Paradigm: Another Emancipatory Myth? **255**
Notes **256**
References **256**

8 **Religio-racialized Taxonomies Based on Comparative Philology** **257**
  1 The Fixation on Creating 'Scientific' Taxonomies of Race **259**
    Biblical Taxonomies **259**
    Ethnographic Explorations **260**
    Comparative Philology **261**
  2 Romantic Musings about Language as the Gateway to the Spirit of People **262**
    Comparative Philology, Grammar, and Race **263**

xii   Contents

3 The Discovery of the Indo-European Language Family **265**
  Oriental Jones and the Indo-European Hypothesis **265**
  The Indo-European Myth as Colonial Ideology **266**
4 Friedrich Schlegel's Comparative Philology and German Romanticism **267**
  About the Language and Wisdom of the Indians **267**
  Inflection and Agglutination **267**
5 Ernest Renan and the Invention of the Semite **270**
  Semitic and Aryan People **270**
  Semitic Monotheism and a Religious People **273**
  Comparing Religions **274**
    On Judaism **274**
    On Christianity **275**
    On Islam **277**
6 Friedrich Max Müller: 'He Who Knows One Religion, Knows None' **279**
  Religion as One and Plural **280**
7 The Task of Classification **282**
  The Religions of the Book and the Rest **284**
8 Conclusion **286**
Note **287**
References **287**

9 The Dialogical Turn beyond Religionization? 291
  1 The World Parliament of Religions in Chicago **292**
    World Fairs **292**
    The Columbian World Fair and National Pride **293**
    The Tripartite Structure of the World Fair **294**
    The Parliament of Religions as Performance of the World Religions Paradigm **296**
      Religion Is One and Many **297**
      Interreligious Brotherhood and Religio-secularization **298**
      The Religions of the World and the Rest: Religio-racialization Exhibited **300**
    Talking Back **302**
    Interreligious Brotherhood as a Depoliticized Discourse **303**
  2 The Second Vatican Council as a Watershed **304**
    Opening the Windows **304**
    Larger Context **305**
    Dialogue as a Key Aspect of Christian Self-understanding **305**
    Nostra Aetate **307**
    The Institutionalization of Dialogue **312**
    The Ritualization of Dialogue **313**
      Changes in the Good Friday Liturgy **313**
      Interfaith Blessings **315**
      John Paul II Visits the Synagogue of Rome **315**
      The Day of Prayer in Assisi **316**
    The Dialogical Turn and the Renegotiation
        of the Religio-secular Divide **316**
    The Dialogical Turn and the Erasure of the Religio-racial Constellation **318**
      The Dismantling of the Religio-racial Constellation **319**
      The Masking of the Religio-racial Constellation **320**
      The Dialogical Turn and the (Non-)Shared Fate of Jews and Muslims in the
          Christian Imagination **321**

Contents **xiii**

3 Dialogue in Post-secular Society **322**
  The Return of Religion **322**
    The Two Faces of Religion **323**
    Interfaith Dialogue and the Performance of Good Religion **325**
  Education, Citizenship, and the Promotion
      of Interfaith Competences **326**
  Islam as Europe's Other **328**
4 Conclusion **329**
Notes **331**
References **332**

CONCLUSION 337
INDEX 339

Text Boxes

Chapter 1

1 Jewish Participation in Pagan Worship? **19**
2 Imaginary Binary Religionized Constructs **20**
3 Ethnoreligious Reasoning as Religionization and the Making of Jewish Others **25**
4 Religionized Boundary Making: What Christians Should Do and What They Did **29**
5 Imaginary Patterns of Religionization and the Messiness of Daily Life **30**
6 Blurring and Constructing Boundaries: Judaizing Christians? **33**
7 One Example of Typological Reading in a Supersessionist Frame: Jacob and Esau **34**
8 Supersessionist Patterns of Religionization between Replacement and Fulfilment **37**
9 Imaginary Constructs: Orthodoxy versus Heresy **42**

Chapter 2

1 On Doctrine and Disputation **47**
2 On the Rhetorical Figure of the Hellene **50**
3 Moving between Past and Present: Reflections on Ecclesiology **53**
4 The Idea of Heresy as Contagious **55**
5 The Myth of Christian Triumphalism **59**

Chapter 3

1 The Gregorian Reform **81**
2 The Meaning of the Term *Reconquista* **84**
3 The Muslim in Christian Medieval Imagination **91**
4 Visigothic Jewry Laws **93**
5 The Jew in Christian Medieval Imagination **97**
6 Naming and Categorizing as Delegitimization **100**
7 The Heretic in Christian Medieval Imagination **103**
8 The Wearing of the Badge **108**

Chapter 4

1 The *Reconquista* **115**
2 On the Compendium **117**
3 Modified Patterns of Religionization Leading to a Changed Social Stratification **127**
4 Shifting Religionized Boundaries **129**
5 Why Blood? **129**
6 The Notion of *Secta* **138**
7 Columbus' Physiognomic Description of the People He Encounters **138**
8 A Religionized Map of the World **139**

Chapter 5

1 The Reformation, Myth Making, and Religionization (1) **150**
2 The Reformation, Myth Making, and Religionization (2) **155**
3 The Modern Devotion and the Reformation **158**
4 Patterns of Religionization in Erasmus' Call for Piety **162**
5 Erasmus, the Jews, and Religio-racialization **163**
6 Patterns of Religionization **171**

Chapter 6

1 Renaming and Relabelling **181**
2 The Embodiment of Meaning, Body Politics, and Deconstructing Imaginary Constructs **186**
3 Naming and Renaming **188**
4 Religious Peace Treaties **191**
5 The Peace of Augsburg and the Redefinition of Religion **194**
6 Beyond Imaginary Constructs: Concepts of Reformation and Counter-Reformation as Patterns of Religionization **195**
7 Real and Imagined Boundaries (1) **198**
8 Real and Imagined Boundaries (2) **200**

Chapter 7

1 Practices of Coexistence **212**
2 The Myth of the Rise of Tolerance **212**
3 Castellio's Plea for Toleration … Not New at All? **214**
4 Patterns of Religionization: Setting a New Norm and a New Tone **219**
5 The Toleration Act of 1689 **221**
6 The Jew Bill of 1753 **223**
7 The Church as Voluntary Society and as Instrument of Salvation **225**
8 The Religio-secular Divide, the Frame of Religious Violence and Christianity's Others **226**
9 Religious Fanaticism and Previous and Current Patterns of Religionization **232**
10 Voltaire's Antisemitism as an Intrinsic Part of His Plea for Tolerance **236**
11 Voltaire, the Logic of Encompassment and Christianity Reinvented **239**

Chapter 8

1 The Modernist Crisis in the Catholic Church **258**
2 Taxonomies **260**
3 On the Notion of Race as a Social Construct **262**
4 Binary Romantic Philological Patterns **264**
5 The Linguistic-racial Project **264**
6 German Romanticism, the Jews, and Antisemitism **269**
7 Laying the Foundation for a New Religionized Map of the World **271**
8 The Semite as a Hermeneutical Figure **272**
9 On the Notion of Antisemitism **274**
10 Algeria, Islam, and Islamophobia **278**
11 Adapting Patterns of Religionization in a Context of Secularized Christianity **278**
12 The Problem of Recognizing Judaism as a Religion, Separate from Christianity **285**

Chapter 9

1 The Problem of Religionized Essentialization in the Context of Interreligious Dialogue **297**
2 The Religio-secularized Norm of Modern Religion and Its Implications for Minorities **300**
3 Religionization at Work: Code of Indian Offences **301**
4 Dialogical Reciprocity and the Interruption of Religionization? **303**
5 The Myth of the Dialogical Turn after the Shoah **306**
6 Finding New Language **307**

7 Religionizing Non-Christians and the Possibility of Dialogical Interruption **309**

8 Finding New Language to Name Muslims **310**

9 Finding New Language to Name Jews and Muslims **311**

10 The Good Friday Controversy **314**

11 The Dialogical Turn as an Interruption of Religionization? **318**

12 Judeo-Christianity **321**

13 The Binary between Good and Bad Religion: An Imaginary Construct **324**

14 Qualifying the Idea of Equality of Religious Freedom **327**

Introduction

Throughout history – in ancient, medieval, and modern times – European Christians have constructed various categories of otherness: 'the Jew', 'the heretic', 'the pagan', 'the Mohammedan', 'the fanatic', and so forth. They did so in an effort to construct and project a normative sense of Christianness: 'it is the Christian thing to...', 'Christians believe...'; 'according to Christian tradition...'. Constructing images of the 'non-Christian' helped to enhance and bolster claims to a normative Christian identity. To know what one *is*, is to know what one *is not*; to know what one *is not*, is to know what one *is*.

Over time, imaginaries of Christianity's others were disseminated, reproduced, and adapted according to changing Christian needs and interests. Thus, a quasi-inexhaustible cultural archive of more than 2,000 years of recurring images, stereotypical categories, invented binaries and normative assumptions, associations and qualifications developed, ready to be tapped by those claiming to represent religious normativity. Following Gloria Wekker, I understand the cultural archive to be 'located in many things, in the way [European Christians] think, do things, and look at the world, in what we find (sexually) attractive, in how our affective and rational economies are organized and intertwined'; in short, it is 'a repository of memory' that affects their heads, hearts, and attitudes (Wekker, 2016, p. 15).[1] While its constructed origins are often forgotten – Wekker speaks about amnesia – the effects of this cultural archive endure to this day.

This book explores how Christians imagined 'non-Christians' and how the resulting cultural archive was used and adapted in changing socio-political contexts. With a specific focus on Western Europe, the book surveys the various processes by which Christianity's others were named and renamed, categorized, essentialized, and governed by those who embody the Christian norm.[2] Taking a *longue durée* approach, it examines imaginaries of Christianity's others in various ecclesial, theological, and literary documents; on occasion it also zooms in on the way boundaries between Christians and non-Christians were ritualized. Special attention, however, goes to legal regulations and disciplinary practices that were put in place to demarcate the borderlines between Christians and non-Christians. While people do not always comply with the law, and while laws are not always enforced, laws do nevertheless give an impression of how European Christian societies intended to regulate religion and how those deviating from the religious norm were treated. This book also shows how the constructed boundary between Christians conforming to the norm, and those deviating from the projected Christian norm, had real effects on the lives of real people.

The book's main interest is the relationship between the shifts in Christian normativity on the one hand and the way Christianity's others were imagined on the other hand. The underlying assumption is that the constructed image of Christianity's others reflected the contemporary concerns and interests that were held by the Christian majority surrounding them. I will therefore ask: Why this label? Why is this particular categorization being made in this context? For what purpose, and by whom? Why is a boundary being drawn here and not elsewhere (Horrell, 2020)? I ask how the image of the religious other, for example the Jew, Saracen, or pagan, has been crafted. What bodily features, moral characteristics, and behavioural patterns are attributed to these hermeneutical figures? What messages do these stereotypical figures of otherness convey? To what audience is this message addressed and with what purpose? How is religious deviance contrasted to Christian normalcy? What deficits and vices are attributed to Christianity's others and what does that have to do with Christian self-understanding in changing circumstances?

I use the term religionization to refer to co-dependent processes of 'selfing' and 'othering' that are predicated on religious difference. The notion of religionization is akin to and intersects with notions like ethnicization, gendering, and racialization. All these terms refer to processes of selfing (the construction of an imagined normative identity) and othering (the

---

Christian Imaginations of the Religious Other: A History of Religionization, First Edition. Marianne Moyaert.
© 2024 John Wiley & Sons Ltd. Published 2024 by John Wiley & Sons Ltd.

2   Introduction

creation of a deviant and hence illegitimate other) that shape or frame the identity of social groups in a manner that creates a hierarchy between the majority and minoritized groups. Critical scholars have pointed out that (i) race, ethnicity, gender, and religion are all ascribed to social groups in a certain way; (ii) this ascription includes the attribution of norms, behaviours, and roles. Furthermore, (iii) people are divided, categorized, and dealt with based on their racialized, ethnicized, gendered, or religionized identity. In brief, these identities have an impact on social relations, namely on how people engage with one another in their personal life, work context, and political relations. (iv) Moreover, the processes of religionization, gendering, ethnicization, and racialization intersect and reinforce one another. With respect to religionization, I will show that religious adversaries were often sexualized and gendered (Drake, 2013; Knust, 2006; Petersen, 2017). Ethnoreligious reasoning also helped to craft claims to true religion (Buell, 2005; Horrell, 2020). In addition, certain physical or biological characteristics were sometimes added to religionized images of self and other, to the extent that religionization would at times intersect with racialization (Jennings, 2010; Kaplan, 2019; Mayerhofer, 2021; Whitaker, 2013).[3] At certain moments in history, religious others were even placed beyond the pale of humanity and were imagined to take on monstrous and bestial characteristics (Strickland, 2003). Certainly, (v) where society is marked by uneven power distribution these processes of selfing and othering facilitate the stratification of society; this means that society is divided and unequal in significant and far-reaching ways along racialized, gendered, ethnicized, and religionized group lines (Sensoy & DiAngelo, 2017). All these categories – religion, race, gender, and ethnicity – play a key part in the way people organize the world they inhabit; they may be imaginary constructs but they nevertheless have the power to affect people's lives. To deviate from the norm – whether gendered, ethnicized, racialized, or religionized – comes at a cost. While some are privileged, others are excluded, discriminated against, or oppressed.

1   On the Notion of Religionization

A growing number of scholars are exploring religionization as a topic of interest (Cuthbertson, 2018; Dreßler, 2019; Nye, 2019; Thatamanil, 2020). These scholars draw on critical theory and work in the field of postcolonial and feminist studies, and critical religious and/or secular studies. They assume a social constructivist approach to religion, 'that recognizes the social reality of distinctions and differentiation with regard to religion, while at the same time being interested in how this reality is being established, thus acknowledging its contingency' (Dreßler, 2019, p. 5). While there is no precise definition of the term yet, scholars tend to agree that religionization refers to the social construction of what 'religion' is. They point out that what is recognized and labelled as 'religious' at any given time reflects the ideas or perceptions of dominant societal groups.[4] When these ideas or perceptions change, the labels may change as well.

Furthermore, the negotiation of the conceptual boundaries of religion goes hand in hand with the process of drawing the boundaries of non-religion: circumscribing what religion is implies defining what it is not, and defining who is religious implies defining who is not religious. The notion of religion and its counterpart(s) are co-constructed and the resulting constructions are context dependent. What counts as religion in our age may not have been recognizable as such in previous historical-cultural settings, even though precisely that versatility tends to be denied, and religion is often projected as a stable category. To study religionization therefore assumes that one takes an interest in the specific historical-cultural expressions of such distinctions. Those exploring the topic of religionization must ask who the cultural agents are in the process of religionization. How do they work out what is to be labelled as religion and what does not count as religion. What is at stake for them and how does that play out for others? This book zooms in on Christians, located in Western Europe, and on their role as the main cultural agents of religionization. The question is how did the construction of Christian identity in terms of true religion contribute to the creation and delegitimization of Christianity's others? If we understand religionization in terms of co-dependent processes of selfing and othering, can we then conclude that a refigured understanding of Christian normativity also impacts the way Christianity's others are imagined and invalidated?

Religionization is a profoundly political process; this means it is related to things people do to gain or keep power or advantage (Nye, 2019, p. 218). Indeed, various social actors in a range of historical-cultural contexts have used the category of religion as 'an ideological weapon to further their own particular colonial, political, and academic agendas' (Cuthbertson, 2018, p. 98). To label one social group and their traditions as 'religious' while denying this label to others can be a way of exerting power. Those who conform to the religious norm are privileged; they enjoy certain advantages (Joshi, 2020). Disadvantage at various societal levels – political, economic, social – befalls those who do not conform to dominant religious norms. That is why one may say that religion is a key category with which to imagine, organize, and govern people and resources. Because religions operate in fields of power, conceptual differences between religion and its counterpart become the blueprint for the embodied realities within which people live (Cuthbertson, 2018, p. 97). The questions that need to be addressed are: How is religious normativity defined? What meanings are attached to it? How is this norm used to create and reproduce boundaries between traditions, people, and communities, and how does religionization feed into the maintenance of unequal power relations?

In general, a reification of conceptual boundaries runs counter to fluid understandings of group and personal identities predicated on religious difference. The outcome of religionization is the essentialization of social groups and their beliefs and practices, as well as hardened constructions of identity, and these conceal overlap, fuzziness, and hybridity. Where the boundaries of religion (and non-religion) are drawn, 'brittle and rigid conceptions of exclusive identity and allegiance' are generated (Thatamanil, 2015, p. 62). While these boundaries are socially constructed and hence context dependent, they are construed as if they were permanent, even natural. They become 'obvious realities that are so obvious that their existence is taken for granted' (Nye, 2019, p. 215). People live in a religionized world; they may conform or contest religious norms, but in either case it affects their social position. Especially those who deviate from the norm will be aware of this and will have to consider how they negotiate the established boundaries.

Up to now, most scholarly attention has been focused on modern processes of religionization and, more specifically, on the co-emergence of the categories of 'the religious' and 'the secular' (the non-religious realm) (Cavanaugh, 2009; Fitzgerald, 2007b). In the work of Markus Dreßler and Ian Alexander Cuthbertson the emergence of the so-called religio-secular divide is approached as an expression of religionization (Cuthbertson, 2018; Dreßler, 2019). I address this modern process of religio-secularization as a form of religionization in the third part of this book and surface how religio-secularization entails a refiguration of Christian normativity as true religion. Other scholars, following the work of Wilfred Cantwell Smith, Tomoko Masuzawa, and Brent Nongbri, have focused their attention on the World Religions Paradigm, which appeared in the nineteenth century. Until recently, the World Religions Paradigm functioned as a scientific explanation of religious plurality (Masuzawa, 2005; Nongbri, 2013). Today, there is a growing consensus among scholars of critical religion that Christianity has functioned as the prototype of this religionized taxonomy (Bell, 2006, p. 28) and that this paradigm remodelled 'non-Christian traditions', which were thus made and remade in the image of Christian religion (Owen, 2011). This reinforced the hegemonic normative position of Christianity. John Thatamanil calls this paradigm, therefore, a particular expression of religionization (Thatamanil, 2020). In the fourth part of the book, the emergence of the World Religions Paradigm will be discussed as a modern religionized taxonomy (Nye, 2019). Yet another line of research focuses on how the discussion of which beliefs and practices count as religious and which do not deserve that label was conducted on modern colonial frontiers, marked by unequal power relations (Chidester, 1996). If to be religious was considered to be a sign of humanity, then to be labelled as not religious (in any way) cast serious doubt on one's human status and,

4 Introduction

especially, on one's rational capacity and potential autonomy (Maldonado-Torres, 2014). In colonial settings, such arguments functioned as a justification for oppression. Here, religionization and racialization intersect and reinforce one another. I will dwell on this in different chapters in Parts 2, 3, and 4.

To understand how the cultural archive of religionized images developed in the context of Western Christian Europe, this book broadens its scope. It applies the concept of religionization to the histories of classification and stratification that have preceded modern expressions of religionization such as religio-secularization, religio-racialization, and the seemingly more benign World Religions Paradigm. These modern expressions of religionization are not a disruption of the past but rather they build on, adopt, and adapt older patterns of religionization that go back to the very first centuries of Christianity and to Latin Christendom. The past has never really *passed*, and modern patterns of religionization were developed in the context of existing webs of meaning, making use of older religionized images of true and false religion. Therefore, this book, taking a *longue durée* approach, explores the way Christians from the very beginning have crafted religionized categories, like that of the 'Jew', 'heretic', and 'pagan', and examines how these categories were institutionalized, embodied, and materialized. This exploration starts in the time of Early Christianity in the Roman Empire, where key religionized categories developed – categories that would have a profound impact on the way Christians, in Western Europe, configured and refigured their identity (and that of Christianity's others) (Part 1). I then take a look at Latin Christendom (Part 2), before examining how the 'splintering' of religion during the Long Reformation set in motion new processes of religionization (Part 3). The thread throughout this exploration is the question: What is the Christian religious norm in specific historical-cultural and socio-political contexts? How is this norm (re)crafted by projecting false, bad, or problematic religion onto Christianity's others? To what extent did these boundaries contribute to the stratification of people?

The book also elaborates on the so-called 'dialogical turn' and sets out to examine if and to what extent the promotion of interreligious dialogue, which was set in motion in the late nineteenth century but only gained traction in the twentieth century, succeeds in disrupting patterns of religionization. Perhaps, the ideal of dialogue itself is at risk of falling prey to a reiteration of religionized patterns of thinking? Which imaginary constructs of true, good, and bad religion permeate lofty dialogical ideals and to what extent do these constructs limit the critical potential of dialogue? To what extent does the past continue into the present?

2   Mechanisms of Religionization

Religionization is a complex form of identity production and it makes use of a range of mechanisms: naming, categorizing, essentializing and, eventually, the governance of those Christians and non-Christians who have been 'constructed' in accordance with or in deviation from the projected norms.

Naming/Renaming

Those singled out as deviating from changing and unfolding Christian religious norms are given a name, for example pagans, Saracens, Cathars, and so forth. Significantly, this process of name-giving is not a descriptive but rather an interpretive (or hermeneutical) process. The given names are not intended to do justice to the self-understanding of Christianity's others; in fact, they tell us little about their particular beliefs, practices, hopes, fears, or values. These names, to the contrary, rename, and hence redescribe the identity of the other so that it fits into a Christian (often biblical-theological) framework. These names, furthermore, function as boundary markers, reinforcing the difference between the norm and its deviance, and thereby concealing any overlap between 'self' and 'other', any fuzziness, and any hybridity. Demarcation is the goal. Finally, the given names tend to be denigrating, insulting, contemptuous, scornful, and so forth. Often, they function as evocative, value-laden, and condensed narratives, which those embodying the norm can read and understand immediately: pagans, Saracens, Christ-killers, infidels, papists, idolaters, Cathars, and so on. They are part of a larger web of meaning, a cultural archive that is ready to be tapped.

Categorization and Classification

Those who have the power to name and rename also have the power 'to mark, assign, and classify'. Giving a group a name, is to engage in a process of constructing categories, 'taxonomies and classifications' (Kahlos, 2020, p. 89). Doing so helps to organize and simplify differences in relation to sameness: it is 'a strategy' to achieve 'some cognitive control over [...] bewildering complexity' (Chidester, 1996, pp. 21–22). In the course of this process, the other (for instance the Jewish other) is assigned a place in the larger scheme of things. Sometimes this other (for instance the Jewish other) will be classified together with other groups (for instance the Muslim other) with which they, according to Christian imagination, share certain characteristics (the nineteenth-century category Semites covers both Jews and Muslims). In another period, however, this classification may change and groups that first occupied a similar or even interchangeable position are allocated opposing positions. In the process of this categorization, the other becomes a 'type', that is a set form of representation, which makes sense in the Christian imagination but does not do justice to the self-understanding of these imaginary others.

Like name-giving, classification is based on power relations: it is a process that serves the interests of the actor's own religious group and delegitimizes other groups. A projected superior image of true Christianity functions as the norm. Sometimes the other is included in a Christian frame, but more often the other is constructed as a negative mirror image of true Christianity. This representation of non-Christian groups as subordinate, inferior, abnormal, and problematic serves the purpose of consolidating the imagined identity of the powerful, here Christian, group. Such 'othering discourses and othering patterns of thinking [...] diminish or entirely ignore common features between the other and the self' (Kahlos, 2020, p. 6). The focus is on establishing a binary or dichotomy between self and other, thereby at once denying any commonalities or overlaps. This does not, however, take anything away from the versatility and instability of taxonomies. Groups may be allocated different places in the Christian imagination, they may be compared or contrasted to different groups, subsumed under a new umbrella or divided into further subcategories.

Essentialization

Religionization also includes the attribution of characteristics to people because they are presumed to belong to this or that group. Stereotypes (from the Greek *stereos*: firm, fixed, stable, and *typos*: model or set) are the outcome of this process. Qualities that are attributed to a particular non-Christian group are contrasted to Christian qualities. In this way, meaning is produced through patterns of differentiation.

Such characteristics are collectively assigned to people simply because they belong to this or that group until belonging to this or that group determines their nature. Often different qualitative attributes interlock and reinforce one another until an entire community is essentialized as fundamentally different. Thus 'Jews' were depicted as stubborn, greedy, and power-hungry; 'Muslims' as violent, untrustworthy, and irrational; 'pagans' are stupid, immoral, and uncivilized and those who embody the Christian norm are innocent, pure, pious, and so forth. Those who do not fit the characterization are projected as the exception confirming the rule, or seen as a mirror, a rebuke to Christians, as is the case with the

6 Introduction

'noble savage', a rhetorical figure who serves the purpose of reinforcing Christian norma-tivity. Stereotypical descriptions of certain groups sometimes take centre stage, but they 'can [also] live a dormant existence for years – sometimes even for centuries – only then to reappear and be reactivated'.[5] When dormant stereotypes reappear, their genealogy tends to be forgotten.

Governance

Religionization is a hermeneutical process of selfing and othering; this, however, does not prevent it from having real and material effects on people's lives, specifically in terms of unequal power distribution. Religionization may not be reduced to religious prejudice. The key idea is that religionized mechanisms of renaming, classification, and essentialization translate into the differential governance of people, resulting in religiously stratified soci-eties. From the perspective of governance, the question to be asked is how a religiously stratified society is put in place? How have societies been re-envisioned, re-organized, and re-created when the Christo-religious norm changed? What patterns of socialization and re-socialization were deployed to that end? Which disciplinary measures were used to instil a sense of religious normativity and to police the boundaries between us and them, self and other? How were religious norms established? How were boundaries between self and other inscribed into the law and how were they materialized into spatial settings and ritually performed? How were people led to appropriate new religious identities according to the expectations of society's religious norm? How were these norms institutionalized, enforced, and controlled?

Usually, different patterns of religionization reinforce one another. On the one hand, attributes assigned to non-Christian groups can function as a legitimization of how these groups are to be governed: they need to be educated, civilized, disciplined, controlled, domesticated, sanctioned, or separated from those who embody the norm and occupy a posi-tion of power. A wide variety of 'practices, institutions, and structures', are put in place to help delineate self and other (Fredrickson, 2002, p. 6) and to establish a hierarchical order in society. On the other hand, this established order, which quite literally separates people, reinforces difference and endorses the religionized taxonomies that already exist.

The governance of religious others may take many forms. It may unfold via formal government, or via the law and law enforcement. For example, those deviating from the norm may be sanctioned with the loss of property rights, denial of access to courts, or with a ban on holding public office. Governance may also take the form of disciplining via sociali-zation, education, or self-governance, that is to say, the interiorization and incorporation of norms, images, and stereotypes. The outcome is that both the norm and its deviation are not only consolidated but also embodied and materialized: a society is created in which imag-ined binaries are made real and have real impact on people's lives. Patterns of religionization define people's legal status, affect the opportunities they have to make a living, impact their social relations, and influence their epistemological status. Whereas some enjoy privileges and benefits, others are faced with various obstacles and disadvantages.

3 The Particular Contribution of This Book

In the past couple of years, several books have been published that seek to trace the way Christians have conceptualized, displayed, and potentially governed religious others, or non-Christians, throughout history and how some of these imaginaries, whose origins have long been forgotten, continue to impact current interreligious relations. Such *longue durée* approaches are usually prompted by the desire to better understand our present time. Therefore, scholars ask to what extent current habits of thinking and behaving are formed and shaped when it comes to religion, religious diversity, and particular religious traditions by the history of Western Christianity's imagination of Jews and Muslims. How do the age-old memories of the violent conflicts between Catholics and Protestants, which ravaged Europe during the sixteenth and seventeenth centuries, impact current ideas about good and bad religion? If it may be said that images of 'us and them' or 'self and other' are always co-constructed and feed on each other, which images of religious otherness circulate in Europe today – a context in which secularized Christianity sets the norm – and to what extent can we trace these images back to past patterns of religionization (Moyaert, 2018)?

Many studies, and this is certainly for reasons of scholarly diligence, are limited to scrutinizing Christian images of a single rhetorical figure of otherness. Some studies concentrate on how Christians, historically speaking, have forged and re-forged the Jew as hermeneutical figure (Cohen, 1999) or how Muslims have featured in Western European imagination (Tolan, 2019). The scholarship of Early Christianity, which explores the co-construction of the binary pair of orthodoxy and heresy (Berzon, 2016; Schott, 2007) and investigates the pagan as Christian counterimage (Jürgasch, 2015) has been important to this study. Here I should also mention the critique of religion which focuses on how the politics of the religio-secular divide continues to affect Christians and non-Christians, both in Europe and beyond (Balagangadhara, 1994; Fitzgerald, 2007a).

This book, however, seeks to broaden the scope of research into various forms of Christian imaginaries of otherness, in an effort at systematization, with all the risks involved (see below). First, rather than focusing on one category, it examines various rhetorical figures of religionized otherness and how they were discursively constructed as 'useful enemies' to think with (Malcolm, 2019): the figures of 'the Jew', 'the Saracen', 'the pagan', 'the heretic', 'the priest', 'the fanatic', and 'the Semite' to mention the most important ones. Furthermore, this book is not limited to one set time period, say the Middle Ages or Modernity, but rather seeks to cover a larger timespan, starting with early Christian apologists and concluding by scrutinizing the so-called dialogical turn in the twentieth century. The question is what role have these figures played in the configuration and refiguration of Christian normativity in changing socio-cultural and political contexts? What Christian questions, concerns, and interests propel the projection of bad, false, or problematic religion onto others? How precisely do these particular others help to buttress a sense of Christian normativity in concrete historical-cultural and socio-political settings? Does the content of what is projected onto these rhetorical figures stay the same or can we notice changes depending on changing historical circumstances, pressures, and events? To what extent do these various rhetorical figures intersect and overlap, or do they rather serve completely different functions in the Christian imagination?

4 The Risk of Systematization and How I Seek to Avoid It

There are several risks attached to this *longue durée* approach and the book's effort at systematization. Here, I limit myself to naming only the most important ones. Below I explain how I have sought to methodologically avert or forestall most of them.

The focus on detecting patterns of religionization may turn into a form of *Hineininterpretierung*, my own hermeneutical framework becoming the guide for how I read and interpret the sources, rather than allowing the sources to speak for themselves. A *longue durée* approach is always in danger of lapsing into a teleological reading of history, which perceives the past as almost necessarily leading up to the present, leaving out contesting perspectives and contingent historic realities. Will I succeed in doing sufficient justice to the concrete motivations and historical contexts of the sources discussed? When does genealogy become teleology?

Second, this book for the most part takes a macrolevel approach to history in its effort to understand past and present patterns of religionization. Such an approach is not that popular anymore among historians, because it often comes in the form of a metanarrative that only looks at the big names and their big ideas and glosses over any local stories that contradict this metanarrative. A work like this does indeed run the risk of glossing over local histories, and of overlooking the messiness of daily interactions in their concrete socio-historical settings; histories which often destabilize and disrupt the grand narratives of history. Especially when dealing with written documents produced by educated Christian elites who undertake to speak on behalf of their tradition and seek to safeguard the communal identity by establishing boundaries between us and them, one might end up with an idealized version of history. Indeed, one might even end up reiterating imagined binary patterns of religionization. Finally, and these are all variations on the same theme, when using concepts like 'the Christian imagination', or 'Christian normalcy', there is the risk of lapsing into generalization, essentialization, and reification, as if all Christians thought alike, as if ideas of Christian normalcy went uncontested. Will this work in its effort to trace patterns of religionization not itself result in an imaginary construct of Christian normativity?

This book does not claim to be exhaustive: it traces how religionization has functioned throughout the history of Christian Western Europe. I am interested in when, where, and how religionization happens. I do this by focusing on how images of religious normalcy and deviation were constructed in certain contexts and places with a specific interest in historical turning points. I hope to be creating some kind of a mosaic, putting together little tiles which, together, produce a picture, albeit incomplete, of the history of religionization.

I embrace the fact that I am looking at history in order to better understand the present and to explore if and to what extent the past continues to impact the way we think about religion, religious diversity, and interfaith relations. Certainly, there is a risk involved in systematization and especially in seeking connections between past and present, but this approach also yields real learning opportunities and enables critical self-reflection. Doing the work of historicization may help to loosen the power of the past and make the past a topic of conversation rather than an invisible and unmarked hermeneutical framework. Clearly, this is only one narrative told with a specific interest in mind, that of charting patterns of religionization; other stories will be different, because they are told from a different perspective and with a different focal point.

Furthermore, this book explicitly deals with imaginary constructs of self and other, and this goes both for the projected ideas about Christian normativity and for the images forged about non-Christians. This is not a study of the social, economic, or political relations between Christians and non-Christians; it is a history of religious image-building and how constructed images have impacted real people (and continue to do so). The focus of the book is on Christianity's images of religious others; the book is not about how these others configured their own self-understanding or how they tried to talk back or sought to subvert Christian normativity. This does not mean that religionized others are only passive victims of hegemonic imaginings. The book is, however, limited to images of 'others', rather than the reaction of 'others' to these images.

Throughout the book, I also make it clear that these imaginary constructs are far removed from reality. I do this by interspersing the process of systematization with local histories that contradict and mess up idealized projections of identity, alterity, and the envisioned clear-cut boundaries, and by setting out the larger political context and the theological and/ or political interests involved in religionization. One reviewer, therefore, called this book a form of macro-history spiked by local micro-stories. Furthermore, from time to time, I show how dominant interpretations of certain historical events, figures, and ideas (e.g. the Modern Devotion seen as a proto-reformatory movement; toleration as a Protestant ideal, etc.) are not only teleological, but are also implicated in the process of religionization. History is never just a reproduction of facts; it is always told from a certain angle and with a certain purpose. Often, the way history is narrated conveys something about 'us' and who 'we' are and how 'we' want to be seen; when this tendency overreaches itself, the stories become mythical. The book scrutinizes some of these mythic stories and shows how they are permeated by patterns of religionization.

I do not claim that my rendering of history is neutral. My approach is pedagogical and in this sense programmatic. I want to contribute to a better understanding of how age-old and ever-changing patterns of religionization are perpetuated in our own age and how they continue to impact not only the way we see and perceive those who believe and practise today, but also continue to influence how we organize our societies. Here I am inspired by David Nirenberg, who once said that 'the peril of fantasizing our freedom from the past is great', and that certainly holds true for the history of religionization (Nirenberg, 2014). As I will argue throughout this book, Eurocentric and Christocentric patterns of religionization have been constructed and gradually built into the fabric of Western European societies for centuries. Revealing and identifying these patterns is of course time-consuming, tedious work that takes us back to long-forgotten discussions and resources that have deeply impacted the way we imagine our world and the people that inhabit it. Such tedious work is important, however, because we need to learn to re-imagine our world, to see and think differently. If we accept that patterns of religionization are socially constructed and therefore made, if we accept that they are historical-culturally dependent and volatile, we ought to believe in the possibility that they can be unmade too.

5   The Use of the Text Boxes

The reader will immediately notice that the text of the different chapters is regularly interrupted by text boxes. These text boxes serve multiple purposes.

- There are what Özlem Sensoy and Robin DiAngelo call 'stop boxes', in which I resume some of the key ideas from previous chapters (Sensoy & DiAngelo, 2017).
- I have also included boxes in which I summarize specific imaginary patterns of religionization and the binary constructs of self and other, for example religion/superstition or Christian/Jew. While I will continue to emphasize this throughout the book, it is important not to forget that these are imaginary social constructs. The Jews, Muslims, pagans, heretics, fanatics, Semites that figure in this book are not real (though real people were affected by these images). They are Jews imagined as Jews, Muslims imagined as Muslims, and so forth. To emphasize this, some scholars argue for the use of inverted commas (Jansen & Meer, 2020, p. 9). I have not done that, as it would not improve the readability of the book, but I agree with the point made. Those boxes which focus on binary patterns of religionization ought not to be read as a simplification of complex local histories of the interactions between Christians and non-Christians. The reader is invited to reflect on the stereotypical nature of these binary constructs and on how little they actually tell us about real people.
- Furthermore, there are also text boxes which zoom in on messy local histories and which explicitly surface the imaginary nature of these patterns of religionization, highlighting the way they remove the complexities of everyday reality. These text boxes often have a title like 'Blurring religionized boundaries'; they are intended to make clear that, while the history that I tell is one of symbolic and real violence, the conclusion ought not to be an affirmation of the impossibility of living together with difference. History provides us with ample examples of the contrary. Quite often the boundaries between Christians and non-Christians were indeed imaginary, and the reality of living together was far messier.
- Some boxes, furthermore, force the reader to step out of the text for a brief moment and seek a more meta-hermeneutical perspective, aimed at highlighting how certain patterns of religionization have profoundly impacted and continue to influence dominant popular teleological readings of history (e.g. the emancipatory history of the rise of tolerance). These boxes are entitled: 'the myth of...'. In these boxes, I do not only mention the key elements of mythic histories, but I also seek to deconstruct them.

6 A Word of Gratitude

This study forced me to step out of my comfort zone. While I have been trained to compare theologies across traditions, regard myself as well-versed in the histories of antisemitism, Islamophobia, and the secular, and might even be called an expert in critical interfaith hermeneutics aimed at uncovering patterns of selfing and othering, I have had to work hard to immerse myself in the historical study of Early and Medieval Christianity as well as in the history of the Long Reformation. While others without any doubt have more expertise in each of these scholarly fields, I hope that this book brings sufficiently new insights to compensate for the flaws it most certainly contains.

This book would not have been possible without the help and critical feedback I received from several colleagues, who have also encouraged me to continue to research and write, especially at times when I felt a bit out of my depth. It is sometimes said that academia is lonely; this is not my experience. I am especially grateful to comparative theologian Michelle Voss and feminist and postcolonial theologian Jeanine Hill Fletcher who read the entire manuscript and provided me with critical feedback, which has really lifted the project to a higher level. I greatly benefited from all the literature suggestions as well as corrections that I received from Mattias Smalbrugge, who specializes in the history of European culture, Violet Soen, who specializes in the history of the Reformation, and from Thomas Jürgash and Stefan Metz, who are scholars of Early Christianity. Amina Nawaz's feedback on chapter 4, dealing with the history of the statues of pure blood, turned out to be of particular value. I am also grateful for the feedback interreligious scholars Hans Gustafson and Rachel Mikva gave on the two final chapters of the book, which deal with the World Religions Paradigm and the dialogical turn. Church historians Wim François, Mirjam van Veen, Anthony Dupont, and Rob Faesen helped me understand particular historical sources and helped me to comprehend their nuances and complexities. Four other colleagues from the field of comparative theology deserve a special mention: Catherine Cornille, Klaus von Stosch, Joshua Ralston, and Daniel Joslyn-Siemiatkoski. I am grateful for their academic rigour, their critical reflections, and their friendship.

A four-month research stay in Tübingen, which was possible thanks to a New Horizons scholarship from the Faculty of Protestant Theology, the Centre for Islamic Theology, and Faculty of Catholic Theology of the University of Tübingen, gave me the time to finish the second draft of the manuscript. I am deeply indebted to the colleagues and students who discussed several chapters during the research colloquia. A word of thanks also to my colleagues and doctoral students of the research group *Decolonizing Interreligious Studies*, Vrije Universiteit Amsterdam; their enthusiasm and support have been priceless. Thanks also to Yolande Jansen, Mariecke van den Berg, Matthea Westerduin, Lieke Schrijvers, Deniz Aktaş, Luca Naus, and Hannah Visser. It is a joy to work with them. I greatly benefited from participating in the Race-Religion network and the Medieval Race reading group, both initiated by my colleague and friend Anya Topolski. Janet Andrewes, once a student in the master's programme *Interreligious Studies* at Vrije Universiteit Amsterdam, corrected my English, gave me valuable feedback with regard to the readability of the manuscript, and more than once saved me from awkward phrasings, jargon, and redundancy.

This is the book that I have been meaning to write for a long time. It is my hope that it addresses a need in our field of critical religious and interreligious studies, (comparative) theologies of religions, and the history of religion. I worked on it for more than five years, and it was the most demanding project that I have undertaken since the start of my academic career. I am acutely aware that this book took away time that I could have and should have spent with my beloved ones, my husband, Michael De Blauwe, and our four beautiful children, Lucas, Norah, Nathan, and Simon. I am sure that, like me, they are happy to see the end of it, but I also hope that they will be proud of the result.

Marianne Moyaert
Pellenberg, 15 May 2023

Notes

[1] Wekker is inspired by Edward Said, who coined this term in his work *Culture and Imperialism* (1993).

[2] My analysis is limited to Western Europe, and more specifically that region which covers what we now call Belgium, France, Germany, the Netherlands, Spain, Switzerland, and, albeit to a lesser extent, the United Kingdom. How the dynamics of what I call religionization play out elsewhere, for example in Eastern or Northern Europe, or in a colonial context, and if the notion of religionization is also applicable to other 'religious' traditions, are questions that require further research.

[3] This formulation suggests that racialization is limited to physical/biological characteristics. Later in this book, I will show that this understanding of racialization is too narrow.

[4] As Timothy Fitzgerald explains, '"Critical religion" is shorthand for the critical historical deconstruction of "religion" *and related categories*' (Fitzgerald, 2015, p. 303).

[5] Anne Frank Stichting. Begin bij jezelf: Kleine uiteenzetting over Stereotypen en Vooroordelen, p. 14 (my translation). www.annefrank.org/nl/downloads/filer_public/ee/f0/eef0eb3b-c48f-47fb-8b25-bf60fee176a7/begin_bij_jezelf_1.pdf.

References

Balagangadhara, S. N. (1994). *'The Heathen in His Blindness...': Asia, the West and the Dynamic of Religion*. Numen Book Series 64. Brill.

Bell, C. (2006). Paradigms behind (and before) the Modern Concept of Religion. *History and Theory*, *45*(4), 27–46.

Berzon, T. S. (2016). *Classifying Christians: Ethnography, Heresiology, and the Limits of Knowledge in Late Antiquity*. University of California Press.

Buell, D. K. (2005). *Why This New Race: Ethnic Reasoning in Early Christianity*. Columbia University Press.

Cavanaugh, W. T. (2009). *The Myth of Religious Violence: Secular Ideology and the Roots of Modern Conflict*. Oxford University Press.

Chidester, D. (1996). *Savage System: Colonialism and Comparative Religion in Southern Africa*. University of Virginia Press.

Cohen, J. (1999). *Living Letters of the Law: Ideas of the Jew in Medieval Christianity*. University of California Press.

Cuthbertson, I. A. (2018). Preaching to the Choir? Religious Studies and Religionization. In B. Stoddard (Ed.), *Method Today: Redescribing Approaches to the Study of Religion* (pp. 96–105). Equinox.

Drake, S. (2013). *Slandering the Jew: Sexuality and Difference in Early Christian Texts*. University of Pennsylvania Press.

Dreßler, M. (2019). Modes of Religionization: A Constructivist Approach to Secularity. *Working Paper Series of the Centre for Advanced Studies 'Multiple Secularities – Beyond the West, Beyond Modernities'*, *7*. Retrieved from www.multiple-secularities.de/media/wps7_dressler_religionization.pdf

Fitzgerald, T. (2007a). *Discourse on Civility and Barbarity: A Critical History of Religion and Related Categories*. Oxford University Press.

Fitzgerald, T. (2007b). *Religion and the Secular: Historical and Colonial Formations*. Equinox.

Fitzgerald, T. (2015). Critical Religion and Critical Research on Religion: Religion and Politics as Modern Fictions. *Critical Research on Religion*, *3*(3), 303–319.

Fredrickson, G. M. (2002). *Racism: A Short History*. Princeton University Press.

Horrell, D. G. (2020). *Ethnicity and Inclusion: Religion, Race, and Whiteness in Constructions of Jewish and Christian Identities*. Eerdmans.

Jansen, Y., & Meer, N. (2020). Genealogies of 'Jews' and 'Muslims': Social Imaginaries in the Race-religion Nexus. *Patterns of Prejudice*, *54*(1–2), 1–14.

Jennings, W. J. (2010). *The Christian Imagination: Theology and the Origins of Race*. Yale University Press.

Joshi, K. Y. (2020). *White Christian Privilege: The Illusion of Religious Equality in America*. New York University Press.

Jürgasch, T. (2015). Christians and the Invention of Paganism in the Late Roman Empire. In M. Sághy, M. R. Salzman, & R. L. Testa (Eds.), *Pagans and Christians in Late Antique Rome: Conflict, Competition, and Coexistence in the Fourth Century* (pp. 115–138). Cambridge University Press.

Kahlos, M. (2020). *Religious Dissent in Late Antiquity, 350–450*. Oxford University Press.

Kaplan, M. L. (2019). *Figuring Racism in Medieval Christianity*. Oxford University Press.

Knust, J. W. (2006). *Abandoned to Lust: Sexual Slander and Ancient Christianity*. Columbia University Press.

Malcolm, N. (2019). *Useful Enemies: Islam and the Ottoman Empire in Western Political Thought, 1450–1750*. Oxford University Press.

Maldonado-Torres, N. (2014). Race, Religion, and Ethics in the Modern/Colonial World. *The Journal of Religious Ethics*, *42*(4), 691–711.

Masuzawa, T. (2005). *The Invention of World Religions, or, How European Universalism Was Preserved in the Language of Pluralism*. University of Chicago Press.

Mayerhofer, K. (2021). Inferiority Embodied: The 'Men-struating' Jew and Pre-Modern Notions of Identity and Difference. In A. Lange, K. Mayerhofer, D. Porat, & L. H. Schiffman (Eds.), *Comprehending Antisemitism through the Ages: A Historical Perspective*, An End to Antisemitism! 3 (pp. 135–159). De Gruyter.

Moyaert, M. (2018). Inter-Worldview Education and the Re-Production of Good Religion. *Education Sciences*, *8*(4), 1–15.

Nirenberg, D. (2014). *Anti-Judaism: The Western Tradition*. W.W. Norton & Co.

Nongbri, B. (2013). *Before Religion: A History of a Modern Concept*. Yale University Press.

Nye, M. (2019). Race and Religion: Postcolonial Formations of Power and Whiteness. *Method & Theory in the Study of Religion*, *31*(3), 210–237.

Owen, S. (2011). The World Religions Paradigm Time for a Change. *Arts and Humanities in Higher Education*, *10*(3), 253–268.

Petersen, S. (2017). 'Women' and 'Heresy' in Patristic Discourses and Modern Studies. In U. Tervahauta, I. Miroshnikov, O. Lehtipuu, & I. Dunderberg (Eds.), *Women and Knowledge in Early Christianity*, Vigiliae Christianae. Supplements 144 (pp. 187–205). Brill.

Said, E. (1993). *Culture and Imperialism*. Knopf.

Schott, J. (2007). Heresiology as Universal History in Epiphanius's *Panarion*. *Zeitschrift für Antikes Christentum*, *10*(3), 546–563.

Sensoy, O., & DiAngelo, R. (2017). *Is Everyone Really Equal? An Introduction to Key Concepts in Social Justice Education*, Multicultural Education Series (2nd ed.). Teachers College Press.

Strickland, D. H. (2003). *Saracens, Demons, and Jews: Making Monsters in Medieval Art*. Princeton University Press.

Thatamanil, J. (2015). How Not to Be a Religion: Genealogy, Identity, Wonder. In M. Johnson-DeBaufre, C. Keller, & E. Ortega-Aponte (Eds.), *Common Goods: Economy, Ecology, and Political Theology* (pp. 54–72). Fordham University Press.

Thatamanil, J. J. (2020). *Circling the Elephant: A Comparative Theology of Religious Diversity*, Comparative Theology: Thinking across Traditions 8. Fordham University Press.

Tolan, J. V. (2019). *Faces of Muhammad: Western Perceptions of the Prophet of Islam from the Middle Ages to Today*. Princeton University Press.

Wekker, G. (2016). *White Innocence: Paradoxes of Colonialism and Race*. Duke University Press.

Whitaker, C. J. (2013). Black Metaphors in the King of Tars. *The Journal of English and Germanic Philology*, *112*(2), 169–193.

PART 1

Religionization in Early Christianity

Christians, Heretics, Jews, and Pagans

In Western Europe, Christianity became the 'prototype for religion' and provided many of the assumptions with which people began to interpret and (de)legitimize different – read non-Christian – traditions and cultures both in Europe and beyond (Bell, 2006, p. 30). In the first part of this book, I explore how Christians began to conceptualize, name, and govern non-Christians. To that end, I focus my attention on the period from the second to the eighth centuries of the common era when Christian *literati* began to construct a normative sense of Christian identity in relation to imagined figures of religious 'otherness'. From this twofold process of 'selfing' and 'othering' a wide range of symbolic figures of religionized otherness emerged, 'the heretic', 'the Jew', and 'the pagan'. These non-Christian others are largely imaginary social constructs that served the purpose of rendering Christian claims to true religion legitimate while delegitimizing the traditions of non-Christians. Many prescriptive, even moral, assumptions were projected onto these figures, until their beliefs and practices became associated with social inferiority, while normative Christianity was projected as superior. Since these figures of otherness function as mere characters in a Christian storyline, we learn little about who these people really are.

In the first chapter, *The Creation of Key Religionized Categories in Early Christianity*, I zoom in on the second and third centuries when Christian apologists, in the sometimes hostile context of the Roman Empire, were tasked with constructing a sense of 'Christianness' against significant non-Christian others. This resulted in binary religionized pairs: religion-superstition; orthodoxy-heresy; new and old people of God. My aim is to retrace the origins of these religionized categories and explore how these categories came to be constructed as symbolic of religious deviation. While some of these categories are new, others already existed but took on a new meaning and significance in the work of Christian apologetics.

Even though we are dealing with imaginary constructs, aimed at establishing boundaries between 'us and them', these religionized categories would go on to have a real impact on the lives of real people, precisely because the societies in which they lived began to organize, classify, and govern their inhabitants on the basis of these same categories (Buell, 2005, p. 33).

Christian Imaginations of the Religious Other: A History of Religionization, First Edition. Marianne Moyaert.
© 2024 John Wiley & Sons Ltd. Published 2024 by John Wiley & Sons Ltd.

In the second chapter, *The Coercive Turn: Institutionalizing Religionized Categories*, I discuss how this came about. Here, I explore how, after the Constantinian turn, the long process of the Christianization of the Roman Empire was set in motion. Against this background, Christian apologetic imaginaries of self (Christian) and other (Jew, pagan, and heretic) were cast into institutionalized structures of exclusion and oppression. Indeed, when Christianity became the official religion of the Roman Empire, the imaginary constructs of Christianity's others became legal categories in Roman jurisprudence. As a consequence, these imaginary, religionized constructs began to be used in the differential and unequal treatment of social groups based on their supposedly deviant beliefs and practices. Thus, religionized categories became real, at least to a certain extent.

Towards the end of the second chapter, I also introduce the Muslims, who enter the stage of history during the seventh century. For a long time, Muslims would not be classified as a separate religious group since, in the European Christian imagination, they were not recognized as a distinct religious challenge. Rather, Muslims were either imagined as heretics or as pagans, and sometimes they were also compared to Jews. It would only be from the thirteenth century onwards that Muslims became a more or less separate (legal) category. Until then, they would be framed into the fourfold Christian *imago mundi* [map of the world], which projects Christianity as the only true faith (*vera religio*) and the others – Jews, pagans, and heretics – as aberrations.

References

Bell, C. (2006). Paradigms behind (and before) the Modern Concept of Religion. *History and Theory*, *45*(4), 27–46.

Buell, D. K. (2005). *Why This New Race: Ethnic Reasoning in Early Christianity*. Columbia University Press.

CHAPTER 1

The Creation of Key Religionized Categories in Early Christianity

In Roman imperial culture before Constantine (r. 306–337), Christianity was a diverse phenomenon (Fredriksen, 2014). Identities were largely 'evolving and fluid' and the distinctions and boundaries between different social groups 'whether those traditionally termed heretical and orthodox, or Jew and Christian' were not yet that clear (Carleton Paget & Lieu, 2017, p. 2). Christianity was a work-in-progress with no official form, and the process of configuring Christianness in a largely non-Christian world was ongoing (Buell, 2005, p. 26). From this perspective, it makes more sense to speak about Christianities, even though precisely that plurality would be denied by those seeking to establish a single Christian norm.

In this setting, where Christians found themselves in a minority position, apologists took on the task of creating a sense of Christian self-understanding. They sought to define what is true and false worship, what is the Christian norm and what deviates from it, who belongs and who does not, and how a Christian ought to live faithfully in a largely non-Christian society (García Soormally, 2019). Operating 'within their particular cultural and rhetorical contexts', they used a variety of discursive strategies they shared with their neighbours, and they did so in ways that served their project of self-making (Knust, 2006, p. 13).

Typically, selfing (the configuration of identity) and othering (the making of alterity) go hand in hand: 'Wherever we look for the emergence of "the self" there looms the spectre of "the other"' (Lieu, 2004, p. 269). This also holds true when we discuss early Christian patterns of religionization understood as the process of selfing and othering predicated on imagined religious difference. Christian apologists constructed and projected their Christian way of life while simultaneously delegitimizing that of others (Stroumsa, 1998, p. 175). That effort of religious (de)legitimization also intersected with ethnicization, gendering, and even sexual slander (Drake, 2013, p. 54). In the course of this process, non-Christians were labelled, categorized, and essentialized as the 'others' of Christianity, while Christianness was imagined as the ultimate religious standard.

Religionization may take varying expressions. One common pattern of religionization follows the logic of dichotomization; the religious other is projected as the reverse image of the self. The emerging traditions of *adversus nationes* [against the nations], *adversus haereses* [against heretics], and *adversus Iudaeos* [against the Jews] contrast 'true' Christianness with respectively 'superstition', 'heresy', and 'Jewishness'. Here, the 'idolater/superstitious fool' (later the pagan), 'the heretic', and 'the Jew' are turned into useful enemies to think

Christian Imaginations of the Religious Other: A History of Religionization, First Edition. Marianne Moyaert.
© 2024 John Wiley & Sons Ltd. Published 2024 by John Wiley & Sons Ltd.

16 CHAPTER 1 The Creation of Key Religionized Categories

with and to contrast with what being a 'true' Christian entails. As mere foils in the service of Christian identity construction they do not tell us a lot about real others or about Christian interaction with those who are labelled as belonging to other religious groups (Kahlos, 2007; Lieu, 2004; Rebillard, 2012). The way Christianity's others are labelled does, however, shed light on those features which early Christians considered salient about their own faith. That also holds true for the second pattern of religionization, which follows a logic of encompassment. While often operating with the same categories as the logic of binary construction, here the 'putatively subordinate category is adopted, subsumed or co-opted (←) into the identity defined and, as it were, owned by those who do the encompassing' (Baumann & Gingrich, 2004, p. 26). According to this logic, the other is projected as an inferior or incomplete, albeit not completely different, version of the self. Here, there is room for overlap between Christians and non-Christians, but this overlap reinforces the truth of Christian tradition. The logic of encompassment seems benign, but also presumes a stratified schema of superiority and inferiority, which is expressed in terms of promise and fulfilment, potential and realization, shadow and light, seed and fruition. At the lower level of knowledge one may find the traces of what is realized, fulfilled, and encompassed at a higher level. Typically, the logic of encompassment elevates a particular term, for example Christian peoplehood or Christian worship, and turns it into a seemingly generic and universal term, which includes everyone, without those who find themselves at a lower level of knowledge realizing that this is the case. Only those who have access to the fullness of truth are in the know. Others tend to remain fixated on what is particular, tribal, or partially true.

Religionization makes us believe that these social categories – Christian, Jew, heretic, superstitious fool/idolater – describe reality as it is (Metz, 2021). These categories are indeed constructed as taken-for-granted categories rather than as malleable categories that are rhetorically forged in the crucible of ideological and sometimes political battles. So there is always a risk that we uncritically adopt these categories of religious difference as 'our categories of social analysis' and that we forget that they actually obscure the multi-layered nature of people's identities and the messiness of social reality (Brubaker, 2002; Rebillard, 2012, p. 2). In the period under scrutiny – the second and third centuries CE – the boundaries between Christian and Jewish social life, Christian and pagan-Roman culture, orthodox Christianity and Christian heresies were anything but clear. Where apologists projected difference and boundaries, social reality did not show discrete religious entities. In fact, apologetic statements about what Christians do or do not do (e.g. attend the games) are usually statements about what they should or should not do to distinguish themselves from others; in reality Christians often did not follow through. The categories of otherness too are discursively created and non-descriptive. Accordingly, when analysing the work of Christian apologists, we have to differentiate between the rhetorical production of difference between Christians and various others and how people actually behaved and what they believed (Lieu, 2004).

The religionized constructs discussed in this chapter form the first basic foundation for the later Medieval Christian map of the world; these constructs will make a profound impact on how Christians imagine, relate to and, in a later stage of history, governed those who deviate from Christian normativity. When power dynamics began to shift, and Christians (or at least those Christians who conformed to the norm) found themselves in the majority, these imagined rhetorical boundaries gradually translated into boundaries of social experience (Lieu, 2004, p. 103). For now, however, let us focus our attention on the time when Christians were one religious minority living in a world full of gods.

1 *Religio* and Its Counterpart *Superstitio*

In their effort to construct a sense of Christianness 'in the midst of great and interconnected diversity' (Carleton Paget & Lieu, 2017, p. 2), early Christian writers made use of existing rhetorical strategies and existing terms, the meaning of which they contested, redefined, and adapted to fit their apologetic goal. Two terms that play a key role in the construction of Christian self-understanding are the contrasting terms *religio* and *superstitio*. To understand how Christian apologists adopted and adapted the distinction between *religio* and *superstitio*, I briefly revisit the shifting layers of meaning in both terms during Late Antiquity and explore how Romans used these terms.

Religio in Antique Times

In antique times, the Latin notion *religio* and its plural *religiones* did not necessarily revolve around beliefs, worship practices, or the gods, namely those things which we would nowadays associate with religion (Nongbri, 2013, pp. 25–30). *Religio* was not limited to some kind of separate realm of human life or a bounded institution or set of institutions; the notion *religio* had a much broader scope. Before it was a system of beliefs, ritual practices, and temples revolving around the gods, *religio* belonged to the realm of experience and emotion (Schilbrack, 2017, p. 833) and it pointed to a sense of restraint, a feeling of having to tread carefully. As Dumézil puts it, '*religio* first pointed to scruple: [...] the concerned hesitation before a manifestation that one must above all understand in order to adapt to it' (Dumézil, 1966, p. 54, my translation).

Religio could also be attributed to any object, person, or place that invoked a sense of awe, restraint, or even anxiety. Anything that caused Romans to act carefully – 'any bond or boundary, any oath, prodigy or omen, any law or tradition or prohibition' – could be *religiosus* (Barton & Boyarin, 2016, p. 27). Especially the uncanny, the unknown, and the perilous could evoke the emotions of *religio* – and could make Romans 'behave with particular circumspection' (Barton & Boyarin, 2016, p. 22): entering a forest, dealing with death. Cultic obligations were also *religiosi* (Smith, 1963, p. 24) and Romans were obliged to observe them, since they were expected to honour the gods and give them their dues. In all of this, neither external authorities – kings or magistrates – nor gods or spirits or other transcendent forces were necessarily seen as the source of the restraint. Further, the transgression of some religious boundaries could evoke a terrible sense of shame or of being tainted. This explains why the Romans 'approached such boundaries as we might approach an electrified fence' (Barton & Boyarin, 2016, p. 22). Those feelings were also called *religio*. Transgression could exclude the transgressor from the community. To overcome this situation of exclusion and to be liberated from the feeling of shame and the taint of transgression, ritualized acts of expiation were needed.

Antiquity and Ethnicity of *Religio*

Over time, however, *religio* came to refer mainly to various worship practices or the performance of ancient rituals to please the gods and to keep the peace (King, 1999, pp. 35–36). Thus, *religio* became more or less synonymous with *traditio*, doing what one's ancestors have always done, with an emphasis on continuity. In *De natura deorum*, Cicero (106–43 BCE) derives *religio* from *relegere*, 'to retrace or re-read' (Cicero, *De natura deorum* II.72, trans. Rackham, 1933). This notion is synonymous with the Greek *álegein*, meaning to heed or to care for. It was an obligation to do as one's ancestors had done, hence the opposition of *relegere* to *neglegere*, to neglect. A religious person is one who keeps the traditions of his ancestors while an irreligious person is one who neglects these traditions (Hoyt, 1912, p. 127). Significantly, the older a *religio/traditio* (the longer its ancestral history) the more authority it had and the more respect it deserved. Thus, antiquity indexed proper *religio*, and piety was the correct attitude towards antique *religio* (Fredriksen, 2006b, p. 235).

Another possible etymological root of *religio* is the verb *religare*, meaning 'to bind together' or 'to tie together', indicating a shared reverence for the same gods. From this perspective, *religio* is a power that holds people together. In ancient Mediterranean culture, *religio* intersected with peoplehood or ethnicity (kinship, genealogy, shared language and/or territory and customs). 'Ancient gods', Paula Fredriksen explains, 'run in the blood' (Fredriksen, 2006b, p. 238). To practise *religio* therefore implied ethnic belonging, and to be 'a Jew, Egyptian, or Greek, or an Antiochene, Athenian, or Roman was to practice the traditional rites of one's ancestors' (Schott, 2008, p. 8). The gods were attached to people and vice versa. So, next to antiquity, ethnicity understood as peoplehood also 'indexed proper religion' (Fredriksen, 2006b, p. 235). People belong together because they share *religio* as *traditio* and this sense of belonging is reproduced by performing ancient rituals together. Peoplehood, therefore, is also made religiously. Given that there are many people, there are also many gods and many ways to worship the gods, and in this sense there was a variety of *religiones*.

Pax Romana, Pax Deorum

In the Roman Empire (from 27 BCE), the term *religio* referred primarily to public rituals performed for the benefit of the state (Cantwell Smith, 2008, p. 9). For the state (and the city) to flourish it was important to maintain good relations with the gods and render them their dues: 'processions, hymns, libations, blood offerings, communal dancing, and drinking and eating – all these public forms of worship expressed and created bonds than bound citizens together and, by establishing or maintaining the necessary relations with powerful numinous patrons (both imperial and celestial), contributed to the common weal' (Fredriksen, 2003, p. 44). *Pax Romana* – Roman peace – depended on *pax deorum* – peace of the gods: 'the concordat between heaven and earth [...] guaranteed the well-being of city and Empire' (Fredriksen, 2006a, p. 601). To refrain from paying respect to the gods was not only an affront but could also endanger the community. Consider in this regard Cicero, who was convinced that

> *in all probability the disappearance of piety towards the gods will entail the disappearance of loyalty and social union among men as well, and of justice itself, the queen of all the virtues* [atque haud scio an pietate adversus deos sublata fides etiam et societas generis humani et una excellentissima virtus iustitia tollatur].
> (De natura deorum *I.4, trans. Rackham, 1933*)

As the Roman Empire expanded, it implemented the policy of absorbing the gods and the *religiones* of other people, rather than destroying or forbidding them. One way to do this was by building temples that incorporated the local tradition into the Roman religion. Thus, Roman deities found their way to the provinces and some local deities travelled to the centre of the empire; for example the cult of Isis, an Egyptian goddess, and that of Mithras, a Persian sun god, became highly popular in Rome. The Roman world was full of gods, and these gods were not only Roman (Stroumsa, 2015, p. 4). This diversity of gods simply reflected the fact that Rome had conquered many people. Romans perfectly understood that different people were bound to different gods (ethnicity) and had to maintain different ancestral obligations (antiquity). For Romans it was even normal to 'show respect to the gods of others too; and in many circumstances – situations calling for political politesse; military or diplomatic engagements; visions of or visitations from divinities other than one's own – such a show of respect was a simple matter of courtesy and common sense. After all, any god is more powerful than any human' (Fredriksen, 2006b, pp. 235–236). While conquered people could continue to practise ancestral cultic traditions, they were also expected to conform to Roman *religio* (Text Box 1).

Text Box 1: Jewish Participation in Pagan Worship?

Jews were a minority living in a world that was full of gods. For a long time, scholars projected the image of Jews as an isolated and perhaps even marginalized people, who did not fully participate in Roman life, which they associated with idolatry. Often this picture entailed understanding the Jewish cult as *religio licita*, that is a legal religion which was tolerated. According to Guy Stroumsa and Paula Fredriksen, both ideas need nuance.

First of all, for Jews idolatry or *idolatreia* is associated with the nations (gentiles, later pagans) and is restricted to a sharply defined domain in contrast to Jewish worship or *latreia* (*avoda* in Hebrew). *Latreia* consists of temple sacrifice or, after the destruction of the temple, prayer, whereas the former refers to sacrifice to or worship of idols, in other words an idol cult (Stroumsa, 1998, p. 179). This restricted definition provided Jews with the space to participate in the Roman world. To be Jewish did not mean isolation. Indeed, social history shows that 'Jews attended theatrical and athletic events, got good gymnasium educations where they could, joined Gentile armies, and lived public lives as municipal leaders. [...] Ancient Jews, as ancients generally, lived in a world congested with gods and they knew it' (Fredriksen, 2003, pp. 44–45). Participating in Rome's social and cultural life implied contact with the gods and, to a certain degree unavoidably, participation in pagan worship. When it comes to actual *latreia*, Jews tended to avoid 'overt public cult'. They did try 'to compensate [for this non-participation] variously through dedications, patronage and prayer' (Fredriksen, 2003, p. 44).

We know that Jews, after 63 BCE, when Judea was conquered, were exempt from participating in the imperial cult and were allowed to keep their own traditions. To explain this exemption scholars often refer to the idea that Jewish religion was *religio licita*. This reference, however, is not helpful. The problem is, first, that *religio* was not a legal category in Roman law prior to the fourth century. So the term is anachronistic. The value of this category for historical analysis is also 'compromised [...] because of its utter wrong-headedness in obscuring the essential connection in antiquity between cult and ethnicity' (Fredriksen, 2006b, p. 239). The exemption of Jews from imperial cult and the acceptance of their cultic exclusivism was, 'for the most part, accepted, because [the *religio* of the Jewish people] met majority culture's twin measure of legal and social respectability, namely, ethnicity and antiquity' (Fredriksen, 2003, p. 42). While Jewish people were sometimes ridiculed as superstitious, a sign of their foreignness (see below), their traditions were nevertheless respected for being old and for being markers of ethnic identity.

Superstitio and *Religio*

Even though Romans recognized many *religiones*, they did distinguish between *religio* on the one hand and *superstitio* on the other hand. The notion of *superstitio* was initially used as a neutral term depicting more personal devotions and oaths. By the first century BCE, however, the word had received a pejorative connotation (see e.g. Cicero, *De natura deorum* I.72, trans. Rackham, 1933; Seneca the Younger [4 BCE – 65 CE], *De clementia*, trans. Basore, 1928 p. 439). It was linked to 'all irrational, improper and perverted credulity as well as unauthorized divination, magic and astrology' (Kahlos, 2007, p. 96). Especially, '[s]orcerers and seers were despised, and all the more so because the majority often came from foreign parts. [...] The Romans, faithful to their official augurs, always condemned any recourse to magic, to divination, to these practices which were regarded as puerile' (Benveniste, 2016, p. 537). *Superstitio* could also be associated with being overscrupulous and overly attached to ritual rules. *Superstitio* was, according to Seneca the Younger, 'the misguided idea of a lunatic [*superstitio error insanientis*]; it fears those whom it ought to love; it is an outrage upon those whom it worships' (Seneca, *Epistle* CCXXIII.16, trans. Gummere, 1925). *Superstitio*, in this sense, was 'not an antithesis of religion', but rather 'a vice that constituted a hyperbole or perverted appendix *inside* the same religious tradition' (Kahlos, 2007, p. 95). Superstitious people participate in exaggerated cults, attach too much importance to prophecies or allow themselves to be swindled by charlatans. The elite often applied this reproach to common people [*vulgus*], to those living in the countryside [*pagani*], to slaves and women. Thus, the distinction between *religio* and *superstitio* was both gendered and classed. Even though the elite ridiculed *superstitiones* and regarded them as contrary to *religio*, in reality these practices were tolerated as long as they were 'harmless to the Roman order' (Kahlos, 2007, p. 97).

Text Box 2: Imaginary Binary Religionized Constructs

The distinction between *religio* and *superstitio* implies a normative judgment, which legitimized some practices and delegitimizes others. *Religio* is appropriate, whereas *superstitio* is not. To call someone superstitious 'amounts to a dismissive way of referring to what in the speaker's opinion appeared excessive, dishonorable, unmanly, sometimes simply new and unfamiliar, sometimes actually wicked, forms of religious action or expression. In other words, the condemnation or distance it asserted was nicely calibrated with the self-image of the Roman politico-social elite in matters relating to religious practice' (Gordon, 2008, p. 77).

Religio	*Superstitio*
State-governed	Chaotic, unruly
Virtue	Vice
Disciplined, ordered, and reasonable cultic obligation	Irrational, improper, and perverted credulity
Proper posture, appropriate, moderate behaviour	Excessive, shameful public behaviour
Citizens	Women, slaves, country-dwellers
A rational, balanced mind	A feeble mind

If the notion of *superstitio* in the first century BCE was mainly reserved for individuals engaging in immoderate religious practices, by the early second century CE it had come to denote the *religio(nes)* of foreigners, and then in a pejorative way (Buell, 2005, p. 193). Roman authors used this label to denigrate foreigners and to demarcate them from Romans. Cicero, for example, emphasized that when it comes to matters of *religio*, Romans were far superior to other people.

> *The fate of these men may serve to indicate that our empire was won by those commanders who obeyed the dictates of religion. Moreover if we care to compare our national characteristics with those of foreign peoples, we shall find that, while in all other respects we are only the equals or even the inferiors of others, yet in the sense of religion, that is, in reverence for the gods [*religione id est cultu deorum*], we are far superior [*multo superiores*]. (De natura deorum II.3, trans. Rackham, 1933)*

This derogatory depiction of the traditions of foreign people also played a role in the genre of Greco-Roman ethnography, which cast foreigners as barbarians, that is as the negative counterimage of civilized Greeks and Romans. 'The Greeks were virile, while Persians were effeminate, Greeks were rational, while Egyptians were irrational; Romans were pious while Jews were impious; Romans were civilized while Germans were savage and so on' (Fredriksen, 2014, p. 24). By calling foreigners superstitious, they were immediately constructed as inferior (Fitzgerald, 2007, p. 115). Druids, Germanic people, the Egyptians as well as Jews were targeted for being involved in magical practices (Pliny the Elder [23/24–79 CE], *Natural History* 30, trans. Rackham, 1938). I call this a form of ethnoreligious othering; when *religio* is considered a marker of ethnicity, delegitimizing a people's *religio* is one way to inferiorize and essentialize them as a whole. Consider in this regard Tacitus (56–117 CE), who in book five of his *Histories* (Tacitus, *Histories*, trans. Moore, 1931), denigrates the Jewish people and their superstitions (book V.8 *superstitionem*), while nevertheless acknowledging the antiquity of their rites. The rhetoric follows the logic of dichotomy, contrasting 'us' and 'them'.

> *The Jews regard as profane all that we hold sacred; on the other hand, they permit all that we abhor* [profana illic omnia quae apud nos sacra, rursum concessa apud illos quae nobis incesta]. (Histories V.4)
> *Whatever their origin, these rites are maintained by their antiquity: the other customs of the Jews are base and abominable, and owe their persistence to their depravity* [Hi ritus quoquo modo inducti antiquitate defenduntur: cetera instituta, sinistra foeda, pravitate valuere]. (V.5)
> *The ways of the Jews are preposterous and mean* [Iudaeorum mos absurdus sordidusque]. (V.5)
> *Those who are converted to their ways follow the same practice, and the earliest lesson they receive is to despise the gods* [contemnere deos], *to disown their country* [exuere patriam], *and to regard their parents, children, and brothers as of little account* [parentes liberos fratres vilia habere]. (V.5)

Typically, such ethnoreligious stereotyping would take on a gendered expression with charges of sexual misbehaviour levelled against others (Drake, 2013; Knust, 2006). Such charges played an important role in the establishment of group boundaries between Romans and non-Romans, civilized people and barbarians. No one can lead a promiscuous sexual life and be in control of their desires, a characteristic of true Romans. Tacitus continues his anti-Jewish slander:

> *They sit apart at meals, and they sleep apart, and although, as a race, they are prone to lust* [proiectissima ad libidinem gens], *they abstain from intercourse with foreign women; yet among themselves nothing is unlawful* [inter se nihil inlicitum]. (Histories V.5, trans. Moore, 1931)

This form of anti-Jewish ethnoreligious rhetoric was 'simply an occasional subspecies of a more general contempt for foreign customs and the obverse expression of Graeco-Roman patriotic pride' (Fredriksen, 2003, p. 47). This example does, however, make clear that religious difference functioned as an identity marker to target ethnic groups and to construct religious boundaries between self and other. Christians too would become the target of such ethnoreligious discourses.

2 Christians as Targets of Religionization

The vast majority of the people among whom Christians lived did not share their religious beliefs and practices. Christian traditions were considered new and did not clearly mark ethnicity. Some Christians kept the Jewish law, others were Romans (or gentiles) but they were all suspect because they did not respect Roman cult. Christian *religio* was frowned upon, mislabelled, and discredited. Some Romans were concerned that Roman Christians (gentile Christians), who did not respect their standing cultic obligations, would threaten the *pax deorum*. This concern may explain the occasional violent outbursts, and even the persecution of Christians for not conforming. Even though persecution was not a constant threat, it

22 CHAPTER 1 The Creation of Key Religionized Categories

was certainly part of the social world in which Christians lived. Thus, Paula Fredriksen and Oded Irshai:

> From the late first to the mid-third century, local pagan resentments and anxieties caused by this Christian lack of respect occasionally burst forth into active aggression: gentile Christians, denounced before magistrates, would be ordered to conform to the religious protocols of the mos Romanorum or face severe sanctions, even death. After 250, imperial initiatives to restore and maintain the pax deorum brought more wide-spread pressure to bear on gentile Christians, to induce them to conform: free to worship Christ as they wished, they nonetheless also had to show honor to the gods. (Fredriksen & Irshai, 2015, p. 120)

Alongside persecution, Christians were also the target of ethnoreligious polemics. Not long after the emergence of the Jesus movement, writers such as Pliny the Younger (61–113 CE), Suetonius (69/70–140 CE), and Tacitus would label it superstitious, thereby at once delegitimizing it as a foreign and excessive practice associated with the feeble minded. Thus, Tacitus in his *Annals*:

> [...] Nero substituted as culprits, and punished with the utmost refinements of cruelty, a class of men, loathed for their vices, whom the crowd styled Christians [Christianos appellabat]. Christus, the founder of the name [Auctor nominis eius Christus], had undergone the death penalty in the reign of Tiberius, by sentence of the procurator Pontius Pilatus, and the pernicious superstition [exitiabilis superstitio] was checked for a moment, only to break out once more, not merely in Judaea, the home of the disease [originem eius mali], but in the capital itself, where all things horrible or shameful in the world collect and find a vogue. (Annals Book 15, V.44; trans. Jackson, 1937)

The fact that Jesus was crucified did not help to raise the status of this novel social group. Crucifixion was a punishment 'reserved for people of low status found guilty of heinous crimes, especially crimes against the *maiestas* of Rome' (Knust, 2006, p. 107). Such public punishment was immediately associated with loss of status and gendered as a sign of diminished masculinity. Followers of Jesus, by implication, were feminized by association, and this would only be reinforced when they themselves were being persecuted and publicly put to trial. The othering of Christian *religio* in terms of *superstitio* was further exacerbated by anti-Christian charges of immoral (un-Roman) behaviour: Christians were accused of cannibalism, child murder, promiscuous behaviour, and even incestuous relations, all of which testified to the potentially dangerous nature of their false and evil religion. Christians, unlike Roman elites, were 'incapable' of controlling themselves (Knust, 2006, p. 27).

Minucius Felix (d. ca. 250), an early Christian apologetic, recorded some of these anti-Christian accusations in his *Octavius* and attributed these accusations to a Roman aristocrat, Cornelius Fronto, who told tales about Christian promiscuities. Thus, he sought to reassert 'the "true" piety of Rome – a piety that leads to sexual and religious decency, not incest and human sacrifice' (Knust, 2006, p. 6). Consider in this regard Fronto on Christians and their lustful religion:

> They recognize one another by secret signs and marks; they fall in love almost before they are acquainted; everywhere they introduce a kind of religion of lust [libidinum religio], a promiscuous 'brotherhood' and 'sisterhood' by which ordinary fornication, under cover of a hallowed name, is converted to incest. And thus their vain and foolish superstition [vana et demens superstitio] makes an actual boast of crime. [...] To say that a malefactor put to death for his crimes, and wood of the death-dealing cross, are objects of their veneration is to assign fitting altars to abandoned wretches and the kind of worship they deserve.
> On the day appointed they gather at a banquet with all their children, sisters, and mothers, people of either sex and every age [cum omnibus liberis, sororibus,

matribus, sexus omnis homines et omnis aetatis*]. There, after full feasting, when
the blood is heated and drink has inflamed the passions of incestuous lust [*incestae
libidinis*]*, a dog which has been tied to a lamp is tempted by a morsel thrown beyond
the range of his tether to bound forward with a rush. The tale-telling light is upset
and extinguished, and in the shameless dark lustful embraces are indiscriminately
exchanged; and all alike, if not in act, yet by complicity, are involved in incest, as
anything that occurs by the act of individuals results from the common intention.
(Minucius Felix, Octavius IX, trans. Glover & Rendall, 1931)*

Such accusations will return at a later stage of our history of religionization when Christians would accuse Jews, heretics, and pagans of similar promiscuous practices.

Christian Apologists and Ethnoreligious Reasoning

Against this background, early second- and third-century apologists tried to construct an account of what it is to be a true Christian, over against others, who sometimes ridiculed them or rejected the legitimacy of their faith claims. These early Christian authors worked 'within their particular cultural and rhetorical contexts, employing tools of rhetoric they shared with their neighbors in ways that served their own persuasive projects' (Knust, 2006, p. 13). They thus started from the existing terms of the debate – *religio/ superstitio* – while modifying their scope and meaning so as 'to include their truth, neatly reversing the terms on their opponents' (Beard et al., 1998, p. 227). That 'ethnicity and antiquity indexed proper religion' was a given (Fredriksen, 2006b, p. 235); how apologists would map their sense of Christianness onto this understanding of *religio* was something they had to creatively figure out. Refuting the charge of newness by claiming antiquity for Christian *religio* was one way to proceed; the other was to claim some sense of Christian ethnicity.

Crafting a Sense of Christian Ethnicity

In early Christian literature, apologists engage in ethnoreligious reasoning and Christians are sometimes called a new people [*laos/genos*], or the real people of God, or the New Israel or the true people of God. As a people they claim shared ancestors (genealogy), shared customs (way of life), shared values, and a shared *religio*. If *religio* constitutes a people and the bond of peoplehood is reinforced by its *religio*, then what brings Christians together [cf. *religare*] is their shared worship of the true God revealed in Christ; as I will explain below, this is a refiguration of the notion *religio* (Buell, 2002, p. 430). Christians also explicitly compared themselves to other peoples, like the Greeks, Romans, Egyptians, and Jews. Sometimes they were termed 'a third race', clearly distinct from Greeks and Jews (Buell, 2005). Consider in this regard Clement of Alexandria (150–211/215), who said:

*Do not worship as the Greeks neither worship as the Jews. But we, who worship
[God] in a new way, in the third way (or form) [genei], are Christians. (Clement of
Alexandria, Stromateis 6.39.4; 41.2; 41.6, quoted in Buell, 2005, p. 42)*

Justin Martyr (100–165) too, in his *Dialogue with the Jew Trypho* (Justin Martyr, trans. Falls, 1948), used ethnic reasoning to establish Christianness as proper *religio*. He emphasizes their shared way of life: members of this Christian people follow Christ's law (123), have faith in Christ (64; 116), and, importantly, change their overall way of life (119). Baptism marks and sets this change in motion; it symbolizes the acceptance of a new way of life and those who are baptized now belong to the Christian people. Here, according to Tertullian (155–220): '[...] we, who were not *formerly* the people of God, have been *made* [God's] people by accepting both the new law [...] and the new circumcision [...]'

(*Adversus Iudaeos* III.13, in Dunn, 2004, p. 75, my emphasis). In a similar vein we read in Justin Martyr's *Dialogue*:

> *Now, since Christ was the First-born of every creature, He founded a new race which is regenerated by Him through water and faith and wood, which held the mystery of the cross. (Dial. 138, trans. Falls, 1948)*

Baptism, while invisible as such, is understood as an indelible spiritual mark branded onto Christian bodies. Like cattle being branded, baptism marks adherence to Christ and thus to God's new people. It changes Christians in their essence, fixates their belonging, and transforms them profoundly and sets them apart (*Dial.* 43, trans. Falls, 1948). This sign cannot be undone; while spiritual, it is a fixed ethnoreligious mark of belonging to Christian peoplehood.

Next to a shared way of life and worship as an ethnoreligious marker, apologists also emphasize how Christians 'are united by common ties of kinship' and blood relations (Buell, 2005, p. 9). Just as the Hellenes projected a genealogy according to which they all stemmed from one common ancestor – Hellas – Christians also claimed a long genealogy; their peoplehood goes way back. Some apologists would project Abraham, Isaac, Jacob, and Judah as the ancestors of Christ, claiming that Christ came to restore the Hebrews and their traditions.

> *Therefore, as your whole people was called after that one Jacob, surnamed Israel, so we who obey the precepts of Christ, are, through Christ who begot us to God, both called and in reality are, Jacob and Israel and Juda and Joseph and David and true children of God. (Dial. 123, trans. Falls, 1948)*

Christians are Hebrews, and Hebrews are the oldest of all people, they even predate the Egyptians and certainly the Greeks (see for example the Pseudo-Clementine *Recognitions*).

Other apologists, while imagining Christians as a distinct and bounded people, would rather emphasize what makes Christian peoplehood unique: this particular people welcomes others from a whole range of nations (gentiles). In so doing, the Christian people promises to achieve the reunification of all people regardless of their particular origins. Here, Christian peoplehood takes on a universal and inclusive stance. Denise Kimber Buell points out, however, that this universal and inclusive Christian claim should not be understood as a break with ethnoreligious reasoning, but rather as an adaptation and reinterpretation of it. Indeed, apologists who emphasized the universal/inclusive dimension of Christianness projected a genealogy that was also able to include gentile Christians. Rather than sticking with a particularly Hebrew genealogy, starting with Abraham or Jacob, apologists, making this universalizing claim, traced Christian peoplehood back to Adam, the first human from which all people stem (marking universality). Such a universalized ethnoreligious line of reasoning claims that at the root or in principle (i.e. in the beginning of creation cf. Genesis 1) there already was a shared connection between all human beings – whether Greek or Jewish – which precedes particular ethnic differences between people. From the very beginning, all humans descend from the same ancestor. Furthermore, within the Christian theological framework, this oneness holds a universalizing promise, that will be fulfilled in the eschaton; all will be united in Christ, the New Adam, the progenitor of a new people. Christ offers the promise of salvation to all people and thus restores them to their original calling.

A variation to this universalizing pattern of ethnoreligious reasoning is the claim that while the incarnation of the Word in Christ was a recent historical event, the *Logos* predates this particular historical event: in the beginning was the Word, and all human beings were created by God's Word and in God's image (cf. Genesis and the Gospel according to John). There can be no older and more inclusive genealogy than that. Consider in this regard Clement of Alexandria in his *Exhortation to the Greeks*:

> *And do not suppose that my song of salvation is new in the same sense as an implement or a house. For it was 'before the morning star' and, 'in the beginning was the Word, and the Word was with God, and the Word was God'. But error is old, and truth appears to be a new thing. Whether then the Phrygians are really proved to be ancient by the goats in the story; or the Arcadians by the poets who describe them as older than the moon; or, again, the Egyptians by those who dream*

that this land first brought to light both gods and men; still, not one of these nations existed before this world. But we were before the foundation of the world, we who, because we were destined to be in Him, were begotten beforehand by God. We are the rational images formed by God's Word, or Reason, and we date from the beginning on account of our connexion with Him, because 'the Word was in the beginning'. Well, because the Word was from the first, He was and is the divine beginning of all things; but because He lately took a name, the name consecrated of old and worthy of power, the Christ, – I have called Him a New Song. (Exhortation to the Greeks *1, trans. Butterworth, 1919*)

This potential Christian inclusivity goes hand in hand with an effort to fix the boundaries of Christianness. While Christianness might in principle be open to all, one only becomes part of Christian peoplehood through the gates of baptism and faith; and that is a hard border (Buell, 2005, p. 46). Universality, inclusion, and the idea of becoming (one can become Christian by becoming in Christ) does not contradict the idea that this is a bounded people of the saved, a people of the righteous, or a God-loving people (*genos*). Only true *religio* (see below) leads to salvation; other forms of *religio* lead to perdition. This exclusivist understanding of *religio* sets boundaries between Christians and non-Christians, baptized and unbaptized; faithful and unfaithful. Hence, the worship practices of Greeks and Jews are projected as finite and inferior. Clearly, universalization does not exclude inferiorization (whether implicit or explicit) and clearly inclusion and exclusion are each other's flipsides (Ricoeur, 2010, p. 37). The pattern of religionization that is being deployed here is that of encompassment or inclusion.

Text Box 3: Ethnoreligious Reasoning as Religionization and the Making of Jewish Others

Typically, Christian anti-Jewish discourses pit Christians over against Jews as Jews. One specific way Jews are made into Christianity's other is by constructing them as tribal and particularistic people in contrast to the Christians, who are cast as inclusivist people, open to all regardless of their ethnicity. Following a logic of dichotomization, the Jewish people is marked primarily as an ethnic group, the Christian community as a group that transcends such ethnic markers. Other religionized binaries get attached to this dichotomy between Jewish ethnoreligious particularism and Christian inclusive universalism: carnal – spiritual, Law – faith, old – new. Jewish law is for Jews only, salvation in Christ is for all people.

David Horrell points out (Horrell, 2020, p. 68) that the Jew-Christian dichotomy is structural. While it may take on various expressions, and its terms may change over time – 'particular and universal', 'exclusive and inclusive', or 'ethnic and trans-ethnic' – at root the dichotomy prevails. Well into the nineteenth century, this anti-Jewish binary of Jewish ethnic particularity versus Christian spiritual universality would contribute to the distinction between national and world religions, as well as to the racialized opposition between Semitic and Aryan religions.

Such dichotomies not only hide more complex realities, but they also hide from view the similarities in the way Jews and Christians constructed their sense of religious belonging and peoplehood. One thing that is lost from view is how the Christian project of universalization adopts and adapts existing patterns of ethnoreligious reasoning (we are also a people, marked by a long genealogy, kinship, customs, worship traditions). At the same time, the fixedness of Jewish peoplehood is essentialized while the fluidity (all may become Christians) is emphasized (Buell, 2005, p. 95). That Christians assume a fixed boundary when it comes to salvation – only Christians may be saved – is downplayed.

By surfacing how both exclusionary and universalizing strategies can draw on ethnoreligious reasoning, simplistic dichotomies are challenged and the boundaries between Jews (as ethnic) and Christians (as universal) blurred. *Religio*, as understood by some Christian apologists, does not transcend *religio*-ethnic bonds, but reaffirms and alters them in accordance with faith in Christ. This is a universalizing move which conceals its own particularity or perhaps ethnicity – all may be included in a particular Christian interpretation of salvific history.

Crafting Christian *Religio* as the Most Ancient

From a Roman perspective, the more ancient the *religio/traditio* the more prestige it had. The Christian movement was new, and that newness was held against them (De Roover, 2014). Again, apologists would develop a counterargument stating that their *religio* was the most ancient of all. To that end, they projected a sacred religious history according to which Christian *religio* predates the birth of Christ and even predates Abraham. Consider again in this regard Justin Martyr, who said to the men of Greece that Christian *religio* was a restoration of ancient knowledge that had been distorted:

> *[...] the advent of our Saviour Jesus Christ; who, being the Word of God, inseparable from Him in power, having assumed man, who had been made in the image and likeness of God, restored to us the knowledge of the religion of our ancient forefathers, which the men who lived after them abandoned through the bewitching counsel of the envious devil, and turned to the worship of those who were no gods. (Justin Martyr,* Exhortation to the Greeks *38, trans. Falls, 1948)*

The strength of this discourse of restoration is that it balances innovation with continuity. Arguing for the antiquity of *religio*, Justin Martyr also emphasized the universal power of the divine *Logos*, operative throughout human history and sowing seeds among peoples and their traditions [*Logos spermatikos*].

> *[Christ] is the Logos of which every genos of humans partakes. Those who lived in accordance with the Logos are Christians, even though they were called godless, such as, among Greeks, Socrates and Heraclitus and others like them; among the barbarians, Abraham, Ananiah, Azariah, and Mishael, and Elijah and many others [...]. (1 Apol. 46.2, trans. Falls, 1948)*

On the one hand, this line of reasoning, which is also known as *consensus gentium*, affirms that even among those who worshipped many gods, rudiments of Christian *religio* could be found. That gentiles worshipped many gods, proved that they actually felt the 'need of some god, the altar with its victims implied convictions of sin, and the lustrations betokened the conscious want of purity' (Eadie, 1869, p. 321). On the other hand, 'because the Christian *logos* was the original source of all truth, anything true was necessarily Christian' (Chidester, 2000). Thus, novelty was tempered by the antiquity and universality of the *Logos* (Buell, 2005, p. 80).

In his *Apologia*, Tertullian too, despite his often antagonizing and polemical language, speaks about the human soul which is by nature Christian, and to underscore this thought, he projected the notion of *testimonium animae naturaliter Christianae:* the soul of man (his claim to universality) is capable of realizing that there is a God creator. Therefore, true worship comes naturally to the soul, even to those who do not regard Christ as their saviour.

> *Yes! the soul, be it cabined and cribbed by the body, be it confined by evil nurture, be it robbed of its strength by lusts and desires, be it enslaved to false gods, – none the less, when it recovers its senses, as after surfeit, as after sleep, as after some illness, when it recaptures its proper health, the soul names GOD, and for this reason and no other, because, if language be used aright, He is the one true God. 'Great God!' 'Good God!' 'Which may God give!' is the utterance of all men. [...] O the witness of the soul, in its very nature Christian [O testimonium animae naturaliter Christianae]! (Tertullian,* Apol. *XVII.5–6, trans. Glover & Rendall, 1931)*

Tertullian even argued that those who call God by the names of Saturn, Jupiter, Mars or Minerva, actually worship the Christian God. A deep desire for the one true God is showcased in this albeit false worship and testifies to the profound innate knowledge of God, that admittedly only belongs to the realm of natural knowledge as distinguished from revelatory knowledge. All human beings have the potential to know God and God's natural laws and all are predisposed to Christian *religio*. '[T]his account both predicted and required the presence of religion among all human groups. As the Creator had given awareness of his existence to humanity, it appeared to have become *theologically impossible* that people without religion could exist' (De Roover, 2014, p. 8, emphasis by the author). At the same time, this notion reaffirmed the general thrust that there is only one true worship and all others are divergences from it. Finally, it asserted that worship of the true God was the oldest form of worship, even predating the actual incarnation. In this way, apologists sought to refute the argument used against Christians that their *religio* was novel.

3   Christians against the Nations: The Distinction between *Religio Vera* and *Falsa*

When Christian ceremonies and practices were being ridiculed by Romans, who called the Christians superstitious (often without distinguishing them from Jews!) and charged them with promiscuous behaviour, early Christian writers, trying to dismiss the charges levelled against them, turned the tables on the Romans and argued that Christian tradition was in fact *religio vera* while Roman traditions were exemplars of *superstitio* or *religio falsa*. Roman charges against the Christians who were accused of angering the gods were reversed, and became Christian charges against those who angered the Christian God with their idolatrous cults and concomitant promiscuity.

Religio as True Worship of the True God

In the course of this process of reversal [*retorsio*] Christian apologists such as Tertullian redefined the distinction between true and false *religio* as a contrast between the worship of true and false gods: Worship of other gods is false worship, coined as *superstitio* or idolatry. In line with Jewish traditions, idolatry would be rhetorically crafted as the primary identity marker of the otherness of the *ethnici* or gentiles. Following this redefinition, the object of worship now became the distinguishing factor between *religio* and *superstitio*. The result of this Christian redefinition is a binary construct in which there is one 'true' *religio* and various forms of *superstitiones* or one '*vera*' *religio* as distinguished from '*falsae*' *religiones* (false worship practices) – false because they worship false or non-existing gods.

In his *Apology*, Tertullian addresses the Roman accusation raised against the Christians that their *religio* was *superstitio*, and that their contempt for the Roman state cult endangered the *Pax Romana*. Tertullian refutes all charges, including those of cannibalism and promiscuity. According to him, Christians, just because they admit to being Christians, are treated unjustly by the Roman juridical system (*Apol.* I.4). They are treated as outlaws and denied the right to prove their innocence (*Apol.* I–II), a right that is normally extended to anyone who stands accused of crimes. Tertullian goes on to make a special plea for freedom of religion and freedom from persecution, arguing in the following way:

> Let one man worship God, another Jove; let this man raise suppliant hands to heaven, that man to the altar of Fides; let one (if you so suppose) count the clouds as he prays, another the panels of the ceiling; let one dedicate his own soul to his god, another a goat's. Look to it, whether this also may form part of the accusation of irreligion – to do away with freedom of religion, to forbid a man choice of deity, [libertatem religionis et interdicere optionem divinitatis], so that I may not worship whom I would, but am forced to worship whom I would not. No one, not even a man, will wish to receive reluctant worship. (Apol. XXIV.5, trans. Glover & Rendall, 1931)

28 CHAPTER 1 The Creation of Key Religionized Categories

However, while making his plea for religious freedom [*libertas religionis*], he also makes a case for the superiority of the true *religio*, which is based on God's revelation in Christ, calling Roman *religio* irreligion (*Apol.* XXIV.3). According to Tertullian, there are no other gods besides the one true God and for that reason the accusation that Christians offended Roman *religiones* was simply nonsensical. Of course, he rhetorically charges, Christians did not pay respect to the Roman gods, why would they honour gods that simply do not exist (*Apol.* X.2)? It follows that 'we [Christians] cannot be thought to injure what we have proved non-existent, the charge of injury is mere madness' (*Apol.* XVII.1). It is Roman worship which revolves around 'profane idols' and 'the deification of human names' (*Apol.* XVII.2). In his words, speaking about Roman *religio*:

> *If they definitely are not gods, then definitely it is not a religion; if it is not a religion because they definitely are not gods, then we are definitely not guilty of injuring religion* [Si enim non sunt dei pro certo, nec religio pro certo est: si religio non est, quia nec dei pro certo, nec nos pro certo rei sumus laesae religionis]. (Apol. *XIV.1, trans. Glover & Rendall, 1931*)

If we follow this line of reasoning, it was not Christians but rather Romans who were guilty of an offence against the true religion of the true God [*veram religionem veri Dei*] (*Apol.* XIV.1).

In the course of Tertullian's argument, we notice a significant shift from emphasizing how one worships to who one worships (the object of worship is the true God); the gentiles [*ethnici*], so he claimed, worshipped nothing but non-existing gods. This is the greatest offence against God: *Atquin summa offensa penes ilium idololatria* (*De spectaculis* II.90). In essence, gentile *religio* is misdirected and therefore idolatrous, and idolatry is ridiculous, stupid, foolish, and irrational. Here Christian charges against *superstitio* intersect with Jewish charges against idolatry. What is more, Tertullian, building on Jewish traditions, linked idolatry to sexual immorality, fornication, and adultery (see *On Idol.* 1). Those who are slaves to idolatry are also slaves to the flesh and to lust. In contrast, Christian *religio* indexed self-control and purity. Christians, so Tertullian claims, do not worship idols; they do not participate in the cult of the emperor and they refuse to sacrifice to the gods or eat from the food offered to idols.

Tertullian not only redefines the boundary between true and false worship in terms of the object of worship, but he also broadens the scope of false *religio* in terms of idolatry. The problem of idolatry is not simply that of idol worship; the problem is that idolatry is all-pervasive. The lure of false gods is everywhere, not just in the temples where the statues are in plain sight, but in everyday Roman life. Remember that Christians lived in a world of many gods. Tertullian regards any sin against God to be a form of idolatry, and interaction with the idolatrous majority implies great risks. Consider in this regard also *De spectaculis*, his work on the games:

> *The whole world is filled with Satan and his angels. Yet not because we are in the world, do we fall from God; but only if in some way we meddle with the sins of the world. Thus if, as a sacrificer and worshipper, I enter the Capitol or the temple of Serapis, I shall fall from God – just as I should if a spectator in circus or theatre. Places do not of themselves defile us, but the things done in the places, by which even the places themselves (as we have argued) are defiled. We are defiled by the defiled* [Loca nos non contaminant per se, sed quae in locis fiunt, a quibus et ipsa loca contaminari [...] de contaminantis contaminantur]. (De spect. *8.94, trans. Glover & Rendall, 1931*)

And further

> *The streets, the market, the baths, the taverns, even our houses are none of them altogether clear of idols. The whole world is filled with Satan and his angels and the places where they are worshiped are sources of defilement.* (De spect. *8.94, trans. Glover & Rendall, 1931*)

Tertullian, starting from the idea that idolatry is difficult to contain and all-pervasive, urges Christians to be careful as they participate in social activities and interact with *ethnici*/gentiles. Boundaries should be drawn between 'us' and 'them', not just in worship but also in social life. In his *Idolatry*, Tertullian makes this even more concrete and formulates clear admonishments concerning what Christians may and may not do and to what extent they may and may not participate in Roman life: no astrology, no participation in the spectacles, no artisan skills for the purpose of manufacturing idols, no pagan festivals, no training of the gladiators, no participation in ceremonies in which respect was given to an idol. Even money lending, because it involved an oath, was forbidden. These are all un-Christian and Christians should do not do such things (Text Box 4). Boundary making is not just about what one believes but also – or even first and foremost – about how one comports oneself (Stroumsa, 1998, pp. 177–178).

Text Box 4: Religionized Boundary Making: What Christians Should Do and What They Did

Tertullian, in his effort to create a sense of Christianness, projects a world in which there are clear boundaries between Christians and *ethnici*/gentiles. While Christians, so he claimed, were good citizens, their participation in daily Roman life ought to be restricted. Especially the contrast between true worship of the true God and idolatry is invoked to separate Christians from non-Christian gentiles and to create, at least to a certain extent, discrete and bounded social worlds.

Tertullian's writings also make clear, however, that not all Christians would have agreed with his broad definition of idolatry and many of the Christians he addressed did not feel compelled to follow his prescriptions. Tertullian is rhetorically making a religionized contrast, which is not matched in real life. Indeed, '[w]hen he evokes everyday situations he consistently decontextualizes them in order to force on them his own agenda about what Christianness should entail. However, the numerous objections he feels compelled to refute show that his point of view was not shared, or at least not shared by all Christians' (Rebillard, 2012, p. 31). While he might claim that it is un-Christian to go to the games, Christians did actually attend and enjoy them.

It is important, furthermore, to realize that Tertullian is speaking to Christians *as gentiles who live among gentiles*. These are people who until recently belonged to the majority culture and participated in what Tertullian is now labelling in the strongest of words, idolatrous. These are people who for much of their lives considered Roman *religio* and its gods to be the norm, their minds and bodies attuned to its practices. These people 'became' Christian and really had to unlearn some practices and acquire a new identity. Their new identity did not come naturally, it had to be built, through participation in Christian life and also by means of polemics, which casts the strongest possible contrast between Christianness and idolatry (Fredriksen & Irshai, 2015).

Tertullian seems to have realized that Christians with a gentile background might import the problem of idolatry into the Christian way of life. This is not the case, of course, for Christ-following Jews. He wants to keep this problem outside the Christian community, realizing it is becoming a problem within.

Tertullian, defending Christians in a context of contestation and persecution, argues that the rejection of idolatry as false worship of false gods does not impede their active participation in Roman society, and therefore Romans ought not to discriminate against Christians. Idolatry is a hard border, but, beyond the scope of idolatry, Christians can still be active citizens. They are really not that different at all.

> [W]e are human beings and live alongside of you – men with the same ways, the same dress and furniture, the same necessities, if we are to live [...]. We remember that we owe gratitude to God, the Lord, the Creator. We reject no fruit of His labours. We are of course temperate – not to use His gifts to excess or amiss. So, not without

30   CHAPTER 1   The Creation of Key Religionized Categories

your forum not without your meat-market, not without your baths, shops, factories, your inns and market-days, and the rest of the life of buying and selling, we live with you – in this world. We sail ships, we as well as you, and along with you; we go to the wars, to the country, to market with you. Our arts and yours work together; our labour is openly at your service. Even if I do not attend your rituals, well, I am a man on that day as much as any other. [...] Nor do I recline to eat in public at the Liberalia, which is the habit of the beast-fighters taking their last meal; but wherever I dine, it is on your supplies. (Apol. XLII.1–5)

Text Box 5: Imaginary Patterns of Religionization and the Messiness of Daily Life

Religionization is the process of selfing and othering predicated on religious difference. Typically binaries are made based on imaginary constructs: true and good religion are contrasted to false and bad religion, here called superstition. The problem of superstition is now projected onto non-Christian gentiles. Their way of worshipping the gods is false religion. There is but one true way of worshipping and that is the worship of the one true God.

Vera religio	*Superstitio/falsa religio*
Christian	Non-Christian
Christians	*Ethnici*
The object of worship: one true God	The object of worship: many false gods
Genuine worship	Idolatry
Purifying	Contaminating

Patterns of religionization produce imaginary constructs which do not describe or match lived experience and the complexities of daily lives. At the time, there was not a 'standard' or 'norm' amongst Christians with regard to the worship of the gods. Some Christians took a firm stance and refrained from any contact with the gods. What they labelled as idol worship was a no-go. Some had a limited definition of idol worship (*idolatreia*), but others were concerned about the contagious effect of any contact with the gods. Remember that the gods were everywhere. There were also Christians who did not see a conflict between their Christian faith and their ancestral traditions and this would remain the case for a long time to come. Thus Fredriksen and Irshai, 'As late as the early fourth century, a council of western bishops felt compelled to condemn baptized Christians who served as priests in the cult of the pagan emperor (Elvira, c. 1); as late as the fifth century, some Christians worshiped the emperor's statue as if it were a god's' (Fredriksen & Irshai, 2015, p. 120). Apologists, like Tertullian, tended to condemn this reality in an effort to create a sense of Christianness. Often we learn about the messiness of daily life and the lack of boundaries precisely by reading these polemical texts and what they claimed a true Christian does and does not do. The fact that such polemics were 'needed' teaches us that the refuted practices were still part of daily life and that few Christians met the projected standard (Rebillard, 2012).

---

4   Crafting the Jew as Un-Christian

Early Christian apologists not only had to craft a sense of Christianness within the framework of Roman *religio*, but they also had to position themselves vis-à-vis the Jewish people and their traditions and this in a highly hybrid context where the boundaries between different religious groups were far from clear. Christians were themselves still arguing about the right way of leading a Christian life. In this process of identity making (selfing), the figure of the Jew would come to function as the anti-Christian (othering). Interestingly, and we already saw traces of this when discussing Christian ethnoreligious reasoning, the contrast between 'the Jew' and 'the Christian', the 'old' and 'new' people of God could also be used when polemicizing against the gentiles and the heretics. Indeed, the rhetorical figure of the Jew is multifunctional. In addition, Jews could also be imagined as heretics; insiders that had gone astray or even as idolaters, 'which is to say the ultimate outsiders' (Freidenreich, 2011, p. 112). This underscores the volatility of these religionized categories and concomitant taxonomies.

As an imaginary construct, the Jew as 'Jew' does not do justice to the lived social reality of Jews, Christ-following Jews, and Christian gentiles. When crafting the contrast between Jew and Christian, old and new people of God, apologists had little interest or concerns about real Jews; their purpose was to make the claim that Christians, rather than Jews, were the true heirs of God's blessings. This does not mean Christians and Jews did not socially interact or maintain friendly relations on a daily basis. The social logic of many apologetical texts suggests that in reality the opposite was true (Schwartz, 2001). Nevertheless, we should bear in mind that

> *Even if, in his inception, in his function, and in his veritable power in the Christian mind-set, the hermeneutical Jew of late antique or medieval times had relatively little to do with the Jewish civilization of his day, his career certainly influenced the Christian treatment of the Jewish minority, the sole consistently tolerated religious minority, of medieval Christendom. (Cohen, 1999, p. 5)*

Jews, Christ-following Jews, and Christians from Gentiles

The first followers of Jesus were Greek-speaking Hellenized Jews and Aramaic-speaking Jews from Judea and other neighbouring provinces, and they shared both the scriptures as well as the Jewish laws regarding food restrictions, festivals, and rituals (Freidenreich, 2011, p. 87). These laws placed boundaries between Jews and gentiles and set Jews aside as a minority in the Roman world. They were foreigners with strange worship practices, often ridiculed, but also respected because their traditions were ancient and marked Jewish peoplehood. Jews, themselves, distinguished between 'holy Jews and mundane gentiles' and their law helped them navigate a gentile world, while maintaining their sense of being a covenanted people of God (Freidenreich, 2011, p. 87).

While the Jesus movement started as a strictly Jewish movement, which upheld Jewish beliefs and practices, many Jews, living under the yoke of the Roman Empire, rejected the claim that Jesus fulfilled the biblical messianic prophecy. Since he did not free them from oppression, Jesus could not be the Messiah. The fact that Christians, who 'claimed to revere as Scripture the same texts as did the Jews' and 'claimed to be the heirs of God's promises through the prophets of the biblical tradition' were contradicted by many Jews, posed a profound challenge (Lieu, 2002, p. 95). Not only did apologists now have to craft a sense of Christianness in a sometimes hostile Roman setting, but they also had to struggle for legitimacy against this Jewish rejection. This rejection was all the more challenging because Jews, ticking the boxes of both ethnicity and antiquity, constituted an ethnoreligious community which was at least recognized as such in the Roman world. While Christian apologists worked hard to claim a similar status and deployed various rhetorical strategies to that end, their own traditions were not recognized as legitimate. Against this background, apologists felt compelled to construct a sense of Christianness while both dealing with this Jewish rejection and making their case vis-à-vis the Roman world. Consequently, the Christian apology against the Jews is never only about the Jews.

There is, however, more. Quite early on in the Jesus movement, there were Christ-following Jews who began to reconsider the relationship between Jews and gentiles. Some believed that gentile Christians, like the so-called God fearers in Jewish communities, while not having to uphold all the Jewish laws, would also not be able to fully participate in the Christian life. Others were convinced that one did not have to be Jewish to obtain full membership or full participation in the community of Christians (cf. the conflict between James, Peter, and Paul). Some sought to maintain a distinction, but others sought to ignore it, stating that in the Christian community there would be 'neither Greek nor Jew' (Rom 10:12), that all would be saved in Christ's name, and that the Jewish law and its prevailing food restrictions, ritual obligations, and festivals had to be reconsidered. As the Jesus movement developed, it also diversified, and evolved into 'Jewish Christianities and Judaizing Gentile Christianities but also purely Gentile forms of Christianity' (Fredriksen & Irshai, 2006, p. 978). This diversification raised multiple questions, theological but also more practical, about what it entailed to be a Christian, and more particularly what this would mean as regards the prevalence of the law. Boundaries were projected and contested.[1]

Adversus Iudaeos

Christians were in disagreement about the 'right way' to be Christian and this disagreement provoked discussions about (i) how to read Scripture and its prophecies; (ii) the meaning and status of the Jewish law and (iii) the relation between Christians, who claimed to be heirs of God's promises, and the Jews who rejected Jesus (Lieu, 2002, p. 95). As apologists sought to defend their respective position, they made their case for what they believed was religiously normative by projecting 'the Jew' as falling outside this norm. 'Christianness' was constructed over against 'Jewishness'. This specific form of religionization gave way to a new genre known as the *adversus Iudaeos* tradition, which produced what Jeremy Cohen has called the 'hermeneutical Jew', an imagined Jew based on Christian-biblical and theological categories rather than on knowledge drawn from personal interaction (Cohen, 1999, p. 3). This 'figure [is] imagined for the purpose of serving as a foil for the construction of Christian identity' (Freidenreich, 2011, p. 114). Once again we are dealing with 'redescription' rather than description.

In crafting this hermeneutical Jew, apologists made use of the tradition of Roman ethnoreligious othering. They also drew on the many prophetic admonishments against Israel, casting the Jewish people as idolatrous and hence unfaithful as well as sinful. Finally, apologists could appeal to some of Jesus' sayings about the Pharisees, scribes, priests, and Sadducees and they could turn to the Pauline corpus, especially those passages in which Paul criticizes his 'apostolic competitors' (see e.g. Romans 11). As Fredriksen has it, 'these Hellenistic Jewish texts, with all their intra-Jewish arguments, were a gold mine for later Christian rhetoric *contra Iudaeos*' (Fredriksen, 2014, p. 24). From them, an image was crafted of a people – the Jewish people – who in principle owned all the resources needed to recognize and accept God's final revelation in Christ but who dismissed the evidence and stubbornly continued to follow the wrong path. This attitude sealed the Jews' downfall as the once beloved, but now rejected, people of God. All the tribulations that befell them, whether the diasporic dispersion, the destruction of the temple or their expulsion from Jerusalem, were now cast as divine punishments for the rejection of Jesus, and to make matters worse, all of this had already been prophesized in their own scriptures.

As a hermeneutical abstraction, the imagined Jew 'contained great power, serving by means of absolute contrast to focus and define the desiderata of orthodox identity' (Fredriksen & Irshai, 2006, p. 984). Following the logic of dichotomization, Christianness was placed over against Jewishness, and seemingly fixed boundaries between identity and alterity were projected. Those Christians who did not accept the projected boundaries were accused of Judaizing (Text Box 6). To call someone a Judaizer, was to accuse that person of engaging in inappropriate practices, thereby at once infecting the entire community. Judaizing was cast as a fall – a lapsing into old habits, a shift from purity into impurity, from spirituality into carnality, from chastity into promiscuity (Drake, 2013, p. 2).

> **Text Box 6: Blurring and Constructing Boundaries: Judaizing Christians?**
>
> For a long time, there were Christians who continued to frequent both church and synagogue and observe festivals from both traditions. In the Levant, minority groups of Christ-following Jews would persist even after the fifth century (Stroumsa, 2015). While most would not have regarded that as contrary to their Christian creed and would perhaps not have considered their identity as 'mixed or hybrid' (Fonrobert, 2001, p. 555), to those Christian apologists charged with forging a sense of true Christian worship and accompanying lifestyle, the drawing of religionized boundaries and the formulation of clear-cut identities was key. The *adversus Iudaeos* literature projected a religious norm and defined 'Judaism in such a way that it falls outside of those norms' (Joslyn-Siemiatkoski, 2022, p. 6). Christian Jews who did not accept and respect these projected boundaries were charged with Judaization.

Anti-Jewish Typologies

The *adversus Iudaeos* tradition is permeated by the idea that Christ functions as the hermeneutical key for understanding the Hebrew scriptures. Jesus is the long-awaited Messiah foretold by the Hebrew scriptures. From this perspective, Christ fulfils the promises of Jewish tradition. To understand this, however, the Scripture should not be read literally but figuratively or *kata pneuma*. One example of such a reading is the hermeneutics of typology, whereby events, figures, or even statements from the Hebrew scriptures prefigure or foreshadow events, figures, and statements from the New Testament.

> *At its most basic level figures set up a reciprocal relationship between two moments in scripture: the first which anticipates and points to the second, and the second which explains the significance of the first. Although this is a theological method of understanding biblical narratives, it operates with historical time and describes material consequences; both figure and fulfillment are understood as actual historical persons and occurrences. A figural interpretation not only construes an incident in the Hebrew Bible as foreshadowing an incident in Christian Scripture, but could also understand the first event as pointing to a future moment beyond the biblical text. (Kaplan, 2019, p. 24)*

Typological reading was not in fact a Christian invention, but was built on the tradition of Midrash; the Rabbis also interpreted 'the Bible figuratively in order to read into it various theological and homiletical ideas made necessary by the contemporary experiences of the Jewish society caught in the whirlpool of great historic changes' (Bokser, 1973, p. 99). Adopting Midrashic hermeneutics, apologists adapted it to their own purpose as a weapon against the Jews (Bokser, 1973, p. 99). Within a Christian theological framework, typological reading contributed to the construction of a fulfilment logic. The Hebrew scriptures, their events and figures, would only be meaningful in light of the Christ event. If the first foreshadows, the latter fulfils and illuminates the deeper meaning and significance of the first. Thus, the Hebrew Bible was transformed into a book of Christian revelation. Irenaeus of Lyon (140–220) states:

> *If anyone, therefore, reads the Scriptures with attention, he will find in them an account of Christ, and a foreshadowing of the new calling. (Adv. Haer. IV.26, trans. Schaff, 1978)*

To drive this point home, Christian apologists depicted the Jews as overly attached to the letter of the text, and this literalist reading supposedly blinded them to the deeper, more spiritual meaning of their texts. Furthermore, Jewish literalist hermeneutics was seen as

34 CHAPTER 1 The Creation of Key Religionized Categories

a direct outcome of their being driven or controlled by fleshly desires. Jews did not read according to the spirit, but rather 'understand everything in a carnal way' [*kata sarka*] (Justin Martyr, *Dial.* 14.2). Their carnal hermeneutics translated into a life of sin and illicit sexual relations and vice versa (*Dial.* 14.2). Again we see how religionization intersects with sexualization. To make matters worse, they even use their literalist hermeneutics to legitimize their vicious life of fornication and idolatry (Drake, 2013, p. 33). Of course, the prophetic charges against Israel's infidelity functioned as a treasury box for Christian apologists like Justin Martyr.

Jewish literal reading of scriptures supposedly also matches their literal understanding of the law and they fail to understand the deeply figurative meaning of their ritual traditions, namely that circumcision prefigures baptism, just as Passover and the sacrifice of the Lamb prefigure Easter and Christ's crucifixion (Justin Martyr, *Dial.* 40), and the meal offerings anticipate the Eucharist (*Dial.* 41). Consequently, this once beloved people of God was now unable to fully experience God's faithfulness and presence. Blind to the true meaning of their own scriptures, they are blind to Gods' plan of salvation. Christians, by contrast, master allegorical readings of Scripture and metaphorical interpretations of ritual.

The reason why the Jews continue to resist the deeper spiritual meaning of the Hebrew scriptures against all evidence is because, according to Justin Martyr, they are a 'stupidly stubborn people' (*Dial.* 123), their hearts are hardened (*Dial.* 18), they are 'idolatrous' and 'sinful' (*Dial.* 18), and ungrateful towards God (*Dial.* 27). For that reason God gave the Jews the law in the first place: to keep them from idol worship and from turning away from God. They are, however, a weak people, and even under the law they did not obey God and did not 'hesitate to sacrifice their children to demons' (*Dial.* 19). Justin Martyr continues:

We, too, would observe your circumcision of the flesh, your sabbath days, and, in a word, all your festivals, if we were not aware of the reason why they were imposed upon you, namely, because of your sins and your hardness of heart (Dial. *18, trans. Falls, 1948).*

The stubbornness lamented by the prophets continues today as the Jews hold on to a law that without faith in Christ has lost all meaning. Christians, thanks to their spiritual hermeneutics, avoid all problems of carnality and live a virtuous spiritual life.

Text Box 7: One Example of Typological Reading in a Supersessionist Frame: Jacob and Esau

Jacob is the son of Isaac and Rebecca and the twin brother of Esau. Genesis recounts how the two brothers struggled with one another even before they were born. Rebecca therefore seeks God's counsel, and He tells her: 'Two nations are in your womb, and two peoples born of you shall be divided; the one shall be stronger than the other, the elder shall serve the younger' (Gen 25:23). This prophecy follows the recurrent pattern in the Hebrew scriptures, according to which the younger son receives the blessing from the father (Cain and Abel, Isaac and Ishmael, Judah and Reuben, etc.). Jacob – incited by his mother Rebecca – swindles Esau out of his rights as firstborn by using a bowl of lentils or, as traditionally translated, red pottage (Gen 25:34). He later deceives his father and receives the blessing Isaac had reserved for Esau. Upon discovering how Jacob has deceived him and his father, Esau becomes filled with great hatred for his brother and swears he will kill him.

This story plays a key role in the theological interpretation of the relation between Jews and Christians. Early on in Christian history, building on Paul's Letter to the Romans, the church fathers placed this story in an anti-Jewish typological supersessionist framework, according to which the church usurps the place of Israel in God's salvific plan. Crucial to the church fathers' interpretation is the identification of Esau (the elder brother) with Israel and Jacob (the younger brother) with the church.

Irenaeus of Lyon ponders the significance of Jacob's name. The Hebrew text contains a wordplay on the name *ya'aqov*, 'Jacob' and the verb *'aqav*, 'to take a hold of and supplant'. Placed in a Christian supersessionist framework, Jacob, the supplanter, foreshadows the coming of Christ who would supplant or supersede Esau, the symbol of the Old People of God: 'If anyone, again, will look into Jacob's actions, he shall find them not destitute of meaning, but full of import with regard to the dispensations. Thus, in the first place, at his birth, since he laid hold on his brother's heel, he was called Jacob, that is, the supplanter – one who holds, but is not held; binding the feet, but not being bound; striving and conquering; grasping in his hand his adversary's heel, that is, victory. For this end was the Lord born, the type of whose birth he set forth beforehand, of whom also John says in the Apocalypse: "He went forth conquering, that He should conquer"' (*Adv. Haer.* IV.21, trans. Schaff, 1978).

Irenaeus' typological reading of this story legitimizes the ecclesiological claim according to which the church, as the new people of God, has superseded Israel, the old people of God. Thus, Esau became the archetype of the Jew, the elder brother who lost his birthright to his younger brother; and Jacob became the prototype of the church, the younger brother, the community of the followers of Christ. The latter are the new people of God; they enjoy God's favour; the younger brother is beloved; the elder brother is rejected.

Some early Christian thinkers even traced the charge of deicide – the most vehement charge ever brought against the Jews (cf. Melito of Sardis) – to this story, stating 'And Esau hated Jacob because of the blessing wherewith his father blessed him. And Esau said in his heart, "The days of mourning for my father are at hand. Then will I slay my brother Jacob"'. Esau's wrath towards Jacob is said to prefigure the Jews' hatred for Jesus and their desire to kill him.

The Supersessionist Logic

Christian apologists developed a sense of Christianness in terms of the new people of God who had inherited God's promises. This translated into fulfilment theologies, which easily slipped into replacement or supersessionist theologies, entailing an abrogation of the first covenant between God and Israel (Moyaert & Pollefeyt, 2010). According to this supersessionist logic, God's plans for the salvation of humanity once had an important part for Israel to play, but this role has now expired because God decided that physical, carnal Israel was to be replaced by the spiritual church. According to Justin Martyr, in his *Dialogue with the Jew Trypho*:

> The law promulgated at Horeb is already obsolete, and was intended for you Jews only, whereas the law of which I speak is simply for all men. Now, a later law in opposition to an older law abrogates the older; so, too, does a later covenant void an earlier one. An everlasting and final law, Christ Himself, and a trustworthy covenant has been given to us, after which there shall be no law, or commandment, or precept. (Dial. *11, trans. Falls, 1948*)

All the blessings and promises that God had once extended to Israel were transferred to the church.

Consider in this regard the work of Melito, Bishop of Sardis (d. ca. 180), near Smyrna. In his *Peri Pascha*, 'a paschal homily, that was [probably] read at Quartodeciman midnight vigils' (Koltun-Fromm, 2009, p. 562), Melito argues that the Jewish people has missed God's

36 CHAPTER 1 The Creation of Key Religionized Categories

visitation and failed to recognize Christ. For that reason, Israel was no longer God's beloved and chosen people. As Israel rejected Christ, so God rejected Israel. Thus, Melito writes:

> *You forsook the Lord, you were not found by him; you did not accept the Lord, you were not pitied by him; you dashed down the Lord, you were dashed to the ground and you lie dead. (On Pascha 99, ed. and trans. Hall, 1979)*

And elsewhere,

> *The people was precious before the church arose and the law was marvellous before the Gospel was illuminated. But when the church arose and the Gospel came to the fore the model was made void giving its power to the truth and the law was fulfilled giving its power to the Gospel [...]. So too the law was fulfilled when the Gospel was illuminated and the people made void when the church arose. (On Pascha 42–43, ed. and trans. Hall, 1979)*

In the end, 'the success of proselytizing efforts among gentiles – the "gentile mission" – determined the fate of the church, as gentiles quickly came to outnumber Jews within the Christ-believing community' (Freidenreich, 2011, p. 87). Against this background, Christians formulate their self-understanding by distancing themselves from the Mosaic law, abandoning Jewish practices such as circumcision, and positing a clear distinction between the elevated spiritual church of belief and the mundane, carnal Israel of ritual observance. Christian rituals were regarded as uplifting and spiritual, Jewish rituals as bloody, tribal, and carnal. One way this played out was through a reinterpretation of the food laws:

> *Just as the Rabbinic Sages define adherence to Biblical dietary laws as emblematic of Jewish identity and employ foreign food restrictions as a means of emphasizing the centrality of these laws, Christian authorities view the anathematization of such laws as emblematic of Christian identity and express this rejection through restrictions on Jewish food. These restrictions remind new and old Christians alike that their identity depends upon the rejection not only of Jewish dietary practices but also of social intercourse with Jews and participation in Jewish festivals. (Freidenreich, 2011, p. 118)*

Belonging to the Christian people – the new spiritual people of God – would entail not upholding Jewish ritual laws, thereby at the same time underscoring the spiritual redundancy of these rituals. Not to participate in Jewish ritual becomes thereby a Christian identity marker. One could call this religious identification through ritual abstention (Colijn, 2019). Over time, commensality between Christ-followers and Jews would even become prohibited.

The Deicide Charge

Though Jesus died on the cross under Pilate (as the creed explicitly states), the gospels (Matthew and Luke more than the earlier gospel of Mark) shift part of the blame for Christ's death from the Roman authorities onto the Jewish authorities. This is especially true of Matt 27:24–27, which has Pilate stating his innocence and the people answering: 'His blood be on us and on our children'. This version of events would go on to have a devastating role and would finally give way to the terrible charge of deicide: that the Jews collectively had killed Christ, Son of God, and for that mortal sin God had turned away from his beloved people. The deicide charge – which names and classifies Jews as Christ-killers and murderers of God – would play a key part in the construction of an idealized bounded Christian self-understanding as the beloved and blessed people of God. One of the first to formulate this deicide charge, holding the Jews responsible for Christ's death, was the just mentioned Melito of Sardis.

You put these things to one side, you hurried to the slaughter of the Lord. You prepared for him sharp nails and false witnesses, and ropes and whips, and vinegar and gall, and a sword and torture as against a murderous thief. You brought forth a flogging for his body, and thorns for his head; and you bound his goodly hands, which formed you from the earth. And you fed with gall his goodly mouth which fed you with life. And you killed your Lord at the great feast. (On Pascha 79, ed. and trans. Hall, 1979)

And while you were rejoicing he was starving. You were drinking wine and eating bread; he had vinegar and gall. Your face was bright whereas his was cast down. You were triumphant while he was afflicted. You were making music while he was being judged. You were proposing toasts; he was being nailed in place. You were dancing, he was buried. You were reclining on a cushioned couch, he in grave and coffin. (On Pascha 80, ed. and trans. Hall, 1979)

And he continues:

O lawless Israel, what is this new injustice you have done, casting strange sufferings on your Lord? Your master who formed you, who made you, who honored you, who called you Israel. (On Pascha 81, ed. and trans. Hall, 1979)

He who hung the earth is hanging. He who fixed the heavens in place has been fixed in place. He who laid the foundations of the universe has been laid on a tree. The master has been profaned. God has been murdered. The King of Israel has been destroyed by an Israelite right hand. (On Pascha 96, ed. and trans. Hall, 1979)

This collective guilt calls for a just response. Thus Melito writes,

You disowned the Lord, and so are not owned by him. You did not receive the Lord, so you were not pitied by him. You smashed the Lord to the ground, you were razed to the ground. And you lie dead, while he rose from the dead, and is raised to the heights of heaven. (On Pascha 99, ed. and trans. Hall, 1979)

The fact that the Romans destroyed the Second temple, which formed the heart of Jewish cultic life, was regarded by Christian communities as a divine sign, as was the subsequent Jewish diaspora. To the mind of many Christ-following Jews, both the destruction of the temple and the Jewish diaspora confirmed their belief that they were the new people of God, in contrast to the Jews who were to live scattered over the earth. This is one of the most violent expressions of selfing and othering. Both guilt and punishment are transferred intergenerationally. To belong to this people is to be guilty and to carry the burden of divine wrath. We are dealing with a form of ethnoreligious reasoning, which projects an anti-Jewish and a Christian genealogy. He who stems from the Jewish line is cursed, he who becomes Christian finds God's blessing. The one people carries the mark of Cain, as Augustine would later call it, the other the mark of baptism.

Text Box 8: Supersessionist Patterns of Religionization between Replacement and Fulfilment

The relation between the Jewish people – Israel – and the Christian people – the church – in terms of religionization is complex. It is clear that anti-Jewish polemics are permeated by a logic of dichotomization, in which the Jew is projected as the negative image of the Christian. Stereotypical thinking here functions by means of types and antitypes. At the same time, it is also clear that the Jews, and especially God's revelation handed to them in their scriptures, is a key building block of Christianness: Christians claim to fulfil and realize the promises given to Israel. Thus anti-Jewish rhetoric tends to vacillate between exclusion and inclusion, replacement and fulfilment, dichotomization and encompassment. To this day, it remains challenging to configure a unique sense of Christianness without lapsing into anti-Jewish patterns of thinking.

Jewish	Christian
Israel	Church
Tribal	Universal
Exclusivist	Inclusivist
Literalist reading	Allegorical reading
Wilful ignorance (stubbornness)	Knowledge
Law	Christ fulfils and supersedes the law
Carnal	Spiritual
Dietary laws excluding gentiles	Commensality with gentile Christians
Jews	No more Greek or Jew
Circumcision	Baptism

Later, we will have to return to the problematic relation between Christians and Jews. For now, suffice it to say that the formation of Christian *religio* as *vera religio* very quickly became entangled with the mislabelling and misrecognition of Jews. Significantly, the hermeneutical Jew only exists in the Christian imagination and does not in any way reflect Jewish self-understanding. In the Christian imagination, Jewish tradition after the destruction of the temple and the expulsion of the Jews from the Roman province of Judea was an anachronism. There was no recognition for the way Rabbinic Judaism, in the course of the next five centuries, continued to develop (shift from temple to synagogue, priest to rabbi, sacrifice to study and prayer) and not unlike Christian tradition undertook a long process of redaction and codification of the oral law (Mishna, Talmud) and Midrash.

While the Jew as anti-Christian is an imaginary construct, this also holds true for projected Christian self-understanding as opposed to Jewish tradition. Indeed, the religionized construction of a clear boundary between Jews and Christians does not match the lived reality. During the first four or five centuries CE, and contrary to this binary pattern of religionization, boundaries between Christian and Jewish communities at grassroots level remained porous. Forging a Christian identity which opposed the Jewish tradition conceals this, and does not reflect the messy reality of that time.

5   Making the Figure of the Heretic

Like the Jew and the idolater, the heretic is the product of religionization; the heretic too is projected as falling outside the realm of *vera religio*, the Christian realm. Typically, heretics are accused of falsely claiming the name 'Christian' for their beliefs and practices. Pretending to be Christian, they poison the one Christian truth with their false and innovative teachings. They are both insiders and outsiders and this makes them particularly dangerous. Consider in this regard Origen (185–253):

I am of the opinion that it is indeed evil for one to err in his manner of life, but far worse to go astray in doctrines and not think in accordance with the most true rule of the scriptures. Since we are to be punished (for indulging) in moral sins, how much more when we sin because of false doctrines? For if a life of good morals sufficed men for salvation, why is it that many philosophers among the gentiles who live continently, and many among the heretics, can by no means be saved, as if the falseness of their doctrine obscured and sullied their manner of life? (Origen, quoted in Williams, 2009, p. xxxii)

The idea that heresy is a deviation from the one orthodox truth is, however, imaginary. The history of Christianity was never one of singularity and uniformity; rather it is a history of diversity, discord, and disunity (Berzon, 2016, p. 14). From the very beginning, there were many communities who claimed to be Christian and there were often disputes about the proper way of leading a Christian life in an otherwise non-Christian world. These communities did not yet have a clearly delineated sense of Christianness, for they were all in the process of identity formation. During the second century this process of selfing would translate into claims of orthodoxy, while those upholding different ideas were cast as heretical. This claimed Christian orthodoxy set the norm over against which deviation is produced, and deviation helps formulate a sense of identity. Irenaeus of Lyon, for example, enlists all the known heresies to defend and sharpen the idea of Christian orthodoxy. He catalogues them by founder, false teachings, corrupt practices and then defines Christian orthodoxy over against these multiple heresies. This is a work of creative and normative theological craftmanship rather than of mere description. Thus, heresy is not a deviation from a previously established, stable, orthodox norm (Berzon, 2016, p. 13); orthodoxy assumes, needs, and feeds on a real (or imagined) heterodox other and vice versa.

The Notion of Heresy

Heresy (*hairésis*) did not always have such a negative connotation. The original Greek word means 'choice', and is used to refer to different schools of thought. These could be either medical or philosophical schools of thought (e.g. the term is applied to Stoics and Pythagoreans) and Flavius Josephus (37–100 CE) applies it to various Jewish groups, like the Pharisees, the Sadducees, the Essenes, and the Zealots (*Ant.* 13.5.9; 18.1.2; *War* 2.8.14). Josephus, while preferring Essenes and Pharisees, does not speak in a derogatory way about these different groups. In Acts, the term is used to refer to the Sadducees, Pharisees, and Christians (see Acts 5:17, 24:5, 24:14, 26:5, 28:22). This word was, however, picked up by second-century Christian apologists to mean deviating opinions which threatened the unity of the Christian community and the continuation of tradition. In Jewish circles, too, heresy would receive a more negative connotation, and Jewish sages called Christians heretics.

The notion 'orthodoxy' is of an even later date. As a specific term it was probably used for the first time in the fourth century in the work by Methodius of Olympus (d. 311/12) *De resurrectione*. Thomas Jürgasch, however, points out that the fixation on what is the 'right teaching and the right belief' rather than the 'right praxis' may already be found in the early Christian communities. According to him,

The question of the correct or 'sound' [hygiaínousa] 'doctrine' [didaché/didaskalía] (cf. Tit 2,1) and its counterpart, 'heresies' [hairéseis] or heterodoxy, was already an important topic as well as a terminological issue in the early church very early on [...]. Already in Paul, we find the admonition to keep away from those who 'against this doctrine' [parà tēn didachēn] cause 'dissent' or 'dispute' [dichostasíai] and 'annoyances/traps', [skándala] (cf. Rom 16,17) which – as it says elsewhere – lead to 'divisions' [schísmata] and 'factions [hairéseis] (cf. 1 Cor 11,17–19; Gal 5,19–21). Especially this warning against the 'heretical man' [ánthropos hairetikós] (cf. Tit 2,1; 3,9–11) standing in contradiction to the right doctrine will subsequently develop into a central and frequently received motif of early Christian anti-heretical literature (cf. also 2 Pet 2,1–3; IgnEph 6,2). (Jürgasch, 2021, pp. 168–169, my translation)

40 CHAPTER 1 The Creation of Key Religionized Categories

Early on in its existence the community of the Christian faithful was imagined as a body, and more particularly as the earthly body of Christ joined together by the love of God. The faithful were like the limbs of Christ's body and the integrity of this body was enacted and enhanced in and through various worship practices and rituals. For the body to remain healthy, all its members would have to dedicate themselves to its moral and spiritual 'hygiene' and to the unity of the community. The apostle Paul expressed his concern about the growing disunity among the Christian communities when he wrote in his first letter to the Corinthians:

> *Now I appeal to you, brothers and sisters, by the name of our Lord Jesus Christ, that [...] there be no divisions [schismata] among you, but that you be united in the same mind and the same purpose. For it has been reported to me [...] that there are quarrels among you, my brothers and sisters. What I mean is that each of you says, 'I belong to Paul', or 'I belong to Apollos', or 'I belong to Cephas', or 'I belong to Christ'. Has Christ been divided?' (1 Cor 1:10–12 NRSV)*

Especially in a context of contestation and persecution, keeping Christian communities together and strengthening Christians' sense of belonging was a difficult challenge. Even some Christians, when put to the test, faltered and rejected their Christian allegiance. Such disunity was seen as threatening and harmful to the community.

During the second century, the problem of disunity was projected onto the notion of heresy, which now became a negative category. A heretic becomes a renegade, someone who harms the community from the inside, by inventing deviating truths. According to Robert Moore, 'in the context of the small and persecuted communities of the early Christians in which the values of fraternity and loyalty must stand supreme' it was assumed that persistent deviation in worship threatened both their intellectual and their social cohesion (Moore, 2007, p. 11). The threat coming from outside (persecution) was matched by a threat coming from inside (heresy). In both cases the menace of the disintegration of the community played a role in the process of identity making. It is a typical pattern of selfing and othering: in times of crisis, the challenge is to strengthen 'right' Christian identity and keep deviation outside.

Building on the metaphor of the body, the threat associated with heresy was first imagined in terms of disease. This is in line with the passages in the gospels where Jesus claims that his opponents need a physician (e.g. Mark 2:17). Heretics were also cast as transgressive, promiscuous, and lustful (Justin Martyr, *1 Apol.* 26). They are enslaved by fleshly desires (or, in contrast, as extremely rigid and ascetic in an effort to control their lust) and they intentionally seek to corrupt feeble women with their treacherous teachings (Irenaeus, *Adv. Haer.* I.6.3). Gendering, sexualization, and religionization intersect.

Adversus Haereses

Apologists who invested their energy in the establishment of a boundary between heresy and orthodoxy are called heresiologists. Daniel Boyarin calls heresiologists the inspectors of religious customs. They 'tried to police the boundaries so as to identify and interdict those who respected no boundaries' (Boyarin, 2004, p. 2). More profoundly, however, they also created and crafted boundaries in a time where these were not so clear. The orthodoxy/heresy binary projects a clearly demarcated truth, understood as single, coherent, and whole, in opposition to falsehood, which is then understood as (i) a deviation and perversion of that single truth, (ii) a wilful and chosen error – malign intent is assumed, and (iii) treacherous, in other words, it often manifests itself under the guise of orthodoxy or under the pretence of orthodoxy, so it is difficult for ordinary people to recognize. The heretic is the enemy within, who tricks and seduces Christians with lies and falsities. Hence, the association with the serpent (cf. the fall of Adam) who poisons the mind and the body of Christ (Irenaeus,

Adv. Haer. I.27.4). Finally, (iv) when one leaves this kind of dissent to fester, it can bring real harm to the Christian body. In the future, accusing a theological opponent of heresy would become a way to discredit him, just like one might accuse a Christian of Judaizing.

Around 180 CE, the heresiologist Irenaeus of Lyon wrote a five-volume book, *Adversus Haereses*, to both refute a wide range of heresies and to convert heretics so that they might find salvation. Anyone who wants to take on this twofold task, Irenaeus writes, 'must possess an accurate knowledge of their [the heretics'] systems or schemes of doctrine. For it is impossible for anyone to heal the sick if he has no knowledge of the disease of the patients' (*Adv. Haer.* IV, preface 2, trans. Schaff, 1978). Using many metaphors, Irenaeus offers an overtly negative image of the nature of heresy, as treacherous, arrogant, and corrupt.

What makes heresy all the more problematic is that it presents itself under the pretence of truth. Thus, Irenaeus writes, 'error [...] is never set forth in its naked deformity, lest, being thus exposed, it should at once be detected'. The error of heresy presents itself as the imitation of a precious jewel, and he continues by stating that heretics are like wolves in sheep's clothing (*Adv. Haer.* I, preface 1.2, trans. Schaff, 1978). Elsewhere, he argues that heresy takes on the form of milk, while it is in fact a mixture of lime and water (*Adv. Haer.* III.17.4). He speaks about the arrogance of the heretics, who claim to have access to knowledge that is beyond their reach, and goes on to object to their 'wicked, although plausible, persuasions' (*Adv. Haer.* I.32.3). Their lies destroy the truth (*Adv. Haer.* I.8.1). Heretics twist the truth and divide it (*Adv. Haer.* I.9.4). They are innovators.

Deviation from the truth translates into moral corruption and especially sexual perversion (Knust, 2006). Heretics 'lead lives of unrestrained indulgence' and they lie and practise adultery. In all of this, one cannot but conclude that 'this class of men have been instigated by Satan' (*Adv. Haer.* I.21.1, trans. Schaff, 1978). They are slaves of desire. Irenaeus was not alone in seeing the connection between heresy and moral corruption. Justin Martyr too, to mention just one other heresiologist, calls heretics demon-inspired sex fiends (*1 Apol.* 26; *Dial.* 35). While 'true Christians' are chaste, false Christians are capable of 'the overturning of the lamp stand and promiscuous intercourse and devouring human flesh' (*1 Apol.* 26.7). Benjamin Kaplan concludes that the

> error [of heretics] [...] was less a product of misunderstanding than a sinful act of malicious will. Pride drove them to claim religious authority; the desires of the flesh drove them to fabricate teachings that licensed immorality. From antiquity onwards, stereotypes circulated casting heretics as hedonistic revelers whose clandestine, nighttime gatherings were excuses for orgies. (Kaplan, 2007, p. 26)

Accusations that were previously raised against Christians were here raised against heretics too. Sometimes, however, heretics would be accused of the opposite, that is of being overly stringent when it comes to the joys of life, including sexuality. Their self-restraint went overboard. That too, could be a sign of heresy.

Heretics furthermore project 'vain' genealogies, which falsify the only legitimate genealogical line of Christians. They are innovators rather than heirs of tradition, born after Jesus' ascension rather than stemming from disciples of Christ, and their origin is demonic rather than divine; Satan is their father. Irenaeus, in an effort to distinguish Christian from heretic genealogy projects Simon Magus (Acts 8:9) as the father of all heresies, all later false teachings (e.g. Marcion) go back to him: 'from [him] [...] all sorts of heresies derive their origin' (*Adv. Haer.* I.13.2, trans. Schaff, 1978). Thus, he wants to emphasize that heresy is a novel invention, an innovation, a deviation, which only 'broke [...] much later' (*Adv. Haer.* III.4.3, trans. Schaff, 1978). Heresy lacks tradition. It does not have a long history and it springs from the 'creative' imagination of arrogant minds. Denying them Christian lineage and excluding them from the one eternal salvific path, Irenaeus gives heretics a non-Christian name: they are Simonians, but also Marcionites and Valentinians, rather than Christians.

Against the genealogical line of heretical corruption and division, Irenaeus places the genealogical line of faithful and apostolic Christians, which is present only in those churches which can guarantee apostolic origin and continuity (Knust, 2006, p. 155).

Since, however, it would be very tedious, in such a volume as this, to reckon up the successions of all the Churches, we do put to confusion all those who, in whatever manner, whether by an evil self-pleasing, by vainglory, or by blindness and perverse opinion, assemble in unauthorized meetings; [we do this, I say,] by indicating that tradition derived from the apostles, of the very great, the very ancient, and universally known Church founded and organized at Rome by the two most glorious apostles, Peter and Paul; as also [by pointing out] the faith preached to men, which comes down to our time by means of the successions of the bishops. For it is a matter of necessity that every Church should agree with this Church, on account of its pre-eminent authority, that is, the faithful everywhere, inasmuch as the apostolical tradition has been preserved continuously by those [faithful men] who exist everywhere. (Adv. Haer. III.2, trans. Schaff, 1978)

The orthodox norm of the apostolic tradition is, so Irenaeus claims, preserved in Rome, thanks to the twofold succession via Peter and Paul (a male line rather than the female line of the heretic). The apostolic tradition guarantees the preservation of Christian orthodoxy, which has been present in the universally founded church from the very beginning. A heretic cannot be a Christian, even though they all claim to be precisely that. Here too, ethnoreligious reasoning is part of religionization.

Text Box 9: Imaginary Constructs: Orthodoxy versus Heresy

The negotiation of the conceptual boundaries of orthodoxy goes hand in hand with the process of defining heresy. To recognize orthodoxy one needs to consider heresy; either term only makes sense in light of the other. This process of demarcation is again one of legitimization/delegitimization. It must not be overlooked that heresy is an etic label: it is a name given by Christians who claim to embody a truthful Christian life in contrast to those who deviate from this projected norm. No heretic would ever call himself thus.

The heretic, like the Jew, is an imaginary religionized construct, but this also holds true for the projected self-understanding that emerges from this binary. The idea that orthodox Christian identity, as embodied in the norm of the apostolic tradition, is marked by stability and coherence, is not confirmed by historical data. It is more correct to acknowledge that even the apostolic tradition itself is pluriform and marked by tension, something Irenaeus certainly would not want to consider. It makes much more sense to argue that plurality or heterodoxy came first, though heresiologists would not agree. For them, fragmentation and plurality are placed outside the realm of orthodoxy. Finally, both orthodoxy and heresy are in the eye of the beholder. All Christian communities considered themselves to be orthodox and others to be heretical. In the sixteenth century, this is exactly the point Castellio would make when arguing for toleration (see Chapter 7).

Heresy	Orthodoxy
Sickness, disease	The healthy body of Christ
Deviance	Norm
Division	Unity
Contamination	Remedy
Falsehood	Truth

6 Conclusion

During the second and third centuries, Christian apologists tried to construct a sense of Christianness in a context of plurality and contestation. To that end, they engaged in a process of selfing and othering predicated on religious difference, which I call religionization. Religionization produces imaginary binary constructs, that follow the demarcation of norm versus deviation. In this chapter, I have specifically examined the following antithetical pairs: *Religio – superstitio*; orthodoxy – heresy; and Christians – Jewish anti-Christians, as well as a series of value-laden oppositions that intersect with these binary constructs. As Christians developed an understanding of *vera religio* as being separate and even opposed to heresy, to Jewish tradition, and to superstitious/idolatrous Roman cults, they strived to create a world that was structured in accordance with their own self-understanding. To bolster their claims to *vera religio*, Christian apologists made use of ethnoreligious reasoning. They also gendered and sexualized their opponents. Furthermore, they claimed that orthodoxy is one, thereby framing plurality as deviation. In the period that I have just discussed, Christians were a minority; their traditions were ridiculed, misunderstood, and rejected and at times, Christian communities were persecuted. Soon, this would change.

In the fourth century, when Nicene Christianity became the official *religio* of the Roman Empire, the long process of Christianization set in. Before Constantine, Christians had remained beyond the fringes of legality (Stroumsa, 2015); now, the Nicene Christian norm would be inscribed into the law, and patterns of religionization that previously figured solely in Christian discourse would become expressed in disciplinary measures with material effects on the relations between Christians on the one hand and Jews, pagans, and heretics on the other.

Note

[1] To get a sense of this intra-Christian diversity, consider Justin Martyr's *Dialogue with the Jew Trypho*. In it, we find an interesting passage in which the relationship between gentile Christians, Jewish-Christians, and Jews is discussed, showcasing the social reality of Christian diversity (47.1–5). The Jew Trypho asks Justin if those Christians who believe Jesus is the Messiah and want to keep the whole law of Moses can also be saved. Justin answers that they can, provided they do not expect all Christians to follow Jewish law. The gentile Christians are not bound by that law. Trypho notes that there are also Christians who disagree about this. Justin admits that there are, and that there are even Christians who do not want to meet in a house with those who keep all of the law. While this is not his personal position, Justin does state that only Jews who recognize Jesus as Messiah can be saved (see Justin Martyr, trans. Falls, 1948).

References

Barton, C. A., & Boyarin, D. (2016). *Imagine No Religion: How Modern Abstractions Hide Ancient Realities*. Fordham University Press.

Baumann, G., & Gingrich, A. (Eds.) (2004). *Grammars of Identity/Alterity: A Structural Approach*. Berghahn Books.

Beard, M., North, J., & Price, S. R. F. (1998). *Religions of Rome*. Cambridge University Press.

Benveniste, E. (2016). *Dictionary of Indo-European Concepts and Society* (Trans. E. Palmer). University of Chicago Press.

Berzon, T. S. (2016). *Classifying Christians: Ethnography, Heresiology, and the Limits of Knowledge in Late Antiquity*. University of California Press.

Bokser, B. Z. (1973). Justin Martyr and the Jews. *The Jewish Quarterly Review, 64*(2), 97–122.

44 CHAPTER 1 The Creation of Key Religionized Categories

Boyarin, D. (2004). *Border Lines: The Partition of Judaeo-Christianity.* University of Pennsylvania Press.

Brubaker, R. (2002). Ethnicity without Groups. *European Journal of Sociology 43*(2), 163–189.

Buell, D. K. (2002). Race and Universalism in Early Christianity. *Journal of Early Christian Studies, 10*(4), 429–468.

Buell, D. K. (2005). *Why This New Race: Ethnic Reasoning in Early Christianity.* Columbia University Press.

Cantwell Smith, W. (2008). Religion in the West. In S. S. Elliott & M. Waggoner (Eds.), *Readings in the Theory of Religion: Map, Text, Body* (pp. 5–40). Equinox.

Carleton Paget, J., & Lieu, J. (2017). Introduction. In J. Carleton Paget & J. Lieu (Eds.), *Christianity in the Second Century: Themes and Developments* (pp. 1–22). Cambridge University Press.

Chidester, D. (2000). *Christianity: A Global History.* HarperSanFrancisco.

Cicero (Trans. H. Rackham) (1933). *On the Nature of the Gods (De natura deorum)*, Loeb Classical Library 268. Harvard University Press.

Clement of Alexandria (Trans. G. W. Butterworth) (1919). *The Exhortation to the Greeks. The Rich Man's Salvation. To the Newly Baptized*, Loeb Classical Library 92. Harvard University Press.

Cohen, J. (1999). *Living Letters of the Law: Ideas of the Jew in Medieval Christianity.* University of California Press.

Colijn, B. (2019). Interrituality in Contemporary China as a Field of Tension between Abstention and Polytropy. In M. Moyaert (Ed.), *Interreligious Relations and the Negotiation of Ritual Boundaries: Explorations in Interrituality* (pp. 227–244). Palgrave Macmillan.

De Roover, J. (2014). Incurably Religious? *Consensus Gentium* and the Cultural Universality of Religion. *Numen: International Review for the History of Religions 61*(1), 5–32.

Drake, S. (2013). *Slandering the Jew: Sexuality and Difference in Early Christian Texts.* University of Pennsylvania Press.

Dumézil, G. (1966). *La Religion romaine archaïque, avec un appendice sur la religion des Étrusques.* Payot.

Dunn, G. D. (2004). *Tertullian.* Routledge.

Eadie, J. (1869). *A Commentary on the Greek Text of the Epistle of Paul to the Galatians.* T&T Clark.

Fitzgerald, T. (2007). *Discourse on Civility and Barbarity: A Critical History of Religion and Related Categories.* Oxford University Press.

Fonrobert, C. E. (2001). Judaizers, Jewish Christians and Others. In A.-J. Levine & M. Z. Brettler (Eds.), *The Jewish Annotated New Testament* (pp. 554–556). Oxford University Press.

Fredriksen, P. (2003). What 'Parting of the Ways?': Jews, Gentiles, and the Ancient Mediterranean City. In A. H. Becker & A. Yoshiko Reed (Eds.), *The Ways That Never Parted: Jews and Christians in Late Antiquity and the Early Middle Ages*, Texts and Studies in Ancient Judaism 95 (pp. 35–63). Mohr Siebeck.

Fredriksen, P. (2006a). Christians in the Roman Empire in the First Three Centuries CE. In D. S. Potter (Ed.), *A Companion to the Roman Empire* (pp. 587–606). Blackwell.

Fredriksen, P. (2006b). Mandatory Retirement: Ideas in the Study of Christian Origins Whose Time Has Come to Go. *Studies in Religion / Sciences Religieuses, 35*(2), 231–246.

Fredriksen, P. (2014). Jewish Romans, Christian Romans, and the Post-Roman West: The Social Correlates of the *contra Iudaeos* Tradition. In I. Yuval & R. Ben-Shalom (Eds.), *Conflict and Religious Conversation in Latin Christendom: Studies in Honour of Ora Limor* (pp. 23–53). Brepols.

Fredriksen, P., & Irshai, O. (2006). Christian Anti-Judaism: Polemics and Policies. In S. T. Katz (Ed.), *The Cambridge History of Judaism, Volume 4: The Late Roman-Rabbinic Period* (pp. 977–1034). Cambridge University Press.

Fredriksen, P., & Irshai, O. (2015). Include Me Out: Tertullian, the Rabbis, and the Graeco-Roman City. In K. N. Berthelot, R. Naiweld, & D. Stökl Ben Ezra (Eds.), *L'Identité à travers l'éthique: nouvelles perspectives sur la formation des identités collectives dans le monde greco-romain* (pp. 117–132). Brepols.

Freidenreich, D. M. (2011). *Foreigners and Their Food: Constructing Otherness in Jewish, Christian, and Islamic Law.* University of California Press.

García Soormally, M. (2019). *Idolatry and the Construction of the Spanish Empire.* University Press of Colorado.

Gordon, R. (2008). *Superstitio,* Superstition and Religious Repression in the Late Roman Republic and Principate (100 BCE – 300 CE). *Past & Present, 199*(3), 72–94.

Horrell, D. G. (2020). *Ethnicity and Inclusion: Religion, Race, and Whiteness in Constructions of Jewish and Christian Identities.* Eerdmans.

Hoyt, S. F. (1912). The Etymology of Religion. *Journal of the American Oriental Society, 32*(2), 126–129.

Irenaeus (Trans. P. Schaff) (1978). *Against Heresies*, Ante-Nicene Fathers 1. Eerdmans.

Joslyn-Siemiatkoski, D. (2022). Towards an Anti-Supersessionist Theology: Race, Whiteness, and Covenant. *Religions, 13*(2), Article 129. https://doi.org/10.3390/rel13020129

Jürgasch, T. (2021). Häresie und Orthodoxie als identitätsstiftende Kategorien in der Alten Kirche und in der frühchristlichen liturgischen Praxis. In S. Kopp & S. Wahle (Eds.), *Nicht wie Außenstehende und stumme Zuschauer: Liturgie – Identität – Partizipation*, Kirche in Zeiten der Veränderung (pp. 160–178). Herder.

Justin Martyr (Trans. T. B. Falls) (1948). *The First Apology. The Second Apology. Dialogue with Trypho. Exhortation to the Greeks. Discourse to the Greeks. The Monarchy or the Rule of God*. Catholic University of America Press.

Kahlos, M. (2007). *Debate and Dialogue: Christian and Pagan Cultures c. 360–430*. Ashgate.

Kaplan, B. J. (2007). *Divided by Faith: Religious Conflict and the Practice of Toleration in Early Modern Europe*. The Belknap Press of Harvard University Press.

Kaplan, L. (2019). *Figuring Racism in Medieval Christianity*. Oxford University Press.

King, R. (1999). *Orientalism and Religion: Post-Colonial Theory, India and 'the Mystic East'*. Routledge.

Knust, J. W. (2006). *Abandoned to Lust: Sexual Slander and Ancient Christianity*. Columbia University Press.

Koltun-Fromm, N. (2009). Defining Sacred Boundaries: Jewish-Christian Relations. In P. Rousseau & J. Raithel (Eds.), *A Companion to Late Antiquity* (pp. 556–571). Wiley-Blackwell.

Lieu, J. (2002). *Neither Jew Nor Greek? Constructing Early Christianity*. T&T Clark.

Lieu, J. (2004). *Christian Identity in the Jewish and Graeco-Roman World*. Oxford University Press.

Melito of Sardis (Ed. and trans. S. G. Hall) (1979). *'On Pascha' and Fragments*, Oxford Early Christian Texts. Oxford University Press.

Metz, S. (2021). *Group Identity and Social Resilience in Early Christianity: The Case of Tertullian's* De Spectaculis *28–30* [Paper presentation]. European Academy for the Study of Religion.

Minucius Felix (Trans. T. R. Glover & G. H. Rendall) (1931). *Octavius*, Loeb Classical Library 250. Harvard University Press.

Moore, R. I. (2007). *The Formation of a Persecuting Society: Authority and Deviance in Western Europe, 950–1250* (2nd ed.). Blackwell.

Moyaert, M., & Pollefeyt, D. (Eds.) (2010). *Never Revoked: Nostra Aetate as Ongoing Challenge for Jewish-Christian Dialogue*, Louvain Theological and Pastoral Monographs 40. Peeters.

Nongbri, B. (2013). *Before Religion: A History of a Modern Concept*. Yale University Press.

Pliny the Elder (Trans. H. Rackham) (1938). *Natural History, Volume I: Books 1–2*, Loeb Classical Library 330. Harvard University Press.

Rebillard, É. (2012). *Christians and Their Many Identities in Late Antiquity, North Africa, 200–450 CE*. Cornell University Press.

Ricoeur, P. (2010). Religious Belief: The Difficult Path of the Religious. In B. Treanor & H. I. Venema (Eds.), *A Passion for the Possible: Thinking with Paul Ricoeur* (pp. 27–40). Fordham University Press.

Schilbrack, K. (2017). Review: Imagine No Religion: How Modern Abstractions Hide Ancient Realities. By C. A. Barton and D. Boyarin. *Journal of the American Academy of Religion 85*(4), 833–835.

Schott, J. M. (2008). *Christianity, Empire, and the Making of Religion in Late Antiquity*. University of Pennsylvania Press.

Schwartz, S. (2001). *Imperialism and Jewish Society, 200 B.C.E. to 640 C.E.* Princeton University Press.

Seneca (Trans. R. M. Gummere) (1925). *Epistles, Volume III: Epistles 93–124*, Loeb Classical Library 77. Harvard University Press.

Seneca (Trans. J. W. Basore) (1928). *Moral Essays, Volume I: De Providentia. De Constantia. De Ira. De Clementia*, Loeb Classical Library 214. Harvard University Press.

Smith, W. C. (1963). *The Meaning and End of Religion: A New Approach to the Religious Traditions of Mankind*. Macmillan.

Stroumsa, G. G. (1998). Tertullian on Idolatry and the Limits of Tolerance. In G. N. Stanton & G. G. Stroumsa (Eds.), *Tolerance and Intolerance in Early Judaism and Christianity* (pp. 173–184). Cambridge University Press.

Stroumsa, G. G. (2015). *The Making of the Abrahamic Religions in Late Antiquity*. Oxford University Press.

Tacitus (Trans. C. H. Moore) (1931). *Histories: Books 4–5. Annals: Books 1–3*, Loeb Classical Library 249. Harvard University Press.

Tacitus (Trans. J. Jackson) (1937). *Annals: Books 13–16*, Loeb Classical Library 322. Harvard University Press.

Tertullian (Trans. T. R. Glover & G. H. Rendall) (1931). *Apology. De Spectaculis*, Loeb Classical Library 250. Harvard University Press.

Williams, F. (Trans.) (2009). *The Panarion of Epiphanius of Salamis: Book 1 (Sects 1–46)*, Nag Hammadi and Manichaean Studies 63 (2nd, rev. and exp. ed.). Brill.

CHAPTER 2

The Coercive Turn

Institutionalizing Religionized Categories

The period following Emperor Constantine's conversion to Christianity in 312 CE was a game-changer for the early Christian movement. After his conversion, the emperor brought an end to the persecutions, and, despite internal rivalries and ongoing power struggles, imperial power joined hands with ecclesiastical power. When the factor of power was added to the mix, apologetic imaginaries of self and other translated into institutionalized structures of exclusion and oppression. Both ecclesial and imperial authorities would argue that the unity of the empire depended on the unity of the church and vice versa. The Edict of Milan (313), which recognizes the church as a corporate body and gave (some) Christians the freedom to worship, presents a key symbolic moment in this historical-political process of transition (Coleman-Norton, 1966, p. 30).

> When I, Constantine Augustus, and also I, Licinius Augustus had met happily at Milan and were conferring about all matters which concerned advantages and public security, among these other matters which we saw would benefit most men – or indeed first and foremost – we have believed that there should be ordained those matters by which reverence [religionem] for the Divinity was contained, that we should concede both to Christians and to all an unrestricted possibility of following which religion each one had wished, whereby whatever Divinity exists in its celestial abode can be placated and propitious to us and to all who are placed under our authority. (Coleman-Norton, 1966, p. 31)

The Christianization of the Roman Empire, however, did not happen overnight and contrary to the assertions made by later Christian scholars in their polemical works, the Constantinian turn did not mark the triumph of the Christian God over the pagan gods (Eusebius, ed. Heinichen, 1830). The empire continued to be populated by many gods. Christianity itself was furthermore fragmented, and multiple Christian groups claimed to practise *vera religio* while labelling dissenting others as heretics.

Constantine struggled to maintain Christian unity and in 325 the emperor convened the First Council of Nicaea, 'to introduce harmony and prevent future ruptures' (Bobrowicz, 2018, p. 94). The council, which sought to solve the so-called Arian crisis, adopted the doctrine of the incarnation as the official normative creed (the Son is begotten not made). The Nicene Creed became *vera religio* and orthodoxy received the title of *Nicaenae fidei* (see *Codex Theodosianus* [henceforth CTh] 16.1.3) (Bobrowicz, 2018, p. 101). Arian Christianity in turn was anathematized. The consolidation of the norm, however, did not end intra-Christian dispute, but rather triggered it: the clearer the norm, the more obvious deviation becomes, and the more likely fragmentation (Text Box 1).

Christian Imaginations of the Religious Other: A History of Religionization, First Edition. Marianne Moyaert.
© 2024 John Wiley & Sons Ltd. Published 2024 by John Wiley & Sons Ltd.

Text Box 1: On Doctrine and Disputation

It is often assumed that the explicit formulation of doctrine settles intra-Christian debates by projecting a clear norm and establishing a boundary between what is true and untrue. For several reasons this does not hold.

First of all, we need to distinguish between implicit and explicit doctrine, or between operational doctrines and official doctrines (Lindbeck, 1984, p. 74). Most doctrines remain implicit, because they are so self-evident and enjoy so much acclaim that there is no need to make them explicit (e.g. God is just or God is love). This means, on the one hand, that there are actually many points of agreement between different Christianities. On the other hand, it implies that dispute is usually the reason that doctrine is made explicit. It follows that 'insofar as official doctrines are the products of conflict, [...] they must be understood in terms of what they oppose and, second, the official doctrines of a community may poorly reflect its most important and abiding orientations or beliefs, either because some of the latter may never have been seriously challenged (and therefore never officially defined) or because points that are under most circumstances trivial may on occasion become matters of life and death' (Lindbeck, 1984, p. 75). Besides, the explicit formulation of doctrine often evokes further contestation. Where a boundary is drawn, sides are taken. Talking about the Council of Nicaea, Paula Fredriksen states that 'the awareness and even the generation of difference were caused by the imperial consolidation itself. Creeds as consensus documents served as occasions for further fracturing' (Fredriksen, 2014, p. 29). Finally, while an orthodox norm is never more than a claimed and therefore contested norm, one of the key characteristics of orthodoxy is that it denies this and projects its version of Christianity as the defining one.

With this Nicene norm in mind, the long process of Christianizing the empire set in, and this 'inevitably implied [...] the conversion of the existing legal system in accordance with Christian values and objectives' (Linder, 2006, p. 144). In the years following the Constantinian and later on, in 380, the Theodosian turn, the Christian norm would be inscribed into laws. These laws set out to defend 'the *insatiabilis honor*, the "boundless claim to honour", of the Catholic Church' (Brown, 1995, p. 33) and aimed at distinguishing orthodox (Catholic) Christians from heretics, pagans, and Jews, who were 'argued to be alien to the Roman order' (Kahlos, 2020, p. 15). In 438, the laws produced after the Constantinian turn were gathered in the *Codex Theodosianus* (Pharr, 1952). '[F]or the first time in the history of Rome, correct religious adherence [became] a requirement for the full enjoyment of the benefits of Roman society' (Brown, 1998, p. 638). Roman and Christian became identical, and those who were not Nicene Christians were not proper Romans.

The authority of the *Codex Theodosianus*, however, should not be bookmarked as 'imperial'. Rather, Christian scholars provided the logic and ideological legitimation for legislation which helped create a stratified society that privileges Nicene Christians and disadvantages others. To be more concrete, the legal work reflected in the *Codex Theodosianus* drew on the perspectives of Christian heresiologists, and Christian heresiologists crafted theologies to authorize the law. This synergy resulted in the rise in status of both heresiology and law. On the one hand, the *Codex Theodosianus* fed on the authority of the scholarly expertise of heresiologists who were defining the religious norm as opposed to deviance. On the other hand, the *Codex* imbued heresiological discourse with the power of imperial pronouncements. As a consequence, heresiology became more powerful: it could now impact the governance of religious difference. As heresiological discourse translated into laws which helped to shape society, the discursive distinction between *vera religio* and various expressions of religious deviation was consolidated as a socio-political and cultural reality. Here we can see clearly how words help create worlds (Hill Fletcher, 2017, p. 83) and how Christian theological categories gradually become lived reality.

1 On Heresiology: Epiphanius' *Panarion*

Heresiology, a product of Late Antiquity, is a particular genre aimed at anatomizing, pinning down, and classifying Christians and those who fall outside of the Christian realm (Boyarin, 2004, p. xi). It divides, labels, classifies, and essentializes various social groups by setting them against the norm of Christian orthodoxy. While presented as a descriptive endeavour, heresiology is a theological project.

One classic example of the heresiological genre is the *Panarion*, written by Epiphanius of Salamis (ca. 310/320–403). Born in fourth-century Palestine of Jewish parents, Epiphanius was one of the driving forces against the condemnation of Origen (Shaw, 2011, p. 217). In his view, the *homoousian* version of Christianity, according to which God the Son and God the Father are of one substance, was the norm, and any deviation from it unacceptable. He projects heretics as enslaved to sexual pleasure and as engaged in various forms of promiscuous behaviour. By gendering them as *concubines*, a trope which he draws from the Song of Songs, Epiphanius subscribes to the stereotype that women are more prone to depravation (Whitley, 2016, p. 241). He also likens the heresies to poisons, which sicken the Christian body, and projects his heresiology as a medicine-chest of antidotes to the poisonous snakebites of heretical sects (*Proem* I, 1, in Williams, 2009b, p. 3). Over against the perversion of heresies, he places the one perfect 'dove' (also from the Song of Songs 6:9): the Church of Christ, which embodies orthodox truth.

In the *Panarion*, Epiphanius combines microscopic and macroscopic ethnographic strategies (Berzon, 2016a, p. 15). Microscopically, Epiphanius claims to describe 80 heretical groups [*haireseis*]. This number corresponds to Solomon's 80 concubines (Song 6:8–9), a finding which highlights that heresiology is not a descriptive undertaking but a theological endeavour: the 'heretic' figures in a story line written for normative Christian purposes. Epiphanius' goal is to organize and refute these heresies, so that none of his fellow Christians goes astray and, if possible, to convince those who had fallen for the treachery of these heresies of the single truth of Christian worship. Therefore, for each sect, he gives an overview of what its followers believe and, where applicable, who their founder is, and he elaborates on how each sect deviates from true religion.

> And to correspond with these [serpents and beasts] I shall give as many arguments, like antidotes, as I can in short compass – one or two at most – to counteract their poison and, after the Lord, cure anyone who wants <to be cured>, if he has fallen, willingly or inadvertently, into these snake-like teachings of the sects. (Proem II, 3.5, trans. Williams, 2009b, p. 15)

The saving remedy comes from 'Christ's [only] holy bride, the Church' (as opposed to the concubines).

Macroscopically, Epiphanius projects a world history that explains both the universal truth of Christian orthodoxy and the ongoing proliferation of heresy (Berzon, 2016a, p. 132). At the heart of this world history, which is really a history of religion, is the idea that 'we are dealing [...] with heretical human opinion which misguided persons have been sowing in the world from man's formation on earth till our own day' (*Proem* II, 2.3, trans. Williams, 2009b, p. 13). None of these heresies, however, is as old as the truth of Christian faith.

The Microscopical 'Ethnographic' Work of Epiphanius

When presenting the 80 heresies systematically, Epiphanius turned them into socially and theologically coherent groups, bound together by beliefs and rituals, and often inspired by a leading figure (cf. Ebion, Marcion, Simon Magus, etc.). Some heresies predate Christianity, but most emerged after Christ's dwelling on earth. Like the Christian Church, named after its founder, these heresies too have a creed, rites and rules, leaders,

On Heresiology: Epiphanius' *Panarion* **49**

and even priests; they were not Christians, however. To highlight this, they were named after their false leader or their false teachings (e.g. Arians, Manicheans, Anomoeans, etc.).

When Epiphanius names these deviant others, for example Marcionites and Ebionites, he is denying them the name of Christians, which most, though not all, would have claimed for themselves.[1] The refusal to name these deviant others Christians is typical of heresiology; it places heretics outside of the salvific promise of Christian worship. Later, 'this kind of alienation outside the Christian community' will be picked up 'in the imperial legislation in which the Christian mainstream was defined as the catholic Christianity, while other Christian inclinations were categorized as un-Christian' (Kahlos, 2020, p. 109).

These heretical groups were in all likelihood imagined constructs, which did not correspond to reality (Stroumsa, 2015, p. 74). Indeed, it is likely that Epiphanius invented some heresies to get to the specific number of 80 (Whitley, 2016, p. 240). He may also have classified several 'heresies' together under one name, just for the sake of systematization. For example, Epiphanius constructed the Messalanians as a coherent social group. These 'heretics' were known as 'the ones who pray', because they refrained from all rituals except prayer, which they believed brought them into direct communication with God. As Daniel Caner explains, 'Epiphanius, having heard of such People Who Pray, simply used the Messalian label to bring together all the practices of disparate ascetic groups that caused him distress. [...] What disturbed Epiphanius was a complex of ascetic practices that could be found diffused in varying shades throughout much of Asia Minor and the neighboring East' (Caner, 2002, p. 101). This example shows how this fourth-century heresiologist turned people that shared certain ideas and practices into '-isms' – docetism, gnosticism, Manicheism, adoptionism, and so on – 'that stand outside established or recognized tradition' (Boyarin, 2004, p. 3). We are seeing the discursive making of heresies. This is characteristic of heresiology as a genre, which was driven by polemical interests: heresiologists self-selectively and self-interestedly mapped, described, and redescribed what best served their theological rhetoric; their study is one of comparative theology, always with the purpose of rendering the true worship of the true God as the only pathway to salvation.

The alleged sexual promiscuity of heretics testifies to this and justified the necessity of boundaries being established between true Christians and heretical others. Consider in this regard what Epiphanius writes about the Simonians and the Carpocratians:

> *[Simon the magician] [...] taught that an unnatural act, sexual congress for the pollution of women, is a matter of moral indifference [...]. He gave his disciples an image of himself in the form of Zeus to worship, and one <in the> form of Athena of the whore named Helen who accompanied him. (Anacephalaeosis II, 21.2–3, trans. Williams, 2009b, p. 59)*
>
> *Carpocratians, founded by one Carpocrates, a native of Asia, who taught his followers to perform every obscenity and every sinful practice. (Anacephalaeosis II, 27.1, trans. Williams, 2009b, p. 59)*

And about the Gnostics:

> *[...] although they have sex with each other they renounce procreation. It is for enjoyment, not procreation, that they eagerly pursue seduction, since the devil is mocking people like these, and making fun of the creature fashioned by God. They come to climax but absorb the seeds of their dirt, not by implanting them for procreation, but by eating the dirty stuff themselves. (Anacephalaeosis II, 26.5.2–3, trans. Williams, 2009b, p. 94)*

The perverse heretical way of life – a life of fornication, adultery, uncleanliness, incontinence, trickery, gluttony – leads to damnation, while the orthodox Christian way of life leads to salvation.

Epiphanius' Universal Account of History

Epiphanius' 'ethnography' also provides a universal account of human history (a macroscopic approach), which explains the historic genesis of heretical plurality in 'opposition to an a-historical orthodoxy that is entirely dissociated from historical processes of cultural development' (Schott, 2007, p. 547). The orthodox norm, he suggests, has always existed. It has been the same from the very beginning and will never change in the future.

Epiphanius' history is permeated by a genealogical classification inspired by Col 3:11: 'Here there is no Gentile or Jew, circumcised or uncircumcised, barbarian, Scythian, slave or free, but Christ is all, and is in all' (NIV). Drawing on this verse, and in contrast to Irenaeus who traced all heresies back to Simon Magus, Epiphanius links the barbarian, Scythian, Greek, and Jew to four mother- or proto-heresies (Schott, 2008, p. 132). He links these to four successive pre-Christian stages of heresy: Barbarism, Scythism (associated with magic), Hellenism (associated with idolatry), and Judaism (of which he gives a supersessionist account). He adds a fifth one, Samaritanism (*Proem* I, 3.1, in Williams, 2009b, p. 4). Together these proto-heresies gave birth to all 80 heresies. Even the contemporary Christian heretical sects, the beginning of which he also attributes to Simon Magus, graft onto these earlier sects: somehow they all reproduce the same errors of previous heresies. In this sense, they are not new.

In Epiphanius' understanding, history shows that there is an endless human impulse for deviation leading to error. This inclination accounts for heretical diversity in the past, that is before the origin of historical Christianity, and for contemporary Christian heresies. Both past and present heresies are the product of that very same impulse. This has two implications. First, it means that even though there are multiple heresies, in the end 'all heresies are a unity of diversity. [...] Their outward difference is superficial, while inwardly they are the same' (Berzon, 2016b, p. 99). All heresy, whatever expression it takes, is poisonous: it is like the poison of the snake bite spreading out rapidly, and if measures are not taken it will destroy the church from within. In addition, it means that, 'contemporary sectarian proponents occupy the same historical and theological space as the heresies of the past. The process of error had not ceased, nor had its essential content changed' (Berzon, 2016a, p. 139).

Text Box 2: On the Rhetorical Figure of the Hellene

Epiphanius writes that Hellenism, 'began from the time of Serug, through idolatry and people's adoption, each in accordance with some superstition, of a more civilized way of life, and of customs and laws. However, when idols began to be set up, the various breeds of men made gods of <the leaders> they <were> then adopting, [...] But then, from the time of Terah the father of Abraham, they also introduced the imposture of idolatry by means of statuary' (*Anacephalaeosis* I, 3.1-2, in Williams, 2009b, p. 9). The Greeks had learned all these 'wicked' things from older cultures. They took over the worship of images and statues from the Egyptians, the Babylonians, Phrygians, and Phoenicians and under the reign of Hellenism idolatry spread wide. In Christian imagination, Hellenism would become a synonym for paganism, the term that would be most commonly used by Christians in the fourth century.

Heresiologists, like Epiphanius, probably inherited such normative usage of Hellenism from Jewish writers, who already referred to the Hellenes as idolaters, that is 'those who were not true Jews in the eyes of the speaker'. This term 'became commonly used as the synonym for non-Christians in Christian literature. It also came to mean those who were not true Christians in the eyes of the speaker. [...] At the Council of Nicaea, members of the opposing party shunned their rivals as Hellenes and accused them of introducing polytheism' (Kahlos, 2020, p. 92). In later periods too, whenever paganism is discussed, Greek 'idol worship' practices would be projected as paradigmatic. Muslims, for example, who were accused of paganism, were depicted as Hellenes worshipping Apollo.

Moving between past, present, and future, Epiphanius defines heresy not as a mere post-Christian development, as one would expect, but rather as radically opposed to orthodoxy. Orthodoxy is truly (i) universal – it transcends previous ethnoreligious kinship boundaries; (ii) singular – there is but one truth and orthodoxy, in contrast to the ongoing multiplication of heresy; (iii) inclusive – through faith all may become members of the Christian people; and finally (iv) ahistorical (Schott, 2007, p. 547). Especially this final idea, namely that orthodoxy is ahistorical, calls for further elaboration.

Orthodoxy, according to Epiphanius, has made several inroads into history but without ever becoming part of history. Indeed, it even precedes the incarnation and the establishment of the church. For all of eternity, above the chaos of human history, 'there was the faith which is now native to God's present day holy catholic church, a faith which was in existence from the beginning and was revealed again' (Williams, 2009b, p. 17). Orthodoxy, therefore, stands above and outside history, and throughout human history it was typologically present in the life of the patriarchs, like the pre-fall Adam, Enoch, Noah, and Abraham. Genealogically, it is from these people that Christ incarnate descends. Consider in this regard the following passage:

> Anyone who is willing <to make an> impartial <investigation can> see, from the very object of it, <that> the holy catholic church is the beginning of everything. Adam, <the> man who was formed at the first, was not formed with a body circumcised, but uncircumcised. He was no idolater, and he knew the Father as God, and the Son and Holy Spirit, for he was a prophet.
>
> Without circumcision he was no Jew and since he did not worship carved images or anything else, he was no idolater. For Adam <was> a prophet, and knew that the Father had said, 'Let us make man', to the Son. What was he, then, since he was neither circumcised nor an idolater – except that he exhibited the character of Christianity? And we must take this to be the case of Abel, Seth, Enosh, Enoch, Methuselah, Noah and Eber, down to Abraham. (Proem II, 2.4-6, trans. Williams, 2009b, p. 14)

Orthodoxy is the antidote to the splintering of heresy. The only distinction that really matters is the binary between orthodoxy and heresy, regardless of its particular forms, because orthodoxy alone holds the promise of reuniting all people in Christ. Notice how Epiphanius combines a logic of encompassment and a logic of dichotomy. All may be united as one Christian people in the Catholic [universal and all-embracing] church – the one and exclusive bride of Christ (in contrast to the 80 concubines), but only through faith in Christ.

2 When Heresiology Intersects with Imperial Law

The classification of the many heresies of the world as developed in the *Panarion* is part of a Christian project of religionization that constructs boundaries, real as well as imaginary, between Christianity and its others, and it does this by means of name-giving, classification, and essentialization. When the classificatory genre of heresiology began to intersect with the disciplinary genre of imperial/legal discourse, the religionized categories found in heresiologies became categories in the law. Subsequently, these imaginary boundaries between Christians and non-Christians were institutionalized, and these imaginary constructs began to impact the social and material realities of real flesh and blood people.

In 380, Emperor Theodosius (r. 379–395) turned the Nicene Creed into the official state *religio* of the Western Roman Empire, and Christianity gradually shifted from a position of persecution to a position of political and cultural hegemony.[2] One of the consequences of this shift was that 'the discourse of heresiology initially forged by earlier Christians [...]

comes to be voiced by Christian bishops who collude, however ambivalently, with imperial power' (Boyarin & Burrus, 2005, p. 443). These bishops often petitioned imperial authorities for a legal translation of what church leaders and councils had already decided on, or they would demand a legal response to a local situation of religious conflict. The counterpart of this evolution was the gradual criminalization of those sects that were deemed heretical, and bishops that belonged to the official *religio* of the empire often slipped the names of those bishops they did not want in their town to the emperor and his magistrates, hoping that they would take action. This shift is sometimes called the 'coercive turn' (Kahlos, 2020, p. 14).

This coercive turn entailed a transition for many people from being subject to name-calling in the genre of polemics to being faced with legal discrimination. Law, 'is, in this sense, constitutive of culture, [it is] a part of the cultural process that actively contributes in the composition of social relations' (Silbey, 1992, p. 41). Three groups were singled out and categorized as being opposed to the Nicene Creed: the heretics, the pagans, and the Jews. All three were cast as enemies of the Christian Empire.[3]

3 The *Codex Theodosianus* and the Criminalization of Heresy

In 380, at the height of the Arian controversy, the *Constitutio cunctos populos* or the Edict of Thessaloniki was promulgated, and Christian worship (following the Nicene Creed) was established as the official state religion. The Nicene Creed became constructed as orthodox, and heresy as an 'illegal mode of existence within a Christianizing world' (Berzon, 2017, p. 130). To practise a deviating expression of Christianity came to be seen as 'one of the gravest transgressions against the state and the emperor, and according to some texts it led to falling out of civilized – Christian and Roman – society' (Kahlos, 2020, p. 30).

The emperor's main concern was to strengthen the unity of the empire (Lokin, 2014, p. 349). In this sense, we are not that far removed from the earlier understanding that the *Pax Romana* depends on upholding good relations with the gods. It was and would continue to be the responsibility of the emperor to ensure the benevolence of the gods and to guarantee the welfare of the empire. The difference, however, is a changed legal definition of 'which cultic acts were to count as *religio* (i.e as licit and thus promoting the health and welfare of the Empire)'. From now on, 'Christianity alone could ensure right relations between men and a single (Christian) God' (Humfress, 2007, p. 235). The *pax deorum* was turned into a *pax Dei or pax Christiana*. Imperial legislators were convinced that the empire would suffer under heretical disunity, therefore orthodoxy had to be defined and enforced (Humfress, 2007, p. 235). Protecting the church and defending the empire are collated, and the enemies of the church are the enemies of the empire. Thus, according to the Edict of Thessaloniki:

> It is Our will that all the peoples who are ruled by the administration of Our Clemency shall practice that religion which the divine Peter the Apostle transmitted to the Romans, as the religion which he introduced makes clear even unto this day. It is evident that this is the religion that is followed by the Pontiff Damasus and by Peter, Bishop of Alexandria, a man of apostolic sanctity; that is, according to the apostolic discipline and the evangelic doctrine, we shall believe in the single Deity of the Father, the Son, and the Holy Spirit, under the concept of equal majesty and of the Holy Trinity.
>
> We command [iubemus] that those persons who follow this rule shall embrace the name of Catholic Christians. The rest, however, whom We adjudge demented and insane [vero dementes vesanosque], shall sustain the infamy of heretical dogmas, their

meeting places [conciliabula] shall not receive the name of churches, and they shall be smitten first by divine vengeance and secondly by the retribution of Our own initiative, which We shall assume in accordance with the divine judgment. (CTh 16.1.2, d. 380)

First, the Edict offers a definition of *religio*, understood in terms of the Trinitarian Creed, which is further legitimized in reference to the apostles and the evangelical doctrine. Using the verb *iubemus* [we order], a dichotomy is crafted between those following the creed and the law, who will be called Catholic Christians, and heretics, who are considered demented and insane [*dementes vesanosque*]. This imperial ordination ordered not only that all should adhere to the Nicene Creed, but also that those who deviate from the norm should bear the infamy of heresy. The notion of infamy [*infamia*] is a legal notion, which 'involved the diminution of the esteem in which a person was held in Roman society (*existimatio*)' (Humfress, 2007, p. 225). Citizens who were labelled *infamia* basically lost their legal rights of Roman citizenship. They could be deprived of their right to conduct economic transactions, own property, receive an inheritance, or enter into public and/or administrative service, act as a witness or make applications in trials. Remarkably, the text continues by saying that the gatherings of heretics are called *conciliabula*, rather than *ecclesia* (Text Box 3). Heretics are not Christians: they do not form churches and may not lay claim to church buildings. This constitution projects the heretics as the 'theological, communal, and criminal counterterm to the *Code*'s professed orthodoxy' (Berzon, 2017, p. 126).

Text Box 3: Moving between Past and Present: Reflections on Ecclesiology

By calling the gatherings of heretics *conciliabula* rather than *ecclesia*, the status of these gatherings is not only lowered to mere 'meetings', but these gatherings are also denied as having any salvific import. *Extra ecclesiam nulla salus* – outside the church there is no salvation.

Denying the name 'church' to opponents is a recurring strategy of religionization throughout history. Under Louis XIV (r. 1643–1715), who revoked the Edict of Nantes and made Protestantism illegal, Protestants were also no longer allowed to speak about their *églises* (churches) and could only use the term 'temple', which evokes connotations of Roman and Greek 'idolatry' or false worship.

Until 1943, in *Mystici Corporis*, the Catholic Church would state that She is [*est*] the church of Christ, the one and only, undivided and universal body of Christ, implying that Protestant churches were not churches. This changed at the Second Vatican Council, where the *est* was changed in *subsistit in*. Thus, Cardinal Walter Kasper stated: 'the Church of Jesus Christ subsists in the Catholic Church, which means that the Church of Jesus Christ is made concretely real in the Catholic Church; in her she is historically and concretely present and can be met. This does not exclude that also outside the visible structure of the Catholic Church there are not only individual Christians but also elements of the Church, and with them an "ecclesial reality"'.[4]

John Locke, whom I will discuss in Chapter 7, in arguing for toleration, would redefine 'the church' as a voluntary organization, which people could opt in or out of. Salvation is an individual concern – every soul is responsible for his or her own salvation and a church is a 'voluntary society of men [*societas libera hominum*], joining themselves together of their own accord in order to the public worshipping of God in such manner as they judge acceptable to him, and effectual to the salvation of their souls' (Locke, *Letter on Toleration*, ed. Shapiro, 2003, p. 220). When exploring the question of whether such voluntary gatherings are not at risk of becoming a setting of rebellion, Locke calls voluntary gatherings *conciliabula*. A term formerly used to deny the Christian, ecclesial nature of the gatherings of heretics is now a term deemed appropriate to refer to churches, divesting them of salvific meaning.

54 CHAPTER 2 The Coercive Turn

The *Codex Theodosianus*: *De Haereticis*

Over time, a legislative body of punitive edicts accumulated; this was later compiled by the grandson of Theodosius I, namely Theodosius II (r. 408–450), and became the sixteenth chapter of the *Codex Theodosianus* (CTh 16.5), *De Haereticis*. It consists of 66 chronologically ordered laws dealing with the problem of heretics. The number of laws already shows the magnitude of the problem of heresy in the early Christian mindset.

We find the following definition of *vera religio* (orthodoxy) as distinct from *falsa religio* (heresy) as follows:

> *that man shall be accepted as a defender of the Nicene faith and as a true adherent of the Catholic religion who confesses that Almighty God and Christ the Son of God are One in name, God of God, Light of Light, who does not violate by denial the Holy Spirit which we hope for and receive from the Supreme Author of things; that man who esteems, with the perception of inviolate faith, the undivided substance of the incorrupt Trinity, that substance which those of the orthodox faith call, employing a Greek word,* ousia. *The latter beliefs are surely more acceptable to Us and must be venerated.* (CTh 16.5.6,2, d. 381)
>
> *Those persons, however, who are not devoted to the aforesaid doctrines shall cease to assume, with studied deceit, the alien name of true religion [*vera religio*], and they shall be branded upon the disclosure of their crimes. They shall be removed and completely barred from the threshold of all churches, since We forbid all heretics to hold unlawful assemblies within the towns. We order that their madness shall be banished and that they shall be driven away from the very walls of the cities, on order that Catholic churches throughout the whole world may be restored to all orthodox bishops who hold the Nicene faith.* (CTh 16.5.6,3, d. 381)

The different edicts brought together in the *Codex Theodosianus* project heresy in negative, uncompromising, and moralizing language. Heretics were insulted with terms such as *sacrilegium, scelus, pollutio, perfidia, furor, criminosa religio*, and *nefaria superstitio*. Categories that were previously used in the Roman Empire to discuss the antonyms of *religio* and 'to blacken those who acted against the claimed public good in a religious or moral context. All now reappear to describe the figure of the heretic, thereby turning him into the epitome of moral evil' (Escribano Paño, 2010, p. 110). The logic of dichotomization is pervasive.

> *We prosecute all heresies [*haereses*] and all perfidies, all schisms and superstitions of the pagans [*omnia schismata superstitionesque gentilium*] and all false doctrines [*errores*] inimical to the Catholic faith [...] and they shall know that, as authors of sacrilegious superstition and as participants and accomplices [*sacrilegae superstitionisque*], they will be punished with proscription, so that if they cannot be recalled by reason from their perfidious false doctrine, at least they may be restrained by terror.* (CTh 16.5.63, d. 425)

Note that the *Codex* follows the taxonomic naming that we have already encountered in the genre of heresiology. Several heretic sects, like the Anomoeans, Macedonians, Arians, Encratites, and Apollinarians are explicitly mentioned in the *Codex*. Rhetorically, this process of name-giving serves several purposes. It denies heretics the name of Christians and projects a clear boundary between 'us' and 'them'. The taxonomic naming also makes the heretical threat real: there are people who have formed a group revolving around false beliefs and practices and who are eager to destroy the church from within and from without. When this taxonomic naming entered into legislation, it allowed '[e]mperors to style themselves as active and vigilant protectors of the empire against the dangerous heretics lurking within' (Humfress, 2007, p. 237).

Many edicts conceptualize heresy as a spatial problem: the heretic is a threat present inside the walls of the city, that is in the imperial orthodox space. That presence needs to be controlled because to allow heretics spatial freedom is 'to permit them to mirror the terms of orthodoxy as a public, legitimate, and sanctioned *religio*' (Berzon, 2017, p. 128). Thus, the laws state that heretics should not be allowed to convene in churches and that any churches they had taken from orthodox Christians would have to be returned. Nor were heretics allowed to own any type of ecclesial space. Kim Bowes points out that even 'private cult is listed time and again as being intrinsic to the heresy itself. Edicts that mention private worship in the context of heresy do so for two reasons: to eliminate all possible venues for heretical gatherings, including private houses, and to provide a further means of identifying heretical behavior' (Bowes, 2008, pp. 197–198): they hide in private places.

Several edicts reaffirm the association between heresy and deceit: heretics are fake; they pretend to be adherents to 'true catholic Christianity'. This idea of deceit was already prominently present in Irenaeus' discussion of the problem of heresy: heretics go by the name of Christians and heresy skilfully mimics true Christianity and operates under the guise of Trinitarian orthodoxy. The fact that heresy was understood to be contagious and poisonous only added to its danger (Text Box 4). Were one to do nothing, it would spread out and infect the entire community. Therefore, the heretic must be driven out from cities and villages (CTh 16.5.13; 16.5.20; 16.5.62), their homes 'confiscated' (CTh 16.5.34), and 'their occupants expelled from the whole world [*orbis terrarum*]' (CTh 16.5.18).

These edicts reveal how 'the social exclusion of dissidents from the Nicene Creed played a decisive role in the creation of Christian identity' (Escribano Paño, 2009, p. 39). The orthodox norm was given space and was made visible, and heretical voices, which in their own understanding were truly Christian, were pushed out. Even though the punishments projected are not consistent and vary from law to law, overall we see that 'late fourth- to sixth-century imperial legislators held that "orthodoxy" had to be defined and enforced, and heresy identified and excluded, if the fabric of empire was not to suffer' (Humfress, 2007, p. 235). Thus, the *Codex Theodosianus* heralded what would become an anti-heretical programme. There is no space for heretics, either in public or in private. Their expulsion 'actualizes [the] imaginary orthodox landscape [...] If the heretics were expelled to the unknown [...] they would be made totally oblivious. Their corrosive chaos could [...] be spatially and thus existentially neutralized within the orthodox world. The heretics, by antipodal association, became nothing' (Berzon, 2017, p. 146). Ideally, however, repentant heretics would convert and return to the Catholic Church.

Text Box 4: The Idea of Heresy as Contagious

The link that was made between heresy and contagious disease would have a terrible impact on the fate of assumed heretics and led to policies of compulsion, containment, expulsion and later even execution (Terpstra, 2015). This association between heresy and contagious disease comes up in Jerome's commentary on Paul's letter to the Galatians. In this commentary, Gal 5:9 plays an especially important part. Here we read: 'A little yeast works through the whole batch of dough' (NIV). In Jewish traditions yeast was already the symbol of moral and spiritual corruption. On the eve of Passover women would clear all traces of it from the house. In Christian communities, under the influence of Jerome (340/7–420), yeast would become a symbol of the corrupting power of heresy. Even the smallest amount of yeast can turn the entire batch of dough bad. Jerome projects another image, namely that of heresy spreading like cancer, throughout the body: 'A little bit of yeast, lightly spread, can change the nature of the loaf, and so "perverse teaching starting first from one man finds scarcely two or three listeners in the beginning", but spreads through the corporate unit just as a "cancer creeps in the body"' (2 Tim 2:17). Jerome, moreover, likens the risk of heretical corruption to the threat posed by the Jews and their fleshly observance of the law, which comes at the cost of a true spiritual reading. A heretic is like a Jew, in other words a non-Christian or an anti-Christian. 'In this conflation, Jerome suggested that the error and the corruption that runs through heretics and Jews was essentially one: an obsessive connection to carnality, and it was contagious' (Barbezat, 2018, p. 44). Orthodoxy was often projected as an antidote that was needed to counteract the sickening false beliefs. Here we may once again bring to mind Epiphanius' *Panarion*, which is presented as a remedy chest against the contagious and poisonous teachings of heresies. Of course, the more 'potent the disease, the stronger the remedies needed to cure it' (Kahlos, 2020, p. 43).

Augustine and the Persecution of Heretics

Against the background of the changed status of Christianity and the development of a body of legal texts criminalizing heresy, Augustine, Bishop of Hippo (354–430) formulated his defence of religious compulsion. This defence came in the form of a theology of intolerance and a pedagogy of fear, both packed as a kind of charitable hatred (Walsham, 2006).

Originally, that is before 400 CE, the church father stated that no one could be forced to embrace the Christian faith against their will and during his first years as a bishop Augustine used only friendly means of persuasion: dialogue, letters, and discussions (Augustine, ed. Schaff, 1996). Augustine believed that forced conversions would lead to inauthentic conversions and he objected to the use of secular power to force a person to return to the church. After 400, however, and inspired by his struggle against the Donatists, Augustine developed a theological blueprint for religious compulsion, based on the idea that only by re-entering the church could heretics be saved. While Augustine recognized that '[i]t is indeed better (as no one ever could deny) that men should be led to worship God by teaching, than that they should be driven to it by fear of punishment or pain', he also held that 'it does not follow that because the former course produces the better men, therefore those who do not yield to it should be neglected. For many have found advantage (as we have proved, and are daily proving by actual experiment), in being first compelled by fear or pain, so that they might afterwards be influenced by teaching, or might follow out in act what they had already learned in word' (Augustine, *The Correction of the Donatists* 6.21, ed. Schaff, 1996, p. 1273).

Several scholars have argued that Augustine's plea for coercion sprang from love rather than from hatred. Concern for the salvation of the sinner's soul makes coercion acceptable and perhaps even required, even if this seems distasteful. Furthermore, Augustine observed that coercion, as projected by various disciplinary laws, worked and was effective. Thus, in 408, he writes in a letter to Vincentius, Bishop of Cartenna and a Donatist:

> *I have, then, yielded to the facts suggested to me by my colleagues, [...] First of all, the case of my own city was set before me, which had been wholly Donatist, but was converted to Catholic unity by the fear of imperial laws, and which now holds your ruinous hatred in such detestation that one could believe it had never existed at all. (Augustine, Letter 93, trans. Parsons, 1953, p. 73)*

From 400 onwards, Augustine claimed that state authorities were 'under an obligation to supplement the work of the ecclesiastical hierarchy in rousing the wayward from their "lethargic sleep" in schism and false belief and awakening them to the salvation which could only be found in the unity of the Catholic Church' (Walsham, 2006, p. 41). If they refrained from using coercion they would fail to fulfil their responsibilities and the heretics would be lost. Since the goal of anti-heretical punishments was conversion (Barnard, 1995, p. 138), coercion is legitimate violence, while execution is illegitimate: to kill a heretic defeats the purpose of saving his soul.

Augustine's defence of persecution had an unmistakably heavy impact on Western Christian history. In fact, his position would function as a key justification for later use of force against heretics and non-believers and remained influential long after his lifetime.

4   The Constantinian Turn and the Destruction of Paganism?

Drawing on the rich biblical tradition of condemning idol worship that came to the Christians via Jewish traditions and Hebrew scriptures, Christians considered the former Roman sacrificial cult as gravely offensive to God, the sole and ultimate object of proper worship (Rubiés, 2006, p. 578). For Christian apologists, participation in the sacrificial cult was a hard border. They also regarded it to be a polluting practice with which they wanted to avoid all contact.

From 360 onwards, non-Christian gentiles were called pagans and the Roman cult was redefined in terms of paganism. This 'redefinition became widely known through Roman society' and would also be institutionalized in the legal system (Salzman, 1987, p. 176). Paganism now refers mainly to 'the series of rituals and actions that characterized the religious life of the Roman empire [...]. In other words, the definition of "pagan" religion here refers principally to cult practices, specifically their traditions, symbols, and infrastructure' (Leone, 2013, p. 6). After the Theodosian turn, in 399, steps were taken to dismantle the Roman cult even though it would continue to exist in the centuries following.

The Pagan as a Hermeneutical Figure

From the second half of the fourth century, *paganus* [country dweller] was the term used by Christians in colloquial language as a '"lump word" for all who were not heretics or Jews' (Brown, 1998, p. 639). That is also when this word started to appear in legal discourse. There is discussion amongst scholars as to why the term 'pagan' came to be used to depict non-Christian gentiles. Various etymological theories have been coined to explain this particular terminology.

One reason that *paganus* came to be associated with idol worship could be because Christianity spread more quickly in larger cities (e.g. Antioch, Alexandria, Rome, Corinth) than in rural areas where ancient 'traditions' continued to exist much longer. Christian thinkers were probably also influenced by Roman culture, where the *paganus* had already been associated with the superstition of the uneducated, foolish peasant, who did not live in the civilized urban Roman realm. The foolishness of the pagan intersects with the foolishness of idol worship. In any case, the notion of the pagan evokes a dichotomy 'between the centre and the periphery, sophistication and crudeness, and even the Roman and the barbarian' (Kahlos, 2020, p. 94).

Thomas Jürgasch finds that the notion *paganus* had an even broader usage, and could for example refer to the contrast between soldiers and civilians understood as non-soldiers. It could also project a contrast between the non-expert or layperson and the specialist or expert. According to Jürgasch, when

> *taking into account all [the] [...] different meanings of* paganus, *we can observe that despite the differences between them, they also display a common feature: The meaning of* paganus *depended on the respective opposite, the antonym the* paganus *was distinguished from in a particular context. To put this point more generally, a* paganus *was someone who was a stranger or an alien with regard to a particular group. (Jürgasch, 2015, p. 118)*

Jürgasch continues:

> *Hence, a* paganus *could be the counterpart of the soldier and therefore a civilian; he could be the counterpart of the townspeople and thus a countryman, and so forth. And what is more, in the course of history he was to become the counterpart to, and the nonparticipant of a group that itself for a long time was considered strange and alien in the Roman Empire – the Christians. (Jürgasch, 2015, p. 118)*

In this view, the notion refers to someone who is an outsider, someone who lives at the fringes of society/community, someone who does not belong. Certainly, from the fourth and fifth centuries onwards, 'the Christians did indeed consider the non-Christians as outsiders or nonparticipants of their own group and that the usage of the term *paganus* reflected their attitude toward the non-Christians' (Jürgasch, 2015, p. 120). Pagans became non-Christians and Christians non-pagans. Put differently, the Christianization of the empire was mirrored in the paganization of the Roman cult (and its practitioners) and vice versa.

58 CHAPTER 2 The Coercive Turn

The Christian logic against idol worship is that images are man-made rather than divine creations: pagans worshipped dead artefacts, like wooden or stone statues, as if they were gods, which is stupid. In Augustine's words:

> *If I say to a pagan, 'Where is your god?' he will show me his image ... 'There you are', he says, pointing with his finger, 'there is my god'. I laugh at the stone. I seize it. I smash it, I throw it away. I hold it in contempt. (Augustine, Sermo 223A.4, trans. Hill, 1993, quoted by Shaw, 2011, p. 210)*

When 'pagans' defended themselves, by arguing that their images were not dead and that what they worshipped was not the material itself but rather the spirits residing in them, Christian polemicists would contend that they worshipped demonic spirits under the guidance of fake priests. Furthermore, false worship supposedly translated into immoral behaviour, and so pagans, time and again, would be depicted as barbaric, wild, savage, drunk, violent, and engaged in perverse sexual practices. These depictions too would prove to be 'remarkably durable and almost infinitely transferable' and malleable (Lipton, 2014).

As a rhetorical figure, the pagan serves several, often overlapping, functions depending on the intentions of the Christian scholars (Kahlos, 2020, p. 95). Christian writers mention the pagan most frequently in polemical anti-heretical literature as a way to slander erring Christians or to discredit a doctrinal opponent or a heretic, somewhat like calling him a Jew or a Judaizer. Consider in this regard Athanasius of Alexandria (295–373), who defamed the Arians (heretics *par excellence*) by calling them pagans:

> *Who would call them even by the name of pagans, much less that of Christians? Would anyone regard their habits and feelings as human and not rather those of wild beasts, seeing their cruel and savage conduct? [...] They are much inferior to the pagans and stand far apart and separate from them. (Athanasius, Hist. Arian. 64, NPNF, modified by Kahlos, 2020, p. 96)*

At the Council of Nicaea, too, opposing parties would accuse one another of Hellenism (a term also used to depict paganism, see Text Box 3). However, Christian authors could also invoke the counterimage of a good and noble pagan to contrast with Christians who showcase immoral behaviour and waste their time on drinking and feasting. No wonder pagans would not convert! In fact, to the eyes of the noble pagan, Christian corruption and perversity was an affront. Here the hermeneutical figure of the pagan functions as a way to encourage Christians to repent and convert. In other contexts, church leaders would sometimes complain about churchgoers who continued to participate in pagan festivities or performed pagan rituals. 'Here the pagan label functioned as a method of chastisement' (Kahlos, 2020, p. 97). In any case, labelling religiously ambivalent people as pagans was a means by which bishops and ecclesiastical authorities tried to police the boundaries of the church and distinguish between insiders and outsiders.

The pagan is a collective, ahistorical, acultural, and imaginary construct. The knowledge produced by this trope does not derive first and foremost from social interaction and makes sense only within (Christian) theological narrative in which there is but one true religion. Consequently, the label 'pagan' functions without having a clear referent. The questions 'Who is the pagan?' 'What do they do?' 'What inspires them?' 'What norms do they uphold?' 'What do they call themselves?' are just not relevant questions within a polemical Christian framework. Similarly, later on, we do not really learn about Celtic, Slavic, Germanic people and their traditions. The assumption was that those people called pagans did not have 'any name for themselves nor conceived of themselves as any kind of unified religious tradition [...]. They neither had a common creed nor aimed at one' (Kahlos, 2020, p. 95). Furthermore, as with the figure of the heretic, the pagan is a trope frozen in time. The pagan of today is in principle the same as the pagan of the past. Paganism never changes. This would explain why contemporary pagan practices were often approached through the lens of ancient Greek, Roman, or sometimes Egyptian polytheistic traditions, or why they were traced back to 'the prototypical episode of idolatry: the forging of the golden calf at the foot of the Sinai while Moses received the laws up above' (Akbari, 2005, p. 34). The message communicated is that paganism is a uniform phenomenon that fundamentally stays the same and therefore may be understood in reference to similar ancient phenomena. This way of thinking about paganism had a long-lasting impact, to the extent that in the eighteenth and nineteenth centuries, when 'comparative scholars' were trying to make sense of the beliefs and practices of newly discovered people, they did so by referencing the Greeks, the Egyptians, the Phoenicians. The idea was that one could learn about ancient pagan traditions by looking at current pagans and vice versa.

The *Codex Theodosianus*: *De Paganis*

After the Constantinian turn, the category of paganism came to function in legal discourse, where it would impact the lives of 'real' pagans, or those perceived as such. The *Codex Theodosianus* 16.10, *Pagans, Sacrifices, and Temples* records 25 chronologically ordered laws aimed at delegitimizing and dismantling pagan cult. These laws also conceptualize paganism as a spatial problem and envision a topography of the Western Roman Empire that has transmuted into a Christian space. For Christians, these laws implied that they 'were able to mingle freely in public space without the risk of encountering a smoking sacrificial altar, a certain source of demonic pollution for Christians, and a truly divisive symbol of the old order' (Brown, 1998, p. 645). For pagans these laws implied serious restrictions.

Text Box 5: The Myth of Christian Triumphalism

Patterns of religionization produce imaginary constructs of self and other. Such imaginary constructs were often captured in mythic accounts of history with ruptures in time, heroes and losers, and grand gestures. That is also the case for the binary pair of Christian/pagan. Christian *literati* frequently portrayed the Constantinian turn as a triumph for Christianity. Accounts of the dismantling of pagan temples were projected as evidence of the defeat of the pagan gods and the victory of the Christian God. Such accounts serve 'an important function in the evolving self-fashioning of Christian identity. Pagan temples were presented as a threat to Christian souls and the community. Bishops and charismatic ascetic leaders were portrayed as saving endangered souls by annihilating and purifying old cult places' (Kahlos, 2020, p. 59). These accounts are part of an effort of Christian *literati* to turn 'Christianity' into the 'ineluctable winner' over rival traditions (Bachrach, 1985, p. 400).

The process of Christianization of 'Europe' spanned several centuries and was never as absolute as is sometimes claimed (Lavan & Mulryan, 2011). The dismantlement of the Roman cult was a slow cultural process and for a long time, new laws notwithstanding, many people at the grassroots level would remain 'impenitently polytheistic in that the religious common sense of their age, as of all previous centuries, led them to assume a spiritual landscape rustling with invisible presences – with countless divine beings and their ethereal ministers. Exclusive loyalty to the One God of the Christians, the dismissal of all ancient gods as maleficent (if not ineffectual) demons, and a redrawing of the map of Roman society in such a way as to see the world in terms of a single, all-embracing dichotomy between Christians and non-Christians; these views were already asserted, at this time, by some Christians; they would enjoy a long future in Byzantium and the medieval west' but in the fifth century despite a growing body of legal texts, these 'were not yet the views of the "cognitive majority" of the Roman world' (Brown, 1998, p. 632). Most continued to live in a world inhabited by many gods.

While the assumption is often put forward that, after the Constantinian turn, Christians used their power to convert the pagans, if necessary by force, in reality this was just not possible in the fourth century because of the large numbers of non-Christians. 'It took a further century of social and religious changes before Justinian could envisage the compulsory baptism of remaining polytheists, and a further century yet until Heraclius and the Visigothic kings of Spain attempted to baptize the Jews' (Brown, 1998, p. 632). For decades Christian as well as pagan groups were involved in a power struggle. Pagan traditions moreover became mixed with Christian practices and after a while some of these practices were simply incorporated in a Christian framework and their pagan origins were forgotten. In this sense, paganism is not just 'the other' of Christianity, it is also part of the history of Christian traditions. Several pagan traditions continued to exist, mainly in more remote rural eras, even after these regions were claimed to have been officially Christianized. 'The names of the days of the week, the months of the year and the constellations in the sky continue to be resolutely pagan, and classical pagan motifs persisted in medieval literature and to a much lesser extent in medieval art; in both, they were, of course, to experience a tremendous expansion at the end of the Middle Ages and thereafter. In Christianity itself, many of trappings of ritual, and the form of buildings, were taken over from the pagan ancient world' (Hutton, 2011, p. 235). Moreover, many people continued to practise 'folk magic', carry amulets, visit 'sacred' trees or wells (to combat infertility for example) while also observing Christian rituals. Curses, spells, and potions were widespread. Fortune tellers and astrologers operated side by side with priests, and pagan deities turned into ghosts, which inhabited people's dreams, visions, and nightmares. It was quite difficult to eradicate such practices from Christianized territories. In the study of religion, such practices are often called vernacular, popular, or folk religion as distinguished from official learned religion (Primiano, 1995, p. 38).

In an almost repetitive fashion the pagan laws call for the abandonment, re-use, or destruction of the altars and the removal of images. When confiscated temples came into the hands of the church, the church would record 'its thanks for the gift by naming the church in honor of its imperial benefactor' (Shaw, 2011, p. 233). Some laws call for the eradication of all superstition but suggest that 'temples outside the walls shall remain untouched' because they are part of cultural heritage (CTh 10.3, d. 346). Sometimes even the statues are to be left alone. They should be 'measured by the value of their art rather than by their divinity' (CTh 10.8, d. 382). In intercultural studies one would call this a form of code-switching – these statues are no longer religious phenomena but have become cultural ones.

The laws detail and forbid a whole range of cultic practices. One shall not 'venerate his lar with fire, his genius with wine, his penates with fragrant odors; he shall not burn lights to them, place incense before them, or suspend wreaths for them' (CTh 16.10.12, d. 392). Such idolatrous practices violated *religio*. Pagan feasts were to be transformed into workdays unless they were somehow integrated into the Christian calendar. Often transgressors would have to pay a fine. Privileges that had been granted by ancient law to priests, ministers, prefects, or hierophants of the sacred mysteries have to be abolished (CTh 16.10.14, d. 396) and those who have been 'polluted by the profane false doctrine of crime of pagan rites [...] shall not be honored with the rank of administrator or judge' (CTh 16.10.21, d. 415).

Especially animal sacrifice or blood sacrifice became the foil over against which Christianity would come to define itself. To the mind of Christians, sacrifice symbolized the wickedness or the madness of paganism. In 312, Constantine banned all blood offerings as the most offensive pagan practice (even though the imperial cult was still retained) and punishments could follow from engaging in such practices (CTh 16.10.2, d. 341). The laws addressing 'pagan cult' are likewise permeated by normative moralizing language setting up a binary between *vera religio* and the falsities of paganism (also called pagan superstition). Both the adjectives and the nouns used to depict pagan cult are negative, ranging from 'abhorrent', 'condemned', 'forbidden', 'deviating from the dogmas of Catholic faith', 'meaningless idols', 'the worse sacrilege', 'execrable', 'insane', honouring 'vain idols', 'criminal'. Paganism is even called 'an outrage against religion'.

[...] the temples shall be immediately closed in all places and in all cities, and access to them forbidden, so as to deny to all abandoned men the opportunity to commit sin. [...] [A]ll men shall abstain from sacrifices. But if perchance any man should perpetrate any such criminality, he shall be struck down with the avenging sword. [...] The governors of the provinces shall be similarly punished if they should neglect to avenge such crimes. (CTh 16.10.4. d. 346, 354, 356)

Nocturnal sacrifices [...] shall be abolished, and henceforth such nefarious license shall be destroyed. (CTh 16.10.5. d. 353)

If any madman or sacrilegious person [...] should immerse himself in forbidden sacrifices [...] and if he should suppose that he should employ, or should think that he should approach, a shrine or a temple for the commission of such a crime, he shall know that he will be subjected to proscription, since [...] God must be worshipped by chaste prayers and not be profaned by dire incantations. (CTh 16.10.7. d. 381)

If any judge also [...] should rely on the privilege of his power, and as a sacrilegious violator of the law, should enter polluted places, he shall be forced to pay into Our treasury fifteen pounds of gold, and his office staff a like sum, unless they opposed him with their combined strength. (CTh 16.10.11. d. 391)

While the enforcement of these laws is uncertain, official support for public cult would gradually be dismantled. The programmes to dismantle paganism were intertwined with internal power struggles and the need to gain control and order. The assumption was that uniformity of practice and belief enhances stability, and that dispute may lead to disorder. From this perspective, Roman Christian rulers were not so different from their Roman, pagan predecessors and their concern for social order. Order in the church and order in the empire were seen to go hand in hand.

During the centuries that followed the Constantinian turn, whether in Visigothic Spain or in the Carolingian Empire or in Anglo-Saxon England, rulers and bishops would continue to combat pagan subcultures and press for the implantation (via the elite) of Christian institutions, practices, habits, and beliefs. On the outskirts of the empire, however, the process of Christianization would take time and for centuries pagan practice and the pagan as 'hermeneutical figure' would continue to figure prominently in written documents, whether theological or juridical.

5 Anti-Jewish Rhetoric and the Establishment of Jewish Tradition as *Religio Licita*

The situation of the Jews in the Western Roman Empire in the fourth and fifth centuries is complex. First, anti-Jewish polemics proliferated and the Jews continued to be projected as the anti-Christians *par excellence*. The anti-Jewish rhetoric (*adversus Iudaeos*) that was fabricated during this period continued to function as a cultural archive for centuries to come; the sermons by the church father John Chrysostom are a case in point (see below). The fourth and fifth centuries are also the time when Augustine developed his influential doctrine of Jewish witness, that would later be invoked by church leaders to protect Jewish communities against violent anti-Jewish outbursts, particularly in the context of the crusades (see Chapter 3). To understand the complexity of Christian-Jewish relations, we must also consider the *Theodosian Code*, which projects the Jews as a third 'group' of non-Christians, next to the pagans and the heretics, thereby affirming and consolidating the Christian map of the world. The legal status of the Jews was different from that of the other two groups however: while heresy and paganism are forbidden, Jewish tradition has the status of *religio licita*, though this does nothing to ameliorate the fact that the *Theodosian Code* rhetorically humiliates the Jews and uses only negative moralizing language to depict them.

Anti-Jewish Rhetorics: Chrysostom as a Case in Point

In the aftermath of the Constantinian turn one notices an increase in anti-Jewish rhetoric. Fredriksen remarks that this is strange, considering that 'these new circumstances represent[ed] a clear victory for "orthodox" Christianity'. Indeed, 'by the mid-fourth century, the Septuagint had empathically become the church's Old Testament; "heresy" had made the transition from being a form of name-calling to being a legal disability; the old Jewish homeland had become the new Christian Holy Land; and the church and its bishops were actively supported by imperial largesse' (Fredriksen, 2014, p. 28). Christians, at least a certain strand of Christians, had, so it seems, finally triumphed. So where did this proliferation of anti-Jewish polemics originate?

According to Fredriksen, intra-Christian dissensus 'goes far in explaining this new bloom of rhetoric *contra Iudaeos*' (Fredriksen, 2014, p. 29). The explicit formulation of Nicene Creed did not halt intra-Christian debate, but rather triggered it and led to further fracturing, and the Constantinian vision of Christian uniformity and stability remained a far-off dream. Polemical texts ranting against Christian heretics enthusiastically made use of the hermeneutical figure of the Jew, understood as the anti-Christian. To call one's opponent a Jew was similar to calling him a heretic or even a pagan. These tropes are versatile. In this regard, anti-Jewish polemics on the part of Christian scholars often had little to do with real Jews or with Jewish traditions. The Jews were constructed in line with the needs of a Christian theological agenda.

Some church fathers, however, did have concrete social realities in mind when writing polemical tracts. John of Antioch, also known as John Chrysostom (347–407) is a case in point. He wrote seven anti-Jewish sermons, which he preached in Antioch in the first two years following his ordination to the rank of presbyter (John Chrysostom, trans. Harkins, 2010).[5] These sermons are not written against the Jews but are aimed at those Christians who continue to mix and mingle with Jews, keep the Shabbat, and participate in Jewish festivities (the so-called Judaizers). Chrysostom's goal was to draw clear boundaries between Christians and Jews and to end the practice of Judaization.[6]

The language Chrysostom uses is incendiary, violent, abusive, full of half-truths, rhetoric misconstruals, excess, and exaggeration (van der Horst, 2000, pp. 228–229). As James Parkes observes, 'in these sermons there is no sneer too mean, no gibe too bitter for him to fling at the Jewish people. No text is too remote to be able to be twisted to their confusion, no argument is too casuistical, no blasphemy too startling for him to employ' (Parkes, 1974, p. 163). Chrysostom calls the Jews 'the most miserable and wretched of all men' and states that they are 'more dangerous than any wolves' (*Jud.* 4.1, trans. Harkins, 2010, pp. 71 and 72) and compares them to dogs. He argues that the Jews carry their snares everywhere and spread their nets to snatch Christians. He depicts the Jews as blind and stubborn, and as having cast away their chance at salvation. Furthermore, he reiterates the deicide charge (cf. Melito of Sardis) and projects the Jews as responsible for Christ's death. They are rejected by God and cursed. To his mind, for all of these reasons, one should avoid any contact with them.

> But do not be surprised that I called the Jews pitiable. They really are pitiable and miserable. When so many blessings from heaven came into their hands, they thrust them aside and were at great pains to reject them. [...] We, who were nurtured by darkness, drew the light to ourselves and were freed from the gloom of their error. They were the branches of that holy root, but those branches were broken. (Chrysostom, Jud. 1.2, trans. Harkins, 2010, p. 5)

> *Nothing is more miserable than those people who never failed to attack their own salvation. When there was need to observe the Law, they trampled it under foot. Now that the Law has ceased to bind, they obstinately strive to observe it. What could be more pitiable than those people who provoke God not only by transgressing the Law but also by keeping it? On this account Stephen said: 'You stiffnecked and uncircumcised in heart, you always resist the Holy Spirit'. (Chrysostom, Jud. 1.2, trans. Harkins, 2010, p. 6)*
>
> *But I must get back again to those who are sick. Consider, then with whom they are sharing their fasts. It is with those who shouted: 'Crucify him! Crucify him', with those who said: 'His blood be upon us and upon our children'. If some men had been caught in rebellion against their ruler and were condemned, would you have dared to go up to them and to speak with them? I think not. Is it not foolish, then, to show readiness to flee from those who have sinned against a man, but to enter into fellowship with those who have committed outrages against God himself? Is it not strange that those who worship the Crucified keep common festival with those who crucified him? Is it not a sign of folly and the worst madness? (Chrysostom, Jud. 1.5, trans. Harkins, 2010, p. 18)*

To Chrysostom's mind, the Jews are a defiled and impure people, because they have shed the blood of Christ. This terrible picture of the Jews as Christ-killers is further enhanced by Chrysostom's use of sexual slander. Jews are a sexually deviant people neighing after their neighbours' wives, while Judaizers are sexual predators, preying on innocent Christians. Their lack of bodily self-control shows that they are a 'base' people.

Chrysostom even calls them *chorous malakōn synagagontes*. According to Dale Martin, this implies their being gendered as feminine, namely as a soft and weak people. Indeed, *malakos* 'can refer to many things: the softness of expensive clothes, the richness and delicacy of gourmet food, the gentleness of light winds and breezes. When used as a term of moral condemnation, the word still refers to something perceived as 'soft': laziness, degeneracy, decadence, lack of courage, or, to sum up all these vices in one ancient category, the feminine' (Martin, 2006, p. 44).

Not only is it an offence to God if Christians celebrate with Jews, participate in their festivals and share practices of commensality; Jewish impurity is also contagious. It may spread and contaminate Christian communities. It is for these reasons that boundaries between Jews and Christians must be upheld.

> *So it is that I exhort you to flee and shun their gatherings. The harm they bring to our weaker brothers is not slight; they offer no slight excuse to sustain the folly of the Jews. For when they see that you, who worship the Christ, whom they crucified, are reverently following their ritual, how can they fail to think that the rites they have performed are the best and that our ceremonies are worthless. For after you worship and adore at our mysteries, you run to the very men who destroy our rites. [...]. Therefore, flee the gatherings and holy places of the Jews. Let no men venerate the synagogue because of the holy books; let him hate and avoid it because the Jews outrage and maltreat the holy ones, because they refuse to believe their words, because they accuse them of the ultimate impiety. (Chrysostom, Jud. 1.5, trans. Harkins, 2010, pp. 20–21)*

Chrysostom's sermons were translated and spread widely. They were popular with the masses and reflected a culture of anti-Jewish denigration (Bibliowicz, 2013, p. 185). Even though the target audience of his sermons were Christians and Judaizing Christians, and even though these sermons deal with an intra-Christian problem, historically speaking it was 'the Jews [who became] its victims' (Gager, 1983, p. 119).

64 CHAPTER 2 The Coercive Turn

Augustine's Doctrine of Jewish Witness: A Different Sound

While Chrysostom's sermons severely impacted medieval perceptions of the Jews, we should also consider Augustine's theology of the Jews. Based on a careful reading of Scripture, particularly the Pauline letters and Genesis, Augustine developed a more moderate view on the Jewish question than that of his contemporaries. In fact, he 'endowed the Jews, their sacred texts, and their presence in Christendom with a new dimension to their purpose, one that has, in various ways, controlled the Western idea of the Jew ever since' (Cohen, 1999, p. 15).

Augustine's original contribution has come to be known as the doctrine of Jewish witness (Cohen, 2009; Fredriksen, 2010). Fredriksen points out he developed this doctrine against the background of his debate with the Manichean Faustus (Augustine, ed. Schaff, 1996). Faustus fiercely attacked the Old Testament and questioned the place of the 'Jewish parts' in the Bible. He also challenged Augustine to explain why he 'still believed in the prophesies of the Old Testament', even when contemporary Christians had moved away from Jewish practice. In his response, Augustine refuted the Manichean rejection of the Old Testament while upholding the triumph and glory of the church. The church father defended the canon, arguing that God had chosen Israel as his elected people, made a covenant with them, and gave them the law. The Old Testament relates this unique history of God and Israel, and all its content is historically true (in the case of narrative) and valid (in the case of prophesy). Furthermore, Augustine states, the Old Testament prefigures the New Testament and the New Testament fulfils the Old. '[A]ll that Moses wrote is of Christ, or relates to Christ, either as predicting Him by words or actions, or as illustrating His grace and glory' (Augustine, *Against Faustus* 16.9, ed. Schaff, 1996, p. 378). Thus, the wisdom of the prophets is an authentic and reliable source of revelation. Seeing this otherwise, as the Manicheans do, would lead to a situation in which the authority of all sacred books becomes questionable: 'If he wrote what was false here, when did he say what was true?' (Augustine, *Letter 40 to Jerome* 3.3, ed. Schaff, 1887a). Augustine, however, also argued that the incarnation is the climax of salvation history and that Christ's life, suffering, and resurrection provide the hermeneutical key with which to read Scripture. The fact that the Jewish people do not recognize Christ precludes them from properly understanding their own scriptures. Tapping into existing anti-Jewish tropes, he calls the Jews blind, stubborn, and hard-heartened. The church, the true bride of Christ, 'knows the difference between the letter and the spirit, or in other words, between law and grace; and serving God no longer in the oldness of the letter, but in newness of spirit, she is not under the law, but under grace' (*Against Faustus* 15.8, ed. Schaff, 1996, p. 255). The Old Testament continues to testify to the truth of Christian *vera religio*. As David Nirenberg puts it: 'Every word of the old Law was good. Every word of it was literally true, even if allegory was necessary for the Christian to find salvation in it. The coming of Jesus and his gospel closed the Law as a path to salvation, but it did not condemn it' (Nirenberg, 2014).

Nevertheless, the question arises: what (if any) is the lasting significance of the Jews and their practice today, now that God has revealed Godself in Christ, now that the church has been established and now that the vast majority of Christians are gentiles? (Cohen, 1998, 1999, 2009). In response to this question, and following an existing typological hermeneutic of Scripture, Augustine compares the status of the Jewish people after the murder of Christ to that of Cain after he killed his younger brother out of jealousy. This typological reading is multi-layered. First, he states that while the Jews of the Old Testament and the first generation of Christ-following Jews were right in upholding the law that had been given to them by God in the first covenant, they were wrong to continue living under the rule of that law. God rejects the Jewish, earth-bound offer and accepts the faithful worship of the church (Abel, the younger brother).

> As Cain's sacrifice of the fruit of the ground is rejected, while Abel's sacrifice of his sheep and the fat thereof is accepted, so the faith of the New Testament praising God in the harmless service of grace is preferred to the earthly observances of the Old Testament. For though the Jews were right in practising these things, they were guilty

of unbelief in not distinguishing the time of the New Testament when Christ came, from the time of the Old Testament. (Augustine, Against Faustus 12.9, ed. Schaff, 1996, p. 214)

Second, he argues that the Jews, like Cain, killed their younger brother, Jesus. If Abel's blood cursed Cain, so does Christ's blood curse the Jewish people. The church has supplanted Israel as God's beloved people. Abel dies in the field; Christ dies on Calvary. Their continued carnal observation of the law does not bring them salvation, because salvation comes only from Christ:

[T]he Church admits and avows the Jewish people to be cursed, because after killing Christ they continue to till the ground of an earthly circumcision, an earthly Sabbath, an earthly passover, while the hidden strength or virtue of making known Christ, which this tilling contains, is not yielded to the Jews while they continue in impiety and unbelief, for it is revealed in the New Testament. While they will not turn to God, the veil which is on their minds in reading the Old Testament is not taken away. This veil is taken away only by Christ, who does not do away with the reading of the Old Testament, but with the covering which hides its virtue. [...] In this way the Jewish people, like Cain, continue tilling the ground, in the carnal observance of the law, which does not yield to them its strength, because they do not perceive in it the grace of Christ. (Augustine, Against Faustus 12.11, ed. Schaff, 1996, pp. 215–216)

To punish the Jews for having killed his Son, God scattered Israel over the earth and condemned them to a life in exile and to a position of subjugation vis-à-vis the church. '[N]o one can fail to see that in every land where the Jews are scattered, they mourn for the loss of their kingdom, and are in terrified subjection to the immensely superior number of Christians' (Augustine, *Against Faustus* 12.12, ed. Schaff, 1996, p. 319). Cursed as they may be, in Augustine's reading God also protects the Jews by giving them the mark of Cain.

No harm should be done to the Jewish people because they serve a twofold vital testimonial function in Christian societies. On the one hand, their subjugated, scattered (cursed) position bears testimony to their guilt. Their survival in exile confirms the dominion of the church, that has replaced them as God's beloved people. On the other hand, their scriptures and rituals testify to the roots of the New Testament in the Old, and to the truth of the prophesies of Christ. Augustine calls them 'our book keepers' (*librarii nostri*).

But the Jews who slew Him, and would not believe in Him, [...] were yet more miserably wasted by the Romans, and utterly rooted out from their kingdom, where aliens had already ruled over them, and were dispersed through the lands (so that indeed there is no place where they are not), and are thus by their own Scriptures a testimony to us that we have not forged the prophecies about Christ. [...] Therefore God has shown the Church in her enemies the Jews the grace of His compassion, since, as says the apostle, 'their offense is the salvation of the Gentiles' (Rom 11:11). And therefore He has not slain them, that is, He has not let the knowledge that they are Jews be lost in them, although they have been conquered by the Romans, lest they should forget the law of God, and their testimony should be of no avail in this matter of which we treat. But it was not enough that he should say, 'Slay them not, lest they should at last forget Your law', unless he had also added, 'Disperse them'; because if they had only been in their own land with that testimony of the Scriptures, and not every where, certainly the Church which is everywhere could not have had them as witnesses among all nations to the prophecies which were sent before concerning Christ. (Augustine, City of God XVIII.46, ed. Schaff, 1887b)

Those who wish to harm the Jews would evoke the wrath of God and would 'bring upon himself the sevenfold penalty under which the Jews lie for the crucifixion of Christ' (Augustine, *Against Faustus* 12.12, ed. Schaff, 1996, p. 216).

Augustine argues that this explains the fact that the Jews enjoyed a special status in the Christian Roman Empire. They are the sole non-Christian minority which deserved protection and should not be hindered in their practices by the new Christian religious laws. Thus Augustine said,

> *all the nations subjugated by Rome adopted the heathenish ceremonies of the Roman worship; while the Jewish nation, whether under Pagan or Christian monarchs, has never lost the sign of their law, by which they are distinguished from all other nations and peoples. No emperor or monarch who finds under his government the people with this mark kills them, that is, makes them cease to be Jews, and as Jews to be separate in their observances, and unlike the rest of the world.* (Augustine, Against Faustus *12.12, ed. Schaff, 1996, p. 320)*

This Augustinian approach to the Jews and Judaism laid the foundation for Christian-Jewish relations and Jewish life in medieval society: on the one hand, the Jews, following God's will, were granted safe and secure existence in Christian society, on the other, they were not allowed to thrive and were to accept their subjugated condition (Chazan, 2016, p. 15). Until the eleventh and twelfth centuries, Augustine's legacy theologically justified the presence of the Jewish communities in Christian societies, where they seem to have flourished, and 'provided authority for later learned churchmen, who used it [...] to deflect and defuse Christian violence against Jews' (Fredriksen, 2010, p. xii).

The *Codex Theodosianus* and the Jews

The laws regulating Jewish life are mostly contained in Chapter 16.8–9 of the *Code*. Like the laws pertaining to the heretics and the pagans, these laws are filled with 'explicit value-laden rhetoric' (Linder, 2006, p. 149), and 'all the adjectives and most of the nouns and verbs that were applied to Jews were negative' (Linder, 2006, p. 149). When discussing the Jews and their practices, the *Code* employs 'several religious composites with oppositional prefixes, such as "incredulity" [*incredulitas*], "impiety" [*impietas*], "the most impious" [*impiissimi*], "nefarious" [*nefarius*], and "sacrilegious" [*sacrilegus*]' (Linder, 2006, p. 149). Furthermore, the Jews are associated with such notions as 'deformity and illness, pestilence, filth, abomination, death, infamy and madness' (Lindner, 2006, p. 149). Generally speaking, the Jews are projected as a threat to the health, purity, sanity, and honour of the Christian Roman Empire. As with the heretics, the Jews are associated with the risk of contagion, with pollution and plague. They defile and corrupt Christian society, which ought to purge itself from this threat. Furthermore, as Roman identity and Christian identity are equated, Jews are presented as alien and hostile to the Roman state (Linder, 2006, pp. 149–150).

This polemical rhetoric, however, does not translate into one-sidedly discriminatory legislation. On the one hand, the Jewish socio-political status was not equal to that of Christians. Jews were theologically inferior and this was matched with their socio-political status of inferiority. They were not allowed to proselytize, namely pollute a Christian or a man of any sect, freeborn or slave, with the Jewish 'stigma' (CTh 16.8.22) nor were they allowed to hold Christian slaves (CTh 3.1.4; 16.8.22; 16.9.1; 2.5): 'For We consider it abominable that very religious slaves should be defiled by the ownership of very impious purchasers' (CTh 16.9.5, d. 423). They were not allowed to hold public office in the government, become advocates, or enter into the imperial service or secret service (CTh 16.8.24) nor were they allowed to build new synagogues. These prohibitions were meant to protect Christians against the threat of Judaizing. Finally, Jews were not allowed to marry Christians (16.8.6 and 3.7.2):

> *It shall be observed that Jews shall not hereafter unite Christian women to their villainy; if they should do so, however, they shall be subject to the peril of capital punishment.* (CTh *16.8.6, d. 339)*

Legally, Jews were awarded a 'recognized, if inferior and, in practice, uncertain place within Christian society' (Stantchev, 2014, p. 68) and these laws do in fact intend to limit social relations between Jews and Christians.

On the other hand, the *Codex Theodosianus* also built on and maintained an entire set of privileges that had previously been granted to the Jews by pagan rulers. Jewish communities had a significant degree of autonomy (Fredriksen, 2014, p. 31). They were allowed to circumcise their sons, celebrate Shabbat and other feasts, and gather in the synagogues. They were also exempt from engaging in activities that profane their religion and Jews had the right not to attend court on Shabbat or any other religious or feast day. Jewish synagogues were not to be destroyed or unlawfully seized. Jews were not persecuted and massive and forced conversion did not belong to the official policy. Even more strikingly, a law dated 416 stated that judges should allow 'men bound to the Jewish religion [who] wish to become associated in the fellowship of the Church for the purpose of evading prosecution for crimes or on account of different necessities, [...] to return to their own law [*ad legem propriam*]' (CTh 16.8.23). Finally, the *Codex Theodosianus* established Jewish worship as a *religio licita* (legal, licit, tolerated practice) and stated that the sect of the Jews is prohibited by no law (CTh 16.8.9). Thus, Jews enjoyed at least a certain degree of legal protection, in a way that neither heretics nor pagans did. Often Christian-Jewish relations were peaceful, close, and friendly.

6   Islam Enters the Scene

In the seventh century, a new movement emerged in the Arabian Peninsula around the prophetic figure of Muhammad, a merchant from Mecca who received several revelations from the archangel Gabriel. During the next two decades, he preached these revelations [*āyāt*], which called for a strict monotheism and submission to God. Eventually these revelations were put in writing in the Qur'an. While the Qu'ran expressed deep respect for the people of the book, at the same time it claimed that the revelation that was handed revealed to Muhammad was a necessary correction of the Hebrew scriptures and the gospels. The Qur'an casts Muhammad as the last in a long prophetic line. Though Jesus is highly regarded as a prophet – he is placed next in line after Muhammad – the Christian claim that he is the Son of God is rejected.

Historians are still struggling to trace the history of the origin of Islam. For a long time, research seems to have 'oscillated between two main options' (Stroumsa, 2015, p. 77). Islam was traced back to either Jewish sources or to Christian sources. According to Sarah Stroumsa, however, neither option does justice to the entangled religious, political, and cultural milieu of the sixth- and seventh-century Near East, which was marked by the free circulation of pagan, Jewish, Jewish-Christian, and Christian beliefs and practices in a dazzling complexity of oral traditions, scriptural sources, and behavioural patterns. In this setting, it is highly unlikely that Islam can be traced back to only one source. It is more appropriate to recognize that 'in this complex intellectual world the ideas flow into each other, brazenly oblivious to communal barriers. The flow of ideas was never unilateral or linear, but rather went back and forth, creating [...] a whirlpool effect' (Stroumsa, 2009, p. xiv).

Early Christian Interpretations of Islam

Initially, Christian commentators had little to say about Muhammad or the Qu'ran as a spiritual development and in their texts we find no trace of the now common terms 'Islam' or 'Muslim'. Early Christian commentators were not interested in the Qur'anic prophecies. Their concern was the expansionary drive and military success of the Arabs, and where

68 CHAPTER 2 The Coercive Turn

Muhammad is named it is in reference to his role as a political leader, not as a spiritual leader. As we shall see, this will become a recurrent theme in Christian dealings with Islam (Green, 2019, p. 36). The religionized ideas about Islam that developed were perhaps more telling about Christians than about Muslims. Islam was approached through the lens of Christianity.

In 637, Jerusalem surrendered to Caliph Umar (r. 634–644), who built a mosque (*al-Masjid al Aqsa*) and a shrine (the Dome of the Rock) which could compete with the grandeur of the churches. In laying claim to this sacred site, the Muslims profiled themselves as the sole legitimate heirs of Abraham, who was neither Jew nor Christian. While Muslim rulers, based on the Qur'an, implemented a policy of toleration vis-à-vis Jews and Christians (the people of the book), Emperor Heraclius (r. 610–641) saw the construction on the Temple Mount as a 'refutation of the Christian vision of history anchored firmly in the bedrock of Jerusalem, spiritual center of the Christian world' (Tolan, 2002, p. 46). Heraclius 'marked the loss of Jerusalem by ordering every Jew within his shrinking empire to be baptized' (Chidester, 2000). The fate of the enemies within and that of the enemies without are joined together.

Christians sought to provide a biblical theological account of what they perceived as a military threat. Sophronius (r. 634–638), the Patriarch of Jerusalem, who surrendered Jerusalem to Caliph Umar in 637, called the invasion of the 'beasty' and barbarous Arabs, who were moreover 'filled with every diabolic savagery', a divine punishment of the church because of its sins. Such a theological interpretation was in line with biblical tradition, where God sends enemies to test his people and make them repent. Sophronius was, however, unaware of there being a new prophet, Muhammad, who claimed access to final revelation. A similar reasoning may be found with Maximus the Confessor (580–662), who likened the Muslims 'to such Old Testament foes as the Philistines and the Amalekites, [...] alleged to indulge in all the evil rites ascribed to gentiles: human sacrifice, idol-worship, sorcery, and devilry' (Lipton, 2014). Some interpreted the ongoing military threat through the apocalyptic literature, which they deployed 'explain the traumatic situation in which they now found themselves and so to provide a model of hope for the future, extending the promise of deliverance to those who stood firm' (Palemer, 1993, p. xxvi).

One of the first to deal with 'Islam' at length was John of Damascus (675/6–749), 'who served in the administration of the Umayyad caliphate in Damascus and subsequently became a monk in the Palestinian monastery of Mar Saba' (Tolan, 2015, p. 174). He wrote the book known as *The Fount of Knowledge*, which consists of three parts: *Dialectics*, *On Heresies* (*De haeresibus*) and *An Exposition of Orthodox Faith* (*De Fide*). John's reaction to Islam may be found in the second heresiological part of his work.

Significantly, John of Damascus almost completely adopts the framework developed by Epiphanius' *Panarion*, with the difference that he adds 20 more recent Christological heresies, one of which is the worship of the Muslims (a term he does not use). He places this false worship last in his enumeration of Christian heresies and from then onwards Islam occupied a place in the Christian imagination as the 'last and worst of all Christian heresies' (Stroumsa, 2010, p. 14). What does he say precisely about Islam in the 100th heresy (here in the translation of Schadler)?

> *There is up to now the still-prevailing people-deceiving practice [θρησκεία] of the Ishmaelites, being the forerunner of the Antichrist. (Schadler, 2018, p. 219)*

The fact that John of Damascus called the adherents of this heresy 'the forerunners of the Antichrist and placed them "in the hundredth and last position, accorded well with the common belief at the time that they were initiators of the coming Apocalypse"' (Schadler, 2018, p. 62). The unfolding of this heresy is, in John's view, a sign 'that ushers in the end time' (Valkenberg, 2005, p. 79). In the hundredth chapter of *De Fide*, the counterpart to his heresiology, John of Damascus, depicts how the Antichrist is overcome by Christ. Clearly, as was the case for Epiphanius and other heresiologists, the intention of John of Damascus is to contrast the norm of orthodox faith from heretical deviation. He continues:

> It takes its origin from Ishmael, who was born to Abraham from Hagar, and for this reason they are called Hagarenes and Ishmaelites. They also call them Saracens, allegedly for having been sent away by Sarah empty; for Hagar said to the angel, 'Sarah has sent me away empty'. (Schadler, 2018, p. 219)

The term 'Ishmaelites' or 'Hagarenes' could be seen as neutral; after all, Muslims claim to be descended from Ishmael, son of Hagar. Both Ishmael and Hagar are figures of faith in Islam. In Islamic tradition, however, Hagar is not a slave woman and the struggle of Hagar in the desert, and especially her relentless search for water for her son, Ishmael, gave rise to an important ritual during the Hajj Pilgrimage. In the Hebrew scriptures, however, Hagar is Sarah's slave woman, sent away with her child into the desert. The offspring of Abraham through Hagar is not blessed and is not part of God's covenant. Ishmael's divine fate was to wander in the desert, invade all the nations and be the enemy of civilization. This biblical and derogatory imagery would become prevalent in Christian imaginary and would lead to the projection of the Muslims as an enslaved people.

Around this same time the Venerable Bede (672/3–735) called the Muslims 'Saracens' in his *Historia ecclesiastica gentis Anglorum*. The term originally – it was already used by the Romans – referred to the 'tent dwellers' – nomadic tribes living in the Syro-Arabian desert. It would however become a derogatory name for Muslims, who 'pretended' to be descended 'from Sara, Abraham's legitimate wife, and not Hagar, her bondwoman, because of their shame – a story that characterized Muslims as *liars*, in the very act of telling a lie about them' (Heng, 2018). Muslims are thus not only an enslaved people, but are also a people of liars.

Interestingly, all three names – Ishmaelites, Hagarenes, and Saracens – are also used by Epiphanius of Salamis, one of John of Damascus' sources. In his *Panarion*, he discusses the Ishmaelites in the following passage about Judaism:

> Before him Abraham had Ishmael by the maidservant Hagar, and Khetura bore him six children. These were dispersed over the land called Arabia Felix – Zimram, Jokshan, Ishbak, Shuah, Medan and Midian. And the 'son of the bondmaid' – as I said, his name was Ishmael – also took up residence <in the wilderness> and founded the city called Paran in the wilderness. He had twelve children altogether; these were the ancestors of the tribes of the Hagarenes, or Ishmaelites, though today they are called Saracens. (Proem II, 4.1, trans. Williams, 2009b, p. 20)

In John of Damascus' *Fount of Knowledge* we read:

> These people worshiped and venerated the morning star and Aphrodite, whom they themselves called Habar in their own language, which means 'great'. Therefore, they were clearly idolaters until the time of Heraclius, from which time a false prophet appeared to them named Muhammad, who chanced upon the Old and New Testaments, and conversing in like manner with an Arian monk, introduced a sect of his own. And on the pretext of having made himself seem a God-fearing person to the people, he reported that a Scripture was brought down to him from heaven by God. So, having put together some sayings in his book, worthy of laughter, he thus handed the object of wonder down to them. (Schadler, 2018, p. 219)

Muslims were also accused of idolatry. This accusation should not be attributed primarily to Christian ignorance. It might also be the outcome of the rhetorical and polemical strategy of reversal, which we already encountered among the early church fathers, when they tried to defend themselves against the Romans. Both Jews and Muslims accused Christians of idolatry because of their adoration of saints, martyrs, icons, and relics, and of polytheism because of their Trinitarian worship, which was understood as a denial of the essential unity of God. John of Damascus was deeply involved in these iconoclastic debates (726–784) and

70 CHAPTER 2 The Coercive Turn

is known as a fierce apologetic of the use of images for worship. To defend Christian iconic tradition against these charges of idolatry, John of Damascus and others would follow his example, projected onto the Ishmaelites 'anxieties about their own problematic relations with sacred images' (Tolan, 2019, p. 21). As such, in his anti-Muslim polemics, John of Damascus turned the accusation of idolatry back upon the anti-Christian accusers as follows:

> *They also slander us as idolaters for venerating the cross, which they despise. And we say to them: 'How, therefore, is it that you rub yourselves against a stone at your Ka'ba, and you worship the stone by kissing it?' (Schadler, 2018, p. 236)*

John of Damascus not only states that adoration of the Black Stone in Mecca is idol worship, but he also refers to slanderous traditions which say that Abraham had intercourse with Hagar on it or that he tied a camel to it when he was about to sacrifice Ishmael. He even argues that the Ishmaelites are reviving pagan idolatry centred around the Greek goddess Aphrodite, 'whose image, according to John of Damascus was carved out in the Ka'aba' (Janosik & Riddell, 2016, p. 203). The message he is sending is that Christians who worship images are not idolaters, while the Ishmaelites are seen as being guilty of the worst kind of idol worship. This 'accusation of idolatry stuck in the Christian imagination and frequently appeared in polemics against Islam' (Chidester, 2000). Indeed, this caricature of Muslims worshipping the Greek pantheon or even their own idol, Mahon or Mahound, would prevail until the late Middle Ages (see Chapter 3).

Moreover, what is interesting about the longer passage quoted above is not only that Islam is seen as a kind of idol worship, but also the very idea

> *that the pagan worship indulged in by worshipers at the Ka'aba is the same as the worship indulged in by those inhabitants of the Roman Empire who had become Christian: in this view, both cultures, Muslim and Christian, share a history of devotion to Aphrodite. While the Christians, however, have turned their backs on the goddess, the Muslims continue to cling to the remnants of this pagan past, disguising their attachment to Aphrodite under the thin covering of monotheism. Idolatry, in the view of the author of* De haeresibus, *remains at the center of Muslim devotion – an idolatry which is, in the end, a fragmentary relic of the spiritual blindness of antiquity. (Akbari, 2009, p. 205)*

The message is clear; all idolaters are in essence the same and there is nothing new under the sun. Islam, like any expression of idolatry, is solidified in time, reified from the outset.

Like the heresies described in the *Panarion*, Islam too has a leader, a false prophet and impostor. In line with the tradition of associating new heresies with old ones, John argues that the source of all this deceit was a heretical Arian monk. Clearly, this is a rhetorical device used to discredit Muhammad: the implication is that Muhammad took his Christological falsities from an unoriginal heterodox source, which likewise lowered the divine status of Christ. This 'new' heresy was thus condemned by association (Schadler, 2018, p. 167). Muhammad invented his own heretical sect.

Jews and Ishmaelites and Their Place in Christian Imagination

While Islam could either be characterized as idolatrous paganism or rationalized as Christian heresy, from a Christian theological point of view, Islam in any case never stood a chance. In the salvation history of Christianity, there was no room for yet another revelation coming after the final revelation of God in Christ. Within this salvific history, which climaxed with Christ's incarnation, Islam had to be pushed back into the past. That is why the 'retrogressive nature' of this newcomer was emphasized time and again. Islam is constructed as yet another expression of idolatry, the origins of which may be traced back to the 'same, collectively and universally [worship] anterior to the advent of Christianity' (Akbari, 2009, p. 227). Similarly, while calling Islam a heresy may make it seem like a dangerous deviation from Christianity, the understanding is rather that the Law of Muhammad is a regression to the Old Law of Moses, namely a return to a legalistic past that had been superseded by Christ and the church. From this perspective, Islam was not really a development from Christianity, but rather a perverse turning back to the Law of Moses. This was exemplified not only in the Muslims' adherence to dietary laws, but especially in their reappropriation of the circumcision of the flesh. From this Christian theological perspective, one may understand why a Muslim would sometimes be depicted as a kind of Jew. In any case, what one blamed the Jews, namely their being legalistic, materialistic, and ritualistic, would also be projected onto the Muslims. The fact that both Jews and Muslims were seen as offspring of the slave woman Hagar (see Paul's letter to the Romans), whose child Ishmael was cast away while his younger brother, Isaac, was blessed, reaffirms how within Christian theological imagination, both non-Christian traditions were expressions of a non-salvific path (see Bede). Thus they shared a similar fate in Christian imagination. The contrasting genealogies of Christian people on the one hand and Jewish and Muslim people on the other, confirmed the Christian theological dichotomous map of the world in which the Christian people of God were opposed to non-Christians. However, other than Judaism, Islam was first and foremost perceived as a military and political threat, and was associated with the problem of violence. This association would never really go away, and Islamic presence would come to be perceived as antithetical to Christian Western Europe. During the next couple of centuries Islam was mostly discussed as an expression of paganism or as an expression of heresy. It would take several centuries before it was recognized as a separate category.

Christian Saracen Law

Christian scholars mainly approached Islam in terms of a military and a political threat, not as a separate ideological threat. In ecclesial law Muslims were called pagans and were regarded as invaders and bearers of power that imperilled Christians in their livelihood and in their faithfulness to their traditions. Christian authorities living in Muslim territories felt the need to respond to the concrete questions and concerns raised by Christians by formulating certain rules. These rules address, for example, the question of whether or not the use of armed force by Christian clergy could be justified (some canons reject such violence, others justify it) and what to do in a case where Christians kill a Muslim out of self-defence. Another issue of concern was the celebration of the Eucharist, which according to canon law required an altar. Exemptions, however, were possible when living in a context of oppression. As David Freidenreich observes, Jacob of Edessa (640–708) allowed for dispensing with proper ecclesiastical procedure in this regard when one is in a '"town of barbarian pagans" [here clearly referring to the Muslims] where there is no altar' (Freidenreich, 2009, p. 90). In addition, there were rules regulating the social relations between Muslims and Christians living under Muslim dominion. Prohibitions were promulgated on the involvement of judges from outside of the church (it seems Christians living in Muslim lands pleaded their case before 'pagan' courts and judges); Christians were not allowed to share a meal with Muslims, have sexual intercourse with them, or marry them. Nor were Christians allowed to undergo circumcision, a practice associated with Jews and with unbaptized pagans. Finally, Christians were not to be sold into slavery to Muslims. Most of the laws applicable to the interaction between Christians and Muslims derived from existing laws regulating the interaction between Christians and pagans (and/or Jews). What was applicable to pagans (and/or Jews) also applied to Muslims.

72 CHAPTER 2 The Coercive Turn

7 Conclusion

The focal point of this chapter has been how, after the Constantinian turn and even more so after the Theodosian turn, Nicene Christianity was transformed into the imperial norm for the Western Roman Empire. Christians conforming to this norm were no longer in a minority position but now gained power. I discussed the *Codex Theodosianus* and the way it projected the Christian norm on the one hand and led to the legal construction of Christianity's others – pagans, heretics, and Jews – on the other. These laws not only express some of the concerns of their promulgators, but they also contribute to the construction, consolidation, and institutionalization of privilege for Christians and of disadvantage for pagans, heretics, and Jews, albeit in varying degrees. Gradually, the religionized distinction between *vera religio* and various expressions of religious deviation were turned into a blueprint for the organization of a stratified Christian society. Religionized categories, that were forged discursively by Christian apologists and heresiologists to craft a sense of Christianness in response to adversaries, now become powerful.

As Nicene Creed (orthodoxy/*vera religio*) was turned into the public, institutional, and imperial norm, heresy was projected as a disturbance of the public order and disruption of the – claimed – Christian unity. Together, both ecclesiastical and imperial authorities would try to enforce this allegedly clear boundary and, as a result, Nicene Christians became privileged and heretics were outlawed. In fact, more Christians were persecuted by the Roman Empire after the Constantinian turn than before. Of course heretics, who suffered marginalization and/or persecution 'under this self-proclaimed Christian empire, questioned the extent to which the empire was truly Christian at all' and challenged the identification of Christian faith with the Nicene Creed (Sanzo & Boustan, 2014, p. 361). To their mind, they were true Christians who lived in a heretical, anti-Christian empire.

Simultaneously, the changed status of Christian worship also changed the status of the Roman cult: it shifted from being normative *religio* to being *superstitio* or paganism. Put differently, the Christianization of the empire entailed the paganization of the Roman cult. Like heresy, the Roman cult would now become criminalized as a form of illicit *religio* and the *Codex Theodosianus* testifies to the gradual dismantling of pagan cult, the shutting down of temples and the prohibition of spectacles. Increasingly, pagans were exposed to the imperial orthodox gaze, and their space to move about in the empire shrank, whereas Christians claimed more and more space for themselves.

Next to heretics and pagans, Jews continued to be viewed as anti-Christians. Polemical discourses targeting the Jews proliferated, but often rhetorical anti-Judaism after Constantine needs to be understood against the background of Christian debates about true *religio*; once again the rhetorical Jew figures mainly as a constitutive element of orthodox identity. The Christianization of the Roman Empire also led to 'ecclesiastical and imperial initiatives' aimed at curtailing 'real contacts between Christians and Jews' (Fredriksen, 2014, p. 29). Whereas Christians, conforming to the Nicene norm, enjoyed a privileged status, Jews faced constraints which were, moreover, institutionalized in Roman imperial law. At the same time, however, the *Theodosian Code* would be the first juridical document which officially turned 'Judaism' into *religio licita*, and this gave Jewish communities protection. Judaism becomes a separate legal category. In contrast to pagans and heretics, the Jews would not face persecution and they were not at risk if they practised their ancestral tradition.

In the last part of the chapter, building on this Christian map of the world and especially on the antithesis between orthodoxy and heresy, I discussed how Christians tried to make sense of a newly emerging 'sect', namely that of the Muslims – or the Ishmaelites or the Saracens as they would also be called. Following patterns previously established by heresiologists, this 'sect' was not regarded as *religio* (after all, there is but one *religio*, *religio christiana*), but rather as a Christian heresy. From this perspective Islam (which was not known as such at the time) was just another heresy and therefore *nil novi sub sole*.

Notes

[1] It is unlikely that the groups in question gave these names to themselves – 'though "Gnostic" may be an exception' (Williams, 2009a, p. xxiii).

[2] In 285, Emperor Diocletian (r. 284–305) divided the Roman Empire, which had become too large to be ruled by one emperor, into two. The Eastern part would flourish until the fall of Constantinople in 1453. The Western Empire, which is the focal point of this chapter, struggled until it fell apart in 476.

[3] Maijastina Kahlos emphasizes that Roman law was first and foremost responsive. Emperors promulgated laws in response to concrete, local problems that were brought to their attention 'by magistrates and delegations from the provinces' (Kahlos, 2020, p. 33). From this perspective, the *Code* does not project a master plan in policy making. Nevertheless, 'taken together' their 'replies suggest a tendency, an inclination, to decide similar things in similar ways, thus finally creating an impression of a considered policy, which, once appreciated, might be articulated in a general law summarizing but also perhaps systematically going beyond individual decisions' (Errington, 2006, p. 9). Furthermore, laws that had originally been drafted in response to local circumstances could later receive a more universal bearing and a more systematic and authoritative character. In fact, this is precisely what happened when these originally 'responsive' laws were compiled in the *Theodosian Code*: 'all of the laws that were included in the Theodosian Code received the status of empire-wide laws', and now transcended their local origin and responsive nature, to become part of a systemic worldview (Kahlos, 2020, p. 38).

[4] Current Problems in Ecumenical Theology. http://storage.cloversites.com/schoolforministry/documents/Problems%20with%20Ecum.%20Card.%20Kasper.pdf.

[5] 'One (*Adv. Iud. or.* 1) was delivered in August/September 386 CE, the remainder (*or.* 4, 2, 5, 6, 7, 8) in rapid succession from 19 August to 19 September 387, all in response to the yearly cycle of major Jewish festivals. *Or.* 6, it is calculated, was in fact delivered during an extraordinary Christian synaxis held on the same day as the Jewish festival of Yom Kippur, deliberately convened as competition' (Mayer, 2019, p. 68).

[6] We do not know if those people participating in Jewish rituals would have called themselves Judeo-Christians, Christians, Jews, and so on or whether they understood their identity as mixed or hybrid. We do know Chrysostom wanted to put an end to what in his mind was a state of undue mixing. Most historians think it is unlikely that he succeeded in that intent.

References

Akbari, S. C. (2005). Placing the Jews in Late Medieval English Literature. In I. D. Kalmar & D. J. Penslar (Eds.), *Orientalism and the Jews* (pp. 32–52). University Press of New England.

Akbari, S. C. (2009). *Idols in the East: European Representations of Islam and the Orient, 1100–1450.* Cornell University Press.

Augustine of Hippo (Ed. P. Schaff) (1887a). *Letters*, Nicene and Post-Nicene Fathers I.1. Christian Literature Publishing. Retrieved from www.newadvent.org/fathers/1102.htm

Augustine of Hippo (Ed. P. Schaff) (1887b). *City of God*, Nicene and Post-Nicene Fathers I.2. Christian Literature Publishing. Retrieved from www.newadvent.org/fathers/120118.htm

Augustine of Hippo (Trans. W. Parsons) (1953). *Letters, Volume 2 (83–130)*, The Fathers of the Church 18. Catholic University of America Press.

Augustine of Hippo (Trans. E. Hill, ed. J. E. Rotelle) (1993). *The Works of Saint Augustine: A Translation for the 21st Century / Part 3, Sermons; Vol. 6, Sermons III/6 (184–229Z) on the Liturgical Seasons.* New City Press.

Augustine of Hippo (Ed. P. Schaff) (1996). *The Writings against the Manichaeans and against the Donatists*, Nicene and Post-Nicene Fathers I.4. Eerdmans.

Bachrach, B. S. (1985). The Jewish Community of the Later Roman Empire as Seen in the *Codex Theodosianus*. In J. Neusner & E. S. Frerichs (Eds.), *'To See Ourselves as Others See Us': Christians, Jews and 'Others' in Late Antiquity* (pp. 399–421). Scholars Press.

Barbezat, M. D. (2018). Fields and Bodies: Toleration and Threat in a Shared Space. In *Burning Bodies: Communities, Eschatology, and the Punishment of Heresy in the Middle Ages* (pp. 35–60). Cornell University Press.

74 CHAPTER 2 The Coercive Turn

Barnard, L. (1995). The Criminalisation of Heresy in the Later Roman Empire: A Sociopolitical Device? *The Journal of Legal History, 16*(2), 121–146.

Berzon, T. S. (2016a). *Classifying Christians: Ethnography, Heresiology, and the Limits of Knowledge in Late Antiquity*. University of California Press.

Berzon, T. S. (2016b). Known Knowns and Known Unknowns: Epiphanius of Salamis and the Limits of Heresiology. *Harvard Theological Review, 109*(1), 75–101.

Berzon, T. S. (2017). Strategies of Containment: Regulatory Rhetoric and Heretical Space in the *Theodosian Code. Studies in Late Antiquity, 1*(2), 124–149.

Bibliowicz, A. M. (2013). *Jews and Gentiles in the Early Jesus Movement: An Unintended Journey*. Palgrave Macmillan.

Bobrowicz, R. (2018). The Inverted Relationship: Constitutive Theory of Law and the Enforcement of Orthodoxy in Book XVI of the Theodosian Code. In J. Giles, A. Pin, & F. S. Ravitch (Eds.), *Law, Religion and Tradition* (pp. 87–118). Springer International Publishing.

Bowes, K. D. (2008). *Private Worship, Public Values, and Religious Change in Late Antiquity*. Cambridge University Press.

Boyarin, D. (2004). *Border Lines: The Partition of Judaeo-Christianity*. University of Pennsylvania Press.

Boyarin, D., & Burrus, V. (2005). Hybridity as Subversion of Orthodoxy? Jews and Christians in Late Antiquity. *Social Compass, 52*(4), 431–441.

Brown, P. (1995). *Authority and the Sacred: Aspects of the Christianisation of the Roman World*. Cambridge University Press.

Brown, P. (1998). Christianization and Religious Conflict. In A. Cameron & P. Garnsey (Eds.), *The Cambridge Ancient History, Volume 13: The Late Empire, AD 337–425* (pp. 632–664). Cambridge University Press.

Caner, D. (2002). *Wandering, Begging Monks: Spiritual Authority and the Promotion of Monasticism in Late Antiquity*, The Transformation of the Classical Heritage 33. University of California Press.

Chazan, R. (2016). Medieval Christian-Jewish Relations in the Writings of Bernhard Blumenkranz. In P. Buc, M. Keil, & J. V. Tolan (Eds.), *Jews and Christians in Medieval Europe: The Historiographical Legacy of Bernhard Blumenkranz*, Religion and Law in Medieval Christian and Muslim Societies 7 (pp. 11–20). Brepols.

Chidester, D. (2000). *Christianity: A Global History*. HarperSanFrancisco.

Cohen, J. (1998). 'Slay Them Not': Augustine and the Jews in Modern Scholarship. *Medieval Encounters, 4*(1), 78–92.

Cohen, J. (1999). *Living Letters of the Law: Ideas of the Jew in Medieval Christianity*. University of California Press.

Cohen, J. (2009). Revisiting Augustine's Doctrine of Jewish Witness. *Journal of Religion, 89*(4), 564–578.

Coleman-Norton, P. R. (1966). *Roman State and Christian Church: A Collection of Legal Documents to A.D. 535*. S.P.C.K.

Errington, R. M. (2006). *Roman Imperial Policy from Julian to Theodosius*. University of North Carolina Press.

Escribano Paño, M. V. (2009). The Social Exclusion of Heretics in *Codex Theodosianus* XVI. In J.-J. Aubert & P. Blanchard (Eds.), *Droit, religion et société dans le Code Théodosien* (pp. 39–66). Université de Neuchâtel.

Escribano Paño, M. V. (2010). Heretical Texts and *Maleficium* in the *Codex Theodosianus* (Cth. 16.5.34). In R. L. Gordon & F. Marco Simón (Eds.), *Magical Practice in the Latin West: Papers from the International Conference Held at the University of Zaragoza, 30 Sept.–1 Oct. 2005*, Religions in the Graeco-Roman World 168 (pp. 105–139). Brill.

Eusebius of Caesarea (Ed. F. A. Heinichen) (1830). *Eusebii Pamphili De vita Constantini libri IV et Panegyricus atque Constantini Ad sanctorum coetum oratio*. Nauck.

Fredriksen, P. (2010). *Augustine and the Jews: A Christian Defense of Jews and Judaism*. Yale University Press.

Fredriksen, P. (2014). Jewish Romans, Christian Romans, and the Post-Roman West: The Social Correlates of the *contra Iudaeos* Tradition. In I. Yuval & R. Ben-Shalom (Eds.), *Conflict and Religious Conversation in Latin Christendom: Studies in Honour of Ora Limor* (pp. 23–53). Brepols.

Freidenreich, D. M. (2009). Christians in Early and Classical Sunnī Law. In D. Thomas (Ed.), *Christian-Muslim Relations: A Bibliographical History, Volume 1 (600–900)*, The History of Christian-Muslim Relations 11 (pp. 99–115). Brill.

Gager, J. G. (1983). *The Origins of Anti-Semitism: Attitudes toward Judaism in Pagan and Christian Antiquity*. Oxford University Press.

Green, T. H. (2019). *The Fear of Islam: An Introduction to Islamophobia in the West* (2nd ed.). Fortress.

Heng, G. (12 August 2018). Race Isn't a Modern Concept. Retrieved from https://historynewsnetwork.org/article/169596

Hill Fletcher, J. (2017). *The Sin of White Supremacy: Christianity, Racism, and Religious Diversity in America*. Orbis.

Humfress, C. (2007). *Orthodoxy and the Courts in Late Antiquity*. Oxford University Press.

Hutton, R. (2011). How Pagan Were Medieval English Peasants? *Folklore, 122*(3), 235–249.

Janosik, D., & Riddell, P. G. (2016). *John of Damascus, First Apologist to the Muslims: The Trinity and Christian Apologetics in the Early Islamic Period*. Pickwick.

John Chrysostom (Trans. P. W. Harkins) ([1979], 2010). *Discourses against Judaizing Christians*, The Fathers of the Church. Catholic University of America Press.

Jürgasch, T. (2015). Christians and the Invention of Paganism in the Late Roman Empire. In M. Sághy, M. R. Salzman, & R. L. Testa (Eds.), *Pagans and Christians in Late Antique Rome: Conflict, Competition, and Coexistence in the Fourth Century* (pp. 115–138). Cambridge University Press.

Kahlos, M. (2020). *Religious Dissent in Late Antiquity, 350–450*. Oxford University Press.

Lavan, L., & Mulryan, M. (Eds.) (2011). *The Archaeology of Late Antique 'Paganism'*, Late Antique Archaeology 7. Brill.

Leone, A. (2013). *The End of the Pagan City: Religion, Economy, and Urbanism in Late Antique North Africa*. Oxford University Press.

Lindbeck, G. A. (1984). *The Nature of Doctrine: Religion and Theology in a Postliberal Age*. Westminster.

Linder, A. (2006). The Legal Status of the Jews in the Roman Empire. In S. T. Katz (Ed.), *The Cambridge History of Judaism* (pp. 128–173). Cambridge University Press.

Lipton, S. (2014). Christianity and Its Others: Jews, Muslims, and Pagans. In J. Arnold (Ed.), *The Oxford Handbook of Medieval Christianity* (pp. 413–435). Oxford University Press.

Locke, J. (Ed. I. Shapiro) (2003). *Two Treatises of Government and A Letter concerning Toleration*. Yale University Press.

Lokin, J. H. A. (2014). The First Constitution of the Codex Justinianus: Some Remarks about the Imperial Legal Sources in the Codices Justiniani. *Subseciva Groningana: Studies in Roman and Byzantine Law, 9*. Retrieved from https://ugp.rug.nl/sg/article/view/28777

Martin, D. B. (2006). *Sex and the Single Savior: Gender and Sexuality in Biblical Interpretation*. Westminster John Knox.

Mayer, W. (2019). Preaching Hatred? John Chrysostom, Neuroscience, and the Jews. In D. de Wet & W. Mayer (Eds.), *Revisioning John Chrysostom: New Approaches, New Perspectives*, Critical Approaches to Early Christianity 1 (pp. 58–136). Brill.

Nirenberg, D. (2014). *Anti-Judaism: The Western Tradition*. W.W. Norton & Co.

Palemer, A. (1993). *The Seventh Century in the West-Syrian Chronicles*. Liverpool University Press.

Parkes, J. (1974). *The Conflict of the Church and the Synagogue: A Study in the Origins of Antisemitism* (2nd ed.). Atheneum.

Pharr, C. (1952). *Theodosian Code and Novels, and the Sirmondian Constitutions*. Princeton University Press.

Primiano, L. N. (1995). Vernacular Religion and the Search for Method in Religious Folklife. *Western Folklore, 54*(1), 37–56.

Rubiés, J.-P. (2006). Theology, Ethnography, and the Historicization of Idolatry. *Journal of the History of Ideas, 67*(4), 571–596.

Salzman, M. R. (1987). 'Superstitio' in the *Codex Theodosianus* and the Persecution of Pagans. *Vigiliae Christianae, 41*(2), 172–188.

Sanzo, J. E., & Boustan, R. S. (2014). Mediterranean Jews in a Christianizing Empire. In M. Maas (Ed.), *The Cambridge Companion to the Age of Attila* (pp. 358–375). Cambridge University Press.

Schadler, P. (2018). *John of Damascus and Islam: Christian Heresiology and the Intellectual Background to Earliest Christian-Muslim Relations*, The History of Christian-Muslim Relations 34. Brill.

Schott, J. (2007). Heresiology as Universal History in Epiphanius's Panarion. *Zeitschrift für Antikes Christentum, 10*(3), 546–563.

Schott, J. M. (2008). *Christianity, Empire, and the Making of Religion in Late Antiquity*. University of Pennsylvania Press.

Shaw, B. D. (2011). *Sacred Violence: African Christians and Sectarian Hatred in the Age of Augustine*. Cambridge University Press.

Silbey, S. (1992). Making a Place for a Cultural Analysis of Law. *Law and Social Inquire, 39*(1), 39–48.

Stantchev, S. K. (2014). 'Apply to Muslims What Was Said of the Jews': Popes and Canonists between a Taxonomy of Otherness and *Infidelitas*. *Law and History Review, 32*(1), 65–96.

Stroumsa, G. G. (2010). *A New Science: The Discovery of Religion in the Age of Reason*. Harvard University Press.

Stroumsa, G. G. (2015). *The Making of the Abrahamic Religions in Late Antiquity*. Oxford University Press.

Stroumsa, S. (2009). *Maimonides in His World: Portrait of a Mediterranean Thinker*. Princeton University Press.

Terpstra, N. (2015). *Religious Refugees in the Early Modern World: An Alternative History of the Reformation*. Cambridge University Press.

Tolan, J. V. (2002). *Saracens: Islam in the Medieval European Imagination*. Columbia University Press.

Tolan, J. V. (2015). Jews and Muslims in Christian Law and History. In G. G. Stroumsa & A. J. Silverstein (Eds.), *The Oxford Handbook of the Abrahamic Religions* (pp. 166–188). Oxford University Press.

Tolan, J. V. (2019). *Faces of Muhammad: Western Perceptions of the Prophet of Islam from the Middle Ages to Today*. Princeton University Press.

Valkenberg, P. (2005). John of Damascus: The Heresy of the Ishmaelites. In B. Roggema, M. Poorthuis, & P. Valkenberg (Eds.), *The Three Rings: Textual Studies in the Historical Trialogue of Judaism, Christianity, and Islam*, Thomas Instituut Utrecht 11 (pp. 71–90). Peeters.

Van der Horst, P. W. (2000). Jews and Christians in Antioch at the End of the Fourth Century. In S. E. Porter & B. W. R. Pearson (Eds.), *Christian-Jewish Relations through the Centuries* (pp. 228–238). Sheffield Academic Press.

Walsham, A. (2006). *Charitable Hatred: Tolerance and Intolerance in England, 1500–1700*. Manchester University Press.

Whitley, T. J. (2016). Poison in the *Panarion*: Beasts, Heretics, and Sexual Deviants. *Vigiliae Christianae, 70*(3), 237–258.

Williams, F. (2009a). Introduction. In F. Williams (Ed.), *The* Panarion *of Epiphanius of Salamis: Book I (Sects 1–46)*, Nag Hammadi and Manichaean Studies 63 (pp. xi–xxxiv) (2nd, rev. and exp. ed.). Brill.

Williams, F. (2009b). *The* Panarion *of Epiphanius of Salamis: Book 1 (Sects 1–46)*, Nag Hammadi and Manichaean Studies 63 (2nd, rev. and exp. ed.). Brill.

PART 2

Body Politics in the Aftermath of the Gregorian Reform

The twelfth century initiated a period of expansion and growth: 'European plows conquered new territories, agricultural productivity increased, trade recovered, and the population grew' (Nirenberg, 2015, p. 18). It was a time of urbanization, of scholastic sophistication, of a renewed interest in the classics and a revival of jurisprudence.

New territories, markets, urban centers, schools, institutions of governance, libraries, varieties of cultural expression, and alternative patterns of Christian self-definition all fostered untold, unprecedented mobility in the society of the Latin West. In a word, the various components of that society scrambled to capitalize on the wealth of new opportunity. (Cohen, 1999, p. 148)

Economically, politically, and culturally, this was a time of prosperity, signalled by new cities, new cathedrals, and new religious orders following a range of monastic rules; Latin Christendom flourished and diversified. Nevertheless, the commitment to the ideal of Christian unity, imagined as a whole body, was never abandoned, just the contrary; '[...] popes, prelates, theologians, and canon lawyers expounded the theoretical ramifications of a Catholic vision for an ideally ordered Christian society with unprecedented determination' (Cohen, 1999, p. 147). The effort to consolidate Christian society and to religionize Christianity's others unfolded in a new direction: Jews, heretics, and Saracens (as pagans) became demonic enemies, out to harm Christian society.

To understand unfolding patterns of religionization during the late Middle Ages we need to elaborate on how most European Christians used the metaphor of the body to describe their community (1 Corinthians 12). This metaphor functioned at local (village), urban (city), and 'national' (kingdoms, empires) levels as well as at an international level. Nicholas Terpstra explains how

the metaphor of the Body had different linked dimensions: the social Body of Christians (Corpus Christianum) drew ultimately on the spiritual Body of Christ (Corpus Christi). This physical metaphor for the social community of believers distinguished

---

Christian Imaginations of the Religious Other: A History of Religionization, First Edition. Marianne Moyaert.
© 2024 John Wiley & Sons Ltd. Published 2024 by John Wiley & Sons Ltd.

78 PART 2 Body Politics in the Aftermath of the Gregorian Reform

> *Christianity from Judaism and Islam, and provided a very powerful imaginative*
> *framework for thinking about what characterized a pure social community and what*
> *threatened it. (Terpstra, 2015, p. 21)*

The *Corpus Christianum* consists of the baptized Christians, whose bodies have been cleansed of what separates them from God. Baptism distinguishes the faithful from the unfaithful, the saved from the unsaved. The eucharistic sacrifice further reinforces this communal sense of being in the presence of Christ. During the Mass, Christians are all ritually incorporated into Christ's body (Cavanaugh, 2001, p. 592). Thus, the Eucharist holds the *Corpus Christianum* together and joins the different Christian bodies into one community, which then participates in Christ's purity. Certainly, during the late Middle Ages and after the doctrine of transubstantiation had become official (Lateran IV, 1215), the metaphor of the body would become increasingly focused on the host, and in time numerous communal celebrations, such as *Corpus Christi* processions (1238), further strengthened the Christian sense of belonging to Christ's body.

The metaphor of the *Corpus Christianum* evokes associations of both wholeness and vulnerability: if one part of the body hurts, the whole body suffers. Understandably, medieval people had a deep sense of the fragility of the body: the mortality rate was high, and the threat of death was everywhere. Bodily suffering was real and tangible, and Christ's bloody, flagellated, and crucified body matched with this all-pervasive sense of pain and death. The metaphor of the body is also an exclusionary one: it casts Christians as insiders and non-Christians as outsiders. Heretics, Jews, or Saracens (as pagans) are not only foreign bodies that do not fit in, but they are also contemporary threats to the integrity of the social body of Christians: just as there were people eager to harm and kill Christ's body at Golgotha so there are now many people eager to bring suffering to the *Corpus Christianum*. As Christ was prepared to suffer for our salvation, so Christians should be prepared to suffer (and fight) to protect Christ's body on earth against menaces coming from various enemies (Bynum, 2002, p. 692).

Furthermore, this metaphor intersects with the multifaceted metaphor of blood. Blood is associated with life: it is the soul of the body, the lifeline of the community. Projected onto the *Corpus Christianum*, blood, too, becomes a token of community. Magical, ritual healing powers were attributed to blood. By participating in the Eucharist and taking in Christ's pure and purifying blood (also present in the host), the Christian community became a life-giving community of blood (Anidjar, 2005, p. 123). Blood, however, is also associated with suffering and death, especially when it flows to excess and does not stay within the contours of the body. While Christ's bloody body holds the promise of the healing power offered to Christians, and Christians who spill blood in the name of Christ (e.g. on the battle field) are martyrs, the blood of those who fall outside the pale of Christianity (e.g. heretics, pagans, and Jews) was seen as overflowing and sick, and hence as a threat to the *Corpus Christianum*. The more Christians formulated their self-understanding in terms of the healing power of the body and blood of Christ (selfing), the more they portrayed the bodies of others as sick, abnormal, and unholy. Religionization takes the form of dehumanizing body politics (othering): the bodies of Christians and non-Christians reflect their soteriological status.

An Ongoing Spiritual Drama

European Christians saw themselves as players in a larger spiritual drama in which the powers of good and evil were engaged in battle; they 'read the body as fundamental to a greater design of correspondences that ordered God's universe' (Burk, 2010, p. 2). More than in previous centuries, this spiritual drama was understood as an ongoing struggle between God and the devil and his army of demons. Both were fighting for the souls of human beings. The militancy of the devil needed to be matched by an increased vigilance of the faithful, because demons could be everywhere, penetrating every corner of life, just waiting to win. In this spiritual drama, God could intervene to punish those who went against his will and bless those who were faithful, while 'every disaster and threat' could be seen as 'a test of obedience and disobedience'. Human faults could have 'eternal consequences' affecting the entire community. Fires, epidemics, drought, famine, or even war could be a divine punishment for human sin and faithlessness (Terpstra, 2015, p. 38). True worship of God, who had given his Son to redeem mankind, was considered conditional to socio-political stability, and deviation was in principle suspicious. The more Christians idealized the *Corpus Christianum*, the more they became conscious of their responsibility to keep the body whole and healthy.

This responsibility translated into an effort to enhance the boundaries of Christian society and reinforce its integrity. Here, we see the mechanisms of religionization unfold again. First, the idea of true Christianness had to be made clear: 'this is who we are, this is what we stand for, this is what we do and how we do it and these are the norms and standards we hold high'. A proliferation of doctrine followed. This effort to create a sense of true Christianness went hand in hand with the crafting of religionized otherness. This translated into an increase in discursive and non-discursive polemics targeting non-Christians – Jews, heretics, and Saracens (as pagans). Finally, we may note a reinvigoration of canon law and law enforcement, which helped to 'define, identify, structure and enforce boundaries between religious groups' (Tolan, 2015, p. 56). Ecclesial authorities, supported by secular authorities, actively and systematically sought to protect Christian society against potential threats, either via containment, segregation, persecution, or even via purgation. The inquisition against the heretics, the crusades to liberate Jerusalem from the Saracens, the *Reconquista*, as well as discriminatory practices targeting Jewish communities, simultaneously affirmed the reality of non-Christians intent on harming the Christian body and helped to reinforce and institutionalize the sense of a communal Christian identity in the context of an otherwise divided Europe.

In this second part of the book, Chapter 3, *Unification, Purification, and Dehumanization,* shows how the centralizing dynamic that pervaded the church negatively impacted the way Christianity's others were imagined and treated. As religionized differentiation gradually attaches itself to the symbols of blood and body, far-reaching measures were put in place to police those who deviate from the Christian norm. In Chapter 4, *The Spanish Catholic Monarchy and Religio-racialization,* I zoom in on the particular case of Spain under the rule of the Catholic monarchs, Ferdinand II of Aragon and Isabella I of Castile. I explore how they adapted and recontextualized existing patterns of religionization for the purpose of nation building, and how in the course of this project religionization takes on the form of religio-racialization.

References

Anidjar, G. (2005). Lines of Blood: Limpieza de sangre as Political Theology. In M. G. Bondio (Ed.), *Blood in History and Blood Histories* (pp. 119–136). Sismel–Edizioni del Galluzzo.

Burk, R. L. (2010). Salus Erat in Sanguine: Limpieza De Sangre and Other Discourses of Blood in Early Modern Spain. Diss. University of Pennsylvania.

Bynum, C. W. (2002). The Blood of Christ in the Later Middle Ages. *Church History, 71*(4), 685–714.

Cavanaugh, W. T. (2001). Eucharistic Sacrifice and the Social Imagination in Early Modern Europe. *Journal of Medieval and Early Modern Studies, 31*(3), 585–605.

Cohen, J. (1999). *Living Letters of the Law: Ideas of the Jew in Medieval Christianity.* University of California Press.

Nirenberg, D. (2015). *Communities of Violence: Persecution of Minorities in the Middle Ages.* New paperback edition, with a new preface. Princeton University Press.

Terpstra, N. (2015). *Religious Refugees in the Early Modern World: An Alternative History of the Reformation.* Cambridge University Press.

Tolan, J. (2015). *Lex Alterius*: Using Law to Construct Confessional Boundaries. *History and Anthropology, 26*(1), 55–75.

CHAPTER 3

Unification, Purification, and Dehumanization

Pope Gregory VII (r. 1073–1085), one of the great popes of the late Middle Ages, initiated a reform programme that would be continued by his successors. The aim of this reform programme was a unified Christendom *in capite et membris* [in head and limbs] (Arnold, 2009, p. 366). The programme included the establishment of papal primacy, the assertion of papal control over the bishops, Roman authority over local tradition, and the restoration of the moral and spiritual authority of the clergy. Educational requirements for clergy were raised, their behavioural standards became stricter and the distance between clergy and laypeople increased. The production of both doctrine and canon law grew significantly. While the success of the Gregorian reform is questionable, and later reformers would again call for reflection, renewal, and restoration, it did initiate a centralizing dynamic; the diffuse episcopal structure of the early Middle Ages gradually gave way to a more consolidated and hierarchically organized structure, featuring the means to take disciplinary action against those perceived as a threat to the uniformity of Christian society. To be sure, Latin Christendom continued to diversify, and historians emphasize the heterogeneous nature of the church at the time and the many different strands of Christianity: the plural expressions of Christian spirituality, the varying theologies, as well as the proliferation of new religious orders with their own monastic rules that enjoyed certain privileges of exemption from the bishop. At the same time, there was also repression of divergence. Medieval people tended to see heresy as a threat and where deviation from the religious norm was perceived to be so great that it would harm Christian society, disciplinary steps were taken to deal with this problem.

Text Box 1: The Gregorian Reform

The Gregorian reform programme initiated a power struggle between ecclesial and secular authorities. As Robert Moore puts it, 'His [Gregory VII] pontificate entrenched the confrontation between the papacy and the (German) Empire, and thence between church and state, which for the next two hundred years largely shaped the political and governmental agendas of Latin Europe and its emerging national monarchies' (Moore, 2014, p. 96). This conflict is known as the investiture controversy (1075–1122).

One of the issues that, according to Pope Gregory VII and other reformers, threatened the integrity and credibility of the church was the widespread practice of simony (the buying and selling of clerical offices). In the eleventh century, bishops, abbots, and priests were usually appointed to their dioceses, monasteries, and churches by noble laymen, a practice known as 'investiture'. Powerful families endowed churches and monasteries, and in return these families expected to be granted the power to govern.

Christian Imaginations of the Religious Other: A History of Religionization, First Edition. Marianne Moyaert.
© 2024 John Wiley & Sons Ltd. Published 2024 by John Wiley & Sons Ltd.

> This practice was made possible because there were no clear ecclesial rules about how to appoint ecclesial authorities. Pope Gregory VII wanted to bring this practice to an end and sent out the message that the church and its clergy could not be bought. To follow up, he attempted to free the church from secular control and developed a vision of papal power that was adopted by the subsequent pontiffs. Challenging the idea that kings and emperors were God's agents on earth, he claimed that 'the Pope was the true "Vicar of Christ" on earth' (Tolan, 2015, p. 67). Temporal authorities were to be subjected to the universal power of the church and their rule was only legitimate in as far as it was in accordance with Christian rule.

The 'move to establish Rome as the guardian of orthodoxy – neatly encapsulated in the apothegm *Hereticum esse constat qui Romane ecclesie non concordat* (a forged text attributed to St. Ambrose but probably composed by Pope Gregory VII) – signified [a] new wave of Roman hegemony' (Gilchrist, 1988, p. 11). Whoever disagrees with the Roman church is a heretic. This effort to solidify a unified Christendom translated into a proliferation of laws distinguishing between Christianity and its others and was matched with polemical rhetoric and exclusionary policies targeting Christianity's others – heretics, Jews, and Muslims – as enemies of Christendom. The Fourth Lateran Council (1215), called by Pope Innocent III (r. 1198–1216), who claimed Rome as the head of the whole world, symbolizes the climax of this enhanced claim to papal authority. This council concerned itself both with 'legislating aspects of the Christian social body within, but also with the delineation and defense of the Christian body vis-à-vis the outside world [;] it has logically come to be seen as a key moment of Christian engagement with non-Christians' (Szpiech, 2019, p. 115). Indeed, against the background of the attempt to reform the Church and strengthen its power, Jews, Muslims, and heretics are increasingly dehumanized and demonized. Religionization takes on new forms, with body politics playing a central role.

1 The Time of the Crusades and Dehumanizing Saracens

In 711, Muslim forces loyal to the Umayyad dynasty conquered Visigothic Spain.[1] By the end of the eighth century, Muslims occupied parts of the Iberian Peninsula, North Africa, the Arabian Peninsula, Persia, and large parts of northern India. Their military and political power was impressive. By the tenth century they had become 'politically dominant in much of the territory formerly controlled by the Byzantine and Persian Empires' and its population was prospering, certainly in comparison to the population of the so-called 'proto-European territories to the North and West, whose mean level of education, literacy, and intellectual awareness was also dramatically lower than in these Islamic lands' (Ballard, 1996, p. 17).

From the eleventh century onwards, however, the church sought to regain control over territories under Islamic rule and this resulted in several centuries of 'Church-sponsored military campaigns against its various enemies' (Latham, 2011, p. 223). These campaigns were aimed at freeing the Holy Land from the 'Saracens' and at reconquering the Iberian Peninsula; these campaigns also fitted in with the centralizing dynamic of the church that had been initiated by the Gregorian reform and continued by subsequent popes (Text Box 2).

The Emergence of Crusading Ideology

Several factors explain why the church began this crusading campaign. First, the invasions of the Huns, the Saxons, and the Vikings had come to an end and the heart of Western Europe had stabilized, providing novel opportunities for Christian expansion. At the same time, there was a large group of warriors that now had little to do. Also, there was the rupture in the Christian church: the Eastern schism in 1054, which entailed a break of communion between the Catholic Church and the Eastern Orthodox churches. Several popes hoped that the crusades would either lead to a reconciliation between East and West or would at least result in an expansion of their influence on Byzantium. Furthermore, the Gregorian reform set out to enhance ecclesial authority and sought to reinforce the core belief that the church had the right to demand support from faithful Christians to fight against the 'Saracen' forces of evil and to liberate territories that had been unjustly claimed by them.

Consider in this regard an encyclical letter written by Pope Gregory VII in 1074, in which he calls for a crusade. He first mentions that 'a pagan race had overcome the Christians and with horrible cruelty had devastated everything almost to the walls of Constantinople, and were now governing the conquered lands with tyrannical violence, and that they had slain many thousands of Christians as if they were but sheep'. The 'murder of so many Christians' ought to fill Christians 'with grief', but grief was not enough: 'the example of our Redeemer and the bond of fraternal love demand that we should lay down our lives to liberate them', just like Christ 'laid down his life for his brethren'. The crucified Christ who was killed by the authorities of the Roman Empire is turned into a call to 'render aid to the Christian empire' (Migne, PL 148, col. 329, quoted in Thatcher & McNeal, 1971, p. 513). Despite his call to arms, Gregory VII himself did not succeed in mobilizing an army. However, when the Byzantine emperor, Alexios I Komnenos (r. 1081–1118), having lost significant territory to the Turks, asked a succeeding pope, Urban II (r. 1088–1099), for his help, Gregory's crusading call was taken up again. Urban, addressing the Council of Clermont on 29 November 1095, invoked the image of a holy army, under the protection of God and church, to help the Greeks liberate Jerusalem from the rule of the Saracens. Calling himself 'prelate over the whole world', Urban II called on his brethren shepherds to 'guard their flock'. Negligence will result in losing God's favour. The pope continued:

> [...] your brethren who live in the East are in urgent need of your help, and
> you must hasten to give them the aid which has often been promised them.
> For, as the most of you have heard, the Turks and Arabs have attacked
> them and have conquered the territory of Romania [the Greek empire] [...]
> They have killed and captured many, and have destroyed the churches and
> devastated the empire. If you permit them to continue thus for a while with
> impunity, the faithful of God will be much more widely attacked by them. On
> this account I, or rather the Lord, beseech you as Christ's heralds to publish
> this everywhere and to persuade all people of whatever rank, foot-soldiers and
> knights, poor and rich, to carry aid promptly to those Christians and to destroy
> that vile race from the lands of our friends. Moreover, Christ commands it.
> (Gesta Dei per Francos, I, ed. Bongars, pp. 382–383, quoted in Thatcher &
> McNeal, 1971, pp. 514–515)

Addressing all Christians, the pope urged them to free Christian lands, assured combatants that they would enter paradise, and gave those who were going to be killed the status of martyrs. He projected the crusade as a new form of piety, mixing pilgrimage with a military project (Tolan, 2002, p. 110). Subsequent popes would even offer full indulgences to those enlisting.

This first crusade was followed by many more. Those crusades that were aimed at reconquering Jerusalem and the Holy Land were – apart from some temporary successes – military and financial failures. Those missions aimed at liberating the Spanish Peninsula from the Muslims were more successful, however. In 1085, Toledo was recaptured, and in later centuries other major cities like Cordoba (1236) and Seville (1248) would follow until finally, in 1492, Granada fell into the hands of the Spanish monarchs, Ferdinand II (r. 1479–1516) and Isabella I (r. 1474–1504).

Text Box 2: The Meaning of the Term *Reconquista*

The term *Reconquista*, which centres on the reconquering of the Iberian Peninsula, implies that this was not about conquering new lands but rather about 'rightfully taking back' lands that were once owned by Christians. The driving idea was that these 'Christian conquests of Muslim held lands rightfully restored territorial ordering of the past' (Remensnyder, 2014, p. 97). This idea of rightfully taking back what belonged to Christians also permeates the campaigns to recapture Jerusalem. In this ideological discourse, crusade became 'a martial instrument for righting injustices and combating evil in the world. More specifically, it defined the crusades as a form of just war whose *moral purposes* were the liberation of Christians, the redress of legal injuries perpetrated against them, the restoration of heretics to the true faith, and the defense of Christendom and the church from attack'. In addition, the crusade was constituted in the medieval imagination as an act of piety, penance, and Christian love. Finally, 'the crusade was constituted as an instrument of *ecclesiastical* statecraft. While secular powers could be (and typically were) mobilized to carry out any given crusade, authority for launching a *bellum Romanum* was reserved exclusively to the papacy' (Latham, 2011, p. 237). This final point affirms how the crusades were not only a response to a threat to Christian society but also served the purpose of unification, and reinforced papal authority. Nothing strengthens authoritative leadership as effectively as a call to arms to fight a mutual enemy.

The Saracen as Pagan

While crusading armies were fighting the Muslims, crusading theologians and chroniclers were producing polemical tracts targeting an enemy they had never met in the flesh. Via sermons, their ideas would spread quickly, but Romanesque architecture, art, plays, and chronicles likewise contributed to the dissemination of anti-Muslim discourses. Through these various channels, negative anti-Muslim imageries made their way into Western Christian imagination. The scope of this propagation 'can only be characterized as an ongoing, church-sponsored propaganda designed to denigrate and discredit' the Muslim, to legitimize and justify the crusades and to strengthen a sense of Christian unity and enhance ecclesial power (Strickland, 2003, p. 13).

Medieval writers used a variety of ethnoreligious terms, like Arabs, Turks, Moors, Hagarenes, and Mohammedans to refer to Muslims. Most often, Muslims would go by the name of Saracens, which as I explained earlier, they supposedly claimed for themselves to deny their proper Ishmaelite lineage and 'falsely claim a genealogy from Sara' (Heng, 2018a, p. 111). The polemical tone of this religionized name is clear: it implied Muslims' untrustworthy and even sly character, but it also made clear that they stemmed from a lineage of slaves that could not claim to be blessed by God; this, of course in contrast to the genealogy of Christians, who claimed to be descendants of Jacob. Sometimes, Muslim lineage was traced back to Cain, who epitomizes the 'unrepentant sinner' (Strickland, 2003, p. 49) and who, together with his descendants, is cursed. Typologically and genealogically, the reference to Cain would immediately evoke the contrast with the Christian, who stems from Abel, the innocent, whose offer is accepted by God but who was slain by his brother Cain. Christians and Muslims have different lineages; they are different people.

Using typological, ethnoreligious reading strategies, both the Christian and the Saracen are reduced to types and in the course of this process all their particularities, differences, and characteristics were flattened out. No difference was made between Umayyads, Fatimids, and Abbasids, or between Arabs and Muslims, Shi'ites and Sunnis, or even Persians and Turks. Different cultural expressions, ethnic differences, various theological schools, none of these differences mattered and all were lumped under the name 'Saracens'. As Christians thought of themselves as the people of the true faith, the Muslims 'were turned into a bad people of the false faith' (Falk, 2018, p. 71).

The Saracen was often religionized as idolater/pagan and infidel, especially when larger audiences were addressed. This depiction provided 'a tangible and satisfying focus for the righteous Christian knight [...]' (Tolan, 2019, p. 28) and it played an important role in the propaganda machinery during the first crusade. Time and again, we encounter the Muslim as a pagan, who worships Venus or Apollo (i.e. the pagan as the Hellene) or Mahound and prostrates himself in front of wooden images. This depiction reinvokes the much earlier 'struggles of ancient Christians against Roman idolaters [...]' and it comforted crusaders to know 'that the risks they undertook were not in vain but were part of an ongoing battle in Christian history to eradicate those enemies of Christ who worshiped false gods and idols' (Green, 2019, p. 53).

Both in literature and artwork, Christians would cry victory by smashing their idols and slaying the Saracen pagan. Once confronted with the power of Christ, these worshippers of the idol 'Mahound', would typically recognize their fault and bow before the cross. Consider in this regard Robert of Rheims (Robert the Monk, 1055–1122), who in his chronicle *Historia Iherosolimitana* [A History of Jerusalem] of the first crusade (1107–1122), has Amiravissus, the pagan lord of Jerusalem, say after having lost on the battlefield:

> *O Mahommed, our Master and protector, where is your strength? [...] Why have you abandoned your people like this to be mercilessly destroyed and dispersed and killed by a wretchedly poor and ragged people, a people who are the scrapings of other races, the lees, rust and slag of the whole human race [...]. Oh, what grief! Everything is turning against us. We have always been the victors, and now others are victorious; we have always lived in a happy frame of mind but are now plunged into misery. [...] O Mahommed, Mahommed, who has ever invested more in the magnificence of your worship with shrines ornate with gold and silver, decorated with beautiful images of you, and with the ceremonies and solemnities of every kind of rite? This is what the Christians say to insult us: that the power of the Crucified One is greater than yours because he is powerful on earth and in heaven. (Robert the Monk, trans. Sweetenham, 2005, pp. 209–210)*

Throughout this work, Robert of Rheims depicts the Muslims as an 'accursed race', 'vile and despised', they are 'barbarians', 'pagans', and 'infidels', 'demon worshippers'. In addition, the Saracen was depicted as someone who lives and dies simply to harm, defile, if not to destroy the integrity of Christian society by dishonouring God and Christ. This was symbolically visualized in the depiction of the Saracen who destroys altars, urinates in the baptismal font, and forcefully circumcises Christian bodies. Once again from *Historia Iherosolimitana* we can read:

> *They throw down the altars after soiling them with their own filth, circumcise Christians, and pour the resulting blood either on the altars or into the baptismal vessels. When they feel like inflicting a truly painful death on some they pierce their navels, pull out the end of their intestines, tie them to a pole and whip them around it until, all their bowels pulled out, they fall lifeless to the ground. (Robert the Monk, trans. Sweetenham, 2005, pp. 79–80)*

In contrast to this Saracen defilement, the crusade and the reconquering of sacred spaces was often imagined in terms of a purification. The biblical image invoked thereby was that of the cleansing of the temple (John 2:15; Matt 21:12–17); indeed the theological significance of the reconquest was frequently seen in those terms (Smith, 2017). Consider in this regard Baldric, the abbot of Bourgueil (1050–1130), who casts the Muslims as filthy pagans:

> *Let us lament, brothers; come, let us lament, and lamenting from the depths of our hearts let us cry out in pain with the psalmist. Wretched and unhappy are we in whose days that prophecy is fulfilled. O God, the heathens are come into thy inheritance; they have defiled thy holy temple [polluerunt templum sanctum tuum]: they have*

86 CHAPTER 3 Unification, Purification, and Dehumanization

made Jerusalem as a place to keep fruit. They have given the dead bodies of thy servants to be meat for the fowls of the air: the flesh of thy saints for the beasts of the earth. They have poured out their innocent blood as water, round about Jerusalem: and there was none to bury them. Woe to us, brothers, we who now are become a reproach to our neighbours: a scorn and derision to them that are round about us *(Ps 78:1–4). (Baldric of Bourgueil, trans. Edgington, 2020, p. 47)*

Another twelfth-century anonymous author writes about the defilement of God's temple in Jerusalem:

*They have humiliated your people and ruined your heritage [*tuum humiliauerunt et hereditatem tuam uexauerunt*]. They have desecrated [*polluuerunt*] your temple and sacred house [*domum sanctum*], of which you said, 'My house shall be called a house of prayer' [*Domus mea domus orationis uocabitur*]. Now, however, it is made not into a den of thieves but rather a temple of demonic idols [*demoniorum idolium*] (Matt 21:13). (France, 1988, p. 648, my translation)*

Just as Jesus was moved to anger when he threw out the merchants, so crusaders are justified in cleansing Jerusalem from the pagans.

The immoral character of the Muslims was, furthermore, underscored by their presumed excessive sex drive and lust, and their unnatural sexual relations, such as polygamy, but also by beastly sex as well as sodomy. Of course, the uncontrollable lust of the Muslims was contrasted to Christian chastity. Once again, a religionized contrast was erected between the spiritual and the carnal: the law of Christ is spiritual, the law of Muhammad is carnal and lust driven. The latter is a perversion of the first. Fighting against the Saracens, the crusaders are going to a frightening place of perversity, to protect the church, Christian purity and, of course, Christian women. All these religionized images contribute to the depiction of the Saracen as profoundly evil; a demonic figure, an agent of Satan. This line of reasoning again enhances the idea that the crusade is a holy war and the crusaders a holy army, fighting for God and Christ against an army of the devil.

One of the ways in which Christian polemicists projected the Saracen as the enemy of Christianity is by placing him 'in the familiar framework of the Christian apocalypse' (Strickland, 2003, p. 212). The military power of the Saracens becomes associated with the apocalyptic forces of evil as described in the Bible. Saracens were trying to lure Christians into following the apocalyptic beast and choosing for a life of material and carnal pleasures. They may even conspire with the Jews or other demonic forces in their plot against Christianity. Pope Innocent III, who also came down strongly on the Jews and the heretics of his time (the Cathars and Waldensians), claimed that Muhammad was the Antichrist. In *Quia Maior*, an encyclical dated 1213, he called for a fourth crusade:

And, indeed, the Christian people possessed almost all the Saracen provinces until after the time of Saint Gregory. But after that time, a certain son of perdition, the pseudo-prophet Muhammad, arose, and he seduced many away from the truth with carnal enticements and pleasures. Even though his perfidy has lasted until the present, still we trust in the Lord who has now made a good sign that the end of this beast, whose number, according to John's Apocalypse [Rev 13:18], counts 666, of which now almost six hundred years are completed, approaches. (Bird et al., 2013, pp. 108–109)

Defiled, Monstrous Black Bodies

In the medieval imagination, a strong relationship was assumed between the external, visible, and physical form and internal, moral, and spiritual character. Physical appearance and biological difference supposedly told a story about the person's religious identity and their moral character. Outer appearance reflected the inner spiritual life. Like names

(Saracen, Ishmaelite, etc.), the bodily depiction of Christianity's others was symbolically meaningful and helped to create religionized boundaries. Exemplary in this regard are the so-called *chansons de geste*, publicly recited poems which told the legends of the era's heroes, Christian knights, who defended Christendom, embraced an attitude of chivalry and fought against the evil and monstrous Saracens. In this literary genre, which developed during the twelfth and thirteenth centuries, ugliness, disfiguration, and even monstrosity symbolized immorality, untrustworthiness, sinfulness, and unfaithfulness. Beauty and fairness by contrast symbolized morality and faithfulness. Alice Colby explains:

> *Upon hearing the portrait of a handsome person, a twelfth-century listener knew immediately that this person was going to play at least a fairly important part in the story, that he was of noble birth and reasonably young, that he was basically of good character and therefore deserved the listener's sympathetic interest in all his undertakings. If, on the contrary, the individual was said to be ugly, the listener had good reason to suspect that he would play an important but unpleasant role in the story and that, being wicked, he merited no sympathy whatsoever. (Colby, 1965, p. 99)*

Typically, the Saracen would be pictured (e.g. in biblical miniatures, stained glass windows, etc.) or described (in literary documents) as blind, referencing his spiritual blindness to the truth of Christ. Often the Saracen would be imagined as a bestial sinner or a demonic monster, with a debased body marked by deformed features, and appalling, terrifying, and exaggerated traits, and a terrible smell (Arjana, 2015). Displayed with dog-heads or horns and tails, the Saracen symbolized the unacceptable, which is to be rejected and hated and contested by all means as a threat to Christian identity (Cohen, 2001, p. 114). This depiction also placed the Saracen beyond the pale of humanity and in the sphere of Satan. Demonization and dehumanization go hand in hand.

In addition to their monstrous features, the Saracen would often be pictured as a black (sometimes blue or purple) figure in contrast to the light-skinned Christian with fair hair (Arjana, 2015). In the medieval mindset, the colour white evoked purity, innocence, and civilization, whereas black symbolized sinfulness and demonic characteristics, and placed the dark-skinned person in the realm of the uncivilized and barbaric – even though it cannot be said that 'everything black was viewed negatively by medieval interpreters'. Consider in this regard the 'black color of the Benedictine habits', which symbolized 'humility and penitence' (Strickland, 2003, p. 84). Nevertheless, generally speaking, whiteness, as an identity marker, also suggested a Christian identity, whereas blackness indicated a non-Christian identity. Together with the disfiguration of bodies, the darkness of skin was the most consistent feature of those who were perceived as enemies of Christianity and the medieval Christian would easily understand this visual symbolization.

In the medieval imagination corporeal difference is not an either/or, black/white dichotomy; skin colour was considered malleable: if one's moral and spiritual character changed, so would the colour of one's skin (Akbari, 2009, p. 160). The sacrament of baptism, for example, which washes away sin, could lead to a transformation of skin colour: the dark dirty Muslim monster becoming a white, pure Christian human. To Christianize is to whiten. Furthermore, a conversion would not only lead to bodily metamorphosis – whitening of the skin colour – but would also transform the character of the Saracen: from being violent and aggressive he would turn into a peaceful and kind-hearted Christian. Such conversion narratives however were exceptional, and usually the Saracen would prefer 'death over a newly Christian life' (Cohen, 2001, p. 121).

The Danger of Blurring Religious Boundaries

While in the Christian imagination the bodies of Christians and Saracens have distinct biological markers expressing their diverging inner spiritual life, perhaps what concerned Christians the most was the actual impossibility of distinguishing between 'real' Christians

88 CHAPTER 3 Unification, Purification, and Dehumanization

and 'real' Saracens, and the fact that this impossibility could inadvertently lead to a blurring of religious boundaries. Social interaction, and especially sexual intercourse, in other words the mixing of flesh and bodily fluids, were to be avoided. There was a fear that such liaisons could lead to apostasy, but there was an even greater fear of the defilement and pollution that would come from mixing bodily fluids. The *chansons de geste* vividly projected the disintegrating consequences of such blurring: children born from such coupling will surely be gruesomely deformed.

The late thirteenth-century English romance the *King of Tars* (Chandler, 2015) is intriguing in this regard. In this romance, the black-skinned Sultan of Damascus (who has a violent and impulsive character) wants to marry the beautiful, fair-skinned, and chaste daughter of the King of Tars, a Christian. The king refuses to give away the hand of his daughter, whereupon the sultan wages war against him. The sultan is the stronger party, and the Christians have to flee. The princess, seeing her people in distress, agrees to marry the sultan. The sultan, however, demands that she convert, and he even threatens to kill her parents if she refuses. After some nights of contemplation, in which she has nightmares about being chased by a black hound (a reference to Ma-hounde, 'a misnomer for Muhammad popular in medieval Christendom that derogatorily combined the name *Mahoun*, for Muhammad, with the oft-used epithet for Muslims, "hounde"' [Whitaker, 2013, p. 183]), she converts, albeit in form only, for in her heart she remains Christian and at night she continues to pray. The child born from this marriage is hideous; it has no clear human contours, a sign of its mixed origin. It is a lifeless lump of flesh, without limbs, bones, or facial features. This deformed child 'terrifies the beholders with its carnal incompleteness and visible lack of any definable identity' (Czarnowus, 2008, p. 471).

> *& when the child was ybore,*
> *Wel sori wimen were therfore,*
> *For lim no hadde it non,*
> *Bot as a rond of flesche yschore*
> *In chaumber it lay hem bifore*
> [When the child was born / The women were very sorry /
> Since it had no limbs / But like a lump cut off from flesh / It
> lay before them in the chamber / Without blood or bones.]

> *For sorwe the levedi wald dye*
> *For it hadde noither nose no eye*
> *Bot lay ded as the ston*
> [The lady wanted to die out of sorrow / For it had neither
> a nose nor eyes, / But it lay dead like a stone.]

> *The soudan com to chaumber that tide*
> *& with his wiif he gan to chide*
> *That wo was hir bigon.*
> *'O dame', he seyd biforn, 'Ogain mi godes thou*
> *art forsworn!*
> *With right resoun y preve*
> *The childe that is here of thee born*
> *Bothe lim & lif it is forlorn*
> *Alle thurth thi fals bileve*
> [On that hour the sultan came into the chamber, / And
> he began to chide his wife / That woe began because of
> her. 'O Lady', he said before her, / 'Against my gods you
> have foresworn, / With the right reason and prayer: / The
> child that is here of thee born / Is devoid of both limbs
> and life / All because of your false beliefs'.] *(Chandler,*
> *2015, pp. 36–37; trans. Czarnowus, 2008, p. 472)*

The sultan blames his wife for being an unbeliever. He thinks the child's deformity is the result of her unbelief or false beliefs. She states that if the gods can bring the lump to life that she will convert. Thereupon, the sultan brings the 'child' to the temple. When his prayers have no effect, he smashes all the idols and returns to his wife. He agrees to convert, if, as she claims, God can bring the child to life. And so it happens: the lump becomes a beautiful child: it is humanized, beautified, and Christianized. Read in this way, '[t]he formless body symbolizes the uselessness of Muslim beliefs, or perhaps even their harmfulness for the health of one's body and spirit. [...] [C]onversion is beneficial in that it may restore things to the "appropriate" shape. Hence the monster constitutes a sign of warning and simultaneously an encouragement to subject oneself to baptism' (Czarnowus, 2008, p. 473). In response, the sultan decides to convert and consequentially, his black skin turns white.

> *His hide, that blac and lothely was,*
> *Al white bicom, thurth Godes gras,*
> *And clere withouten blame.*
> *And when the soudan seye that sight,*
> *Then leved he wele on God almight.*
> [His skin, that had been black and loathsome, became all
> white, through God's grace, and was spotless without
> blemish. And when the sultan saw that sight, well he
> believed on almighty God.] *(Chandler, 2015, p. 45; trans.*
> *Hahn, 2001, p. 15)*
> *Unnethe hir lord sche knewe.*
> *Than wist sche wele in hir thought*
> *That on Mahoun leved he nought*
> *For chaunged was his hewe.*
> [Scarcely did she (his wife) recognize her lord. Then
> she well knew in her mind that he did not believe at all
> in Mohammed, for his color was entirely changed.]
> *(Chandler, 2011, p. 87; trans. Hahn, 2001, p. 15)*

King of Tars had a moralizing function. Its purpose is not only to imagine the battle between Christians and Saracens, how the latter would be vanquished by the rule of the only true God, and how God would conquer all forms of paganism. It also visualizes the incompatibility of Christian faith and pagan faith as expressed in the lifeless child. Physical mixing and blurring spiritual boundaries translate into deformity. Furthermore, life comes through the Christian faith, whereas the pagan/Saracen faith contributes nothing. *King of Tars*, however, is also a story about the transformative power of conversion: (i) to whiten (purify) a black (bad, immoral, un-Christian) heart and (ii) to bring life where there was no life, form where there was no form, beauty where there was only ugliness. The grace of baptism transforms the impure soul into a pure soul, and this spiritual transformation is matched by a physical transformation (Chandler, 2015, p. 11). It may even be argued that this story invites Christian listeners/readers to contemplate and bolster their own faith. They are encouraged to ponder the Saracen (black, impure) aspects of their own faith identity and drive them out by turning to God.

The Conflation of Jew and Muslim

Underscoring the fact that the Saracen is a mere hermeneutical figure, the violent Saracen (the enemy far off) became increasingly conflated with the figure of the Jew ('the enemy-at-home in the heartlands of Europe' (Heng, 2018a, pp. 112–113). The lines between these two groups become blurred as both are projected as enemies that are intent on harming the mystical and integral unity of the church. Thus, the Saracen not only functions as a stand-in for the Greco-Roman pagan but also becomes interchangeable with the eminent anti-Christian,

90 CHAPTER 3 Unification, Purification, and Dehumanization

the Jew (Strickland, 2003, p. 160). Both are religionized as enemies of Christianity, and the threat posed by one is reinforced by the threatening image of the other.

David Freidenreich and Veronique Plesch refer to the thirteenth-century wooden Beam of the Passion, displayed at the Museu Nacional d'Art de Catalunya in Barcelona, as one unique example of such conflation. Unexpectedly, this version of the passion, which was created in Iberia for display above the eucharistic altar, includes black-skinned Muslims, with hooked noses and angry-looking faces. They wear turbans on their heads – a distinguishing sign of Saracens in thirteenth-century art. In various scenes they are depicted as mocking Christ, flagellating him, and turning away from Christ hanging on the cross.

The Muslims on the beam represent the gospel's Jewish characters. From a historical perspective, this depiction is out of place; the Saracens are placed in a gospel story where they do not belong. However, Freidenreich and Plesch note, that

> [t]he artist evidently intended his viewers to recognize as an anachronism his visual conflation of ancient Jewish priests and elders with present-day Muslims: we can be certain, after all, that thirteenth-century Iberian Christians understood the difference between Jews and Muslims. These viewers likely recognized the anachronistic nature of other depictions of Muslims in biblical and early Christian scenes as well. [...] These viewers could recognize Christ's enemies both as first-century Jews and as present-day Muslims; by the same token, they could recognize themselves in Christ's first-century followers. (Freidenreich & Plesch, 2020, pp. 120–121)

As the Jews were responsible for killing Jesus in the past and continued to bring harm to his contemporary body, so too the Saracen, in line with biblical prophecy, lived only to raise his hand against the viewer's blessed brethren, that is the church (Genesis 16). Like the Jews, the Saracens are considered to be 'crucifiers' of Christian martyrs, who were fighting to recover Christian lands.

The beam, however, does not depict the Saracens as the actual killers of Christ but rather as disbelieving priests and elders. Above the heads of the Saracens is written *Quid ad nos* (What is it to us?). In placing this dismissive statement above their heads, the painter depicts the Saracens as those who reject the Christian truth about Christ's divinity and his salvific death. According to Freidenreich and Plesch, the 'Beam of the Passion suggests that the ongoing conflict between Christians and Muslims is nothing less than a battle over the significance of the Crucifixion' (Freidenreich & Plesch, 2020, p. 122). This battle is further reinforced by the spiritual strength of the holy women (the three Marys) who are depicted on the other side of the cross and lean towards it. The contrast between these pious women who recognize Christ's passion and the dark Saracen figures underscores the struggle about the salvific power of the cross. Selfing and othering once again go hand in hand.

The beam would have hung above the altar, where the Eucharist was celebrated, and where bread and wine were transformed into Christ's body and blood. Christ's cross as depicted on the beam, and positioned as it was, refers to Christ's body present in bread and wine, offered to the Christian community that has gathered around the altar. By depicting Christ's suffering against the background of the crusades and projecting Christianity's current enemies as Christ's past torturers, the truth of the doctrine of transubstantiation, the idea that bread and wine become Christ's body and blood during communion, is reinforced. Christ is ready to sacrifice himself time and again; he died at Golgotha and he continues to sacrifice himself now for our salvation, just as his enemies, whether Jews or Saracens, continue to bring harm to his body and to all that are part of that body. 'By contrasting Christ's grotesque and despicable enemies with his faithful and visually pleasing followers, the Beam of the Passion inspires revulsion toward those who reject Christian doctrines and identification with those who model adherence to them' (Freidenreich & Plesch, 2020, p. 115). As was the case with the *Kings of Tars*, here too an appeal goes out to the spectators to answer the question: Where do you stand? On the side of the unbelievers or the side of the faithful? To which community do you belong? To the community that is healed thanks to Christ's salvific sacrifice or to the disintegrating body of those who deny the salvific power of his sacrifice, as symbolized in the Eucharist.

Text Box 3: The Muslim in Christian Medieval Imagination

All these distorted images were 'spread throughout every stratus of society', becoming popular in oral and material culture, for example via Romanesque architecture, which often used decorations depicting battles between crusaders and demonic Saracens, or in the *chansons de geste*. This ongoing dehumanization and even demonization of the Muslim as Saracen went so far that Bernard of Clairvaux (1090–1153), co-author of the Rule for the Order of the Templars, could say 'that the killing of a Muslim wasn't actually homicide, but malicide – the extermination of incarnated evil, not the killing of a person' (Heng, 2018b).

Christian	Saracen
Christ	Mahmout
Isaac/Abel	Ishmael/Cain
Christ-followers	Christ-killers
Blessed	Cursed
Benign, moral	Malign, immoral
Spiritual	Carnal
Pious	Sex driven
Innocent	Intentionally guilty
White	Black, purple
A pure and whole human body	A disfigured, bestial, demonic body
Sanctifying and purifying	Polluting and profaning

2 The Deteriorating Fate of the Jews

Early on in its existence, the church developed its self-understanding as the people of God and heir to God's promises by denying Israel a lasting place in God's plan of salvation. Because the Jews refused to embrace the gracious gift of salvation offered to them in Christ, God turned away from Israel and revoked his promises to them. Israel was no longer his beloved people. According to supersessionist theologies, the Jewish people were marked by Cain's curse. These theologies promised little good for Jewish communities in Christian societies. In reality, however, at least until the eleventh century, it seems that the Jews, despite some violent outbursts, were fairly well integrated.

From the eleventh century onwards, and even more so during the centuries that followed, Jews suffered various forms of exclusion as well as eruptions of violence, and to make matters more complex, the 'holy' war against the Muslims became a justification to turn on the Jews. 'The culpability of the Jew steadily increased in Christian eyes. Medieval Christianity eventually demonized him' (Cohen, 1999, p. 16). If the Jews were previously cast as 'living letters of the law', testifying (however unwillingly) to the truth of Christian faith, now they were cast as intent on harming Christ's body and eager to bring pain to the Christian community. They are not just blind; they are also evil and their malign intent is apparent in their revulsive actions. Religionization takes on new forms. As the Middle Ages wore on the situation of the Jews living in European societies deteriorated, popes would, however, continue to speak out to protect the European Jewish population (see *Licet Perfidia Iudaeorum*).

Flashback: The Jews and the Legacy of Antiquity

The position of the Jews after the Constantinian turn was complex and ambiguous. Following Roman law, their worship cult was *religio licita* (legal, licit, tolerated practice). Jews were allowed to visit their synagogues; they were not persecuted, and massive and forced conversion did not belong to the official policy. Legally, Jews were awarded a 'recognized, if inferior and, in practice, uncertain place within Christian society' (Stantchev, 2014, p. 68). The *Justinian Code* (529, 534) – a codex developed during the rule of the Byzantine emperor Justinian between 529–565 – would further affirm their ambivalent position. This code compiled the laws which had been collected in earlier codes as well as those laws that had been promulgated since the *Theodosian Code* in 438. It contains 33 Jewry laws, which may be found in Chapter 9, entitled *De Iudaeis et Caelicolis* and Chapter 10, *Ne Christianum mancipium haereticus vel paganus vel Iudaeus habeat vel possideat vel circumcidat* (Linder, 1987). While previous laws were mainly upheld – Jews could not own Christian slaves, employ Christian servants in their houses, marry Christians, nor hold public office – new laws were added. Justinian was the first emperor to order the conversion of existing synagogues to churches and to prohibit the construction of new synagogues (Brewer, 2005, p. 131). He also disqualified Jews from bearing testimony in Christian courts against Christians. The emphasis on the hierarchical relations between Christians and Jews, and the subordinate position of the latter vis-à-vis the first, matched with Augustine's doctrine of witness.

> *Jews were tolerated as long as, and* only as long as, *they* served *Christian aims. Toleration was conditional on Jews being* useful *to Christian society. Jews were expected to recognise that their place in Christian society was contingent on their subservience to Christians. Judaism was deemed to have been superseded by Christianity; Jews were supposed to serve Christians and not Christians Jews. That was the prevailing theory in medieval Christian thinking. (Abulafia, 2017, p. 12, emphasis by the author)*

Justinian's *Corpus iuris civilis* remained in force in the Eastern Roman Empire until the ninth century, but it had little impact on daily life in the West. In any case, after the fall of the Roman Empire in 476, local law would prevail, and few rulers, secular or ecclesiastical, felt the need to enforce Jewish subordination. For years Justinian's *corpus* was lost from sight, until it was rediscovered during the Gregorian reform. From the twelfth century onwards, with the renaissance of Roman law, 'it displaced the Theodosian Code as the main source of information about ancient Roman legislation' (Linder, 1987, p. 47).

The Jews under the Frankish Merovingians and the Carolingians

Under the Frankish Merovingians, who ruled between the fifth and eighth centuries, 'Jews and Christians [...] engaged each other across a larger spectrum of relationships and experiences (Text Box 4). Jews were deeply integrated into the rhythms of these local worlds, living as natural participants in the culture, politics, and societies of early medieval Europe' (Elukin, 2007, p. 11). Jewish people had Latin names and expressed themselves in the vernacular, speaking Hebrew only in the synagogue. They did not distinguish themselves in their appearance, for example by dressing in a particular manner, and mainly worked as traders; they were an accepted part of the Merovingian towns. Under Carolingian rule, which lasted from the eighth until the tenth century, this 'Frankish Convivencia' (Elukin, 2007, p. 136) seems to have continued. Jews were granted liberal conditions of settlement; they were exempt from certain feudal obligations, and they received fiscal privileges. Furthermore, the restrictions against Jewish slave ownership were softened and certain charters protected them against the threat of ecclesial persecution. Thanks to these policies Jewish communities seem to have done well. Jews took on commercial roles; they traded in slaves and luxury goods, like silk (Malkiel, 2003, p. 54). Furthermore, Jews, because of their focus on the study of the Torah and Talmud, were far more educated and literate than most Christians at the time, which probably explains why they were often called upon as advisors and diplomats. Many lords, lay and ecclesial, included Jews among their entourages, as doctors, suppliers, tax collectors, and even as friends. Generally speaking, Jews simply participated in cultural, economic, and political life and Christian-Jewish relations were governed less by ideology or rhetoric than by custom, convenience, and circumstance.

> **Text Box 4: Visigothic Jewry Laws**
>
> The position of the Jews under the Frankish Merovingians (fifth–eighth century) and that of Carolingians (eighth–tenth century) was that of a rather well-integrated minority with a more or less stable place in society. The fate of the Jews in Visigothic Spain (fifth–eighth century), however, was significantly different and the prevailing Jewry laws promulgated by the consecutive councils of Toledo bear witness to an all-pervasive mistrust not only vis-à-vis the Jews, but also vis-à-vis Jewish converts. Jews were converted by force (which was contrary to canon law). They were not allowed to trade, celebrate their festivals, or circumcise their children, and this under the threat of severe punishments. Furthermore, Freidenreich notices that 'Visigothic Canons refer to converts from Judaism as Jews even after they have become Christian' (Freidenreich, 2013, p. 83). The Fourth Council of Toledo (633) calls them 'baptised Jews' (c. 60), in a similar vein, the Twelfth Council of Toledo (681) refers to converted Jews as 'Jews' and urges them to 'be good Christians' (c. 9). There are doubts about the depth of their conversion and they are suspected of clinging to their old traditions. While these Jewry canons should not be conflated with the blood purity laws of the fifteenth century, it is clear that the Visigothic bishops were already convinced that 'there is something intrinsic to Jews that makes them especially prone to reject the teachings of the church even after their conversion' (Freidenreich, 2013, p. 84). The fact that many Jews had been forced to convert increased mistrust about Jewish sincerity. This would be no different in the fifteenth century (see Chapter 4).

Some ecclesial authorities (e.g. Agobard, Bishop of Lyon, ca. 779–840) did oppose the leniency that developed under the Carolingian rule (Moore, 2007, p. 27) because it went against the Augustinian theology of Jewish witness. They were especially sensitive to the right order of relations and considered situations whereby the roles were reversed and Christians regarded Jews as a thorn in their flesh. Social mixing between Jews and Christians also concerned them; they felt that social barriers had to be maintained and at times ecclesial authorities even protested against the 'privileged' position of the Jews in Carolingian society. These protests had little impact but they are interesting because they show a world in which Jews and Christians interacted on a daily basis, as friends, business partners, and servants. Just like early church fathers, who, at a time when the boundaries between Christian and Jewish communities were still porous, developed polemical anti-Jewish discourses to establish clear-cut boundaries, so too anti-Jewish protests during the Carolingian era provide us with a glimpse of a society in which Jews and Christians are found living together as part of each other's world (Elukin, 2002, p. 63).

The Jew: From Unwilling Witness to Enemy, Child Murderer, and Usurer

From the twelfth century onwards, however, Jews are increasingly confronted with violent outbursts, daily vexations, and discrimination. The anti-Jewish tone harshens to the extent that Jews are demonized and placed outside the realm of humanity. Three factors need mentioning here: the crusades, anti-Jewish mythologies (such as blood libels), and the money connection. Step by step the Jew is religionized as a malign enemy of the pure, integral *Corpus Christianum* – an internal enemy, out to harm Christians, whether out of bloodthirst (literally) or out of greed.

94 CHAPTER 3 Unification, Purification, and Dehumanization

Crusading Ideology and the Jew as Christianity's Internal Enemy   During the first crusade (1096–1099) European Jewish communities became the victim of unbridled violence that took local Jewish communities by surprise. These violent outbursts were mainly the work of a badly disciplined army of warriors, who looted and plundered. Many secular and ecclesial rulers tried to protect the Jews in their local societies from these mobs, just as there were Christian neighbours to whom Jews turned for help. Nevertheless, 'floating crusaders, sympathetic burghers and aroused rural folk could on occasion join forces and form temporary active and destructive groupings alongside the crusading militias' (Chazan, 2009, p. 297). As time went by, the animosity spread by crusade preachers stimulated anti-Jewish hatred and the holy war against the Muslims became a justification to turn on the Jews (Kessler, 2010, p. 108). While Muslims were polluting the distant Holy Land, Jews were polluting Christian territories at home. While Muslims were fighting Christ's army of warriors, Jews stood opposed to Christ's mystical family, the church (Stow, 1994, pp. 106–107). Anti-Jewish violence became a pattern during the ensuing campaigns, resulting in massacres in Reims, Worms, Trier, and Rouen. But also in England 'a trail of blood followed the coronation of the famed hero [...], Richard Lionheart, in 1189, when Jews were slaughtered at Westminster, London, Lynn, Norwich, Stamford, Bury St. Edmunds, and York' (Heng, 2018a, p. 15).

Jewish communities would call upon the popes for protection: Pope Alexander II (r. 1061–1073) tried to defend the Jews while at the same time legitimizing the crusades. In *Dispar nimirum est* (1063), a fragment of a letter Pope Alexander II wrote to praise the bishops of Spain for protecting the Jews, he argued that the fate of the Jews and Saracens [*Iudeorum et Sarracenorum*] was clearly distinct: the Saracens sought to drive Christians out of their homes, but the Jews, on the contrary, were servants of Christians – even though their rejection of Christ condemned them to perpetual servitude. Those who 'are saved by God's mercy' may not be destroyed. The pope commended those who rallied against the Muslims for their restraint vis-à-vis the Jews. This fragment was later included in Gratian's *Decretum* and thus received canonical status. From the twelfth century onwards, popes promulgated formal statements, known as *Constitutio pro Iudaeos*, to protect Jewish communities against violent outbursts. Jews should not suffer any attacks upon their life, ought not to undergo forced conversions, their cemeteries had to be respected as well as their worship practices (Grayzel, 1933, p. 77). Many local bishops and secular rulers, recalling Augustine's 'protective' theology of Jewish witness, argued as well that it would be unacceptable to kill those who are under the protection of God. However, these pleas had little impact.

While the violence unleashed by the crusades was not permanent, and Jewish communities usually recovered after a while from the immediate threat, the crusading ideology and the 'heightened awareness of others outside the fold went hand in hand with growing sensitivity to difference, disagreement, and deviation from within'. These 'attacks upon Jews during the Crusades undoubtedly awakened Christian society to the anomaly of the Jews' position: enemies/killers of Christ whose lives and errant religion God had protected for the greater good of Christendom' (Cohen, 1999, pp. 149 and 151). The fact that, this being the time of the Renaissance, Christians were gaining more and more access to Hebrew texts and were learning that the Jews were not simply 'librarians of the Hebrew letters' but continued to develop their own living interpretive traditions, enhanced the sense that the Jews were out of place in Christian society. The Augustinian theology of witness was reaching a turning point and even in the papal letters aimed at protecting the Jews there is a change of tone towards the start of the thirteenth century. Pope Innocent's III *Constitutio* (1199), for example, written almost a century after Alexander II's letter, stated clearly that only those Jews would be protected, who did not plot against the Christians [*qui nihil machinari praesumpserint in subversionem fidei christianae*] (Denzinger et al., 1996, p. 277). This qualification reflects and encourages a 'growing suspicion in the late twelfth and early thirteenth centuries that many Jews in Europe were deliberately seeking to undermine and harm the "societas Christiana"' (Rist, 2007, p. 290).

Jews and Usury   When, in the twelfth century, the money economy began to burgeon and the gap between rich and poor began to grow, money came to be seen as the devil's substance, and moneylending became a mortal sin. The church reiterated and reinforced its position on this issue in the canons of the Second (1139) and Third (1179) Lateran Councils, both of which threatened usurers with excommunication. At the same time, however, there was a need to raise capital for business projects, and since canon law does not apply to non-Christians, who were not subject to ecclesial punishments, Jews were approached on this matter. Still more strikingly, '[m]any princes throughout Europe adopted the habit of playing host to Jewish communities so that the local Jews could practice moneylending to the benefit of local trade, industry and war-making' (Dorn, 2016). This only added to the existing negative image of the Jews as enemies of Christians. Christians started to 'imagine usury as a mode for Jews to wreak vengeance on contemporary Christians, a vengeance to be persistent, perennial, and all consuming' (Mell, 2018, p. 48). The image of the 'carnal Jew' as contrary to the 'spiritual Christian' takes on new interpretations. Against the background of the crusades, which were costly and needed financing, Jewish usury came to be seen as a pact between Christianity's internal others – the Jews – and its external others – the Saracens – to thwart the 'holy war' and to inflict harm once again on Christ's body, the church. In this context, the story of Jesus' cleansing of the temple functioned as a way to condemn the moneylending activities of the Jews as profane and polluting. A single story functions as an interpretive master key to delegitimize both Jews and Saracens as enemies of the *Corpus Christianum*, and to justify actions aimed at containing the problem of contamination.

Blood Libels From the twelfth century onwards, the ancient deicide charge (initiated by Melito of Sardis) came to play a more prominent role, not only in theological documents but also in ritual practice, dramatic performances, popular culture, and architecture. According to Sara Lipton, this projection of Jews as Christ-killers had to do with a shift in Christian devotional culture, which started to focus more on Jesus' humanity, his suffering, and death rather than on his divine and elevated nature. This focus on Christ's passion, his wounded body, and sacrificial death was liturgically matched by a new eucharistic piety revolving around the idea that Christ is present in bread and wine and that Christians partake in his salvific sacrifice when receiving communion. The more the body of Christ was turned into 'an auratic object', the more Jews were singled out as the ones seeking to harm it. By extension, the more *Societas Christiana* was envisioned as Christ's integral body on earth, the more Jews were singled out as those perpetual enemies trying to sicken it, defile it, disunite it, and so on. While salvation was imagined as coming through the body and blood of Christ, Satan and his accomplices were imagined to be obsessed with bringing harm to Christ's blood and body. Several anti-Jewish myths projected an image of Jews as intentionally wanting to harm the *Corpus Christianum*. Jews were portrayed as 'murderers of God, haters of truth, minions of Satan, and enemies of Christendom' (Resnick, 2000, p. 242).

One particularly nasty myth accused Jews of kidnapping, torturing, and murdering innocent Christians. It related to the murder of William of Norwich (1132–1144), a young leather apprentice, who was supposedly kidnapped by prominent Jews, subjected to all the tortures of Christ, and subsequently killed (1144) (Thomas of Monmouth, 2011). Jews were later accused of similar deeds in Gloucester (1168), Bury St. Edmunds (1181), and Winchester (1192) (McClymond, 2016, p. 69). We know that such myths sometimes translated into violent anti-Jewish pogroms.

Then there were the ritual murder charges, according to which the Jews killed Christian infants for their blood, which was thought to have healing power.

Jews were believed to employ Christian blood during the rite of circumcision, and also at Passover when they used it in mixing the wine and baking the unleavened bread. They were also said to need it to, allegedly, make aphrodisiacs and magical potions; to prevent or cure epilepsy; to paint the bodies of the dead; to cover the foetor Judaicus – *the stench that connotated them; to ease labour pains; to cure haemorrhoids; to redden their typical pallor; to heal skin diseases, sores and scrofula; to cure the blindness that was said to afflict all Jews at birth; to make children fertile; to remove the monstrous parts that distinguished Jewish infants, such as two small fingers, so similar to the Devil's horns, attached to their foreheads; and to stop haemorrhages and the copious menstruation that affected both Jewish women and men. (Matteoni, 2008, pp. 190–191)*

Scholars have argued that these myths only make sense against the background of the medieval understanding of the Eucharist in terms of transubstantiation. A changed understanding of Christian normativity (Christian self-making) translates into new images of deviation (crafting of otherness).

While the debates about the nature of the Eucharist and the extent to which the elements of bread and wine were transformed into Christ's body and blood go back to the ninth century, they proliferated in the twelfth century, until the Fourth Lateran Council decided the matter by promulgating the doctrine of transubstantiation.

These theological developments helped in turn to give rise to new mythical structures into which traditional Christian anti-Judaism could be channeled: ritual crucifixion (the notion that contemporary Jews crucified and killed innocent Christian boys, just as their ancestors had killed the innocent Christ); ritual cannibalism (the notion that Jews murdered Christians and consumed their blood for magical and ritual purposes); and host desecration. (Stacey, 1998, p. 14)

These blood libels thus tell us more about the construction of Christian identity than about the Jews. Some scholars even argue that these mythical blood libels were spread in order to enhance and strengthen the Christian belief in the power of the sacrament of the Eucharist, which became the sacrament of Sacraments. It is telling in this regard that the Feast of *Corpus Christi* (1264) was instituted by Pope Urban IV (r. 1261–1264) just at that moment when the myth of host profanation began to spread, and Jews were being targeted as the main enemies of Christ(ians). Some think that these myths emerged amongst the populace and were a mere 'negative by-product of the very increase in popular Eucharistic piety [...] By profaning the Host and causing it to bleed and by extracting blood from Christian children for ritual purposes they were literally "substantiating" Christian belief in transubstantiation and in the spiritual efficacy of blood' (Biale, 2007, p. 112). Whatever the precise explanation for the emergence of these blood libels, the harm they caused to Jews was significant. Myths, plays, artwork, miniatures, stained glass windows, and literary documents exaggerated Jewish 'defiance and hostility, and [...] assigned collective and transhistorical guilt' to the murderous and bloodthirsty 'Jewish people' (Lipton, 2014). Together, they created an image of the Jew and the Jewish people as satanic and monstrous, intent on harming Christians and the church.

Blackness, Disfiguration, and Bodily Afflictions

In line with medieval imagination, Jewish spiritual difference translated into bodily difference (Mayerhofer, 2021, p. 135). Christians imagined the Jew as black, dark-skinned, or even purple, and displayed him with bestial characteristics, grotesque facial and physical deformities (horns and tails). As with the 'Saracen', the Jew too is as ugly as sin. Besides his blackness and bodily deformity, there are three other symbolic identity markers that were widely used during the late Middle Ages to link Jewishness and evil. First, the hooked nose signifies 'voraciousness, arrogance, and wantonness' and is a sign of the Jew's perverted character. It projects one more condensed narrative of Jewish diabolic nature. Second, the goat beard, which is associated with lasciviousness: the goat is 'so full of lust that his eyes look sideways' (Strickland, 2003, p. 78). Finally, Jews were said to be born with two smaller fingers, symbolizing the small horns of the devil.

The body, however, does not only mirror inner character, but it is also negatively impacted by bad character. Hence the assumption that Jews, because of what 'they' had done to Christ, suffered from bodily afflictions, like (extreme) menstruation, haemorrhoids, eye ailments, bloodletting, epilepsy, and so on. The body and blood of the Jews are different from those of the Christian: their bodies disintegrate (Matteoni, 2008, p. 195). Consider in this regard *Historia Orientalis* written by the French Dominican, Jacob of Vitry (ca. 1160–1240). He wrote the following about the Jews and their bodies:

> *Finally, there are other Jews, the descendants of those who have cried out 'His blood be upon us and upon our children!' They have become unwarlike (imbelles) and weak (imbecilles) like women [quasi mulieres]. Therefore, they suffer from blood flow every month, as one says [unde singulis lunationibus [...] fluxum sanguinis patiuntur]. For God smote them in the hinder parts and put them to a perpetual reproach. After they killed their brother, the true Abel, they became wanderers and fugitives like the cursed Cain, so they have a trembling head, which means an anxious heart, and fear for their lives day and night. (Jacob of Vitry, ed. Donnadieu, 2008, p. 328, my translation)*

Religious difference and inferiority – the Jews are punished by God for having killed Jesus – are here written onto the Jewish body (Maor et al., 2021). Religious difference is biologized, at least to a certain extent. Furthermore, the afflictions written onto the Jewish body also imply a feminization of the Jew as Jew. The Jewish body is weak, sick, and not in control of its fluids. Femininity connoted powerlessness. Jews are feeble and womanish and this in contrast to the ideal image of Christianness in terms of 'morally and spiritually edified, and, above all, male' (Mayerhofer, 2021, p. 147).

To be cured of all their afflictions, Jews needed innocent Christian blood: a blind Jew could learn to see again after smearing the blood of a monk on his eyes; Christian blood would cure the wound of circumcision or the typical Jewish disorder of male menstruation (cf. the blood libels). The integral, whole body of the Christian and its pure and innocent blood promised to heal the black deformed Jewish body. The outcome is the dehumanization of the Jew and a reaffirmation of the redemptive power of Christ's blood and body.

Suzanne Akbari adds that the individual Jew represents 'on a microcosmic level, the uncleanliness of Synagoga herself, for the entire community of the Jews was believed to have become unclean [...] at the time of the crucifixion' (Akbari, 2009, p. 152). His/her inferior, disfigured body and flowing blood imply the threat of disintegration, transgression, and decay. This disfigured, bleeding, and stinking body presents a threat to the *Corpus Christianum*. To avert the risk of pollution, the threat posed by the Jew had to be contained, and to that end mechanisms of demarcation would have to be put in place – hence the need to separate Jews from Christians, to limit their social interactions, to prohibit any corporal mixing and, in extreme cases, to persecute and expel them from Christian territories.

Text Box 5: The Jew in Christian Medieval Imagination

Christian body/Church	Jewish body/Synagogue
Christ	Antichrist
Christians	Christ-killers
Believer	Idolater
Blessed	Cursed
Benign, moral	Malign, immoral
Innocent	Guilty
White	Black
Whole, healed bodies	Disfigured, bestial, demonic, sick bodies
Blood that purifies/saves	Blood that contaminates/curses
Wholeness	Disintegration
God's helpers	Satan's helpers

3   The Return of the Problem of Heresy

The long list of heresies, as written down by heresiologists, testify to the Christian preoccupation with the binary of orthodoxy/heresy, and they also point to the way the heretic – like the Jew, the pagan, and the Saracen – functions as a hermeneutical figure of religionized otherness in the process of Christian identity construction. Even when 'real' heretics were absent from Christian society, that is when the problem of heresy is not perceived as a pressing problem, heretics would continue to figure in Christian imagination as wicked enemies within, determined to weaken and destroy the church. During the late Middle Ages, this dreadful image would become prevalent again.

Flashback on Heresiology

Heresiologists did not so much describe different 'heretic communities', but rather named, categorized, and hierarchized them within a particular Christian theological narrative, thereby fashioning and reshaping them at the same time. Reading about heresies teaches us more about the concerns of those claiming the orthodox norm than about the heresies themselves. The degree of coherence of certain heresies was by all likelihood heightened if not exaggerated in order to enhance both the problem of heresy and the solution of orthodoxy. Heresiologists *crafted* otherwise scattered and fragmented beliefs and practices into more or less coherent and systematic ideologies (Arianism, Manicheism, Donatism, etc.) and communities, inspired by a leader (a false teacher), with their own rites, teachings, and even structures, all of which contested and perverted *vera religio*. By contrast, Christian apologists projected a clear-cut understanding of orthodoxy as self-evident, pristine, and *au fond* universal (Catholic), even though it was itself under construction, contested, and context dependent.

That Nicene Christianity emerged after the Constantinian turn as 'orthodox' had much to do with power and the support of imperial rulers. This particular expression of Christian worship became conditional for Roman citizenship. The general thrust was that orthodoxy ensured the stability of the *Societas Christiana*, while heresy embodies the threat of disorder. If one allowed deviant groups to flourish, one could provoke the wrath of God and bring destruction upon all. This worldview entailed the responsibility of both ecclesial and secular authorities to enforce the Christian orthodox norm. This attitude is known as charitable hatred (Walsham, 2006).

The Disappearance and Return of the Problem of Heresy

While occasional accusations of heresy would continue to go back and forth, as opponents sought to name and shame one another, by the late sixth century the problem of heresy had lost something of its urgency. At least, it was no longer considered to be the kind of problem that would get you killed (Fernández-Armesto & Wilson, 1996, p. 45). A notable resurgence of heresy came in the first half of the eleventh century and 'produced a flurry of accusations and allegations of popular heresy' (Moore, 2002, p. 8). There was an increase in the number of heresy trials, which had been absent in the previous centuries (Moore, 1975). What the heretics of the time seem to have had in common, was a deep dissatisfaction with the state of the church. They questioned the church's corruption, challenged the laxity of ecclesial authorities and their attachment to worldly wealth – whether they were bishops, monks, or priests – and demanded a return to the purity of the gospel. Those ecclesial authorities which did not want to change the status quo denounced the most vocal of those critics by charging them with heresy. Such a charge was one of the more effective ways of discrediting opponents. Moore, however, notices that when the goal of these critical voices began to coincide with the goal of the Gregorian effort to reform, the problem of heresy gradually waned. The efforts of the church to raise the standard of behaviour for clergy and, especially, to end the practice of simony, became accepted as the ecclesial norm. What was previously rejected as heretical, now became inscribed in church policy.

In the twelfth century, the problem of heresy returns, precisely at that moment in history when the Latin church was investing in the establishment of a more centralized ecclesial structure and in doctrinal and liturgical unification. Most of the so-called heretical movements disagreed with the project of Latin Christendom, papal monarchy, and clerical hierarchy as well as with the material and political power these bodies wielded. Their 'heretical' programme often included 'variations on three key points: challenging the spiritual powers and special status of the clergy, making the central sacrament of Communion more inclusive, and putting the Bible into the hands of ordinary believers' (Terpstra, 2015, p. 49). That some of these movements seem to have had a wide popular appeal and were able to stir up faith and action in ordinary people concerned those defending the orthodox norm. Certainly some ecclesial authorities were worried about their own authority, but many were also deeply concerned that the *Corpus Christianum* was threatened by the rapid spread of heretical doctrines (Rist, 2009, p. 4).

> It was order they [the authorities in church and state] were worried about, and when order in church and state was directly challenged, they responded harshly. Sacred and secular authorities believed that they had a duty to preserve the Corpus Christianum against infections that would sicken it, or against temptations that would lead simple believers to disobedience and hell, triggering God's judgment on a whole city or society. (Terpstra, 2015, p. 51)

This overall concern is notable in the explosion of textual treatments dealing with the problem of heresy, ranging from polemical tracts to texts for edification, long lists of heresies and their mistakes, canon law texts, and later also inquisition reports (Sackville, 2011, p. 10).

The Cathars and Waldensians

Two groups that symbolize the problem of heresy in the twelfth century are the Cathars and the Waldensians. The first, the Cathars or *Katharoi*, meaning 'the pure ones', a popular name used by the enemies of this movement, were dedicated to poverty and chastity (Text Box 3). The Cathars considered themselves to be good men and women, good Christians, or friends of God, who hoped to reach heaven by upholding an ascetic lifestyle. They are said to have held dualist beliefs, regarding the spiritual world as created by a good god and the material world by an evil one. These dualist beliefs led them to reject the idea that Christ ever had a human body, and from this it followed that they took issue with the sacrament of the Eucharist and the idea that Christ's body and blood were present in wine and bread. This rejection of the Eucharist by the Cathars was considered to be a direct threat to Christian society: where there is division about Christ's body and blood, there is a division in the *Corpus Christianum*. In addition, the rejection of the Eucharist shook the hierarchical order of the church, for the idea of the Mass as a sacrifice made on behalf of members of the church underlies the Catholic tradition of the priestly office and its exclusive responsibility for performing this ritual. In 1179, Pope Alexander III (r. 1159–1181) convened the Third Lateran Council which anathematized the heresy of the Cathars and strongly condemned anyone lending support to this movement. The relevant canon 27 states that Christians were not allowed to trade with heretics, nor entertain social relations with them and that those who did so nevertheless could be excommunicated. Heretics, furthermore, were not to receive communion nor a Christian burial. They were cast outside the *Corpus Christianum*.

Text Box 6: Naming and Categorizing as Delegitimization

While the name 'Cathars' has become common place, its members preferred the terms good men and women or simply Christians. The name 'Cathars' is a religionized manipulation of their self-understanding and is part of the ecclesial effort to classify this movement, using earlier heresiological sources, as a return of the heresy of ancient Manichean dualism, which had already been condemned. Indeed, the name 'Cathars' is not new, but stems from John of Damascus, who used it to denote heretic groups. John of Damascus, in turn, was inspired by the heresiology of Epiphanius of Salamis. The Cathars, the pure ones, were followers of Mani, the leader of the Manicheans. The name Cathars was also used to depict the Novations, who upheld deviant ideas about baptism and the readmission of 'lapsed Christians'. Of course, it is possible that the Cathars from the twelfth century were inspired by the fourth-century Manicheans or the third-century Novations and that they sought to reinvigorate the legacy of these ancient heresies. However, and since most of our sources about the Cathars are polemical, it is more likely that, in line with the tradition of heresiology, an effort was made to delegitimize this movement by classifying it as an expression of an ancient heresy that had already been condemned at the Council of Nicaea in 325.

Another group of dissidents were the so-called Waldensians, who called themselves the Poor of Lyon, even though they later spread out to Germany and North Italy (Biller, 2009, p. 175). They were followers of Peter Waldo (1140–1218), also known as Valdes, a merchant from Lyon, who left behind his old life in order to live a Christian life of chastity, poverty, and preaching. Valdes based his vision of Christian life on the Bible and he believed that all Christians should have access to Scripture. He therefore commissioned translations of the Bible from Latin into the vernacular. The Waldensians, furthermore, rejected the apostolic authority of the Roman Church, denounced ecclesial hierarchy, and claimed that anyone with the right Christian spirit could be a priest. What concerned the pope the most, was the fact that Waldensians challenged the clergy's monopoly on preaching; they regarded the Bible as the Word of God and felt that it was there to inspire everyone, not only those who had been ordained. In 1179, just before the Third Lateran Council (see below), Waldo met Pope Alexander III and requested his approval. While Pope Alexander III approved the Waldensians' dedication to a life of poverty, he did not allow them to preach unless they received permission from their bishop or local clergy. The latter, however, were not keen to give permission to preachers who openly challenged their moral and spiritual authority. The Waldensians continued to preach without an episcopal licence and in 1184, Pope Lucius III (r. 1181–1185), with the support of Emperor Frederick I (r. 1155–1190), condemned them in the papal bull *Ad Abolendam* (Kras & Panz-Sochacka, 2020, p. 19).

Polemical Depictions of Heresy

The first 'weapon' against heresy was the production of polemical texts, which depicted the heretics in a negative light. These texts tapped into a whole reservoir of negative descriptions, developed by the church fathers, of *haeretica pravitas* [heretical perversion], while also projecting horrible new images aimed at inciting terror. Over time, these depictions would also function as a justification of oppression, persecution, and penalization.

Heretics as Foxes   In line with previous traditions, heretics would continue to be projected as secretive (they operate in dark places, hiding from broad daylight), sanctimonious and feigned (they pretend to be something – Catholic – which they are not), and malign (driven purely by the desire to harm the church). This cluster of ideas functions as a thread running through various polemical and other texts.

During the twelfth century, and especially under the influence of the Cistercian abbot Bernard of Clairvaux, one other image, that of the foxes in the vineyard, became highly influential in sermons, bulls, and even canon law. This image stems from two scriptural passages; the first, Judg 15:5, narrates Samson's destruction of the Philistine harvest by tying firebrands to the tails of foxes and sending these burning foxes into the fields, and the second, Song 2:15, has the bride say to her beloved 'catch us the little foxes that destroy the vine'. In his *Sermones super Cantica Canticorum* (1144), Bernard of Clairvaux had already used the image of the little foxes to reference people who, in his own community, were undermining monastic life. Later however, particularly in sermons 64–65, he applied this same image to the secretive and destructive power of heretics.

Typologically, the vineyard symbolizes the church and the little foxes the heretics, who are out to destroy the vineyard. In his commentary, Bernard of Clairvaux expresses his concern that the vineyard is not sufficiently protected against the many out to bring harm to it:

> *I refer to that vineyard which has covered the whole earth, and of which we ourselves are a portion, an exceedingly great vineyard, planted by the Hand of Christ, redeemed with His Blood, watered with His teaching, propagated by His grace, fertilised by His Spirit. [...] But I now feel impelled to espouse its cause on account of the multitude of its despoilers, the paucity of its protectors, and the difficulty of its defence. What makes the difficulty is the fact that the despoilers are concealed from us. (Bernard of Clairvaux, trans. by a priest of Mount Melleray, 2016, Sermon 65)*

It is the secrecy of the heretics that concerns Bernard of Clairvaux the most. For him, this secrecy distinguishes the new heresies from the old ones, and makes them more dangerous. Old heretics, so he claims, preached in the open, eager to win the argument, but these new heretical movements display a new kind of secrecy, which makes it almost impossible to uncover them. They are evil disguised as good, falsehood dressed up as truth, heresy as religion. The abbot especially takes issue with the way these popular new heretics pretend to follow the highest moral standards, which one normally associates with the religious (i.e. monastic) life. Behind their apparent chastity, piety, humility, and purity lies a malign desire to mislead people and make them turn away from God, who has given himself for their salvation.

> *The recent destruction of the vines tells us unmistakably that the fox has been busy there. But the wily beast has so cleverly covered his footprints by I know not what artful device, that human intelligence cannot easily discover at what point he entered or where he made his way out. The mischief done is manifest enough, but the author thereof cannot be detected, so cunningly does he conceal himself and his wickedness under an exterior of affected innocence. Examine one of these heretics concerning his faith and you will find him perfectly orthodox. Listen to his conversation and you will never hear anything in the least worthy of censure. Yea, he even proves by his actions the sincerity of his words. You may see him bearing testimony to his faith by frequenting the churches, showing honour to the priests, offering his gifts, making his confession, and approaching the holy table. What greater proof of fidelity can you require? Then, as regards his life and morals, he overreaches no man, he circumvents no man, he does violence to no man. His face is pale and wan from rigorous fasting, and far from eating his bread idle, he earns his livelihood by the labour of his hands. Where now is the fox? We had him secured just a moment since, and lo! he has slipped from our grasp. How has he disappeared so suddenly?*
>
> *But let us give instant chase. Let us follow his footprints. By his fruits we shall know him. Certainly, the destruction of the vines proves him to be a real fox. For what do we behold? Wives forsaking their husbands and husbands abandoning their wives in order to join themselves to these sectaries! Clerics and priests, old and young, having deserted their churches and people, are often to be seen amongst them side by side with weavers, male and female! Is not this a dreadful destruction of the vines!*

102 CHAPTER 3 Unification, Purification, and Dehumanization

Have we not here the work of the foxes? (Bernard of Clairvaux, trans. by a priest of Mount Melleray, 2016, Sermon 65)

This commentary displays a growing concern about the discrepancy between the outward form and the inner reality of heretics. One cannot trust what one sees. This discourse about the secretive nature of heresy soon translated into a discourse about the necessity of taking action, geared towards stripping away heretical falsehoods and revealing their 'true nature' and 'true intentions'. John Bilodeau explains,

When you begin with the hypothesis that a person is an untrustworthy liar, it is difficult to establish the proper means of acquiring evidence about their beliefs. The only way to discern the thoughts of another person is, one assumes, for the person to volunteer them. It is difficult to imagine the situation in which you could trust the confession of a known liar. (Bilodeau, 2010, p. 30)

To uncover heresy and surface pretence, one needs to learn to read the signs and inquire, if necessary by force, into the level of belief, motivation, and intention. Even though one may never know for certain if a liar is telling the truth, one can establish an inquisition, an inquiry into the lives of suspects: observe their behaviour (What do they eat? Drink? What clothes do they wear? Do they participate in the ritual life of the church?, etc.), What do their neighbours say? Their family and friends?, etc. What do they themselves say? Which words do they use? If necessary, one may resort to physical coercion to make them confess (see the papal bull *Ad Extirpanda*, 1252).

The image of the foxes would be repeated time and again, it even appeared in papal bulls to justify using force. Consider in this regard, Pope Gregory IX's (r. 1227–1241) decretal, *Ille Humani Generis* (1231):

Although the heretics have lain concealed for a long time, scuttling about in hiding like crabs and, like little foxes, attempting to destroy the vineyard of the Lord of Hosts, now, however, their sins leading them on, they rise up in the open [...]. Wishing to entrap some of the faithful in their wiles, they have made themselves teachers of error, who once were students of truth. Wherefore it is fitting that we rise up against them manfully, so that the faith of Christ may flourish and this heresy of theirs be confounded [...]. (Trans. Miola, 2007, p. 480)

Against this background, a nuance is in order. Even though the charges of secrecy certainly are part of the rhetorical construction of 'the heretic', more is at stake here. First, in a context where heretics would be tracked down, questioned, tortured, and even put to death, secrecy and simulation are also a survival strategy. Where there is no room for dissent and control is increased, going underground and pretending to be something one is not may be the only thing left to do (Sackville, 2011, p. 171). Second, and approaching the charges of simulation from another angle, one may consider the fact that heretics themselves claimed to be the true heirs of the gospel in all its purity. In fact, they charged those belonging to the Catholic Church, with its hierarchical clerical institutions, with having strayed from the straight and narrow path while pretending to be true Christians. Polemicists defending the Catholic Church and its institutions reversed this critique and projected it onto those movements that were critical of the church. As mentioned in the first chapter, everyone claims to belong to the true church, and everyone sees the deviating other, who questions this claim to normativity, as heretical. Leaving aside any substantial discussion of these claims, the significant difference consists of course in the power imbalance between these different social groups.

Heretics as Morally and Sexually Perverse Creatures in the Service of Satan
When the problem of heresy returned, tales of nocturnal orgies 'were revived and applied to various religious outgroups in medieval Christendom' (Cohn, 1977, p. 17). Heretics were accused of unnatural (i.e. unproductive) sexual relations, like homosexual

sex, bestiality, and incest. Even though the association between heresy and perversity was not new, in the course of the late Middle Ages these fantastic tales took on unseen proportions. Next to their absolute promiscuous behaviour during nocturnal orgies, heretics were also said to engage in child murder and cannibalism, an allegation which amounts to saying that heretics are 'an incarnation of the anti-human'. They fall outside the realm of humanity, and their 'relationship to mankind as a whole can only be one of implacable enmity' (Cohn, 1977, p. 12). While some of these tales go way back, the 'morbid fascination', the preposterous proportions, and the fixation on the power of the devil of these late medieval accusations are new, and this time round the accusations really gained a foothold and became commonplace. They may be found in polemical tracts and theological treatises as well as in papal bulls. Norman Cohn observes, 'as so often, by dint of repetition fictions were coming to be accepted as fact' (Cohn, 1977, p. 22).

In 1233, in his influential bull *Vox in Rama*, Pope Gregory IX, in line with this polemical tradition, depicted heresy as a demonic attack on the church, which is expressed and symbolized by the rituals they perform: they kiss toads and exchange saliva, they share a meal with a cold skinned man and engage in a perverted version of the Litany of the Saints. Such charges need to be understood against the background of medieval discussions about the eucharistic ritual and the nature of the consecrated bread and wine. If participation in the eucharistic ritual symbolized and reinforced the unity of the *Corpus Christianum*, participation in this satanic and perverse ritual promised to do the opposite: it joined the heretics together in a state of sin and invited evil to do its work. Their shared meal, 'a clear antithesis to the sacramental meal at the heart of the Christian mass, articulates the heretical community around it. That this community, outside of and opposed to the Christian community, is the same as that of the Devil cannot be doubted' (Barbezat, 2018, p. 67). Those who participate unknowingly also fall into the clutches of these evil powers. The heretics' perversion 'reflected how they had turned away from the spiritual unity of God and believer for an internal immersion in a fallen understanding' and worship of Satan (Barbezat, 2016, p. 415). Clearly, heretics by their own choice had cut themselves off from the redemptive unity in the body of Christ and had established another community in the service of the devil. The image that emerges is that of 'a dangerously secretive and conspiratorial society, battening ruthlessly on the most vulnerable members of society and performing the most inhuman, repellent, and sacrilegious acts' (Price, 2003, p. 53). By lending papal authority to these accusations, *Vox in Rama* transformed these tales into truths and legitimated future inquisitions. In time, 'each new persecution [...] lent fresh credibility and authority to the fantasies that had stimulated and legitimated it, until those fantasies came to be accepted as self-evidently true – first by many of the educated, and in the long run by the bulk of society' (Cohn, 1977, p. 77).

Text Box 7: The Heretic in Christian Medieval Imagination

Corpus Christianum **Christian society**	*Corpus Heretici* **Conspiracist society**
God	Devil
Benign, moral	Malign, immoral
Innocent	Guilty
Spiritual	Lust-driven, carnal
Eucharist	Cannibalism
Pure	Impure
Honest	Untrustworthy
Wholeness	Disintegration

The War on Heresy

To root out the problem of heresy three disciplinary strategies were deployed, one more successful than the others: preaching, crusades, and inquisition.

Preaching Two different religious orders were formally established to counter the heresies of the Cathars and Waldensians: the Dominicans and the Franciscans. The first order was established by the Spanish priest Dominic de Guzmán (1170–1221); it was to fight heresy by educational and legal means. The friars contributed to the development of 'theological studies, preaching, and sustained investigation as key tools' (Terpstra, 2015, p. 48) to counter the proliferation of heretical movements. The second, the Franciscans, were followers of the Italian Francesco di Pietro di Bernadone (1181–1226), who had turned away from a life of wealth to embrace the virtues of charity, poverty, chastity, and obedience. The Franciscans were to counter the idea that all clergy were blinded by power and riches. Over time, however, these orders, whose initial mission had been to counter heresy through their preaching and their pious lifestyle, became deeply implicated in the inquisition. A 'later pun on the Dominicans as "domini canes" appropriated earlier imagery of the preacher as a "dog" frenetically sniffing out the heterodox "little foxes" wherever they may, or may not, be present' (Perron, 2009, p. 35).

Crusading In 1209, after the murder of Pierre de Castelnau (1170–1208), the papal legate in the region of Languedoc, Pope Innocent III called for a crusade against the Cathars. Just as the Holy Land had to be defended against the Saracens, so Christianity had to be defended against those who attack the Catholic faith and the honour of the Holy Trinity (Rist, 2009, p. 67). Innocent III not only expanded the notion of the crusade from being outward reaching to becoming introspective, but he also linked the two projects together, arguing that failure in the Holy Land against the Saracens was a consequence of the defilement of Christian society. Therefore, an army of Christian knights had to be mobilized to defend the Christian faith, whether to fight in faraway lands or nearby. The heretic nearby threatens the integrity of the *Corpus Christianum* and jeopardizes the crusade against the Saracens.

To gain support from worldly authorities, Innocent III went further than any pope had previously gone by promising the 'same plenary indulgence for the campaign against heresy as popes traditionally granted for taking part in a crusade against Muslims in the Holy Land' (Rist, 2010, p. 96) and he offered the heretics' lands to anyone who would sincerely strive to suppress the heresy. In his letter, *Ne nos eius* (1208), addressed to the Bishops of Narbonne, Aix-en-Provence, and Arles, he states

> *But for those who, inflamed with zeal for the orthodox faith to vindicate just blood which ceases not to clamour from earth to heaven until the God of Vengeances shall descend upon the earth, should manfully gird themselves against pestilential persons of this kind who at the same time together fight both peace and truth, you may securely promise the remission of their sins conceded by God and by His vicar, that a labour of this kind for the performance of the work may be sufficient for them on behalf of those offences for which they shall have obtained contrition of heart and true oral confession to the true God. (Trans. Rist, 2009, p. 65)*

This message was also sent to all the nobles, knights, and subjects of France, communicating clearly that it was the responsibility of 'the whole French political community' to support the church in its endeavour to maintain the unity of the *Corpus Christianum*, while at the same time making this task as attractive as possible. They were all called to go to war and wipe out the heretics, and in return they would be rewarded with land and the remission of their sins. When the papal legate, Arnaud Amaury (d. 1225), was asked how crusaders would have to distinguish between heretics and orthodox Christians, he told them not to worry about this.

> Those who realized that Catholics and heretics were mixed together, said to the Abbot: 'What shall we do, my lord? We cannot discern between the good and the evil'. Both the Abbot and the rest feared the heretics would pretend to be Catholics, from fear of death, and afterwards return again to their perfidy; so he is reported to have said: 'Kill them. For the Lord knows who are his'. (Quoted in Bryson & Movsesian, 2017, p. 224)

The Albigensian crusade (1209–1229) has been called one of the most savage wars of the Middle Ages. The massacre of Béziers, especially, symbolizes the cruelty that was displayed by the crusaders. The city was burned down and allegedly 20,000 citizens were killed. In the long run, however, the crusade against the heretics had less effect than the establishment of the inquisition, which attacked heresy using legal procedures.

The Inquisition   The foundation for the inquisition was gradually put in place. The papal bull *Ad Abolendam*, which was issued by Pope Lucius III at the Synod of Verona, in 1184, is often mentioned as a turning point. This bull opens by stating that,

> In order to put an end to the evil of various heresies which has begun to break forth in modern times [modernis coepit temporibus pullulare] in most parts of the world, the power of the Church ought to be aroused; when, indeed, with the sanction of imperial power, both the insolence of heretics, in their attempts to promote falsehood, may be put down, and the truth of Catholic unity, shining forth in the Holy Church, may display her, free from all charge of false doctrine. (Trans. in Peters, 1980, p. 170, doc. 129)

This bull gives archbishops and bishops the responsibility to actively search for heretics and make them confess and repent. Those who refused to do so would be handed over to secular authorities to carry out punishment. Neighbours were involved in this process and were actively encouraged to identify and betray people they suspected of heresy. Thus, the bull states,

> that every archbishop or bishop, by himself, or his archdeacon, or by other trustworthy and fit persons, shall twice, or once, in the year go round any parish in which it shall have been reported that heretics reside; and there call upon three or more persons of good credit, or, if it seem expedient, on the whole neighborhood, to take an oath that if anyone shall know that there are heretics in the place or any persons holding secret conventicles or differing in life and manners from the common conversation of the faithful, he will make it his business to point them out to the bishop or archdeacon. Moreover, the bishop or archdeacon shall cite the accused to appear before him, who, unless they shall clear themselves from the charges brought against them to their satisfaction, according to the custom of the country – or if, after such clearance, they shall relapse into their error – they shall be punished by the judgment of the bishop. If, however, any of them, through damnable superstition, denying the lawfulness of oaths, shall refuse to swear, they are from that very circumstance to be adjudged heretics, and to be subjected to the punishment aforesaid. (Trans. in Peters, 1980, p. 172, doc. 129)

In 1215, Innocent III established a new legal procedure, called *inquisitio ex officio*, which replaced the older legal procedure of *accusatio*. This new procedure required an accuser to come forward and bring charges against a suspect in front of a judge; it was more proactive and gave more power to special judges to prosecute anyone thought to have deviant beliefs.

While the first targets of this new procedure were clergy suspected of simony or concubinage, from 1230 onwards this new procedure was also employed to prosecute heretics. The

106 CHAPTER 3 Unification, Purification, and Dehumanization

first papal inquisitors were appointed by Pope Gregory IX. Starting in 1231, the Dominicans and to a lesser degree the Franciscans became the main inquisitors. Because heresy was regarded as a threat to the social order, and thus akin to treason, the papal bull promulgated by Pope Innocent IV (r. 1243–1254), *Ad Extirpanda* (1252), established that those persecuting heretics were allowed to use extraordinary means, like torture, to gain evidence and confessions. A culture of suspicion and fear took hold of targeted communities. While 'inquisitors aimed for repentance and conversion more than punishment', they 'worked together with secular authorities in the event that an unrepentant prisoner required removal from the *Corpus Christianum*' (Terpstra, 2015, p. 95). Since heresy was a form of treason, the death penalty, to be executed by secular authorities, could be asked for.

4 The Fourth Lateran Council

The Gregorian reform initiated a centralizing and governing dynamic and turned Christian Europe into a society that was not only conscious of the threats to the *Corpus Christianum*, but also ready to take action to protect Christian society against those threats. The Fourth Lateran Council (1213–1215) represents the culmination of centuries of ecclesial efforts to gain more power and control over Latin Christendom.[2] To this day, the council is considered to have been the greatest of the Middle Ages, gathering 400 bishops and 800 abbots, as well as representatives of secular power. It produced a wide range of tools with which to screen and govern Christians, heretics, Jews, and Muslims and to consolidate ecclesial power. Held during the pontificate of Pope Innocent III, a lawyer and legislator, Lateran IV 'generated seventy canons – more than double the number issued by any of the three previous Laterans of the preceding century, and more than triple those of Lateran I', and it led to 'a massive codification of rules on a vast array of subjects' (Heng, 2003, p. 69). This significantly strengthened the reach of the church.

The Lateran decrees 'opened with a declaration of faith' (Moore, 2007, p. 7), clearly defining what it entails to adhere to the church and maintaining that for those who do not belong to the church there would be no salvation. We may understand this in terms of religionized selfing.

> *There is indeed one universal church of the faithful, outside of which nobody at all is saved [*Una vero est fidelium universalis Ecclesia, extra quam nullus omnino salvatur*], in which Jesus Christ is both priest and sacrifice. His body and blood are truly contained in the sacrament of the altar under the forms of bread and wine, the bread and wine having been changed in substance, by God's power, into his body and blood, so that in order to achieve this mystery of unity we receive from God what he received from us [*cuius corpus et sanguis in sacramento altaris sub speciebus panis et vini veraciter continentur, transsubstantiatis pane in corpus, et vino in sanguinem potestate divina*]. (Lateran IV, canon 1)[3]*

The confession of faith, stating 'this is who we are', further references ordained priesthood, baptism, penitence, and marriage. This was followed by strong condemnations of all those heresies that went against the one true, faithful, and salvific church. The conciliar decrees condemned the Cathars and Waldensians explicitly, but simultaneously maintained that all heresies, while different in their manifestation, are at root the same: 'They have different faces indeed but their tails [a reference to the image of the foxes] are tied together inasmuch as they are alike in their pride' (canon 3). Being the same at root, heretics may expect equal treatment: they should all be excommunicated, punished, and dispossessed. Archbishops and bishops were called upon to actively track down heretics who lived in their diocese. If they failed to do so, they would be regarded as inept and would be replaced by a more efficient leader. Moreover, the council also called upon secular authorities 'if they wish to be reputed and held to be faithful, to take publicly an oath for the defense of the faith to the effect that they will seek, in so far as they can, to expel from the lands subject to their jurisdiction all heretics designated by the church in good faith' (canon 3). Those who failed to 'cleanse his territory of this heretical filth, he shall be bound with the bond of excommunication by the metropolitan and other bishops of the province'. Catholics, on the other hand, 'who take the cross and gird themselves up for the expulsion of heretics shall enjoy the same indulgence, and be strengthened by the same holy privilege, as is granted to those who go to the aid of the Holy Land'.

Next to the heretics, the Lateran decrees single out two other groups requiring special attention: the Jews and the Muslims, both perceived as a threat to the *Societas Christiana* – the first present an internal threat, the latter an external threat. Canons 67–71 are an attempt to further codify and systematize existing negative attitudes towards them. The council knew that it had no authority over Jews and Muslims, therefore it adopted 'two strategies to enforce their ruling: [First,] they call on Christian rulers to oblige Jews and Muslims to respect these rules (and hence to translate these conciliar canons into secular law) [...] [Next] they oblige Christians, under pain of ecclesiastical censure, to abstain from commerce with Jews, thereby denying Jews material benefits, and the resources needed to make a proper living. In other words, if the Churchmen have no legal power to oblige Jews and Muslims to respect this legislation, they can punish them indirectly by preventing Christians from doing business with them' (Tolan, 2018, p. 13).

Canon 67 associates Jews with usury. Stating that Christians are restrained from engaging in such practices, it claims that 'the perfidy of the Jews [does] grow in these matters so, that within a short time they are exhausting the resources of Christians'. To protect Christians against Jewish extortion, it is ruled that 'if Jews in future, on any pretext, extort oppressive and *excessive* interest from Christians, then they are to be removed from contact with Christians until they have made adequate satisfaction for the immoderate burden'. This canon would be referenced to justify both the ghettoization of Jewish communities and even the expulsion of the Jews from several countries and regions: England (1290), France (fourteenth century), Germany (1350s), Portugal (1496), Provence (1512), and the Papal States (1569). It also stated that the Jews would have to compensate the church financially for 'tithes and offerings due to the churches, which the churches were accustomed to receive from Christians for houses and other possessions, before they passed by whatever title to the Jews, so that the churches may thus be preserved from loss'.

Canon 69 calls the Jews blasphemers and states that Christians may not serve Jews and that the latter be removed from public offices, thereby reiterating old rulings. The same holds for pagans; it is assumed that this implies the Muslims.

Canon 70 states that those who converted to Christianity had to give up their old rites and that any sort of mixing had to be prohibited.

> *Certain people who have come voluntarily to the waters of sacred baptism, as we learnt, do not wholly cast off the old person in order to put on the new more perfectly. For, in keeping remnants of their former rite, they upset the decorum of the Christian religion [christianae religionis] by such a mixing. Since it is written, cursed is he who enters the land by two paths, and a garment that is woven from linen and wool together should not be put on, we therefore decree that such people shall be wholly prevented by the prelates of churches from observing their old rite, so that those who freely offered themselves to the Christian religion [christianae religioni] may be kept to its observance by a salutary and necessary coercion.*

Those who had willingly accepted the Christian faith had to be prevented, if need be by a 'salutary and necessary coercion', from returning to their old rites. 'For it is a lesser evil not to know the Lord's way than to go back on it after having known it'.

Canon 68 applies to both Jews and Muslims (Text Box 8). They are told to dress differently so as to be distinguishable from the Christians among whom they live (the need for such a sign makes clear that in reality one cannot easily distinguish a Christian from a Jew or even Muslim). The canon did not give further details or instructions and exhorted local ecclesial and secular authorities to implement the canon. This visible sign, which is not further defined, provided external evidence of an internal state of damnation. It also functioned as a public humiliation, giving expression to the fact that neither Jews nor Muslims belonged to Christian society and that their status was one of inferiority. This message was clearly received by those who wore the visible sign and those who observed it. This canon was probably also inspired by an increased concern about protecting the 'the physical and spiritual purity of Christians [...]. The Christian had to be kept free from the polluting contact of the infidel subject: sexual contact was above all to be avoided' (Tolan, 2002, p. 196). The resulting situation is one of ambivalence. On the one hand, both Jews and Muslims are increasingly seen as different from Christians, not only in terms of religious orientation but also in terms of bodily appearance. On the other hand, it is clear that this difference is mainly constructed and imagined, as clothing regulations are needed to visualize an otherwise unnoticeable difference.

Text Box 8: The Wearing of the Badge

Some countries ordered Jews to wear specific head coverings, outer garments, or shoes. Eventually, however, virtually every country under papal authority required a fabric badge, though these differed in appearance. The law directed the shape, size, and colour of the badge and where on the clothing the badge was to be worn. England became the first country to enjoin the Jewish badge in 1218, then Spain in 1219. France followed in 1234, Italy in 1257 and Hungary in 1279. Over the next 250 years, Portugal, Germany, Switzerland, and Austria replaced what they had initially compelled Jews to wear with a badge. Some countries ordered it to be worn on the waist or the back, but the left breast, upper arm, or shoulder were the most common positions for the Jewish badge.

'Badge laws remained in effect for centuries, even for countries in which Jews were no longer permitted to live. Though Mannheim had abolished Jewish badges in 1691, the rest of Germany did not follow suit until 1781 [...] The Jewish badge was eliminated after the French Revolution in France in 1789 and in Rome in 1798. As late as 1812, badges were mentioned in a Prussian edict, though whether they were still being worn is of question. In all, badge laws were in effect in some parts of Europe for more than 500 years' (Jablon, 2015, p. 44).

The final canon, number 71 which is also the longest, returns to the issue of the crusades, and reiterates what we have called the crusading ideology. The canon explains again why it is justified for Christendom to recover the lands that have fallen into the hands of infidels, why a new expedition is needed and how it ought to be organized. Here too, the Jews living in Christian society are targeted. Thus canon 71:

> *We order that Jews be compelled by the secular power to remit interest, and that until they do so all intercourse shall be denied them by all Christ's faithful under pain of excommunication. Secular princes shall provide a suitable deferral for those who cannot now pay their debts to Jews, so that after they have undertaken the journey and until there is certain knowledge of their death or of their return, they shall not incur the inconvenience of paying interest. The Jews shall be compelled to add to the capital, after they have deducted their necessary expenses, the revenues which they are meanwhile receiving from property held by them on security. For, such a benefit seems to entail not much loss, inasmuch as it postpones the repayment but does not cancel the debt.*

As for the Muslims, the canon threatens any Christian who sells them material (ships, iron, weapons) or gives them advice that would help them in their fight against the church with excommunication. Moreover, those who violate this prohibition will be severely punished: they are to be deprived of their possessions 'and are to become the slaves of those who capture them'.

5 Conclusion

During the late Middle Ages, religionization took the form of body politics. European Christians used the metaphor of the body [*Corpus Christianum*] for the social community of believers. Christianity's others – Jews, Muslims, and heretics – were projected as foreign bodies that did not fit in. They were, furthermore, increasingly dehumanized and demonized: the bodies of those falling outside the realm of the (imagined) *Corpus Christianum* also fall outside the realm of humanity. They are projected as posing a threat to the integrity of the Christian body and as having a body that is qualitatively different from that of a Christian. Their disfigured bodies, the illness of their blood and the blackness of their skin reveal that they are agents of Satan and that their beliefs and practices are not only misdirected, but even demonic and monstrous. In brief, 'they were ugly as sin' (Strickland, 2003, p. 29). Again, the construction of an ideal integral Christian society went hand in hand with an increased production of negative discourses about those who were imagined as posing a threat to this unity. These threats, coming from both within and without, were projected as infections, which when left unchecked would spread throughout the body of Christ. From this perspective, the bodies of non-Christians are not simply alien, but also impure, contagious, and potentially life-threatening (Terpstra, 2015, p. 1). It would not be uncommon for non-Christian bodies to be cast as tumours that needed to be removed. Clearly, this kind of medical rhetoric not only arouses fear but also calls for immediate remedies.

The patterns of religionization discussed in this chapter included naming and renaming, hierarchical categorization, and essentialization, and also various governmental measures: the inquisition, marital law, trade law, and clothing prescriptions, and these all helped to mould a stratified society. The Christian norm and the delegitimization of Jews, Muslims, and heretics were institutionalized and this seriously impacted the societal position of these groups as well as their mutual relationships. In the next chapter, we shall see this confluence of developments exemplified in the nascent nationalist ambitions of the Spanish Catholic monarchs, Isabella I and Ferdinand II.

Notes

[1] The Visigoths were one of many Germanic tribes who settled in Spain. The capital of their kingdom was Toledo. Originally Arian Christians, they converted to Catholicism when King Recarred (r. 586–601) became Catholic.

[2] www.papalencyclicals.net/councils/ecum12-2.htm#3.

[3] All council texts are taken from: www.papalencyclicals.net/councils/ecum12-2.htm.

References

Abulafia, A. S. (2017). Gratian and the Jews. *European Journal for the Study of Thomas Aquinas*, *36*(1), 8–39.

Akbari, S. C. (2009). *Idols in the East: European Representations of Islam and the Orient, 1100–1450*. Cornell University Press.

Arjana, S. R. (2015). *Muslims in the Western Imagination*. Oxford University Press.

Arnold, J. (2009). Repression and Power. In M. Rubin & W. Simons (Eds.), *The Cambridge History of Christianity, Volume 4: Christianity in Western Europe, c.1100–c.1500* (pp. 355–371). Cambridge University Press.

Ballard, R. (1996). Islam and the Construction of Europe. In W. A. R. Shadid & P. S. van Koningsveld (Eds.), *Muslims in the Margin: Political Responses to the Presence of Islam in Western Europe* (pp. 15–51). Kok Pharos.

110 CHAPTER 3 Unification, Purification, and Dehumanization

Barbezat, M. D. (2016). Bodies of Spirit and Bodies of Flesh: The Significance of the Sexual Practices Attributed to Heretics from the Eleventh to the Fourteenth Century. *Journal of the History of Sexuality, 25*(3), 387–419.

Baldric of Bourgueil (Trans. S. B. Edgington; Introd. S. J. Biddlecombe) (2020). *Baldric of Bourgueil 'History of the Jerusalemites': A Translation of the 'Historia Ierosolimitana'.* Boydell.

Barbezat, M. D. (2018). The Beginning at Orleans in 1022: Heretics and Hellfire. In *Burning Bodies: Communities, Eschatology, and the Punishment of Heresy in the Middle Ages* (pp. 61–80). Cornell University Press.

Bernard of Clairvaux (Trans. by a priest of Mount Melleray) (2016). *Saint Bernard of Clairvaux Collection.* Aeterna.

Biale, D. (2007). *Blood and Belief: The Circulation of a Symbol between Jews and Christians.* University of California Press.

Biller, P. (2009). Christians and Heretics. In M. Rubin & W. Simons (Eds.), *The Cambridge History of Christianity, Volume 4: Christianity in Western Europe, c.1100–c.1500* (pp. 170–186). Cambridge University Press.

Bilodeau, J. (2010). 'Secrecy and the Social Construction of Heresy in Medieval Languedoc'. Diss. Concordia University.

Bird, J. L., Peters, E., & Powell, J. M. (2013). *Crusade and Christendom: Annotated Documents in Translation from Innocent III to the Fall of Acre, 1187–1291.* University of Pennsylvania Press.

Brewer, C. (2005). The Status of the Jews in Roman Legislation: The Reign of Justinian 527–565 CE. *European Judaism, 38*(2), 127–139.

Bryson, M., & Movsesian, A. (2017). *Love and Its Critics: From the Song of Songs to Shakespeare and Milton's Eden.* Open Book Publishers.

Chandler, J. H. (2011). 'The King of Tars'. Diss. University of Rochester.

Chandler, J. H. (2015). *The King of Tars.* Medieval Institute Publications, Western Michigan University.

Chazan, R. (2009). 'Let Not a Remnant or a Residue Escape': Millenarian Enthusiasm in the First Crusade. *Speculum, 84*(2), 289–313.

Cohen, J. (1999). *Living Letters of the Law: Ideas of the Jew in Medieval Christianity.* University of California Press.

Cohen, J. J. (2001). On Saracen Enjoyment: Some Fantasies of Race in Late Medieval France and England. *Journal of Medieval and Early Modern Studies, 31*(1), 113–146.

Cohn, N. (1977). *Europe's Inner Demons: An Enquiry Inspired by the Great Witch-Hunt.* New American Library.

Colby, A. (1965). *The Portrait in Twelfth-century French Literature: An Example of the Stylistic Originality of Chrétien de Troyes.* Droz.

Czarnowus, A. (2008). 'Stille as Ston': Oriental Deformity in 'The King of Tars'. *Studia Anglica Posnaniensia: An International Review of English Studies, 44*, 463–474.

Denzinger, H., Hünermann, P., & Hoffmann, J. (1996). *Enchiridion symbolorum, definitionum et declarationum de rebus fidei et morum.* Cerf.

Dorn, N. (2016, 20 May). The Consilia of Alessandro Nievo: On Jews and Usury in 15th Century Italy. Retrieved from https://blogs.loc.gov/law/2016/05/the-consilia-of-alessandro-nievo-on-jews-and-usury-in-15th-century-italy/

Elukin, J. (2002). Judaism: From Heresy to Pharisee in Early Medieval Christian Literature. *Traditio, 57*, 49–66.

Elukin, J. (2007). *Living Together, Living Apart: Rethinking Jewish-Christian Relations in the Middle Ages.* Princeton University Press.

Falk, A. (2018). *Franks and Saracens: Reality and Fantasy in the Crusades.* Karnack Books.

Fernández-Armesto, F., & Wilson, D. (1996). *Reformatie: Christendom en de wereld 1500–2000.* Anthos.

France, J. (1988). The Text of the Account of the Capture of Jerusalem in the Ripoll Manuscript, Bibliothèque Nationale (Latin) 5132. *The English Historical Review, 103*(408), 640–657.

Freidenreich, D. M. (2013). Jews, Pagans, and Heretics in Early Medieval Canon Law. In J. Tolan, N. de Lange, L. Foschia, & C. Nemo-Pekelman (Eds.), *Jews in Early Christian Law: Byzantium and the Latin West, 6th–11th Centuries*, Religion and Law in Medieval Christian and Muslim Societies 2 (pp. 73–91). Brepols.

Freidenreich, D. M., & Plesch, V. (2020). What Is That to Us? The Eucharistic Liturgy and the Enemies of Christ in the Beam of the Passion. *Studies in Iconography, 41*, 104–130.

Gilchrist, J. (1988). The Perception of Jews in the Canon Law in the Period of the First Two Crusades. *Jewish History, 3*(1), 9–24.

Grayzel, S. (1933). *The Church and the Jews in the XIIIth Century: A Study of Their Relations during the Years 1198–1254, Based on the Papal Letters and the Conciliar Decrees of the Period.* The Dropsie College for Hebrew and Cognate Learning.

Green, T. H. (2019). *The Fear of Islam: An Introduction to Islamophobia in the West* (2nd ed.). Fortress.

Hahn, T. (2001). The Difference the Middle Ages Makes: Color and Race before the Modern World. *Journal of Medieval and Early Modern Studies, 31*(1), 1–37.

Heng, G. (2003). *Empire of Magic: Medieval Romance and the Politics of Cultural Fantasy*. Columbia University Press.

Heng, G. (2018a). *The Invention of Race in the European Middle Ages*. Cambridge University Press.

Heng, G. (2018b, 12 August). Race Isn't a Modern Concept. Retrieved from https://historynews network.org/article/169596

Jablon, S. (2015). Badge of Dishonor: Jewish Badges in Medieval Europe. *International Journal of Fashion Design, 8*(1), 39–46.

Jacob of Vitry (Ed. J. Donnadieu) (2008). *Histoire orientale. Historia orientalis*, Sous la Règle de saint Augustin 12. Brepols.

Kessler, E. (2010). *An Introduction to Jewish-Christian Relations*. Cambridge University Press.

Kras, P., & Panz-Sochacka, M. (2020). *The System of the Inquisition in Medieval Europe*. Peter Lang.

Latham, A. A. (2011). Theorizing the Crusades: Identity, Institutions, and Religious War in Medieval Latin Christendom. *International Studies Quarterly, 55*(1), 223–243.

Linder, A. (1987). *The Jews in Roman Imperial Legislation*. Wayne State University Press.

Lipton, S. (2014). Christianity and Its Others: Jews, Muslims, and Pagans. In J. Arnold (Ed.), *The Oxford Handbook of Medieval Christianity* (pp. 413–435). Oxford University Press.

Malkiel, D. (2003). Jewish-Christian Relations in Europe, 840–1096. *Journal of Medieval History 29*, 55–83.

Maor, N. R., Roguin, A., & Roguin, N. (2021). Medieval Roots of the Myth of Jewish Male Menstruation. *Rambam Maimonides Medical Journal, 12*(4), 1–6.

Matteoni, F. (2008). The Jew, the Blood and the Body in Late Medieval and Early Modern Europe. *Folklore, 119*(2), 182–200.

Mayerhofer, K. (2021). Inferiority Embodied: The 'Men-struating' Jew and Pre-Modern Notions of Identity and Difference. In A. Lange, K. Mayerhofer, D. Porat, & L. H. Schiffman (Eds.), *Comprehending Antisemitism through the Ages: A Historical Perspective*, An End to Antisemitism! 3 (pp. 135–159). De Gruyter.

McClymond, K. T. (2016). *Ritual Gone Wrong: What We Learn from Ritual Disruption*. Oxford University Press.

Mell, J. (2018). *The Myth of the Medieval Jewish Moneylender* (Vol. 2). Palgrave Macmillan.

Miola, R. S. (2007). *Early Modern Catholicism: An Anthology of Primary Sources*. Oxford University Press.

Moore, R. I. (1975). *The Birth of Popular Heresy*. Edward Arnold.

Moore, R. I. (2002). The Birth of Popular Heresy: A Millennial Phenomenon? *Journal of Religious History, 24*(1), 8–25.

Moore, R. I. (2007). *The Formation of a Persecuting Society: Authority and Deviance in Western Europe, 950–1250* (2nd ed.). Blackwell.

Moore, R. I. (2014). *The War on Heresy: Faith and Power in Medieval Europe*. Profile Books.

Perron, A. (2009). The Bishops of Rome, 1100–1300. In M. Rubin & W. Simons (Eds.), *The Cambridge History of Christianity, Volume 4: Christianity in Western Europe, c.1100–c.1500* (pp. 22–38). Cambridge University Press.

Peters, E. (1980). *Heresy and Authority in Medieval Europe*. University of Pennsylvania Press.

Price, M. L. (2003). *Consuming Passions: The Uses of Cannibalism in Late Medieval and Early Modern Europe*. Routledge.

Remensnyder, A. G. (2014). *La Conquistadora: The Virgin Mary at War and Peace in the Old and New Worlds*. Oxford University Press.

Resnick, I. M. (2000). Medieval Roots of the Myth of Jewish Male Menses. *Harvard Theological Review, 93*(3), 241–263.

Rist, R. (2007). Papal Protection and the Jews in the Context of Crusading, 1198–1245. *Medieval Encounters, 13*(2), 281–309.

Rist, R. (2009). *The Papacy and Crusading in Europe, 1198–1245*. Continuum.

Rist, R. (2010). Salvation and the Albigensian Crusade: Pope Innocent III and the Plenary Indulgence. *Reading Medieval Studies, 36*, 95–112.

Robert de Monk (Trans. C. Sweetenham) (2005). *Robert the Monk's History of the First Crusade: Historia Iherosolimitana*. Routledge.

Sackville, L. J. (2011). *Heresy and Heretics in the Thirteenth Century: The Textual Representations*. York Medieval Press.

Smith, K. A. (2017). The Crusader Conquest of Jerusalem and Christ's Cleansing of the Temple. *Commentaria, 7*, 19–41.

Stacey, R. C. (1998). From Ritual Crucifixion to Host Desecration: Jews and the Body of Christ. *Jewish History, 12*(1), 11–28.

Stantchev, S. K. (2014). 'Apply to Muslims What Was Said of the Jews': Popes and Canonists between a Taxonomy of Otherness and *Infidelitas. Law and History Review, 32*(1), 65–96.

Stow, K. R. (1994). *Alienated Minority: The Jews of Medieval Latin Europe.* Harvard University Press.

Strickland, D. H. (2003). *Saracens, Demons, and Jews: Making Monsters in Medieval Art.* Princeton University Press.

Szpiech, R. (2019). Saracens and Church Councils, from Nablus (1120) to Vienne (1313–1314). In M.-T. Champagne & I. M. Resnick (Eds.), *Jews and Muslims under the Fourth Lateran Council: Papers Commemorating the Octocentenary of the Fourth Lateran Council (1215),* Religion and Law in Medieval Christian and Muslim Societies 10 (pp. 115–137). Brepols.

Terpstra, N. (2015). *Religious Refugees in the Early Modern World: An Alternative History of the Reformation.* Cambridge University Press.

Thatcher, O. J., & McNeal, E. H. (1971). *A Source Book for Medieval History: Selected Documents Illustrating the History of Europe in the Middle Age.* AMS Press.

Thomas of Monmouth. (Ed. and trans. A. Jessop & M. R. James) (2011). *The Life and Miracles of St William of Norwich.* Cambridge University Press.

Tolan, J. V. (2002). *Saracens: Islam in the Medieval European Imagination.* Columbia University Press.

Tolan, J. V. (2015). Jews and Muslims in Christian Law and History. In G. G. Stroumsa & A. J. Silverstein (Eds.), *The Oxford Handbook of the Abrahamic Religions* (pp. 166–188). Oxford University Press.

Tolan, J. V. (2018). Introduction. In M.-T. Champagne & I. M. Resnick (Eds.), *Jews and Muslims under the Fourth Lateran Council: Papers Commemorating the Octocentenary of the Fourth Lateran Council (1215),* Religion and Law in Medieval Christian and Muslim Societies 10 (pp. 11–22). Brepols.

Tolan, J. V. (2019). *Faces of Muhammad: Western Perceptions of the Prophet of Islam from the Middle Ages to Today.* Princeton University Press.

Walsham, A. (2006). *Charitable Hatred: Tolerance and Intolerance in England, 1500–1700.* Manchester University Press.

Whitaker, C. J. (2013). Black Metaphors in the King of Tars. *The Journal of English and Germanic Philology, 112*(2), 169–193.

CHAPTER 4

The Spanish Catholic Monarchy and Religio-racialization

At a time when the church was working hard to get a stronger hold on Christian societies and was trying to implement a culture 'in which institutions of control [were] expanded, intensified, and refined', one can also see 'a fractionalizing, partitioning drive at work in the European polity that powered nascent nationalisms' (Heng, 2003, p. 70). The dominance of the universal Christian church did not prevent the development of national consciousness in Europe, rather 'territorial nationalisms coalesced within Christendom' (Heng, 2018, p. 32).[1] Mechanisms of religionization applied by the universalizing church to consolidate its power also proved useful for the purpose of nation formation.

Any project of nation building revolves around the imaginative configuration of a sense of peoplehood. People are brought together by the idea that their communion is exclusive and unique; they share history, territory, language, and ancestry (Anderson, 2006). This sense of peoplehood must be reiterated narratively, performed ritually, and consolidated via societal institutions like the law, education, and so forth. Ethnoreligious reasoning, too, is typically part of this process: religion marks peoplehood. In the realm of Latin Christendom and in line with the metaphor of *Corpus Christianum*, ideas about 'true' Christianness were integral to discourses of medieval nationalism: one king, one law, one faith. Both rulers and subjects considered unity of faith 'the best antidote to sedition and subversion and a preservative against internal dissolution, both being indirect manifestations of the wrath of the Almighty against iniquitous nations. Accordingly, tolerance of [deviation] was anathema, a recipe for chaos and anarchy' (Walsham, 2006, p. 2). People deviating from the norm of Christianness posed a socio-political threat; Jews, heretics, and Muslims were often framed as posing such a threat.

Nascent national communities could draw upon a long-established archive of patterns of religionization to reinforce a sense of communion ('us') while triggering deep feelings of distrust vis-à-vis non-Christians ('them'). An entire reservoir of religionized images was there to be tapped, and this included the interlocking discourses of spiritual and bodily differences discussed in the previous chapter. In the context of nation formation, bodily markers of spiritual difference were easily turned into bodily markers of national difference and religionization developed in the direction of a religio-racial project. When this happens, religious differences are understood 'to be inherent and passed genealogically'; they are essentialized as biological differences, resistant to spiritual transformation (Delgado & Moss, 2018, p. 45). Nature – what one is – trumps religion – who and how one worships.

Christian Imaginations of the Religious Other: A History of Religionization, First Edition. Marianne Moyaert.
© 2024 John Wiley & Sons Ltd. Published 2024 by John Wiley & Sons Ltd.

114 CHAPTER 4 The Spanish Catholic Monarchy

If the societal goal is unity and purity, 'foreign' people who cannot change, pose a problem. Here too, the centralizing and hierarchizing church offered governmental tools that could be employed, ranging from polemics, separation, and containment, to inquisition and persecution (Heng, 2018, p. 32). Emerging medieval nation states could even use such measures as exile and expulsion as deliberate policy tools to build a unified and purified nation.

To showcase how these mechanisms played out in a concrete historical-cultural context, I focus on the Spanish *Reconquista*, which reached a climax under the rule of the Catholic monarchs Ferdinand II of Aragon and Isabella I of Castile.[2] Their royal marriage implied 'the joining of the two largest Iberian kingdoms', and marked the beginning of early modern Spain in terms of 'a [composite] political entity' (Cowans, 2003, p. 1). In as far as they framed their project as a continuation of the crusading ideology, they envisioned a Catholic society free from non-Christians and with the support of a local inquisition tribunal (1478) they were able to implement this vision. In 1492, after the reconquest of Granada, their project of nation building culminated in the expulsion of the Jews, and in that same year they instructed Christopher Columbus (1451–1506) to search for an alternative route to the West Indies. The subsequent 'discovery' of the new world marked the beginning of the colonial expansion of the Spanish Empire, which they framed as an extension of their project to spread the Catholic faith (Saxonberg, 2020, p. 114). In 1494, and in recognition of the way they had defended the Catholic faith against its enemies, Pope Alexander VI (r. 1492–1503) gave Ferdinand II and Isabella I the title of 'Catholic monarchs' (*Los reyes católicos*).

The Spanish Catholic project of nation formation was 'charted symbolically onto the body' in an unprecedented way. Blood and more specifically (im)purity of blood became the crucial element to determine both Spanish and Catholic identity and to distinguish between who belongs and who does not. Just as the gods had once run through the blood of people, Spanish national religious identity was mapped onto an 'internal differential, a difference in bodies located in the blood' (Burk, 2010, p. 10). As a consequence, religious identity alone (Christianness) no longer sufficed to belong; biological identity (the purity of blood) mattered too. This fixation on purity of blood gave way to new religionized categories and new classifications, which also transformed Christian self-understanding. As the norm of 'blood purity' was incorporated into the statutes of many Spanish secular and religious institutions, it became a condition for gaining access to 'certain professions, public offices, university colleges, military and religious orders, convents, guilds and so forth' (Johnson, 2010). Some benefited from this norm; others experienced oppression. The end result was a society organized around religio-racial stratification.

To understand how this happened, I revisit the long period of *Reconquista*, which spanned several centuries, lasting from the eighth to the fifteenth century with 1492 as the symbolic end date, and focus on how, during this period, a sense of pure, authentically Spanish, Catholic identity was constructed over against Jewish and Muslim otherness.

1 The *Reconquista* and the Re-Christianization of the Iberian Peninsula

In 711, Arabs and Berbers who served the Umayyad caliphs of Damascus began to conquer the Iberian Peninsula. The territories that came under Muslim rule, Al-Andalus (Muslim Iberia) were marked by great diversity. Here, Muslims, Jews, and Christians lived closer together than they did anywhere else in Europe. From the eighth until the eleventh century, these three communities lived under specific rules laid down by the Muslim rulers of the Umayyad dynasty. Christians and Jews were considered *dhimmis*, people of the book/law (*Ahl al-Kitab*); as custodians of Scripture, they occupied a special place between infidels and believers and deserved protection as long as they submitted to the Islamic ruler. According to Sharia (the laws of Islam), they were free to follow their own worship practices and laws (e.g. in matters of marriage and divorce), go to their own courts to settle disputes about divorce or inheritance cases, and discuss theological matters amongst themselves. They were even allowed to drink wine and eat pork. In brief, they enjoyed considerable religious freedom. Islam was, however, the dominant tradition and set the norm regarding worship and morality. Blasphemy and insults to Islam were not tolerated. The law considered non-Muslims as inferior to Muslims and they had to accept various regulations which decreased their influence in society and at the same time confirmed Islamic superiority.[3] 'They [Christians and Jews] had a second-class status and had to pay a separate tax. In any case, they were not allowed to have any authority over a Muslim. A Christian could not be a presiding judge in a case that involved Muslims or an officer in the Muslim army. Their voice as a witness counted only half of that of a Muslim' (Berger, 2022, episode 3). While the law projects an ideal society from a certain point of view, it does not reflect reality and people's behaviour often deviates from the established rules. This was no different in Al-Andalus. On the one hand, some *dhimmis* did indeed rise to high positions in various fields of life, becoming ambassadors, physicians, intellectuals, merchants, and artisans. We also know cases of Christians, who, looking for martyrdom, blasphemed publicly, but who received an entirely different response than they hoped for: they were simply ignored. On the other hand, some rulers overstepped the mark and persecuted Jews and Christians or discriminated against them in ways that were not covered by the law. On the whole, however, Christians, Jews, and Muslims lived comfortably together but apart.

As might be expected, these centuries of *convivencia* produced a diverse and hybrid culture: architecture, language, and various other cultural expressions, such as dress, cuisine, and art, were shared across religious communities and testify to the cultural hybridization that developed in Al-Andalus. Over time, the Iberian Peninsula became 'a place where bishops spoke Arabic, imams Ladino, and Jewish viziers advised caliphs and gave dinner parties for Muslim poets in their presidential gardens' (Almond, 2009, p. 28). Regulations notwithstanding, it would not have been easy to distinguish between conventions of Catholics, Jews, and 'Moors', a name used by European Christians to designate the Maghreb Muslims who had conquered the Iberian Peninsula.[4]

Starting in the eleventh century, the power of the Umayyad dynasty began to wane and Christian kings who still held territory in the North of the Iberian Peninsula gradually managed to take territory away from Al-Andalus and brought it under Christian rule. Reconquering territory is one thing; re-Christianizing these territories another. Centuries of Islamic rule cannot simply be undone; it requires much effort to re-establish Christianity as norm. To achieve this goal, Christian victors made use of various tried and tested strategies. Here I limit myself to two: mosque conversion and law making.

Text Box 1: The *Reconquista*

The *Reconquista* was a long period spanning several centuries, in which Christian rulers, with the help of the church and crusading armies, step by step recovered the Iberian Peninsula from the hands of the Muslims, who according to Christians occupied these lands unlawfully. Toledo was the first major city to be recaptured, in 1085, but the *Reconquista* only gained momentum in the thirteenth century, when the the cities of Cordoba (1236), Valencia (1238), Seville (1248), and Cadiz (1260) were recovered. By the end of the century Muslim power in the Iberian Peninsula had been broken (Yovel, 2009, p. 29). However, it would only be in 1492 that Isabella I and Ferdinand II received the keys of Granada, thereby unifying the 'Spanish territories' under Christian rule for the first time since 711, the year that the Umayyad Muslims overthrew the Spanish Visigothic monarchy of Toledo.

116 CHAPTER 4 The Spanish Catholic Monarchy

Reclaiming Space: Converting and Cleansing Mosques

When Christian rulers reconquered territory, they sought to re-establish the religionized norm of Christendom and to materialize the victory of the Christian god over the god of the 'pagan' Moors. To that end, a new religious landscape had to be created and various strategies were employed to achieve this. New church buildings were constructed, while Moorish sites were destroyed or stripped of their religious meaning, to be used as stables or housing for the conquerors. Existing religious sites were often refashioned to suit the conquerors' cultic needs.

Reclaiming ownership over sacred space was a particularly powerful symbolic action of religionization, which fitted the *Reconquista* ideology. Mosques had to be handed over to the church and would be purged and converted. As Amy Remensnyder explains, 'congregational mosques – those large and often splendid buildings where Muslim communities gathered as a whole for worship – rarely stayed in Muslim hands for longer than a year or so after Christian conquest; typically, Christians converted them into cathedrals almost immediately' (Remensnyder, 2016, p. 125). This is what happened with the mosques of Toledo (1086), Cordoba (1236), Jaén (1246), Seville (1248), and Murcia (1266) and finally Granada (1492). Indeed, in almost all of the captured cities the principal mosque was seized and became the new episcopal see (Bueno Sánchez, 2022). Capturing the central mosque was considered to be a public manifestation of Christian victory, even when there were hardly any Christians to fill the newly established church (Kroesen, 2008). Renewed mastery over the religious landscape helped to establish Christianness as the norm, with Muslims (and by extension Jews) as the others.

This Christian reclamation of space also entailed rituals of purgation. In line with the ideology of purgation, the conversion process consisted of purging the 'filth' of the pagan cult or even the demon worship of the Moors and subsequently celebrating the first Mass. Julie Harris explains, '[w]hen the conversion of a mosque to a church is described [...] the phrase "*eliminata spurcitia Mahometi*"' will often be used. 'In the Vulgate, the term *spurcitia* appears in Numbers 19.13 and Matthew 23.27. In both instances, the word refers to a contamination associated with dead bodies. In mosque conversion texts, the term *spurcitia* is often followed by the modifier *paganorum* or *Machometi* and most easily translates as "filth"' (Harris, 1997, p. 162). This is for example the case in the twelfth-century anti-Islamic writings produced by Bernard of Clairvaux, who called the Muslims 'enemies of the cross' [*crucis adversarii*] and 'pagan filth' [*spurcitia paganorum*] (Kroemer, 2012, pp. 55–56). Recall in this regard that one of the key biblical images used to capture the import of the *Reconquista* was that of Jesus evicting the moneylenders from the temple (Matt 21:12–17) (Lapina & Morton, 2017). Thus, the following was said about the conversion of Huesca's mosque in 1097:

> *And where the sacraments of the lord's body and blood were celebrated, the heinous fictions of the demons and the filthiest Muhammad were worshiped [*atque ubi dominici corporis et sanguinis celebrata fuerant sacramenta nefanda demonum spurcissimique Mahomat colebantur figmenta]. *Here, in the city Huesca, to restore the head of the ancient pontificate, I, Pedro of Aragón, have given to the bishop of all, the most splendid mosque of the Spanish cities, [and] I have dedicated [it] as a church in honor of the lord Jesus of Nazareth, as well as to the most blessed Peter, first among the apostles, to Holy Mary, mother of God and the holy John the Baptist and evangelist.* (Diploma Petri I regis Aragoniae et Navarrae [1097 IV 5], ed. Durán Gudiol, 1965, pp. 89–91, no. 64, my translation)

Often the conversion of mosques to churches went hand in hand with myth making: a converted mosque was claimed to have originally been a church, used by the Christian Visigoths before it was desecrated and profaned by the Moors. Now, thanks to the *Reconquista*, it could be restored to its ancient glory on the condition that the impure space was purified and reconsecrated; only then could it become a place worthy of celebrating the Eucharist again. Just as the reconquest is typologically cast as the cleansing of the temple by Jesus, so the ritual purgation of the demonic presence from sacred spaces symbolizes the re-Christianization of Spanish territories and the concomitant paganization of Islam. Ideas of profanation and re-sacralization go hand in hand, both in the ideology of the reconquest as well as in the ritual of mosque conversion.

Law Making

Reclaiming territory and symbolic sacred sites is one way to establish a Christian religious norm; the more complex question is how the new Christian rulers would actually govern the population, which was still a mixture of Muslims, Jews, and Christians. Here Christian rulers had to strike a balance: while trying to re-establish Christian society, they also had to maintain order and economic stability. Upheavals and revolts were therefore to be avoided. This explains why most combined an ideology of religious purgation with political and legal pragmatism and even a policy of toleration. It also seems that Christian rulers liked to present themselves as being as 'tolerant' as the Muslim rulers had been, and initially they continued the ideal of *convivencia*.

During the *Reconquista*, policies 'were [often] devised on the spot by means of treaties, terms of surrender, or laws that had been applied to Jews in the Christian rulers' homelands' (Berger, 2014, p. 84). These policies were aimed at reshaping society and reorganizing the hierarchies between the different communities such that Christian supremacy was reaffirmed. No Christian should be the inferior of a Muslim (or a Jew for that matter). At the same time, Christian rulers granted the Jews and Moors a certain freedom to worship and practise their own tradition. The legal Compendium (1265), *Las Siete Partidas* (Seven divisions of law) of King Alfonso X (r. 1252–1284) is a case in point (Text Box 2). Inspired by Roman law, Visigothic law, and canon law, it envisions a re-Christianized, stratified society based on religionized difference and revolving around an imperial monarch, whose legislative will and sacred identity command loyalty (Menjot, 2017, p. 85). At the same time, we still find traces of a 'more tolerant and pragmatic' policy in this Compendium.

Text Box 2: On the Compendium

While the Compendium was finalized in 1265, it would only be implemented in 1348 because of the ongoing strife and chaos. The 'chief cause' for this delay was the fact that the Spanish territory continued to be torn apart by battles being waged against the Moors, so that 'Spain' was not prepared to accept any orderly regulation. However, this code did eventually have a major impact, as it would 'spread with the spreading Spanish Empire, taking root in the Americas, the Philippines, and in surprising ways even in the United States' (Burns, 2002, p. 46).

Las Siete Partidas touched on a large number of topics, including natural law, public and military law, judicial organization, domestic relations, contracts, and criminal law. Only in the seventh part, *On criminal law*, does the Compendium discuss 'the large communities of Jews and Moors in [the] kingdom, devoting just over four pages to each' (Burns, 2002, p. 46). Here, King Alfonso X lays out his vision of a society based on Christian normativity, which simultaneously enables a *modus vivendi* between the different communities. The latter requires at least 'a few basic ground-rules for [Jews and Moors'] external relations with the [Christian] community' (Burns, 2002, p. 48). Both religionized minorities were entitled to certain protections under the law, but they were to be closely monitored and disciplined. Indeed, the laws dealing with the Jews and Moors appear under the chapter on criminal law because 'the crown feared two kinds of serious crime extrinsic to the situation of these minorities but omnipresent – apostasy by Christians, and conversely mistreatment or coerced conversion of the guest communities to the detriment of public order and Christian belief' (Burns, 2002, p. 49).

On the Jews (*De los judíos*)

The Jews, according to *Las Siete Partidas* (trans. Scott, 2001), are a people 'who do not believe in the religion of our lord Jesus Christ' [*no creen en la fe de nuestro señor Jesucristo*]. They are a 'party who believes in, and adheres to the law of Moses [...] [*cree y tiene la ley de Moisé*] as well as one who is circumcised, and observes the other precepts commanded by his law [*ley suya*]' (7.24.2). The presence of Jews in Christian lands is justified by the centuries-old Augustinian doctrine of living witness: 'The reason that the Church, emperors, kings and princes, permitted the Jews to dwell among them and with Christians, is because they always lived, as it were, in captivity, as it was constantly in the minds of men that they were descended from those who crucified Our Lord Jesus Christ' (7.24.2). This theology, formulated by Augustine against the background of the Christianization of the Roman Empire, remained intact for the time being, even though, in the Iberian Peninsula as elsewhere, it would be undermined in the course of the following centuries. The Jews were Christ-killers, rejected by God, 'exiles' in Christian society, and their prophecies were living witness to the truth of the Christian faith. Considering that the Iberian Peninsula hosted the largest and one of the oldest Jewish communities at that time, it is striking that the Compendium simply reiterates theological and legal commonplaces. The fact that Alfonso's legal team was inspired mainly by the *Codex Theodosianus* and *Justinianus* (as compiled in the Gratian Decree of 1234) might explain this conservatism. However, *Las Siete Partidas* does convey 'a degree of social integration and interaction between Jews and Christians that was not found elsewhere in Europe at this time' (Simon, 1987, p. 84). The Jews were allowed to 'live among the Christians', 'quietly and without disorder'; they could practise their law, though they were not allowed to offend Christian faith (7.24.2), to preach, or proselytize (7.24.1); they might also gather in the synagogue and even construct new synagogues – as long as the new one was not 'higher, larger, or better decorated than the old one' (7.24.4). Furthermore, the Compendium states that because the

> *synagogue is a place where the name of God is praised, we forbid any Christian to deface it, or remove anything from it, or take anything out of it by force; except where some malefactor takes refuge there; for they have a right to remove him by force in order to bring him before the judge. Moreover, we forbid Christians to put any animal into a synagogue, or loiter in it, or place any hindrance in the way of the Jews while they are there performing their devotions according to their law. (7.24.4)*

In addition, Jews may rest on Shabbat (7.24.5), and no force should be used to convert Jews (7.24.6). Also, and this is in sharp contrast to the later statutes of pure blood:

> *after any Jews become Christians, all persons in our dominions shall honor them; and that no one shall dare to reproach them or their descendants, by way of insult, with having been Jews; and that they shall possess all their property, sharing the same with their brothers, and inheriting it from their fathers and mothers and other relatives, just as if they were Jews; and that they can hold all offices and dignities which other Christians can do. (7.24.6).*

That this law explicitly states that Jews who become Christian ought to be treated as Christians, probably means that this was not always the case and that Jewish converts in their daily lives were confronted with defamation (Gebke, 2020, p. 68). This law thus already heralds a new social stratification that would be central to the Catholic Spanish religio-racial project and which distinguishes between Jews, new Christians, namely Jews who converted to Christianity [*conversos*] and old Christians, in other words Christians with a long Christian lineage. Jews, furthermore, should not outrank Christians (7.24.3); a Christian who becomes a Jew shall be put to death (7.24.7); intermarriage (7.24.8) or intercourse is prohibited (7.24.9); Jews may not hold Christian slaves (7.24.9). Finally, the clothing regulations of Lateran IV were to be implemented. Such visual signifiers are meant to avoid sexual and social mixing.

Las Siete Partidas also mentions, and thereby gives credibility to, the terrible blood libels that were told about the Jews at the time.

> *Because we have heard it said that in some places Jews celebrated, and still celebrate Good Friday, which commemorates the Passion of Our Lord Jesus Christ, by way of contempt; stealing children and fastening them to crosses, and making images of wax and crucifying them, when they cannot obtain children; we order that, hereafter, if in any part of our dominions anything like this is done, and can be proved, all persons who were present when the act was committed shall be seized, arrested and brought before the king; and after the king ascertains that they are guilty, he shall cause them to be put to death in a disgraceful manner, no matter how many there may be.*
>
> *We also forbid any Jew to dare to leave his house or his quarter on Good Friday, but they must all remain shut up until Saturday morning; and if they violate this regulation, we decree that they shall not be entitled to reparation for any injury or dishonor inflicted upon them by Christians. (7.24.2)*

On the Moors (*De los moros*)

While the Jews settled down in cities, where they became key economic and political players, functioning as traders, administrators, translators, tax collectors, or physicians, the Moors progressively fell back into rural communities, sometimes by expulsion and sometimes to enjoy religious solidarity. Their presence, however, 'was more widely diffused, not only as more numerous in most of early modern Spain but because a skilled Moorish agricultural tenant brought serious profit, as expressed in the common proverb "No Moor, no money" [*Quien no tiene moro, no tiene oro*]' (trans. Scott, 2001, p. xxxiii).

The acceptance of the Moors had less to do with theology (cf. the Jews in Christian society) than with the legally binding treaties of surrender after the reconquest and with pragmatism. To enable orderly coexistence in the context of Christian society, the Compendium would protect minorities and guarantee some religious freedom, while re-emphasizing Christian supremacy. Nevertheless, as is the case in the canons of the Fourth Lateran Council (1215), most laws obtaining to the Jews are also applied to the Muslim communities that remained after the reconquest. Their status is both similar to and different from that of the Jews. *Las Siete Partidas* 7.25.1 opens by stating that the term Moor has the same connotation as the Latin term *Sarracenus* [*Sarracenus en latin tanto quiere decir en romance como moro*]. The Moors are described as

> *a people who believe that Muhammad was the Prophet and Messenger of God, and for the reason that the works which he performed do not indicate the extraordinary sanctity which belongs to such a sacred calling, his religion is, as it were, an insult to God. Wherefore, since in the preceding Title we treated of the Jews and of the obstinacy which they display toward the true faith, we intend to speak here of the Moors, and of their foolish belief by which they think they will be saved. (7.25.1)*

To the extent that the Moors' status is similar to that of the Jews, the Compendium states that 'We decree that Moors shall live among Christians in the same way that we mentioned in the preceding Title that Jews shall do, by observing their own law and not insulting ours'. Just like the Jews, Alfonso is willing to accommodate the Moors, guaranteeing their safety, and protecting their legal rights.

> *Although the Moors do not acknowledge a good religion, so long as they live among Christians with their assurance of security their property shall not be stolen from them or taken by force; and we order that whoever violates this law shall pay a sum equal to double the value of what he took. (7.25.1)*

Some laws applying to the Moors were more severe, probably because the *Reconquista* was ongoing, and the Moors were military adversaries, both in the Iberian Peninsula and elsewhere, and also because there was no theological framework for ensuring the Moors' ongoing existence. Therefore, unlike the Jews, the Moors were not allowed to have mosques in Christian towns and any 'mosques which they formerly possessed shall belong to the king; and he can give them to whomsoever he wishes' (25.7.1). The Compendium continues, thereby at once insinuating that the Moors are pagans, that they may not perform 'their sacrifices publicly in the presence of men' (25.7.1).

The main legal concern, however, related to conversion and apostasy; seven of the 11 laws deal with this issue. No Christian should convert to Islam, though Moors who convert to the Christian faith should be treated with respect and ought not to meet with any form of contempt, as this could make them return to their former faith. Intermarriage (7.25.4) is forbidden as is mixed sexual intercourse (7.25.6). Punishments await those who transgress these laws: confiscation of property, stoning, flogging, and even burning and execution. The concern seems to have been mainly about a Moor having sexual relations with a Christian virgin or married woman, not so much that of a Christian man having sexual relations with a Moorish girl/woman.

Based on a combination of pragmatism and *Reconquista* ideology, the societal ideal projected in *Las Siete Partidas* is that of a Christian society in which parallel communities have as little contact with each other as possible, especially in the private sphere, and with both Jews and Muslims kept in a position of subordination in relation to the Christians. To avoid conflicts and contamination, communities are to be separated. Nevertheless, a system of parallel communities in a society where one of those communities embodies the norm and enjoys various privileges can easily lead to a situation where minority groups are subject to contempt and discrimination. This in turn leads to tensions and conflicts.

2 The Long Road towards Blood Purity Laws

The big question now is how this religiously stratified society changed into a society that was out to purge itself of all religious minorities with impure, un-Christian, non-Spanish blood. How may we understand this transition from religionized segregation to cleansing and purgation based on ideas and ideals about blood purity? While more research needs to be done and there is still much we do not know, we do know that the construction of the Spanish community as a religio-racialized blood community emerged in a 'specific political and social climate in early modern Spain [but has] a place in larger religious-theological and cultural developments at work throughout Europe' (Burk, 2010, p. 16). Several factors need to be reckoned with: (i) the crusading ideologies, which created a sense of Christian identity that feeds on the subjugation of non-Christians (Castillo, 2017, p. 8); (ii) the overall rise of anti-Jewish sentiments in Europe, which also impacted the Iberian Peninsula; (iii) the socio-economic motives; and (iv) political instability, which led to the production of new discriminatory anti-Jewish discourses and actions. To unpack these different aspects, I take another jump into history, and return to an imagined and pure past, prior to the Moorish occupation.

Crusading Ideology and the Ideal of Christian Visigothic Descent

Centuries of projecting a 'holy war' – a spiritual battle between the Christian armies of God and Satan's army – left its traces on the mindset of Christians both in the Iberian Peninsula and elsewhere in Latin Christendom. The war against the Muslims was not only framed as a sacred conflict against Christianity's enemies, but also as a *Reconquista*, implying that it was not simply a matter of conquering new land, but rather about reconquering land that had illegitimately been taken from its earlier, legitimate Visigothic Christian rulers (sixth to eighth centuries) and unlawfully occupied by Umayyad rulers. To underscore their legitimate claim to the land, the monarchs of the Christian kingdoms 'of Castile (and, on occasion, Aragon and other Mediterranean kingdoms)' used ethnoreligious reasoning: they claimed 'an uninterrupted descent from the Goths who had ruled from Toledo, sometimes even styling themselves, as Enríquez del Castillo does for Henry IV, "Gothic" kings' (Devereux, 2006, p. 3). Indeed, during and after the *Reconquista*, the Visigothic rulers were romanticized as the first rulers that had succeeded in creating a united and independent Christian kingdom in the Iberian Peninsula. Visigothic peoplehood and Catholic identity intersect.

This admiration for the Visigoths goes back to the popular writer St Isidore of Seville (560–636), who has been called the 'chief apologist' for the Visigoth era (Roth, 1994, p. 14), and to his *Historia Gothorum* [History of the Goths] (Isidore of Seville, trans. Donini & Ford, 1966). This work would later inspire Rodrigo Jiménez de Andrada (1170–1247), Archbishop of Toledo for almost 40 years, when he wrote *Historia de rebus Hispaniae* [A History about the Iberian Peninsula] (1243). This work turned Visigothic Christian culture into a romantic source of inspiration for the Spanish elite both during and after the reconquest. Making use of ethnoreligious reasoning, many legitimized their status and authority by basing it on their alleged Visigothic lineage. For example, when the above-mentioned King Alfonso X succeeded to the throne, he commissioned the *Primera crónica general* [The first general chronicle], aimed at relating the history of Spain starting from biblical times until the present reign of Ferdinand III (Furtado, 2012, p. 100). This work consists of four parts: the first focuses on Roman history, the third on the *Reconquista*, and the fourth on the rise of the Castilian and the Leonese monarchies. The entire second part zooms in on the Visigothic Christian rulers, from whom these monarchies claim their descent (Furtado, 2012).

Christian rulers not only claimed Visigothic ancestry, but they also tried to reinvigorate Visigothic traditions, like the right of investiture, which was contested elsewhere.

When the ancient sees were reclaimed from Moorish control, Spanish Christian kings operated according to Visigothic traditions, which recognized the monarch as the head of the Church and elected bishops both directly and indirectly through local cathedral chapters [...]. At the coronation of a new monarch it was customary that he take an oath to respect the ecclesiastic privilege as part of 'a mutual compromise of fidelity between the monarchy and the Church'. The bishops then responded in kind, making an oath of homage to the monarchs. These vows were further reinforced by the tradition of investiture, or royal installation of clergymen to episcopal offices. After a clergyman swore his loyalty, the king would bestow the symbols of the position; for a bishop, these were the pastoral staff and ring, for a priest, the keys to the Church. (Castillo, 2017, p. 19)

Much later, the Catholic monarchs Ferdinand II and Isabella I, who likewise claimed to be heirs of the Visigoths, came to believe that it was their responsibility to reconquer the last occupied territories (Granada) so that all the land that had once belonged to the Visigoths would be restored.

The Visigoths were idealized as a military people who were allegedly the first to have unified and Christianized Hispania, a region as large as the Roman diocese of Spain and which included Mauretania in North Africa. The figure of the *hidalgo*, which means son of a Visigoth (*hijo de godo*), embodies the ideal of the Spanish reconquering mentality: dedicated to serving God and king, while being of pure Catholic lineage (unpolluted by foreignness). The term *hidalgo* was first used during the twelfth century in Castile and Portugal to refer to the knights of the reconquest, who legitimized their right to the reconquered land based on their Visigothic lineage. A *hidalgo* is a noble man, who abides by values such as chivalry, loyalty, and courage and is dedicated to the protection of Latin Christendom. As Kathleen Deagan explains:

Values evolved over those seven centuries of holy war idealized the hidalgo *man who built a livelihood on service to God and king (as opposed to labor or trade), and acquired property and wealth as rewards for honor, valor, and military success.*

122 CHAPTER 4 The Spanish Catholic Monarchy

The hidalgo was furthermore of pure Spanish (i.e. Christian) lineage, without taint of Muslim of Jewish lineage. (Deagan, 2001, pp. 185–186)

In time, a fixation on pure Visigothic, Christian lineage became an integral part of the Spanish national consciousness. To be 'Spanish' is to have reconquered Christian (Visigothic) land from foreign Islamic powers, who furthermore were supposed to have colluded with the Jews.

Isabella I and Ferdinand II would continue this crusading ideology of reclaiming what had once been theirs and presented their political project as a re-unification of what had once been one before the shattering rule of the Moors. When, in 1492, they finally conquered Granada, this was considered the end of the war against the infidel and the ultimate victory of Christian faith. The reconquest of Granada thus symbolized the final eradication of Islamic power.

Increasing Anti-Judaism

The reconquest did not immediately mean the end of the deep-rooted culture of *convivencia*. For quite some time, 'the three religions coexisted peacefully, as is illustrated by the fact that the Castilian kings Fernando III of Castile (1217–1252) and Alfonso X of Castile (1252–1284) both described themselves as "king of the three religions"' [*rey de las tres religiones*] (Kroesen, 2008, p. 115). Like their Islamic predecessors, they wanted to be seen as tolerant and as rulers over three religions. Nevertheless, starting from the thirteenth century, anti-Jewish sentiments began to extend over the Iberian Peninsula. The hardening tone elsewhere in Europe, and the concrete effort to purge Christian society from impure bodies (see for example the expulsion of the Jews from England in 1290 and in France in 1306) also impacted the Iberian Peninsula, and its Christian rulers began to copy this trend and adopt the anti-Jewish policies that were in place in French, German, and English territories. How did this come about?

The Conversionist Programme of the Mendicant Orders First of all, mention should be made of the mendicant orders: the Dominicans (founded by the Spanish priest Domingo de Guzmán) and the Franciscans. Both invested their energies in combating heresy and deviance by preaching and distributing polemical tracts. These orders set up a missionary programme which the Jews, especially, were made to undergo. Rather than leaving the Jews to themselves, they invested in an assertive, if not aggressive, conversionist programme. They preached in synagogues and used the court of the inquisition to intimidate and stir up the populace. A key aspect of their programme was to set up public disputations between friars and Jews. Such disputes were not open conversations between equal partners but rather intended as a demonstration of 'Christian intellectual superiority [...]. Its antagonists were carefully chosen, its agenda determined, its direction planned and its conclusion foreseen before the first step was taken to translate the idea of a disputation into a reality' (Cohen, 1964, p. 161). The Jewish counterpart had no way of refusing to participate.

The most famous of these was the four-day disputation held at the Royal Palace and the Cloister of Barcelona, convoked by King James I of Aragon (r. 1231–1276), in July in 1263. On this occasion, the leading medieval Jewish scholar Nahmanides (1195–1270) was ordered to take on the Dominican Friar Pablo Christiani (d. 1274), who had converted from Jewish to Christian worship. They discussed the nature of the Messiah. Even though Nahmanides had been promised that he would be allowed to speak freely, he was later, in 1265, brought before the court of the inquisition on the charge of blasphemy. Thereupon Nahmanides left the Iberian Peninsula and emigrated to Palestine. As for Pablo Christiani, everywhere he went he would continue to compel the Jews to listen to his polemical speeches and to engage with him in debate. Realizing that he was not achieving his aim, he turned to Pope

Clement IV (r. 1265–1268) for help, asking him to denounce the Talmud. In 1264, the pope issued a bull coercing 'by [threat of] excommunication the King of Aragon and his nobles to force the Jews to deliver up their Talmuds and other books to the Inquisitors for examination when, if they contained no blasphemous statements, they might be returned to them, but, if otherwise, they were to be sealed up and kept securely' (Wright, 1925, p. 203). Subsequently, a commission, led by Christians, was appointed to examine and censor those passages in the Talmud that were hostile to Christian faith.

Conspiracy Theories: Treason, Ritual Murder, and Poisoning Around the thirteenth century, stories began to circulate depicting the Jews as allies of the Moors. Jews were described as traitors: it was their duplicity that had led to the Muslim conquest of Visigothic Spain in 711. A conspiracy between these two non-Christian enemies – the Jews and the Moors – was imagined. One example is the *Chronicon Mundi* written by Lucas de Tuy (d. 1249) around 1196, which describes how Toledo was captured by the Muslims with the help of Jews who rebelled against the Christians and betrayed them.

> *While the Christians on Palm Sunday had come together in the church of St. Leocadia outside the royal city [...] to hear the Word of God, the Jews, who had given the sign of treason to the Saracens [*Iudaei qui proditionis signum dederant Sarracenis*], closed the gates to the Christians and opened the gates to the Saracens [*Christianis claudentes portas Sarracenis aperuerunt*]. Therefore, the faithful people of Toledo, who were found unarmed outside the city, came to be destroyed by the sword. (Quoted in Roth, 1976, p. 156, my translation)*

This idea of Jewish collaboration, which is very much a thirteenth-century creation, would contribute to the marginalization of the Jews in Spanish society and later help to legitimize their degradation, their conversion, and finally their expulsion.

Also in the course of the thirteenth and fourteenth centuries, the first accusations of Jews practising black magic and ritually murdering children made their appearance on the Iberian Peninsula. Several myths circulated. The best known is that of the choirboy, Dominguito del Val, who in 1250 was allegedly ritually murdered by the Jews of Zaragoza, in the Spanish kingdom of Aragon. The choirboy, so the legend went, infuriated the Jews with his beautiful religious chants. The Jews, therefore, kidnapped the child, tried to persuade him to blaspheme, and, when he refused to do so, crucified him. While it is uncertain whether the child ever existed, the cult of the choir boy who suffered at the hands of the Jews continues to this day.[5]

Finally, there was a growing anxiety vis-à-vis Jewish medical practitioners. On the one hand, Jewish doctors had a good reputation. They were more skilled and better educated than Christian doctors and they were therefore called upon more often. That they also charged less certainly contributed to their popularity. On the other hand, growing anti-Jewish sentiments and policies aimed at restricting the social interaction between Jews and Christians were also affecting the Jews in their professional activities as doctors. There were fears about homicidal Jewish doctors and there was particular anxiety surrounding Jewish apothecaries: what if the 'Jews would adulterate their remedies in order to poison and injure or kill Christians' (Soyer, 2019, p. 145).[6]

Economic Motives

The strong, albeit ambiguous, economic and social position of many Jews aroused resentment among Christians. Many Jews were economically well-off; they provided 'financial, technical, and administrative services' to the new Christian monarchs 'much as they had previously provided the same services to Moslem rulers' (Friedman, 1987, p. 7). In addition, they were 'involved in the production of goods and foodstuffs (owning vineyards, mills,

124 CHAPTER 4 The Spanish Catholic Monarchy

and oil presses), in local commerce as well as long-distance trade, working in skilled occupations such as blacksmiths and other forms of metalwork' producing clothes, footwear, furniture, tools, and weapons (Soyer, 2019, p. 233). While involved in a wide variety of economic activities, in the end, 'it was trade, moneylending [...] and tax-farming that came to characterise the economic role of Jewish in the eyes of many medieval Iberian Christians' (Soyer, 2019, p. 233).

Christian nobility, active in the cities and in charge of trade and commerce, considered the Jews to be competitors. At the same time, they were interested in having access to the wealth of the Jews. Peasants frequently had dealings with the Jews in their role as moneylenders. As Teofilo Ruiz notes, 'agricultural production often required an outlay of capital that would not be recovered until the harvest was completed'. If the harvest failed, peasants would have to find money to pay off their debts.

> *In fourteenth-century northern Castile, judicial agents of small towns and villages confiscated farms and auctioned them off to ensure payment of outstanding debts to Jews. [...] It was precisely this type of transaction that fed popular rancour against Jews, and that anti-Jewish [...] sentiment manifested itself most violently among the lower social groups. (Ruiz, 2002, p. 71)*

Monarchs found Jewish advisors especially interesting: they offered much-needed skills, for example literacy skills, but there was no chance of them ever being able to rise to independent power; their position would always have to be inferior to that of the Christian. Many operated as the Crown's tax collectors. Yirmiyahu Yovel tellingly pictures their position as that of the 'King's political eunuchs' (Yovel, 2009, p. 32). Their 'privileged' position did, however, evoke resentment and their role as tax collectors easily angered people. While the violence against the Jews in their role as royal tax collectors sprang from anger vis-à-vis royal authority, the Jews as a social group paid the price. The anti-Jewish image that circulated elsewhere in Europe, of the Jews as greedy usurers, gradually rooted itself and found its way into the collective imagination of Spain.[7]

Political Instability

In 1348 and again in 1351, there was a massive outbreak of the plague. The devastating impact of this epidemic should not be underestimated. It has been calculated that over 30 million people died in Europe including one third of the population in what is today Spain. This was a time of utter uncertainty and distress, economic instability, and the absence of order. Many believed that God 'was punishing Christians for sheltering his enemies, and that He would not rid them of the plague until they had rid themselves of Jews' (Terpstra, 2015, p. 60). Others saw it as a sign of the omnipresence of the devil, out to bring harm to the *Corpus Christianum*. Many in Europe, furthermore, believed the Jews were responsible for spreading the plague. They were accused of having 'poisoned the well'. As Nicholas Terpstra comments, 'here the concept of contagion was both literal and metaphorical' (Terpstra, 2015, p. 59). Jewish communities suffered greatly because of these accusations. For some time, destruction, mob violence, and expulsions were a daily occurrence. Even though Jewish communities recovered, the image of the Jew as an enemy of Christians never disappeared.

Matters got out of control when a dispute over the throne between Peter I of Castile and Leon (r. 1350–1369) and his half-brother Henry (1334–1379) turned into civil war. Whereas Peter I had 'set up a semi-Jewish administration and had allegedly brought Jewish power in Castile', Henry successfully exploited anti-Jewish bias among the population and called upon them to kill Peter 'and his Jews'. When Peter I was later killed, the Jews suffered gravely. This situation of socio-political and economic instability was a fertile breeding ground for a renewed demonization of the Jews, preparing the ground for a more systematic anti-Jewish attack later on. Previously, anti-Jewish measures had been more or less ad hoc and disorganized; what would now follow was a pogrom of unseen dimensions.

3 Forced Mass Conversions

On 6 June 1391, the situation exploded: socio-political insecurity, economic rivalry, and deeply rooted anti-Jewish bias conflated and led to pogroms, first against the Jews in Seville, who were presented with the choice of death or baptism. Many were killed, but most were forcibly baptized. Soon, these riots spread from town to town, resulting in a wave of forced mass conversions to Catholicism among the Jewish population in Toledo, Valencia, Barcelona, and so on. There is ample evidence that this was far more than a mere eruption of anti-Jewish violence. What we are looking at is a more systematic attempt to free this Christian society of any Jewish presence: the beginning of an ethnic cleansing that would see its dramatic climax a century later in 1492 with the expulsion of the Jews. Both 'citizens and civic leaders' expressed the idea that it would be a structural improvement of society if all Jews were 'eliminated' (Nirenberg, 2014a). Thousands were killed and tens of thousands forced to convert. Reuven, the son of Rabbi Nissim Gerund, survived the massacre, and described the damage as follows:

> *Wail, holy and glorious Torah, and put on black raiment, for the expounders*
> *of your lucid words perished in the flames. For three months the conflagration*
> *spread through the holy congregations of the exile of Israel in Sepharad. The fate*
> *[of Sodom and Gomorrah] overtook the holy communities of Castile, Toledo,*
> *Seville, Mallorca, Cordoba, Valencia, Barcelona, Tàrrega, and Girona, and sixty*
> *neighbouring cities and villages [...] The sword, slaughter, destruction, forced*
> *conversions, captivity, and spoliation were the order of the day. Many were sold as*
> *slaves to the Ishmaelites; 140,000 were unable to resist those who so barbarously*
> *forced them and gave themselves up to impurity [that is, converted]. (Hershman,*
> *quoted in Nirenberg, 2014a)*

The whole process of mass conversion would later be repeated in the years 1412–1415 when the Dominican friar Vincent Ferrer (1350–1419) 'with support from the papal court in Avignon and the crowns of Aragon and Castile, travelled around the Spanish territories. While doing so he held sermons aimed at getting Jews to convert' (Saxonberg, 2020, p. 117).

Questions about Authenticity

The phenomenon of mass forced conversion resulted in a dramatic change in the religious demography of the Iberian Peninsula. It also impacted socio-economic boundaries and social relations. These rapid societal changes led again to instability and insecurity, especially amongst those who felt that their privileged position was at risk. In the aftermath of these forced conversions, existing concerns about the sincerity of Jews converting, about the depth of the converts' faith, and about their continuing attachment to former Jewish traditions were exacerbated (Jennings, 2010, p. 33). Willie Jennings suggests that there was a concern that if *conversos* continued to secretly practise Jewish traditions, they were endangering the Christian body from within (Jennings, 2010, p. 33). Jewish converts were increasingly seen as heretics, or at least potential heretics, in other words as 'disobeyers within the fold' (Burk, 2010, p. 13). These prejudices incited anxieties about whether it is even possible to change Jewish nature; is baptism strong enough to transform the deeply problematic nature of Jews? Should one not make a distinction between Christians whose religious identity can claim a long lineage, and those who have only just now converted, perhaps under pressure or because of economic motives? Even when there was no doubt as to the motive of the converts, would baptism alone suffice to bring about change in the nature of the stubborn Jew? Would not a period of transition be needed, perhaps of one or two generations of conversion, before Christian transformation could really occur? Against this background, the bodies of Jews came to be seen as recalcitrant – resisting the power of baptism. The salvific possibility of *conversos* was in doubt (Jennings, 2010, p. 35).

Conversos Destabilize Boundaries

Thanks to their new religious affiliation, *conversos* were freed from previous repressive exclusionary legislation; now they could participate in most aspects of life, acquiring wealth, property, and status. They were eligible for public and ecclesial offices that had previously been off-limits. They were also allowed 'to live outside of Jewish quarters [*juderias*] and to stop wearing distinctive clothing' and they could marry other Christians (Martinez, 2008, p. 27). Many of them found routes to societal success and power. The prevailing power dynamics in society were altered and this heightened social tensions. Focusing on Cuenca, a city in Castile, Lu Ann Homza notes how

> *[a]ntagonism towards the* conversos *was inflamed by their social success since many* converso *families deftly climbed a social hierarchy that had been off-limits before their baptism.* Conversos *came to occupy 85 percent of the positions on the city council in Cuenca, held prominent positions at the royal courts and could achieve remarkable success in the church. (Homza, 2006, p. xvi)*

Over time, *conversos'* increased commercial and social status led to clashes with 'old' Christians, who did not want to give up their privileged position in society. The latter resented the rapid socio-economic advancement of the *conversos*, their ability to secure public positions and ecclesial appointments, and their swift integration into old noble families. When privileges are under pressure, violence lurks around the corner. However, there is more.

The *conversos* also destabilized the clear and bounded religious identities, or as David Nirenberg puts it, they initiated 'a crisis of classification and identity' (Nirenberg, 2002, p. 11). In previous chapters, I have discussed how the religionized understanding of self and other are closely intertwined and how historically speaking Christian self-identity was imagined time and again in opposition to its imagined and constructed others; others that are clearly different, inferior, and separated from those who embody the prevailing Christian norm. The relations between Christians and their others were restricted and regulated, especially in as far as social interaction was concerned. Laws were implemented to that end, until separation became the normal habitus: one does not eat with, sleep with, or marry non-Christians. Against this background, we may also understand why the effort to liberate Spanish society and render it 'Jew-free' by means of forced conversions turned out to be highly unsettling:

> *Not Jews anymore, but unable to disappear into the mass of Christian subjects either, these new Christians troubled the category of 'Jew' and that of 'Christian' by embodying an indeterminacy of status and identity that had the potential to put the categories* Christian *and* Jew *into crisis. Unsurprisingly, the potential for crisis peaks exponentially when power is recognized to be at stake: when a convert is authorized to sit in judgment over Christians and levy sentences involving the life and limb of Christians, or when a generational descendent [sic] of a convert might occupy the throne of St. Peter and exercise panoptic power as the supreme head of all Latin Christendom. At such moments, the horror of category crisis peaks spectacularly, and the resultant drama lodges itself in the cultural record of ideological writing. (Heng, 2018, p. 78)*

Christians had always imagined their identity over against the Jew, who was seen as un-Christian or even anti-Christian. The question arose, 'how would Christianity define itself if the living exemplars of that difference vanished?' (Nirenberg, 2014a). This question is intriguing, because it shows that it is not so much visible difference that is unsettling, but rather the disappearance of visible difference: here, difference that goes underground, that can no longer be distinguished, contained, or set apart, arouses suspicion and distress. It is difference that manifests itself as sameness that unnerves, alterity that comes under the guise of identity.

While the church accepted these conversions as real and made no distinction between 'old' Christians and *conversos*, suspicion grew nevertheless; suspicion about what *conversos* said, did, and really believed; were they not secretly continuing with their Jewish traditions?

Misgivings that had up to now been formulated vis-à-vis heretics were now raised against the *conversos*. Rather than being accepted as baptized Christians, the masses came to see them as deviant Christians who hide their true identity: they are baptized Jews, crypto-Jews, or Judaizers and charged with all things heretic: 'apostasy, [...] love of novelty and dissention, ambition, presumption and hatred of peace' (Burk, 2010, p. 13). Perhaps, we are dealing here with the return of a distinction that was previously projected by Visigothic rulers: the distinction between baptized Jews and unbaptized Jews.

Imaginations about Jewish infiltration, contamination, and Judaization came to intersect with ancient essentializations about the untrustworthy character of the Jews, their hunger for power and their greed. Jewish nature impedes true conversion: the effort to wipe out Jewish presence by means of forced conversions failed, because their Jewish nature resisted transformation. These baptized Jews would be called *Marranos*, namely pigs. Some scholars argue that the name refers to the fact that baptized Jews – assimilated Jews, Christian Jews – had difficulties with eating pork, which points to their lingering Jewish inclination. Whatever may be the case, *conversos* came to be seen as a particular 'type of convert, never fully able to rid themselves of their ancestral beliefs and therefore never capable of becoming fully realized Christians' (Martinez, 2008, p. 52).

These prejudiced social anxieties and religious fears would finally give way to new expressions of religionization based on an altered taxonomy, which distinguished between (i) *Cristianos viejos*, that is Christians who could pride themselves on their long Christian lineage, (ii) *Cristianos nuevos* or *conversos* (sometimes also called *Marranos*, i.e. pigs), (iii) Jews and (iv) Muslims. This taxonomy would be biologized *and* naturalized in the legal statutes of pure blood, which assumed that the blood of old Christians is essentially different from the blood of Jews, converted or not. The result was a hierarchically organized Spanish society, which ranks people based on these new religionized categories (Text Box 3).

Text Box 3: Modified Patterns of Religionization Leading to a Changed Social Stratification

When Jews began to convert and were thus disappearing as a visible presence in society, contemporaries worried that it would now be impossible to distinguish between converted Jews and Christians and that it would no longer be possible to separate both social groups (Nirenberg, 2014b). In that concern both economic, political, and religious motives interlock and turn into a dangerous derailment of identity or *déraison identitaire* (Ricoeur, 2000). Concerns expressed by 'old Christians' latched on to the age-old demonization of Jews, now claiming that they had only converted out of 'ambition for office' or worse out of 'carnal lust for nuns and [Christian] virgins', and that *converso* physicians 'poisoned their Christian patients in order to get hold of their inheritance and offices, "marry the wives of the Old Christians they kill" [...]' (Nirenberg, 2014a). Different myths circulated, feeding mistrust.

Old Christians	New Christians	Jews
Visigothic lineage	New lineage	Jewish lineage
Christians	(Potential) heretics/Judaizers	Jews
Spanish citizens (men)	Inferior to Christians	Inferior to Christians
Loyal subjects	Traitors	Poisoners, usurers, Child murderers
Pure blood	Impure blood	Impure blood
Christians by nature	Jews by nature (thus everything that is said of Jews is applicable to them – see column on the right)	Jews by nature

128   CHAPTER 4   The Spanish Catholic Monarchy

4   Law Making: *Limpieza de Sangre*

From the mid-fifteenth century onwards, broad social and religious anxieties about the authenticity of *conversos* led to violent outbursts, which caused new societal unrest. In 1449, in order to restore stability, Pedro Sarmiento (1375–1464), the mayor of Toledo, promulgated 'a civic ordinance' prohibiting *conversos* from entering public or clerical positions in his city, which at that time was one of the most important cities in Castile (Ingram, 2012, p. 16). I quote from the statutes (Martín Gamero, 1862, pp. 1036–1040):

> [We] pronounce and declare that, insofar as it is well-known, both by canon and civil law, that the converts of Jewish lineage, being of doubtful faith in our Lord and Saviour Jesus Christ, onto which they frequently spew forth their shallowness, [still] practicing [Jewish law], may not hold public or private offices or benefices where they may effect injuries, harms or ill treatments to pure [lindos] Old Christians, nor may they serve as witnesses against them. (Modified translation from Hering Torres, 2012, p. 16)

The statutes of pure blood (*limpieza de sangre*: purity of blood) made a connection between lineage, blood, and religious identity. These laws formalized and institutionalized anti-*converso* discourses that had already been circulating in society: that *conversos* could not claim equal status or authority as old Christians with a pure Christian lineage, that *conversos* were dishonourable [*infames*] and should therefore not be allowed to access positions of power, authority, and standing. Such positions ought to be restricted to people with unsullied blood, namely old Christians with a long Christian lineage. As Max Hering Torres puts it:

> Consequently, a new legal definition of the Jewish convert, the converso, was formulated, in order to make visible what was no longer visible: their past, i.e., their origin, which could only be traced in terms of blood. Due to the attempts at Christian homogenization, religious affiliation was no longer the reason for exclusion; religious origins instead became a new motive for discrimination [...]. The core argument was the following: despite their Christian affiliation, the Jewish converts still bore Jewish blood in their bodies and this continued to have a negative influence on their morality and conduct. According to some Old Christians, the influence of blood in the neophytes was such that, while they were nominally Christians, they still acted like Jews. To put it another way: the pseudo-causal relationship between lineage and behavior had been perpetuated and inscribed in the bodies of Christians with Jewish ancestry. (Hering Torres, 2012, pp. 15–16)[8]

The purity of blood statutes, thus institutionalized 'discrimination toward those who could not claim "Old Christian" status', and biologized religionized difference (Delgado & Moss, 2018, p. 45). Now, people's nature – who they essentially are and what they are capable of – would be determined by their religious genealogy, and it is furthermore their religious genealogy that determined the purity or impurity of their blood and, inescapably, their reproduction of stable, essential, visible, and invisible human attributes. The assumption is that a Jewish lineage produces miserable people and there is no escaping from this: origin determines. Those who stem from a damaged line *are* damaged. Anyone with at least one Jewish ancestor (either father or mother) was himself still a *converso*, because he bore Jewish blood in his body, which would continue to negatively impact his faith, morality, and conduct. Furthermore, 'if mixed with Christian blood, the Jewish blood would contaminate subsequent generations and would continue to do so indefinitely. Jewishness, then, was not a statement of faith or even a series of ethnic practices but a biological consideration' (Friedman, 1987, p. 15). Jewish impure blood made both Jews and *conversos* a threat to Christians. Even the sacraments of baptism and the Eucharist were no longer powerful enough to purify a bad blood lineage and the attendant characteristics.

Text Box 4: Shifting Religionized Boundaries

Gradually, the identity of these Jewish converts changed (i) from being Jews separated from Christians through various restrictions, (ii) to being baptized as Christians, (iii) to being new Christians who are still rather weak in their Christian faith and liable to lapse back into old traditions, (iv) to being Judaizers and heretic Christians, to being (v) Jewish by nature – religious identity runs in the blood. Blood impurity implies that one has Jewish ancestors, whereas blood purity is the absence of such antecedents. However, this preoccupation with Jewish lineage went hand in hand with an ever-increasing fixation on proving the purity of one's Christian lineage. The Christian community was transformed into a religio-racialized blood community. Gradually, a society obsessed with genealogy, blood purity, and Christian lineage emerged. Anxieties about mixture exploded.

Appearing for the first time in Toledo in 1449, the *limpieza de sangre* laws began to spread widely and infiltrated into the different bodies of society: monastic orders, schools, universities, governmental bodies, and so on. Everyone accepted these laws and organized themselves around them. They led to the discrimination criminalization of *conversos*, who were suspected of heresy; they also helped restore the privilege and status of old Christians. While the assimilation of the *conversos* had previously threatened their position and status, now the 'spread of blood distinctions potentially provided every Christian Spaniard with a claim to a kind of nobility. [...] Every peasant who could claim Old Christian status gained honorable standing, conveying moral-cultural capital if not explicit legal rights' (Burk, 2010, p. 20).

Soon a deep distrust spread and took hold of Spanish society with a dramatic and endless fixation on blood purity and ancient lineage: how can one know who is a true Christian and who is not? How can one tell the difference between an old and a new Christian? Who can say if one's neighbour is not Judaizing? Who can legitimately claim access to position and status? This culture of fear and suspicion provided the Spanish Crown with the perfect excuse to reinforce state control. At the level of society at large, furthermore, these laws transformed the identity of the *Corpus Christianum* into a religio-racialized, blood-based community (Text Box 5).

Text Box 5: Why Blood?

Scholars are still pondering the issue of why blood (which is invisible, hidden, and quite difficult to distinguish) became the *topos* to differentiate, hierarchize, and separate social groups. How did blood latch onto religious difference, how did religious difference attach itself to blood? Why did blood purity, religious genealogy, and Spanish identity form a nexus? While there are still lacunae in our understanding, the genealogical turn to blood certainly did not come out of nowhere: blood already was a multi-layered and evocative symbol that functioned in various significant contexts.

(i) Mention should be made of the late medieval idea of the Christian community as *Corpus Christianum* with Christ's blood as its lifeline. By participating in the sacrament of the Eucharist, the Christian community was transformed into a blood community. (ii) The idea that religious difference is written onto the body is not new: in the medieval imagination, spiritual difference and biological difference intersect. The body reflects the quality of spirituality and vice versa and the quality of one's spiritual life manifests itself in bodily features. (iii) Focusing even more closely, we know that the quality of blood was one of the signs of religious difference; remember that Jews (male and female) menstruated excessively and needed pure Christian blood to be cured. (iv) We already discussed the interconnection between religious deviance, disease, and contamination, hence the importance of avoiding mixture, and the relevance of the hereditary nature of religious deviance and its concomitant stain (cf. the curse of Cain). (v) Another factor that certainly played a role in the development of the *limpieza* statutes was the connection between lineage and status. The nobility (*hidalgua*), especially, took pride in their ancestry and were obsessed with keeping their noble bloodline pure, by marrying nobility (rather than outside the social group) and avoiding offspring from mixed relations. Commoners were regarded as inferior in relation to their lineage. However, as religious blood purity was not fixed (baptism could transform mind, soul, and body), nobility too, even though it was considered to be hereditary, could be earned. As Maria Elena Martinez writes: 'Kings could bestow *nobleza de privilegio* (nobility of privilege) on a worthy commoner, for instance, and allow the status to be passed down from father to son. On the third generation, *nobleza de privilegio* became *nobleza de sangre* (nobility of blood), the most valued noble status in Spanish society because it implied being part of a privileged lineage since 'time immemorial'. The strong Spanish belief in nobility as a natural condition, as an 'essence' transmitted by blood, thus did not preclude the possibility that it could be acquired through the paternal line of descent and, after a few generations, transformed into a permanent status' (Martinez, 2008, p. 49).

Finally, mention should be made of the term *raza* (race), which links character and behaviour to lineage and nature. This term, according to Nirenberg, came into use in the fifteenth century and it meant something like a family tree. When discussing horse breeding, the *raza* – the pedigree – of a horse is of utmost importance, as foals tend to take after their *father* as far as character, beauty, and strength goes. A similar line of reasoning was applied to human beings: where the son takes after the father, it is seen as impossible to transcend or deviate from one's origins. This was considered common sense. As Alfonso Martínez del Mora, who lived in Toledo in the fifteenth century, put it: 'The son of an ass must bray. This can be proven, he suggests, by an experiment. If one were to take two babies, the one a son of a laborer, the other of a knight, and rear them together on a mountain in isolation from their parents, one would find that the son of the laborer delights in agricultural pursuits, while the son of the knight takes pleasure only in feats of arms and equestrianship: "Esto procura naturaleza"' (quoted in Nirenberg, 2008, p. 78).

Quite quickly, when discussing people, *raza* would come to have a negative connotation and would be applied to people from Jewish or Muslim descent, their blood is tainted, whereas the blood of the old Christian is without the taint of the Moorish or Jewish race. Here in the words of Sebastián de Covarrubias (1539–1613): 'the caste of purebred horses, which are marked by a brand so that they can be recognized [...]. Race in [human] lineages is meant negatively, as in having some race of Moor or Jew' (quoted by Nirenberg, 2014b).

5 The Catholic Monarchs and the Purgation of the Spanish Monarchy

In 1469, Isabella I of Castile (1451–1504) and Ferdinand II of Aragon (1452–1516) were married. Their marriage laid the basis for the unification of the two largest Iberian kingdoms. The 'kingdoms' they inherited, however, were 'torn by civil war and internal strife [...]' (Rae, 2002, p. 57). The challenge that awaited them was to contain the chaos and upheaval (Moore, 2007, p. 100) and to impose political stability. They also faced the challenge of gaining 'legitimacy among a population which until recently lived under different kingdoms' (Saxonberg, 2020, p. 114).

Ferdinand and Isabella exploited the *converso* issue in their attempts to bring together disparate kingdoms in the Iberian Peninsula under the banner of a shared Catholic tradition. To that end, they deployed a state apparatus in which the inquisition played a key part, and they reinvigorated a myth of pure Visigothic Christian lineage which fed on age-old anti-Jewish prejudice. What we are witnessing here is state violence, made possible by a dangerous cocktail of economic uncertainty, political instability, social change, and ingrained anti-Jewish (and anti-Muslim) bias.

In 1477, the Catholic monarchs asked Pope Sixtus IV (r. 1471–1484) to allow them to establish an inquisition, under their authority. In line with the Visigothic tradition of investiture, the monarchs would name the inquisitors, who were to investigate charges of heresy among Christians and *conversos*. The task of this inquisition would be to maintain Catholic orthodoxy in Castile and Aragon by rooting out the problem of secret Judaizers and other forms of so-deemed heresy. The pope replied by suggesting that an inquisition be established under the authority of his papal nuncio in Castile and Aragon, an offer that was rejected by the royals, because it 'contradicted their political project' (Yovel, 2009, p. 158). The pope eventually gave in, and a royal inquisition was established in 1478. Other than the medieval, papal inquisitions, the Spanish inquisition became an instrument in the hands of the Crown. As Martinez puts it:

> *In theory, the pope exerted some influence on the choice of inquisitor general, but he too was presented by the monarchs. Because the crown ultimately determined the inquisitors, a number of historians have regarded the Holy Office as more of a royal than ecclesiastical tribunal, as an instrument of civil power, and even as an expression of Spanish absolutism. (Martinez, 2008, p. 34)*

The Spanish Crown used the inquisition as an instrument to support their absolute and centralizing regime, increase their royal power, and create a religio-racial-national identity based on the exclusion of Jewish (and later Islamic) elements.

Administrative and bureaucratic measures were taken, tribunals established, higher officials and councils appointed, and procedures were formulated to inquire into the authenticity of the *conversos*. The inquisition, targeting baptized Jews, always presumed guilt and always acted upon an accusation. Their inquiry, aimed at rooting out all Judaizers, focused on investigating whether the accused was still practising Mosaic Law. Inquisitors not only examined whether *conversos* knew the creed and were able to recite it, but also what the *conversos* did, namely their practices. An investigation would often be set in motion by an 'anonymous report' of suspicious behaviour: washing at the wrong moment, not eating pork, not resting on Sunday, lighting candles on the Sabbath, eating meat during Lent, speaking Hebrew, the purchase of certain ingredients at certain moments (aubergines or chickpeas) around Passover, cooking in olive oil rather than pork fat, and so on. Any of these practices could be turned into a sign of heresy, justifying an exploration of the genealogy of the accused and whether they were descended from Jews or converted Jews.

The inquisition, however, would also become tasked with investigating people – acclaimed old Christians – who were soliciting for public office or wanted access to certain institutions (monastic orders, schools, universities, army). Only people who could prove that they were third-generation Christians and could demonstrate their pureness of blood were granted access to honourable societal, ecclesial, and royal occupations.[9]

> *Any Jewish or Muslim ancestry in one's genealogy became a proof of dubious Christianity, converso status, and blood impurity. In practice, certificates of blood purity attesting three generations of Catholicism for one's mother and father, backed by 'pure' Christians' letters of recommendation, became compulsory to join brotherhoods and corporations, to apply to civil, military, and church positions, to the university, to non-manual professions, and to all grants and honors. Other inherited requirements were added, such as legitimate birth and non-manual-degrading work. (Helg, 2017, p. 79)*

132 CHAPTER 4 The Spanish Catholic Monarchy

An ever more complex bureaucratic system of legitimization and control was established to inquire and control claims to old lineage. The applicant, on the one hand, had to submit *probanzas* or *informaciones de limpieza de sangre* [proof or information about purity of blood], including genealogical information, sworn testimonies of family members, and long-term residents of the applicant's birthplace. Control mechanisms were put in place to check the legitimacy of these *probanzas* and a commission was appointed to that end. This could take weeks, months, and even years. While it was possible to challenge an undesirable outcome, the procedure was difficult and hardly ever successful.

The establishment of the inquisition together with the juridical procedures it entailed contributed to the making of a new society, one in which socio-economic and political relations are organized according to religio-racial difference. Soon the categories of old and new Christians entered 'into the realm of the habitus, a form of mediation that by making certain social practices seem natural, part of a common-sense world, turns history "into nature, i.e., denied as such"' (Martinez, 2008, p. 62).

The desire for purity and national unity, however, did not stop there and in 1492, Ferdinand and Isabella decided to expel all Jews who refused to be baptized. The official reason for their expulsion was that by their mere presence the Jews contributed to the problem of Judaizing, namely the problem of heresy (or crypto-Judaism) among the *conversos*. Later, a similar treatment awaited converted Muslims, called Moriscos. Between 1502 and 1525, the Muslims were baptized *en masse*. The first baptism decrees were in Granada in 1502, with the Muslims given a choice of exile, baptism, or death. The other major cities soon followed and by 1525 most areas in the Iberian Peninsula had undergone forced baptism. The Moriscos presented a similar problem to that of the Marranos, and the inquisition would also target them, questioning the sincerity of their conversion and accusing them of secretly maintaining Islamic practice. In their case too, circumstantial evidence supposedly gave them away. As Mauritz Berger explains,

> *These alleged 'Islamic' practices could take on many different forms: the failure to observe holidays or to go to mass or confession; the use of Arab names in addition to the Christian names given at baptism; the refusal to have representations of saints in their homes; the refusal to drink wine or eat pork; the habit of regularly washing (an indication that one might prepare for Islamic prayer). And if the evidence was insufficient, confessions were extracted by means of torture.*
> *(Berger, 2014, p. 126)*

Edicts were promulgated prohibiting the Arabic language, traditional clothing, amulets, and jewels, the practice of circumcision, ritual slaughtering, and Islamic marriage, as well as Zambra dancing and singing. All the public baths were destroyed. Moriscos were obliged to leave their front doors open and women had to unveil (Berger, 2014, p. 127). Throughout the century, while a few Moriscos became sincere converts to Catholicism, the vast majority continued practising Islam. After much debate within the Spanish church about how best to eradicate Islam from these Morisco communities, they were finally expelled from Spanish soils in 1609 and 1614; this meant the final eradication of Muslims and Jews from the Iberian Peninsula.

Expulsion, however, did not succeed in solving the problem of the *conversos* altogether, and for centuries to come the inquisition would continue its activities in Castile, Aragon, and their direct dependencies, concerning itself principally with the problem of Judaizing *conversos* and with monitoring the documentation of an applicant's pure bloodline that was needed to obtain certain hierarchical positions. In time, the idea of 'blood purity extended beyond its initial life as a legal mechanism and grew into a full-fledged culture-wide preoccupation' (Burk, 2010, p. 13) and this blood-fixated culture would be exported to the Americas. Only missionaries and *conquistadores* of pure blood would be allowed to travel to the Americas to acquire land and settle down (Fredrickson, 2002, p. 33). Thus the racialized understanding of religious identity became part of the Spanish colonizing project.

6 The Religio-racial Project of the Spanish Catholic Monarchy: An Exceptional Case?

The religio-racial project of the Spanish Catholic monarchy based on the naturalization of religious difference in terms of physiological/biological difference (blood) is often projected as exceptional and as a radical break with the past. Approaching this history through the lens of religionization, I would rather emphasize both its continuity and its novelty. First of all, let us look at continuity.

In terms of continuity, the ideal of the *Corpus Christianum*, which took a central place in the way European medieval Christians imagined their society, is key. This ideal projects religious difference, understood as deviation from Christian faith, as an insult to God and a threat to the socio-political order. The idea of the non-Christian as an enemy of Christian faith and a potential enemy of the state had already been made explicit in the *Theodosian Code (pax Romana, pax Dei)*. It became more prominent during the late Middle Ages when more active policies were put in place to protect the Christian body against internal and external threats. Christian society became a persecuting society.

Furthermore, in the Christian medieval imagination, body, mind, and soul were interconnected, and physiological and spiritual differences intersected. From this perspective, it made perfect sense that the risk of societal disintegration was charted onto non-Christian bodies. The problem of haemorrhaging – from which Jews suffered – is a case in point. Christians, conversely, by partaking in the sacrament of the Eucharist, were integrated into Christ's redemptive body and form one blood community. Christ's body and blood heal and make whole, whereas non-Christian bodies bring harm. Jewish and Muslim bodies furthermore were portrayed as black, disfigured, and sometimes they even smelled. All of this signified their distorted relation to God. Christian piety in contrast translated into white, perfect, and beautiful bodies.

Then there was the idea of transgenerational collective guilt projected onto the Jews, which Augustine elaborated on. This form of ethnoreligious reasoning suggests that merely by being born, Jews were already guilty. Generation after generation, they carry the burden for having killed Christ; they are marked by Cain's curse. To be Jewish is to be guilty. Centuries of religionized stereotyping, linking Jewish identity to certain moral attributes, only added to the idea that there is something wrong with Jews as Jews: they are untrustworthy, greedy, stubborn, and so forth. It is hereditary and it is in their nature; it runs in their blood.

Beyond ideas that were part of the Christian European cultural archives, the Spanish project of nation building could also build on a wide range of ecclesial governmental tools to cure the *Corpus Christianum* from the sickness of heresy (Terpstra, 2015, p. 21). Epiphanius' *Panarion*, had already projected orthodoxy as the best medicine for the sickness of heresy, but during the late Middle Ages European Christians began to actively protect the pure Christian body against threats – whether those threats came from within, namely heretics rejecting Catholic doctrine or Jews rejecting Christ as Son of God, or from without, that is the Saracens aiming to take over dominion. Various laws were in place to ensure that Christian and non-Christian bodies would not mix and, where necessary, the latter could be traced, contained, or even expelled.

What is new at this time, however, is the essentialization of religious difference in an unchangeable, natural, and 'stable' biological difference, at least for three generations. Up to now, any natural traits that were associated with religious difference 'were by no means rendered immutable' (Martinez, 2008, p. 48). The blurring of 'biology or physiology' and spirituality did not preclude change. If heretics, Jews, or Moors converted, their bodies would likewise transform: the colour of their skin whitens, their faces turn beautiful, and their disfigurement is overcome; such was the power of being part of Christ's body, such was the power of the sacraments of baptism and the Eucharist. However, in the context of Spanish nation building, where being Spanish implies being Catholic and vice versa, a further essentialization of the nature of Christian/non-Christian bodies occurs: religious difference translates into 'innate, indelible, and unchangeable' body properties and

134 CHAPTER 4 The Spanish Catholic Monarchy

character traits (Fredrickson, 2002, p. 5). One of the consequences is that a Jew may never become a true Christian, even after baptism. Their salvific potential is turned into a question (Jennings, 2010, p. 35). Whereas previously the concern may have been that Jews might incite or inspire or lure Christians into leaving their tradition (even though this was always more an imagined concern than a real one) now a fear of contamination is projected revolving around Jewish nature being essentially different. Even baptism could not alter this. This explains the fixation on genealogical investigation in order to ascertain that a person's parents and grandparents had all been old Christians. The essentialization/naturalization of the 'religious' other reached a new level in the Spanish project of nation building; that is why we speak about religio-racialization.

This also had implications for Christian self-understanding: the sacramental power of the church – especially the transformative power of baptism and Eucharist – to make Christians, to redeem, whiten, and heal bodies, is undermined by the pure blood laws. Physiological identity markers (here blood purity) were now essentialized, and this undermined the 'principled Pauline equality' of the Christian community – 'there will be no more Jew nor Greek, no more slave nor free, no more male nor female; for all of you are one in Christ Jesus'. Against this background, Gil Anidjar states that 'the true "New Christians" [*cristianos nuevos*]' were not the Jewish and Muslim converts, but 'the old Christians', who now understood themselves in a novel way, that is as belonging to 'a community of blood, of pure [*lindos*] blood, a community brought together by the bonds of blood that would come to define kinship and group identity, as well as citizenship [...]' (Anidjar, 2014, p. 170).

In time, the religio-racialized social hierarchy as developed in the Spanish Catholic Monarchy travelled to the colonies where Spanish policies on emigration to the Americas, bureaucratic requirements, and the inquisition's investigative mechanisms 'all contributed to the spread and reproduction of the discourse of *limpieza de sangre* in the Hispanic Atlantic world' (Martinez, 2008, p. 267). Discussions about the nature of both the natives and African slaves likewise came to be framed in terms of their potential for religion and salvation, namely their potential to embrace and be transformed by Christian faith. 'Old World Iberian Christians' prejudices against Jews and Muslims served as a blueprint for Europeans' racialization of Native Americans and Africans in the New World' (Delgado & Moss, 2018, p. 40).

7 Columbus, New Worlds, and the Question of Religion

We have already seen how the notion of Christianity as the sole true religion became entangled in violent exclusionary political projects like the crusades, the *Reconquista,* and the process of nation building as exemplified in Castile and Aragon (Daggers, 2010, p. 965). In 1492, the same year as the expulsion of the Jews, this Catholic monarchy pioneers a new part of the European colonial project. This date marks the beginning of a violent era of foreign explorations, discoveries, and colonization, first of the Azores, the Americas, and then of South and East Asia and Southern Africa (Stroumsa, 2010, pp. 15–16). When the era of colonization began, a fourfold religionized map of the world distinguishing Christians from Jews, Muslims, and pagans was in place. Columbus sailed to the 'Indies' with this *imago mundi* in mind, as is made clear in his diary, where he addresses the Catholic monarchs who sponsored his journey, Ferdinand and Isabella. The people he encountered, however, did not fit in with this *imago mundi*. The question of who these people were, what qualities and capacities they have (and whether they had souls to begin with), would occupy the minds of many in the years that followed.

In the opening pages of his journal, Columbus describes how the Spanish king and queen, the 'enemies of all idolatries', having conquered the Moors and expelled the Jews, gave him orders to go to India to propagate the holy Catholic Christian faith, and how in India the people had been waiting for the Christian faith eager to convert. In fact, in the passage below, Columbus connects his journey with the repeated request from the Grand Khan to be instructed in Christian religion. Columbus rhetorically links all these events together: the reconquest of Granada, the expulsion of the Jews, and his missionary journey to India, commissioned by the kings of this emerging nation that went by the motto: one king – one faith – one law.

> *Because, O most Christian, and very high, very excellent and puissant Princes, King and Queen of the Spains and islands of the Sea, our Lords, in this present year of 1492, after your Highnesses has given an end to the war with the Moors who reigned in Europe, and had finished it in the very great city of Granada, where in this present year, and on the second day of the month of January, by force of arms, I saw the royal banners of your Highnesses placed on the towers of Alfambra, which is the fortress of that city, and I saw the Moorish King come forth from the gates of the city and kiss the royal hands of your Highnesses, and of the Prince my Lord, and presently in that same month, acting on the information that I had given to your Highnesses touching the lands of India, and respecting a Prince who is called Gran Can, which means in our language King of Kings, how he and his ancestors had sent to Rome many times to ask for learned men of our holy faith to teach him, and how the Holy Father had never complied, inasmuch that many people believing in idolatries where lost by receiving doctrine of perdition. Your Highnesses, as Catholic Christians and Princes who love the holy Christian faith, and the propagation of it, and who are enemies of the sect of Mahoma and to all idolatries and heresies, resolved to send me, Cristobal Colon, to the said parts of India to see the said princes, and the cities and lands, and their disposition, with a view that they might be converted to our holy faith. [...].*
>
> *Thus, after having turned out all the Jews from all your kingdoms and lordships, in the same month of January, your Highnesses gave orders to me, that with a sufficient fleet I should go to the said parts of India. (Columbus, ed. and trans. Markham, 1893, pp. 15–16)*

Later in his journal (26 December), Columbus would express his hope of bringing home barrels of gold to cover the costs of the final conquest of Jerusalem. Again, he links his pursuit of wealth to a missionary zeal and the ideology of the crusades (Ward, 2003, p. 36). His quest for India and its resources was also a quest for Jerusalem.

First Encounters

Columbus' first reaction when he set foot on land at the island of Guanahani, and encountered the people who lived there, would 'set the tone for the manner in which Europeans from many nations would regard the indigenous people they met' (Beebe & Senkewicz, 2015, p. 5). At the same time however, his reaction and the way he interpreted what he saw was inspired by a wide range of existing and familiar Christian, theological, biblical, and ethnogeographic ideas. Relating the unfamiliar with what he already knew, Columbus tried to make sense of this whole new world and the people he encountered did not fit into the more common map of heretics, Jews, Muslims (Moors), and pagans.

Upon his arrival, on 12 October 1492, Columbus notices that these people, the Arawak people, walked naked, without shame, and were in fact 'very well made, with very handsome bodies and very good countenances'. He observes that they wear their hair long, paint their faces and bodies and are fair skinned, 'neither black nor white'. Their hair is 'not curly but loose, and coarse like horse hair'. On 6 November, he again notices that they were not very black, even less so than the Canarians, and in the same sentence, he links the colour of their skin to their character: they are perfectly respectful.

136 CHAPTER 4 The Spanish Catholic Monarchy

On several occasions, Columbus mentions that they carry no weapons. As the days pass, he continues to write down his observations, noticing that they have beautiful eyes, long legs, and are overall well-formed, but 'simple minded'. Later he would remark that they not only carried no weapons, but also did not know governmental structures, private property, or laws. They did not have a money system and would trade anything they owned. He seems to perceive them as savages (a word which derives from *silva*, meaning forest) placing them in nature as opposed to civilization and culture, 'living in the wild, outside the bonds of communication and the responsibilities of human society' (Brickman, 2018, p. 18) or as primitives, living in a paradise-like environment, innocent and uncorrupted by sin. They seem not to know shame. The nudity of the inhabitants might be understood as a sign that they lived in some kind of prelapsarian state. It may be that Columbus was thinking of the first human couple, Adam and Eve, who lived naked, in their idyllic garden of Eden. It is also possible that their nudity meant that they were uncivilized.

In any case, Columbus (still with his royal sponsors in mind) judges that because their nature is gentle, sweet, and kind 'they would make good servants'. The 'Indians' appear intelligent to Columbus, as he sees them to be absorbing everything he says. He believed, therefore, that they would readily become Christians (11 October, 16 October, 6 November). The image that emerges is that of innocent children living in nature and 'receptive to tutelage in civilization and Christianity' (Fredrickson, 2002, p. 36). Columbus immediately added, however, that with 50 people he could easily subjugate them (14 October). One example in this regard is the diary entry for 16 December, where Columbus almost lyrically describes the land as 'the best words can describe'. It is cool and fertile. There are luxuriant trees, and valleys and rivers (compared to Spain, which was rather dry, this clearly made a positive impression). In this setting, he again describes the people as having no weapons, going naked, and as being so timid that 'a thousand would not stand before three of our men. So that they are good to be ordered about, to work and sow and do all that may be necessary to build towns, and they should be taught to go about clothed and to adopt our customs'. Later on in his journey, however, he would encounter other islanders, who were hostile and 'were written off as "cannibals"' and who therefore had to be 'subdued by force or exterminated' (Fredrickson, 2002, p. 36). Clearly, Columbus, and later other explorers, traders, and settlers who followed this lead, contributed to the creation of the distinction between the noble savage, who had 'the natural goodness of the uncivilized' and who 'lived in innocence and peacefulness, without want, conflict, property or laws', and the wild savage, who is more bestial. The emerging identity of the 'Indian', whether noble or savage, is as imaginary as that of the pagan, the Saracen, or the Jew. It is one more hermeneutical figure that only exists in the Christian European imagination and does not do justice, nor intend to do so, to 'heterogeneous identities that existed in the Americas before the arrival of the Europeans' (Grosfoguel, 2013, p. 82). Any understanding of complex societies, political organizations, social hierarchies, trading systems, ceremonies, and rituals, unique communication means, ... is forgotten or obliterated. This imaginary construct better serves the expansionary and missionary interests of Christian Europeans.

No Religion

Historically, Christian understanding of religious normativity played a central part in the way people were named, classified, essentialized, and governed. From this perspective, the question of what Columbus thought about these people in terms of their 'religion' is relevant to the question of how he perceived and depicted them and what his attitude towards them should be. Several scholars have focused their attention on various diary entrances, where Columbus states 'I do not detect in them any *secta y crea*'.

Exemplary in this regard are the diary entries on 10 October 1492:

> *I believe that they would easily be made Christians, as it appeared to me that they had no religion [*que ninguna secta tenían*]. (Columbus, ed. and trans. Markham, 1893, p. 38)*

Columbus, New Worlds, and the Question of Religion **137**

and 12 November 1492:

*The Admiral says that, on the previous Sunday, the 11th of November, it seemed
good to take some persons from amongst those at Rio de Mares, to bring to the
Sovereigns, that they might learn our language, so as to be able to tell us what there
is in their lands. Returning, they would be the mouthpieces of the Christians, and
would adopt our customs and the things of the faith. I saw and knew (says the
Admiral) that these people are without any religion, not idolaters [no secta ninguna
ni son idólatras], but very gentle, not knowing what is evil, nor the sins of murder
and theft, being without arms, and so timid that a hundred would fly before one
Spaniard, although they joke with them. They, however, believe and know that there
is a God in heaven, and say that we have come from heaven. At any prayer that
we say, they repeat, and make the sign of the cross. Thus your Highnesses should
resolve to make them Christians, for I believe that, if the work was begun, in a little
time a multitude of nations would be converted to our faith, with the acquisition of
great lordships, peoples, and riches for Spain. (Columbus, ed. and trans. Markham,
1893, p. 73)*

On 27 November 1492, Columbus writes again that it will be easy to convert the Indians
to Christianity because *ellos no tienen secta ninguna ni son idolatras.*

An interesting scholarly discussion has unfolded regarding these passages and how to
understand them. Clearly, to Columbus' mind, these people were neither Christians nor
Jews nor Muslims. Columbus, however, does not seem to regard them as pagan idolaters
(*idolatras*), since they do not appear to worship idols. Neither are they heretics, namely
those who worship God in deviant ways (*secta*). But what are they? The very fact that we,
together with Columbus, are asking the question shows that these natives fell outside of
the 'religious categories' of the fourfold map of the world. They presented something of a
mystery, bursting open the familiar classifications (Stroumsa, 2010).

Several scholars have translated the phrase *secta y crea* as 'they had no religion'.
This translation implies that not only were these people neither heretics nor pagans (nor
Christians), but also that Columbus saw them as falling outside of the realm of 'natural
religion'. Remember that from a classical Christian theological perspective, despite the
dehumanization and demonization of Christianity's others, *religio* tended to be considered
universal, transcultural, and transhistorical and that even idolaters had an innate and natural
sense of the divine, however undeveloped or corrupted (logic of encompassment). The early
church fathers already spoke about the *testimonium animae naturaliter Christianae*. While
emphasizing the discontinuity between *vera religio* and *superstitio* (or *falsa religio*), they also
saw a certain continuity (Nongbri, 2013, p. 87).

If we translate, as many have done, the passages that speak of *secta y crea* as stating that
these people had no religion, this would amount to saying that they had no soul and were
not human. According to Nelson Maldonado-Torres this is indeed the way we should read
this passage:

*To refer to the indigenous as subjects without religion removes them from the
category of the human. Religion is universal among humans, but the alleged lack of
it among natives is not initially taken to indicate the falseness of this statement, but
rather the opposite: that there exist subjects in the world who are not fully human
[...] Columbus' assertion about the lack of religion in indigenous people introduces
an anthropological meaning to the term. In light of what we have seen here, it is
necessary to add that this anthropological meaning is also linked to a very modern
method of classifying humans: racial classification. With a single stroke, Columbus
took the discourse on religion from the theological realm into a modern philosophical
anthropology that distinguishes between different degrees of humanity through
identities fixed into what would later be called races. (Maldonado-Torres, 2014,
pp. 641 and 658)*

138 CHAPTER 4 The Spanish Catholic Monarchy

> **Text Box 6: The Notion of *Secta***
>
> The notion of *secta* or *sectatores* referred to organized heresies, with places of worship, priests, rituals and ceremonies. Despite all the negative connotations projected onto these sects, they were also seen as a sign of civilization. The absence of sects was the sign of a lack of civilization (Johnson, 2006, p. 601).

This is indeed the way Columbus' remarks have been received, namely as saying that the Amerindians were subhuman, and these remarks have been deployed to legitimate various forms of oppression. David Chidester discussing the colonial project in the African continent notices how European Christian colonizers, upon their arrival, time and again stated that the 'natives' had no religion, thereby casting doubt on their human nature (Chidester, 1996). The binary religion/no religion played a key part in the construction of asymmetrical power relations in colonial contact zones. That being said, I am not convinced that one should understand this Columbian passage as saying that these people had 'no religion' and therefore no soul. There are several reasons for my hesitation.

First, although Columbus states that these people have no precise conceptualization of the divine, they do seem to think that Columbus and his companions came from heaven. He interprets their behaviour as giving thanks to God. He continues to claim that they have some notion of God and are eager to learn about Christianity. Moreover, it makes more sense to read Columbus' claim that they had no *secta y crea* as a positive judgement: because they are not influenced by *sectas de perdición*, like the Jews and Muslims, and are not idolaters either, they would not have to be convinced about the wrongness of their ideas and practices and would be – as Columbus admits – 'more open to the idea of conversion to Christianity than either Muslims or Jews, who belonged to *sectas de perdición*'. I think it makes more sense to argue, like Graham Ward does, that these people, in Columbus' imagination 'stood prior to idolatry, representing some kind of "natural religion": a state of innocence, *tabula rasa*, unused pieces of wax naturally prepared for receiving the impress of "custom" and "matters of the Faith"' (Ward, 2003, p. 41).

> **Text Box 7: Columbus' Physiognomic Description of the People He Encounters**
>
> Columbus' descriptions of the Amerindians and of these newly discovered territories are interest driven; he is conveying the message to the Spanish sovereigns that there is much of value to be found here (even though he has not yet discovered any gold) and that the Amerindians would be easily Christianized and subdued. Columbus is not merely engaged in description, but also in redescription. It should not be forgotten that Columbus at the time still thinks he is in India, and he depicts the people he comes across as fitting in with that assumption, namely as Asian. To that end, he seems to make use of the semiotics of physiognomy, according to which the form of the body – colour of skin, hair texture, bodily proportions, eyes, facial expressions – is expressive of inner character, all that matters in this symbolic realm. Bodily parts mirror moral dispositions and reflect group characteristics: they are timid, generous, no sense of possession, ... Their coarse hair tells us they are savages, their nudity relates their innocence (they are like children) and possibly sexual drift. Their beautiful eyes and well-shaped faces speak of their intelligence. The fact that they feel no shame for being naked would later raise the question of whether or not they were participants in Adam's sin and whether or not they carried the burden of it. In trying to make sense of the people he encounters, Columbus is making small forays into comparative physiognomy, comparing the bodies of the Amerindians (the colour of the Canarians) to black and white bodies, the latter being a sign of civilization and refinement, the former more associated with negative character traits and, increasingly, with the incapability of salvation (Jennings, 2010, p. 34).

While Columbus may not have removed the indigenous people from the category of the human, his descriptions of them, of their habitat, appearance, lack of organization, and their lack of *secta y crea*, show that he did regard them as inferior, placing them on a lower level than Christians. They are subhuman and incapable of running their own land, unable to value gold, and incapable of protecting themselves. In fact, Columbus already considered them 'subjects to the Spanish Crown' and potential 'Christians' (cf. one king – one faith – one law). This judgement paved the way for their brutal treatment as well as for their dispossession. On 4 May 1493, the papal bull *Inter Caetera* launched the doctrine of discovery, granting the Spanish Crown ownership of this newly discovered world, its inhabitants, land, and resources. This 'discovered' land was regarded as *terra nullius*: no man's land. Not much later, on 4 May 1493, on Columbus' return, Pope Alexander VI issued a papal bull granting ownership of the newly discovered territories to Ferdinand and Isabella and calls upon them to convert its inhabitants:

> We of our own motion, and not at your solicitation, do give, concede, and assign for ever to you and your successors, all the islands, and main lands, discovered; and which may hereafter, be discovered, towards the west and south; whether they be situated towards India, or towards any other part whatsoever, and give you absolute power in them. (Quoted in Southey, 1968, p. 22)

Text Box 8: A Religionized Map of the World

Jew	Saracen/Moor	Savage
Lost land as a divine curse	Occupied lands that formerly belonged to Christians or that had been promised to Christians	No land
Displaced from Jerusalem		No socio-political organization, no economic system, no legal system, no '*secta y crea*'
Covenantal promise of the land revoked as the first covenant had been abrogated	This legitimizes crusades and reconquest	
The promise of the holy land has passed on to Christians		This is *terra nullius* or *vacuum domicilium* (land belonging to no one, waiting to be made useful)
The Jew is doomed to wander, finding no place to settle down, remaining a permanent political stranger in Christian lands		Doctrine of discovery
Dispersed and scattered		
Belong nowhere, while they may be found everywhere		

---

8 Conclusion: Blurring Boundaries between Racialization and Religionization

Throughout history and in a range of periods and settings, Christian normalcy has been a key factor in the process of social stratification. Social groups were categorized and ranked in a hierarchy based on how people were imagined to position themselves vis-à-vis Christian normativity. What we are dealing with is not simply prejudice, but institutionalized prejudice with concrete material consequences for the people involved. Throughout this book, I call this religionization: the naming, categorization, stratification, essentialization, and governance of people predicated on religious difference. The outcome is inequality. In this chapter, and building on the previous chapter, I explored how the fixation on protecting the pure *Corpus Christianum* against the threats coming from impure 'others' played out in the context of the *Reconquista* and Spanish nation building. This history is particularly important because it brings to the surface the intersection of religionization and racialization and counters a common contemporary assumption that religion is fundamentally different from race.

Often race and religion are seen as two utterly different and even separate categories. Religion, so this line of reasoning goes, revolves around beliefs, transferred via tradition and celebrated in the community. It is a matter of the interior, spiritual life expressed in various ritual, legal, and ethical practices. The particular tradition one adheres to is a personal choice: it is something that one may change if, for whatever reason, one becomes inspired by another way of life. It is something that may be altered. Race, on the other hand, supposedly refers to certain external visible and inherited features, which one cannot change. Race belongs to the visible, rather than the invisible realm; it refers to the involuntary (colour, ethnic features, etc.) in contrast to the voluntary; and it implicates those features that cannot be changed. Race, as a category, refers to what one is, not to what one believes and does.

Building on this distinction, the understanding is that patterns of religionization and racialization are also qualitatively different: the first is discrimination based on what a person believes and practices; the second is discrimination based on what a person is. One example of this line of reasoning is the distinction that is often made between anti-Judaism and antisemitism, a distinction we will deal with in later chapters.

While I agree it makes sense to distinguish between religionization and racialization, what I have tried to show here is that the categories of race and religion are twinned concepts (Nye, 2019): historically they have largely overlapped and both have functioned as important ways in which to classify, hierarchize, and govern people. In my understanding, the distinction between racialization and religionization is relative rather than absolute, and where '"race" ends and "religion" begins' is not always that clear (Nye, 2019, p. 231).

To begin with, both religion and race have functioned and continue to function as imaginative categories which construct difference in an essentialized way, and both have been pivotal in stigmatizing and discriminating against people based on their (assumed) adherence to a group. Both race and religion are imagined social constructs (Nye, 2019, p. 214), which feed on a wide variety of narratives and symbols that have become sedimented in our cultural archive. Symbols that derive from a theological/biblical framework and feed patterns of religionization may at another stage be recycled in patterns of racialization. Both have been expressed in practices, laws, institutions, and structures which validate and naturalize the normative distinction between legitimate and illegitimate difference (laws and governmental institutions help shape worlds). Both have been pivotal to naming, classifying, and essentializing social groups as fundamentally and absolutely different. Both do the work of establishing a hierarchical order in which the licence to exert power by one group over another is distributed unequally.

Furthermore, the well-known claim that race is a modern, pseudo-scientific invention, while patterns of religionization are theological, not only makes religionization less serious, but also tends to make patterns of religionization 'irrelevant' for understanding 'modern race' (Westerduin, 2020). This separation between religion and race ignores not only how, historically, patterns of religionization have functioned in similar ways to patterns of racialization, but also how patterns of racialization in fact feed on patterns of religionization while also adapting them to new needs.

The category of race is intimately tied up with Christian theological language. Recall in this regard how, starting from the thirteenth century, a fixation on blood purity emerges; a fixation that needs to be understood against the background of Christian theologies about the redemptive nature of sacrifice, the eucharistic liturgy with its doctrine of transubstantiation and the medieval understanding of the church in terms of a pure and mystical body that has to be protected against contamination. We also looked at how Jewish and Islamic bodies were perceived as disfigured, disintegrated, sick, and polluting, while Christian bodies were considered whole, pure, and purged. This distinction served theo-political interests; the blessed Christian body needs to be protected against a projected cursed internal *Fremdkörper* (the Jews), and against a threat coming from elsewhere (the Saracens). The doctrines of pure blood, which emerged in early modern Spain in the fifteenth century, build on these patterns of religionization and take them in a new direction by essentializing the impure nature of the Jew, until it becomes immutable and hereditary (Hoyt, 2016, p. 39). A converted Jew would still be a Jew, his nature unchanged by baptism. The doctrines of pure blood, which functioned against the background of Spanish nation formation 'align[ed] religion to ancestry, foreignness and political disloyalty to the state and the church' (Westerduin, 2020, p. 140). This is when religious difference (religionization) transforms into immutable biological difference (racialization). But again, one should not understand this difference between religionization and racialization in terms of a historical rupture. The much older idea that Jews were collectively and intergenerationally guilty of the murder of Christ and that they were a sinful group of people, stubborn, arrogant, greedy, and so on is really not that far removed from these later patterns of 'biological' racialization.

The idea that race is about external features and religion about internal beliefs ignores the way in which, in the medieval mindset, external features were deemed to express an inner character. Inner and outer mirrored each other. Dark skin expressed sinfulness; white was the colour of innocence. External visible features were heavily charged with symbolic meaning. Sometimes external features which were invented to symbolically express a certain characteristic of otherness that made sense in a particular theological framework (e.g. the hooked nose, an imagined feature of the Jews expressing 'voraciousness, arrogance, and wantonness'), later became an assumed feature of the Semite, but was still charged with a similar meaning.

This brings me to my next point, namely that both religionization and racialization are processes of the imagination: both the religionized and the racialized person is a hermeneutical figure that exists only in the eye of the beholder. In addition, how the other is imagined depends to a large extent on how the identity of self is imagined. Selfing and othering are co-constitutive processes and the formation of identity feeds on the construction of alterity. This also means that both patterns of religionization and of racialization are interest driven and context-dependent, and that who counts as other, and what characteristics are ascribed to him/her are part of this imaginative process. Religious differences and racial differences are not fixed and bounded, but malleable and adaptable.

I have one final remark. Focusing on how racialization is a modern phenomenon that is connected to state formation (cf. early modern Spain) may lead one to conclude, erroneously, that patterns of racialization gradually replaced patterns of religionization. This assumes that when religion (contrary to race) was finally recognized for what it 'essentially is' – a personal affair (choice), that pertains to the interior, spiritual realm – race began to do the work previously done by religion. As I will show in the next chapters, this is a problematic assumption, for the understanding of religion as personalized, interiorized, and spiritualized is also a historical-cultural construct. It served certain socio-political interests and it was matched with changed spiritual sensitivities. In fact, I will argue that interiorization introduces us to yet one more chapter in the history of religionization and continues, albeit in novel ways, the work of delegitimizing certain people who do not fit in with this normative, personalized understanding of religion.

Notes

[1] Until recently, scholarly consensus stated that nation building was a modern project ushered in by the Enlightenment or even earlier by the Protestant Reformation. Medievalists have begun to question this periodization, pointing at the discourse around medieval nationalism for example in England and Spain. See Hastings (1997) and Heng (2003).

[2] In her book, Geraldine Heng (2018) explores medieval England as a case in point.

[3] 'Islamic law obligates Muslim authorities to abstain from acts of hostility toward *dhimmīs*, to accord them various rights, and to protect them from attack by Muslims or foreigners. It further grants to *dhimmīs*, including the slaves and wives of Muslim masters, the right to freely exercise their religion in private. *Dhimmīs*, in turn, must acknowledge their subservience to Muslim authorities and adhere to Islamic laws governing *dhimmīs*. Non-Muslims who refuse to accept these terms or who renege on their commitments forfeit the right to live as non-Muslims in the lands of Islam' (Freidenreich, 2009, p. 102).

[4] Mudéjar is a name given to Muslims who remained during and after the *Reconquista*; meaning subjugated.

[5] François Soyer mentions that 'While the cults of other ritual murder saints like Simon of Trent and Anderl von Rinn have been officially suppressed by the church in the wake of the Second Vatican Council, the cult of Dominguito de Val endures in Spain alongside that of another child martyr in neighboring Castile: the Holy Child of La Guardia' (Soyer, 2021, p. 168).

[6] In his *Las Siete Partidas*, King Alfonso X, ruled that the Jews were not to make medicines for Christian patients; medicines were to be made by Christians, who could nevertheless follow the instructions of Jewish doctors. In 1322, the Council of Valladolid decided that Christians could visit neither a Jewish nor a Muslim doctor: 'no Christian shall take any medicine [...] made by a Jew; but he can take it by the advice of some wise person, only where it is made by a Christian' (7.24.8).

[7] Exemplary in this regard is 'one of the early thirteenth-century pier capitals of the cloister of the Cathedral of Tarragona' which 'depicts the legend of Saint Nicholas punishing a Christian who had deceitfully sworn an oath in the Saint's name to a Jewish moneylender' (Soyer, 2019, p. 234).

[8] Etymologically the notion of *limpieza* stems from the Latin *limpidus*, meaning clear, bright. '*LIMPIO. Viene del nombre latino, no muy usado, limpidus, da, dum, por cosa limpia, no tiene suciedad, mancha ni mota ni otra cosa que lo afee o turbe. Mujer limpia, mujer aseada [...] Limpio se dize comúnamente el hombre cristiano viejo, sin raza de moro ni judío*' 'Cleansed. It comes from the Latin name, not widely used, *limpidus, da, dum*, for a clean thing, it has no dirt, stain or speck or anything else that makes it ugly or cloudy. A clean woman, a neat woman [...] Clean is commonly called the old Christian man, without the race of Moor or Jew' (Sebastián de Covarrubias Orozco, quoted and translated in Burk, 2010, pp. 98–99).

[9] In the sixteenth century this became standard procedure.

References

Almond, I. (2009). *Two Faiths, One Banner: When Muslims Marched with Christians across Europe's Battlegrounds*. Tauris.

Anderson, B. (2006). *Imagined Communities: Reflections on the Origin and Spread of Nationalism* (Rev. ed. [with a new afterword]). Verso.

Anidjar, G. (2014). *Blood: A Critique of Christianity*. Columbia University Press.

Beebe, R. M., & Senkewicz, R. M. (2015). *Lands of Promise and Despair: Chronicles of Early California, 1535–1846*. University of Oklahoma Press.

Berger, M. S. (2014). *A Brief History of Islam in Europe: Thirteen Centuries of Creed, Conflict and Co-existence*. Leiden University Press.

Berger, M. S. (2022). History of Islam in Europe, podcast, episode 3, Living together. Retrieved from https://open.spotify.com/show/1SXaa6hjR2bT8hQ5pun1d1

Brickman, C. (2018). *Race in Psychoanalysis: Aboriginal Populations in the Mind*. Routledge.

Bueno Sánchez, M. (2022). Rituals of Victory: The Role of Liturgy in the Consecration of Mosques in the Castilian Expansion over Islam from Eleventh to Thirteenth Centuries. *Religions*, *13*(5), Article 379. https://doi.org/10.3390/rel13050379

Burk, R. L. (2010). Salus Erat in Sanguine: Limpieza De Sangre and Other Discourses of Blood in Early Modern Spain. Diss. University of Pennsylvania.

Burns, R. I. (2002). Jews and Moors in the Siete Partidas of Alfonso X the Learned: A Background Perspective. In R. Collins & A. Goodman (Eds.), *Medieval Spain: Culture, Conflict and Coexistence. Studies in Honour of Angus MacKay* (pp. 46–62). Palgrave Macmillan.

Castillo, A. E. (2017). Constructing Race: The Catholic Church and the Evolution of Racial Categories and Gender in Colonial Mexico, 1521–1700. Diss. University of Houston.

Chidester, D. (1996). *Savage System: Colonialism and Comparative Religion in Southern Africa*. University of Virginia Press.

Christopher Columbus (Ed. and trans. C. R. Markham) (1893). Journal of the First Voyage of Columbus. In *Journal of Christopher Columbus (during His First Voyage, 1492–93), and Documents Relating to the Voyages of John Cabot and Gaspar Corte Real* (pp. 15–193). Hakluyt Society.

Cohen, M. A. (1964). Reflections on the Text and Context of the Disputation of Barcelona. *Hebrew Union College Annual, 35,* 157–192.

Cowans, J. (2003). *Early Modern Spain: A Documentary History.* University of Pennsylvania Press.

Daggers, J. (2010). Thinking 'Religion': The Christian Past and Interreligious Future of Religious Studies and Theology. *Journal of the American Academy of Religion, 78*(4), 961–990.

Deagan, K. A. (2001). Dynamics of Imperial Adjustment in Spanish America: Ideology and Social Integration. In S. E. Alcock, T. N. D'Altroy, K. D. Morrison, & C. M. Sinopoli (Eds.), *Empires: Perspectives from Archaeology and History* (pp. 179–194). Cambridge University Press.

Delgado, J. L., & Moss, K. C. (2018). Religion and Race in the Early Modern Iberian Atlantic. In P. Harvey & K. Gin Lum (Eds.), *The Oxford Handbook of Religion and Race in American History* (pp. 40–60). Oxford University Press.

Devereux, A. (2006). Royal Genealogy and the Gothic Thesis in Medieval Iberian Historiography. *Foundations 2*(1), 3–26.

Durán Gudiol, A. (Ed.) (1965). *Colección diplomática de la Catedral de Huesca 1 (CSIC. Fuentes para la historia del Pirineo 5: Escuela de estudios medievales. Textos 34.* Publicaciones de la Sección de Zaragoza 10. Escuela de estudios medievales.

Fredrickson, G. M. (2002). *Racism: A Short History.* Princeton University Press.

Freidenreich, D. M. (2009). Christians in Early and Classical Sunnī Law. In D. Thomas & B. Roggema (Eds.), *Christian-Muslim Relations: A Bibliographical History, Volume 1 (600–900),* The History of Christian-Muslim Relations 11 (pp. 99–115). Brill.

Friedman, J. (1987). Jewish Conversion, the Spanish Pure Blood Laws and Reformation: A Revisionist View of Racial and Religious Antisemitism. *The Sixteenth Century Journal 18,* 3–30.

Furtado, R. (2012). Isidore's Histories in the Mozarabic Scholarship of the Eighth and Early Ninth Centuries. In P. Farmhouse Alberto & D. Paniagua (Eds.), *Ways of Approaching Knowledge in Late Antiquity and the Early Middle Ages: Schools and Scholarship,* Studia Classica et Mediaevalia 8 (pp. 264–287). Traugott Bautz.

Gebke, J. (2020). *(Foreign) Bodies: Stigmatizing New Christians in Early Modern Spain.* Verlag der Österreichischen Akademie der Wissenschaften.

Grosfoguel, R. (2013). The Structure of Knowledge in Westernized Universities: Epistemic Racism/Sexism and the Four Genocides/Epistemicides of the Long 16th Century. *Human Architecture: Journal of the Sociology of Self-Knowledge, 11,* 73–90.

Harris, J. A. (1997). Mosque to Church Conversions in the Spanish Reconquest. *Medieval Encounters, 3*(2), 158–172.

Hastings, A. (1997). *The Construction of Nationhood: Ethnicity, Religion, and Nationalism.* Cambridge University Press.

Helg, A. (2017). Slave But not Citizen: Free People of Color and Blood Purity in Colonial Spanish American Legislation. *Millars. Espai i Història, 42,* 75–99.

Heng, G. (2003). *Empire of Magic: Medieval Romance and the Politics of Cultural Fantasy.* Columbia University Press.

Heng, G. (2018). *The Invention of Race in the European Middle Ages.* Cambridge University Press.

Hering Torres, M. S. (2012). Purity of Blood: Problems of Interpretation. In M. S. Hering Torres, M. E. Martínez, & D. Nirenberg (Eds.), *Race and Blood in the Iberian World* (pp. 11–38). Lit.

Homza, L. A. (2006). *The Spanish Inquisition, 1478–1614: An Anthology of Sources.* Hackett.

Hoyt, C. A. (2016). *The Arc of a Bad Idea: Understanding and Transcending Race.* Oxford University Press.

Ingram, K. (2012). The Converso Phenomenon and the Issue of Spanish Identity. In M. J. Rozbicki & G. O. Ndege (Eds.), *Cross-Cultural History and the Domestication of Otherness* (pp. 15–38). Palgrave Macmillan.

Isidore of Seville (Trans. G. Donini, & G. B. Ford) (1966). *Isidore of Seville's History of the Kings of the Goths, Vandals, and Suevi.* Brill.

Jennings, W. J. (2010). *The Christian Imagination: Theology and the Origins of Race.* Yale University Press.

Johnson, C. L. (2006). Idolatrous Cultures and the Practice of Religion. *Journal of the History of Ideas, 67*(4), 597–621.

Johnson, P. J. (2010, 8 January). Tracing the Roots of Discrimination. *USC Dornsife: College of Letters, Arts and Sciences.* Retrieved from https://dornsife.usc.edu/news/stories/659/tracing-the-roots-of-discrimination/

Kroemer, J. (2012). Vanquish the Haughty and Spare the Subjected: A Study of Bernard of Clairvaux's Position on Muslims and Jews. *Medieval Encounters, 18*(1), 55–92.

144 CHAPTER 4 The Spanish Catholic Monarchy

Kroesen, J. E. A. (2008). From Mosques to Cathedrals: Converting Sacred Space during the Spanish Reconquest. *Mediaevistik*, *21*, 113–137.

Lapina, E., & Morton, N. (2017). *The Uses of the Bible in Crusader Sources*, Commentaria 7. Brill.

Maldonado-Torres, N. (2014). AAR Centennial Roundtable: Religion, Conquest, and Race in the Foundations of the Modern/Colonial World. *Journal of the American Academy of Religion*, *82*(3), 636–665.

Martín Gamero, A. (1862). *Historia de la ciudad de Toledo*. Imprenta de Severiano López Fando.

Martinez, M. E. (2008). *Genealogical Fictions: Limpieza de Sangre, Religion, and Gender in Colonial Mexico*. Stanford University Press.

Menjot, D. (2017). Taxation and Sovereignty in Medieval Castile. In Y.-G. Liang & J. Rodriguez (Eds.), *Authority and Spectacle in Medieval and Early Modern Europe: Essays in Honor of Teofilo F. Ruiz* (pp. 84–103). Routledge.

Moore, R. I. (2007). *The Formation of a Persecuting Society: Authority and Deviance in Western Europe, 950–1250* (2nd ed.). Blackwell.

Nirenberg, D. (2002). Mass Conversion and Genealogical Mentalities: Jews and Christians in Fifteenth-Century Spain. *Past & Present*, *174*, 3–41.

Nirenberg, D. (2008). Race and the Middle Ages: The Case of Spain and Its Jews. In M. R. Greer, W. D. Mignolo, & M. Quilligan (Eds.), *Rereading the Black Legend: The Discovery of Religious and Racial Difference in the Renaissance Empires* (pp. 71–87). University of Chicago Press.

Nirenberg, D. (2014a). *Anti-Judaism: The Western Tradition*. W. W. Norton & Co.

Nirenberg, D. (2014b). Was There Race before Modernity? The Example of 'Jewish' Blood in Late Medieval Spain. In Neighboring Faiths: Christianity, Islam, and Judaism in the Middle Ages and Today. University of Chicago Press, 2014. Chicago Scholarship Online, 2015. https://doi.org/10.7208/chicago/9780226169095.003.0009.

Nongbri, B. (2013). *Before Religion: A History of a Modern Concept*. Yale University Press.

Nye, M. (2019). Race and Religion: Postcolonial Formations of Power and Whiteness. *Method & Theory in the Study of Religion*, *31*(3), 210–237.

Rae, H. (2002). *State Identities and the Homogenisation of Peoples*. Cambridge University Press.

Remensnyder, A. (2016). The Entangling and Disentangling of Islam and Christianity in the Churches of Castile and Aragon (11th–16th Centuries). In D. Wolfram & C. Scholl (Eds.), *Transkulturelle Verflechtungsprozesse in der Vormoderne*, Das Mittelalter: Perspektiven mediävistischer Forschung. Beihefte 3 (pp. 123–140). De Gruyter.

Ricoeur, P. (2000). Fragile identité: respect de l'autre et identité culturelle. Paper Presented at the Congress of the Fédération Internationale de l'Action des Chrétiens pour l'Abolition de la Torture, Prague, October 2020.

Roth, N. (1976). The Jews and the Muslim Conquest of Spain. *Jewish Social Studies*, *38*(2), 145–158.

Roth, N. (1994). *Jews, Visigoths, and Muslims in Medieval Spain: Cooperation and Conflict*, Medieval Iberian Peninsula 10. Brill.

Ruiz, T. F. (2002). Trading with the 'Other': Economic Exchanges between Muslims, Jews, and Christians in Late Medieval Northern Castile. In R. Collins & A. Goodman (Eds.), *Medieval Spain: Culture, Conflict and Coexistence Studies in Honour of Angus MacKay* (pp. 63–78). Palgrave Macmillan.

Saxonberg, S. (2020). *Pre-Modernity, Totalitarianism and the Non-Banality of Evil: A Comparison of Germany, Spain, Sweden and France*. Spring International Publishing.

Scott, S. P. (Trans.) (2001). *Las Siete Partidas, Volume 5: Underworlds: The Dead, the Criminal, and the Marginalized (Partidas VI and VII)*. University of Pennsylvania Press.

Simon, L. J. (1987). Jews in the Legal Corpus of Alfonso el Sabio. *Comitatus: A Journal of Medieval and Renaissance Studies*, *18*(1), 81–97.

Southey, T. (1968). *Chronological History of the West Indies* (Vol. 3). Cass.

Soyer, F. (2019). *Antisemitic Conspiracy Theories in the Early Modern Iberian World: Narratives of Fear and Hatred*, The Iberian Religious World 5. Brill.

Soyer, F. (2021). From Medieval Ritual Murder to Modern Blood Libel: The Narrative of 'Saint' Dominguito de Val in Spain. *Antisemitism Studies*, *5*(1), 139–174.

Stroumsa, G. G. (2010). *A New Science: The Discovery of Religion in the Age of Reason*. Harvard University Press.

Terpstra, N. (2015). *Religious Refugees in the Early Modern World: An Alternative History of the Reformation*. Cambridge University Press.

Walsham, A. (2006). *Charitable Hatred: Tolerance and Intolerance in England, 1500–1700*. Manchester University Press.

Ward, G. (2003). *True Religion*. Blackwell.

Westerduin, M. (2020). Questioning Religio-secular Temporalities: Medieval Formations of Nation, Europe and Race. *Patterns of Prejudice*, *54*(1–2), 136–149.

Wright, D. (1925). The Burnings of the Talmud. *The Open Court*, *39*(4), 193–218.

Yovel, Y. (2009). *The Other Within: The Marranos, Split Identity and Emerging Modernity*. Princeton University Press.

PART 3

The Long Reformation

During the sixteenth century calls for reform began to sound louder in all layers of society. Several, often disparate, voices called upon the church to relinquish its attachment to power and to rediscover the purity of the primitive Christian community. The desire to return to a more truthful understanding of the gospel, a more purified sense of Christianness and a better organization of the church, eventually led to the splintering of Latin Christendom. Such calls for spiritual and structural reforms were not new, nor was critique of clericalism and the papacy. Besides, in the past, several councils had already aimed at ecclesial renewal and restoration (e.g. the Council of Pisa, 1409, the Council of Constance, 1414). In the sixteenth century, religious, cultural, political, and economic factors, however, interlocked such that the pleas for change gathered momentum. While 'Christians had never been a wholly united group, the Christian factions breaking away from the Catholic church [...] [received] material [political and popular] support that allowed them to have a much greater effect on the intellectual landscape than had the dissidents who preceded them' (Nongbri, 2013, p. 85). By the end of that century, the world that had been was no more: Christian religion had splintered and fragmented and Europe had changed dramatically. In his comment on the book of Daniel (1530) Luther put it as follows:

> *Everything has come to pass and is fulfilled: the Roman Empire is at the end, the*
> *Turk has arrived at the door, the splendor of popery has faded away, and the world*
> *is crackling in all places, as if it is going to break apart and crumble. (Quoted in*
> *Hsia, 2006, p. xii)*

The Reformation was a long and complex process, but it certainly revolved around the question of what true worship of God is and what it means to be a disciple of Jesus. As Latin Christendom began to fragment, new religious identities had to be forged. From there being simply Christians, now there would be Lutherans, Calvinists, Roman Catholics, and so forth; all of them claimed to be the only true Christians. But what does it mean to be Lutheran, Calvinist, or Anabaptist; how can one be a Catholic after the splintering of the *Corpus Christianum*? How could these respective groups justify their exclusive claim to true religion? What distinguished them from others and how might this distinction be made real? The effort to fashion novel religious identities set in motion new religionized processes of selfing and othering: those deviating from the Christian norm were labelled, categorized, and essentialized as heretics, with this difference that this norm itself was contested as never before. Once again we will encounter the different mechanism of religionization: framing, renaming, essentialization, classification, and finally the unequal treatment of those deviating from the newly established religionized norm.

Christian Imaginations of the Religious Other: A History of Religionization, First Edition. Marianne Moyaert.
© 2024 John Wiley & Sons Ltd. Published 2024 by John Wiley & Sons Ltd.

In Chapter 5, *The Turn Inwards*, I focus on different (Catholic and Protestant) reformers – Geert Grote, Erasmus of Rotterdam, and Martin Luther – who projected a refigured understanding of true religion based on a reinterpretation of the relationship between the spiritual and the material (Eire, 1986, p. 2). While their thinking is different in many ways, a common thread in their effort to purify the church is the idea that true *religio* is less about outward manifestations and more about a voluntary personal dedication to God; piety really has no need for public displays, external rules, or images. Their call to turn inwards builds on a normative binary between interior (spiritual) and exterior (ritual, material). This binary is reminiscent of the Pauline binary between the spirit and the flesh, used by Christian apologists to delegitimize Jews, as well as pagans and Muslims. The spirit/flesh binary functions as some sort of master key in religionized processes of selfing/othering overall, and reformers too found it useful to enhance their argument for a more purified Christian faith. The reformers' suspicion of material and ritual practices targeted Catholic superstition first and foremost; it would, however, also impact the way Jews as well as native Americans were imagined and how they were dealt with from a legal point of view (Pagden, 1982). Intra-Christian disputes once again affected Christianity's *other* others – the Jews, Muslims, and pagans. Their fates are interwoven.

After the splintering of Latin Christendom, Christian communities had to be re-imagined, re-invented, and re-shaped based on emerging confessions, creedal statements that clearly state the beliefs of Lutheran, Catholics, Calvinists, and so forth (Reinhard, 1999; Rodrigues, 2017; Schilling, 2004). How would those who confessed to adhering to let's say the Lutheran creed display their faithfulness to the gospel – ritually, spatially, and doctrinally; how would Calvinists, Anabaptists, and Catholics? Based on imagined confessional (religionized) differences, identities had to be refigured, communities remade, and boundaries between orthodoxy and heresy redefined. This process of making confessional identities – confessionalization – went hand in glove with a process of territorialization: each ruler tried to maintain the medieval ideal of the pure *Corpus Christianum* in his own territory and each tried to submit his subjects to the religion of his choice and to enforce religious uniformity/purity. This required an immense project of social disciplining: people had to unlearn previous religious norms, ritual traditions, and beliefs and become acquainted with the new normal in their territory – or leave. In Chapter 6, *The Fragmentation of Religion and the Re-creation of Society*, I elaborate on the different aspects of this twofold project of confessionalization/territorialization with a specific interest for how the institutionalization of confessional norms was accompanied by the oppression of those deviating from this norm. This was a violent period.

Finally, in Chapter 7, *Reconfiguring True Religion in Terms of Toleration*, I deal with the same period of the Reformation, but now from another perspective, namely that of several key thinkers spread across three centuries – Sebastian Castellio, John Locke, and Voltaire – who in the face of confessional intolerance argued for the possibility of toleration based on a religio-secular divide. They in effect projected a counter-narrative to bolster the dual effort of confessionalization/territorialization. Going against the grain, they argued that it was un-Christian (i.e. not in line with true religion) to persecute people for their beliefs and practices. These voices for tolerance, however, constructed their argument for toleration by means of religionization. In their understanding, true religion is apolitical, interiorized, and adogmatic; and to rhetorically support their argument they projected false religion, understood as political, legal, and ceremonial, onto problematic others who were thereby placed beyond the limits of toleration, namely in a place of delegitimization. To that end, they drew on a deeply established repertoire of religionized tropes and representations. Judaism, Islam, and even Catholicism would be projected as symbolic carriers of false religion.

References

Eire, C. M. N. (1986). *War Against the Idols: The Reformation of Worship from Erasmus to Calvin.* Cambridge University Press.

Hsia, R. P.-c. (2006). Introduction. In R. P.-c. Hsia (Ed.), *A Companion to the Reformation World* (pp. xii–xvi). Blackwell.

Nongbri, B. (2013). *Before Religion: A History of a Modern Concept.* Yale University Press.

Pagden, A. (1982). *The Fall of Natural Man: The American Indian and the Origins of Comparative Ethnology.* Cambridge University Press.

Reinhard, W. (1999). Pressures towards Confessionalization? Prolegomena to a Theory of the Confessional Age. In C. S. Dixon (Ed.), *The German Reformation: The Essential Readings* (pp. 169–192). Blackwell.

Rodrigues, R. L. (2017). Confessionalization Processes and Their Importance to the Understanding of Western History in the Early Modern Period (1530–1650). *Tempo, 23*(1), 1–21.

Schilling, H. (2004). Confessionalization: Historical and Scholarly Perspectives of a Comparative and Interdisciplinary Paradigm. In J. M. Headley, H. J. Hillerbrand, & A. J. Papalas (Eds.), *Confessionalization in Europe, 1555–1700: Essays in Honor and Memory of Bodo Nischan* (pp. 21–36). Ashgate.

CHAPTER 5

The Turn Inwards

In this chapter, I discuss three thinkers who argued for a purer Christian piety: Geert Grote (1340–1385), Desiderius Erasmus (1466–1536), and Martin Luther (1483–1546). Significantly, all three believed that purity was to be found in the early church, that is, the church before the Constantinian turn and before the long period 'of stagnation and corruption' set in (McGrath, 2012, p. 4). While they all agreed that reforms were needed, the extent of the reform they envisioned differed, especially as it pertained to the relation between the material and the spiritual and the place of various material and ritual practices in Christian worship. Typically, reformers – both Catholic and Protestant – projected a vision of Christian piety that implies a turn inward that privileged individual, 'interior' spirituality over the bodily performance of ritual and the engagement with material things. In their view, true *religio*, true Christianness, is less about outward manifestations and more about a personal dedication to God in Christ, rooted in the sources of Scripture. On the one hand, this turn inwards would give way to new practices of piety, like private prayer, self-reflection on personal unworthiness, confession of fault, acceptance of penance, and scriptural meditation. On the other hand, practices which revolved around the cult of the saints and related devotional practices, especially the use of relics and images in worship, became a topic of debate, as did pilgrimages to saints' shrines (Scase, 2004, p. 18). Debates about sacramentality – the idea that outer signs (symbols and rituals) can mediate and make present God's grace in a tangible way – proliferated and impacted both sacramentalia and later also the sacraments. Of course, opinions varied widely as to the 'problem' of material and ritual practices. Some believed that such practices could guide and edify the laity and could support their worship and the formation of their inner self, while others believed that such practices served no soteriological purpose, but also did no harm. Still others felt that both the proliferation of these popular devotional practices as well as their physical and tactile nature were expressions of superstition, understood as exaggerated or excessive religious expressions. These practices harboured the risk of misoriented worship, a problem that could, according to some, be remedied by reintroducing people to the gospel and making it accessible to all. Reformed Protestants, who stressed the radical transcendence of God, took particular issue with any attempt to contain the sacred within the realm of the profane: *Finitum non est capax infiniti* [the finite does not (or cannot) comprehend the infinite]. They directly associated the ritual and material aspects of religion with malign idolatry, exposing the hand of the devil. This conviction would lead them to start a crusade against idolatry and the cult of the saints: relics and images had to be taken down.

To bolster their argument for a turn inwards and to discredit the Catholic principle of sacramental mediation, reformers – Catholic and Protestant – invoked the old Pauline division between spirit and flesh. In one fell swoop, anti-Jewish patterns of religionization entered into reforming discourses: to misunderstand the proper relationship between the inner and the outer is to relapse into Jewish customs or to Judaize. Papists – a pejorative term for Catholics – were like Jews and vice versa. Overall, the Reformation is a time that

---

Christian Imaginations of the Religious Other: A History of Religionization, First Edition. Marianne Moyaert.
© 2024 John Wiley & Sons Ltd. Published 2024 by John Wiley & Sons Ltd.

150 CHAPTER 5 The Turn Inwards

witnessed an increase of anti-Judaism with Luther's fierce attack against the Jews as a sad climax. These intra-Christian discussions about true worship, however, also affected the way Christians imagined the recently discovered people in the Americas and their traditions. Questions about the juridical status of the indigenous people and how they should be treated were framed theologically as questions about the precise nature of their traditions. The theological 'finding' that Amerindians were idolaters provided one justification for the colonial project. The fate of Christianity's near and faraway others is intertwined.

Before exploring the ways in which the above-mentioned figures made their case for a turn inwards, I begin by elaborating on some of the larger issues that were at play in the late Middle Ages. Doing so will help to understand the concerns of the reformers and their focus on the interiorization of religion. It will also help to better grasp how this turn inwards depended on a critique of the material and ritual expressions of worship. At the same time, it will help us understand the transformation that this turn inwards set in motion.

Text Box 1: The Reformation, Myth Making, and Religionization (1)

The Reformation is often associated exclusively with the Protestant Reformation and Luther's symbolic act of nailing his 95 theses about faith, grace, and indulgences on the door of the castle church of Wittenberg. This act speaks to the imagination and it is often viewed as a foundational act with almost mythic proportions: 'it implies something had "begun", with unstoppable momentum behind it' (Marshall, 2017). Even though Luther did not intend to begin a Reformation in 1517, historians today believe that the process of mythmaking had already started during his lifetime. Luther himself seems to have believed that he was 'a prophet and apocalyptic witness [...] charged with a divine and historical mission to liberate the true religion from the obscurity and thralldom in which it had been kept by the anti-Christian papacy for nearly a millennium' (Walsham, 2015, p. 227). The fact that he changed his father's name, Luder, meaning cadaver, to the Greek *Eleutheros*, meaning the free one (later standardized to Luther) is telling in this regard. His name contained his programme to also free others from Catholic corruption. Within this mythic framework, Protestant Reformation is contrasted to and placed above Catholic tradition. This binary is itself a religionized imagery, which does little justice to more complex historical processes.

According to the myth of the Reformation, Luther's symbolic act of nailing the 95 theses on the church door set in motion the division of the Latin Western Church into two opposing camps with contrasting interests and irreconcilable doctrinal convictions: the Protestant churches on the one hand and the Roman Catholic Church on the other. In line with this, the Protestant Reformation is projected as initiating a much-needed transformation away from papal corruption, ecclesial perversion, 'white magic', and the prohibition of lay people from reading the Bible in the vernacular. Indeed, part and parcel of this process of Protestant mythmaking was the idea that the Protestant Reformation 'efficiently swept away the spiritual apathy, superstition, and credulity into which the papacy and priesthood had allowed the European populace to sink'. Protestantism became 'an instrument and agent of progress' and liberation. The result of this myth is a religionized binary between the Protestant Reformation and Catholic Counter-Reformation. Protestantism came to be associated with progress, liberation, and over time with Enlightenment and tolerance. Catholicism came to embody oppression, conservatism, and the continuation of the dark Middle Ages and intolerance (Walsham, 2015, pp. 227–228).

While the Reformation is rightfully regarded as a watershed in Western history, this conflictual and oppositional reading of history is too one-dimensional and anachronistic; it is the result of a modern pattern of religionization. It creates an imaginary dichotomy between Catholicism and Protestantism which hides from view (i) how reformation, understood as a return to a purer Christianity in line with the gospels and the early traditions of the church, was in many ways a shared concern among Catholic and Protestant reformers (Mullett, 1999, p. 2). (ii) Furthermore, such a reading of history tends to one-sidedly and mistakenly attribute certain developments to Protestantism – for example a focus on a more personal relationship with God or translations of the Bible into the vernacular – thereby overlooking how similar developments were already occurring in the late medieval Catholic Church. For one thing: if 'there hadn't been a huge interest in the Bible among medieval Catholics' and if there had not been a desire for a purer spirituality, 'Reformation ideas would have struggled to get traction' (Marshall, 2017). (iii) Moreover, this binary reading of history projects the schism in the Western Latin Church as ideologically necessary, whereas it was just as much the result of ecclesial politics and contingent circumstances. (iv) Last but not least, it leads to a reading of history according to which reforming voices that predate 1517 are understood as proto-Reformatory movements paving the way for Luther, Calvin (1509–1564), and Zwingli (1484–1531), rather than as reforming movements embedded in the Catholic Church. Along with Felipe Fernández-Armesto and Derek Wilson, I seek to emphasize that '[i]n the Catholic, Protestant and Orthodox worlds, the era of the Reformation was defined by the reorientation of religious life towards the personal and individual quest for God: a liberation of the soul, encouraging the Christian to pursue a personal relationship with God, without neglecting his fellow Christians. The disagreements distinguishing the Catholic and Protestant traditions arose in the course of the joint venture' (Fernández-Armesto & Wilson, 1996, p. 24, my translation).

1   Mediation, Fear of Death, Excess, and Corruption

In the year 1348, the plague erupted in Europe, leading to a decimation of the population and a collapse of the economy and agriculture. Death hovered over the century. These calamities happened at a time when Christian understanding of the meaning of death had been changing, a change that instigated both a process of personalization and a further development of the mediating role of the church in God's economy of salvation. Some excesses relating to the cult of saints and to the practice of distributing indulgences need to be seen against this background.

The Church and the Mediation of Salvation

From the patristic era, Christian tradition has given an important place to the church in God's economy of salvation. Often reference is made to scriptural passages which project an intimate relation between Christ and his communion, suggesting that the *ekklesia* [church], when it comes together to eat his body (bread) and drink his blood (wine), does not simply gather around Christ Jesus, but 'abides in him as He in them' (cf. John 6:56). The elements of bread and wine mediate Christ's sacred presence: the faithful are in his presence and Christ becomes present in them. Within this framework, salvation is a communal affair: in and through that table fellowship the ecclesial community participates in God's economy of salvation. Outside the church there is no salvation. As tradition developed, this sacred presence came to be conceptualized in terms of the doctrine of transubstantiation and *presentia realis* (Fourth Lateran Council, 1215).

Especially since the Gregorian reform, the ordinary faithful were expected to obey papal authority and to accept ecclesial, priestly mediation. This hierarchical, ecclesial mediation is manifest in the sacramental life of the church. When rightly celebrated, sacraments were considered to be visible channels of invisible grace, through which God in Christ seeks to restore the world to Godself. These sacraments were said to be available only in the one true church and, thanks to priestly mediation, Christians are able to share in God's spiritual gifts; in its sacramental life the church brings Christ tangibly near (van Veen, 2012, p. 12).

The ecclesial community consists of both the living and the dead, the sinners and the saints. The dead are not separated from the living; on the contrary, they continue to be part of Christ's living body, even after they have passed away. The saints reside at the heavenly court, with Mary, whose virtuous way of life exemplifies what it means to be a Christ-follower, as the foremost saint. As powerful figures, they are 'capable of hearing the prayers of the living and acting upon such prayers as if they had never died' (Cooper, 2018, p. 71). They can be invoked, and they can intercede on behalf of the faithful. Salvation is a communal affair, which concerns both the living and the dead.

The cult of saints gave way to a remarkable extension of the sacramental principle of mediation. Early on in church history, relics – either bodily remains, like bones, body parts, and even hair (primary relics) or objects touched by the saints, like books and clothing (secondary relics) – 'associated with the lives of Christ, Mary, and the saints, were sought with fervor as special sources of divine grace' (Eire, 1986, p. 15). Strong supporters of relics, like Augustine, John of Damascus, and Thomas Aquinas (1225–1274), emphasized how relics function as tangible points of contact, where heaven and earth, life and death meet. This may explain why,

> for [...] Catholicism during the European Middle Ages, constructing a church [...] required the physical remains of saints. Since they acted as patrons, protectors, and intercessors between the material and spiritual worlds, the saints had to be present in a church. In fact, their bones had to be located within the most sacred center of the church, the altar, in order for the building itself to be sanctified. (Chidester, 2018, p. 81)

With its rituals the church sanctified the entire society. It brought people together and transformed society into one community dedicated to God in Christ. Its rituals and ceremonies blessed places and guilds, and marked the rhythm of time. Carlos Eire captures this as follows:

> In 1509, when John Calvin was born, Western Christendom still shared a common religion of immanence. Heaven was never too far from earth. The sacred was diffused in the profane, the spiritual in the material. Divine power, embodied in the Church and its sacraments, reached down through innumerable points of contact to make itself felt: to forgive or punish, to protect against the ravages of nature, to heal, to soothe, and to work all sorts of wonders. Priests could absolve adulterers and murderers, or bless fields and cattle. During their lives, saints could prevent lightning from striking, restore sight to the blind, or preach to birds and fish. Unencumbered by the limitations of time and space, they could do even more through their images and relics after death. [...]. The map of Europe bristled with holy places; life pulsated with the expectation of the miraculous. In the popular mind and in much of the official teaching of the Church, almost anything was possible. One could even eat the flesh of the risen Christ in a consecrated wafer. (Eire, 1986, p. 1)

The principle of sacramentality expresses God's sensitivity to the bodily nature of humans, their desire to relate intimately to God, and their sensory way of knowing and imagining (Vásquez, 2011, p. 30). The medieval world was an enchanted world marked by a varied devotional life, where communities and individuals could establish intimate, corporeal, and sensory relations with the sacred. In any case, 'late medieval religion was not in terminal decline. It had a remarkable vitality, vigour, and inventiveness and retained the respect and loyalty of perhaps the vast majority of the laity' (Walsham, 2008, p. 502).

Death, Purgatory, and Intercession

Charles Taylor notes that the late Middle Ages were characterized by increasing fear of death as a personal concern. In the earlier ages of Christianity, the focus was on 'the notion of a common judgment, englobing everyone, at the end of time [...]' (Taylor, 2007, p. 67). Death was part of life, a fate awaiting everyone. Judgement would happen at the end of times, collectively.

> *In the later Middle Ages, [however], the church begins to give currency to the idea that each individual will face as well his/her own judgment, immediately on their death. This [...] made more urgent the whole issue of my 'dossier' at the moment of my demise. Previously, the belief in a Last Judgment could be added on, as it were, to older, pre-Christian ideas of death as part of the round of life. The ultimate transformation was put off into a deeper distance, where the issue of its articulation onto our present experience of death can be left vague. The new belief in immediate individual judgment brought it up close, sometimes terrifyingly so. (Taylor, 2007, pp. 67–68)*

The fear of death connected with this individual judgement led to an increased focus on the necessity of personal confession and penance. The Fourth Lateran Council (1215) made this an explicit part of doctrine by obliging the faithful to individually and privately confess serious sins to a priest at least once a year and to complete the imposed penance (Cameron, 1999, 2013, p. 82). This focus on personal fault, personal confession, and a personal judgement immediately after one's passing away contributed to individuation. There is no escaping judgement and one's whole life will be placed on the scales after one has died. Those souls that were not perfect, and therefore would not go to heaven – but had not committed mortal sin so therefore would not go to hell either – were believed to go to purgatory, the antichamber to heaven, where their souls would be purged of their guilt before entering heaven. This belief in purgatory was made official at the Second Council of Lyon in 1274. That same council also taught that souls undergoing purification could benefit from the prayers of those still alive. So, together with this increased focus on personal responsibility in the face of death and judgement, 'a new solidarity of intercession' began to emerge, in line with the principle of ecclesial mediation. The 'living can pray for and otherwise bring relief to the souls of the dead. The terrifying individual destiny can be met by mutual help' (Taylor, 2007, p. 69). Adding to this sense of communal responsibility, people also believed that those already in heaven could come to their aid if called upon. Sinful humans were unable to remedy their own faults, but the 'intercession of the saints helped them on the way to bliss' (Watkins, 2018). The personalized understanding of death and judgement together with the doctrine of purgatory, thus, gave a new impulse to the cult of saints. Gradually an 'enormous patronage network' emerged, 'which extended to particular nations, regions, or peoples, to trades and crafts, or to activities such as travelling or childbearing. Alternatively, they were given particular duties in helping and healing particular ailments' (Cameron, 1999, 2013, p. 86).

The cult of saints gave way to an explosion of devotional practices and celebrations. The many medieval saints and feast days became excessive and distractive, and, increasingly, popular devotion overshadowed the key themes of Christian worship: Christ's life, death, and resurrection. Furthermore, an economy of bogus relics, far-fetched miracles, and even fictive saints emerged. It is this seemingly endless proliferation of saints and the excesses related to devotional ceremonies that would become an object of ridicule. And that was not all. There were also concerns about the role and status of the religious authorities, who played a key part in the ecclesial mediation of salvation.

Corruption, Abuse, and the Practice of Indulgences

Between 1378 and 1417, the church was hit by one of the greatest crises in its history: the so-called Western Schism (Mullett, 1999, p. 2). For about 40 years, two, and later three, popes simultaneously claimed the *sedes* [the papal seat]. The spectacle of rival popes created confusion among the faithful: if salvation is dependent on participation in the sacramental life of the church and on the ordinance of the priests, people asked, which church administers the sacraments rightfully (Flanagin, 2009, p. 337)? This crisis 'opened the doors for the great cultural debates about religious reforms and values that were to take place during the sixteenth century and that resulted in the Protestant and Catholic Reformations' (García Soormally, 2019, p. 20). Many felt that the church was distracted by the lure of worldly goods and by the appeal of power. At the same time, the disconnect between the church's claim to mediate grace on the one hand and the corrupt behaviour of some religious authorities on the other hand was increasingly criticized.

Especially the unbridled practice of indulgences came to symbolize 'everything' that was wrong with the church. Indulgences, which had already been on offer to the crusaders from the eleventh century onwards, were now even more widely available and became a lucrative business. This practice was based

> *on an idea called the treasury of merits, which said that Christ and the saints, through their virtue, had accrued merits that they did not need. An indulgence, then, used the merits of the saints and applied them toward the spiritual demerits of sinners. In the late Middle Ages, the claims of indulgences were expanded. Some indulgences were said to forgive not only the penalty of sin but also the guilt of sin, which was previously forgiven only by the absolution of a priest. Indulgences also began to be given for money instead of good works, and they were claimed to be transferrable to souls already in purgatory. (Whitford, 2012, p. 418)*

Here, the church gave the impression of having the power to open or close the gates of heaven, taking over God's role as the judge of the living and the dead.

Catholic Piety under Critique

In various layers of society, one could notice an increasing uneasiness vis-à-vis the idea of sacramental mediation. Especially the relation between inner and outer, the spiritual and the material, faith and ritual was being scrutinized. Reformers – to varying degrees – criticized the materiality of Catholic worship as false worship, because it confused the spiritual and material, the sacred and the profane. Many 'religionized images', which Christians had previously used to discredit non-Christians, were now put to work to delegitimize (excessive) medieval piety. Some critics labelled excessive medieval Catholic practices, especially those revolving around the cult of saints, as superstitious or even idolatrous. Thus, calling for reform also questioned the performative power of ritual and associated ritual with external pomp and mindless repetitive behaviour. Edward Muir states, that during the Long Reformation ritual became a negative term implicated in the process of religionized othering: it was used to 'describe the disreputable practices of somebody else: what I do is ordained by God and is "true religion"; what you do is "mere ritual", at best useless, at worst profoundly evil' (Muir, 2005, p. 9). Of course, this perspective also entailed a profound criticism of the clerical hierarchy and the priest's monopoly of sacramental power. Even though the Reformation was a diverse movement, generally speaking it brought about a process of 'excarnation', namely 'the steady disembodying of spiritual life, so that it is less and less carried in deeply meaningful bodily forms, and lies more and more "in the head"' (Taylor, 2007, p. 771).

Suspicion about the material and ritual dimensions of Christian worship went hand in hand with a call to 'turn to a more inward and intense personal devotion' (Taylor, 2007, pp. 75–76). Cornerstone of a truly pious life had to be Scripture, which people could read and ponder or receive through preaching. Many also believed that the initiative for this reform had to come from the faithful themselves (van Dijk, 2012, p. 135) and they advocated 'for the priesthood of all believers' (Vásquez, 2011, pp. 31–32). By the second half of the sixteenth century, 'it was no longer possible to take [the] intermingling of spiritual and material for granted' (Eire, 1986, p. 1).

Text Box 2: The Reformation, Myth Making, and Religionization (2)

The Long Reformation redefined age-old traditions of piety as superstition and/or idolatry. Boundaries of proper religion were redrawn and ideas of good and bad religion, true and false worship were refigured. Idea(l)s about what it entails to be a true Christian were enhanced by delegitimizing the beliefs and practices of others. As is typically the case with religionized imaginaries of self and other, they shield from view the messiness of the daily interactions between people as well as the continuities, overlaps, and homologies between their beliefs and practices. In redefining what is true and false worship, what is the Christian norm and what deviates from it, who belongs and who does not, and how a Christian ought to live faithfully, reforming apologists accentuated boundaries, rather than highlighting nuance. They projected an ideal that was not necessarily realized.

The idea that the Reformation radically broke with the Catholic past is the result of an imaginary religionized binary pitting Protestant reform over against Catholic perversion. Historically, it is more accurate to say that the Reformation was both initiated and continued within Catholic milieus. Many Catholics had concerns about abuses and sought to spiritualize traditions of piety, while pruning away 'the dubious accretions and corruptions Christianity was perceived to have accumulated in the course of [...] the preceding half-millennium' (Walsham, 2008, p. 501). Reversely, several of the beliefs and practices which reformers criticized as too carnal were continued in Protestant milieus. Certainly, reforming discourses about the interiorization, personalization, and even textualization of religion initiated a process of de-materialization and de-ritualization, but in practice, the idea of the mediation of the sacred and embodiment of meaning – key to Catholic imagination – was not foreign to Protestants either. Despite their criticism of the cult of saints, for example, many Protestants believed bodies could mediate sacred presence: 'in the guise of martyrs who had sacrificed their lives for the faith and charismatic preachers who were the centre of popular cults of celebrity the Reformation not entirely unwittingly perpetuated the tendency to regard some living human beings as set apart or specially chosen by God. [...] Famously, Martin Luther himself was represented and posthumously revered in a manner that was highly reminiscent of the medieval cult of saints' (Walsham, 2008, pp. 510–511). In addition, 'Protestantism [...] seems to have found room for hallowed objects, [...] [and] although it severely pruned the calendar of saints and dispensed with dozens of former "holy days" it would be a mistake to suggest that the Reformation completely demystified or neutralized the concept of time' (Walsham, 2008, pp. 512–513).

When thinking about the Reformation, we modern scholars sometimes tap into a mythological story of progress and emancipation, which leads us to forget that this story is part of religionized polemics, which contrasts dark and light, flesh and spirit, true and false worship, Protestant critique and Catholic excess.

2   The Modern Devotion

Protestant reformers were not the first to criticize the Catholic fixation on relics, saints, and images and various excessive devotional practices that could be labelled superstition. This problem occupied the minds of many during the late Middles Ages already, and 'from Iberia to the Low Countries and from Paris to Vienna [theologians, clergy and monastics, and lay people] turned their attention to this topic' (Bailey, 2009, p. 633). Next to a concern about excessive (popular) devotional practices, there was an even stronger concern about misdirected worship, which entailed the risk of idolatry (wrongly performed worship or worse: worship of non-divine entities). Thomas Aquinas already expressed his unease about misdirected worship by clearly distinguishing between different expressions

156 CHAPTER 5 The Turn Inwards

of devotion. *Latria* is an act of adoration or reverence due to God understood as Trinity. God alone is worthy of worship. Next, there are acts of veneration, which are intended for Mary. Because she is the mother of God [*theotokos*], she receives higher veneration than the other saints. Mary, however, is not worshipped. Acts of reverence aimed at the saints and angels, who may intercede on behalf of believers are called *dulia*. Relics, finally, were to be venerated but not to be worshipped. Only God is worshipped. Whether or not this distinction was always known to ordinary people is open to discussion, just as the difference between what was orthodox and heretical was not always clear.

Later thinkers like Jean Gerson (1363–1429) pleaded for a renewed theology of piety and a life of profound spirituality. On several occasions, Gerson expressed his concern for the excesses of popular devotional practices, which really had no salvific power. Reiterating a classed distinction, Gerson considered the problem of superstition to be mainly a problem of the uneducated, and while he admitted that such superstitious practices entailed the risk of lapsing into paganism, in the end he seemed not too concerned. He was pragmatic enough to realize that such corruption from true worship could never be completely rooted out amongst lay people; he also felt that 'cases of devotional deviancy [could] be salvaged through proper intention' (Hobbins, 2006, p. 61). If these devotional practices were done in good faith, they would probably do no harm. In his *De erroribus circa artem magicam* [About the errors of the art of magic] (1402) we read the following:

> *I confess, we cannot deny that many things have been introduced among simple Christians that it would be holier to omit. Yet they are tolerated because they cannot be destroyed root and branch, and because the faith of the simple, while it may not understand very well in some matters, is yet ruled and in a certain manner rectified and saved in the faith of their superiors. [The simple] presuppose this faith in all their observances, at least in general intention, if they understand piously and humbly – that is, in a Christian way [christiane] – and if they are ready to obey the revealed pattern of truth (10.83–84). (Translated and quoted in Hobbins, 2006, p. 59)*

Gerson did not intend to abolish such popular practices, nor did he mean to put an end to the cult of saints. He merely sought to point out abuses and express his concern that such popular devotional practices catered to human weakness.

The effort to develop a more personalized approach to piety with an emphasis on Scripture was also supported by the lay movement *Devotia Moderna*. The modern devout, as the adherents of this movement were called, believed that reform of the church begins with reform of the self. They advocated an inwards turn towards the self [*conversio*], which was, in fact, a turn towards God [*devotio*] (Van Engen, 2008b, p. 37). The true mark of an authentic Christian life is 'an intimate union with Christ and personal contact with God' (Faesen, 2019, p. 71).

Geert Grote: The Fountain of Modern Devotion

A key figure in this movement is Geert Grote of Deventer, a city in what is now the Netherlands (1340–1384). For many years, he pursued an academic itinerary and subsequently a career in the service of the church. He had obtained appointments as a canon in Aken (1362) and Utrecht (1372) and he was looking for more ecclesial revenues and benefices (van Dijk, 2012, p. 137). According to his own account, he lived a dissolute life. This would change when, in 1372, he fell seriously ill, had a conversion experience (1372) and decided to turn his life around. Grote left his former ways and his well-paid clerical positions to adopt a more ascetic way of life. In 1379, he was ordained as a deacon, which provided him with a licence to preach publicly about his vision for reform. Going from city to city, he called for penance and criticized those bishops and priests who were more interested in power, money, and sex, than in setting an example of piety. Beyond critique, he argued that every Christian was responsible for the whole of the church as a mystical body and he called on everyone to convert to a life of piety that would revolve around an intimate relationship with God (van Dijk, 2012, p. 249). In 1383, after being silenced by the Bishop of Utrecht,

Grote retreated to a monastery in Woudrichem, where he dedicated his time to his 'personal spiritual direction' (Faesen, 2019, p. 72) until he died of the plague in 1384.

During his lifetime, Grote inspired a whole group of people, who began to gather voluntarily in private houses, where they dedicated themselves to a life of piety (Van Engen, 1988, p. 12). After his death, these Brothers (and later Sisters) of the Common Life, as they came to be known, became increasingly popular, and Modern Devotion spread rapidly, especially in the regions around Groningen, Münster, and Ghent. The movement flourished until 1500, 'only to be shut down by Protestants and Catholics alike in the 1560s' (Van Engen, 2008a, p. 261).

The Brethren of the Common Life and the Reinterpretation of *Religio*

The Brethren of the Common Life lived in a 'community of goods' modelled on the life of the early Christians; they lived in houses, rather than in monasteries and convents, and dwelled in towns rather than in rural areas (Van Engen, 1988, pp. 21–22). These communities advocated 'a life without vows and therefore without official monastic rules as prescribed by canon law' (Van Engen, 1988, p. 2), and they did not wear the monastic habit. Rather than being a new religious order, the Brethren of the Common Life was rooted in free association and a voluntarily chosen way of life. Their models were not the church fathers or the hermits and they organized their community around the ideal of the *Ecclesia primitiva*, 'the apostles and disciples gathered around Mary – in a word, the original Apostolic community' (Mixson, 2016, p. 322). This is an important development, which shatters existing categories and in fact results in a situation whereby the laity comes to occupy 'a status alongside those bound by formal religious vows'. They insisted that a pious way of life leading to knowledge of God and personal salvation was possible for the farmer as well as the scholar and the clergyman as well as the lay person (Magill, 2017, p. 39). But this meant that every single person ought to be personally concerned about the reshaping of his or her soul; no one should hand over this responsibility to others, like for example to the monks in the monasteries who prayed night and day for the spiritual welfare of others. Even the Sisters of the Common life were allowed to read and discuss Scripture, albeit under male supervision.

By opening up the age-old monastic ideal of a devout spiritual life to laypeople, Grote extended the meaning of the word *religio*. During the Middle Ages, this Latin word was hardly used, but when it was used it referred to religious life.[1] 'Religious' people were people who had entered a religious order and had taken solemn vows – of poverty, chastity, and obedience for example – to lead a life dedicated to God. At the time, when 'a plurality of religions' was mentioned, that plurality referred to the various religious orders recognized by canon law: the Benedictines, the Franciscans, the Dominicans, the Augustinians, and so forth (Cavanaugh, 2009, p. 64). The communities of the Brethren of Common Life offered the possibility of a religious life that was not regulated by solemn vows and separated from secular life (cf. also the semi-religious life of the Beguines and the Beghards). *Religio*, so Grote argued, should not be defined as 'an *ordo*, but as a virtue, even as the highest of virtues apart from faith, hope, and charity' (Goudriaan, 2016, p. 90). He took *religio* to mean 'the quality of devoting one's life entirely to God'. Religious people are, therefore, fully committed to serve God and practise the virtue of religion regardless of whether they do this in a monastery or elsewhere. Monks and nuns may have solemnly promised to lead a life 'devoted to the effort of reaching perfection', this does not mean that they are indeed perfect (Goudriaan, 2016, p. 91). By contrast, people who do not belong to a religious order may also reach this perfection. What matters is the quality of devotion not what we see on the outside or what people perform publicly.

Especially in his work *De Simonia ad beguttas*, Grote reacts against those who claim that religion 'is found only in the life of those that are called *religiosi* officially: monks and nuns'. Grote formulates the following rebuttal:

> *If devout women separate themselves from the world and try to serve God in the privacy of their homes, without taking monastic vows, they are just as 'religious'*

as the nuns in their convents. To love God and worship him [sic] is religion (religio),
not the taking of special vows. [...] If it is, therefore, one's aim to live a religious life,
one's way of living becomes religious in God's opinion, and according to the judgment
of one's own conscience. (Gro(o)te, ed. De Vreese, 1940, p. 5)

There are many who are not protected by the name religio, and yet they may be
more religious than those whom the Church calls religious. (De Simonia, p. 30)

The virtue of *religio*, in Grote's understanding, is an unconditional love of God. Such love is not dependent on formal rules, but can be cultivated by all people in various settings, if one sets one's heart on it. Inner resolutions, not external obligations, form the heart of religious life. Spiritual progress, furthermore, requires a never-ending process of personal conversion, whereby the human will voluntarily submits to God's will.

Cultivating a personal relationship with God in Christ [*religio*] requires, according to Grote, a wide variety of humbling spiritual exercises [*exercitia*] aimed at breaking down self-assertion. In this sense, for Grote, there was no contradistinction between inner and outer spiritual life, quite the contrary. One reforms the inner life by reorganizing the outer life (Asad, 1993). This explains why the modern devout engaged in a particular regimen of disciplinary practices such as fasting, confession, chastisement from their brothers and sisters, but they also did good works, such as almsgiving. The overall goal was 'to induce in individuals a state of perpetual self-examination and self-confession, checking one's faith, one's doubt, one's pride, one's avarice...' (Van Engen, 2008b, p. 269). While it is true that the modern devout 'did not seek to overturn external religion, [they did] help make it suspect and vulnerable among its adherents at the end of the Middle Ages' (Eire, 1986, p. 22) and they certainly contributed to an understanding of true religion as personalized and spiritualized.

Implied in this understanding of true religion is an emerging critique of *empty* ritualism. Taylor captures this as follows,

to take my religion seriously is to take it personally, more devotionally, inwardly,
more committedly. Just taking part in external rituals, those that don't require
the kind of personal engagement which, say, auricular confession, with its
self-examination and promises of amendment, entails, is devalued on this
understanding. This isn't what religion is really about. (Taylor, 2002, p. 11)

Text Box 3: The Modern Devotion and the Reformation

Scholars have sometimes seen the modern devout through the prism of the sixteenth-century schism between Protestant and Catholic reformers (see for example Hyma). Indeed, it cannot be denied that the spirituality of the modern devout echoes some of the concerns that Protestant reformers, and also Renaissance Humanists for that matter, would later formulate: the return to the early church, a scriptural turn, the focus on a personal relation with God, as well as the opening up of a life of piety and devotion for all the faithful. To say, however, that these concerns were somehow alien to the Catholic context in which this movement emerged is an anachronism and ignores the many ways in which the Modern Devotion movement was profoundly Catholic. This anachronistic frame is a product of religionized imaginary that contrasts the Catholic and Protestant Reformation (see Text Boxes 1 and 2 in this chapter). Van Engen even suggests that if modern devouts were forerunners of some kind, 'the closest links may well be to certain aspects of the Counter-Reformation' (Van Engen, 1988, p. 10). The later Catholic Jesuit movement, which was established in 1540 by Ignatius of Loyola (1491–1556), may in many ways be considered as a continuation of the spiritual movement of the Modern Devotion. As I said above, both Catholics and Protestants shared concerns about abuses and sought to spiritualize traditions of piety.

3 Christian Humanism

Desiderius Erasmus (1467–1536) was the illegitimate child of the daughter of a physician and a monk, a legacy with which he struggled throughout his lifetime. He was educated in Deventer in one of the Latin schools of the Brethren of the Common Life. After the death of his parents, Erasmus entered the Augustine monastery of Steyn in Gouda (1488) and became a priest in 1492. He loved the library of the monastery, but he found the monastic life itself, and especially its manifold rules and obligations, suffocating and stultifying. Thanks to his extraordinary knowledge of classical languages, he was able to leave his monastery and become secretary of the Bishop of Cambrai. In the years that followed, Erasmus studied in Paris at the Collège Montaigue, travelled to the Italian Peninsula, where he came into contact with Renaissance thinkers such as Lorenzo Valla (1407–1457), and received a doctoral degree from Turin University. We also know that he stayed in England for a long time (1509–1514). A poet, a satirist, a theologian, and a textual critic, he was deeply committed to the Christian faith and was convinced of the need for a re-Christianization of Europe. Eire notes that 'few men in Europe had done as much to discredit the materialism of medieval piety as had Erasmus' (Eire, 1986, p. 28). Thus, he contributed to the emerging modern religionized binary of piety and ritual.

In Praise of Folly

Inspired by the humanistic spirit, Erasmus studied patristic texts, which represented the Golden Age of the early church and sought literary emendation and emulation of them. His work is permeated by a historical consciousness: the past became the measuring stick for the present, which emerged as excessive and corrupt. By contrasting the current state of Christian life with the model of the early Christian church, Erasmus sought to achieve a religious rebirth. If the study of language and original texts (*ad fontes*) enabled Erasmus to return to an ideal beginning, then satire and humour were his instruments to challenge ecclesial corruption. His pamphlet, 'In Praise of Folly' [*Moriae Encomium*, 1511] (Erasmus, trans. Radice, 1986a) is a good example: it unmasks the worthlessness of the indulgences and mocks the lust for power of popes, cardinals, and people of the cloth – the hierarchical church – and its exaggerated claims to authority. Erasmus ridicules the fixation of ecclesial authorities on external pomp and ceremonial matters, as well as the fact that they behave like secular rulers (Erasmus, trans. Radice, 1986a). He also mocked scholastic theologians who lost themselves in abstract speculations and had no sense of humility vis-à-vis the Divine mystery.

> *Then there are the theologians, a remarkably supercilious and touchy lot. I might perhaps do better to pass over them in silence [...], lest they marshal my words. If I refuse they'll denounce me as a heretic on the spot, for this the bolt they always loose on anyone to whom they take a dislike [...]. They interpret hidden mysteries to suit themselves: how the world was created and designed; through what channels the stain of sin filtered down to posterity, by what means, in what measure, and how long Christ was formed in the Virgin's womb; how, in the Eucharist, accidents can subsist without a domicile [...]. Such is the erudition and complexity they all display that I fancy the apostles themselves would need the help of another Holy Spirit if they were obliged to join issue on these topics with our new breed of theologian. (Erasmus, trans. Radice, 1986a, pp. 126–127)*

Erasmus was convinced that 'reflective Christians' ought to acknowledge just 'how limited [...] their ability to reach unquestioned Truth or unqualified certainty over all matters of doctrine' is (Toulmin, 1990, pp. 24–25). To be a Christian had little to do with assenting to doctrinal statements, performing devotional – superstitious – rituals or obeying ecclesial authorities. He rather envisioned a simpler life of piety and pleaded for people 'to become the monitors of their own worship and, instead of relying on the vigilance of the institutions

160 CHAPTER 5 The Turn Inwards

[...]'. Each would have to 'take control of his own practice' (García Soormally, 2019, p. 22). Already during his lifetime, 'In Praise of Folly' was condemned by various instances, among which the Parisian theologians in 1532. In 1559, all his works ended up on the *Index Librorum Prohibitorum*, the list of forbidden books in the Catholic Church.

Erasmus' satire shows his growing impatience with many devotional practices, which in his view, express 'a misplaced faith in the external forms of religion' (Eire, 1986, p. 37). He disliked excessive public exhibitions of religiosity, especially when those claiming to be followers of Christ displayed so little authentic piety. The cult of saints, the worship of relics, and the practice of indulgences were especially problematic in his eyes, as they often went together with immoral behaviour.

> *Now what am I to say about those who enjoy deluding themselves with imaginary pardons for their sins? They measure the length of their time in Purgatory as if by water-clock, counting centuries, years, months, days, and hours as though there were a mathematical table to calculate them accurately. Then there are people who rely on certain magic signs and prayers thought up by some pious imposter for his own amusement or for gain – they promise themselves everything: wealth, honours, pleasure, plenty, continual good health [...] and finally a seat next to Christ in heaven. [...] Take for example some merchant [...] who believes he has only to give up a single tiny coin from his pile of plunder to purify once and for all the entire [...] morass he has made of his life. All his perjury, lust, drunkenness... killings [...] and treachery he believes can be somehow paid off [...] in such a way that he's now free to start afresh on a new round of sin [...]. (Erasmus, trans. Radice, 1986a, pp. 114–115)*

People were too focused on externalities while they should be cultivating personal piety and moral virtue. Thus he stated in his 'Handbook of a Christian Soldier' [*Enchiridion Militis Christiani*, 1515] rule five: 'perfect piety is the attempt to progress always from visible things, which are usually imperfect or indifferent, to invisible, according to the division of man discussed earlier. This precept is most pertinent to our discussion since it is through neglect or ignorance of it that most Christians are superstitious rather than pious, and except for the name of Christ differ hardly at all from superstitious pagans' (Erasmus, trans. Fantazzi, 1988, p. 65). Therefore, he called upon Christian soldiers to wage a war against the externalization of religion. A shift was needed from visible worship to invisible piety; from externality to interiority; from materiality to spirituality; from doctrinal disputes to moral virtue without however demanding the abolition of symbols, statues, or rituals. Rituals had their functionality; they could aid the weak in faith, just as long as excess was avoided, and outward ceremony was accompanied by inward disposition.

To bolster his ideal true Christianness – true piety – Erasmus used anti-Jewish patterns of religionization: he contrasted the *religio* of Jesus to the external religion of the Jews and reprimanded contemporary Christians for lapsing back into Jewish ways. The contrasts between inner and outer, spirit and flesh, *religio* and *superstitio*, mystery and things, mind and body, matter and word (Scripture) were projected onto the binary of Christian and Jew:

> *You gaze with awe at what is purported to be the tunic or shroud of Christ, and you read the oracles of Christ apathetically? You think it an immense privilege to have a tiny particle of the cross in your home. But that is nothing compared to carrying about in your heart the mystery of the cross. If such things constitute religion, who could be more religious than the Jews? Even the most impious among them saw Jesus living in the flesh with their own eyes, heard him with their own ears and touched him with their own hands. [...] So true is it that the flesh is useless without the spirit that it would have been of no use even to the Virgin Mary to have borne Christ of her own flesh if she had not also conceived his spirit through the Holy Spirit. (Erasmus, trans. Fantazzi, 1988, pp. 72–73)*

> *But to worship Christ through visible things for the sake of visible things and to think of this as the summit of religious perfection; [...] to be alienated from Christ by those very things that should be employed to lead us to him – this would be to desert the law of the gospel, which is spiritual, and to sink into a kind of Judaism [...].*
>
> *How hard Paul, [...] defender of the spirit, had to toil in all his travels to woo the Jews away from their faith in works and spur them on to spiritual things! And yet I see that the common run of Christianity has reverted to this again [...]. (Erasmus, trans. Fantazzi, 1988, p. 74)*

Elsewhere, Erasmus stated that many Christians, in their this-worldly attachments and fleshly worship, were more like pagans than the pagans themselves: they are Christians in name only, devoid of the Spirit, enmeshed in silly ceremonies and superstitious practices (Erasmus, trans. Fantazzi, 1988, p. 71). Still, he never advocated the abolition of the cult of saints or the use of images and statues and in fact, he abhorred the iconoclastic waves that were spreading over Europe.

Scripture as the Cornerstone of Christian Life

For reform to become possible, Erasmus maintained, both laity and clergy would have to strengthen their religious life by collectively turning to Scripture, listening to God's word, and obeying the *lex Christi*, the law of Christ, that is, the New Testament. Any person, whether clergy, lay, or religious, committed to reading and contemplating may attain a profound and authentic spiritual life. To him Scripture was a 'clear fountain or source (*fons*) from which everyone can draw for his or her refreshment and comfort [...]' (François, 2008, p. 93). Erasmus suspected ecclesial authorities of monopolizing access to biblical sources, which was contrary to the attitude of Jesus himself who 'did not address his *euangelica philosophia* to scholars in the first instance, but rather to ordinary men and women'. Therefore, it would be wrong to prevent such people from reading Scripture. Consider in this regard his *Paraclesis* (1516).

> *I disagree entirely with those who do not want divine literature to be translated into the vernacular tongues and read by ordinary people, [...] Christ desires his mysteries to be known as widely as possible. I would like every woman to read the Gospel, to read the Epistles of Paul. [...] I wish that the farmer at his plough would chant some passage from these books; that the weaver at his shuttles would sing something from them; that the traveller would relieve the tedium of his journey with stories of this kind, that all the discussions of all Christians would start from these books, for our daily conversation reflects in large measure what we are. (Erasmus, trans. Dalzell, 2019, pp. 410–412)*

From at least 1505 onward, Erasmus applied critical philological methods of text study to the Vulgate. He carefully studied the various New Testament manuscripts and realized that Jerome's Vulgate had been poorly translated and distorted by numerous additions. In his view, this had led to the current corrupt understanding of Christian faith. In response, Erasmus set out to compile a new critical edition of the Greek New Testament, entitled *Novum Instrumentum omne* (1516). Erasmus hoped that his audience, seeing the differences between the Vulgate and the original Greek text, would conclude that the Vulgate was unreliable and in need of revision. Erasmus also researched the theological implications of his text-critical work for the Latin Vulgate tradition. He was convinced that philology would help return the gospel to its purity; it is via the study of language that one gains access to God, not via bodily practices.

Erasmus' text-critical work contributed to the sense that the development of tradition does not necessarily lead to deeper understanding and can run the real risk of leading away from the purity of the original. Tension grows between origin and tradition, between Scripture and doctrinal/liturgical development. To understand what it means to be a Christian entails

162 CHAPTER 5 The Turn Inwards

going back to the beginning of Christianity, and this in turn entails liberating Scripture from the added – often corrupting – layers that it has accrued over the years. As critical text study developed further, this fixation on historical validity increased: only here would one find authenticity, purity, and truth. Compared to the purity of the early church medieval piety came across as overloaded with external practices, like pilgrimages, the veneration of saints, the cult of images and relics, which were nothing but a deviation from the original simple worship of God in Christ.

Erasmus also contributed to a shift that was already underway and that would accelerate under the impulse of the Protestant reformers: the shift from seeing the Bible as a sacred material object venerated in the context of the liturgy to viewing it as an object through which God speaks to all of the faithful. This shift exemplifies the transition from a materialized, ritualized understanding of Christianity revolving around embodied, communal practice, to a textualized understanding of Christianity focused on hermeneutics. Intimacy with God passes through understanding via the mind (reading, hearing), rather than via embodied and sensory contemplation (touching, smelling, tasting). Scripture needs to be understood and explained rather than venerated. In the Protestant imagination, the Bible would clearly differ from any other material object, such as 'a crucifix or religious painting because language did not share their material qualities'; and because 'the Word did not engender illusions, and the Bible, as a providential presence, was properly "spiritual" and not "material" or "physical"' (Engelke, 2007, p. 21). The emphasis was put on Scripture as 'a kind of immaterial presence' (Engelke, 2007, p. 21). It is engaged through (contemplative) reading aimed at reaching a deeper understanding. Hermeneutics takes precedence over sacramental mediation. People had to read, listen, pray, and even sing in their own language, rather than touch, smell, and taste to find God.

Text Box 4: Patterns of Religionization in Erasmus' Call for Piety

Erasmus was committed to reforming the church by advocating Christian piety, which he understood as an inward dedication to God inspired by the gospel. Erasmus' others are the superstitious populous (absorbed by outward exhibitions of 'religiosity'), the scholastic theologians (with no sense of relativism and moderation), and popes, cardinals, and bishops (who have succumbed to the attractions of wealth and power). As he targets corruption and perversions, his plea for a return to a pure spirituality and personal devotion tends to be associated with emancipation from undue claims to authority and with the freedom of the critical mind. Thus, he certainly contributed to the association of ritualized, materialized religion with the vices of inauthenticity, pretence, and outward show and superstition.

True Worship	False Worship
Piety	Outward show
Scripture accessible to all	Ecclesial hierarchy dictates scriptural meaning
Morality	Rituality
Internal motivation (or conversion)	External obligation (or coercion)
Humility	Power
Scriptural theology	Scholastic theology

Erasmus on Judaism

Erasmus' criticism of external ritual practices as lacking piety returns in the way he religionizes Jews and even questions their capacity to become fully Christian. Erasmus regards Jewish law as being overly attached to externalities (rites) and lacking inspiration. He is not critical of Jewish rites as such, but of the fact that Jews relied on them without devotion: 'God', he writes, 'rejects the Jews, not because they observed the rites of the Law but because, foolishly puffed up by keeping them, they neglected what God especially requires of us. Saturated with greed, pride, theft, envy, and other sins, they thought God much in their debt because they frequented the temple on holy days, offered burnt sacrifices, abstained from forbidden foods, and fasted occasionally' (Erasmus, trans. Thompson, 1997, p. 188). Jewish religion understood in terms of ceremonialism is contrasted to true piety. Judaism is projected as the 'antinorm' of true Christianity. Notice also the connection between Jewish religion and the supposed immorality of Jews.

However, Erasmus is not primarily concerned about Jews and Judaism as such. He is instead targeting Christians who are enmeshed in external forms of religion. To use an old trope, he is interested in Christians who are Judaizing. Consider in this regard the following passage from *Declarationes ad censuras Lutetiae* [Clarifications concerning the Censures Published at Paris in the Name of the Theology Faculty], 1532, where he explicitly says as much:

> But since the Jews attributed a great deal to bodily observances, I use Judaism to
> mean not the ungodliness of the Jews but prescriptions concerning external things
> such as clothing, food, or fasts, which have some similarity with the observances of
> the Jews. And in observing them (though they were established to promote piety)
> many Christians have a Jewish outlook, either resting content with them and
> neglecting the things of the spirit, or else, by a topsy-turvy judgment, attributing more
> to those externals than to true godliness, which consists in a state of mind. (Erasmus,
> trans. Miller, 2012, p. 179)

Erasmus used this ready-made religionized image of the Jews to criticize impious Christians and to project the ideal of authentic, pious Christian worship. 'In branding Christians as Jews and in criticizing their religious observances as Judaic rites, he is indirectly disparaging Judaism while he attacks the superstitions of his fellow Christians' (Pabel, 1996, p. 21). In the end, he believed that the more 'we' become spiritual the more 'we' become Christians, and the more 'we' turn to external ceremonies the more 'we' become like Jews.

Text Box 5: Erasmus, the Jews, and Religio-racialization

Erasmus uses Jewish religion, which he calls the most irreligious of all religions, as a negative trope to bolster true Christian piety. He is, however, also convinced that there is something wrong with Jewish nature. In his work inferior religion and inferior nature go hand in hand. The Jewish people were a murderous people, who pretended to be innocent of Christ's death (Erasmus, trans. Phillips, 1991, p. 205). Because they were responsible for killing Christ, Jews had called eternal ruin upon themselves. They are marked by a hereditary stain passed from one generation to the other. Hence, once a Jew always a Jew. While Erasmus does not talk about blood purity, he doubted whether Jewish nature could ever be really transformed through baptism. Indeed Erasmus, who made explicit his desire that all would convert to Christianity, seriously doubted whether conversion would suffice to alter and transform the inner nature of the Jew (Ron, 2019, pp. 147 ff.). Their inferior 'religion' makes them a people not capable of salvation. This is especially clear from the harsh claims he made vis-à-vis the converted Jew and Dominican Johann Pfefferkorn (1469–1523) and other converted Jews. While many of his claims may be understood against the background of the Reuchlin-Pfefferkorn controversy, nevertheless he clearly expresses his disquiet about Jewish converts, depicting them as *turncoats* out to harm Christian unity, hiding their true nature behind the mask of their conversion (Markish, 1986). A Jew who converted was still a Jew of some sorts. Jewish nature could not be washed away by baptism and therefore Erasmus calls converted Jews 'half Jews', rather than Christians. Here Erasmus shows an

164 CHAPTER 5 The Turn Inwards

attitude of pervasive suspicion about the real intentions of converts, who are thought to be hiding their true nature behind the mask of their Christian religion. He also seems to question the power of baptism. When it comes to Jews, race trumps religion:

'There has lately arrived here one Matthaeus Adrianus, by race a Jew but in religion a Christian of long standing, and by profession a physician, so skilled in the whole of Hebrew literature that in my opinion our age has no one else to show' (Erasmus, *Letter 686, to Gilles de Busleyden*, 1517, trans. Mynors & Thomson, 1979, p. 155).

'That *product of the circumcision*, who started as a criminal in the ghetto and is now a greater felon since he became, I will not say a Christian but *a Christian ape*, is said to have published a book – [...] in which, they tell me, he attacks all the learned world by name. [...] In heaven's name, what a tool they have chosen, those who behind their masks would overthrow religion! This *half-Jew Christian* by himself has done more harm to Christendom than the whole cesspool of Jewry' (Erasmus, *Letter 713, to Reuchlin*, 1517, trans. Mynors & Thomson, 1979, pp. 203–204).

'And then just look at the tool [Pfefferkorn] selected by these very far from true champions of true religion [...] What better instrument could the devil hope to find, the *eternal enemy of the Christian religion*, than *an angel of Satan like him, transformed into an angel of light*, who under the most utterly *false pretence of defending true religion* overthrows everywhere what is the chiefest and best thing in our religion – the public unity of the Christian world? [...] Now for the first time he is playing the part of a real Jew, now that he has donned *the mask of a Christian*; *now he lives up to his breeding*. [...]. He could render to his fellow Jews no service more welcome than to pretend he is a *turncoat and betray the Christian polity to its enemies* [...]' (Erasmus, *Letter 694, to Willibald Pirckheimer*, 1517, trans. Mynors & Thomson, 1979, pp. 167–169).

'As it is, this *angel of Satan transformed into an angel of light is attacking us under our own colours* and rendering his colleagues of the circumcision the same service that Zopyrus did to Darius, the father of Xerxes. My life upon it, you would *find in his bosom more than one Jew*' (Erasmus, *Letter 700, to Jacopo Banissio*, 1517, trans. Mynors & Thomson, 1979, p. 179).

'My life upon it, if he could be opened up, you would find in *his bosom not one Jew but a thousand*. One must be on one's guard against an *angel of Satan transformed into an angel of light*. If only the old saying were not so true, that *a bad Jew always makes worse Christians*!' (Erasmus, *Letter 701, to Johannes Caesarius*, 1517, trans. Mynors & Thomson, 1979, p. 181).

'My learned friends tell me that one Pfefferkorn, once *a damned Jew and now a most damnable Christian*, has published a book in German in which like a mad dog he tears the whole learned world to pieces, and me with it. [...]: [A]s a Jew in disguise he could throw peace among Christians into confusion' (Erasmus, *Letter 697, to Johann Poppenruyter*, 1517, trans. Mynors & Thomson, 1979, p. 175).

4 Martin Luther

The Protestant Reformation is inextricably related to the figure of Martin Luther (1483–1546), a Catholic Augustinian monk and professor at the University of Wittenberg. Like so many of his contemporaries, Luther was burdened by a deep fear of death of the Last Judgement. He relates that he entered the monastery to calm his anxieties regarding divine judgement but became frustrated by the rules of his order because they were unable to relieve his sense of sinfulness and his fear of death. While in the convent, Luther tried to make peace with God by obsessively following the prescribed religious duties of his order: he confessed daily (sometimes more than once) and fasted (sometimes several days in a row). Nothing, none of these works, could bring him comfort however. Under the guidance of his mentor, Johannes von Staupitz (1460–1524), who directed him to the idea of 'God's objective grace', based on the merits of Christ rather than on the works of believers, Luther turned to Scripture, to the Psalms, and to the Pauline epistles. This eventually led, in his own words, to an 'experience of conversion', the so-called Tower experience, which took place somewhere between 1515–1519. A profound meditation on Paul's epistle to the Romans made him realize that there is nothing he could do, other than accept his fate and turn to God in Christ. It is not the law that will save, but God through faith. The fallen human is utterly helpless and can do nothing about his fate by himself. The utter helplessness of the human is contrasted to the greatness, power, and mercifulness of God, who is willing to save this unworthy creature. Thus, Luther writes

> *At last, by the mercy of God, meditating day and night, I gave heed to the context of the words, namely, 'In it the righteousness of God is revealed', as it is written, 'He who through faith is righteous shall live'. There I began to understand that the righteousness of God is that by which the righteous lives by a gift of God, namely by faith. And this is the meaning: the righteousness of God is revealed by the gospel, namely, the passive righteousness with which merciful God justifies us by faith, as it is written, 'He who through faith is righteous shall live'. (Luther, 1545, 1960, p. 337)*

Today, most historians question the 'sudden' character of Luther's conversion and emphasize that the Tower experience was in all likelihood the outcome of a longer period of study, which gradually led Luther to a ground-breaking and novel understanding of the salvific relation between God and humankind. Nevertheless, it is a story that continues to fascinate and helps us to comprehend key aspects of Luther's theology.

On 31 October 1517, the day before the feast of All Saints, and now commemorated as Reformation day, Luther supposedly nailed his 95 arguments to the door of the castle church in Wittenberg, also known as the All Saints church (Luther, 1517, 2012).[2] Luther, who opposed the excessive practice of selling indulgences, 'collected in [this] document the general dissatisfaction that had been felt for a long time in many sectors of the Catholic Church' (García Soormally, 2019, p. 23). He presented his arguments as an invitation to theological debate, not as a call for an ecclesial schism. In an earlier time, Luther's invitation might not have had such a great impact. However, thanks to the printing press (the new communication technology from 1450), to the fact that he spoke to a widespread dissatisfaction with the fraudulent excesses of the Catholic Church and capitalized on a profound antipapist and anticlerical mood, and thanks to the support he received from certain German princes, his theological arguments circulated quickly, leading to a major ecclesial crisis and finally to an ecclesial schism. In 1520, the universities of Cologne and Louvain had already offered 'well-examined condemnations and censures of Luther's teachings' (Soen, 2017, p. 38). Rome followed this lead and declared Luther's theses as heretical *ad litteram*. In a bull (1520) *Exsurge Domine* – in Germany known as the *Bannandrohungsbulle* – the church finally calls all faithful Christians to 'rise up for the foxes have risen to destroy your vineyard' and threatens Luther with excommunication. This bull was distributed widely; it is estimated that 60,000 copies were printed. In 1521, Emperor Charles V (r. 1519–1556), summoned Luther before the Diet of Worms, an assembly of nobility and princes of the Holy Roman Empire. He refused to refute his statements to comply with Roman censorship and communication. Luther was convicted and banned. The reformer now became a heretic and his books were burnt.

A Reformed and Purified Christian Norm

In contrast to Erasmus, Luther upheld a pessimistic anthropology, emphasizing the fallen nature of the human being and his/her proclivity towards sin, thereby denying him/her any role of significance in God's plan of salvation. All human beings are sinners, and both their moral compass and their intellect have been severely harmed by the fall. Furthermore, as sinners, the only thing human beings deserve is punishment; they deserve nothing else. However, while sinfulness marks human nature, God, out of the pureness of God's grace, does not hold it against the faithful who acknowledge this sinful nature and who accept that

166 CHAPTER 5 The Turn Inwards

their fate is completely in his hands. God generously offers salvation to those who have faith. Salvation is God's free gift to humanity, made possible through Christ's atoning death and resurrection (Luther, 1522, 2012).

Significantly, in Luther's work too, Jewish tradition symbolized problematic religion: the Jews do not understand God's grace; they are driven by fear of punishment but lack faith. They observe the law (outward behaviour), while hating it (inward attitude). This makes them all hypocrites; they are not what they claim to be:

> *For even though you [the Jews] keep the law outwardly, with works, from fear of punishment or love of reward, nevertheless you do all this unwillingly, without pleasure in and love for the law, but with reluctance and under compulsion [...]. The conclusion is that, from the bottom of your heart, you hate the law. What point is there then in your teaching others not to steal, if you yourself are a thief at heart and would gladly be one outwardly if you dared? Though, to be sure, the outward work does not lag far behind among such hypocrites! (Luther, 1522, 2012, p. 77)*

Luther opposed the idea that Christians could somehow gain access to salvation based on their own efforts, by doing good works or performing certain rituals: God saves those who have faith in Godself.

Luther was also reacting to the (Catholic) practice of indulgences, which gave the impression that Christians could buy their way into heaven. What matters in a life of piety is not so much the social, externalized dimension of religion, but rather its interiorized, personalized devotion, inspired by Scripture, which ensures true spiritual advancement. All this external pomp leads to nothing:

> *The soul receives no benefit if the body is adorned with the sacred robes of the priesthood, or dwells in sacred places, or is occupied with sacred duties, or prays, fasts, abstains from certain kinds of food or does any work whatsoever that can be done by the body and in the body. [...] [S]ince the things which have been mentioned could be done by any wicked man, and such works produce nothing but hypocrites. On the other hand, it will not hurt the soul if the body is clothed in secular dress, dwells in unconsecrated places, eats and drinks as others do, does not pray aloud, and neglects to do all the things mentioned above, which hypocrites can do. (Luther, 1520b, 1957)*

Proper worship of God has no need of frills, bells, churches, ornaments, special clothes, and so forth, God does not care for these, and they may even distract. Luther would simply declare most of these material practices *adiaphora*, namely a matter of indifference. Clearly, it would be better to do without all these things, but they do no real harm, because they are neither holy nor unholy. They are in no sense sacred, and carry no inherent sacrality. These are inessential practices, which serve no soteriological purpose. While he opposed iconoclasm, he did disempower most of Catholic liturgy by stripping material and ritual practices of their mediating role. Thus Luther: 'One thing and one only is necessary for Christian life, righteousness, and liberty. That one thing is the most holy Word of God, the Gospel of Christ' (Luther, 1520b, 1957). God speaks directly to human beings by means of the Bible, therefore all have the right and duty to read and study the Bible devoutly and prayerfully. According to Luther, 'Scripture alone is the true Lord and master of all writings and doctrine on earth'.

5 Erasmus and Luther: Profound Disagreements

Erasmus and Luther were contemporaries, who shared several concerns. Both had been exposed to the influence of the *Devotio Moderna* and its plea for self-reflection and introspection, scriptural meditation, and prayerful piety. Erasmus was educated in Deventer and

Luther in Magdeburg. Both became Augustinian monks – Erasmus in Stein and Luther in Erfurt, and both struggled to follow the rules of their monastic order. Both men, who communicated with one another via letters, were convinced about the need for ecclesial reform. Luther would even rely heavily on Erasmus' critical edition of the New Testament when drafting his 95 theses (though not when he translated the Bible into German). Nevertheless, they disagreed profoundly about the future of the church. Erasmus rejected Luther's revolutionary ideas and the harshness of his words, which, he feared, could lead to violence. So Erasmus wrote in reaction to Luther:

> *I have never entered your churches, but now and then I have seen the hearers of your sermons come out like men possessed, with anger and rage painted on their faces ... They came out like warriors, animated by the oration of the general to some mighty attack. When did your sermons ever produce penitence and remorse? ... Do they not make more for sedition than for piety? (Erasmus, quoted in Smith, 1962, pp. 391–392)*

According to Erasmus, such rage was irreconcilable with a Christian mindset. 'A preacher', so Erasmus stated, 'tempers his speech so as not to provoke powerful men needlessly and thereby harm the cause of the gospel' (quoted in Rummel, 2004, p. 104). Erasmus believed in reform from within and he accepted that this would take time; he preferred intellectual revolution above a social one. He detested uproar, conflict, and violence and envisioned a united and peaceful *Societas Christiana*. Following the example of Christ, Christianity would triumph by believing in the power of the word (Erasmus, trans. Radice, 1986b, p. 309). While Luther too was appalled by the iconoclasts and would remain open to the use of material objects in ritual life as long as they were regarded with indifference, Erasmus considered Luther's polemicizing co-responsible for the outbursts of violence.

The difference between the two reformers, however, was about more than difference in style. Erasmus, and here he showed himself a true humanist, believed that by means of education and with trust in divine mercy, Christians could perfect themselves, thereby setting the church at large in the direction of much-needed reform. Better educated men would turn into better educated Christians. Clearly, Erasmus started from a more optimistic anthropology, according to which the will and intellect may have been harmed by the fall, but not completely corrupted. It is all the more remarkable therefore that he had such doubts about the educability of the Jews and their capacity to convert and to become proper Christians. To his mind, the human will is and remains free, freedom being in his view the 'power of the human will by which man may be able to direct himself towards, or turn away from, what leads to eternal salvation' (Erasmus, trans. McCardle, 1998, p. 21). Erasmus, furthermore, argued that he had tradition on his side:

> *I would remind readers that, if Luther and I seem to be evenly matched on the basis of scriptural testimonies and sound arguments, they should then take into consideration [...] [that] [f]rom the apostles' times to this day, there has not been a single writer who has completely denied the power of free will. (Erasmus, trans. McCardle, 1998, p. 15)*

This is, he argues, the authoritative position of the Catholic Church, which he accepts.

Luther, on the other hand, was more pessimistic and claimed that the Catholic Church has underestimated the seriousness of sin. He speaks of the enslaved will (*de servo arbitrio*) and argues that man cannot return to God based on his own free choice. In his reading, Scripture depicts the state of 'man' in terms of corruption, and what is more, man seems to be entirely oblivious of this. Free will is completely abolished by the fall. To be reconciled to God, Christians must acknowledge their sinfulness; they must come to God as lost beings, rather than approaching God through their own merits or good works. Guided by reason, humans will always (re)turn to works rather than faith to reach justification. While Luther may have acknowledged that all human beings, even the pagans, were capable of knowledge of God, with reason alone humans could never attain eternal life; rather it would plunge them 'out of heaven (as happened to Lucifer) and into the abyss of hell' (Luther, 1539, 2012, p. 41). Without the gospel, Satan would easily lure people into idolatry.

Reforming Christian Faith and Projecting False Religion onto the Enemies of God

As Luther set out to redefine true Christian faith (selfing), he also redescribed Christianity's others and their errors (othering). His projection of a Christian norm centred on faith, Scripture, and grace went hand in hand with the projection of deviation onto papists and clerics, the Jews and the Turks, who despite their differences suffered from the same ills: works without faith. This viewpoint creates a religionized boundary between Christian faith and its others: Jews, Turks (Ottomans), papists, and all sorts of sectarians.

> *If the doctrine of the justification is lost, the whole of Christian doctrine is lost. And those in the world who do not teach it are either Jews or Turks or papists or sectarians. For between these two kinds of righteousness, the active righteousness of the law and the passive righteousness of Christ, there is no middle ground. (Luther, 1522, 2012, p. 90)*

Orthodoxy is one, and deviation, while taking on multiple expressions, at heart is also one. Luther even returns to the image of the foxes to make his point:

> *Jews, Turks, papists, radicals [...] All of them claim to be [...] God's people in accord with their conceit and boast, regardless of the one true faith and the obedience of God's commandments through which alone people become and remain God's children. Even if they do not all pursue the same course, but one chooses this way, another that way, resulting in a variety of forms, they nonetheless all have the same intent and ultimate goal, namely, by means of their own deeds they want to manage to become God's people. [...] They are the foxes of Samson whose heads turn away in different directions. (Luther, 1543, 1971, p. 175)*

Similarly, he writes,

> *However, I am no longer amazed by either the Turks' or the Jews' blindness, obduracy, and malice, since I have to witness the same thing in the most holy fathers of the church, in pope, cardinals, and bishops. (Luther, 1543, 1971, p. 177)*

To serve God by relying on one's own strengths and works is idolatry. For Luther idolatry, therefore, is not something that only pagans fall prey to, but also implicates Christians when they are attached to externalities and hierarchies rather than to God. Luther thus considerably broadens the scope of idolatry; it is not only the worship of a god other than the one God, rather it is the human endeavour to seek God by means of works rather than faith. Furthermore, idolatry is no longer the problem of a distant other, but is a Christian problem first and foremost. It is also not just a societal problem; it is a personal problem. Faith is personal, but so is the problem of idolatry: it proliferates in one's heart. The remedy (or medicine) is not submission to external ecclesial authorities who claim orthodoxy, but faith.

> *Thus it is with all idolatry; for it consists not merely in erecting an image and worshiping it, but rather in the heart, which is intent on something else, and seeks help and consolation from creatures, saints or devils, and neither accepts God, nor looks to him for good to such an extent as to believe that he is willing to help; neither believes that whatever good it experiences comes from God.*
>
> *Besides, there is also a false divine service and extreme idolatry, [...] upon which also all ecclesiastical orders are founded, and which alone concerns the conscience, that seeks in its own works help, consolation, and salvation, presumes to wrest heaven from God, and reckons how many institutions it has founded, how often it has fasted, attended Mass, etc. [...]. What is this but reducing God to an idol, yea, [a fig image or] an apple-god, and elevating and regarding ourselves as God? (Luther, 1529, 2018, p. 18)*

Luther called Catholics – here he is mainly thinking of members of the secular and regular clergy, bishops, and cardinals – who accepted the authority of the pope papists (who put their thrust in the pope), rather than Christians (who have faith in Christ). In one sweep, he classified them as idolaters. He speaks about their greed, their superstition, their power lust; he calls the Roman pontiff, 'the fount and source of all superstitions', states that the Romanists 'persist in their hypocrisy', lose themselves in 'external pomp', 'grasp for money', and deny ordinary people access to the gospel. The vows taken by monks are a mere 'ceremonial law' with no scriptural basis, and therefore 'fraught with danger'. Idolatry is a moral and spiritual danger. The church of true Christians cannot be the visible Roman Catholic Church:

> Therefore, he who says that an external assembly or unity creates Christendom speaks his mind arbitrarily. And whoever uses Scripture to support this brings divine truth down to the level of his lies and makes God a false witness, which is what this miserable Romanist does when he brings everything that is written about the Christendom in the level of the external pomp of Roman power. But he cannot deny that the majority of this mob, particularly in Rome itself, is not in spiritual unity. (Luther, 1520a, 1970, pp. 66–67)

According to Luther, the one true church is a spiritual community of believers in Christ, not a bodily assembly held together by rituals, ceremonies, and rules (external works). The papist idolatry is not simply an expression of ignorance; Luther took on a fiercer point of view: the papists' idolatry expressed their true nature as servants of the devil. In the most violent and vulgar treatise to issue from Luther's pen, 'Against the Papacy at Rome, Founded by the Devil' (1545), as well as in other writings, Luther 'bestializes' and thereby dehumanizes the papists, 'likening them to pigs or asses, or called them liars, murderers, and hypocrites' (Edwards, 1983, p. 127). Furthermore, he depicts them as antichrists who claim to lead men to heaven, while their actions close heaven to them. By associating papists with the Antichrist, Luther makes clear that they are working against the will of God and inciting men to lead a sinful life. They are no longer Christians; their church is a synagogue of the devil.

The fundamental error of the papists is that they consider the pope as the head of the church, and worship him as God, while there is only one head, and that is Christ. Furthermore, they trust their fate to their good works rather than to Christ and listen to ecclesial authority rather than to the Word of God as revealed in Scripture. In so doing, they reintroduce the veil of Moses, which Christ had lifted.

> Not only do they [the pope, bishops and priests] never preach this Spirit, indeed, they do not even explain the letter correctly. Instead, they [preach] their own law, canon law, and nothing but human teaching – consecrated salt, water, vigils, masses, and whatever other tomfoolery like this you can name. They fill the world with them, obscure the law of God, and replace the veil of Moses which the apostles had lifted. [...]. But the pope does not only reintroduce Moses (which would still be a favor), but also replaces the veil before his eyes and, indeed, with his innumerable laws builds a stone wall before him so that now neither Spirit nor letter is recognized or preached [...]. (Luther, 1521, 2012, p. 63)

Luther is particularly harsh on the papists because they are guilty of wilful unbelief: they have access to all the necessary sources to know the truth (Scripture) and still they turn away from it, thereby blaspheming and raging against God. In this regard, papists are like Jews: they stubbornly close their eyes to their own prophecies and do not want to hear the Word of God even when it is spoken directly to them. They read Scripture according to the flesh and not according to the Spirit. Luther also aligns the papists in their attachment to 'works' with the 'legalism' of the Jewish Pharisees. The crimes of the Jews are now the

170 CHAPTER 5 The Turn Inwards

crimes of the papists and a new typology unfolds in which he reads the crimes of the papists through the mould of the Jews and vice versa. David Nirenberg explains:

> If the Jews deserve death for stabbing the host with little knives in their attempts at desecration, he writes in his lectures on the epistle to the Hebrews (1517/18: his allusion is presumably to the host desecration trial held in Brandenburg in 1510), how much worse do the Roman priests deserve for murdering the faithful, that is, the living children of God? And if the Jews' mistaken faith is based on their perversion of circumcision, he writes in 'On the Jews and their Lies' (1543), is the Papists' perversion of the sacraments not exactly the same error? (Nirenberg, 2014)

For all of these reasons, Luther urged the authorities to expel the papists from their territories, and he regretted that many did not follow this through.

Luther was also particularly harsh on the Jews themselves. Initially, he approached them with a certain generosity. Luther could not hold it against them that they did not fall for the falsities of the papists; he seemed to have believed that Jews would be convinced by Protestant arguments. When this did not happen, his position hardened and he wrote a book *On the Jews and Their Lies,*

> so that I [Luther] might be found among those who opposed such poisonous activities of the Jews who warned the Christians to be on their guard against them. I would not have believed that a Christian could be duped by the Jews into taking their exile and wretchedness upon himself. However, the devil is the god of the world, and wherever God's word is absent he has an easy task [...]. (Luther, 1543, 1971, p. 137)

Luther draws on a deeply established repertoire of anti-Jewish tropes and representations: they are blind, stubborn, untrustworthy, and so on. Furthermore, they rob, steal, and kill Christians. It is their intention to corrupt the faith of Christians and they live solely to blaspheme; this shows that they are servants of the devil. He also does not believe in their capacity to reason. Entering into a conversation with them or trying to convert them will amount to nothing. Again we see how, in this case Luther, sows doubt about the Jewish capacity to embrace true worship and their capacity to be saved (Jennings, 2010, p. 35).

> From their youth they have been so nurtured with venom and rancor against our Lord that there is no hope until they reach the point where their misery finally makes them pliable and they are forced to confess that the Messiah has come, and that he is our Jesus. Until such a time it [...] is useless to argue with them [...]. (Luther, 1543, 1971, p. 139)

Christians ought to take measures to protect themselves against the Jews, whose malign intent makes them a danger to Christian society. In Luther's imagination, these measures take on unseen proportions and would have devastating effects on Jewish communities in Europe:

> First, to set fire to their synagogues or schools and to bury and cover with dirt whatever will not burn, so that no man will ever again see a stone or cinder of them. This is to be done in honor of our Lord and of Christendom, so that God might see that we are Christians, and do not condone or knowingly tolerate such public lying, cursing, and blaspheming of his Son and of his Christians. [...] Second, I advise that their houses also be razed and destroyed. [...] Third, I advise that all their prayer books and Talmudic writings, in which such idolatry, lies, cursing and blasphemy are taught, be taken from them. Fourth, I advise that their rabbis be forbidden to teach henceforth on pain of loss of life and limb. [...] Fifth, I advise that safe-conduct on the highways be abolished completely for the Jews. For they have no business in the countryside, since they are not lords, officials, tradesmen, or the like. [...] Sixth, I advise that usury be prohibited to them, and that all cash and treasure of silver and gold be taken from them and put aside for safekeeping. [...] Seventh, I commend putting a flail, an axe, a hoe, a spade, a distaff, or a spindle into the hands of young,

strong Jews and Jewesses and letting them earn their bread in the sweat of their brow, as was imposed on the children of Adam [...]. [...] No, one should toss out these lazy rogues by the seat of their pants. (Luther, 1543, 1971, pp. 268–272)

Text Box 6: Patterns of Religionization

In Luther's imagination, true worship is one; deviation takes many forms but at root remains the same. Through the lens of religionization, it makes sense that Luther compares Jews, papists, and Turks and contrasts them with Christians deserving of that name.

True religion	False religion
Christians	Turks, papists, Jews
Christian faith	Idolatry
Christ	Antichrist
God's work	Devil's work
Reliance on faith, grace, and Scripture	Reliance on works, reason, and ritual
Spirit	Letter

---

6 The Colonial Project and the Question of True Religion

The developments in Europe and especially the debates about true Christianness did not happen in isolation from developments in the newly 'discovered' and eventually colonized territories of the Americas. As people travelled back and forth, ideas, concepts, and frameworks travelled with them. Soon theological discussions about true and false worship, about invisible and visible piety, about superstition and idolatry became a key part of theo-political discussions about the status of the indigenous people and the (il)legality of their subjugation. Debates about the nature of their worship traditions went hand in hand with discussions about the nature of the natives living in America and questions about how they ought to be treated. Once again, people's religious status was in 'a mutually constitutive relationship with developing systems and relations of racial [...] power' (Delgado & Moss, 2018, p. 53). The fate of the distant others and that of the near others of Christianity intersect.

Context

Clearly, 'few conquerors [...] argued that their right to rule over a defeated people was based simply on limitless greed, the joys of naked aggression, or the desire to exercise power for personal pleasure' (Pike, 1969, p. 217). While the Portuguese and Spanish Empires and *conquistadores* as well as missionaries were conquering territory and people at a rapid pace, questions were raised about if and to what extent their domination in the 'new world' was justified. Also, 'by what right had the crown of Castile occupied and enslaved the inhabitants of territories to which it could make no prior claims based on history?' (Pagden, 1982, p. 27).

First, the encounter with the indigenous people evoked debates about their human status (Maldonado-Torres, 2014, p. 700). This debate about their nature – who are these people compared to 'us' – was framed in terms of whether or not they were religious, namely whether or not they were marked by 'an innate human propensity towards God'. By analogy to early

172 CHAPTER 5 The Turn Inwards

Christians debating the 'religious' status of non-Christian gentiles, the question of religion was also the dominant frame used by theologians trying to make sense of the indigenous people. This question was not just a theological-anthropological affair, on the contrary. If the indigenous people fell outside the realm of natural religion, they were non-human and could be enslaved but if, by contrast, it could be established that they shared the natural propensity to worship God, and therefore were religious, it would be sinful to enslave them. Thus, legal discussions were framed as theological discussions, and theological categories (and religionized images) co-determined the juridical status of indigenous people and how they were to be treated.

Second, and intersecting with the debate about the scope of religion, there was the question as to the nature of the indigenous people's (symbolic) practices. The ongoing European discussions about material and ritual practices, and especially the Protestant polemics against the idolatry of the papists, would affect the way the Americas were incorporated into European Christian imaginaries. While Columbus could still say that the natives he first encountered were innocent, and were neither idolaters nor heretics, at a later stage, when Protestant reformers defined Catholic symbols and rituals as idolatrous, Catholic missionaries began to use similar language when talking about the indigenous people: all they encountered was idolatry; all they encountered was worship of false gods and a misguided attachment to religious externalities. Thus Eire says,

> *In the sixteenth century, one man's devotion was another man's idolatry. It is good to keep in mind that at just about the same time that the soldiers of Charles V replaced the 'horrible idols' of the Aztecs with 'beautiful' crosses and images of Mary and the saints in the New World, Protestant iconoclasts were wreaking havoc on these Catholic objects in lands nominally ruled by him in Europe. (Eire, 1986, p. 5)*

According to some, the indigenous people's idolatry was the result of ignorance (so no fault of their own) and lack of evangelization; others, however, saw nothing but the hand of the devil.

In 1550, after learning about the mistreatment of the natives by the conquistadors and colonists, the Holy Roman emperor, king of Spain (Aragon and Castile) and lord of the Netherlands, Charles V, gathered together a *junta* [a jury] consisting mainly of academics and theologians to discuss one single, legal issue: whether it was just to wage war on the Native Americans and to subjugate them as slaves. The emperor ordered that conquests in his name ought to cease, until the matter was settled. The main proponents of this debate, held in Valladolid (1550–1551), were Bartolomé de las Casas, Juan Ginés de Sepúlveda, and later José de Acosta.

Juan Ginés de Sepúlveda

Juan Ginés de Sepúlveda (1490–1573) was a Spanish priest and historian, but also confessor of the emperor, philosopher, theologian, and epistolary friend of Erasmus. Following Aristotle (384–322 BCE) in his *Politics* (Book I), he divided and ranked people into different categories based on their rational capacities: masters, women, children, and natural slaves. In his *Tratado sobre las justas causas de la Guerra* [Just War Theory and the Conquest of America, 1548], Sepúlveda argues that inferior people, marked by irrationality, must submit to more civilized and human people and that civilized people had the duty to direct the fate of those deemed uncivilized or barbarian (Sepúlveda, ed. Menendez y Pelayo, 1941).

> *Those who surpass the rest in prudence and intelligence, although not in physical strength, are by nature the masters. On the other hand, those who are dim-witted and mentally lazy, although they may be physically strong enough to fulfill all the necessary tasks, are by nature slaves [...]. (Translation by Pike, 1969, p. 218)*

While previously, native Americans had been likened to innocent children, Sepúlveda imagined the relationship between the Spanish and natives along the lines of a master/slave dichotomy. The Spanish were clearly superior because they lived according to natural law, implanted by God in all humans. Their strength, intellect, justice, and *religio* makes them natural masters. The indigenous people, on the other hand, lack culture, science, do not have written laws, and no art; they also do not know the principles of just war, and did not develop a monetary economy. Their customs are barbarous. Clearly, they are uncivilized. Or as according to Sepúlveda, one will find in them hardly 'any vestiges of humanness'. Furthermore, their idolatry is so barbarian that it is clear that they worship the devil.

> *[...] Until now we have not mentioned their impious religion and their abominable sacrifices, in which they worship the Devil as God, to whom they thought of offering no better tribute than human hearts. [...] Interpreting their religion in an ignorant and barbarous manner, they sacrificed human victims by removing the hearts from the chests. [...] They also ate the flesh of the sacrificed men. (Pike, 1969, pp. 228–220)*

The overall picture was that of the native American as 'a half-man creature whose world was the very reverse of the "human" world of [those who by their] magnanimity, temperance, humanity and religion' (Pagden, 1982, p. 118). That Sepúlveda likened the indigenous people to monkeys and pigs further contributed to their dehumanization. Falling prey to essentialization, Sepúlveda categorized all natives as inferior people or natural slaves and concluded that the Spanish could wage just war against them.

This war was justified as punishment for their crimes against natural law, especially their crimes of idolatry and human sacrifices. This war was also justified as serving a civilizing and moralizing purpose, namely to convert them. Thus, the scope of Christian religion could be broadened. Implied in this project is the idea that to be Christian is to be civilized and human; to be pagan is to be uncivilized and inhuman:

> *It will always be just and in conformity with natural law that such people submit to the rule of more cultured and humane princes and nations. Thanks to their virtues and the practical wisdom of their laws, the latter can destroy barbarism and educate these [inferior] people to a more human and virtuous life. And if the latter reject such rule, it can be imposed upon them by force of arms. (Pike, 1969, p. 218)*
>
> *War against these barbarians can be justified not only on the basis of their paganism but even more so because of their abominable licentiousness, their prodigious sacrifice of human victims, the extreme harm that they inflicted on innocent persons, their horrible banquets of human flesh, and the impious cult of their idols. [...]. (Pike, 1969, p. 220)*
>
> *What is more appropriate and beneficial for these barbarians than to become subject to the rule of those whose wisdom, virtue, and religion have converted them from barbarians into civilized men (insofar as they are capable of becoming so), from being torpid and licentious to becoming upright and moral, from being impious servants of the Devil to becoming believers in the true God? (Pike, 1969, p. 220)*

Bartolomé de las Casas

Dominican friar Bartolomé de las Casas (1484–1566) was horrified by the domination and oppression of native Americans in the *encomienda* system and strongly disagreed with Sepúlveda's justification of the subjugation of the indigenous people. He became an important defender of the rights of the indigenous people without rejecting the 'civilizing' mission in the New World.

In his *Apologetica Historia*, and likewise relying on Aristotle's *Politics*, he denied that they were barbarians and went to great lengths to show that the indigenous people were not that different from the people who lived in pre-Christian civilizations of the 'old world', like Greece, Rome, and Egypt. They were neither brutal, irrational, nor barbaric, but were guided by the voice of natural law and were capable of religion [*capax religionis*] (Stroumsa, 2010, p. 18). Rather than seeing their lack of civilization, he pointed to their social and political achievements, which showed that they were free human beings, capable of self-governance. Therefore, they ought to be treated as such (see Las Casas, *Memorial de Remedios para las Indias* [In Defence of the Indians, 1516]) (Las Casas, ed. Tudela Buesco, 1958, pp. 6–27). As to their worship traditions, he also took a different point of view. Inspired by the logic of encompassment embraced

174 CHAPTER 5 The Turn Inwards

by the early church fathers, Las Casas insisted that their idolatry was in fact natural and a sign of their religiosity and humanity: it is human, so he said, to worship idols. He considered the indigenous people in terms of a *praeparatio evangelica* and demonstrated that, like the pagans in the past, they too detected God's presence in nature. For 'whatever nobility, whatever excellence and virtue is to be found in created things [...] is nothing other than a trace, a light and gentle footprint, of divine perfection' [*apologetica historia*]. Here we may recall Tertullian, who argued that pagans showed their longing for the one true God in their (false) worship practices and testified to knowledge of God, that belong to the realm of natural knowledge (as distinguished from revelatory knowledge). When left uncultivated and unenlightened by the proclamation of the gospel, this natural thirst for God develops in the wrong direction, and that is precisely what happened in the 'New World', which had not yet been exposed to Christianity. That they sacrifice is a sign that they follow natural law – since to sacrifice is a basic commandment of natural law. That they execute their sacrifices to God wrongly, is not their fault; they are innocent in their misguidedness. To Las Casas' mind, the idolatrous practices of these natives were simply the result of their invincible ignorance; this is the state in which a person cannot overcome their ignorance, and cannot be blamed for the acts resulting from their state of ignorance.[3] Only through education could the thirst for God become knowledge of God: 'Idolatry, supposed corruption of human nature without guide for the doctrine or grace of God, is natural because that which all or most people do without having been taught seems natural' (Las Casas, translated and quoted by García Soormally, 2019, p. 13).

Las Casas believed in the indigenous people's salvific potential: they were ready and open to conversion. If they were educated properly, and with God's grace, they would come to know God and Christ. Even though he also saw a connection between their idolatry and their degree of civilization, he rejected the idea of waging war against the indigenous people to Christianize and civilize them. Faith cannot be imposed; only by means of gentle persuasion will they be convinced to leave behind their idolatrous traditions and come to embrace Christian faith. Those who are invincibly ignorant simply cannot be 'obliged to believe unless the faith is fully presented and explained to them by suitable ministers' (Las Casas, trans. Poole, 1974, pp. 133–134). Violent subjugation will only result in their detesting Christianity. He continues, 'A great many unbelievers are excused from accepting the faith for a long time and perhaps for their whole lifetime, no matter how long it lasts, so long as they see the extremely corrupt and detestable conduct of the Christians'. Only peaceful means should be used to stop the indigenous people's idolatries, change their way of living, and finally bring them to the Christian faith. In sum, idolatry is a sign of their religiosity (natural longing for God) and their humanity (it is human to worship idols), but it is also a sign of their not being fully civilized and their need to be Christianized.

José de Acosta

As the conflict between Catholics and Protestants escalated, and Catholics were losing ground to Protestants who rejected their traditions as idolatry, the question about the nature of the indigenous people, and the related question about the nature of their worship practices, continued to be asked. In 1590, the Jesuit José de Acosta (1539–1600), who lived the greater part of his life in Peru, published *Historia natural y moral de las Indias* [Natural and Moral History of the Indies], in which he ponders these questions (Acosta, ed. Beddall, 1977). Like Las Casas, he was struck by the natural goodness of the natives, and considered their practices as a sign of their natural desire for God (Logic of encompassment). He was, however, less optimistic about their capacity for conversion and was, after several decades of missionizing activities and mass conversions, doubtful about the authenticity of the natives' embrace of Christian worship. What concerned him deeply, however, were the striking similarities between Catholic rituals and the practices of the natives. Especially disconcerting, in view of the conflict between Protestants and Catholics, were the similarities between eucharistic rituals (which were contested in Europe too) and indigenous rituals. Indeed, Acosta writes about processions that resembled the feast of *Corpus Christi*; communal banquets where the natives 'ate the body of their idol' and drank wine from a cup, and so forth. Comparing their rituals to

Catholic ceremonies created what Robert Orsi has called 'an anxiety of ontological proximity' (Orsi, 2016, p. 33). How could this be explained in a way that did not lead to the paganization of Catholic sacraments? How could sense be made of these similarities without playing into the hands of Protestant reformers. If what native Americans did was idolatry, how was this not the case for Catholics? Intra-Christian debates and the process of religionized selfing (identity-making) heightened concerns about ritual similarities. That these 'pagans' resembled pre-Christian civilizations is one thing; that their ceremonies resembled Catholic practices that were already under attack was a different matter and made Catholics vulnerable to Protestant critics, who were already comparing Catholic rituals to pagan idolatries.

Acosta resolved his problem by arguing that this blasphemous parody of Catholicism could only be the result of the work of the devil, who had instituted sham imitations of Catholic sacraments to defy God. Idolatry was not innocent or natural. It was rather the result of demonic manipulation. The very fact that the devil chose this form of ritual mimicry actually testifies to the divine nature of Catholic rituals. Thus according to Acosta:

> *the Divell strives to imitate and to pervert, to bee honoured, and to cause men to be damned: for as we see the great God hath Sacrifices, Priests, Sacraments, Religious Prophets, and Ministers, dedicated to his divine service and holy ceremonies, so the Divell hath his sacrifices, priests, his kinds of sacraments, his ministers appointed, his secluded and fained holinesse, with a thousand sortes of false prophets [...]. There is scarce any thing instituted by Iesus Christ our Saviour in his Lawe of his Gospel, the which the Divell hath not counterfeited in some sort, and carried to his Gentiles, as may be seene in reading that which we hold for certaine, by the report of men worthie of credite, of the customes and ceremonies of the Indians, whereof we will treate in this Booke. (Acosta, ed. Markham, 2010, pp. 324–325)*

Protestant reformers, however, were not convinced and reversed the arguments formulated by Catholics to discredit Catholic sacramental tradition. Thus, they exploited Las Casas' suggestion that the natives were keen to embrace Catholic tradition in order to argue that Catholicism was akin to the savagery of 'Indian' traditions. The indigenous people's readiness to convert to Catholicism pointed to a family resemblance: both are nothing but idolatry. At the same time, Protestants readily accepted Acosta's finding that certain indigenous ceremonies resembled eucharistic rituals and argued that both of these rituals deviate from the only true Christian worship, which is based on Scripture (Shullenberger, 2010, p. 90).

Overall, idolatry, whatever its precise scope and nature, became the category European Christians used to make sense of native Americans and their traditions and to justify their imperial expansion in terms of civilization and evangelization. As a religionized category, it was 'used by the colonizers to alienate the *others* and unite them in an artificial category defined by what Spaniards were not' (García Soormally, 2019). The mere existence of the problem of idolatry gave missionaries a reason to continue to invest in the colonial project and to destroy idolatry in the new world, while trying to fend off similar accusations raised against their traditions in the old world. The trope of idolatry cast natives as slaves by nature, barbarians, or uncivilized people in need of education. In all of these cases, idea(l)s about proper worship combined with idea(l)s about what counts as civilized, functioned as the norm to categorize, essentialize, and govern Amerindian pagans. While Christians reformulated their religion in interiorized terms, they were all too eager to project the problem of religion in terms of exteriority onto others.

7   Protestantism and the Rejection of the Principle of Mediation

Reformers – Catholic and Protestant – projected a new sense of Christian normativity, understood as interiorized, spiritualized, hermeneutical, and personal. This is a shift away from the principle of mediation, which had long functioned as the norm in Europe.

176 CHAPTER 5 The Turn Inwards

Within late medieval imagination, sacred presence was mediated via a wide variety of channels and radiates out from the incarnation, which sanctified creation 'along a network of routes, images, stories and memories' (Orsi, 2016, p. 68). From this perspective, it made perfect sense that the faithful invoke the saints, want to be exposed to the healing power of relics, venerate the sacrament of sacraments (and fear to participate in holy communion), just as it makes sense that the priestly class is surrounded by an air of ritual power. The picture that emerges here is that of a community in which all members endeavour to achieve and earn God's grace (Fernández-Armesto & Wilson, 1996, p. 98). During the Long Reformation, this understanding came to be seen as 'a presumptuous and blasphemous refusal to acknowledge the sole and entire contribution of God to our salvation. It was an arrogant attempt to fetter God's unlimited sovereignty' (Taylor, 1989, p. 216). Protestant reformers would argue especially for the dismantling of key Catholic principles: ecclesiology, clerical hierarchy, and especially the principle of sacramental mediation of salvation.

While in the Catholic tradition the priests claimed a monopoly on ritual power, Protestants for their part would advocate a priesthood of all believers (Vásquez, 2011, p. 31); while salvation in the Catholic imagination was a communal concern and responsibility, salvation would now become a personal concern; while salvation relied on the proper administration of the sacraments by ordained priests, salvation would now depend on faith and God's grace; while the establishment of an intimate relationship with God could be facilitated by means of material mediation engaging all the senses, now that relationship would be facilitated primarily through listening to the Word. No priest could help to establish the salvific relation between God and man. No saint could intercede for the sinner and no good deed could somehow help the doer to enter into God's good graces. The individual stood alone before the face of God with nothing but Scripture. She is entirely helpless and completely surrendered to God's grace, and that experience of laying one's fate in the hands of God is, in the Protestant mind, utterly redemptive.

The whole widely branched Catholic ecclesial system of mediation now became associated with an air of faithlessness, superstition, idolatry, and magic. Over time, 'Protestant [...] churches swept away pilgrimages, venerations of relics, visits to holy places, and a vast panorama of traditional Catholic rituals and pieties. And along with the sacred went the medieval Catholic understanding of the Church as the locus and vehicle of the sacred. As a consequence of this, in turn, the central mediating role of the Church ceased to have any meaning' (Taylor, 1989, p. 216) and became associated with a papist theology of achievement. In the wake of the Protestant Reformation, a process of de-materialization and de-ritualization set in, or to put it in Taylor's words, a process of 'excarnation', namely 'the steady disembodying of spiritual life, so that it is less and less carried in deeply meaningful bodily forms, and lies more and more "in the head"' (Taylor, 2007, p. 771). Importantly, this excarnation was projected as liberation from superstition, from magic, and ecclesial authority and a return to pure faith and internal faith based on God's word. Interior spirituality is privileged over bodily performance and ritual practices that engage materiality – handling objects, touching statues, cherishing relics, worshipping the wafer – become questionable. Soon, reforming efforts would turn into a polemic among Protestants, while Catholics raged over rituals and other outward forms of piety (Stroumsa, 2010, p. 8). As Bellah writes,

> *[a] great deal of cosmological baggage of medieval Christianity is dropped as superstition. The fundamentally ritualist interpretation of the sacrament of the Eucharist as a reenactment of the paradigmatic sacrifice is replaced with the anti-ritualistic interpretation of the Eucharist as a commemoration of a once-and-for-all historical event. (Bellah, 1991, p. 37)*

A de-ritualizing tendency began to emerge; it placed the stress on 'faith, an internal quality of the person, rather than on particular acts clearly marked "religious"' (Bellah, 1991, p. 37). Form is placed over against meaning; ritual against the spiritual; the outer against the inner; mind against body. The assumption is that true religiosity detaches people from their material and ritual forms and liberates them from the risks of empty formalism and inauthenticity.

In the eyes of Protestant reformers, ritual (and the handling of material objects) turned into a negative term describes 'the disreputable practices of *somebody else*: what I do is ordained by God and is "true religion"; what you do is "mere ritual", at best useless, at worst profoundly evil' (Muir, 2005, p. 9, my emphasis). Rituals came to be associated with (the risk) of inauthenticity (think of empty formal ritualism or mindless repetitive behaviour), of idolatry (worshipping something that was not God), and of magic (as if rituals had any efficacy or influence on God). Ritual (magic, idolatry, manipulation, inauthenticity) and sincerity (faith, devotion, trust, authenticity) are thus placed in a religionized antithetical scheme (Seligman et al., p. 9); it is now associated with all the faults of paganism and idolatry (the misguidedness, the stupidity, the foolishness at best or at worst the work of the devil).

In reaction to Protestant Reformation, Catholics faced the challenge of both sharpening their creed and sacramentology and reforming their tradition without giving the impression that they were bending to Protestant critique. Problematizing and delegitimizing the practices of the 'pagan' native Americans were part of the effort to bolster the legitimacy of Catholic tradition. Simply put, they bought into some of the new definitions and now projected the critique formulated against their tradition onto faraway others.

8 Conclusion

The Reformation was inspired by a desire to return to a more truthful understanding of the gospel, a more purified sense of Christianness. This effort to restore the church to its early purity gave way to a typically modern pattern of religionization which pits a material/ritual understanding of religion against an interiorized and personalized understanding of religion. Notions of empty ritualism/legalism, external pomp, power lust, financial gain, but also magic (hocus pocus) and idolatry clustered together and became expressions of bad religion. More than ever before, the accent falls on what is happening on the inside: sincerity, belief, and the inner motives of religious people. A tension between ritual and sincerity took hold and the emphasis was placed on pure intention. Without faith, rituals are empty of meaning at best and idolatrous at worst; they are in any case only effective if one's believing heart is in them. What one sees on the outside is not always to be trusted; it can be belief or false pretence, as was the case for example with the *conversos* in early modern Spain.

To make their case for a more interiorized and purified Christianness (selfing), reformers projected false religion onto Christianity's others, the Jews in the first place, but also the Turks and the papists. These groups symbolize outward religion, that is fixated on material stuff and ritual practices. They lack faith, true faith. Anti-Jewish patterns of religionization, especially, were ready to be tapped by polemicists of the Reformation, and reproaches of paganism and idolatry went back and forth. These intra-Christian discussions, however, also impacted the indigenous people living in the Americas. Their beliefs and practices, their traditions were also read against the background of European discussions about the proper way to worship. At the same time, the finding that some indigenous practices showed certain resemblances to Catholic ritual traditions, also gave concern. Protestant reformers used this resemblance to further delegitimize the Catholic tradition of the Eucharist especially as 'pagan'; Catholics from their part, in trying to defend their traditions against Protestant attacks, claimed that this resemblance could only be attributed to the work of the devil. In the midst of all this turmoil, groups were religionized and their traditions redescribed, essentialized, and categorized.

The turn inwards, the effort to reshape *religio* and to refigure Christianness, would finally result in increased efforts – Catholic and Protestant – to educate people about the gospel so that they would not get confused about the proper relation between the inner and the outer. Thus, reform goes hand in hand with a civilizing and evangelizing discourse aimed at saving souls and conforming to the religionized norm of true piety. The next chapter, which deals with religionization as confessionalization and the effort to resocialize Christian society based on a changed understanding of *religio* further elaborates on the profound impact of the Reformation on real people.

Notes

[1] The notion of *religio* was hardly used after the fourth century and it only came into use again during the late Middle Ages. Reflecting on this finding, Wilfred Cantwell Smith suggests the following: 'It would seem that there is perhaps a correlation between the frequency of usage of this word and the historical situation of religious pluralism and rivalry, where there were many "religions" of which the Christian was one – a situation that had not been known before in the Latin world. By the fifth century, when the Christian church had virtually eliminated its rivals, the term was less actively in use, and in fact almost disappeared. But in the meantime its meaning had evolved and the word had become incorporated into the Christian tradition from which modernity has inherited it' (Cantwell Smith, 2008, pp. 24–25).

[2] This dramatic act symbolically marks the beginning of the Protestant Reformation and to this day it is celebrated as Reformation day. It is doubtful that this event took place. Luther, who on other occasions did enjoy a certain level of drama, never really mentions it and the only person who does mention it, Melanchton (1497–1560), was not and eyewitness. Even if Luther 'nailed' his theses to the church door, originally it would not have been received as such a theatrical gesture. At the time: 'it was the normal way to announce a debate at a medieval university, and the job was undertaken by lowly beadles, not senior professors' (Marshall, 2017).

[3] 'This notion emerged in the twelfth century. But while medieval theologians elaborated such a notion, they nonetheless stressed that in reality no one could be guiltlessly ignorant of natural and divine law. The arrival of the Spaniards to the Americas triggered the awareness that entire nations could, in fact, be invincibly ignorant of Christianity' (Toste, 2018, p. 283 abstract).

References

Acosta, J. de (Ed. B. G. Beddall) (1977). *Historia natural y moral de las Indias.* Valencia Cultural.

Acosta, J. de (Ed. C. R. Markham) (Trans. E. Grimston) (2010). *The Natural and Moral History of the Indies, Volume 2: The Moral History.* Cambridge University Press.

Asad, T. (1993). *Genealogies of Religion: Discipline and Reasons of Power in Christianity and Islam.* Johns Hopkins University Press.

Bailey, M. D. (2009). A Late-Medieval Crisis of Superstition? *Speculum, 84*(3), 633–661.

Bellah, R. N. (1991). *Beyond Belief: Essays on Religion in a Post-Traditionalist World.* University of California Press.

Cameron, E. (1999, 2013). Power of the Word: Renaissance and Reformation. In E. Cameron (Ed.), *Early Modern Europe: An Oxford History* (pp. 63–101). Oxford University Press.

Cantwell Smith, W. (2008). Religion in the West. In S. S. Elliott & M. Waggoner (Eds.), *Readings in the Theory of Religion: Map, Text, Body* (pp. 5–40). Equinox.

Cavanaugh, W. T. (2009). *The Myth of Religious Violence: Secular Ideology and the Roots of Modern Conflict.* Oxford University Press.

Chidester, D. (2018). *Religion: Material Dynamics.* University of California Press.

Cooper, D. (2018). *Sinners and Saints: The Real Story of Early Christianity.* Kregel.

Delgado, J. L., & Moss, K. C. (2018). Religion and Race in the Early Modern Iberian Atlantic. In P. Harvey & K. Gin Lum (Eds.), *The Oxford Handbook of Religion and Race in American History* (pp. 40–60). Oxford University Press.

Edwards, M. U., Jr. (1983). *Luther's Last Battles: Politics and Polemics, 1531–46.* Cornell University Press.

Eire, C. M. N. (1986). *War against the Idols: The Reformation of Worship from Erasmus to Calvin.* Cambridge University Press.

Engelke, M. (2007). *A Problem of Presence: Beyond Scripture in an African Church.* University of California Press.

Erasmus, D. (Trans. R. A. B. Mynors & D. F. S. Thomson) (1979). *The Correspondence of Erasmus: Letters 594–841 (1517 to 1518),* Collected Works of Erasmus 5. University of Toronto Press.

Erasmus, D. (Trans. B. Radice) (1986a). In Praise of Folly / *Moriae encomium.* In A. H. T. Levi (Ed.), *Literary and Educational Writings 5 and 6,* Collected Works of Erasmus 27 (pp. 77–154). University of Toronto Press.

Erasmus, D. (Trans. B. Radice) (1986b). A Complaint of Peace Spurned and Rejected by the Whole World / *Querela pacis undique gentium ejectae profligataeque.* In A. H. T. Levi (Ed.), *Literary and Educational Writings 5 and 6,* Collected Works of Erasmus 27 (pp. 289–322). University of Toronto Press.

Erasmus, D. (Trans. C. Fantazzi) (1988). The Handbook of the Christian Soldier / *Enchiridion militis christiani*. In J. C. Olin (Ed.), *Spiritualia: Enchiridion – De contemptu mundi – De vidua christiana*, Collected Works of Erasmus 66 (pp. 1–128). University of Toronto Press.

Erasmus, D. (Trans. J. E. Phillips) (1991). *Paraphrase on John*, Collected Works of Erasmus 46. University of Toronto Press.

Erasmus, D. (Trans. C. R. Thompson) (1997). The Godly Feast / *Convivium religiosum*. In C. R. Thompson (Ed.), *Colloquies*, Collected Works of Erasmus 39 (pp. 171–243). University of Toronto Press.

Erasmus, D. (Trans. P. McCardle) (1998). A Discussion of Free Will / *De libero arbitrio διατριβή sive collatio*. In C. Trinkaus (Ed.), *Controversies*, Collected Works of Erasmus 76 (pp. 1–90). University of Toronto Press.

Erasmus, D. (Trans. C. H. Miller) (2012). The Censures of the Paris Faculty of Theology about the Propositions of Erasmus. In C. H. Miller (Ed.), *Controversies*, Collected Works of Erasmus 82. University of Toronto Press.

Erasmus, D. (Trans. A. Dalzell) (2019). The Paraclesis of Erasmus of Rotterdam to the Pious Reader / *Erasmi Roterodami paraclesis ad lectorem pium*. In R. D. Sider (Ed.), *The New Testament Scholarship of Erasmus*, Collected Works of Erasmus 41 (pp. 393–422). University of Toronto Press.

Faesen, R. (2019). Tentamen vitae contemplativae in actione: The Doctrine of the Devotio Moderna. In G. Melville, S. Close, & J. Ignasi (Eds.), *Lutero 500 anni dopo: una riletura della Riforma luterana nel suo contesto storico ed ecclesiale* (pp. 69–89). Libreria Editrice Vaticana.

Fernández-Armesto, F., & Wilson, D. (1996). *Reformatie: Christendom en de wereld 1500–2000*. Anthos.

Flanagin, D. Z. (2009). Extra Ecclesiam Salus Non Est – Sed Quae Ecclesia? Ecclesiology and Authority in the Later Middle Ages. In J. Rollo-Koster & T. M. Izbicki (Eds.), *A Companion to the Great Western Schism (1378–1417)*, Brill's Companions to the Christian Tradition 17 (pp. 333–374). Brill.

François, W. (2008). Erasmus' Plea for Bible Reading in the Vernacular: The Legacy of the Devotio Moderna? *Erasmus Studies*, *28*(1), 91–120.

García Soormally, M. (2019). *Idolatry and the Construction of the Spanish Empire*. University Press of Colorado.

Goudriaan, K. (2016). *Piety in Practice and Print: Essays on the Late Medieval Religious Landscape*. Verloren.

Gro(o)te, G. (Ed. W. De Vreese) (1940). *De simonia ad beguttas. De Middelnederlandsche tekst opnieuw uitgegeven met inleiding en aanteekeningen*. Nijhoff.

Hobbins, D. (2006). Gerson on Lay Devotion. In B. P. McGuire (Ed.), *A Companion to Jean Gerson*, Brill's Companions to the Christian Tradition 3 (pp. 41–78). Brill.

Jennings, W. J. (2010). *The Christian Imagination: Theology and the Origins of Race*. Yale University Press.

Las Casas, B. de (Ed. J. P. Tudela Buesco) (1958). *Obras escogidas de Fray Bartolome de Las Casas, V: Opusculos, cartas y memoriales*, Biblioteca de autores españoles 100. Atlas.

Las Casas, B. de (Trans. S. Poole) (1974). *In Defence of the Indians*. Northern Illinois University Press.

Luther, M. (1517, 2012). The Ninety-five Theses, or, Disputation on the Power of Indulgences (LW 31:25–33). In T. F. Lull & W. R. Russel (Eds.), *Martin Luther's Basic Theological Writings* (3rd ed.) (pp. 8–13). Fortress.

Luther, M. (1520a, 1970). The Papacy at Rome. In E. W. Gritsch (Ed.), *Church and Ministry I*, Luther's Works 39 (pp. 55–104). Fortress.

Luther, M. (1520b, 1957). On the Freedom of a Christian. In H. J. Grimm (Ed.), *Career of the Reformer I*, Luther's Works 31 (pp. 333–337). Fortress.

Luther, M. (1521, 2012). Concerning the Letter and the Spirit (LW 39:175–203). In T. F. Lull & W. R. Russel (Eds.), *Martin Luther's Basic Theological Writings* (3rd ed.) (pp. 53–70). Fortress.

Luther, M. (1522, 2012). Preface to the Epistle of St. Paul to the Romans (LW 35:365–380). In T. F. Lull & W. R. Russel (Eds.), *Martin Luther's Basic Theological Writings* (3rd ed.) (pp. 76–85). Fortress.

Luther, M. (1529, 2018). *Martin Luther's Large Catechism* (Trans. H. E. Jacobs). Lutheran Library 194TC. United Lutheran Publication Society.

Luther, M. (1539, 2012). Preface to the Wittenberg Edition of Luther's German Writings (LW 34:283–288). In T. F. Lull & W. R. Russel (Eds.), *Martin Luther's Basic Theological Writings* (3rd ed.) (pp. 36–42). Fortress.

Luther, M. (1543, 1971). On the Jews and Their Lies, in F. Sherman (Ed.), *The Christian in Society IV*, Luther's Works 47 (pp. 137–306). Fortress.

Luther, M. (1545, 1960). Preface to the Complete Edition of Luther's Latin Writings. In L. W. Spitz (Ed.), *Career of the Reformer, IV*, Luther's Works 34. Muhlenberg.

Magill, R. J. (2017). Turn Away the World: How a Curious Fifteenth-Century Spiritual Guidebook Shaped the Contours of the Reformation and Taught Readers to Turn Inward. *Christianity & Literature*, *67*(1), 34–49.

Maldonado-Torres, N. (2014). Race, Religion, and Ethics in the Modern/Colonial World. *The Journal of Religious Ethics*, *42*(4), 691–711.

Markish, S. (1986). *Erasmus and the Jews*. University of Chicago Press.

Marshall, P. (2017, 30 October). 9.5 Myths about the Reformation. *Academic Insights for the Thinking World*. https://blog.oup.com/2017/10/9-myths-reformation/.

McGrath, A. E. (2012). *Reformation Thought: An Introduction* (4th ed.). Wiley-Blackwell.

Mixson, J. D. (2016). The 'Devotio Moderna' and the New Piety between the Later Middle Ages and the Early Modern Era. In K. Elm & J. D. Mixson (Eds.), *Religious Life between Jerusalem, the Desert, and the World*, Studies in the History of Christian Traditions (pp. 317–331). Brill.

Muir, E. (2005). *Ritual in Early Modern Europe*, New Approaches to European History 11. Cambridge University Press.

Mullett, M. A. (1999). *The Catholic Reformation*. Routledge.

Nirenberg, D. (2014). *Anti-Judaism: The Western Tradition*. W. W. Norton & Co.

Orsi, R. A. (2016). *History and Presence*. The Belknap Press of Harvard University Press.

Pabel, H. M. (1996). Erasmus of Rotterdam and Judaism: A Reexamination in the Light of New Evidence. *Archiv für Reformationsgeschichte*, *87*, 9–37.

Pagden, A. (1982). *The Fall of Natural Man: The American Indian and the Origins of Comparative Ethnology*. Cambridge University Press.

Pike, F. B. (1969). *Latin American History: Select Problems. Identity, Integration, and Nationhood*. Harcourt, Brace & World.

Ron, N. (2019). *Erasmus and the 'Other': On Turks, Jews, and Indigenous Peoples*. Palgrave Macmillan.

Rummel, E. (2004). *Erasmus*. Continuum.

Scase, W. (2004). Lollardy. In D. Bagchi & D. C. Steinmetz (Eds.), *The Cambridge Companion to Reformation Theology* (pp. 15–21). Cambridge University Press.

Seligman, A. B., Weller, R. P., Puett, M. J., & Simon, B. (2008). *Ritual and Its Consequences: An Essay on the Limits of Sincerity*. Oxford University Press.

Sepúlveda, J. G. de (Ed. M. Menendez y Pelayo) (1941). *Tratado sobre las justas causas de la guerra contra los Indios*. Fondo de cultura economica.

Shullenberger, G. (2010). Analogies of the Sacrament in Sixteenth-Century French and Spanish Ethnography: Jean de Léry and José de Acosta. *Romance Studies: A Journal of the University of Wales*, *28*(2), 84–95.

Smith, P. (1962). *Erasmus: A Study of His Life, Ideals, and Place in History*. Ungar.

Soen, V. (2017). Arise, O Lord (Exsurge Domine). In M. Lamport (Ed.), *Encyclopedia of Martin Luther and the Reformation* (pp. 38–39). Rowman & Littlefield.

Stroumsa, G. (2010). *A New Science: The Discovery of Religion in the Age of Reason*. Harvard University Press.

Taylor, C. (1989). *Sources of the Self: The Making of the Modern Identity*. Harvard University Press.

Taylor, C. (2002). *Varieties of Religion Today: William James Revisited*. Harvard University Press.

Taylor, C. (2007). *A Secular Age*. The Belknap Press of Harvard University Press.

Toste, M. (2018). Invincible Ignorance and the Americas: Why and How the Salamancan Theologians Made Use of a Medieval Notion. *Rechtsgeschichte: Zeitschrift des Max-Planck-Instituts für Europäische Rechtsgeschichte*, *26*, 284–297.

Toulmin, S. (1990). *Cosmopolis: The Hidden Agenda of Modernity*. Free Press.

Van Dijk, R. (2012). *Twaalf kapittels over ontstaan, bloei en doorwerking van de Moderne Devotie*. Verloren.

Van Engen, J. (1988). *Devotio Moderna: Basic Writings*. Paulist Press.

Van Engen, J. (2008a). Multiple Options: The World of the Fifteenth-Century Church. *Church History: Studies in Christianity and Culture*, *77*(2), 257–284.

Van Engen, J. (2008b). *Sisters and Brothers of the Common Life: The Devotio Moderna and the World of the Later Middle Ages*. University of Pennsylvania Press.

Van Veen, M. G. K. (2012). *De kunst van het twijfelen: Sebastian Castellio (1515–1563): Humanist, calvinist, vrijdenker*. Meinema.

Vásquez, M. A. (2011). *More Than Belief: A Materialist Theory of Religion*. Oxford University Press.

Walsham, A. (2008). The Reformation and 'the Disenchantment of the World' Reassessed. *The Historical Journal*, *51*(2), 497–528.

Walsham, A. (2015). Reformation Legacies. In P. Marshall (Ed.), *The Oxford Illustrated History of the Reformation* (pp. 227–268). Oxford University Press.

Watkins, C. (2018). Saints and Martyrs in Late Medieval Religious Culture. In P. Linehan (Ed.), *The Medieval World* (pp. 385–402). Routledge.

Whitford, D. M. (2012). *T&T Clark Companion to Reformation Theology*. T&T Clark.

CHAPTER 6

The Fragmentation of Religion and the Re-creation of Society

In the aftermath of the Reformation, Latin Christendom fractured, or as we will read in the Augsburg Peace Treaty promulgated in 1555: religion was divided [*Spaltung der Religion*]. This European reality once again triggered processes of religionization, understood as selfing (configuration of identity) and othering (the making of alterity) predicated on religious difference. Christianity splintered as never before, and old identities had to be unmade, new identities forged, and different communities shaped. Once again, Christian *literati* sought to define what is true and false worship (*religio*), what is 'the' Christian norm and what deviates from it, who belongs and who does not (García Soormally, 2019). Group boundaries between 'us' and 'them' had to be imagined, established, and policed not just with respect to worship but also as regards social life. After the fragmentation of religion, religionization took the form of confessionalization, because so many confessions or creeds were produced at that time. These confessions clearly defined what true Christians believed. In order to enforce the boundary between those who adhered to the true confession/religion and those who followed a false path, various forms of social discipline were introduced, ranging from polemics to the propagation of the true faith, and finally to the suppression of those who deviated from the projected religionized/confessionalized norm (e.g. the Augsburg Confession or *Confessio Augustana*, 1530).

> **Text Box 1: Renaming and Relabelling**
>
> The names that these new religious identities would go by were often the outcome of a 'renaming' or re-labelling process. All claimed to be Christians, namely followers of Christ, but were denied this name by their adversaries. Following a long tradition in heresiology, heretics were named after their 'misguided' leader or after their misguided teaching. Over time, groups would adopt and embrace these labels to distinguish themselves from others. Thus, they became Lutherans, Calvinists, Anabaptists, Anglicans and ... Roman Catholics. The latter qualification of Roman was necessary as too many heretics laid claim to catholicity. Leonard Lessius (quoted in Parker, 2008, p. 8), writes: 'Again the Religion that should be judged as the true Religion of Christ is the one which was always customarily called Catholic... But only the Roman has been called Catholic and only its worshippers Catholics: therefore only the Roman Religion is the true Religion of Christ'.

Christian Imaginations of the Religious Other: A History of Religionization, First Edition. Marianne Moyaert.
© 2024 John Wiley & Sons Ltd. Published 2024 by John Wiley & Sons Ltd.

Remarkably, after the splintering of religion, the binary framework of orthodoxy and heresy lost none of its appeal (Text Box 1). In the mind of most reformers – Catholic or other – there could only be one true Christian way of life, and truth continued to be imagined as one and undivided. The fragmentation of Latin Christendom also did not change the 'equation of the civic and sacral community' (Kaplan, 2007, p. 50) and the medieval ideal of the *Corpus Christianum* survived both the Catholic and the Protestant Reformations. Faith, in any case, was not yet a mere personal choice and the prevailing idea was that 'every community, great or small, formed an organic body, governed by a single mind, in which the well-being of every member depended vitally on all the others' (Luebke, 2016a). Deviating from the norm could have dramatic consequences and could endanger the entire community. In this sense, at least, the bodily image of society had not changed.

This bodily understanding of society and politics would deeply impact the way early modern Europeans handled the drama of the rupture of Latin Christendom and how they coped with dissent. It explains why Europe's rulers tried to make their choice of faith official in their own territory, why they projected confessional allegiance as one of the defining aspects of socio-political identity and why they invested in disciplinary measures to purge their society of heretics (Lotz-Heumann, 2013, p. 34). As before, ecclesiastical and secular powers would join hands to institutionalize newly imagined ways of being Christian and to reorganize society around confessional boundaries. Identities had to be made, unmade, and remade, practices had to be created, learned, and unlearned, and boundaries had to be drawn and redrawn. Old and new patterns of religionization were deployed to that end with a real impact on the lives of real people.

The process of unmaking Latin Christendom and recreating Christian societies based on newly forged Christian ideals was not realized overnight. People not only had to unlearn old habits, but they also had to acquire new ones. Confessional identities were not fixed at the beginning of the process of religionization. They had to be constructed and thought through in terms of their practicality. While boundaries between 'us' and 'them' would be projected as fixed, the reality at grassroots levels was fuzzier and hybrid. Indeed, patterns of religionization typically disguise if not deny the 'ambiguous or interstitial spaces between opposed categories [and social groups] so that [acknowledgment and the reckoning with] overlapping becomes impossible' (Mambrol, 2017). On closer inspection, those overlappings are not only noticeable when we zoom in on what people who adhered to different confessions believed and did, but also when we look at the mechanisms they used to religionize and craft boundaries between self and other.

1 Polemics and the Dehumanization of Religious Others

The Protestant and Catholic Reformations shattered the religious unity of Europe: from there being one 'orthodox' Christian norm, which both secular and ecclesial authorities were supposed to protect, now the Christian norm itself was contested in ways never seen before. Throughout this process, the body remained the most important metaphor with which to imagine the integrity of Christian society. However, '[i]n place of one body of the faithful there was now a number of different bodies all claiming to be the one true *corpus mysticum* devolved from the age of the Apostles' (Dixon, 2016a, p. 69). This rupture of the *Corpus Christianum* initiated a period of profound antagonism and created an explosive situation (Benedict, 2016, p. 86). Catholic and Protestant reformers all claimed to be orthodox and hardly anyone 'was willing to extend legitimacy to dissenters' (Dixon, 2016b, p. 34). There was little space in Christian imagination at the time to think about plurality as a good thing and only a few were able to consider the possibility of toleration as something beneficial to society. To maintain the coherence of the *Corpus Christianum*, reformers at all ends of the spectrum made use of various, by now familiar, mechanisms to create boundaries between 'us' and 'them', the first being the production of polemical discourses.

Theologians and clergy were faced with the task of admonishing the faithful and condemning error. Against the background of a fragmented *Corpus Christianum*, this task 'unleashed a torrent of polemical [works] by all confessional groups' (Parker, 2008, p. 7). Different parties showed themselves to be true heirs of a firmly established Christian polemical tradition. As in the past (cf. *Adversus Haereses*), the goal was not so much to change 'heretical' minds, but rather 'to galvanize those who had already "owned" a confessional label but whose allegiance was shallow, or conditional' (Morrissey, 2015). Polemicists grabbed every chance to sharpen their pens and pencils and to paint a picture of their confessional adversaries that would evoke repulse and shock. When the other (and his practices) evokes disgust, boundaries are put in place more easily. Preaching in churches or on the town square, printing polemical tracts, or distributing vicious wood paintings, apologists left little to the imagination. To repudiate each other, they opened all the registers of the cultural archive and its stock images. What had previously been said of the Arians, the Nestorians, the Cathars, and the Waldensians – and also of Jewish and Islamic bodies – was now being projected onto Catholics, Lutherans, Calvinists, and others. Polemicists on all sides accused one another of false religion and demonized/dehumanized those with whom they disagreed.

Interestingly, for all their assumed confessional differences, Christian polemicists – even those who were intent on shattering the intermingling of the spiritual and material – shared a worldview in which spirit and body were entangled and in which transcendent forces continued to be present in the material world (see Text Box 2). This becomes obvious in the way both 'Catholic' and 'Protestant' polemicists employed sexual slander to discredit one another, as well as in their dealings with 'impure heretical bodies'.

Sexual Slander

Reformers on both sides imagined their conflict in terms of a fight between the forces of good and evil. 'Catholics considered it obvious that Luther had been inspired by the devil' (Kaplan, 2007, p. 35). Protestants in turn declared Catholics accomplices of the Antichrist and called the Catholic Church 'Satan's Synagogue', an accusation Catholics eagerly threw back in their faces. Heretics were regarded as evil incarnate and embodiments of satanic transcendent forces. While God abhors heretical lies, the devil takes delight in them. Back and forth, reformers on both sides accused each other of sacrilege, idolatry, criminality. Of course, such accusations would intersect with charges of immorality. Having concluded a pact with the devil, the heretic falls prey to gluttony and greed. They are animals, dogs, and worse than savage beasts (dehumanization). The images of the monk-calf and pope-ass are a well-known example in this regard. The shattering of Latin Christendom and the European *Corpus Christianum*, as well as the subsequent bloodshed, was often understood as a sign of the end of times and the coming of the Antichrist. In this apocalyptic setting, testimonies of monstrous births proliferated. Especially in Germany, both Catholic and Protestant polemicists deployed monstrous births to stir up fear and repugnance. At the time, such births would have been understood in terms of punishment from God: society was degenerating and judgement was near.

Here too religionization intersected with the sexualization of others. Sexual slander continued to be a way of delegitimizing the other and projecting a clear moral boundary between us and them. Excessive sexuality or sexual perversity implied a lack of control over one's carnal desires; this could be a sign that a person was in the power of Satan and had fallen prey to the lure of a sinful life. Heresy is a work of the flesh and the flesh is weak. Finally, by casting the other as impure, one legitimized strategies of purgation.

Fixation on the carnality of Catholic superstition translated into a Protestant preoccupation with imagining the sexual and moral perversion of Catholics, who fell prey to earthly longings. Monks, nuns, priests, and bishops were depicted as pretending to lead a life of piety

184 CHAPTER 6 The Fragmentation of Religion and the Re-creation of Society

while being driven by earthly desires. Here, Protestants could of course fall back on earlier polemics against promiscuity and fornication in the Catholic Church; they could draw on a deeply established repertoire of tropes and representations about Catholic clergy seduced by the lure of the world. In the Protestant imagination the pope, especially, was the pre-eminent hate figure and the papacy was projected as serving only the carnal interests of the church. So numerous were the depictions of the pope-antichrist, that they developed into a condensed trope that signified gluttony, perversity, immorality, lust, and whoredom. The image of the pope as male prostitute was commonplace. At a time when there was a great fear of outbreaks of syphilis, this disease was called *Roman pox*. While, '[t]hese representations often conveyed a theological message, they were also intended to shock and repel – to make people squirm at the foulness of their confessional enemies' (Oldridge, 2005, p. 142).

Catholic polemicists reacted, claiming that it had been Luther's unbridled sexual desires that had brought him to rupture the church. Unable to obey the rules of sexual abstinence, he married a former nun, dismantled the rule of celibacy for clergy, and ended the long tradition of monasterial living – all out of lust. Women who married former priests or monks were depicted as whores. Catholic saintliness was placed over against Protestant worldliness (Spinks, 2009). The fact that the Protestants gave themselves over to the desires of the flesh was cast as a testimonial to the fact they were all in the power of Satan. For all their talk about piety and true worship, they were clearly driven by carnal desires.

Corrupted Souls and Diseased Bodies

The polemical othering of heretics also followed the path of negative bodily depictions. Recall how in the medieval imagination there was a close interconnection between bodily, moral, and spiritual welfare. Catholics, Lutherans, Calvinists, and others all shared the assumption that the state of the soul was reflected in the body. Moral and spiritual disorder translated into physical afflictions, and spiritual perfection into a purified and healed body. The body thus functioned as an important signifier of religious difference. The body is a book from which one can read whether or not a person was leading a pious life. A healthy, beautiful (Christian) body would have pointed to a pure soul, and that purity could be enhanced by engaging in 'devotional practices such as praying to the patron saints of specific diseases or believing in the healing power of relics' (Celati, 2014, p. 12). Stories about martyrs, especially, made use of body politics to pit adherents of true religion against those deemed heretical and/or idolatrous. These stories – whether written by Protestants or Catholics, projected the bodies of martyrs, through whose veins ran the blood of truth, as being pure and unsullied. Consider in this regard Theodore Beza (1519–1605), student and later the successor of Calvin in Geneva and author of the *Histoire ecclésiastique des églises réformées* [Ecclesiastical History of Reformed Churches] (de Bèze, 1841). In this historical work, the reformed Christian relates the miraculous story told about the brothers de Mouvans, who were killed because of their religion. I quote him here at length:

> *Here I add a memorable event, [...] that happened immediately after the death of the eldest brother of de Mouvans. [What happened is] that two of those who were also killed by those of Castellance, after the said of de Mouvans, were buried at the bend of the river that passed. Those bodies, after they had been uncovered by the force of the water after more than three months surfaced without having been corrupted at all [...].*

When they were finally buried,

> *something admirable, and otherwise incredible [occurred]: the wounds of one of the bodies found, at the time of their final burial, [were] as fresh and with blood as red as if they had been killed at the same time. (de Bèze, 1841, p. 240, my translation)*

Enemies of true religion, on the other hand, were imagined as possessing 'a tangible, physical pathology' (Parker, 2008, p. 7). Engaging in heretical activities and giving into moral and spiritual depravity would eventually lead to the disintegration and even deformation of the body. Beza continues his remarkable story by recounting what happened to the captain in charge of guarding the bodies of the brothers de Mouvans:

> On the contrary, it is said [about] a captain, one of the guards of those bodies, who had been killed during those troubles, and who had only been lying there for a half day, that his body was so rotten and infected that one could no longer approach it: it was such that the crawls and dogs were eating from it, before his companions could arrive to give him a burial. (de Bèze, 1841, p. 240, my translation)

Clusters of ideas that we first encountered in Early Christianity and also later in the Middle Ages – think of the bodies of heretics, Jews, and Muslims – were now adapted to fit the polemics against 'Christian' others, who were afflicted by disease, stench, blood loss, and incontinence. Despite the fact that the reformed sections of the Christian community projected a worldview which disentangled the material and the spiritual, the idea that corruption of the soul would affect the body remained intact. An example is the story told by Jean Crespin (1520–1572), a French reformed martyrologist, who in his *Histoire des martyrs: persécutez et mis à mort pour la vérité* [History of the Martyrs: Persecuted and Put to Death for the Truth], gives several dramatic accounts of what happened to the bodies of those who persecuted 'true' Christians. Here, he tells the story of a Catholic who persecuted reformed Christians. While he seemed to flourish, he soon became afflicted by a *flux du sang* [a blood flow], which 'moved his shameful parts, and caused him to become fleshly and to retain urine; [he] died with horrible cries and vexations, feeling a fire that burnt him from the navel upwards, with extreme infection of his lower parts' (Crespin, 1619, ed. 1885, p. 534, my translation).

However, such accounts may also be found in Catholic literature, which shares the understanding of the body as a signifier of morality and spirituality. Franciscus Costerus, a first generation Jesuit (1532–1619) who lived in Flanders and was labelled *haereticorum malleus* [hammer of heretics] theorized that Protestants were dominated by wet and cold humour, which makes them weak (like women).

> Though they had previously been members, they were transformed (how sad!) into phlegm and into a deadly abundance of humors that usually afflict the stomach, and since the stomach is not a place of filth, but naturally desires wholesome food, these are people who have too little waste, too much juice, and are able to collect blood too easily. Finally, like the filthy dregs that flowed out through the outhouse, they also flow along, one sullied with a harlot, one sullied with thieving, and another with crimes. Because this is what ordinarily happens to those who are overcome with phlegm and excessive pituitia, just as if religion became sick and vomited them out [superne a congressu Sanctorum velut vomitu Religionis nauseantis exsputi]. (Coster 1599, 48–49, quoted and translated in Parker, 2014, p. 1283)

Because they lacked the healing power of the Eucharist, they could not recover. The Jesuit Peter Canisius (1521–1597) was also convinced that turning away from the Catholic Church would harm the soul and sicken the body.

In line with their fixation on the depraved Catholic body, Reformed Christians emphasized the profoundly polluting nature of Catholic ritual life – the 'diabolical magic of the Mass' (Zemon Davis, 1973, pp. 58–59). The Catholic body, that is to say, the Catholic worshipping community, was coined as seriously ill because its members continued to feed on the sickening and polluting idolatrous idea of transubstantiation. This practice made Catholics sick to their stomach, precisely the point where body and soul were deemed to intersect (Parker, 2014): the false beliefs of 'cannibalistic' Catholics which climaxed in the Eucharist – the eating of the body of Christ – were polluting them and in one step the entire body of Christ. An act that held healing power to Catholics (also remember the accusation against the Jews that they would steal the host to heal their sick bodies) was polluting in the eyes of others.

Finally, heresy continued to be regarded as extremely contagious, 'even in very small concentrations' (Suerbaum, 2016, p. 131). Left to itself, it would spread insidiously, like cancer, and threaten 'the *Heil* of entire communities' (Kaplan, 2007, p. 71). In a similar vein, heretics, through their disgusting smells, infectious sounds, and malformed bodies, could spread and infect the entire *Corpus Christianum*. The use of such dangerous metaphors as cancer, pollution, and contamination incited members of their communities to sever 'gangrenous' members from the Christian body, so that order could be restored. This called for radical measures to purge the community from dissenters. Therefore,

> [r]eligious leaders and institutions ought to be the spiritual doctors who could halt this contagion [...]. A Body thus weakened needed strong purgative medicines to restore it to health: doctors cut into the veins of sick patients to release bad and infected blood, gave emetics to trigger violent vomiting, enemas to empty the bowels, and diuretics to clear the bladder. The source of sickness had to be eliminated from the body before healing could begin. (Terpstra, 2015, pp. 21–22)

These bodily images place 'other' Christians, here religionized as heretics, outside the realm of the *Corpus Christianum*; even stronger, they are projected as a threat to the wholeness of Christian society. The sickness of their bodies symbolizes the sickness of their beliefs and practices; as their bodies disintegrate so their presence might lead to the disintegration of Christian society. These people are not Christians and they do not belong to Christian peoplehood. The dehumanization that is part of this work of religionization facilitated the disciplinary actions that would be taken to solve the problem of heresy after the splintering of religion.

Text Box 2: The Embodiment of Meaning, Body Politics, and Deconstructing Imaginary Constructs

In the preceding chapter, I focused on the way the Reformation projected a changed understanding of true religion, an understanding that challenged the medieval Catholic understanding of sacramental mediation of Christ's presence. This new understanding of true religion had profound consequences for the objects, rituals, and spaces 'designed to accommodate Christ's presence, as well as for the purpose and the power of the clergy and Church that facilitated that presence' (Dixon, 2016a, p. 70). The Catholic understanding of sacramental mediation, which revolves around the embodiment of meaning (assuming the intertwining of the spiritual and material realms), was set apart from a more symbolic, figurative, or expressivist understanding of divine presence (Moyaert, 2015). The relation between the spiritual and material realm was profoundly altered. While Lutherans were less radical in their call for ritual reformation and held the middle ground, reformed Christians such as Zwingli and Calvin would react fiercely against any effort to contain the infinite in the finite [*Finitum non est capax finiti*]. Reformed Christians would attack Catholic religion as false worship, and they would unleash a war against idolatry. The cult of saints, the veneration of relics, and the accompanying clerical system were repugnant. The idea that the sacred could be contained, touched, smelled, caressed, and so forth was an affront. A vigorous attack on religious externalities resulted. '[W]herever those who held these views acquired enough power, churches were sacked, images smashed and burnt, relics destroyed, sanctuaries desecrated, altars overturned, and consecrated hosts fed to dogs and goats. The religion of immanence was replaced by the religion of transcendence' (Eire, 1986, p. 2). In this regard, the Reformation set in motion a de-materialization and de-ritualization of religion (see also Chapter 5). The turn inwards implied a turn away from mediation in terms of the embodiment of meaning. This is true, but also needs further nuancing.

The making of self and other predicated on religious difference produces imaginary constructs, which tend to hide from view more complex realities and hybrid identities. To be sure, the Reformation paved the way for a changed understanding of religion, one that emphasized personal piety and worship and the remodeling of the interior life of the religious person. The religionized boundaries that were projected and imagined during this shift, however, were not real. The reality was more nuanced.

First, it is important to realize that Catholics also embraced this more interiorized understanding of religion, before as well as after the Reformation (cf. the modern devout on the one hand, and the Jesuits on the other hand) and this was in alignment with various religious sensitives at the time. Our discussion of the modern devout made clear that interiorization and mediation are not necessarily contradictory. Furthermore, the idea that the Protestant Reformation said goodbye to the embodiment of meaning is also increasingly questioned. The way Protestant reformers imagine their Christianness in contrast to Catholics and the way they make use of religionized binary patterns of selfing and othering to that end, hides from view the material dimensions of their religion. We are, again, dealing with a projected boundary which does not match lived reality. Scholars in the field of material religion have been identifying the material dimension of the Protestant Reformation and the way spaces, rituals, and objects (the outer) helped to shape religious faith and spirituality (the inner) (Houtman & Meyer, 2012). For example, they have begun to identify how even Protestant communities, mainly Lutheran, created their own cult of sainthood. Finally, historians with a specific interest in gender and sexuality also point out that the understanding of the body as a signifier of virtue and vice, of orthodoxy and heresy, of piety and impiety – that is as a symbolic carrier of meaning – was shared across confessional divides. For both Catholics and Reformed, the body carried meaning, and both holy and demonic powers could take hold of the body or could become present in the body. Thus, one could touch, smell, or even see divine or demonic presence in the bodies of the faithful and the unfaithful. The connection of flesh and spirit remained entangled in the minds of both Catholics and Protestant reformers and they agreed that the body signified heresy and idolatry as well as orthodoxy and piety. As Charles Parker puts it, 'The body also continued to serve as a barometer of the soul because corporality remained integral to perceptions of religious difference in an age of confessional conflict and epistemological uncertainty' (Parker, 2014, p. 1292).

2 Protecting the Socio-political Order: Expulsion, Confiscation, Torture

Polemics surrounding disgusting heretical bodies legitimized violent acts of purgation. Heretics had to be brought back into the fold, if necessary by using force. There was no charity in letting them go to hell because of their beliefs and practices, nor could anything good come from calling down God's wrath and endangering the community. It was better to treat heretics harshly, so that they might come to their senses and return to the flock. Harsh treatment was an expression of charitable hatred (Walsham, 2006). Tolerance, on the other hand, was nothing but a loser's creed. Many reformers agreed and this conviction was also widely accepted under the larger population, and subscribed to by secular authorities. Given, however, that heretics were stubborn and that their hearts had hardened under the influence of Satan, many considered it difficult if not impossible to convert heretics, so that persecution, exclusion, and even extermination, 'of those who wilfully persisted in soul-destroying doctrinal error [was regarded as] a divinely imposed duty' (Walsham, 2015, p. 229). Many questioned if heretics were even capable of conversion and hence capable of being saved.

Ecclesial authorities and lay people 'expected the civil authorities to legally purge the most offensive heretics from the community' (Zemon Davis, 1973, p. 52). We know from the historical archives that the latter accepted this responsibility and tried to repress heresy. Francis I (r. 1515–1547), the 'most Christian King of France', has been recorded saying that he wanted heresy to be rooted out 'in such a manner that if one of the arms of my body was infected with this corruption, I would cut it off, and if my children were tainted with it, I would myself offer them in sacrifice' (Diefendorf, 1991, p. 47).

Text Box 3: Naming and Renaming

The Huguenots were French Calvinists, who suffered at the hands of Catholics during the sixteenth century. They were massacred during St. Bartholomew's night in 1572. The origin of their name is under discussion. Some have argued it was 'evocative of pestilential bodies: "Huguet" was a contemporary nickname for ghosts who rose from purgatory, bodies neither living nor dead, but sinister and dangerous. The Huguenots were frequently accused of carnal impurity, their night meetings characterized as orgies, where Protestant "whores and sluts" seduced good Catholics. [...] The Huguenots were thus religionized as a kind of material impurity within France and her church, their physical persons the embodiment of pollution' (Osborn, 2018, p. 329).

In Reformation Europe, heresy trials began around 1523, and their number peaked around 1560 (Monter, 1996, p. 56). Heretical bodies were tortured, publicly humiliated, and executed. In view of the ideology of contamination/purgation, it is relevant to note that heretical bodies would either be drowned, the water having the power to cleanse souls or exorcise harmful souls, or burnt, fire having the power to completely destroy the heretical body and thus to finally purge the community from the threat of heretical bodies. The aim was 'literally burn, wash and sweep' the heretic's body from the *Corpus Christianum* (Osborn, 2018, p. 139). 'The records of their trials were burned along with them and the ashes scattered to the winds, thereby preventing their burial [...]. Unlike other criminals, whose bodies could be exposed and left to rot, the heretic had to be utterly destroyed' (Nicholls, 1988, p. 50). According to William Monter, some 3,000 people were executed for heresy between 1520 and 1565 (Monter, 1996, p. 49).

To maintain the coherence of Christian society, authorities often expelled dissenters from their territories. The example set by Catholic monarchs Ferdinand and Isabella in 1492, when they expelled the Jews from their lands, was followed by many European rulers in the centuries that followed. The first Reformation exile was Luther: in 1521 he was placed under an imperial ban after he had refused to renounce his views at the Imperial Diet. This ban made him an outlaw. No one in the empire was allowed to protect him or spread his heretical views – we know that Frederick the Wise (1463–1525), elector of Saxony ignored this prohibition and protected Luther against the church.

Some dissenters left voluntarily and went into exile; others were formally expelled. Several scholars state that these religious turbulences sparked an unprecedented refugee crisis with thousands of displaced families. Exiles were forced to leave their homes and belongings and would not be allowed to return. Their property would be confiscated, and their furniture often sold. Their family and social relations were severely damaged, as were their financial means. This was a traumatic experience, which affected refugees and exiles in their very livelihood. Both the number of expulsion edicts and bans and the number of refugees and exiles grew as doctrinal disputes became more and more interwoven with political interests, and local rulers became the protectors of a particular creed in their territory.

Rituals of Purgation

Heresy persecution was a legal affair: it was a joint responsibility of secular and ecclesiastical authorities. It was not up to the common people to take matters into their own hands. However, when authorities refrained from taking action, polemical preachers would sometimes incite the masses and claim that it was their community's responsibility to take action and defend God's honour (Benedict, 2016, pp. 80–81). When the crowd 'took over' or temporarily appropriated the role of the authorities, riots sometimes erupted. While these actions were illegal, 'the crowds believed [they] were legitimate' (Zemon Davis, 1973, p. 66). Often, these actions were legitimized after the fact.

Natalie Zemon Davis' research has shown that the violence committed by rioters was not random or blind, but seems to have functioned as some sort of ritualized defence of true doctrine, a performative rejection of heresy, and an empathic appropriation of a true Christian self-understanding. Besides, this violence also had the goal of purging society from the source of pollution and defilement. It acted upon the metaphor of the *Corpus Christianum* and assumed the interlocking of the material and the spiritual. Thus, she states,

> *[i]t is not surprising, then, that so many of the acts of violence performed by Catholic and Protestant crowds have [...] the character either of rites of purification or of a paradoxical desecration, intended to cut down on uncleanness by placing profane things, like chrism, back in the world where they belonged. (Zemon Davis, 1973, p. 59)*

These rites of violent purgation could target both objects (resulting in iconoclasm, which often went together with mockery or the execution of clergy) and bodies (resulting in such actions as execution or the desecration of those graveyards where filthy heretical bodies were buried).

Iconoclasm Iconoclasm – 'removing, breaking, or defacing of religious statues, paintings, and symbols' (Muir, 2005, p. 188) – was one specific expression of Protestant ritualized violence aimed at Catholic culture. Such iconoclastic actions continued the work of anti-heresy polemics and assumed the rhetoric of purgation. Reformed Christians, especially, believed that Catholic tradition was 'polluted doctrinally, and that these heresies were embodied in physical articles of the Catholic faith' (Osborn, 2018, p. 133). Precisely those things that Catholics considered sacred were considered by them to be blasphemous and idolatrous. The most immediate goal of iconoclasm was to stop people from engaging in idolatrous practices, which offended God and could provoke God's wrath. Material objects could not mediate the sacred or bring about its presence. The holy bodies of statues and saintly relics repulsed them. Carly Osborn, however, argues that these material objects actually 'stood in proxy for Catholicism itself, imagined as a poison of which true Christians needed to be purged' (Osborn, 2018, p. 133).

Iconoclasm took the form of a threefold rite of purification. According to Robert Scribner, it began with a desegregation of the statue from the sacred space by taking it to a profane place, often a marketplace, a tavern, or even a brothel. Next, during the transitional phase, the statue would be humiliated and tortured, while being 'interrogated' and asked to prove its sacred power. After failing the test, humiliation or punishment would follow. In the third stage, the material of the statue, now profaned and clearly powerless, could be used as building material or to light a fire (Scribner, 1987). During the process, these statues were treated as heretical bodies, removed from their home (church), dragged through the streets, interrogated, humiliated, and mutilated.

For Catholics, iconoclasm was a fierce attack on the economy of the sacred. Often, the objects under attack were material embodiments of the sacred and carriers of social memories; they were valuable goods and people were often very attached to them, both personally and collectively. Seeing them harmed and destroyed was a painful experience for the Catholic faithful. This in turn legitimized Catholic violence against Protestant iconoclasts.[1]

When the latter were overcome, the violence used against them likewise took on a ritualistic character: public processions would be organized to show renewed veneration for profaned objects, Protestants were forced to forsake their faith and participate in the Eucharist. Such rituals of purgation have to be understood in the light of the understanding of society in terms of *Corpus Christianum*; the presence of heretics [here Protestants] poses a threat to the community.

Humiliating, Killing, and Exhuming Heretical Bodies
During a riot, Protestants tended to target people of the cloth, who were considered to be symbolic embodiments of the Catholic culture of mediation; Catholics, on the other hand, would not make this distinction. Mimicking official executions, heretics would be humiliated, tortured, and corporally punished. They would be dragged through the streets, mocked, and harmed. Since the goal was to obliterate all traces of the heretic, heretical bodies were often drowned in the river. Sometimes, however, even this would not be sufficiently cleansing and 'the bodies had to be weakened and humiliated further' (Zemon Davis, 1973, p. 83), which is why the bodies would also be 'thrown to packs of dogs, dismembered, disfigured and disembowelled' and finally burnt (Osborn, 2018, p. 140).

Funerals and graveyards also became the battleground for members of the Catholic and Reformed faiths (Korpiola & Lahtinen, 2015, p. 27). Protestants refused to bury Catholics in the churchyards and vice versa. In brief, they denied one another a Christian burial. Catholics especially were disgusted by the heretical body being buried within their sacred space. This disgust points once again to the fear of pollution spread by heretical corpses. Every 'trace of their contaminated bodies had to be removed from the company of the righteous' (Tait, 2002, p. 96). Sometimes crowds would demand that bodies be dug up again, and hanged on the gallows, only to be buried anew outside of the churchyard, where the criminals lay. Sometimes the deceased would be stoned, dismembered, or executed *post mortem*, and sometimes the exhumed body would even be burnt, so that it did not come back to haunt the living.

In all of the violence that erupted, whether legal or illegal, we see the metaphorical ideal of human society as Christ's social body and the ideological dichotomy of purity (orthodoxy) and impurity (heresy) at work. It is a dangerous metaphor, reiterated in polemical works and acted upon by various social agents. We also see that the idea of transcendence continued to hold power, regardless of confessional differences.

3 The Legal Establishment of the Fragmentation of Religion

While efforts to herd the heretics back into the fold continued, attempts were also made to reconcile the different parties so as to establish eternal peace and to undo the rupture in the one true church. Councils and colloquies were convened. Church leaders and theologians weighed in, trying to come together on key doctrinal questions. Such reconciliations, or *concordia* as they were called, depended on a careful distinction between what is essential to true Christian faith and what is 'adiaphoral' (*adiaphora* are religious matters of indifference because they are neither commanded nor forbidden in the Bible).

Efforts to reconcile the various parties by finding a theological compromise of some sort bore little fruit, however. Catholic and Protestant reformers found themselves on opposites sides, unable to settle such complex doctrinal issues as infant baptism, grace, predestination, natural and supernatural revelation, and the nature and extent of human sin. The fiercest debates revolved around the question of whether the mystery of the Eucharist should be conceived in terms of transubstantiation, consubstantiation, or as an *in memoriam*. The symbol par excellence of the Christian community became a point of division, a boundary that to this day remains difficult to cross. While many continued to call for a universal council hoping that it would bring reconciliation, such calls were in vain, and 'None of the three major religious conferences organized between 1540 and 1541 in Haguenau, Worms, and Regensburg succeeded in bridging the differences between Catholics and Lutherans, even if the notable progress made in Regensburg on the central problem of justification for a time augured a decisive success' (Christin, 1997, p. 23, my translation). Most of the peace treaties that were concluded in the face of conciliatory disillusion nevertheless mentioned this hope for eternal peace explicitly.

Civil rulers also fell short. It was their responsibility to ensure socio-political stability by protecting the one Christian norm against heresy. The 'traditional' legal measures of admonition, persecution, expulsion, and even execution did not make the catastrophe of growing dissent go away. Civil rulers were unable to contain the proliferation of heretical movements and halt the splintering of Latin Christendom. The effort to suppress dissent evoked protest and incited more violence, creating even more unrest and instability. Furthermore, vehement oppression created martyrs, whose suffering was refigured as a sign of piety. Inspired by the example of early Christians, a true Christian is one who is willing to undergo persecution and follows Christ unto death. The 'choice to die for the faith' and hence imitate Christ, became 'a way to prove one's steadfastness, piety and sacrifice' (Janssen, 2011, p. 479). Persecution evoked a sense of pride rather than shame, and often those who were persecuted because of their confession became yet more radical.

Secular rulers sought to protect the true faith in their own regions, sometimes out of piety, sometimes motivated by political, territorial, and/or economic considerations but they still profoundly disagreed about the identity of that 'true faith'. Some embraced the old (Catholic) religion and others followed Luther's path or that of Calvin. As conflicts became military in nature, they also turned increasingly grim. Territories were turned into battlefields.

This situation left

sovereigns to confront their own powerlessness: not only had they failed to maintain or restore religious unity within their states either by violence or by negotiation, but their attempts had only increased the distance and mistrust among adversaries everywhere. Neither the edicts of persecution nor the military violence nor the efforts at doctrinal reconciliation had led to the expected results or filled the growing gaps between confessions. (Christin, 2004, p. 427)

Peace Treaties and the Redefinition of the Binary of Orthodoxy/Heresy

To resolve conflicts and restore socio-political order, European rulers, starting from the middle of the sixteenth century, 'embarked on an unfamiliar path' towards religious coexistence by concluding peace treaties (Text Box 4). Significantly, peace only came after disillusion (Christin, 2004, p. 427). These peace treaties formalized the 'procedures to mediate or

Text Box 4: Religious Peace Treaties

Mention should be made of the Peace of Kappel, Switzerland (1529), the Peace of Augsburg, Holy Roman Empire (1555), the Peace of Amboise, France (1563), the Pacification of Ghent (1576), and the Religious Peace of 1578, the Low Countries. At a later stage, we may think of the Edict of Nantes (1598), the Edict of Grace of Alès (1629), Bohemian Maiestas Rudolphina (1609), and finally the Westphalian Peace Treaty (1648). These peace treaties became something of a new *genre:* the resemblances between them are significant. Generally speaking, they consisted of a solemn pact in which adversaries agreed to renounce violence for religious reasons and accepted the legal principles established in the pact.

192 CHAPTER 6 The Fragmentation of Religion and the Re-creation of Society

adjudicate conflicts', which simultaneously 'activated religious boundaries' (Te Brake, 2017, p. 11). Indeed, these treaties turned the fragmentation of religion (*Spaltung der Religion*) into a legal reality. This was a dramatic change. At least from a legal perspective, it meant that the ancient binary of orthodoxy/heresy was profoundly redefined: from now on there would be two and later three legitimate confessions/religions.

The establishment of religious plurality by law, however, did not mean that pluralism was embraced in principle (*de iure*). Even in these treaties, the ideal of the *Corpus Christianum* lost nothing of its appeal and most rulers tried to preserve and duplicate the medieval ideal of the *Corpus Christianum* by creating territorial theo-political wholes: *cuius regio eius religio*. The Peace of Augsburg is a key example of this development towards the institutionalization of religious difference.

The Peace of Augsburg The Peace of Augsburg (25 September 1555) was an agreement between Emperor Charles V (1500–1558), represented by his brother Ferdinand, and the Schmalkaldic League, and dealt with the problem of *Religionsspaltung* (§15).[2] The final text consists of 144 articles, of which 24 (articles 7–30) deal directly with the problem of religion and how to handle conflicts related to the religious schism. The opening paragraph of the treaty makes clear that this peace is concluded because the parties involved were tired of war and the conflict had reached a stalemate. Their state of 'weariness and resignation' made the parties finally accept the reality of religious plurality (Te Brake, 2017, p. 58), albeit grudgingly (§1).[3] The goal of the treaty was to protect 'the Nation, our beloved fatherland' from ruin by calling for an immediate ceasefire: 'We therefore establish, will and command, that from henceforth no one [...] shall engage in feuds, make war upon, rob, seize, invest or besiege one another'. Furthermore, the treaty projects an ideal of Christian love, stating that 'everyone shall love the other with true friendship and Christian love' (§14). While the treaty has not given up the hope that the various parties involved would reach theological agreement on doctrinal, liturgical, and scriptural issues, it acknowledges that, at least for the time being, this was an unrealistic goal (§9). The only option left was to settle for a political peace without giving up on the ideal of religious unity for the Roman Empire (§25). Thus, we read:

> If such a [theological] reunion cannot be obtained by way of a General Council, a National Council, colloquies, or the Imperial Diet, the agreement in all of the above points and articles shall nonetheless remain in force until the final agreement in matters of religion and faith. Accordingly, in this and in other forms, a durable, permanent, unlimited, and eternal peace should be established and agreed upon and remain in force. (§25)

In fact, Ferdinand never gave up hoping for future theological reconciliation and 'up until his death in 1564, lobbied so that the third period of the Council of Trent briefly engaged with the desiderata of the imperial princes' (Soen, 2017a, p. 562). This is the reason that the Augsburg peace has been called a 'truce without end', rather than being seen as a principled embrace of religious plurality.

The treaty established the principle of mutual recognition and security: on the one hand the Confession of Augsburg is projected as an established and licit religion and the electors, princes, and estates of the empire promise not wage war against it. On the other hand, those estates which embraced the Augsburg Confession agreed to allow (tolerate) electors, princes, and estates that adhere to the old religion. Thus, the splintering of Christian *religio* (§13) was recognized as a legal and political reality and, at least within this framework, rulers would refrain from regarding and treating each other as heretics. By writing the religious schism into the imperial constitution, the treaty alters the one-on-one relationship between religious uniformity and socio-political order: stability no longer depends exclusively on uniformity and might even require the recognition of more than one religion in one and the same territory, provided that there is a legal framework setting the rules of engagement.

From now on (and up until theological reconciliation might be reached) none of the princes or estates would wage war on account of religion (§15) nor would they interfere with other estates for religious reasons. The sovereignty of the estates was to be respected and this includes matters of religion (see below *ius reformandi*). Religious difference was eliminated as *casus belli* [a legitimate reason for war].

Next, the Peace of Augsburg establishes the principle of *ius reformandi* (§24), which gave regional rulers – rather than the emperor or the ecclesial authorities – the authority to choose the public religion and to determine the freedom or repression of other religious groups. Importantly, the regional rulers could only choose between the old religion or the *Confessio Augustana* (i.e. the creed Lutherans agreed upon in Augsburg in 1530); all other 'traditions' were excluded. Later, Greifswald law professor Joachim Stephan (1544–1623) would call this the *cuius regio eius religio* principle. The sovereign would also have the power to allocate ecclesial properties and rights (who gets to worship where). '[R]ulers such as Count Ottheinrich of the Palatinate called it [the *ius reformandi*] the "highest" such attribute (*höchstes Regal*)' (Kaplan, 2007, p. 103). The peace treaty certainly testifies to the sovereign's increased control over religious matters even though this shift came with restrictions, for example the ecclesiastical provision that church property within an imperial diocese was exempt from re-assignment. As we know, most rulers tried to impose uniformity on their territories in an effort to bind their subjects more firmly to their authority and to one another, and also because they were convinced that their confession would please God (Kaplan, 2007, p. 102). In their own territories, the ideal of the *Corpus Christianum* was therefore maintained.

The new understanding of fragmented religion in combination with the *ius reformandi* principle contributed to a re-arrangement of the European map and the establishment of a new international political order. Power in religious matters shifted from the pope and the emperor to territorial and even local sovereigns. Consequently, the religious map of Europe would thus be organized like 'a leopard skin', consisting of multiple sovereign monoconfessional regions (Christin, 2004, p. 432). To this day, Europeans feel the reverberation of this treaty (and others like it) in their cultural heritage, for example in their architecture and calendar.

Subjects with a deviating religion were given the right to emigrate (§24) and take their family and belongings to a territory of their own confession [*ius emigrandi*].

> It may happen that Our subjects or those of the electors, princes, and other estates, either of the old faith or the Confession of Augsburg, wish to leave Our lands or those of the electors, princes, and estates of the Holy Roman Empire, together with their wives and children, and settle elsewhere. They shall be permitted and allowed to do so, to sell their goods and possessions, after having paid a reasonable sum for freedom from servile obligations and for taxes in arrears, such as has everywhere been customary for ages. [...] (§24)

This was a step forward from the earlier policy, which simply confiscated the belongings of heretics, but nevertheless the impact on the inhabitants was severe, and in reality the emigration right was often interpreted by rulers as the right to expel dissenting voices (Brady et al., 2006, p. 97).

Another principle was the *reservatum ecclesiasticum*, which protected the special status of the ecclesiastical states. If the prelate of an ecclesiastical state changed his religion, the inhabitants of this state did not have to change with him. Rather, the prelate was expected to leave his position and resign. The intention of this principle was to avoid the secularization of ecclesiastical principalities and curb the expansion of Lutheranism. Ecclesiastical princes converting to 'the other religion' would lose their position, their preferential treatment, and their revenues to newly appointed Catholic officials (Soen, 2017a). It should come as no surprise that Protestant parties strongly opposed this principle as it 'ensured that Catholicism was sustained throughout a significant part of the empire' (Soen, 2017b, p. 771). Their protests eventually led to the insertion of a highly contested addendum known as the *Declaratio Ferdinandea*; this *Declaratio* 'granted religious toleration to corporations within

194 CHAPTER 6 The Fragmentation of Religion and the Re-creation of Society

ecclesiastical territories', that had been practising the Augsburg Confession 'for many years [*lange zeit und jar*]' (Luebke, 2016b, p. 135).

While this peace treaty continued to be based on the assumption that peace is more stable if the area is 'confessionally pure', cleansed, and homogeneous (Zulehner, 2014, p. 609), the Peace of Augsburg basically turned the Holy Roman Empire into a bi-confessional empire. Thus it 'saved the theory of religious unity for each state while destroying it for the Empire' (Wedgwood, 1944, p. 42). The Holy Roman Empire was no longer whole in religious terms, but the ideal of the *Corpus Christianum* was not relinquished. Some estates followed the rule of the old religion and others the Augsburg Confession but all of them tried to recreate their territories in accordance with this ideal and to maintain a semblance of unity.

The principle of the *ius reformandi* had severe consequences for the people who were affected by it. 'In the context of the Counter-Reformation and the struggle between Lutherans and Calvinists for Protestant ascendancy, the religious identities of the German princes were often fluid, creating a heightened state of religious insecurity for their peoples' (Reus-Smit, 2013, p. 100). To make matters more complicated, Ferdinand also exempted the free imperial cities (*Reichsstädte*) of the Holy Roman Empire – Augsburg, Cologne, and Nuremberg – from having to comply with the norm of religious uniformity. In these cities, the *jus reformandi* was suspended and religious coexistence within one city was legalized. Here, Catholics and Lutherans could live together in peace, and (§27) both Catholics and Lutherans had members on the city council. Inhabitants could publicly practise according to their creed.[4]

> *In many free and Imperial cities, both religions – Our old religion and that of the Augsburg Confession – have for some time been practiced. They shall continue to exist and be maintained in these cities. The citizens and other residents of these free and Imperial cities, both of clerical and lay estates – shall continue to live peacefully and quietly with another. Neither party shall venture to abolish or force the other to abandon its religion, usages, or ceremonies. On the contrary, according to the provisions of this peace, each party shall leave the other to maintain in a peaceful and orderly fashion its religion, faith, usages, ordinances, and ceremonies, together with its possessions, just as is mandated above for the estates of both religions.*

From a legal and political perspective, this treaty symbolizes the beginning of the end of the empire understood as one sacred community. The historical reality of fragmented Christian reality was confirmed by law and there were now two religions permitted: the old religion and the Augsburg Confession. 'All others, however, who are not adherents of either of the aforementioned religions are not included in this peace but shall be altogether excluded from it' and continue to be regarded as heretics (§17). This placed a bomb under the peace treaty (Christin, 1998, pp. 504–505) and would lead to new conflicts and new peace treaties.

Text Box 5: The Peace of Augsburg and the Redefinition of Religion

It is not entirely clear what the notion of religion implies in the Augsburg Peace Treaty (Feil, 1986). Its usage points in diverging directions. Sometimes *religio* is mentioned in a longer enumeration next to 'faith, usages, ordinances, and ceremonies...' Here *religio* may refer to the medieval understanding of *religio* as virtuous worship of God (piety/*pietas*). In other places, however, the Augsburg peace seems to use the term *religio* as an all-encompassing term, qualified by an adjective: 'the old religion' or 'the other religion', 'the religion affiliated with the Augsburg Confession', or 'any of the aforementioned religions'. *Religio* here seems to function as a synonym of *confessio*, meaning creed and by extension churches following a specific creed (see below), hence the claim of several scholars who state that this era turned religion into a belief system. This fixation on *religio* as confession should not, however, detract from the fact that the fragmentation of *religio* was mainly a ritual concern and touched upon the question:

how do we maintain the body social, which is a sacred body, when we may not celebrate together. The splintering of religion is the splintering of ritual. From this perspective, *religio* also means something akin to the Roman understanding of tradition, namely the rituals that had to be performed to give the gods their dues and maintain the Roman civic order. *Pax Romana est pax deorum.*

Der Spaltung der Religion **Two legal religions**		**Heresy** **Illegal religion**
Old religion	Other religion/ Augsburg Confession	All others who are not adherents of these religions are excluded from the peace treaty
Catholic	Lutheran	
Has its own *religion, faith, usages, ordinances, and ceremonies*	Has its own *religion, faith, usages, ordinances, and ceremonies*	
In territories where the old religion is the legal norm, the Augsburg Confession becomes illegal with material consequences for its followers	In territories where the Augsburg Confession is the legal norm, the old religion becomes illegal with material consequences for its followers	They become outlaws in the Holy Roman Empire

4 Religionization as Confessionalization

While the process of identity formation and border demarcation accelerated after the Augsburg peace, it had started earlier, in the first half of the sixteenth century, when different churches began to produce written confessions of faith (*confessio fidei*), declarations containing their main doctrines. These confessions served not only the 'purpose of synthesizing in *formulae* the doctrines considered basic for the Christian faith' (Rodrigues, 2017, p. 2), they also contributed to a hardening of the divisions in Europe (Marshall, 2009, p. 66). All the churches that emerged in the sixteenth century produced such confessions and they all exhibited three tendencies: 'the internalization of church teachings, the drawing of sharp dichotomies, and the quest for 'holy uniformity' (Text Box 6). Each fuelled intolerance' (Kaplan, 2007, p. 29). Because of the significance of the confessions, the early modern process of religionization took the form of confessionalization. However, as we shall see below, confessionalization was about so much more than written statements; it refers to a broad socio-cultural process in which ritual, space, and control all played an important part.

Text Box 6: Beyond Imaginary Constructs:
Concepts of Reformation and Counter-Reformation as Patterns
of Religionization

For a long time, Protestant historians considered the sixteenth and seventeenth centuries in terms of a Protestant Reformation and a Catholic Counter-Reformation. They understood the Counter-Reformation as an effort on the part of the Catholic Church to react, counter, and reverse the Reformation. Usually, the Council of Trent (1545–1563) was projected as the symbolic embodiment of the Counter-Reformation. Within this hermeneutical framework, the Protestant Reformation sets the norm and functions as the default position over against which Catholicism is defined as reactionary. First, the Catholic Church of the Middle Ages is projected as having left behind nothing but spiritual fallow land, in need of Protestant (re)-Christianization. Next, Catholic reform efforts are understood as making sense only in the light of the Protestant Reformation and only as backward-looking, defensive and conservative. Especially from the nineteenth century onwards, the Reformation was projected as a progressive, emancipatory movement that initiated the victory of liberalism and the triumph of modern civilization over 'blind prejudice and barbarous persecution' (Walsham, 2006, p. 6). The general thrust was that Protestants set in motion a 'gradual move away from the grip of closed medieval tribalism to an enthusiasm for the liberties and freedoms popularized by Enlightenment philosophy' (Dixon, 2016b). One example in this regard is Hegel (1770–1831), who considered the Reformation as the 'all-illuminating Sun, which follows that daybreak at the end of the Middle Ages'. To his mind, Luther was the first 'great exponent of individual conscience and human freedom. [...] He stood against the authoritarian darkness and superstition of the Middle Ages and so helped his fellow Europeans break through to civilizational maturity' (George, 2019). Within this binary framework:

> *Protestantism correlates with* Scripture, reasonableness, mature faith, the emancipation of the individual, enlightened modernity, disenchantment, tolerance, freedom of religion, democracy;
> *Catholicism correlates with* ritual, magic, immature faith, authoritarian structures, dark middles ages, intolerance, persecution, theocracy.

Some Catholic historians were far from happy with this one-sided depiction and tried to claim the notion of 'Catholic Reformation', to which Protestant church historians strongly objected, largely because they did not want the term 'Reformation' to be used for anything other than the Protestant Reformation. Protestant historians, therefore, continued to use the term 'Counter-Reformation' (Lotz-Heumann, 2013).

In recent years, however, this binary hermeneutical framework of action and reaction has been criticized as being overly simplified and as articulating a Protestant bias in historiography. I consider it to be an example of how patterns of religionization, which feed on imaginary constructs, find their way into scholarship. First, this binary framework continues the problematic assumption that Reformation is a purely Protestant endeavour and ignores how reforming movements not only preceded the Protestant Reformation but also how these reforming movements were at heart Catholic and not simply 'proto-Reformations'. Besides, this antithetical paradigm frames all Catholic reform efforts after 1517 as reactionary, as if they only make sense when placed against the Protestant Reformation. Third, it taps into the logic of setting progressive, emancipatory Protestantism in opposition to reactionary, conservative Catholicism. Fourth, it ignores how *la déraison identitaire* – as Paul Ricoeur calls it, the attempt to define who we are in juxtaposition to imagined others – was happening simultaneously within the Catholic Church and among Protestant communities (Lutheran, Baptist, Calvinist, Zwinglian, etc.).

Today, the preferred term among historians is that of confessionalization, a more 'neutral term which could be applied to all churches' (Lotz-Heumann, 2013). Historians note that the Protestant churches and the Catholic Church all invested more or less simultaneously in confessionalization. Put differently, for all the differences and points of contention that bitterly divided them, in some respects the churches of early modern Europe were developing in parallel to one another. Whether we speak about Lutheran, Calvinist, or Catholic *Konfessionsbildung*, the dynamic was more or less the same (Rodrigues, 2017, p. 4). Just as the reforming efforts started long before the Protestant Reformation, the effort to consolidate, standardize, and institutionalize confessional difference was a metaconfessional process, which finally resulted in various confessional churches.

Confessionalization and the Making of Bounded Communities

The production of competing confessions of faith played an important role in the formation of clearly bounded communities that all claimed to be Christian (Puff, 2018, p. 46). In the period between 1530 and 1647, Lutherans united around the Augsburg Confession (1530) and the Book of Concord (1580). The Reformed accepted the Helvetic Confessions of 1536 and 1566, the Heidelberg Catechism (1563), and the formulae of Calvinist orthodoxy from the 1619 Synod of Dort. The Roman Catholic Church promulgated the decrees of Trent (Marshall, 2009, p. 66). The basic objective of these creedal statements was to define the most important articles of faith that are accepted, affirmed, and subscribed to by the members of that confession, for example the Reformed Church (selfing), while simultaneously anathemizing those who confessed differently.

The practice of writing creeds has a long history in church tradition. However, contrary to earlier conciliar documents that stem from the period of the church fathers or from the early medieval period, which had a more limited scope – addressing specific doctrinal issues, for instance issues related to Christology, Trinity, and so on – these documents tended to be broader in scope and they were longer and more explanatory than previous creeds. Their 'intention was to formulate the global corpus of doctrines considered essential by the ecclesiastic group that produced them' (Rodrigues, 2017, p. 2). To take one example, the Belgic confession *The Summary of the Doctrine of God and of the Eternal Salvation of Man* contains 37 articles of faith. Each article starts with 'we believe' or 'we confess', or 'we believe and confess' that, and so on. Understanding one's creed, knowing why one believes the various items, and being able to explain the reasoning behind them became increasingly important in the context of the Reformation. In this age of fragmentation, identity confusion was to be avoided, and people were expected to know to which community they belonged and why.

This confessional focus presented a change from the previous situation when one was simply a Catholic Christian.

> *In medieval Europe, ordinary laypeople knew little church doctrine. They received no formal religious instruction, and their pastors rarely preached. [...] They could establish their orthodoxy simply by declaring they 'believe as their priests bids them'. Such ignorance did not matter greatly in a world where everyone was by default Catholic. It did after Europe split into competing 'confessions', each propounding a rival truth. As each church began to define its identity in terms of its unique teachings, doctrine took on an unprecedented importance, and the expectation [...] began to build that church members know what their church taught and how it differed from other churches. [...] Catholic reformers too began to demand that ordinary church members internalize the teachings of their church. Religion itself thus came increasingly to mean belief in a particular creed, and a life lived in accordance with it. (Kaplan, 2007, pp. 30–31)*

From now on, Christian discipleship is not just about participating in the sacramental life of the church and performing the communal rituals that bind the Christian community together; it is about knowing, understanding, and consenting to certain beliefs and practices, and about evaluating one's life in the light of the respective confessional standard. This also explains the importance most Protestant communities attach to 'the specific act of the *profession of faith* as a conscious commitment assumed by the believer who, having been baptized in infancy and having received, later, catechetical instruction, becomes through this profession a full member [...]' (Rodrigues, 2017, p. 3). Religion takes the form of confession.

The Propagation of True Christianness

On their own, the promulgation of confessional statements and the implementation of disciplinary measures would never be enough to transform a community altogether. True Christian faith, captured in creed, first had to be disseminated, so that all who belonged would not only know why they adhered to this or that confession, but would also feel a deeper connection and affinity with the confession. This required a massive pedagogical campaign (Kaplan, 2007, p. 31). People who had always considered themselves to be Christian would now have to learn to identify as Roman Catholic, Lutheran, Reformed, or Anabaptist. Confessions would need to become identity labels, from cradle to grave. Confessionalized boundaries had to be made concrete.

> ### Text Box 7: Real and Imagined Boundaries (1)
>
> Confessionalization fed on the heightening of differences, the establishment of boundaries, and the policing of borders. Where a Lutheran, Calvinist, or even Catholic identity was envisioned and desired, it was simultaneously contrasted with the undesirable identity of an imagined inferior, which was often demonized: the other's presumed difference was blown up out of all proportion, his/her assumed deviation from the one true faith emphasized, his/her alleged perversity accentuated. Again, we see how building group cohesion and identity seems to require a process of othering: enhancing self-understanding by creating a negative mirror image (Must, 2017, p. 13). To be a Lutheran is to empathically not be a Catholic or a Calvinist and vice versa.
>
> The process of religionization as confessionalization may remind us of Early Christianity and the then synergistic construction of orthodoxy and heresy. The all too real confusion or unclarity about what it means to be a 'Lutheran' is covered up by a passionate and straightforward rejection of the non-Lutheran. During the sixteenth and seventeenth centuries also, orthodoxies and heresies co-emerged. The words uttered by Erasmus in 1523 speak volumes: 'the more there are dogmas, the more material there is for heresies' (Chomarat, 1981, p. 1131). The more errors were rejected and the more enemies were anathemized, the more detailed confessions became.
>
> As the pursuit of a sacred uniformity continued, the boundaries between different confessional blocks would be policed with increasing efficiency and a variety of mechanisms of exclusion and rejection were put in place. The blurring of boundaries or fluidity of Christian identities became intolerable. In 1579, one author captures the confessional mood of the time saying 'either the Reformed religion is good or it is bad; there is no middle, since the affairs of heaven permit no averages ... truth and falsehood are as much at odds as Belial and Christ and hence there is little in common between the Reformed teaching and Roman fantasies as there is between white and black' (Fredericq, *Het Nederlandsch proza*, [1907], pp. 107–108, quoted in Kaplan, 2004, p. 491). Against this background, the mild scepticism that was displayed by some Renaissance humanists, like Erasmus, would become anathema, for it was seen as endangering the need for clear boundaries (Rummel, 2000).
>
> Significantly, the process of confessionalization covers up the fact that at grassroots level, people (i) had not yet embraced their new confessional identities and (ii) the confessional rituals, liturgies, and spaces had yet to crystalize out of the messiness of the Reformation. Many continued to practise as they did before, mixing ritual practices and engaging in ceremonies which they were 'supposed' to reject as idolatrous, attending weddings and funerals of neighbours who adhered to another confession. Authorities claim identities and boundaries before they exist. The construction of the rhetorical/hermeneutical other goes hand in hand with the construction of self as bounded and clear-cut.

The printed media played a key part in confessional dissemination campaigns. It allowed people to spread information to massive groups faster than ever before. During the confessional age, Bibles and psalters were in high demand as well as prayer books, books of private devotion, homilies, lives of saints, and sermons. In addition, confessional and catechetical works written by clergy and professors as well as the above-mentioned creedal statements were also propagated widely. The same technology that helped to spread information about true faith was used to propagate polemical disinformation about others and to incite fear, revulsion, and hatred for them.

Music proved to be another important medium for guiding the public towards orthodoxy. Songs, which were easy to remember, proved particularly effective (Fernández-Armesto & Wilson, 1996). While Protestant reformers rejected visual culture, they did make use of music, and especially hymns and songs, to educate ordinary believers and gather them together into one community. Especially in Germany, Lutherans produced songs at a rapid pace in an effort to win the hearts of ordinary people. Often these songs were 'scandalous cries of anger at the papacy, at the clergy, at the merchants who benefited from the Catholic Church's downfall', but many of them 'expressed high ideals and deep faith' (Wagner Oettinger, 2001, p. 1).

Ritual Rituals, especially, were critical in the process of confessionalization. People do not simply take on a new religious identity. They have to be persuaded, and the embodied, repetitive nature of ritual provided an apt means to do so. Both Protestant and Catholic reformers realized that the repetition of symbolic acts could forge a sense of community and could facilitate 'shared acceptance' of core beliefs (Karant-Nunn, 2017, p. 422). By introducing people to a particular 'tempo-spatial continuum', confession becomes enfleshed, its truth embodied, the identity of the ritualist reshaped (O'Donnell, 2015) and boundaries established. In time, differences between confessions were reflected in distinct ritual performance: what, how, and with whom one celebrates matters, even when one does not always understand why.[5]

Beyond their aim of creating a sense of community, Protestant reformers were deeply committed to the purification of the liturgy. If worship is not done properly and if it is misdirected, it may very well distort the relationship between the community and God as well as between the individual believer and God; in their view, such distortion was exactly what had happened in the Catholic liturgy (Moore-Keish, 2008, p. 37). To return to the *ecclesia primitiva*, they had to purge their liturgies from all the papist ritual traditions and restore worship to its right order so that it could convey the approved theology (Karant-Nunn, 2017, p. 411). This had a tremendous impact, also on social life, as many of the ceremonies that people used to celebrate together, and which sacralized the secular realm, would now be off-limits (e.g. processions, blessings, etc.). To not participate in certain rituals that were now deemed 'Roman Catholic' and thus *heretical*, became a Protestant identity marker (to not kneel when a procession came by; to not close one's shop on a religious holiday, etc.). One could call this religious identification through ritual abstention (Colijn, 2019).

Luther rejected the doctrine of transubstantiation and embraced the doctrine of consubstantiation – 'after the consecration, the substances both of the body and the blood of Christ and of the bread and the wine coexist in union with each other' (Daly, 2014, p. 160). Accordingly, while preserving many parts of the Catholic Mass, Luther introduced some significant changes in line with his theological rejection of the sacrificial nature of the eucharistic sacrament. Not only did he eliminate the 'sacrificial prayers and actions of the Mass – offertory, Canon, and fraction' (Schattauer, 2014, p. 216), he also encouraged both clergy and laity to receive communion under both kinds, which he argued, based on Scripture, was theologically legitimate. This practice reaffirmed and ritually re-enacted the priesthood of all believers. The presiding cleric should dress modestly.

Calvin truly wanted a return to the simplicity of the liturgy of Early Christianity. He was convinced that God was 'meant to be [...] above palpability' (Karant-Nunn, 2017, p. 418). To his mind, the purpose of the Lord's supper was threefold: '(1) spiritual nourishment, in which we are united with Christ, (2) incitement to gratitude for all God's goodness to us, and (3) exhortation to holy living and to mutual love' (Moore-Keish, 2008, p. 37). Every trace of Catholic liturgy had to be removed and this would translate into the whitewashing of church interiors. Liturgical objects – think of 'priestly gowns for the Mass, choir robes, cowls, tonsures, flags, candles, altars, gold and silver', – had to be banned, since in Calvin's view they hinder and pervert proper worship or even lead to idolatry, just as images and pictures had to be banished from our holy congregation (The First Helvetic Confession of 1536 in Cochrane, 1966, p. 109). Of course, they would also get rid of the special Catholic liturgical vessels needed to support the doctrine of the transubstantiation, like thc pyx (for storage of consecrated hosts) and the monstrance (for showing the host to the people). Psalms, prayers, and sermons formed the heart of the Reformed liturgy.

In response to the liturgical simplification of the Lutherans and the iconoclastic tendencies of the Reformed, Catholics began to enrich their liturgies and to increase the sense of mystery surrounding the Eucharist. They retained the sacrificial nature of the Eucharist, reaffirmed the doctrine of transubstantiation, and continued to promote the veneration of the host by all believers. Increasingly, the Eucharist turned into a dramatic spectacle, announced by ringing bells, and everyone knew that they were witness to a miracle. Catholic priests would continue to re-enact not only the Last Supper but also Christ's crucifixion by extending their arms during the ritual of transubstantiation. Post-Tridentine Catholicism would only intensify the devotion of the consecrated host, 'carried in public procession on its feast day of *Corpus Christi,* or displayed and venerated in churches in the new 'Forty Hours' devotion' (Marshall, 2009, p. 57).

This discussion about how to celebrate the Eucharist played a major role in the process of confessionalization *and* the demarcation of self and other. While it may be true that for most people the complex theological differences between transubstantiation and consubstantiation remained incomprehensible, they would nevertheless have immediately noticed when their weekly church service changed in its form, and they soon realized that their confessional identity depended on how they worshipped. The eucharistic table became an especially clear dividing line between Lutherans, Calvinists, and Catholics; participation in the rituals of other confessions became prohibited. Given that the Eucharist – the sacrament of communion – had always been the key identity marker of the Christian community, bringing everyone together in the one body of Christ, the impossibility of celebrating together – of enjoying commensality – now cast other 'Christians' as outsiders, and in fact as non-Christians. Notice how confessional boundaries are established by means of food restrictions; other 'Christians' are no longer fellow diners.

Text Box 8: Real and Imagined Boundaries (2)

Confessionalization was a long-winded process; new and previously non-existent confessional identities had to be formed and new demarcations had to be established. What it meant to be Lutheran or Catholic or Reformed had to be invented and reinvented. People had to learn how to pray, how to celebrate, when to gather and with whom, which gestures to perform and which not to perform; their bodies had to learn new things and unlearn other things. Furthermore, confessionalization, demarcation, and segregation was a slow cultural process, and it took several generations before people learned to disidentify as Christian, learned to identify as Lutheran, Reformed, or Catholic, unlearned the old ritual practices and interiorized the newly established boundaries. Hybrid practices and fuzzy boundaries had to be suppressed and practices of accommodation rooted out. That did not happen overnight. While in many communities emotions ran high and violence erupted, certainly in smaller villages and towns, where there were strong kinship and neighbourhood relationships, cutting social bonds by refraining from community ritual practices was no easy matter. People were dependent on each other, relied on one another, were connected to each other and often they did not fully understand the complex doctrinal debates that led to the fragmentation of Christian religion.

In previous chapters, I discussed how the projection of bounded identities did not match the messiness and fluidity at the grassroots level. Time and again, I explained how the other was turned into a hermeneutical figure, serving the purpose of defining and superiorizing Christian normativity. The identity of Christianity's other – whether pagan, heretic, Jew, or Muslim – was imaginary rather than real. However, that also holds true for the identity of those who claim to embody the norm. The boundaries that are projected reflect a powerful ideal, but one which is not necessarily realized on the ground. I mentioned this when discussing the so-called parting of the ways between Jewish and Christian communities, which took much longer than many realize. Polemicists, who aggressively agitated against Christians celebrating Shabbat, actually offer us an insight in the fluidity of Jewish-Christian relations at a time when the Jew was already depicted as anti-Christian. I also mentioned that the so-called Christianization of the Roman Empire was a slow cultural process, and that many 'pagan' traditions became mixed with Christian practices. After a while, some of these traditions were simply incorporated in a Christian framework and their pagan origins were forgotten. Something similar happened when Latin Christendom splintered in many confessions, which were supposed to be clearly bounded and demarcated. Certainly, in the early stages of the Reformation, in many towns across the Holy Roman Empire, Catholics and Protestants, who were supposed to hate each other, found ways of living together and accommodating one another's needs. Where the old religion was the norm, Protestants continued to get married according to the Catholic rite and did not object to their children being baptized by a priest, as long as the latter did not object to Protestant godparents. Such practices continued well into the seventeenth century. Some parish priests also experimented with the eucharistic liturgy, trying to reconcile Catholic and Lutheran sensitivities. While some were willing to kill and die because of theological differences, there were also many who tried to accommodate difference in an effort to hold the community together and maintain the bonds of kinship and neighbourhood. The norm they established was that of accommodation and compromise (Luebke, 2016a). This troubled the authorities and they would pressure overly accommodating priests to perform rituals in accordance with the normative confession. As the process of religionization as confessionalization continued, experiments and efforts to compromise came under increasing pressure. Confessional identities became more firmly established and gradually it became impossible to cross ritual borders or deviate from the liturgical norm. Stricter oversight, persuasion, and education rooted out fuzziness and orthodoxy triumphed. Eventually, the 'executors of orthodoxy succeeded in enforcing confessional criteria for civic inclusion and exclusion' and people could no longer imagine celebrating with their confessional adversaries (Luebke, 2016a).

Space   In this age of confessionalization, buildings functioned as confessions in stone and wood (Terpstra, 2015, p. 281). Especially Christians who were perhaps not fully conversant with the dogmas could be strengthened in their faith by the design and decor of the church (Fernández-Armesto & Wilson, 1996, p. 118). This highlights once more how the shaping and reshaping of the interior life requires serious investment in the shaping and reshaping of the exterior dimensions of spiritual life and it holds true both for Catholics and for Protestants. Space matters. It orients the body and mind in a certain direction, steers ritual comportment, and helps to interiorize specific confessional attitudes. Furthermore, these buildings visualized the power and appeal of a particular confessional identity in towns and cities. The erection of a church building sent the message: this ground is ours and signifies the defeat of our opponents. In this regard, the same strategies of spatial acquisition that were used to transform Late Roman society into medieval Christendom or to re-catholicize reconquered Spanish territories were now reiterated in the process of confessionalization: property seizure, destruction, renovation, and new construction plans.

While Protestant spatio-material purgation took on many forms, it was on the whole aimed at a rejection of the Catholic sense of the mediation of the sacred. God would no longer be present in the same way as before. The churches in predominantly Lutheran regions 'preserved medieval liturgical furnishings [...]. Side altars, which were not needed, were generally dismantled but not always'. Some Lutheran churches required the removal of images, but not all of them did. As long as images did not become the focus of worship, it was often decided to keep them as decoration. The 'few images still in place, [however] were not to be the objects of devotion. No candles burned before them. [...] Not paintings, statuary vestments, or the much-depleted equipment of the eucharist any longer possessed God's genius. It did no good to see them, touch them, or be in their presence' (Karant-Nunn, 1997, p. 184). A different picture emerges, however, in Reformed regions, where the impact on church buildings was greater. Often, existing buildings would be renovated and Reformed sympathizers would whitewash 'over the frescoed walls and ceilings', and cover wall carvings with plaster, remove rood screens and any remaining statues (Terpstra, 2015, pp. 274, 281).

Protestant churches, generally speaking, repositioned the community to understanding the centrality of the Word, and this translated into a suppression of all other religious symbols and signs. Confessional booths were removed as well as private chapels and chantry altars. Often baptismal fonts would be moved to the front of the church. The most obvious and best-known element of course would be the centrality of a large pulpit, which 'sanctified the worship space with the immediate presence of God [...] As they cleared saints' bones in silver and gold reliquaries from their churches, Protestants of most all confessions replaced them with printed Bibles on elaborate brass stands as the physical manifestation of God's power and immediate presence' (Terpstra, 2015, p. 278).

The Reformation also evoked an extensive, mostly urban, Catholic building programme. Everywhere, new churches, monasteries, schools, and hospitals were erected, spreading a sense of ecclesial triumphalism, which profoundly changed the look of these towns (Schilling, 2004, pp. 33–35). Baroque became the house style of the Catholic Reformation (Mullett, 1999, p. 197). Other than Protestant churches, baroque churches drew attention to the main altar, the heart and soul of ecclesial life. The Mass became a spectacle for everyone to view. In line with this, the tabernacle of the Eucharist came to hold a central place on the main altar. While 'medieval reserved hosts had been kept in wall cupboards (aumbries), hanging images, often of doves (pyxes), or in freestanding towers (sacrament houses) [...] now a visual association was made between devotions to the consecrated Host and the liturgical experience of the Mass' (White, 2003, p. 4). After the Council of Trent however, conscious of the importance of the Word, Catholics too started to give an increasingly central position to the pulpit.

Education   Both ecclesial and secular authorities understood the tremendous potential of education as a disciplinary instrument for transmitting the key values, beliefs, and norms of their culture while simultaneously discouraging what is deemed unfit, inappropriate, or abnormal. The goal was to streamline the educational system such that it would ensure conformity to the norm (Wriedt, 2018, p. 316).

Various confessions began to invest in the training of their clergy. For *Konfessionsbildung* to work, clergy would have to meet whole new levels of knowledge, conduct, competencies, and behaviour, which they would then be expected to transfer to their parishioners (Reinhard, 1999, pp. 179–180). Consequently, clerical personnel of all denominations were trained 'with an unprecedented degree of thoroughness and sophistication [...]' and schooled in rival theologies and pastoral pedagogies (Harrington & Smith, 1997, p. 79). This increased emphasis on the importance of theological training not only led to the broadening of the distance between clergy and laity, but also again between the different confessional communities.

Besides this, there was also a massive expansion of grammar and Sunday schools, where future schoolteachers would be trained according to the perceived confessional standards, ready to instruct children and adolescents, 'either at school or through special catechism classes' (Kaplan, 2007, p. 31). Here, the emphasis was on dogma, Bible study, and moral education. Children would be taught civilized manners, piety, proper behaviour. They learned what they were supposed to believe, how their beliefs differed from the beliefs of others and how they were to comport themselves as members of society. From this perspective, education was not simply an investment in the personal development of everyone, rather it was used to change Christian society and produce civilized subjects (Ehrenpreis, 2006, p. 43).

While the catechisms already existed in the fifteenth century, they began to be used more widely during the confessionalization period. They became an important tool in this educational endeavour and supported the widespread struggle for religious conformity and uniformity. By means of a question-and-answer format, the catechism explained basic confessional principles. Children were expected to learn these by heart and to be able to reproduce the answers when asked. Rui Luis Rodrigues draws our attention to how catechisms were organized and how they matched the disciplinary mood of the confessional age.

> *an instrument generally chosen to make the learning of the confession of faith by the believer feasible, not only had a structure which, based on repetitions and on questions and answers, fit well with teaching that was above all oral; this structure was, after all, presented as an interrogation, something which must have been understood, in the highly polemical context of the sixteenth and seventeenth centuries, in a different way from the perspective which medieval catechists and catechumens had of this practice. Catechism not only instructed and with this prepared for the* professio *before the religious community (the moment of full reception as member of a Church), but also prepared for a broader* professio, *confession before the rest of society. The unstable nature of the epoch meant that, even in apparently safe situations, in which the confessional group was not at the periphery of secular power, religious education was a constant preparation for external testimony.* (Rodrigues, 2017, pp. 4–5)

Censorship Propagation of true faith was matched with censorship, which had to ensure that wrong ideas would be kept from contaminating pure faith. Various means were put in place to correct the behaviour and mould the beliefs of ecclesial members. While censorship has always been around, the arrival of the printing press added a new sense of urgency to the need to contain the world of ideas. Books came to be seen as silent heretics, because they were held responsible for spreading dissident thought. The battle against heresy became a battle against the book (Fishburn, 2008). In 1487 a papal bull, *Inter Multiplices*, was issued by Pope Innocent VIII (r. 1482–1492), stating that every new book had to mention the name of the author, date of publication, as well as an authorization by the local bishop. Some bishops prohibited books which they believed would undermine true faith (Fernández-Armesto & Wilson, 1996, p. 41).

Theologians played a key role in determining the degree of error contained in a book. After studying a suspicious book, they made a list of *errores excerpti*. Each of these errors received a qualifying label *falsa, erronea, scandalosa*, or *heretica*. These lists often formed the basis for a more formal condemnation. The most famous condemnation to arise from this decree was the 1520 prohibition of Martin Luther's books which even included his future works, with the penalty of excommunication attached. During the sixteenth and seventeenth centuries, because of the rapid proliferation of printing, authorities felt the need to organize themselves more effectively. From 1557 onwards, the Catholic Church would place condemned books on the *Index Librorum Prohibitorum*.

Censorship, however, was not confined to Catholics. Protestant reformers too regarded it as an effective and legitimate instrument of control; in general, there was a 'broad consensus that Christian authorities' both secular and ecclesial, were responsible before God for the salvific fate of their community', and that they therefore 'had not only the right but also the duty to police opinion and belief' (Creasman, 2012, p. 14). In fact, during this period, there was not a single region in Europe where ecclesial and political rulers did not try to contain the proliferation of ideas.

Discipline Church discipline, the formation of confessional identity, and the demand for uniformity in dogma and religious practice were combined with a general effort to impose extensive social discipline and to create an obedient community, firm in its belief and faithful to the political regime. Confessions functioned as instruments of socio-religious disciplining: they offered ecclesial and secular authorities standards for assessing who conforms to the norm and who departs from it.

Especially people in so-called strategic positions – think of theologians, pastors, teachers, as well as secular authorities – would be required to meet the standards of religious orthodoxy. To this end, various control mechanisms were deployed. There was, for example, the requirement that applicants for public office were to be examined on their orthodoxy or were explicitly asked to swear to uphold the respective confession. Projecting the ideal of uniformity in dogma and religious practice, those presumed to be dissidents would be excluded from such public positions, if not from society at large. In time, ordinary members of the community would also be submitted to control mechanisms. In this context of turmoil (mass conversions, migrations), some authorities were concerned about the sincerity of conversions and their profundity. Was the faith of converts authentic? Did they not secretly remain attached to their old practices and beliefs and what if they lapsed back to their old ways? One may remember that we encountered these questions when discussing the phenomenon of the Spanish *conversos*. Authorities, both ecclesial and secular, wanted to control their subjects and ensure their conformity. Wolfgang Reinhard mentions that 'lists of communicants were kept, and registers of baptisms, marriages and funerals, not for statistical purposes but to control life in the confession' (Reinhard, 1999, p. 181).

When suspicion ran high, stronger measures of social discipline and control were put in place involving 'episcopal and inquisitorial visits in Catholic territories; ecclesiastical supervision visits in Lutheran territories; the diligent action of consistories in Reformed-Calvinist territories' (Rodrigues, 2017, p. 10). These consistories were tasked with examining all accusations of moral and religious lapses, accusations which were usually triggered by observed deviant behaviour. Penalties could range from reprimands and fines to excommunication, being expelled from the community altogether, which would also entail losing one's civil and political rights (Terpstra, 2015). Against this background, we can understand how the notion of 'confession of faith' gained an extra meaning, that of providing testimony of one's confessional loyalty not only for the religious community but also for the religious authorities. Indeed, members of a confession would have to learn their creed by heart (hence the emphasis on education), so that they would at all times be ready to publicly testify to their faith and prove their membership to the one true confession.

5 The Parting of the Ways and Confessional Identity Markers

Gradually, markers of identity sprang up across innumerable aspects of life and almost any facet of public and private life could become a sign of confessional difference. Protestant reformers set out to rid the liturgical year of Catholic exuberances and papist inventions, that had no scriptural grounding and were injurious departures from the will of God. This not only meant the abolition of such practices as the feasts of *Corpus Christi* and All Saints; all the feasts and processions related to patrons, which often had a rather local character, as well as the many medieval feasts devoted to the life of Mary (the Annunciation, the Assumption, the Immaculate Conception of Mary in the womb of Anna, her visit to Elisabeth, etc.) were done away with. Furthermore, 'for reasons of discrimination, even confessionally neutral achievements by other confessions were rejected' (Reinhard, 1999, p. 181). One example in this regard was the conflict over the calendar. In 1582, Pope Gregory XIII (r. 1572–1585) decided to replace the ancient Julian calendar with the Gregorian calendar, a decision that had nothing to do with confessional strife and everything with scientific reasoning. Protestant reformers were suspicious however, and most European states, by then Protestant, only accepted the revised calendar around 1700, with Britain and Sweden following even later, in 1750. Even time had become confessionalized and politicized.

Confessionalization continued and issues such as when to fast, what to eat when fasting (fish, meat, or neither), how to dress, how to curse, which jokes to crack (humour always feeds on stereotypes), almost everything, even when it was theologically indifferent, could be interpreted in terms of confessional identity and could arouse suspicion. Certainly, in public life, where one could be seen by others, it was particularly important to demonstrate one's confessional identity and behave according to the written and unwritten norms and standards. Thus *Konfessionsbildung* profoundly impacted every corner of people's lives.

Names offered one of the more powerful means to signal confessional identity and difference, even to children. Obviously, across all confessions, New Testament names would be maintained, but Protestants tended to reach back to Old Testament figures, whereas Catholics preferred saints' names, and these were unacceptable in Reformed areas. But even before the birth of a child, there were laws prohibiting marriage across confessional lines. Just as marriages between Jews and Christians had long been outlawed, authorities now sought to establish control over interconfessional unions. Such mixed unions were seen as a deformity, which would seriously threaten the unity of the *Corpus Christianum*. Cecilia Cristellon, discussing the Catholic position on intermarriage, notes how 'canon lawyers, theologians and polemists inserted mixed marriage into the category of carnal crimes. To their minds, the severity of mixed marriage was such as to render it comparable, in doctrine, to rape (*stuprum*), since it constituted the "admission of an extraneous body" into the ecclesiastical body, rendering it impure and even analogous to violent rape, since through mixed marriage the Catholic Church (that is, the bride of Christ) had been "raped with express violence by heretical dogma"' (Cristellon, 2017, p. 608). Harsh rulings against intermarriage reaffirm once again how, theologically speaking, there was no awareness of there being multiple Christianities; one true Christianity and multiple Christian heresies was the only possibility. Nevertheless, according to the Catholic canon law a mixed marriage that had been concealed was deemed to be valid.

6 Conclusion

During the era of Reformation, anti-heresy polemics built on previous patterns of religionization, patterns that projected one single orthodox norm and understood deviation in terms of contamination, disease, and perversion. The medieval ideal of the purity of the *Corpus Christianum* and the concomitant ideology of purgation remained largely unchanged; the idea that there could be multiple ways of being Christian or even multiple Christianities made little sense. The dominant idea shared by all contesting parties was that there is one true Christian faith and multiple heresies. This logic of dichotomy, which contrasts of orthodoxy and impure heresy, paved the way for both legal and illegal violent actions to purge society of dissenters.

The Treaty of Augsburg (1555), which is widely known for its principle *cuius regio eius religio,* is an example of the way rulers were trying to find a way out of the violence. This treaty is particularly interesting because it provides us with an insight into the emergence of a new legal and political framework for dealing with the fragmentation of the religious norm. Fragmentation was legalized and multiple religions/confessions were recognized. If the *Codex Theodosianus* had supported the Christianization of the empire (by inscribing one religious norm – the Nicene creed – into the law), now the Augsburg Treaty paved the way for the territorialization of religion by legalizing a range of religious norms. Within their own territories, rulers would implement their own religion as the norm for all subjects. Once again we clearly see that religionization is political; it is 'a strategy from a position of power' and *vera religio* is turned into 'an instrument of governmentality' (Dreßler, 2019, p. 11).

Through various processes of political and social governance, known as confessionalization, people slowly began to interiorize the fragmentation of religion and began to structure their lives accordingly. This process started when reform movements began to produce written confessions of faith (*confessio fidei*), with the aim of formulating their key beliefs – 'this is who we are', 'this is what we believe' – and clarifying how these beliefs were orthodox and not heretical; 'synthesizing in *formulae* the doctrines considered basic for the Christian faith' (Rodrigues, 2017, p. 2). The production of these confessions initiated an unprecedented process of systematization and standardization of beliefs and practices (Burke, 2005, p. 16) and transformed religion into confession. This required a wide range of disciplinary measures, pedagogical campaigns, and liturgical transformations before 'ordinary people' began 'to own the religious labels that the officially agreed confessions [...] were creating' and learned to behave accordingly. Taking pride in these identities, people often also grew to detest confessional adversaries (MacCulloch, 2003, p. 338). Here too, the appropriation of confessional identities went hand in hand with an appropriation of antagonisms and with the institutionalization of dichotomics. Religionization is never only about prejudice.

From the perspective of religion, it is not just that the outlook of Christendom changed, or that new forms of Christianity emerged, or even that Christian plurality became institutionalized; the significance of religionization as confessionalization also exists in the way it contributed to the 'emergence of the modern "believer" out of medieval Christian man. In other words, a person who is linked to the Church not only by (child) baptism and by participating in cults and sacraments, but also by a *professio fidei*, by a profession of faith which stops being simple participation in the creed of Christian tradition' and becomes 'adhesion and faithfulness sworn to the ecclesiastic institution to which the individual belongs' (Prodi, 2005, pp. 237–238). From then onwards, to be a church (a confession) would become understood in terms of gathering around a creed. To be a Christian would come to mean being a believer, and religion would come to be understood as 'a set of internalized dogmas rather than "a ritual method of living"' (Walsham, 2008, p. 498). The new type of Christianity emerging from this process is known as 'confessional' (Kaplan, 2007, p. 29). Mack Holt even speaks about 'a definitional shift of the Christian religion altogether, from a body of people to which one belonged and with whom one worshipped together, to a body of doctrines and beliefs that one not only believed but could be memorized even by young children in the form of a catechism' (Holt, 2015). By 1700 the Christian world knew multiple, competing religions/confessions. This reality of confessional plurality, together with the expectation that believers should be able to explicitly profess their faith, turned being Christian into a more informed and percipient affair (Kaplan, 2007, p. 47). Undoubtedly, the confessional age helps to explain why to this day, we ask people what they 'believe' if we want to understand their religious way of life. In Chapter 8, we will see how the remaking of religion as confession also impacts how Christianity's others – the Jews, Muslims, and pagans – are imagined.

Notes

[1] On the one hand, iconoclasm is about exposing the fraudulent nature of images by showing 'that the statues [people] worshipped were just pieces of wood, that the relics might well be animal bones, and that the Blessed Sacrament was a little circle of baked dough' (Benedict, 2016). From this perspective, iconoclasm is about showing that people have erred and that they have misdirected their worship. On the other hand, however, some of the particular iconoclastic actions did more than simply expose the real nature of these statues. The iconoclastic actions could also be interpreted as an effort to break them, diminish their power, and render them powerless. Indeed, the real problem was not so much that these images were in reality powerless, but rather that they were too powerful, 'too irresistible, too diverting in luring the laity back into the world of traditional ritual behaviors' (Muir, 2005, p. 210). They were anything but impotent; they claimed authority and people were drawn to them. Iconoclasts

would subject statues to a humiliating ritual of desacralization/profanation aimed at making these images powerless by showing that they were nothing but innate matter. While there were rituals to change the character of material objects into sacred objects, iconoclastic rituals reversed this process, however, both breaking and reaffirming the power of the statues and concomitantly denying and reasserting the idea of the embodiment of meaning.

[2] Source of English translation, Reich (1905).

[3] While the Treaty of Augsburg would have a historic impact on the transformation of Europe and its dealings with religious plurality, it should also 'be contextualized as a short-term reaction to a renewed military conflict that had begun in 1552' (Soen, 2017b, p. 771).

[4] Significantly, these cities at the time consisted of a Lutheran majority (Szepesi, 2016, p. 17) and therefore lost to the Old Catholic religion. This means that Ferdinand used the exemption of the free imperial cities and the principle of biconfessionalism to 'reintroduce a religion (Catholic) that the local populace had largely rejected and to give its adherents power disproportionate to their numbers' (Kaplan, 2004, p. 494). From this perspective, biconfessionalism had little to do with an embrace of religious parity and all the more with an imperial effort to re-establish the old religion where it had become marginal.

[5] This was particularly challenging for Protestant reformers finding the balance between devising new rituals, which would convey the central tenets of their belief (or express their confession), while simultaneously maintaining that rituals were not soteriologically significant and therefore only of secondary importance.

References

Benedict, P. (2016). Were the French Wars of Religion Really Wars of Religion? In W. Palaver, H. Rudolph, & D. Regensburger (Eds.), *The European Wars of Religion: An Interdisciplinary Reassessment of Sources, Interpretations, and Myths* (pp. 67–92). Ashgate.

Brady, T., Cameron, E., & Cohn, H. (2006). The Politics of Religion: The Peace of Augsburg 1555: A Roundtable Discussion. *German History, 24*(1), 85–105.

Burke, P. (2005). *Towards a Social History of Early Modern Dutch.* Amsterdam University Press.

Celati, A. (2014). Heresy, Medicine and Paracelsianism in Sixteenth-Century Italy: The Case of Girolamo Donzellini (1513–1587). *Gesnerus, 71*(1), 5–37.

Chomarat, J. (1981). *Grammaire et rhétorique chez Érasme,* Études 10. Les Belles Lettres.

Christin, O. (1997). *La Paix de religion: l'autonomisation de la raison politique au XVIᵉ siècle.* Seuil.

Christin, O. (1998). L'Europe des paix de religion: semblants et faux-semblants. *Bulletin de la Société de l'Histoire du Protestantisme Français (1903–2015), 144,* 489–505.

Christin, O. (2004). Making Peace. In R. P.-c. Hsia (Ed.), *A Companion to the Reformation World* (pp. 426–439). Blackwell.

Cochrane, A. C. (Ed.). (1966). *Reformed Confessions of the 16th Century.* Westminster.

Colijn, B. (2019). Interrituality in Contemporary China as a Field of Tension between Abstention and Polytropy. In M. Moyaert (Ed.), *Interreligious Relations and the Negotiation of Ritual Boundaries: Explorations in Interrituality* (pp. 227–244). Palgrave Macmillan.

Creasman, A. F. (2012). *Censorship and Civic Order in Reformation Germany, 1517–1648: 'Printed Poison & Evil Talk'.* Ashgate.

Crespin, J. (1619, ed. 1885). *Histoire des martyrs persécutez et mis à mort pour la vérité de l'évangile, depuis le temps des apostres jusques à présent.* Édition nouvelle précédée d'une introduction par Daniel Benoit. Société des livres religieuses.

Cristellon, C. (2017). Between Sacrament, Sin and Crime: Mixed Marriages and the Roman Church in Early Modern Europe. *Gender and History, 29*(3), 605–621.

Daly, R. J. (2014). The Council of Trent. In L. Palmer Wandel (Ed.), *A Companion to the Eucharist in the Reformation,* Brill's Companions to the Christian Tradition 46 (pp. 159–182). Brill.

de Bèze, T. (1841). *Histoire ecclésiastique des églises réformées au Royaume de France.* Leleux.

Diefendorf, B. B. (1991). *Beneath the Cross: Catholics and Huguenots in Sixteenth-Century Paris.* Oxford University Press.

Dixon, C. S. (2016a). *The Church in the Early Modern Age.* Tauris.

Dixon, C. S. (2016b). Introduction. In C. S. Dixon, D. Freist, & M. Greengrass (Eds.), *Living with Religious Diversity in Early-Modern Europe,* St Andrews Studies in Reformation History. Routledge.

Dreßler, M. (2019). Modes of Religionization: A Constructivist Approach to Secularity. *Working Paper Series of the Centre for Advanced Studies 'Multiple Secularities – Beyond the West, Beyond Modernities', 7.* Retrieved from www.multiple-secularities.de/media/wps7_dressler_religionization.pdf

Ehrenpreis, S. (2006). *Kaiserliche Gerichtsbarkeit und Konfessionskonflikt: Der Reichshofrat unter Rudolf II. 1576–1612*, Schriftenreihe der Historischen Kommission bei der Bayerischen Akademie der Wissenschaften 72. Vandenhoeck & Ruprecht.

Eire, C. M. N. (1986). *War against the Idols: The Reformation of Worship from Erasmus to Calvin.* Cambridge University Press.

Feil, E. (1986). *Religio: Die Geschichte eines Neuzeitlichen Grundbegriffs.* Vandenhoeck & Ruprecht.

Fernández-Armesto, F., & Wilson, D. (1996). *Reformatie: Christendom en de wereld 1500–2000.* Anthos.

Fishburn, M. (2008). *Burning Books.* Palgrave Macmillan.

García Soormally, M. (2019). *Idolatry and the Construction of the Spanish Empire.* University Press of Colorado.

George, T. (2019). What the Reformers Thought They Were Doing. In K. L. King, E. E. Hindson, & B. K. Forrest (Eds.), *Celebrating the Legacy of the Reformation* (pp. 9–25). B&H Academic.

Harrington, J. F., & Smith, H. W. (1997). Confessionalization, Community, and State Building in Germany, 1555–1870. *The Journal of Modern History, 69*(1), 77–101.

Holt, M. P. (2015). Belief and Its Limits. In H. Scott (Ed.), *The Oxford Handbook of Early Modern European History, 1350–1750, Volume 1: Peoples and Place* (pp. 720–744). Oxford University Press.

Houtman, D., & Meyer, B. (Eds.) (2012). *Things: Religion and the Question of Materiality.* Fordham University Press.

Janssen, G. H. (2011). Quo vadis? Catholic Perceptions of Flight and the Revolt of the Low Countries, 1566–1609. *Renaissance Quarterly, 64*(2), 472–499.

Kaplan, B. J. (2004). Coexistence, Conflict and the Practice of Toleration. In R. P.-c. Hsia (Ed.), *A Companion to the Reformation World* (pp. 486–505). Blackwell.

Kaplan, B. J. (2007). *Divided by Faith: Religious Conflict and the Practice of Toleration in Early Modern Europe.* The Belknap Press of Harvard University Press.

Karant-Nunn, S. C. (1997). *The Reformation of Ritual: An Interpretation of Early Modern Germany.* Routledge.

Karant-Nunn, S. C. (2017). The Reformation of Liturgy. In U. Rublack (Ed.), *The Oxford Handbook of the Protestant Reformations* (pp. 409–430). Oxford University Press.

Korpiola, M., & Lahtinen, A. (2015). Cultures of Death and Dying in Medieval and Early Modern Europe: An Introduction. In M. Korpiola & A. Lahtinen (Eds.), *Cultures of Death and Dying in Medieval and Early Modern Europe* (pp. 1–31). Helsinki Collegium for Advanced Studies.

Lotz-Heumann, U. (2013). Confessionalization. In A. Bamji, G. Janssen, & M. Laven (Eds.), *The Ashgate Research Companion to the Counter-Reformation* (pp. 33–53). Ashgate.

Luebke, D. M. (2016a). *Hometown Religion: Regimes of Coexistence in Early Modern Westphalia.* University of Virginia Press.

Luebke, D. M. (2016b). A Multiconfessional Empire. In T. M. Safley (Ed.), *A Companion to Multiconfessionalism in the Early Modern World*, Brill's Companions to the Christian Tradition 28 (pp. 127–154). Brill.

MacCulloch, D. (2003). *Reformation: Europe's House Divided, 1490–1700.* Allen Lane.

Mambrol, N. (2017, 2 October). Binarism in Post-colonial Theory. *Literary Theory and Criticism.* Retrieved 21 April 2019 from https://literariness.org/2017/10/02/binarism-in-post-colonial-theory/

Marshall, P. (2009). *The Reformation: A Very Short Introduction.* Oxford University Press.

Monter, W. (1996). Heresy Executions in Reformation Europe, 1520–1565. In O. P. Grell & B. Scribner (Eds.), *Tolerance and Intolerance in the European Reformation* (pp. 48–64). Cambridge University Press.

Moore-Keish, M. L. (2008). *Do This in Remembrance of Me: A Ritual Approach to Reformed Eucharistic Theology.* Eerdmans.

Morrissey, M. (2015). Confessionalism and Conversion in the Reformation. In J. Simpson (Ed.), *Oxford Handbooks Online: Literature, Literary Studies – 1500 to 1700.* https://doi.org/10.1093/oxfordhb/9780199935338.013.73

Moyaert, P. (2015). Touching God in His Image. *Heythrop Journal, 56*(2), 192–202.

Muir, E. (2005). *Ritual in Early Modern Europe*, New Approaches to European History 11. Cambridge University Press.

Mullett, M. A. (1999). *The Catholic Reformation.* Routledge.

Must, N. (2017). *Preaching a Dual Identity: Huguenot Sermons and the Shaping of Confessional Identity, 1629–1685*, St Andrews Studies in Reformation History. Brill.

Nicholls, D. (1988). The Theatre of Martyrdom in the French Reformation. *Past & Present* (121), 49–73.

O'Donnell, E. (2015). *Remembering the Future: The Experience of Time in Jewish and Christian Liturgy*. Liturgical Press.

Oldridge, D. (2005). *Strange Histories: The Trial of the Pig, the Walking Dead, and Other Matters of Fact from the Medieval and Renaissance Worlds*. Routledge.

Osborn, C. (2018). Rites of Expulsion: Violence against Heretics in Early Modern Catholic France. In S. Cowdell, C. Fleming, J. Hodge, & C. Osborn (Eds.), *Does Religion Cause Violence?: Multidisciplinary Perspectives on Violence and Religion in the Modern World*, Violence, Desire, and the Sacred 7 (pp. 129–146). Bloomsbury Academic.

Parker, C. H. (2008). *Faith on the Margins: Catholics and Catholicism in the Dutch Golden Age*. Harvard University Press.

Parker, C. H. (2014). Diseased Bodies, Defiled Souls: Corporality and Religious Difference in the Reformation. *Renaissance Quarterly, 67*(4), 1265–1297.

Prodi, P. (2005). *Uma história da justiça: do pluralismo dos foros ao dualismo moderno entre consciência e direito*. Martins Fontes.

Puff, H. (2018). Belief in the Reformation Era: Reflections on the State of Confessionalization. *Central European History, 51*(1), 46–52.

Reich, E. (Trans.) (1905), *Select Documents Illustrating Mediaeval and Modern History* (pp. 226–232). P. S. King & Son, revised and with additional articles by Thomas A. Brady Jr. Retrieved 22 May 2003 from https://germanhistorydocs.ghi-dc.org/pdf/eng/Doc.67-ENG-ReligPeace-1555_en.pdf

Reinhard, W. (1999). Pressures towards Confessionalization? Prolegomena to a Theory of the Confessional Age. In C. S. Dixon (Ed.), *The German Reformation: The Essential Readings* (pp. 169–192). Blackwell.

Reus-Smit, C. (2013). *Individual Rights and the Making of the International System*. Cambridge University Press.

Rodrigues, R. L. (2017). Confessionalization Processes and Their Importance to the Understanding of Western History in the Early Modern Period (1530–1650). *Tempo, 23*(1), 1–21.

Rummel, E. (2000). *The Confessionalization of Humanism in Reformation Germany*. Oxford University Press.

Schattauer, T. H. (2014). From Sacrifice to Supper: Eucharist Practice in the Lutheran Reformation. In L. Palmer Wandel (Ed.), *A Companion to the Eucharist in the Reformation*, Brill's Companions to the Christian Tradition 46 (pp. 205–231). Brill.

Schilling, H. (2004). Confessionalization: Historical and Scholarly Perspectives of a Comparative and Interdisciplinary Paradigm. In J. M. Headley, H. J. Hillerbrand, & A. J. Papalas (Eds.), *Confessionalization in Europe, 1555–1700: Essays in Honor and Memory of Bodo Nischan* (pp. 21–36). Ashgate.

Scribner, R. W. (1987). *Popular Culture and Popular Movements in Reformation Germany*. Hambledon.

Soen, V. (2017a). From the Interim of Augsburg until the Treaty of Augsburg (1548–1555). In A. Melloni (Ed.), *Martin Luther: A Christian between Reforms and Modernity (1517–2017)* (pp. 548–564). De Gruyter.

Soen, V. (2017b). Treaty of Augsburg. In M. A. Lamport (Ed.), *Encyclopedia of Martin Luther and the Reformation* (pp. 770–772). Rowman & Littlefield.

Spinks, J. (2009). Monstrous Births and Counter-Reformation Visual Polemics: Johann Nas and the 1569 *Ecclesia Militans. The Sixteenth Century Journal, 40*(2), 335–363.

Suerbaum, A. (2016). Language of Violence: Language as Violence in Vernacular Sermons. In A. Suerbaum, G. Southcombe, & B. Thompson (Eds.), *Polemic: Language as Violence in Medieval and Early Modern Discourse*. Routledge.

Szepesi, I. (2016). Biconfessionalism and Tolerance: The Peace of Augsburg in Three Imperial Cities. Diss. University of Waterloo.

Tait, C. (2002). *Death, Burial and Commemoration in Ireland, 1550–1650*. Palgrave Macmillan.

Te Brake, W. P. (2017). *Religious War and Religious Peace in Early Modern Europe*. Cambridge University Press.

Terpstra, N. (2015). *Religious Refugees in the Early Modern World: An Alternative History of the Reformation*. Cambridge University Press.

Wagner Oettinger, R. (2001). *Music as Propaganda in the German Reformation*. Ashgate.

Walsham, A. (2006). *Charitable Hatred: Tolerance and Intolerance in England, 1500–1700*. Manchester University Press.

Walsham, A. (2008). The Reformation and 'the Disenchantment of the World' Reassessed. *The Historical Journal, 51*(2), 497–528.

Walsham, A. (2015). Reformation Legacies. In P. Marshall (Ed.), *The Oxford Illustrated History of the Reformation* (pp. 227–268). Oxford University Press.

Wedgwood, C. V. (1944). *The Thirty Years War*. Jonathan Cape.

White, J. F. (2003). *Roman Catholic Worship: Trent to Today* (2nd ed.). Liturgical Press.

Wriedt, M. (2018). Founding a New Church? The Early Ecclesiology of Martin Luther in the Light of the Debate about Confessionalization. In A. Beutel & D. Bohnert (Eds.), *Scriptura loquens: Beiträge zur Kirchen- und Theologiegeschichte des Spätmittelalters und der Reformationszeit* (pp. 309–326). Evangelische Verlagsanstalt.

Zemon Davis, N. (1973). The Rites of Violence: Religious Riot in Sixteenth-Century France. *Past & Present, 59*, 51–91.

Zulehner, P. M. (2014). Early Modern Religion Peace Agreements: Their Effects on the Ideological Development of Europe. *Society, 51*(6), 605–612.

CHAPTER 7

Reconfiguring True Religion in Terms of Toleration

The history of religionization as confessionalization explains why the sixteenth, seventeenth, and eighteenth centuries are often depicted as having been marked by intolerance. It also explains why, at least from a macro-historical perspective, the European map is more or less organized according to confessional boundaries. The dynamics of confessionalization notwithstanding, this was also a period when religious plurality became a lived reality with which people had to make do, however grudgingly. Travellers, traders, merchants, diplomats, soldiers, and so forth knew that wherever they went there could be different customs (Dixon et al., 2016). Depending on the context, the confessional norm and concomitant practices would vary, and many learned to adapt their behaviour accordingly so as not to give any offence. Religious refugees or economic migrants who packed up their belongings to start anew elsewhere had similar experiences (van Veen & den Hollander, 2019). Besides, those who lived in frontier zones between two confessional territories were confronted daily with religious differences. Finally, several villages and cities were more diverse than the textbook maps suggest. Sometimes local authorities did not have the military power to impose the religion of their choice and religious minorities simply 'could not be persecuted out of existence' (Marshall, 2009, p. 112).

In some free imperial cities, moreover, bi-confessionalism had been established as the legal norm. Here 'both Protestants and Catholics had equal claims on the sacred and the profane' (Dixon, 2007, p. 9). This novel reality of plurality confronted people, in all layers of society, with such questions as: How does one relate to people of different confessions? How could one be kin, friends, or neighbours with them? How can 'a town act out its cohesion as a civic community in the absence of a single unifying faith?' Is community possible when there is no eucharistic communion? (Luebke, 2016). Thus, toleration became an urgent subject for many people who in the messiness of everyday life managed, by trial and error, to develop ad hoc practices of coexistence (Text Box 1), slowly but steadily

> the notion that ideological diversity was a certain recipe for political chaos and social anarchy began to wither in the face of tangible evidence that toleration could work as a strategy for bringing peace to bitterly divided cities, regions, and nations. Reluctant steps started to be taken towards a society in which the formal coexistence of men and women who held different beliefs was enshrined in law [...].
> (Walsham, 2015, p. 230)

Christian Imaginations of the Religious Other: A History of Religionization, First Edition. Marianne Moyaert.
© 2024 John Wiley & Sons Ltd. Published 2024 by John Wiley & Sons Ltd.

212 CHAPTER 7 Reconfiguring True Religion in Terms of Toleration

> ### Text Box 1: Practices of Coexistence
>
> Social historians have described the ambivalent practices of toleration and coexistence as *Auslauf* (when those who belong to a 'deviant' confession march out to practice their religion outside the boundaries of the town), *schuilkerken* (semi-clandestine churches), and *Simultankirchen* (shared churches). Typically, these practices tried to maintain the medieval ideal of the *Corpus Christianum* (uniformity) while at the same time challenging that ideal by providing scope for a certain degree of religious freedom (plurality).

Practices of toleration, however, were not necessarily supported by a principled embrace of tolerance. On the contrary, even up to the eighteenth century most people still operated from an ideal of religious uniformity, and tolerance remained a loser's creed, 'the party cry of the disappointed, the dispossessed, or the seriously confused' (Pettegree, 1996, p. 198). There were some people, however, mostly 'outsiders in both religious, political [and] social terms' (Grell, 1996, p. 4), who questioned the ideal of the *Corpus Christianum* and took issue with the culture of persecution that followed from it. Going against the grain, they developed a counter-narrative in which the ideal of tolerance would take centre stage.

The number of thinkers who wrote on toleration during this period is vast. In this chapter, I limit myself to three of them, spread over three centuries and living in different West-European regions: Sebastian Castellio, John Locke, and Voltaire. All three were closely confronted with the devastating effects of intolerance. To support their plea for tolerance, they formulated a reconfigured understanding of true Christianness and projected a vision of a society based on the separation of the religious and secular realm. Today we welcome these thinkers as progressive minds, who directed 'us' – Europeans – beyond the dark and intolerant Middle Ages towards the light of modernity (see Text Box 2). From this perspective, one might expect these voices of toleration to have interrupted the endeavour of religionization. This is, however, too simple. These thinkers were not atomistic individuals who simply went against the grain, they too worked within their particular cultural and rhetorical contexts and developed their argumentation in such a way that it would be intelligible to their contemporaries. To make their case for toleration, these thinkers also made use of older patterns of religionization while modifying their scope and meaning. Castellio, Locke, and Voltaire, albeit in different ways and with varying intensity, gauged a normative understanding of good/true religion to be apolitical, interiorized, and adogmatic; the negative counter-image they thereby constructed – false/bad religion – was projected onto those problematic others who were now positioned on the far side of the limits of tolerance, that is in a place of delegitimization. True religion respects the boundaries between the religious and the secular. Religionization takes the form of religio-secularization (Dreßler, 2019).

> ### Text Box 2: The Myth of the Rise of Tolerance
>
> The myth of the rise of tolerance belongs to the cultural archive of Western liberal democracies and enables Europeans to this day to construct a dichotomy between civilized, progressive, and modern people (who embrace the virtue of tolerance) and those who are yet to be exposed to the critical effects of the Reformation and, by extension, of the Enlightenment. This myth is (i) a story of progress, emancipation, and liberation; (ii) it connects the Protestant Reformation with tolerance; (iii) it sees a direct correlation between the Enlightenment and tolerance; (iv) it regards the emergence of tolerance as the achievement of intellectuals (a history of ideas); (v) it locates the practice and theory of tolerance in the West; 'in locales outside of the Occident where tolerant practices and principles are evident, the common explanation for their occurrence

is contact with Westernizing (essentially) liberal ideals and values' (Nederman, 2011, p. 348); (vi) it one-sidedly associates religion with violence and frames the separation of the secular and religious realms as the solution to violence.

While the story of the rise of tolerance continues to be related in textbooks, it is a myth, which does not match the complexities of history. It is, furthermore, a self-congratulatory story, which self-declared progressive voices reiterate while simultaneously contrasting their tolerant identity with those intolerant (non-Western) others (Brown, 2006). This oft-repeated story of the rise of tolerance feeds on and perpetuates binary patterns of religionization in which an ideal of tolerant religion is imagined over against intolerable/intolerant others – Jews, Muslims, Catholics, and pagans. In these new binary patterns of religionization, older patterns of legitimization/delegitimization resonate, albeit in a transformed way.

(i) Contrary to the myth of the rise of toleration, 'there was no high road to toleration, signposted from the Reformation. Religious pluralism in early-modern Europe was a set of muddy and winding streets, most of them not one way, in which perceptions, appropriations, dialogue, debate, unexpected reversals, and sacrifice are the landmarks on the wayside' (Greengrass, 2009, pp. 283–284). (ii) Both Protestant and Catholic reformers contributed to the process of confessionalization/territorialization and most reformers mimicked 'their medieval forebears': they 'put considerable numbers of heretics to death and utilized the machinery of ecclesiastical and civil justice to coax and discipline others' (Walsham, 2015, p. 229). (iii) Advocates for tolerance built their argument by projecting the trope of the 'intolerable' onto religionized others: papists, Jews, and Muslims, who are increasingly coined as fanatics, incapable of tolerance. Delegitimization of 'imaginary' problematic religious others forms one of the key building blocks for the argument in favour of tolerance. (iv) Toleration was a practice before it was an ideology. (v) This myth of tolerance as a 'distinctively Western phenomenon', glosses over non-Western practices and theories of tolerance, for example in the Ottoman Empire, Persian tolerance during the time of Cyrus, and Eastern arguments for tolerance (Nederman, 2011, pp. 249–250). (vi) Most importantly, this story oversimplifies the relation between religion and violence. That the division of religion played an important role in the wars that ravaged Europe is clear. Stating, however, that religious fracture was the sole cause of these conflicts is reductive. These conflicts were certainly not motivated solely by confessional disagreements; rather they were the result of a mixture of religious, political, and economic issues (Diefendorf, 2014, p. 554). Furthermore, the separation of church and state did not end violence. People have committed and continue to commit the greatest atrocities in the name of secular motives: economic, political, and others (Cavanaugh, 2009).

1   Sebastian Castellio: Beyond Coercion

Sebastian Castellio (1515–1563), was a French Reformed biblical scholar, humanist, and school teacher. Like many reformers at the time he wanted to renew and purify the church. This would also entail a radical reconstruction of the existing societal structures and relations between church and state (van Veen, 2012, p. 7). Castellio's effort to reform the church led him to systematically deconstruct the argument for heresy persecution and become an advocate of toleration. In this regard, he was far more radical than John Calvin, who continued, albeit based on reformed principles, to replicate the medieval ideal of the Christian society. Calvin's urge for confessional uniformity is well-documented and the operation of the Genevan consistory as counterpart to the Catholic inquisition was alluded to in the previous chapter. While friends and colleagues at an earlier stage of their lives, Calvin and Castellio clashed, and their conflict was fought out publicly in a 'pamphlet war'.

214 CHAPTER 7 Reconfiguring True Religion in Terms of Toleration

Context

The immediate cause for Castellio's condemnation of persecution was the execution of the humanist, Michael Servetus (1511–1553). Servetus was a Spanish physician and lawyer who denied that the doctrine of the Trinity (and child baptism) had any scriptural basis; Jesus was not God incarnate, but a prophet. Because of this, at the time outrageous, claim, Servetus was sentenced to death by the Viennese Catholic authorities. While he first managed to escape his execution, he was later caught in Geneva, where, on 27 October 1553, the city council, instigated by Calvin himself, carried out the death penalty: Servetus was burnt alive together with his books. The Catholic Church of Vienna reacted with relief when they realized that the Reformed Protestants, despite their own heretical beliefs, drew the line at anti-trinitarian ideas, and several Lutheran theologians from Weimar likewise sent their support. In Geneva too, the execution met with little resistance.

Still, some people protested against Servetus' treatment and this led Calvin to write an apologetic pamphlet *Defensio orthodoxae fidei de sacra Trinitate, contra prodigiosos errores Michaelis Serueti Hispani* [The Defence of the Orthodox Faith in the Holy Trinity against the Prodigious Errors of Michael Servetus: Where it is Shown that Heretics Rightly are to be Coerced by the Sword] (1554). According to Calvin, civil authorities were obliged to protect the church and to punish those heretics who threaten the unity of faith. I quote one passage, which captures Calvin's point of view and which underscores the power of the ideal of the *Corpus Christianum*:

> *But when religion is shaken to the core [*Sed ubi fundamentis convellitur religio*], when horrible blasphemy is directed at God, when souls are led to their perdition by way of impious and baneful teachings [*impiis et pestiferis dogmatibus*] and when men attempt openly to turn others away from their God and his pure teachings [*puraque eius doctrina*], then extreme measures must be used to stop the deadly poison from spreading. (Calvin,* Defensio *31, ed. Kleinstuber, 2009, p. 25)*

Castellio, who had already fallen out with Calvin, was appalled by this defence of coercion and expressed his protest first in a direct reaction to Calvin, entitled *Contra libellum Calvini* [Against the Libel of Calvin] (1554) (Castellio, ed. Barilier, 1998). Here, he formulated his famous sentence, that 'to kill a man is not to defend doctrine, but is to kill a man' [*Hominem occidere non est doctrinam tueri, sed est hominem occidere*] and claimed that the Genevans did not defend doctrine, but simply killed Servetus.

In a tractate that appeared soon after, entitled *De haereticis an sint persequendi et omnino quomodo sit cum eis agendum doctorum virorum tum veterum tum recentiorum sententiae* [Concerning Heretics, Whether They Should Be Persecuted and How They Should Be Treated] (1554),[1] Castellio continues his protest against heresy persecution. This tract consists of a preface addressed to Count William of Hesse, known for his commitment to the mitigation of persecution; a dedication to the Duke of Württemberg and a compilation of opinions of 'learned men' on the topic of toleration. Fearing for his own life, Castellio published this work under the pseudonym of Bellius (Text Box 3).

Text Box 3: Castellio's Plea for Toleration ... Not New at All?

The third part of Castellio's work is a compilation of texts by key figures who argue against persecution. Castellio inserted arguments formulated by early church fathers like Hilary, Lactantius, Chrysostom, Augustine, and Jerome, many of whom were themselves persecuted in their time. In Castellio's view, being persecuted is a sign of faithfulness: Christ and his followers were persecuted and persecuted no one. By compiling Christian arguments in favour of toleration, he makes clear that what he is saying is not new but belongs at the heart of the Christian tradition; before the Constantinian turn, toleration was indeed the norm. However, once they were no longer persecuted themselves, Christians began to turn on their fellow Christians who held diverging ideas. The lure of power turned Christians into servants of the devil rather than followers of Christ, who himself died because of his faith. Castellio is adamant: compelling people to 'come in', is not charitable hatred; it is not the Christian thing to do; it is not a sign of love, but misguided behaviour. Early church fathers, so he argues, share this point of view.

Castellio also selected texts from modern thinkers. Interestingly, he not only inserted arguments from modern thinkers like Desiderius Erasmus and Sebastian Franck (1499–1542), known advocates of tolerance, he also referenced Martin Luther and John Calvin, who in their early writings, namely before they had become widely known and powerful, had argued against persecution. Castellio states that their earlier writings have more credibility because they were written in a time of tribulation, when they, like Christ and his followers, were persecuted and pleaded for meekness and goodness (Castellio, trans. Joris & Bainton, 1965, p. 20).

Castellio's work is laced with religionized contrasts: body/spirit; word/sword; followers of Christ/followers of Satan; piety/external pomp; essential beliefs/non-essential beliefs; dogmatic disputes/inner conversion. Playing with these terms, this Christian humanist seeks to recast the heresy/orthodoxy binary and sets in motion a re-humanization of heretics, an interiorization, personalization, and moralization of religion, and a hereticization of intolerant religion. The heretic is not he who deviates from orthodoxy, but he who uses violence against others who go by the name of Christian.

During the sixteenth century and long afterwards as well, Castellio embodied the minority voice. While his work was translated into several languages and influenced likeminded thinkers, it soon fell into oblivion and was only rediscovered in the twentieth century, when Calvin, once the charismatic leader of the Reformed Church, had gained the reputation of being a *Prinzipienreiter* [a dogmatic person] (van Veen, 2012, p. 8).

Preface Dedicated to Count William of Hesse

The preface opens with a dedication to Count William of Hesse (1743–1821), which is headed by a quote from Paul's letter to Galatians: 'He that was born after the flesh persecuted him that was born after the Spirit'. In this preface, Castellio builds an argument for the separation of the religious and political realm based on the distinction between the power of the Word and the power of the sword on the one hand and that of the free spirit/heart and the body/flesh on the other hand. Princes should refrain from persecuting people because of their 'faith and religion' [*foi et religion*], which above all else is 'free' (Castellio, trans. Joris & Bainton, 1965, p. 136). Faith does not belong to the body but to the heart, and the heart is beyond the reach of the sword. Sins of the heart, like unfaithfulness, hate, envy, and heresy, have to be addressed by God's word.

> *If anyone disturbs the commonwealth by an assault under color of religion [*battant, ou frappant aucun sous couleur de religion*], the magistrate may punish such a person not on the score of religion, but because he has done damage to bodies and goods, like any other criminal. If anyone conducts himself amiss in the Church, both in his life and in his doctrine, the Church should use the spiritual sword [*du glaive spirituel*], which is excommunication, if he will not be admonished. (Castellio, trans. Joris & Bainton, 1965, p. 137)*

Castellio continues by adding another binary to this mix, namely that of dogmatic hair-splitting and fixation on ritual externalities on the one hand and the acceptance of

216 CHAPTER 7 Reconfiguring True Religion in Terms of Toleration

uncertainty on the other. In his later work, he would speak about true faith in terms of *Ars dubitandi* [Art of Doubting] (Castellio, ed. Feist-Hirsch, 1981). Those who are unable to tolerate doubt resort to literalism (i.e. reading according to the letter rather than according to the spirit) and power abuse. Castellio crafts a contrast not only between dogma and true religion, but also between ritual externalities and true religion. This binary would also have resonated with the flesh/spirit dichotomy, as an antithesis between the outward and the inward, the manifest and the latent, the body and the soul, Christian and Jewish. In addition, he contrasts power and true religion; he even warns against those who pretend to protect the Republic by 'hitting' others under the guise of religion [*sous couleur de religion*]. Here Castellio seems to be suggesting that those who claim to protect the *Corpus Christianum* by using force are in fact heretics (who typically act under false pretences), a point he will make more strongly at a later point in his text.

In the second part of *Concerning Heretics*, and now writing under the name of Basil Montfort, Castellio continues his argument, stating that the use of power works against the spiritual church, because it encourages blind obedience rather than pious commitment. To reinforce his argument, Castellio makes use of an anti-Jewish trope:

> *Nothing is too monstrous to teach the people when doubt is prohibited, since if you doubt or do not believe, you are put to death. Hence, the power of the Scribes and Pharisees, who exclude from their synagogue those who dare to speak of Christ. Hence the tyranny of him who in our day has been unmasked and is rightly held in detestation. He could never have attained his tyranny if he had left religion free, nor would he have introduced so many errors had he not deprived men of the power of judgment. (Castellio, trans. Joris & Bainton, 1965, p. 248)*

Castellio, still under the pseudonym of Montfort, continues his typological reading of good and bad religion, by projecting a contrasting genealogy revolving around Cain and Abel, who each led an army – an army of the good and an army of the bad:

> *If you are not able to distinguish the true shepherds from the false, employ the test: paint a picture of an army, of the good and the bad. On the left portray an elder and powerful prince, named 'Cain', with a red banner and a wolf as emblem. The device is, 'Let us lay in wait for blood'. The watchword is 'Crucify'; the escutcheon, 'unbelief'; the girdle, 'a lie', and the sword, 'violence'. Let this figure be followed by his progeny with fire and sword, the giants, the Sodomites, Ishmael, Esau, the Egyptians, Saul, the false prophets, the Babylonians, Scribes, Pharisees, tyrants, and all the host of the powerful of the world. Paint on the right side a younger and weaker prince, by name Abel, with a white banner and a sheep as emblem. The motto is, 'All that will live godly in Christ Jesus shall suffer persecution'; the watchword, 'patience', the escutcheon, 'faith'; the girdle, 'truth'; the breastplate, 'justice'; the greaves, 'swiftness to aid a neighbor', and the word, the 'Word of God'. Above the two armies place a judge. Inscribe on his left in letters of fire these words; 'O Cain, where is thy brother?' [...]. 'Woe unto you Scribes and Pharisees, hypocrites!' 'O thou wicked servant, I forgave thee all that debt, because thou desirest me: Shouldest not thou also have had compassion on thy fellowservant, even as I had pity on thee?' 'Depart from mee, ye cursed, into everlasting fire'. But on the right side, let these words be written: 'Blessed is he that considereth the poor'. [...] 'Blessed are the meek. Blessed are they which do hunger and thirst after righteousness. Blessed are the pure in heart. Blessed are the peacemakers [...]. (Castellio, trans. Joris & Bainton, 1965, pp. 249–250)*

In other works, Castellio makes his position even more clear. In his *Libel against Calvin*, he argues that Calvin was 'inspired by the Jews, who chose to crucify Jesus between two thieves' (Castellio, ed. Barilier, 1998, p. 237, my translation). Furthermore, just like the Pharisees who used force against those who upheld deviant beliefs, Calvin is the tyrant of his day. He, Calvin, remains overly attached to the rigidity of Mosaic law and its fierce ruling against blasphemy. In this sense, he is like a Jew who reads the Mosaic law with 'a veil before his eyes' (2 Cor 3:15) and who does not understand that Christ signifies the end of the law (Castellio, ed. Barilier, 1998, p. 238, my translation). Continuing along these lines, Castellio writes: 'who would bear to have Christ snatched away from him to return to Moses, in the company of Calvin? Let Calvin, with his Jewish friends, be the disciple of Moses. For us, the Messiah has come. He is our legislator, and it is his law that we want to obey' (Castellio, ed. Barilier, 1998, pp. 245–246, my translation).[2] Thus, Castellio employs an anti-Jewish trope to criticize the tyranny of the sword (exemplified by Calvin and the Genevan Church) and the bondage of the externalities of religion; he seeks to project an interiorized and spiritualized pious Christian faith. The trope of the Jew, which evokes a rich palette of contrasting meanings, works to project true Christian religion (tolerant, free, spiritual, with room for doubt) – against false religion (carnal, legalistic, oppressive, violent). This pattern of religionization will return regularly in the Enlightenment's pleas for toleration: those who are solely concerned with power, and with ritual externalities and dogma, are overly focused on the law and not on the spirit (Yelle, 2011).

In *Concerning Heretics*, we find yet another important distinction, namely between what is essential to true religion [*les principaux points de la vraie Religion*] – those things that are necessary to ensure salvation – and what is inessential [*adiaphora*] – those doctrines, which are ambiguous and transcend human understanding. For Christians, Castellio argues, it is sufficient to find agreement on what is essential. The number of essential beliefs is limited: that there is one God; that God is the source of goodness; that man is condemned because of the disobedience of the first man and saved by the obedience of the second man, Jesus Christ, who is our saviour. Agreeing on the principal elements of true religion, there is no need for Christians to fight one another on more ambivalent ([*ambigu et douteux*] doctrines, like the Trinity, whether we eat Christ's blood and body during communion, whether we should baptize our children, and so forth (Castellio, trans. Joris & Bainton, 1965, p. 139).

Castellio is writing at a time when confessional communities were producing their detailed creeds and when any difference could become an identity marker: nothing seemed exempt in the process of boundary making. Castellio opposes this process, and rhetorically suggests that only those who agree with this distinction between what is essential and what is non-essential are capable of toleration, while those who do not agree, and remain fixated on penultimate ritual externalities and dogmatic differences, are intolerant. This effort to limit himself to the principal elements of faith makes Castellio 'a central figure in a process that might be termed the valorisation of doubt: a growing conviction that God is not honoured by the dogmatic gesture; that Christ is no friend of formula' nor of ceremonial acts (Erdozain, 2017, p. 483).

Castellio's use of binaries is reinforced in his other work, *L'impunité des hérétiques* [*De haereticis non puniendis*] (1554–1555) (Castellio, ed. Becker & Valkhoff, 1971), in which he distinguishes between two churches, the carnal and the spiritual church. He places the distinction between the two churches in a typological framework which had previously served the purpose of distinguishing between old and new Israel. Just as Cain persecuted Abel, Ishmael Isaac, Esau Jacob, the Pharisees Christ, so the carnal law persecutes the spiritual law and the carnal church persecutes the spiritual church. Thus, while he is targeting the Genevan Church, he does so by deploying the anti-Jewish typological imaginary of the Jews as carnal, legalistic, materialist, and ceremonial.

> So today that carnal Church, void of charity, swollen with the outward signs of
> sermons and sacraments and armed with the sword of the magistrate, assaults the
> spiritual; which being poor, humble, scattered and fugitive, puts nothing in front
> of him except humility and does not try anything else than to appease him for the
> salvation of one and the other. (Castellio, ed. Becker & Valkhoff, 1971, my translation)

Castellio even prophesies that a church that resorts to persecution will call upon itself the curse that has fallen on the Jews, who killed Jesus. Their kingdoms, republics, cities, souls, and bodies will be wiped out and they will be reduced to the same ruin and misery as the Jewish people.

218 CHAPTER 7 Reconfiguring True Religion in Terms of Toleration

Later, in his *Conseil à la France désolée* [Advice to a Desolate France] (1562), Castellio stated that the Genevan Church was no better than deceitful, hypocritical, and oppressive popery (Castellio, ed. Alazard et al., 2017). The evils once perpetuated by the Catholic Church were now continued by the Reformed Church and a once persecuted church had turned into a persecuting church. The Reformed had become like papists and were now also driven by carnal lust for power. Here Jews, papists, and Genevan Calvinists take almost interchangeable positions; all of them symbolize bad, external, carnal religion, and ever since the church 'abandoned the spiritual arms for the carnal, everything has gone wrong' (quotation form Counsel to France, p. 263, in Castellio, trans. Joris & Bainton, 1965, p. 262).

Dedication to Duke Christoph of Württemberg

Castellio's dedication to Duke Christoph of Württemberg (1515–1568) opens with a parable (Castellio, trans. Joris & Bainton, 1965, pp. 121–135). In this parable, the duke tells his subjects that he would come back at an uncertain time, and he asks of them that they, when he returns, wear white robes. During his absence, his subjects enter into endless discussions about the precise whereabouts of the duke, when he will be returning, how he will return and whether he will come alone or with an entourage. The discussion gets out of hand, and they start to fight each other, claiming to do so in the name of the duke. Surely, Castellio argues, the duke, upon his return, would be upset by the conduct of his subjects: they do not do as they were told, they lose themselves in endless discussions about doctrinal questions and engage in violence. In a similar vein, Christ also left this world, prophesized that he would come back at an uncertain hour, and asked his followers to prepare for his return by living a Christian life, loving one another, without falling prey to disputes. Like the duke, Christ too would be displeased when he sees how his followers quarrel about all sorts of dogmatic issues while forgetting to follow Christ's example. What matters, Castellio suggests, is not the doctrine of the Trinity, predestination, God, the nature of angels, or even the state of our souls in the afterlife, but rather whether we have a pure heart [*le coeur net*], for none of the issues listed above will make us better human beings (p. 122).

Furthermore, Castellio notes, too often Christians focus all their attention on disputing these doctrinal issues about which they simply cannot reach any certainty. It would be better to await the judgement of God on these questions. Castellio, highlighting the hypocrisy of persecution, continues by asking how we, who are steeped in sin ourselves, can pretend to be the judge of others. Would it not be more appropriate to focus on improving our own way of living instead of condemning others (p. 125)? Here, Christ set the example: he did not condemn those who killed him but forgave them. If Christ was so benign, then what gives us the right to sentence people to death because they follow their conscience? What is more, one can only be saved by one's own faith. I quote Castellio here:

> But I dare not violate my conscience lest I offend Christ who has forbidden by his servant Paul that I do anything about which I am in doubt whether it is good or bad. I must be saved by my own faith and not by that of another. (Castellio, trans. Joris & Bainton, 1965, p. 124)

Castellio, furthermore, notes that Christ himself, as well as the first Christians, were killed because they were accused of holding the wrong beliefs. This leads him to ask how we can decide who is a heretic and who is a true follower of Christ. Is there not a great risk that we will wrongly condemn people as heretics?

Castellio in fact regards the varying confessions as context-determined; their differences are relative, and thus certainly not a reason for persecution.

> [*W*]e regard those as heretics with whom we disagree [que nous estimons hérétiques tous ceux qui ne s'accordent avec nous en notre opinion]. *This is evident from the fact that today there is scarcely one of our innumerable sects which does not look upon the rest as heretics, so that if you are orthodox in one city or region, you are*

held for a heretic in the next. If you would live today, you must have as many faiths and religions as there are cities and sects. Just as he who travels from country to country must change his money from day to day [autant de fois et religions, qu'il est de cités, ou de sectes: tout ainsi que celui qui va par pays a besoin de changer sa monnaie de jour en jour], *since the coin which is accepted in one place is rejected in another, unless indeed the money be gold, which is valid everywhere regardless of the imprint. (Castellio, trans. Joris & Bainton, 1965, p. 129)*

Interestingly, Castellio broadens the scope of his reflections, when stating that Christians, Jews, and Turks can agree that there is but one God, while disagreeing on many other issues, just like Christians among themselves. The problem is that 'the Catholics, the Lutherans, the Zwinglians, the Anabaptists, ... and others – end up killing one another more cruelly than they would kill Jews and Turks. Should it come as a surprise that, when we treat each other like beasts, no Jew or Turk wants to become Christian? Who would want to serve Christ, when he runs the risk of being burned alive for holding a diverging opinion from those who are in power' (p. 133). One cannot hold it against them that they do not want to become Christian, that they do not see how Christian faith leads to salvation, when all Christians do is bring harm to one another. Rather than killing one another, Christians should instruct Jews and Turks and teach them the gospel by leading an exemplary life marked by piety and virtue; that will be the only way to convince them of the virtues of the true Christian faith. Mutual love is the 'bond of peace' until we reach 'unity of faith' (p. 133). Castellio continues by saying that something similar goes for the way we live together with other Christians. The only way to avoid disputes and conflicts is to focus on what is essential, to avoid mutual condemnation, to invest in mutual charity, just like Christ did, and to spread the gospel in word and deed.

Text Box 4: Patterns of Religionization: Setting a New Norm and a New Tone

Castellio crafts a new understanding of true Christian religion that is set over against false or un-Christian religion.

He (i) redefines both orthodoxy and heresy. Not only does he recognize the relativity of the binary orthodoxy/heresy – heretics are people who deviate from 'our opinion' – he also rehumanizes them: to kill a heretic is to kill a man, as he famously argued. (ii) In addition, he associates being a true Christian with leading a life of charity, meekness, and piety and he refutes the established understanding that compelling heretics to enter the fold is a Christian thing to do. Persecution is un-Christian. (iii) The heart of religion is ethics, not dogma. He moves away from a confessional dogmatic understanding of religion to a moral soteriology. (iv) Furthermore, a true Christian knows the difference between what are essential or foundational beliefs shared by all Christians and what are uncertain doctrinal claims. (v) Confessional difference is historically and culturally determined, and hence relative and of secondary importance to what is essential: Christian love. (vi) Finally, he mentions that Christians, Jews, and Turks share the belief in one God. Perhaps, it is because Castellio does not consider the doctrines of the Trinity or the incarnation to be essential that he is capable of including Jews and Turks. Significantly, Castellio is crafting a counter-discourse. At that time, his understanding of toleration was not normal/normative nor was it supported by the civil and ecclesial powers. In time, however, this understanding of 'meek' religion would become dominant and would become the norm against which confessions/religions, also of 'non-Christians', were to be measured. Indeed good religion would be religion which matches the worldview to which the religio-secular divide had given rise.

True Christian religion	False Christian religion
Tolerance	Intolerance
Meekness	Cruelty
Love	Violence
Following Christ	Following Satan
Living a moral life	Hypocrisy
Following personal conscience	Following authority
Purifying one's heart and comportment	Focus on doctrinal disputes rather than on moral behaviour
Christ was persecuted	Persecutors are followers of *Satan*
A heretic is someone who morally misbehaves or persecutes others	A heretic is one who deviates from us; persecution is a valid reaction

2 John Locke on Toleration

John Locke (1632–1704) was a physician and a political philosopher who experienced up close the religious turmoil and political chaos in England and the consequences of religious oppression. He wrote several works on the topic of toleration. These works focused mainly on the 'situation of Protestant dissenters under the Anglican monarchy'. Nevertheless, he also considered the possibility of the toleration of Jews, Muslims, and pagans and pondered their 'religious and legal needs' (Matar, 1993, p. 45). As the secretary to the Council of Trade and Plantations and the Lords Proprietors of Carolina (Armitage, 2004, p. 601), 'he devoted much thought and attention to the settlement and governance of colonies' (Armitage, 2012, p. 86), and was one of the legal drafters of the Fundamental Constitutions of Carolina (1669 and later revisions). This '*Constitution* enshrined toleration for all theists, including "heathens", Jews, and other dissenters from the purity of the Christian religion' (Armitage, 2012, p. 87).

Locke's understanding of the scope of toleration changed significantly during his career. I focus here on his *Epistola de tolerantia* [Letter concerning Toleration] (Locke, ed. Goldie, 2010), which I complement with insights from his other works. Locke wrote the *Letter* in 1685 while in exile in what is now the Netherlands, after he had participated in subversive political activity. The *Letter* may be read as a reaction to contemporary political events, like the revocation of the Edict of Nantes, the violent persecution of the Huguenots, and the effort of the Catholic King James II to repeal the Test Acts (1673), and also as a reflection of his first-hand experience of the relatively tolerant Dutch Republic (Gorham, 2011, pp. 104–105).

In this *Letter*, Locke develops a vision of the commonwealth based on the principle of toleration and the separation between the religious and the political realm. In support of his societal vision, he puts forward an interiorized, apolitical, and personalized understanding of religion. Thus Locke:

> *The care of Souls cannot belong to the Civil Magistrate, because his Power consists only in outward force: But true and saving Religion consists in the inward persuasion of the Mind; without which nothing can be acceptable to God. (Locke, ed. Goldie, 2010, p. 13)*

To further enhance the plausibility of this understanding of religion he cast both priestly religion and the Jewish religion as symbolic carriers of problematic religion.

> **Text Box 5: The Toleration Act of 1689**
>
> In the same year that Locke's *Letter* was published, the so-called Toleration Act was promulgated. While the act in principle led to the toleration of Protestant dissenters, it still maintained that the Anglican Church was the established and institutionalized church in England and Wales, which gave it a position of power in society with significant legal repercussions and material effects. Mark Goldie sums these up in the following passage, 'Citizens remained obliged to pay church taxes known as tithes; it was difficult to conduct marriage and burial outside the official church; and bishops were crown appointees who sat in the House of Lords. Furthermore, the Test Acts remained in place, by which citizens were disabled from holding public office unless they were communicant members of the Anglican Church. Although the Tests were often evaded in practice, they were not formally repealed until 1828. The separation of religion from public institutions proved a long, slow, and incomplete process, and in national schooling, for example, it has never fully occurred' (Goldie, 2010, pp. xiii–xiv). A religionized norm is institutionalized resulting in unequal power dynamics between those who conform and those who deviate.

Toleration as a Characteristic of Being a True Christian

In the opening pages of his *Letter*, Locke projects toleration as the 'chief characteristical mark of the True Church' (Locke, ed. Goldie, 2010, p. 7). Being a 'true Christian' requires an attitude of 'Charity, Meekness, and Good-will towards all Mankind; even to those that are not Christians' (p. 8). Leading a Christian life has little to do with boasting of 'the Antiquity of Places and Names', 'the Pomp of Outward Worship' [*externam pompam*] or claiming 'the Orthodoxy of [one's] faith', because in the end, 'every one is Orthodox to himself' (p. 7). According to Locke, all these things 'are much rather Marks of Men striving for Power and Empire over one another, than of the Church of Christ' (pp. 7, 8). Imposing the Christian religion on others makes no sense, certainly not when one has not yet embraced Christian religion in one's own heart (p. 9). The only war Christians should wage is on their 'own Lusts and Vices', for moral conduct is necessary to achieve eternal salvation. Disclosing the hypocrisy of so many Christians, Locke continues to ask why it is that men are so eager to 'deprive' others of their 'estates', to 'maim them with corporeal Punishments, starve and torment them in noisome Prisons, and in the end even take away their Lives' all because they supposedly are concerned about their 'salvation', while at the same time they remain unconcerned about the vicious lives so many lead; lives of 'Whoredom, Fraud, Malice, [...] and Heathenish Corruption', which are so clearly against 'the Glory of God, [...] the Purity of the Church, and ... the Salvation of Souls' (p. 9).

In brief, persecution is un-Christian and persecutors are nothing but power-hungry hypocrites, who operate under the 'pretence of religion' (pp. 8, 23, 40). Previously the problem was that heretics acted under the guise of religion and created disorder and chaos in the community. Now the problem is fiery zealots acting under the pretence of religion. Here, the 'reader is [...] encouraged to contemplate both the excesses of the Catholic inquisition and the rigors of the Republic of Geneva' (Lacorne, 2019, p. 16). Locke continues by saying that anyone who is 'indulgent to such Iniquities and Immoralities' (Locke, ed. Goldie, 2010, p. 10) while being 'cruel and implacable towards those that differ from him in Opinion', does not deserve to be called a Christian. However, it is a sign of true Christian faith to use the pulpit to call upon the Christian community to embrace the virtue of tolerance and to contribute to peace (p. 24).

True and False Religion

As in Castellio's work, Locke associates fixation on the ceremonial dimension of religion with power lust (Yelle, 2011, p. 32). Together with the privatization and individualization of religion, de-ritualization and de-materialization constitute key rhetorical building blocks of Locke's plea for tolerance. Besides, Locke's *Letter* exhales a 'stridently anticlerical tone' (see also, Locke, *The Reasonableness of Christianity*). Locke is suspicious of wicked priests, who were more interested in 'the tricks of religion' than in leading a virtuous life. In so doing, he evokes the typical enlightened trope of priestcraft (a new category), which charged 'priests, ministers, prelates, and popes [...] [across traditions] with having systematically deceived common people through fraudulent, cunning, and exploitative means' (Lancaster & McKenzie-McHarg, 2018, p. 1). Popery and priestcraft are carriers of false (carnal, ritual, external) religion. Under the guidance of imposturous priests who are obsessed with externals and privilege the carnal body over spirit, works over faith, law over grace, temporal power over piety, and ceremonial performance over inner conviction, people fall away from true religion (Gow & Fradkin, 2017, p. 276).

In his earlier, unpublished work, *Two Tracts on Government* (1660), Locke also projected problematic religion onto the Jewish people, and he represented Judaism as the inverse of his understanding of true religion, which is personal, ethical, and apolitical. In line with traditional supersessionist patterns of religionization, he 'characterized Judaism as a religion based on submission to law' (Ilany, 2020, p. 123). He was critical of the Mosaic Law as too ceremonial, too detailed, and excessively rigorous, and the same applies to the God of the Old Testament: he even 'descended to the lowest actions and most trivial utensils, not leaving out the very snuffers and firepans of the sanctuary' (Locke, ed. Abrams, 1967, p. 133). Indeed, the God of the Old Testament goes so far as to create 'an outward form of worship cumbered with more ceremonies and circumstances than I believe ever any in the world' (Locke, ed. Abrams, 1967, p. 163). Consequently, the Jewish religion makes it impossible to distinguish between what is essential and what is non-essential [*adiaphora*], and to identify what is necessary for salvation and of penultimate importance (Russo, 2002). Locke, reiterating a supersessionist framework, writes: '[E]ven until now when the writings of Moses are read, the veil remains upon their [the Jews'] hearts, they see not the spiritual and evangelical truths contained in them' (Locke, ed. Wainwright, 1987, I, p. 280). Within this unfree (read ritualistic/legalistic) religion, Jewish scribes and Pharisees become the archetypes of perverted and corrupt priestcraft (Goldie, 2018). Thus, the hermeneutical figure of the scribe intersects with the trope of priestcraft. Finally, Locke depicts Israel as symbolizing the ancient ideal of theocracy, which errs in mixing the religious and political realms.[3] In a theocracy, there is no space for religion understood as free, and therefore it is contrary to Christian religion and to a Christian organization of society.

This negative depiction of the Israelite political model of theocracy popped up regularly in enlightened philosophical works projecting the ideal of tolerance and it played a key role in the projection of problematic or dangerous (read political, legal, ceremonial) religion, that is to say, religion that 'can be related to religious fanaticism, which in turn can motivate violent political action' (Jansen, 2011, p. 998). While in Locke's work, this negative counterimage served the purpose of rhetorically reinforcing the process of secularization (i.e. the division of church and state), and while Locke included Jews as legal subjects in the scope of toleration (see below), it is not hard to imagine how this problematization of the Jewish religion (and by extension any religion that reeks of priestcraft) would eventually evoke questions as to whether or not the religion of contemporary Jews (and by extension that of Catholics) was to be tolerated. Might those who follow the Jewish religion (or a similar religious expression) be trusted? Do they not form a risk for society (and those who do keep the separation of church and state) (Text Box 6)? Might they not bring harm to the key principles of our liberal society? Do they deserve citizenship? And, if this suspicion holds, would it not make sense for the magistrate, who may resort to disciplinary measures in cases of worldly harm, to intervene (McClure, 1990, p. 380).

Text Box 6: The Jew Bill of 1753

In 1753, the Jewish Naturalization Bill was introduced in the House of Lords. This bill allowed 'persons' who had been born outside of England and who professed 'the Jewish religion' to become naturalized, without having to receive the 'Sacrament of the Lord's Supper'. The bill was approved by the House of Lords and returned to the House of Commons without much dispute. However, it evoked enormous popular outrage, which found its way into pamphlets, songs, and prints. Age-old anti-Jewish stereotypes were reiterated. Next to economic concerns, Jews would drain British resources and threaten the material well-being of the people. Political concerns were expressed: the sacrament functioned as a token of fidelity and loyalty to the state, without that token the state, imagined as a whole body, would disintegrate. Jews are not British. They are foreigners and rebels unwilling to pledge loyalty to the state, unwilling to receive the sacrament, and unwilling to accept Christ. The threat of division (religious wars) was projected onto the Jews as a nation within the nation. More importantly, the state would eventually be 'completely taken over and ruled by the Jews and transformed into a Jewish state – *Nova*. The British were warned that with the passage of the bill they would become foreigners and second-class citizens in their own land' (Gossman, n.d.). As such, the threat posed by the Jews was comparable to the threat posed by the intolerable and traitorous Catholics. It is the threat of treason and division. Dana Rabin elaborates on this political motive as follows, '[t]he prints and pamphlets reveal discomfort surrounding the perception by Christians, Anglicans in particular, that both individual Jews and the Jewish community as a whole had a fixed, cohesive singular identity' (Rabin, 2006, p. 168). In this setting, however, the Jew was not projected as feminine (cf. menstruating Jew) or as feeble, but rather as marked by aggressive sexuality, which targeted innocent, pious British women. As Rabin explains, 'the violent, militant, and sexually dangerous nature attributed to Jews suggests a physical threat to the nation. Given that the number of Jews in England stood at only 8,000 and that most English Jews in the eighteenth century were poor peddlers, the image of a potential for harm could not have been founded on any real threat to property or politics. The threat seems to have been based on anxiety about difference: a fear of being taken unawares, fear of an infiltration by the Jews as well as a fear that universal circumcision would erase the distinction between different groups and erode their particularity as Christians, as Anglicans, and as Britons' (Rabin, 2006, p. 160). Eventually, the so-called Jew Bill was repealed. Only in 1858, the Houses of Parliament promulgated the Jewish Relief Act, which enabled Jews to pursue their political and civil rights, albeit with continuing restrictions.[4]

The Magistrate

At the heart of Locke's argument is the necessary separation of 'the business of Civil Government from that of Religion' (Locke, ed. Goldie, 2010, p. 12). This separation hinges upon a clear definition of the Commonwealth on the one hand and the church on the other. The commonwealth is a society of men established with the purpose of 'procuring, preserving, and advancing of their own Civil Interests' (p. 12). Those civil interests are 'Life, Liberty, Health, and Indolency of Body, and the Possession of outward things, such as Money, Lands, Houses, Furniture, and the like' (p. 12). The jurisdiction of the magistrate only pertains to these civil concerns (p. 12), which revolve around the body, earthly possessions, and the impartial execution of laws. The magistrate may use the fear of punishment and force to discipline his subjects. However, '[t]he care of Souls cannot belong to the Civil Magistrate, because his Power consists only in outward force: But true and saving Religion consists in the inward persuasion of the Mind; without which nothing can be acceptable to God' (p. 13). Belief makes outward worship and the profession of creed acceptable to God and no force can ever produce belief. Furthermore, Locke argues, if one were obliged to conform to the religion of one's sovereign, and we accept that there is only one way to salvation, that would mean that all those who are so unlucky as to have been born in the wrong region cannot reach salvation, for there is but one right way to salvation.

> *For there being but one Truth, one way to heaven; what hope is there that more*
> *Men would be led into it, if they had no other Rule to follow but the Religion of the*
> *Court; and were put under a necessity to quit the Light of their own Reason; to oppose*
> *the Dictates of their own Consciences; and blindly to resign up themselves to the*
> *Will of their Governors, and to the Religion, which either Ignorance, Ambition,*
> *or Superstition had chanced to establish in the Countries where they were born?*
> *(pp. 14–15)*

The magistrate, therefore, may not impose his own religious norm, or rituals or ceremonies onto his subjects, who, based on their own conscience and faith, ought to worship God as they believe would please Godself. This also holds for those things indifferent.

> *To impose such things [...] upon any People, contrary to their own Judgment, is*
> *in effect to command them to offend God; Which, considering that the end of all*
> *Religion is to please him, and that Liberty is essentially necessary to that End,*
> *appears to be absurd beyond expression. (p. 33)*

The magistrate has no authority to interfere in religion, except, however, when religious beliefs and practices cause worldly injury and harm.

What Is a Church?

Locke continues by asking what then is a church (Text Box 7). He provides us with the following definition:

> *A Church then I take to be a voluntary Society of Men [*libera & voluntaria Societas*],*
> *joining themselves together of their own accord, in order to the publick worshipping*
> *of God, in such a manner as they judge acceptable to him, and effectual to the*
> *Salvation of their Souls. (p. 15)*

People are not born into a church; religion is a choice and no one can ever be bound to a church. People become members of a church because they are convinced that its worship pleases God and that it will lead them to salvation. If a person concludes that he or she had been mistaken in their hope to reach salvation in a particular church, he or she should be free to enter another church (p. 26). After all,

> *I may grow rich by an Art that I take not delight in; I may be cured of some Disease*
> *by Remedies that I have not Faith in; but I cannot be saved by a Religion that I*
> *distrust, and by a Worship that I abhor [...]. Faith only, and inward Sincerity, are the*
> *things that procure acceptance with God. (p. 32)*

A church, like any society, will be governed by certain laws, for without them it would simply dissolve. However, a church, may never use force to discipline members, because force belongs to the realm of the magistrate. Within the ecclesial realm, the only 'arms' one may resort to are 'many Exhortations and Arguments' (p. 43) and if this is to no avail, one may cut a member loose. Excommunication, however, can never entail the confiscation of earthly goods, because to do so belongs to the responsibility of the magistrate. In this regard it is important to bear in mind that any claim to orthodoxy is in the end nothing but a claim, for as Locke notes (cf. Castellio above): '[...] every church is Orthodox to itself; to others, Erroneous or Heretical' (p. 21).

Text Box 7: The Church as Voluntary Society and as Instrument of Salvation

Locke's argument for the division of the religious and the secular realm assumes a reinvention of religion and *mutatis mutandis* of the true nature of the church. His privatization and individualization of religion in terms of a personal choice to believe, implies a theological shift in the understanding of the role of the church in the economy of salvation: from an ecclesiocentric soteriology – an economy of salvation based on ecclesio-sacramental practice – to soteriology in terms of personal faith and moral conduct. The repudiation of ritual is an intrinsic part of the refiguration of the relation between church and state. In fact, this difference in the understanding of the proper role of the church in the economy of salvation still separates Catholic and (liberal) Protestant Christians.

Within the Catholic-Christian imagination, the ecclesial community consists of both the living and the dead, the sinners and the saints. The dead are not separated from the living, on the contrary, they continue to be part of Christ's living body, even after they have died. The saints, with Mary as the foremost saint, whose virtuous way of life exemplifies what it means to be a Christ-follower, reside at the heavenly court (Orsi, 2016). They can be invoked, and they can intercede on behalf of the faithful. Clearly, salvation is not an individual concern and interests all, the living and the dead. This understanding of the church as an instrument of salvation differs significantly from Locke's understanding of the church as a voluntary society, which one may opt in or out of. This is one of the reasons that scholars will say that a (liberal) Protestant understanding of church and salvation undergirds Locke's plea for toleration.

Church as voluntary society	Church as instrument of salvation
Salvation is an individual responsibility	Salvation is a collective ecclesial responsibility
Every person is responsible for his own soul	Salvation is not an individual concern, but interests all, the living and the dead, the sinners and the saints
Faith is conditional to salvation	God offers grace via the sacraments and with the proper disposition they work *ex opere operatis*
The church is a voluntary association	The church is God's salvific instrument on earth
The church is not necessary for salvation	No salvation outside of the church
Rituals are outward expressions of inward faith	Ritual practices (outward) mould and shape the inner person and incite faith

Locke, finally, makes clear that church and state need to be clearly separated. Any mixing of these two realms, any mixing of Heaven and Earth, is a recipe for violence (Text Box 8). The boundaries between ecclesial and secular powers have to be respected. They are fixed and unchangeable. The realm of religion is not the realm of the secular and vice versa.

226 CHAPTER 7 Reconfiguring True Religion in Terms of Toleration

> **Text Box 8: The Religio-secular Divide, the Frame of Religious Violence and Christianity's Others**
>
> In Locke's work one already sees a typically modern religionized frame at play, a frame which links religion on the one hand and violence on the other hand. The idea is that religion is particularly prone to violence and must therefore be contained. The religio-secular divide, which enables tolerance, assumes that religion harbours the problem of fanaticism – an idea which will be even more central to Voltaire's work on toleration – and that the separation of word and sword, church and state, is the answer to this problem. In the previous chapter, I described in some detail the confessional dimension of intolerance by zooming in on the metaphor of the *Corpus Christianum* and the oppressive regimes that emerged when ecclesial and secular authorities joined hands to protect the wholeness of the Christian body. However, viewing the religio-secular divide as a *lens* through which to approach the 'wars of religions' is a form of *Hineininterpretierung*, which does not do justice to the complex whirlpool of factors – confessional, material, territorial, economic, and others – which impacted the unfolding of violence during the confessional age (see also (vi) in Text Box 2). Put differently, it one-sidedly associates violence with religion, while ignoring the violence in the secular. This imaginary binary construct subsequently becomes a justification for governing religion, especially when suspected of turning violent. Following the religio-secular divide, the key-question becomes: how does one tell when religion runs the risk of turning violent? How does one discern religious fanaticism and distinguish it from meek, peaceful, and tolerant religion? How might one read the signs of growing intolerance? How might one tell if a 'religion' is capable of conforming to the religio-secular divide?
>
> In keeping with a pattern we encountered when discussing the Inquisition's treatment of the Moriscos and the Marranos, and following the established pattern of religionization that pits spiritual religion against carnal religion, religions are considered suspect when their adherents show an 'excessive' attachment to ceremonialism, legalism, and particularism, namely those practices that show 'religions' to be different from the secularized, interiorized, and spiritualized Christian norm.
>
> The religio-secular expectation that religion ought to be privatized and interiorized in order to be tolerated stimulates new expressions of inquisitive religionization.[5] During the eighteenth and nineteenth centuries, Jews and Catholics in particular (depending on the country) would find themselves subject to suspicion. In the twenty-first century, Muslims have become the carriers of problematic religion, with the veil, circumcision, and halal slaughter as signs of concern. The religio-secular divide and its presuppositions about religious violence is to this day, and since the 1990s with increasing vigour, the framework used to interpret and measure the 'integration' of Muslim minorities in Europe. Following the fallacy of the single narrative, this limits our understanding of the socio-economic, political-historical, intercultural, and inter-ethnic challenges that Muslims in Europe encounter (Jansen, 2017). What we see happening here is once again that a changed understanding of Christianness affects the fate of Christianity's others and the legitimacy of their presence in Europe. In this regard, the Jewish question, the Catholic question, and later the Muslim question are all really expressions of the Christian European question. The lens of religionization shows that these are entangled questions.

The Scope of Tolerance: Jews, Muslims, and Pagans

In his *Letter concerning Toleration*, and based on what the gospel commands, Locke extends the scope of tolerance to Jews, Muslims, and even pagans. He considers their opinions to be 'false and absurd', but he sees no reason to place them outside the scope of toleration. In his words,

Nay if we may openly speak the Truth and as becomes one Man to another; neither Pagan, nor Mahumetan, nor Jew, ought to be excluded from the Civil Rights of the Commonwealth, because of his Religion. The Gospel commands no such thing. [...] And the Commonwealth, which embraces indifferently all men that are honest, peaceable, and industrious, requires it not. (Locke, ed. Goldie, 2010, p. 59)

Religion – whether that of the Jews, Muslims, or pagans – cannot provide grounds for discrimination in the secular realm, not even when it concerns non-Christians. Locke gives several arguments to substantiate this claim. First, that people (and this also holds for non-Christians) are responsible for the salvation of their own soul. Second, as long as people's beliefs and practices cause no worldly harm, the magistrate may not interfere. Pagans, Jews, or Muslims who worship according to their own customs do not in any way endanger the state (p. 59). Finally, Locke mentions the principle of reciprocity. If one licenses the magistrate to impose his religious norm onto all his subjects, one must realize that this will also affect one's co-religionists who happen to live under a magistrate belonging to a different religion: Christians will suffer intolerance from a 'Mahumetan or a pagan prince'.

Extending Toleration to the Pagans As secretary to both the Lord Proprietors of Carolina (1668–1675) and the Council of Trade and Plantations (1673–1675), Locke had various economic interests in America. He served on several governmental bodies tasked with overseeing the colonial empire, and part of his income came from his work as a colonial servant and from personal investments in the empire. In this capacity 'he defended the right of the Indians to practise their religion' (Matar, 1993, p. 52), stating that '[n]ot even Americans, subjected unto a Christian Prince, are to be punished either in Body or Goods, for not embracing our Faith and Worship' (Locke, ed. Goldie, 2010, p. 39). Locke also contributed to the drafting of the constitutions for the Carolinas, which stated that the beliefs and practices of the indigenous people was not a legitimate argument to interfere in their earthly condition and material belongings. Like all human beings, they are responsible for their own soul, therefore the magistrate may not interfere. 'Idolatry, ignorance, or mistake, gives us no right to expel, or use [the Natives of Carolina] ill'. In Carolina, there would be no undue mixing of religious and secular (this includes political and economic) motives.[6] Nabil Matar notes how Locke, in this context, considered the conquest of Canaan by the Israelites. He viewed that biblical act as an expression of colonial expansion: the Israelite march into the land, their extirpation of the native inhabitants and their settlement there were models quite similar to what English colonizers were doing in New England. But Locke warned that he drew attention to the theocratic colonialism of the Israelites for the sole purpose of refuting it as a precedent. He wanted to show why and how the English, and for that matter any other colonizing people, should never see themselves as successors to the Israelites. 'You will not make', he warned his reader, 'everything laid down by law for the Jews into an example for all'. As far as he was concerned, the Israelite model was unique because Israel had been a theocracy, unlike any Christian commonwealth (Matar, 1993, p. 52).

The Limits of Toleration Theoretically, Locke regarded tolerance to be a universal right, in reality he also saw the need to limit the scope of tolerance. First, Locke states that those who do not 'teach and own the duty of tolerating men in matters of religion' are not to be tolerated. For such people are simply waiting to seize control of the government and 'possess themselves of the estates and fortunes of their fellow subjects'. He explicitly excludes those Muslims who are 'bound to yield a blind obedience to the Mufti of Constantinople; who himself is entirely obedient to the Ottoman Emperor'. This also goes for those churches whose adherents pledge allegiance to a foreign prince. In his Amendment to *A Letter concerning Toleration,* we read:

That Church can have no right to be tolerated by the Magistrate which is constituted upon such a bottom, that all those who enter into it, do thereby, ipso facto, *deliver themselves up to the Protection and Service of another Prince. For by this means*

the Magistrate would give way to the settling of a foreign Jurisdiction in his own
Country and suffer his own People to be listed, as it were, for Soldiers against his own
Government. (Locke, ed. Goldie, 2010, p. 52)

Most scholars, however, assume that Locke has Catholics in mind too, even though he
does not mention them (in fact he hardly mentions them at all in the letter). In his earlier
Essay concerning Toleration (1667), he takes a more explicit stance against the Catholics.
Catholicism would present no problem if its followers were capable of separating politics
from religion. Locke, however, doubts that 'papists' are capable of such separation. For one
thing, Catholics do not behave as subjects who possess freedom of conscience because they
pledge allegiance to a foreign prince, who is our enemy. Catholics are considered to function
as a state within the state, a nation within a nation:

*It being impossible either by indulgence or severity to make papists, whilst papists,
friends to your government, being enemies to it both in their principles and interest, and
therefore considering them as irreconcilable enemies of whose fidelity you can never
be secured, whilst they owe a blind obedience to an infallible pope, who has the keys
of their consciences tied to his girdle, and can upon occasion dispense with all their
oaths, promises and the obligations they have to their prince, especially being a heretic,
and arm them to the disturbance of the government, I think they ought not to enjoy the
benefit of toleration.* (An Essay concerning Toleration, *Locke, ed. Goldie, 2010, p. 123*)

Furthermore, should Catholics come to power, they would refuse to tolerate Protestants.
Matar reads the refusal to extend toleration to Catholics against the background of the
political context of the time. Especially after the Glorious Revolution (1688–1689), Locke
feared that the religious obedience of Catholics vis-à-vis the pope would prevent them from
loyalty to the Crown.

Locke also places atheists outside the scope of tolerance. Following the common sense of
the time, atheists, because they do not fear God and his punishment, were deemed untrustworthy. One simply cannot build a society based on moral and legal principles without the
recognition of the existence of God and the warning of his chastisement. Atheists risk plung-
ing society onto a path of immoral private behaviour and public anarchy.

Crafting Judaism, Islam, and Paganism as 'Religions': Legal and Political Consequences in Europe and Beyond

Locke argues that Jews, Muslims, and
pagans are also entitled to toleration, based on his understanding of the nature of religion.
Religion, to his mind, is personally and voluntarily adopted belief. The goal of all religion is
to please God and to reach salvation. Even though there is but one true way to salvation, one
could say, in a Lockean reading, that all religions claim to offer a path to salvation, a path
that pleases God. Furthermore, since all men are responsible for their own soul, they may
not be forced in any way to leave their own path and follow that of the sovereign.

Locke's extension of the realm of toleration (or religious freedom) is made possible by
a redefinition of what (Christian) religion is and by a re-description of 'non-Christian' traditions based on this refigured understanding. This refigured understanding of religion is
not neutral, universal, or timeless, but is a particularly 'modern, European creation, and
a Protestant one at that' (Batnitzky, 2011, p. 1). Religion is belief, namely a personally
chosen belief unfettered by authority. It is not only personalized, but also depoliticized, de-
ritualized, and de-materialized. Toleration is contingent on this normative understanding of
religio, which is a social construct. It is the product of religio-secularization.

When Judaism, Islam, and even pagan traditions are cast as 'religious' and included in
the realm of 'religion', they are simultaneously made in the image of this modern, European,
and Christian understanding of religion: they are assumed to revolve around belief and the
prime concern of the religious person is first and foremost the salvation of his/her own soul.
Too much attachment to the ceremonial and ritual dimensions (external pomp) of religion is
suspect and may be a sign of bad religion (practising under the guise of religion, cf. heresy).

In any case, the political does not belong to the nature of true religion. Whether this aligns with the self-understanding of other traditions is not considered relevant; that question only becomes central after the so-called dialogical turn (see Chapter 9). The promise of toleration presupposes that people refigure their traditions according to this religious norm. There is freedom of religion for those who comply and integrate, but surveillance and discipline for those who do not (or who are suspected of being incapable of doing so). A key question in modern societies, that are structured around the religio-secular divide, is: are religious minorities capable of refiguring their traditions according to this religious norm? Are they capable of 'integration'? If the answer is yes, their traditions are deemed religious (in a good sense) and hence tolerable, if the answer is no, their traditions are suspected of going under the cover of religion, while actually serving political goals, in which case these traditions fall outside the scope of tolerance.

In eighteenth- and nineteenth-century Europe, for example, this refigured understanding of religion would confront Jews seeking emancipation with the challenging question of 'whether or not Judaism can fit into a modern, Protestant category of religion', while Christian and liberal thinkers debated whether Jews would ever be able to liberate themselves from their 'culture, law, and peoplehood', a prerequisite to their being given citizenship (Jansen & Meer, 2020, p. 4). The Jewish law especially and its ritual prescriptions met with suspicion (Judd, 2011). Religion, understood in this modern sense, may be integrated, but traditions that deviate, and remain stubbornly legalistic, ritualistic, materialistic, and political, can have no place in modern, secularized society. Liberal Judaism emerged in this socio-political context (Text Box 6).

This modern Christian understanding of religion and the distinction between the religious and the secular would also become the optics through which other colonized people and their traditions were observed, analysed, and governed. Not only would Christianity 'often be conceived as the religious formation most attuned with modernity and the secular organization of society', but other traditions would also only gain legal recognition if they became religions in this modern sense; when they became de-politicized, de-materialized, and de-ritualized belief systems. This often implied a restructuring of ancient traditions. This is why scholars working in the field of critical secular studies and the critique of religion will point out that toleration and religious freedom comes at a cost. Nelson Maldonado-Torres states in this regard: 'Coloniality [...] takes place not only when certain practices are excluded from the category of religion, but also when they are included in it' (Maldonado-Torres, 2020).

While extending toleration to different religions is a benign measure in some regard, and undoubtedly to be preferred over persecution, it is also a disciplinary measure. Indeed, certainly in a colonial setting, the religio-secular divide, and the concomitant understanding of religion, functions as a means of reorganizing people and their traditions, and it has functioned as a governmental tool of disempowerment: it requires traditions to become personal and apolitical (Yountae, 2020). Those religions that are deemed political – and thus not truly religious – need to be monitored, disciplined, and perhaps even oppressed, as has for example been the case with Islam under the French colonial regime in Algeria (Amer Meziane, 2021). A civilizational discourse of bringing toleration to the world can play out as a method of ruling through division. Several scholars have been exploring how the religio-secular divide and the modern understanding of religion in terms of personal, politically irrelevant belief aimed at salvation played out in various colonial settings. They identified how the religious-secular divide, while claiming to protect 'religion' against political interference, became a governmental discourse in the hand of colonial powers and was used to regulate people and their traditions (Jansen, 2017, p. 371).[7]

3   Voltaire and the Problem of Fanaticism

I now consider the work of the eighteenth-century philosopher Voltaire (1694–1778). Buried in the Pantheon in 1794, this *philosophe* [a freethinker)], poet and playwright is one of France's national heroes (Sutcliffe, 2000). Voltaire was a fierce advocate of toleration, and

230 CHAPTER 7 Reconfiguring True Religion in Terms of Toleration

this advocacy went hand in hand with a profound critique of revealed religion and every-thing he associated it with – priestcraft, dogmatism, absolutism, and so forth. Revelation is nothing but superstition (false religion): it does not match with the emancipation of the Enlightenment and imprisons people in a premodern era of darkness. With his satirical pen, Voltaire intended to liberate human reason from religious restrictions. To that end, he exposed contradictory scriptural claims, nonsensical dogmas, theological bogus arguments, clerical hypocrisy, and so forth.[8]

Voltaire's primary target was Christianity, and more specifically the hierarchical, clerical, and sacramental body of the Catholic Church. However, he also took the measure of both Judaism and Islam, which he projects as symbolic carriers of the problems of revealed reli-gion. He depicted these religions as antithetical to the spirit of tolerance, reason, and true religion, and coins their central figures – Moses and Muhammad – as archetypes of fanati-cism (Blijdenstein, 2021, p. 32). In his overall programme to emancipate religion, Muslims and Jews function as 'useful enemies' (Malcolm, 2019). Over against problematic, if not dangerous, religion, Voltaire places the deistic ideal of reasonable religion, namely 'the reli-gion that God had poured into the heart of every human being' and which passes the test of rational critique (App, 2010, p. 32). Exhaling the orientalist mood of the time, he also turned to India to destabilize false religion, to enhance his critique of Judaism, Christianity, and Islam, and to restore religion to its original purity. In the philosopher's imagination, India's religious tradition became the symbolic carrier of the most antique, reasonable, tolerant, and peaceful religion.

Context

Just like other European regions, France too had been affected by the splintering of religion and by the concomitant conflicts. Here too, the rival camps had tried to end the violence by organizing theological colloquies and establishing peace treaties, the most famous being the Edict of Nantes in 1598, which legally recognized both Catholics and Huguenots. The Edict of Nantes, however, was revoked in 1685 and, to the joy of the king, France was finally again *toute Catholique* [completely Catholic]. John Renwick scrutinizes how '[i]n the fifteen years following the Revocation, the government – having to deal with considerable num-bers of recalcitrant Protestants who now had no legal status – embarked upon a combined policy of persecution, repression and vexatious *dragonnades*'.[9] Protestants were faced with unjust 'fines, confiscation of property, imprisonment, flogging, branding, the galleys, death' (Renwick, 2009, pp. 180–181). However, protest against the policies of intolerance was growing and, by Voltaire's time, there was concern that the absolutist regime of France was harming social order, political stability, and economic progress.

Like Castellio, Locke, and others, Voltaire was convinced that matters of faith ought to be kept separate from all other human realms that concern politics, commerce, industry, and so forth (Renwick, 2009, p. 186). The drama of the history of intolerance stems from the endless entanglements of religious and secular powers. Any confusion of these two realms leads to *le système le plus monstrueux* [the most monstrous system] (*Prêtres*, in Voltaire, 1764–1785, ed. 2020).

The Case of Jean Calas

Voltaire's fight for the cause of tolerance reached its climax when he took an interest in the case of Jean Calas (1698–1762). The latter was a Huguenot from Toulouse who had been accused of killing his son, Marc Antoine, supposedly because he could not accept his son's conversion to Catholicism. The son in all likelihood had committed suicide. Anti-Huguenot hysteria got the upper hand and after a trial Jean Calas was executed and his family lost the right to inherit his property and possessions. In the meantime, the body of the son was exhumed and reburied in consecrated ground to be venerated as a Catholic martyr.

Voltaire, who was outraged, set up a campaign to clear the name of Jean Calas and restore justice to his family. Part of this campaign was his book *Traité sur la tolérance* [Traitise on Tolerance] (Voltaire, 1763, ed. 2013) where he depicts the family of the 'innocent Jean Calas' as being 'delivered up to the hands of fanaticism' (Nicholls, 2002, p. 444). The unrelenting cries of abuse of religion finally led to the demand for 'blood', Calas' blood (Voltaire, 1763, ed. 2013, Chapter 1). Voltaire not only recounts the circumstances leading up to Calas' death sentence and the failure of the judicial system but also sketches a terrible picture of the religious fanaticism of the Catholics in Toulouse. Intolerance 'destroys all societal ties' (Voltaire, 1763, ed. 2013, Chapter 1).

In the body of the book, Voltaire makes his case for tolerance, with reference to historical examples drawn from Greece, Rome, China, and India, and he turns the 'individual drama of Jean Calas into a matter for general human concern with political repercussions' (Renwick, 2009, p. 187). He argues that intolerance is a Christian European problem and that tolerance has been far more common in the rest of the world. 'The fury of the dogmatic spirit' has been the cause of so much blood spilling, indeed, the history of Christianity has been permeated by intolerance: persecution of heretics, iconoclasm, the inquisition, and the sad climax of the St Bartholomew massacre (24–25 August 1572), which showcased that of all European countries France was lagging the farthest behind (Voltaire, 1763, ed. 2013, Chapter 2). In contrast, elsewhere, rulers do not have a problem with religious diversity, and tolerance is not seen as a threat to society. On the contrary, Greece, Rome, India, Persia, Japan, China are all great cultures and empires which show that diversity is not a problem and that tolerance is possible (Voltaire, 1763, ed. 2013, Chapter 4).

Voltaire's campaign was successful and after three years, Calas' name was posthumously cleared. However, it was not until 1787 and the Edict of Tolerance that Protestants would be granted freedom of conscience and that the Huguenots would be legally recognized.

The Fanatic as a Rhetorical Figure

The Calas case provided Voltaire with an occasion to combat religious *fanaticism*; this would become an important label for problematic religion. But what exactly does Voltaire mean by fanaticism? In his *Dictionnaire philosophique* [Philosophical Dictionary] under the entrance of 'Fanaticism' (Voltaire, 1764–1785, ed. 2020), we read:

> FANATICISM is to superstition what delirium is to running a temperature, or rage is to feeling cross. People who have ecstatic visions, or mistake their dreams for reality and the heated products of their imagination for prophecy, are what we call 'enthusiasts'. Fanatics are people whose madness is fuelled by murder [...] The most loathsome example of fanaticism is that of the burghers of Paris who on the night of St Bartholomew ran hither and thither murdering, defenestrating, and hacking to pieces those among their fellow citizens who did not attend mass. Some people are cold-blooded fanatics: they're the judges who condemn to death those whose only offence is to think differently. [...] Once fanaticism has infected the brain, the illness is all but incurable [...]. The only cure for this pandemic malady is the philosophical cast of mind which, as it spreads from one person to another, eventually makes us gentler in our ways and forestalls all attacks of this evil; because, as soon as the illness starts making progress, we have to flee and wait for the air to clear. Religion and the law are inadequate as a defence against the bubonic plague of the spirit; far from being health-giving nourishment for the soul, in infected brains religion morphs into a poison. (Voltaire, trans. in the ed. of Cronk, 2011)

Voltaire depicts fanaticism as superstition that is out of control. It is explosive and violent. Fanatics are mad and ugly, their brain infected, their passions excessive: in brief, they are beyond the reach of reason. Notice how Voltaire links fanaticism with the image of the worst pandemic ever, that of the bubonic plague. He is suggesting that fanaticism is a disease that may infect entire societies. Religious fanaticism is a form of a boundless rage

232 CHAPTER 7 Reconfiguring True Religion in Terms of Toleration

that cannot stop itself. In connecting religion and fanaticism in this way, Voltaire certainly reinforces modern discourses about the problem of religious violence.

In his dictionary entry, Voltaire traces back the etymology of the word fanaticism to the Latin word *Fanum*, namely the temple where oracles were pronounced, occasions which sometimes went together with bloody rituals. In ancient Rome too, seers who interpreted the oracles were called *fanatici*. Voltaire connects this original meaning of fanaticism with that of enthusiasm, which comes from 'Greek *enthusiasmos* denoting the in-pouring or in-breathing of the divine, as performed by the inspired pythoness at Delphi' (Toscano, 2017, p. 112). In Voltaire's age, enthusiasts were those who claimed to have been directly inspired by God or who were convinced that God has spoken to them via visions or dreams. According to Voltaire, enthusiasts are wrong in their belief to have privileged access to divine truth. They mistake 'heated products of their imagination for prophecy' (see 'Fanaticism', in Voltaire, ed. Cronk, 2011). They take their dreams and their visions to be reality (cf. phantasy vs. reason). Voltaire also draws our attention to the danger of enthusiasm: 'such persons [enthusiasts] are fully convinced that the holy spirit which animates them is *above all laws*; that their enthusiasm is the only law they must obey' (see 'Fanaticism', in Voltaire, ed. Cronk, 2011). Thus, they pose a danger to societal order. Fanaticism is enthusiasm gone wild. Against this background we may understand Voltaire's infamous slogan: *écrasez l'Infâme*, which he repeatedly used to sign off his letters to friends. This phrase 'encapsulated the Enlightenment project of rooting out error, superstition and intolerance by means of reasoned argument, common sense, and often a healthy dose of biting irony' (Brewer, 2009, p. 206). What is intolerable must be crushed, eradicated, and whipped out.

Text Box 9: Religious Fanaticism and Previous and Current Patterns of Religionization

Voltaire is known for 'his vehement and persistent critique of the intolerance and reactionary influences of the old Church' (Levin, 2011, p. 124). However, in formulating his critique, he remains profoundly indebted to established patterns of religionization. His plea for emancipation makes use of binary patterns and rhetorical figures that stem from the 'intolerant' past, from which he seeks emancipation. Below, I shall discuss how he adapts the figure of the Jew and the Muslim to deal with revealed religion in general and with clerical Christianity more specifically. Here, I highlight how religious fanaticism builds on, combines, and reorganizes elements from both heresy and superstition in a manner that fits the construction of Voltaire's Enlightenment ideal.[10]

On the one hand, we may notice the divisive and destructive power of the fanatic, who is projected as being able to destabilize communities and plunge them into destruction and violence. This makes the fanatic akin to the heretic. Fanaticism, like heresy, spreads, contaminates, and sickens. It evokes Voltaire's repulsion and needs to be contained. However, whereas heresy is placed over against orthodoxy and is understood in terms of malign distortion of 'the' truth (understood as single), fanaticism is placed over against reason and rationality. This is an important shift: whereas the destructive nature of heresy consists in its divisive nature – it threatens the unity, purity, and integrity of the *Corpus Christianum* and thus brings about societal disintegration – the destructive power of religious fanaticism consists precisely in its desire to impose unity and to disallow difference and plurality. This desire springs from the belief in absolute, non-negotiable religious truth. From this perspective, fanaticism correlates with dogmatism and absolutism, two aspects of bad or problematic religion.

On the other hand, fanaticism understood as 'enthusiasm gone crazy', evokes the phenomenon of superstition, here understood as exaggerated frantic worship of the gods. We may recall here the *superstitiosi*, who engaged in ridiculous and mad ritualized actions in an embarrassing effort to please the gods (see Chapter 1). They were enslaved by fear and tied down by ritual. Akin to this notion is that of the idolatrous pagan, who worships natural elements or man-made statues rather than the one God. The pagan is confused. He mingles the ultimate with the penultimate. To put it in modern terms, his gaze follows a dark rather than an enlightened path. The figure of the pagan – the superstitious and/or idolatrous fool living in the countryside – resonates in the contrast between the fanatic (who, like the enthusiast, takes his dreams to be real) and the *philosophe* who is guided by reason. However, other than the pagan or the superstitious person, the fanatic (cf. the heretic) is not just foolish but also mad, dangerous, violent, and bloodthirsty: the fanatic may destabilize society and cause real harm, as the St Bartholomew massacre had shown or the case of Jean Calas. For that reason, fanaticism is intolerable.

In his 'telegraphic way of staking claims' (Brewer, 2009, p. 205), Voltaire launched charge after charge against what he considered to be dangerous religion and in so doing he contributed to the creation of new patterns of religionization, which to this day impact the Western imagination. Indeed, many of the ideas that crystallized in Voltaire's work have become almost natural assumptions of the modern age: Voltaire's devastating picture of religious fanaticism resonates with current popular ideas about religion and violence, the fraudulent nature of priests, the magic of rituals, the absurdity of Scripture, the irreconcilability of religion and reason (Sutcliffe, 2003, p. 4). The figure of the religious fanatic, especially, has entered into our collective imagination as a figure who embodies all that 'we' as modern, emancipated, and enlightened people do not want to be and with whom dialogue simply is not possible. For example, in the aftermath of the terrorist attacks on Charlie Hebdo, Voltaire's polemics against religious fanaticism were suddenly rediscovered and retrieved from French literature. As one author puts it: 'That day, two French djihadists, the Kouachie brothers, murdered eight newspaper collaborators and injured eleven others before managing to flee, after having shouted: "We have avenged the Prophet". Here we see the new form taken by religious fanaticism today. In the evening, many French people gathered at the Place de la Bastille to reflect and they waved their copies of a symbolic work: a treatise on toleration by Voltaire, which then immediately topped the sales charts for French books, showing both the importance of this work and the values it advocates' (Apasu, 2019, p. 1, my translation).

Refuting Theological Religion

Voltaire significantly broadens the scope of the problem of enthusiasm. In his understanding, enthusiasm is not simply a problematic expression of religion (a deviation, excess, an aberration), but the problem is far more profound: there simply is no revealed religion that can stand the test of reason. The entire construction of revealed religion – the idea that God has spoken to a people, via prophets, to make known his will to them, that God directs history towards a redemptive goal, and that Scripture contains the divine moral and ritual prescripts which only a select elite may interpret and perform – is nothing but nonsensical superstition. Especially when the leaders of different theological sects start to quarrel about doctrinal differences and ritual performances, fanaticism lurks around the corner. In Voltaire's words, 'theological religion [...] is the source of all conceivable foolishness and trouble; it is the mother of fanaticism and civil discord; it is the enemy of mankind' (*Religion*, in Voltaire, 1764–1785, ed. 2020, my translation). This also means that 'if the content of religious commitment is superstition and the presence of superstition [enthusiasm] is a necessary condition of fanaticism, then fanaticism must "pollute" the whole pool of religious believers' (Nicholls, 2002, p. 488). While it does not necessarily follow that all religious believers are fanatics, it does follow that they are all potentially fanatical. In one sweep, Voltaire has incriminated almost all religious people. Vice versa, only those who do not

234 CHAPTER 7 Reconfiguring True Religion in Terms of Toleration

'believe in any religious superstition lack, *ex hypothesi*, the potential to become a fanatic' (Nicholls, 2002, p. 488). As we shall see below, only deists meet this standard.

Ideally, the problem of fanaticism could be eradicated by means of emancipation. However, because of the credulity of the masses, Voltaire was not convinced that philosophical enlightenment would be able to curb the problem of fanaticism. That is why Voltaire deemed it legitimate for the sovereign to impose his religion, to use his power to root out the madness of fanaticism and to establish good, civilized, enlighted religion. Especially theologians, who keep adding ridiculous doctrines and practices to religion, must be silenced because their dogmatic and ritual hair-splitting only fans the flames of religious conflict.

> *A good and honest religion [...]. A religion which has been established by an act of the court, and which is totally subordinated to the sovereign, that is what we need, and let us tolerate all others. We are only happy when we are free and tolerant. (Voltaire, ed. Lefèvre, 1985, p. 64, my translation)*

Against this background, we may better understand his relentless attack on Christianity, and by extension Judaism and Islam, which he depicts as religions of 'priestcraft' and 'imposture' (Marshall, 2018, p. 167).

Christianity Voltaire lashed out against the Christian religion, which was supposed to inspire tolerance but which ended up being the most intolerable of all (*Tolérance*, in Voltaire, 1764–1785, ed. 2020). This is nothing but a 'sanguinary sect, maintained by hangmen and surrounded by funeral piles; a sect which could find no admirers but among those to whom it communicated wealth and power' (Voltaire, 1736, trans. 1841, p. 45). It is a religion which all should loathe. Strike after strike, he expressed his conviction that 'every sensible man, every honest man, ought to hold' this religion 'in abhorrence' (Voltaire, 1736, trans. 1841, p. 45). In a letter to the Prussian king, Frederick II (1712–1786), dated 5 January 1767, he writes 'As long as there are impostors and fools, there will be religions. Ours is without a doubt the most ridiculous, the most absurd and the most bloodthirsty that has ever infected the world' (Voltaire, ed. de Pompéry, 1889, my translation).

Even more specifically, Voltaire loathed the Roman Catholic Church, which embodies everything that is wrong with revealed religion and which is, with all its rituals, dogmas, and ceremonies, the very opposite of the religion of Jesus. Catholicism is a concatenation of scriptural absurdities, magical rituals, and nonsensical dogmas, which are all kept alive by a cast of imposturous, immoral, and power-hungry priests – popes, Jesuits, inquisitors, monks – who intentionally trick ordinary people and deliberately keep them stupid and feed their fanatical mindset. The trope of the priest figures prominently in Voltaire's work and evokes both fanaticism in belief, hypocrisy in lifestyle, and the cunning deception of ordinary, foolish people. In brief, priests set out to deceive the masses with their ritual hocus pocus, while they themselves lead immoral lives. Next to the priests, church leaders too are targeted for having concocted an ever-growing body of totally absurd dogmas, which they then declare to be 'orthodox' and for which theologians subsequently have to invent similarly nonsensical explanations in an effort to rhyme the incongruities. Theologians in turn pretend to be scholars, but are in reality unscientific, irrational, poisonous, and dangerous. They occupy themselves with the most ridiculous and absurd questions, while claiming to work in a scholarly fashion (Voltaire, ed. Lefèvre, 1985, p. 63).

Considering that (Catholic) Christianity drew 'its authority and intellectual underpinning from the Bible', Voltaire especially set out to discredit the Bible (Gargett, 2009, pp. 194, 197). In dozens of texts, he argued that on closer inspection the blindly revered book is full of grotesque imagery and immoral or completely nonsensical stories, and that no unbiased reader can seriously assume that it is in any sense God's word (Pelckmans, 2020, p. 33). By pointing out mistranslations, absurdities, and contradictions, and by making use of rabbinic commentaries which contest basic Christian assertions about the Virgin Birth and the nature of the Jewish Messiah, he undermines the idea that the second part of the Bible fulfils the prophecies of the Old Testament (Ages, 1966). He disputes the historical reliability of the gospels by showing that they contradict one another, even on the basic historical facts ascertaining to Christ's life: his birth, earthly life, crucifixion, and resurrection. Christ was a simple man, and he only became God under the influence of later Platonists, who turned this carpenter into a God.

Judaism   Given his commitment to tolerance, one might have expected that Voltaire would entirely reject the European legacy of anti-Jewish patterns of religionization. This is, however, not the case (Brustein & Roberts, 2015, p. 11). Voltaire had nothing but contempt for the Jews and he grounds his plea for toleration in a reiteration of the vilest anti-Jewish patterns of religionization. Indeed, when he frames his vision of Enlightenment as a battle between reason and religion, between philosophy and fanaticism, and between tolerance and intolerance, he projects the figure of 'the Jew' (any Jew, past, present, or future) as an irrational, intolerant fanatic, belonging to the past and lacking enlightenment. Thus Voltaire showed himself a true heir of the teaching of contempt (Isaac et al., 1964): he taps into centuries of anti-Jewish discourse, which he moulds according to his own needs and inscribes into his redemptive narrative of Enlightenment reason. Judaism becomes a symbolic carrier of fanatic religion which is entirely contrary to the values of the Enlightenment and to enlightened religion.

The God of the Jews is the true culprit: this is a barbaric God, a jealous despot, a cruel tyrant, always irritated and angry because his people fall short. The Jewish people themselves are abominable and detestable, ignorant and immoral, stubborn, blind, and irrational. They are usurers and liars, and he even recalls the idea that they smell bad. In fact, they are 'the most abominable people on earth' (*Anthrophages*, in Voltaire, 1764–1785, ed. 2020).

To discredit the Jews and to decentre the place of Jewish tradition in history, Voltaire uses similar strategies to those used when discussing Christianity. The Old Testament is not the written account of the history of God and 'his' elected people; rather this 'petty ignorant people' has crafted its own history, claiming a leading role for themselves which contrasts to the 'historic reality' of their being 'a wretched Arabic tribe without art or science, hidden in a small, hilly and ignorant land'. Mocking the pivot of their redemptive story, he relates that the Jews were not freed from Egypt by God under the guidance of Moses, but rather expelled because they had leprosy (continuing the association between Jewishness and contagious disease). Moses, the key figure in Jewish history, is nothing but a charlatan, an impostor. Considering that not a single historian mentions him or the exodus it is even possible that Moses never existed (*Moïse*, in Voltaire, 1764–1785, ed. 2020). Furthermore, Voltaire mocks Jewish law as arbitrary and nonsensical (Blijdenstein, 2021, p. 37), and he condemns the Jews of his time for unthinkingly accepting these illogical rules and abiding by them. Even worse, Jewish laws are proof of the profound immorality of the Jewish people; the commandment of circumcision was introduced only to keep the Jews from masturbation and the fact that the Bible repeatedly reiterates the prohibition of bestiality is a sign that this abominable people is particularly susceptible to this immoral practice. Just as the laws are irrational and immoral, so too the people who accept them as their guide to life are nothing but a superstitious lot. More fundamental, however, is that the Jews are a cruel and barbarous bunch of fanatics, who hide behind the claim that they are simply doing as God commands them. Indeed, they do the most horrendous things 'in God's name', whether it is the violence against the Midianites, the savage barbarous treatment of young women, Samuel's slaughter of Agagor, or Israel's extermination of the Canaanites. Comparing Jewish tradition with the norm of reasonableness, he claims the Jews are the lowest of the low.

> I [...] know the mores of this people. [...] they are the most brutal people of all,
> detested by all their neighbours, they detest everyone. [They have] always been
> robbers or robbed, bandits or slaves, murdered or murderers. [...] They are born with

236 CHAPTER 7 Reconfiguring True Religion in Terms of Toleration

the rage of fanaticism in their heart, like the Germans and English with blond hair. I would not be surprised if this nation would one day prove to be fatal for human kind. (Voltaire, 1772, p. 8, my translation)

In whatever nation the Jews live, their asocial, immoral, and irrational laws make it impossible for them to fit in. Therefore, they are rightfully treated as 'a nation opposed to all others' or expelled because the ruin they brought to society was intolerable. Should it really come as a surprise that they are 'hated by the whole human race'? Consider in this regard the following passage from *Essai sur les mœurs et l'esprit des nations*. This people

dares to spread an irreconcilable hatred against all nations [...] it revolts against all its masters. Always superstitious, always greedy for the good of others, always barbarous, creeping in misfortune, and insolent in prosperity. (Voltaire, 1785, ed. 2020, chap. 41–42, my translation)

Besides, Voltaire had little hope that the Jews would change (Text Box 10). Who they are is captured in the Old Testament: they are unable to evolve, unable to progress, unable to change, unable to diversify: once a Jew always a Jew and the Jew of the past is the Jew of the present (Sutcliffe, 1998, p. 110). Finally, Voltaire states, the Jewish people have never in their entire history contributed anything original to culture; they are incapable of doing so because they are an 'enslaved' people, which imitates its masters (Voltaire, 1736, trans. 1841, p. 12). The Jews are nothing but plagiarists and imitators in everything they do. In an era that was obsessed with detecting the origins of history and culture, being called out as a forgery or an imitation was an important strategy of delegitimization. While claiming to occupy centre stage in human history, while claiming the status of God's elected people, while claiming to be the instrument via which God acts in the world and communicates his divine will, the Jewish people are in fact meaningless, futile, a remark in the margins of universal history, which encompasses Islamic, Chinese, Indian as well as European civilization.

Text Box 10: Voltaire's Antisemitism as an Intrinsic Part of His Plea for Tolerance

Voltaire's condescending and offensive language is striking, especially because Voltaire is known as one of the main eighteenth-century advocates for tolerance. His contempt for the Jews casts a problematic shadow over his commitment to universal toleration, understood as a human right. Furthermore, Voltaire's antisemitism is not a minor issue in his otherwise tolerant philosophy, nor is it a mere remnant of the intolerant Middle Ages, an issue that would be transcended as soon as the Enlightenment progressed. The pattern of religionization that pits Enlightenment, tolerance, and deism (see below) against revealed religion forms one of the key building blocks of modern enlightened self-understanding: this is who we are in contrast to whom we do not want to be, to whom we reject, to what we have left behind (Sutcliffe, 2003). The problem of fanaticism is constructed as a problem of revealed (theological, priestly) religion – Judaism, Christianity, and by extension (see below) Islam. Tolerance, by contrast, belongs to good religion, namely enlightened, progressive religion, which is deist religion. Tolerance as an ideal is attainable only for those who free themselves from superstition (enthusiasm). Jews are unable to do so. They cannot free themselves from their fanatical nature and they cannot become philosophers. Emancipation, Enlightenment, and reason are beyond their reach. They cannot become philosophers [*philosophes*].

Even the Jewish claim to be central to European history as Judeo-Christian history is overstated: the Jews are not European; they are Asiatic, their contribution is not original and, in the end, the roots of European history are Greco-Roman rather than Judeo-Christian. From this perspective, the Jews do not belong in Europe. Thus, Adam Sutcliffe explains, Voltaire 'thought of the Jew not as a people within history, but rather as standing outside or even against history, stuck in a non-rational mindset of myth, superstition, and uncritical obedience to arbitrary laws' (Sutcliffe, 2017, p. 1069). In fact, it is doubtful whether the Jews, who form a particular people, can ever be loyal to the nation in which they live. Thus, he writes in a letter to Cardinal Dubois (28 May 1722):

> *Sir, I am sending Your Eminence a brief memo of what I have been able to unearth concerning the Jew of whom I had the honor of speaking to you. If Your Eminence deems the matter important, may I dare to suggest to you that a Jew, being of no country except the one where he earns money, can just as well betray the king for the emperor as the emperor for the king? (Voltaire, 1721–1730, Letter 55, my translation)*

For all these reasons, the Jews were excluded from the universal scope of enlightened reason. One cannot be enlightened and be Jewish. One may not be a *philosophe* and be Jewish. One may not be incorporated into modern tolerant society and be Jewish. For Jews to reach some form of emancipation they would need to transcend their tribalism and their attachment to law; it would entail leaving behind their particular Jewish identity. European Jews had long been charged with stubbornness for having refused to accept Christianity, now Jewish particularism was imagined as being out of sync with the hope 'for a more universalistic and progressive society' (Brustein & Roberts, 2015, p. 12).

Islam   As was the case with his critique of Christianity and Judaism, Voltaire's critique of Islam served the purpose of countering 'the hypocrisies of organized religion and its associated ills: superstition, dogma, and fanaticism' (Santing, 2007, p. 79). The philosopher was not ignorant about Islam, and he had access to more nuanced views about this tradition. With a few positive exceptions, as when expressing his admiration for Muhammad as the 'sole religious legislator who had courage' to found 'a great empire' (*Philosophical Dictionary*), Voltaire considered Islam in terms of fanaticism and depicted 'Mahomet [...] as a despotic Oriental Other who was defined by his lack of Enlightenment and who belonged to the past' (Levin, 2011, p. 139). More subtle portraits of Islam did not fit in his binary narrative of reason versus unreason, philosophy versus fanaticism, and enlightenment versus religion.

In his *Philosophical Dictionary*, he identifies Muhammad as a brigand, a charlatan, and an impostor, who intentionally and for personal gain deceives his ignorant people by claiming to be a prophet who speaks on behalf of God (*Arabes*, in Voltaire, 1764–1785, ed. 2020, my translation). The Qur'an, 'is a collection of ridiculous revelations and vague and incoherent preaching' (*Alcoran*, in Voltaire, 1764–1785, ed. 2020, my translation). It consists of 'contradictions, absurdities, and anachronisms' (Chapter 7 sur l'Alcoran, in Voltaire, 1785, ed. 2020, my translation). In his *Essai sur les mœurs* [Essai on Morals], Voltaire dedicates one chapter to Muhammad (Chapter 4: *De l'Arabie et de Mahomet*) of whom he states that he deliberately instilled a sense of enthusiasm in the Arabs.

> *It is to be believed that Mahomet, like all enthusiasts, violently struck by his ideas, at first spouted them in good faith, strengthened them by daydreams, deceived himself by deceiving others, and finally supported [...] a doctrine which he believed to be good. (Voltaire, 1785, ed. 2020, my translation)*

This is not a new image. On the contrary, the deceptive nature of Muhammad is one of the oldest accusations made by Christian polemicists and is simply reiterated by Voltaire.

The fixation on Muhammad's carnality, and more specifically his unbridled lust and 'abnormal' sexual interests, likewise, pass the review. Especially in his satirical play *Le Fanatisme, ou Mahomet le prophète* [Fanaticism, or Mahomet the Prophet], this image comes out: Muhammad's unhealthy interest in Palmire, a young slave girl (hinting towards paedophilia), who regards him as a father figure (incest), brings the prophet to the most terrible deeds. Furthermore, Voltaire reinvokes the association between Islam, power, and violence, which goes 'all the way back to anti-Islamic polemics authored by medieval Christians writing within the framework of a biblical historical meta-narrative' (Levin, 2011, p. 144). This image of Islam as a religion of the sword functions as the anti-figure in his progressive narrative that pits religious fanaticism against enlightened reason.

As he did when criticizing Judaism and Christianity, Voltaire deploys several strategies to question Islam's claim to a unique revelatory status. He questions the historic veracity of some of the so-called 'established facts' about the prophet, 'with the aim of destabilizing the historical singularity of the prophet as an unschooled Arabian who could not have possibly relied on acquired knowledge to devise a path to prophecy' (Fatih, 2012, p. 1076). The Qur'an does not contain God's word; rather Muhammad, the impostor, has crafted his so-called 'direct revelation' from existing sources. Thus, he writes, this

> religion, although it has some good points, such as worship of the great Being, and the necessity of being just and charitable, is otherwise nothing but a rehash of Judaism and a tedious collection of fairy tales. If the archangel Gabriel had brought the leaves of the Koran to Mahomet from some planet, all Arabia would have seen Gabriel come down: nobody saw him; therefore, Mahomet was a brazen impostor who deceived imbeciles. ('Reason', in Voltaire, 1785, trans. 2006)

The Qur'an is a jumble of suras with no chronological order, and the events described in the Qur'an are fabulous and ridiculous. Voltaire often refers to the story of 'Mahomet' putting half the moon 'in his sleeve' as an example in this regard. When asking why it is that someone comes to believe such ridiculous stories, Voltaire answers:

> It is through fear. He has been told that if he did not believe in this sleeve, his soul, immediately after his death, when passing over the pointed bridge, would fall for ever into the abyss. [...] All this terrifies the good Arab, his wife, his sister, all his little family into a state of panic. [...] But does our Arab believe in fact in Mohammed's sleeve? No. He makes efforts to believe; he says it is impossible, but that it is true; he believes what he does not believe. ('Common Sense', in Voltaire, 1785, trans. 2006)

It was, furthermore, priests and theologians – here imams and muftis – who, according to Voltaire, made up these absurd beliefs, instilling fear into the Arabs and preventing all criticism by threatening to punish them (Marshall, 2018, p. 174). In brief, the problem of Islam is comparable to that of Judaism and Christianity.

Deism/Theism

The French satirist had a vision of an era in which humanity would be guided by reason and enlightened by 'philosophy' and would embrace a simple, pure, and universal religion, *théisme* (deism): 'The only gospel we should read is the grand book of nature, written with God's own hand, and stamped with his own seal. The only religion we ought to profess is, "to adore God, and act like honest men"' (Voltaire, 1736, trans. 1841, p. 45). Voltaire's deist 'manifesto' figures in his *Sermon de cinquante* [Sermon of the Fifty], a prayer book for a society of 50 reasonable men; they voluntarily come together (cf. Locke) to worship the one God, who rewards those who live a good life, and punishes those who go astray.

> My brothers, religion is the secret voice of God who speaks to all men it has to unite all rather than divide them. It follows that every religion which belongs to only

one people is false. Ours in principle the religion of the entire universe; because we adore a Supreme Being like all the nations, we practice justice like all the nations teach and we reject all the lies which people reproach one another. [...] Religion has to conform to morality and be universal. (Voltaire, 1749, p. 4, my translation)

This religion, moreover, is 'the oldest and the most widely spread, because the simple adoration of God has preceded all the systems of the world. It speaks the language which all people hear, when they do not understand one another' (*Théisme*, in Voltaire, 1764–1785, ed. 2020, my translation). Deism revolves around a minimal credo, a sort of common ground, an original core, which could be shared across religions among all reasonable people. This common core consists of the notion of a (i) Creator God, who had equipped the world with (ii) natural laws, which this God respects. This means God does not intervene in the world; miracles destabilize natural order and were considered unreasonable. (iii) The God-given moral law is engraved in the conscience of every person and one does not need revelation to know how to lead a good life. (iv) The only way to honour the Creator God is by respecting moral law and leading a good life. Clearly, we are returning here to a kind of natural religion, which comprises those religious truths which may be attained by reason, rather than through revelation.

Deism is religion purified from dogmatic claims and ceremonial externalities. It is devoid of mystical addenda, ridden of revealed elements, and free from priestly mediators. This is what religion deep down is, has always been, and should be. Furthermore, no people can claim the monopoly of this religion; it is universal, precisely because it comes naturally to human beings and is common to all, notwithstanding the distortions and corruptions it has historically suffered. Voltaire was convinced that this stripped-down creed provided an answer to the problem of intolerance: if only everyone limited themselves to this shared, reasonable creed, there would be no more ridiculous doctrinal disputes, no further need to defend the honour of God against blasphemy, and no more confessional identities to be defended. Deists do not fight, and they may even help to reconcile quarrelling parties. In brief, reasonable religion is tolerant religion and this religion, which is religion in its essence, becomes the norm with which to measure all other religions (Text Box 11).

Text Box 11: Voltaire, the Logic of Encompassment and Christianity Reinvented

Throughout his work, Voltaire describes the concept of true religion as universal and natural religion. As mentioned above, this religion is the original religion and can be found among all people. Elsewhere, he claims that deism is the metal ring that holds all religions together. Voltaire's projection of an original and pure religion that may be found amongst all people is a typical expression of the logic of encompassment. As I explained elsewhere, while the logic of encompassment seems benign and welcoming, it also presumes a religionized schema of superiority and inferiority. This is certainly clear in Voltaire's work. Indeed, to his mind, while all religions go back to this original, universal religion, most of them have, under the influence of 'imposturous priests' and theologians, become corrupt. They are inferior expressions of this originally pure deist religion to which all are called to return. Furthermore, when criticizing revealed religion, Voltaire resorts to a logic of dichotomy pitting reasonable, enlightened religion (deism) over against revealed religion, philosophers over theologians, universality over particularity, religious fanaticism over tolerant religion.

In Voltaire's work, Christian orthodoxy is no longer the measuring stick for other traditions; rather Christianity is itself placed under critique, and is compared to other problematic (read revealed and theological) religions. On closer inspection, however, the deist norm against which the different traditions are judged, remains deeply indebted to Christian tradition. Indeed, this universal (true) religion as distinct from false (fanatical) religion emerges from and reiterates Christian theological notions like natural religion and natural theology (understanding God through reading the book of nature or making use of reason). Besides this, it reinforces the Pauline binary of spirit/law. Voltaire's disdain for the ritual priestly Catholic tradition, furthermore, has to be understood against the background of the Long Reformation. In any case, the fingerprints of Christian patterns of religionization are all over his re-description of true and false religion.

Therefore, one might argue, deism is still Christianity, albeit Christianity reinvented: it maintains Christian tradition, but is stripped of those elements that are now deemed irrational. Jenny Daggers would call this 'Christianity transcended' (Daggers, 2010): re-imagined, reasonable Christian religion remains the criterium with which to categorize and hierarchize different traditions.

This Christianity reinvented or transcended becomes the religious norm implicated in legitimization/delegitimization. Over against this norm, deviation is projected as problematic. Enlightened religion is placed over against the religion that stems from the dark Middle Ages; at that stage, problematic religion was bloody, violent, intolerant, fanatical, irrational, tribal, dogmatic, ritualistic, legalistic, and so forth. As we have seen happen with previous patterns of religionization, the hierarchical categorization of religions intersects with other binary constructs, like the one which sets the learned elite over against ordinary people.

True religion	False religion
Deism	Judaism, Christianity, Islam
Universal religion	Tribal religion
Rational religion	Superstition, fanaticism
Purified religion	Ceremonial/traditional religion
Unites	Divides
Light of reason	Darkness of tradition
Tolerance	Intolerance
Natural religion	Revealed religion
Moral religion	Ritualistic, legalistic, dogmatic religion
Religion of the philosophers	Religion of theologians, priests, religious leaders

Deism, Orientalism, and the Construction of the Religion of India

Voltaire was intent on finding traces of this original and most pure religion. Urs App captures Voltaire's reasoning as follows: 'If a good creator God had, like a supreme mechanic, fashioned a world as he intended it to remain, that is, a world without any need for further intervention and maintenance, then the religion and morality he had endowed humanity with needed somehow to show up in history' (App, 2010, p. 67). However, rather than identifying this most original religion with Christian religion (or one of its expressions), Voltaire, who had never travelled outside Europe, turned to Asia, and more particularly to the religions of the 'Orient'. If Christian missionaries at the time were trying to integrate Oriental traditions into the biblical historical framework, Voltaire coined China and later India as the cradle of all (true) religion in an effort to decentre biblical tradition (App, 2010, p. 34).

> *In placing the land of the most ancient origins outside the parameters of the biblical Orient, Voltaire sought to demonstrate that the biblical narrative was geographically and temporally parochial. He thus deftly integrated an assault on the Bible with a cosmopolitan narrative of history that incorporated parts of the world far removed from Europe. (Kang, 2012, p. 3)*

Initially, Voltaire directed his enthusiastic attention to 'the religion of China', and he became convinced that the teachings of Confucius came closest to deism. It is a religion rooted in the light of reason. Consider in this regard his *Philosophical Dictionary*, where he claims that 'there has been only one religion in the world which has not been polluted by fanaticism and that is the religion of the learned in China' ('Fanaticism', in Voltaire, 1785, trans. 2006). The same idea may be found in his *Essai sur les mœurs*, where, in the chapter on China, he writes that the religion of the Chinese was *simple, sage, auguste, libre de toute superstition et de toute barbarie* [simple, wise and free of any superstition and barbarity] (Voltaire, 1785, ed. 2020). Confucius, furthermore, never introduced new ideas, rites, or doctrines. He did not claim to be inspired nor suggest that he was some sort of prophet; he was a wise magistrate, who did not preach mysteries, but merely virtue. That is why, Confucius was a theist, a moral teacher who taught pure ethics with no claim to revelatory status; his teachings pre-date and precede Christian tradition, which in comparison is nothing but a flawed and faded version of this original universal religion.

Voltaire, however, soon lost his interest in Chinese tradition and turned to India and the Vedic religion of the Brahmans, which, he claimed, was even more ancient than that of China. In his imagination, India was the cradle of civilization, the source of antique wisdom. Thus Voltaire asked, '[i]s it not probable that the Brahmins were the first legislators of the earth, the first philosophers, the first theologians?' ('Brahmins', in Voltaire, 1785, trans. 2006). He contrasted the learned Brahmans to the corrupt, perverse, and fanatical priests; where the latter failed, the Brahmans embodied pure spirituality and deep morality. Their lifestyle was one of detachment and meditation instead of ritual and dogma. They were guardians of the most ancient religion, which revolved around worship of a sublime Being, which has created everything, including a pure moral system. In contrast to the reports that came back from missionaries, which tended to emphasize the backwardness of India and categorized Indian traditions as pagan and idolatrous, Voltaire projected Indians as law-abiding, chaste, mild, sweet, kind, and peaceful by nature. In contrast, for example, to Columbus, he did not use their mildness as an argument for their weakness or their childlike nature, but rather relates these characteristics to their high moral character. Any corruption/superstition came from outsiders, from foreigners; in its *Urform*, Vedic religion was deism. Consider in this regard the following passage:

> *Their annals make no mention of any war undertaken by them at any time. [...] One remarks a singular contrast between the sacred books of the Hebrews, and those of the Indians. The Indian books announce only peace and gentleness; they forbid the killing of animals: the Hebrew books speak only of killing, of the massacre of men and beasts; everything is slaughtered in the name of the Lord; it is quite another order of things. ('Brahmins', in Voltaire, 1785, trans. 2006)*

Voltaire's primary source for the knowledge he produced about the Vedic religion was the *Ezour-Vedam*, a Jesuit 'work that was supposedly an abbreviated version of the most ancient Indian holy book, [the Hindu Veda] but was actually a forgery' (Kang, 2012, p. 29). This manuscript was transmitted as a French translation of a Sanskrit original, which supposedly predated the Bible. The translation was written by a Father Martin, a Jesuit missionary, who wrote it with a missionary purpose: he hoped that it would help Christian missionaries to preach the gospel and lead Hindus to conversion. Voltaire himself received

242 CHAPTER 7 Reconfiguring True Religion in Terms of Toleration

this manuscript in 1760 from Comte Maudave (1725–1777), who had brought its existence to Voltaire's attention around 1758. While it was long thought that Voltaire was not aware of the dubious nature of this manuscript and that he assumed it to be authentic, we now know that Comte Maudave expressed his doubts about the authenticity of the manuscript to the French philosopher. Maudave knew that the translator of the text was a French Jesuit and this made him somewhat suspicious about its authenticity. Furthermore, Maudave was concerned about the overlap between the *Ezour-Vedam* and the Bible, especially with regard to the unity of God and the creation of the universe. He suspected that the Jesuit 'translator' may have had a hand in this conformity. Nevertheless, he sent a copy of the manuscript to Voltaire, whom he greatly admired (App, 2010, p. 63). Rather than approaching the *Ezour-Vedam* with his typical critical mindset – as he did with the Bible and the Qur'an – Voltaire did quite the opposite. He ignored the evidence that was in front of him and 'enhanced' the status of the text by false claiming that 'Maudave had received the *Ezour-Vedam* from a Brahmin who was a correspondent of the French Compagnie des Indes and had translated it' (App, 2010, p. 51); an 'entirely fictional' story (App, 2010, p. 52). Later, he would call it 'possibly the oldest book in the world'. The only conclusion possible is that Voltaire deliberately and knowingly 'created a narrative to serve a particular agenda' (App, 2010, p. 53) and actively 'misled' his readers. He deleted passages and added content and basically 'massaged' the *Ezour-Vedam* until it supported his claim that 'a form of monotheism uncorrupted by idolatry [...] had flourished in India prior to the culmination of the Christian revelation' (Sweetman, 2021). Thus, Voltaire became one of the proponents of the modern craze for the East, a made-up image of Indian deist religion which is compatible with his vision of a tolerant society.

Comparing Religions in Voltaire's Work: Decentring and Recentring Christianness

Voltaire projects a new norm/standard by which all religious traditions are to be judged and constructed. We may notice a shift away from Christian normativity (orthodoxy) and its focus on truth (as single, uniform, and pure) to enlightened, deist normativity with a focus on reason/rationality. The binary is no longer orthodoxy/heresy (true religion/false religion; truth/untruth; true worship/false worship) but deism/revealed religion (true religion/false religion; rationality/irrationality; tolerance/superstition →fanaticism). In the course of this comparative process, he refashions categories that were in use in the seventeenth and eighteenth centuries and reconstructs them as cutting across traditions: priestcraft, impostor, enthusiasm, superstition, fanaticism. The key figures in these traditions – Abraham/Moses, Jesus/Paul and Muhammad are all three comparable in their deceit. In all three traditions priests and theologians scheme, and put together creedal and ritual systems based on the fear of God, the Lord of the creation, and history. The idea of deceit or imposture, for example, which was previously projected mainly onto the Muslims and heretics, now becomes a cross-cultural category, applicable to all three theological traditions. The same upholds for the figure of the priest and that of the fanatic. In his effort to delegitimize revealed religion (and legitimize deism), Voltaire applies the same critical strategies: he questions the historicity of key figures and events; exposes the mythic and fabulous nature of biblical and qur'anic passages; surfaces scriptural contradictions; ridicules ritual practices and cultic law; uncovers hypocrisy and immoral behaviour and zooms in on the problem of religious violence (massacres, murder, war, persecution, etc.). Voltaire constructs these three religions in terms of quasi interchangeable tropes: what is projected onto one tradition, may just as well be projected onto the other, and to drive home his point (the problem of fanaticism), Christians, Jews, and Muslims all function as useful enemies. Just as Voltaire turns to Islam, Christianity, and Judaism as useful enemies for explaining his critique of fanaticism, so too he imagines and constructs Indian religion, by means of the *Ezour-Vedam*, to render it the embodiment of ideal religion in all its purity. This reasonable, moral, and natural religion is universal and authentic; it is what religion deep down is and should be; the religion to which humankind ought to return. It is the precondition for tolerance and peace. One final remark regarding the status of Christianity in this pattern of religionization: on the one hand, Christianity becomes one false religion amongst other false religions. From this perspective, Christianity loses its previous status as the measure against which other traditions are judged. This is a degradation. On the other hand, one could also argue that the projected deist/theist norm is in fact a reinvention of Christianity. As Daggers notices: 'It was but a small step from Christianity as the absolute and universal religion, absorbing all others within itself, to the notion of an absolute religion transcending Christianity, and incorporating all the religions' (Daggers, 2010, p. 969). In theory, Christianity is no longer the measuring stick for other traditions, but is now being measured. In reality, deism re-establishes Christian normativity, albeit in a refashioned way.

4 Conclusion

A recurrent theme in the work of Castellio, Locke, and Voltaire is the refiguration of society and especially the readjustment of the power relations between religious and secular authorities. This reconfiguration of society had a vast influence on the understanding of religion and its legitimate place in society. Religion was re-made and re-defined 'in a manner that is commensurate with modern sensibilities and modern modes of governance' (Mahmood, 2009, p. 837). Thus we may notice a shift from salvation being a collective affair to it being an individual affair; from church membership being compulsory to it being voluntary; from spiritual matters being the joint responsibility of church and magistracy to a clear division of responsibilities between the two parties. While for centuries intolerance of difference and the compulsion of dissenters to enter into the one true church had been projected as proper Christian behaviour, now some would argue the complete opposite. If previously secular and ecclesial authorities had been co-responsible for the well-being of the *Corpus Christianum*, now the domains of the religious and the secular would become clearly demarcated: the secular is the non-religious and vice versa. They are not to be mixed. Religion, as a separate realm, is to be protected from the interference of the magistracy, and vice versa. This separation, which would become one of the cornerstones of modern society, is the product of religio-secularization: the making of 'true religion' by assigning it a space that is clearly distinct from the realm of the secular.

Significantly, the religio-secular divide and the projection of tolerant religion emerged partly through a refiguration of a particular self-understanding of Christianity (Yelle, 2011). Gil Anidjar would even go as far as stating that Christianity reinvented itself as secularism (Anidjar, 2006). I would rather say that religionization in terms of religio-secularization remakes true religion (proper Christianness) in terms of tolerant religion (that is religion that is interiorized, personalized, adogmatic, and apolitical; religion that recrafted following the religio-secular divide). Immediately, the claim is projected that this tolerant religion is Christianness properly understood; it restores Christian faith to its origins. This re-imagination of the Christian norm went hand in hand with a re-imagination of problematic others, namely those who supposedly deviated from this norm or whose beliefs and practices could not be reconciled with the changed norm. True/good religion would now be understood as a set of beliefs that was 'privately held, spiritual and non-political' (Nongbri, 2013, p. 6), whereas bad/false religion would come to be associated with material and ritual pomp as well as with political ambition. Religion is a matter of the spirit, belief, and faith, not of body, law, politics, or ritual. This contrast between good and bad religion, true and false religion, however, builds on patterns of religionization that were 'established in earlier periods [and] remained in evidence, even as reworkings of these patterns were inscribed over them' (Sutcliffe, 2020, p. 92). Our advocates for tolerance resorted to and made use of the trope of 'the Jew', 'the Mohammedan', and by extension 'the papist' as a negative counter-image of enlightened tolerance and modern religion. Their spiritualized understanding of true religion is assumed to have restored Christianity to its true meaning, coining Catholic Christianity as paganopapism (being too material, too ritual, too carnal), superseding Jewish law that was cast into the 'dustbin of history', and projecting Islam as political religion. Thus, once again, the hermeneutical figures of the past are refigured to serve new purposes. The institutionalization of this religio-secular norm in Europe (and beyond), thus implied the redefinition and transformation not only of Christianness but also of the traditions of several other peoples as well.

Notes

[1] I will be using Castellio, ed. Gounelle and Choisy (2009). For the English translation: Castellio, trans. Joris & Bainton, 1965. When mentioned explicitly, I use my own translation.

[2] Elsewhere, Castellio writes differently about Moses and in fact casts him as an example. Just like Moses who did not enter in the promised land, Christians should accept that they live in eschatological expectation about the settlement of doctrinal conflicts.

[3] It also happened that the theocracy of Israel was invoked as a positive example with which nascent nations could identify; Adam Sutcliffe mentions how both the Dutch Republic and England rhetorically self-identified with the Ancient Jews, who also had to fight off enemies and oppressors in order to establish themselves (Sutcliffe 2003, pp. 27, 45).

[4] The emancipation of Catholics, who for a long time had been seen as a political threat to the unity of Great Britain, proceeded gradually. The first Relief Act (1778) gave Catholics the right to acquire real property, like land. In 1791, they received the freedom to practise their religion without risking civic penalties. In 1829, the Emancipation Act allowed Catholics to stand in parliamentary elections and pursue careers in the judiciary and the civil service. In 1871, Catholics were allowed to study at the universities of Oxford and Cambridge after the removal of religious tests.

[5] For the notion of inquisitive racialization see Jansen & van der Steen (2023, forthcoming).

[6] That being said, it is clear that Locke considered the colonial project legitimate and it was again a specific interpretation of Scripture and Christian doctrine that informed his thinking on this issue. Christian theological discourses infused the colonial project and they were transferred to and consolidated in the legal structures. Theologically justified legal conceptualizations become social realities affecting the lives of real people. In Locke's mind, God gave the world to all men and they were to cultivate it. Dominion fell to those who, following the commandment of Genesis 1:28, were capable of cultivating the land to its fullest capacity (Pagden, 1998). Second, every man owns his own body and may appropriate what is held in common through labour (Locke, ed. Shapiro, 2003, p. 111). Third, God gave the world to the industrious and the rational. The English are more industrious and rational than the Amerindians, who leave the land to waste, fail to cultivate 'the wild woods [...] of America' and do not use the riches of it. While the English may claim as property the land they cultivate, they were not entitled, however, to land that was already cultivated by Amerindians. At the very least this makes clear that the separation of church and state and the redefinition of religion in terms of a private affair does not lead to a rejection of the colonial project, which may be legitimized on a variety of grounds. Even when all people are projected as created in the image of God and hence of 'the same rank', there may be theologically justified reasons for some to dominate others and claim territory. Colonial law with regard to property and the rights of native inhabitants is informed by theological reasoning and by religionized patterns of thinking: we are dealing with a manifestation of the Christian mission to bring all of creation into the domain of Christendom. The idea that God had destined Christians to populate the land served as a legitimation of the colonial project (Hill Fletcher, 2017; Jennings, 2010; Newcomb, 2008).

[7] David Chidester focused on South Africa (Chidester, 1996); for India, Balagangadhara & De Roover (2007) and De Roover et al. (2011) ought to be mentioned; for Japan, I refer to Josephson (2012) and for the United States the books by Shakman Hurd, Khyari Y. Joshi, and Jeannine Hill Fletcher are recommended (Hill Fletcher, 2017; Hurd, 2017; Joshi, 2020).

[8] For the French version of Voltaire's work, unless indicated differently, I use Voltaire 1763, ed. 2013.

[9] A 'dragonnade' was the forced lodging of dragoons, the king's soldiers, in Huguenot homes which were looted and mistreated until they renounced their faith. https://museeprotestant.org/en/notice/the-dragonnades-1681-1685/.

[10] As far as the notion heresy is concerned, Voltaire follows the line of reasoning that we already encountered in Castellio, namely that everyone is orthodox to oneself and regards those who deviate heretical. Those who rise to power set out to impose their norm as orthodoxy and persecute those who uphold other opinions as heretics.

References

Ages, A. (1966). Voltaire, Calmet and the Old Testament. *Studies on Voltaire and the Eighteenth Century, 41,* 87–187.

Amer Meziane, M. (2021). *Des empires sous la terre: histoire écologique et raciale de la sécularisation.* La Découverte.

Anidjar, G. (2006). Secularism. *Critical Inquiry, 33*(1), 52–77.

Apasu, M. (2019). L'Intolérance et le fanatisme religieux dans l'œuvre de Voltaire. Diss. University of Saskatchewan.

App, U. (2010). *The Birth of Orientalism.* University of Pennsylvania Press.

Armitage, D. (2004). John Locke, Carolina, and the Two Treatises of Government. *Political Theory, 32*(5), 602–627.

Armitage, D. (2012). John Locke: Theorist of Empire? In S. Muthu (Ed.), *Empire and Modern Political Thought* (pp. 84–111). Cambridge University Press.

Balagangadhara, S. N., & De Roover, J. (2007). The Secular State and Religious Conflict: Liberal Neutrality and the Indian Case of Pluralism. *Journal of Political Philosophy, 15*(1), 67–92.

Batnitzky, L. (2011). *How Judaism Became a Religion: An Introduction to Modern Jewish Thought.* Princeton University Press.

Blijdenstein, A. (2021). Liberalism's Dangerous Religions: Enlightenment Legacies in Political Theory. Diss. University of Amsterdam.

Brewer, D. (2009). The Voltaire Effect. In N. Cronk (Ed.), *The Cambridge Companion to Voltaire* (pp. 205–218). Cambridge University Press.

Brown, W. (2006). *Regulating Aversion: Tolerance in the Age of Identity and Empire.* Princeton University Press.

Brustein, W. I., & Roberts, L. (2015). *The Socialism of Fools? Leftist Origins of Modern Anti-Semitism.* Cambridge University Press.

Calvin, J. (Ed. J. Kleinstuber) (2009). *Defensio orthodoxae fidei de sacra trinitate contra prodigiosos errores Michaelis Serueti Hispani.* Droz.

Castellio, S. (Trans. D. Joris & R. H. Bainton) (1965). *Concerning Heretics, Whether They Are to Be Persecuted and How They Are to Be Treated: A Collection of the Opinions of Learned Men, Both Ancient and Modern,* Records of Civilization 22. Octagon Books.

Castellio, S. (Eds. B. Becker & M. Valkhoff) (1971). *De l'impunité des hérétiques. De haereticis non puniendis.* Droz.

Castellio, S. (Ed. D. Feist-Hirsch) (1981). *De arte dubitandi et confidendi, ignorandi et sciendi,* Studies in Medieval and Reformation Traditions 29. Brill.

Castellio, S. (Ed. E. Barilier) (1998). *Contre le libelle de Calvin après la mort de Michel Servet.* Zoé.

Castellio, S. (Eds. A. Gounelle & E. Choisy) (2009). *Traité des hérétiques: a savoir, si on les doit persécuter, et comment on se doit conduire avec eux, selon l'avis, opinion, et sentence de plusieurs auteurs, tant anciens, que modernes.* Ampélios.

Castellio, S. (Eds. F. Alazard, S. Geonget, L. Gerbier, P.-A. Mellet, & R. Menini) (2017). *Conseil à la France désolée.* Droz.

Cavanaugh, W. T. (2009). *The Myth of Religious Violence: Secular Ideology and the Roots of Modern Conflict.* Oxford University Press.

Chidester, D. (1996). *Savage System: Colonialism and Comparative Religion in Southern Africa.* University of Virginia Press.

Daggers, J. (2010). Thinking 'Religion': The Christian Past and Interreligious Future of Religious Studies and Theology. *Journal of the American Academy of Religion, 78*(4), 961–990.

De Roover, J., Claerhout, S., & Balagangadhara, S. N. (2011). Liberal Political Theory and the Cultural Migration of Ideas: The Case of Secularism in India. *Political Theory, 39*(5), 571–599.

Diefendorf, B. (2014). Were the Wars of Religion about Religion? *Political Theology, 15*(6), 552–563.

Dixon, C. S. (2007). Urban Order and Religious Coexistence in the German Imperial City: Augsburg and Donauwörth, 1548-1608. *Central European History, 40*(1), 1–33.

Dixon, C. S., Freist, D., & Greengrass, M. (Eds.) (2016). *Living with Religious Diversity in Early-Modern Europe*, St Andrews Studies in Reformation History. Routledge.

Dreßler, M. (2019). Modes of Religionization: A Constructivist Approach to Secularity. *Working Paper Series of the Centre for Advanced Studies 'Multiple Secularities – Beyond the West, Beyond Modernities'*, 7. Retrieved from www.multiple-secularities.de/media/wps7_dressler_religionization.pdf

Erdozain, D. (2017). Jesus and Augustine: The God of Terror and the Origins of European Doubt. *Journal of Religious History, 41*(4), 476–504.

Fatih, Z. (2012). Peering into the Mosque: Enlightenment Views of Islam. *The French Review, 85*(6), 1070–1082.

Gargett, G. (2009). Voltaire and the Bible. In N. Cronk (Ed.), *The Cambridge Companion to Voltaire* (pp. 193–204). Cambridge University Press.

Goldie, M. (2010). Introduction. In J. Locke *A Letter concerning Toleration and Other Writings* (pp. xi–xxiv). Liberty Fund.

Goldie, M. (2018). John Locke, the Early Lockeans, and Priestcraft. *Intellectual History Review, 28*(1), 125–144.

Gorham, G. A. (2011). Spinoza, Locke, and the Limits of Dutch Toleration. *Macalester International, 27*, 104–118.

Gossman, L. (n.d.). The History of Jews in Great Britain: The 'Jew Bill' of 1753. Retrieved 20 October 2021 from https://victorianweb.org/religion/judaism/gossman4.html

Gow, C. A., & Fradkin, J. (2017). Protestantism and Non-Christian Religions. In U. Rublack (Ed.), *The Oxford Handbook of the Protestant Reformations* (pp. 274–300). Oxford University Press.

Greengrass, M. (2009). Living Religious Diversity. In C. S. Dixon, D. Freist, & M. Greengrass (Eds.), *Living with Religious Diversity in Early-Modern Europe*, St Andrews Studies in Reformation History (pp. 281–296). Ashgate.

Grell, O. P. (1996). Introduction. In O. P. Grell & B. Scribner (1996). *Tolerance and Intolerance in the European Reformation* (pp. 1–12). Cambridge University Press.

Hill Fletcher, J. (2017). *The Sin of White Supremacy: Christianity, Racism, and Religious Diversity in America*. Orbis.

Hurd, E. S. (2017). *Beyond Religious Freedom: The New Global Politics of Religion*. Princeton University Press.

Ilany, O. (2020). Christian Images of the Jewish State: The Hebrew Republic as a Political Model in the German Protestant Enlightenment. In I. Aue-Ben David, A. Elyada, M. Sluhovsky, & C. Wiese (Eds.), *Jews and Protestants* (pp. 119–136). De Gruyter.

Isaac, J., Weaver, H., & Bishop, C. H. (1964). *The Teaching of Contempt: Christian Roots of Anti-Semitism*. Holt, Rinehart and Winston.

Jansen, Y. (2011). Secularism and Religious (In-)Security: Reinterpreting the French Headscarf Debates. *Krisis, 2*, 2–19.

Jansen, Y. (2017). Beyond Comparing Secularisms: A Critique of Religio-secularism. In P. Zuckerman & J. R. Shook (Eds.), *The Oxford Handbook of Secularism* (pp. 369–386). Oxford University Press.

Jansen, Y., & Meer, N. (2020). Genealogies of 'Jews' and 'Muslims': Social Imaginaries in the Race-religion Nexus. *Patterns of Prejudice, 54*(1–2), 1–14.

Jansen, Y., & van der Steen, N. (2023, forthcoming). Inquisitive Racialisation or Race 'after' Secularisation: A Critical Phenomenological and Cultural Analytical Approach. *Identities: Global Studies in Culture and Power*.

Jennings, W. J. (2010). *The Christian Imagination: Theology and the Origins of Race*. Yale University Press.

Josephson, J. (2012). *The Invention of Religion in Japan*. University of Chicago Press.

Joshi, K. Y. (2020). *White Christian Privilege: The Illusion of Religious Equality in America*. New York University Press.

Judd, R. (2011). *Contested Rituals: Circumcision, Kosher Butchering, and Jewish Political Life in Germany, 1843–1933*. Cornell University Press.

Kang, T. S. (2012). *The Place of India in Enlightenment and Post-enlightenment Philosophies of History*. Cornell University Press.

Lacorne, D. (2019). Tolerance according to John Locke. In *The Limits of Tolerance* (pp. 11–30). Columbia University Press.

Lancaster, J. A. T., & McKenzie-McHarg, A. (2018). Priestcraft: Early Modern Variations on the Theme of Sacerdotal Imposture. *Intellectual History Review, 28*(1), 1–6.

Levin, P. T. (2011). *Turkey and the European Union: Christian and Secular Images of Islam*. Palgrave Macmillan.

Locke, J. (Ed. G. W. Ewing) (1965). *The Reasonableness of Christianity as Delivered in the Scriptures*. Regnery Publishers.

Locke, J. (Ed. P. Abrams) (1967). *Two Tracts on Government*. Cambridge University Press.

Locke, J. (Ed. A. W. Wainwright) (1987). *A Paraphrase and Notes on the Epistles of St. Paul: To the Galatians, 1 and 2 Corinthians, Romans, Ephesians*. Clarendon.

Locke, J. (Ed. I. Shapiro) (2003). *Two Treatises of Government and A Letter concerning Toleration*. Yale University Press.

Locke, J. (Ed. M. Goldie) (2010). *A Letter concerning Toleration and Other Writings*. Liberty Fund.

Luebke, D. M. (2016). *Hometown Religion: Regimes of Coexistence in Early Modern Westphalia*. University of Virginia Press.

Mahmood, S. (2009). Religious Reason and Secular Affect: An Incommensurable Divide? *Critical Inquiry, 35*(4), 836–862.

Malcolm, N. (2019). *Useful Enemies: Islam and the Ottoman Empire in Western Political Thought, 1450–1750*. Oxford University Press.

Maldonado-Torres, N. (2020, 3 March). Religious Studies and/in the Decolonial Turn. Retrieved from https://contendingmodernities.nd.edu/decoloniality/religiousstudiesdecolonialturn/

Marshall, J. (2018). Voltaire, Priestcraft and Imposture: Christianity, Judaism, and Islam. *Intellectual History Review, 28*(1), 167–184.

Marshall, P. (2009). *The Reformation: A Very Short Introduction*. Oxford University Press.

Matar, N. I. (1993). John Locke and the Jews. *The Journal of Ecclesiastical History, 44*(1), 45–62.

McClure, K. M. (1990). Difference, Diversity, and the Limits of Toleration. *Political Theory, 18*(3), 361–391.

Nederman, C. (2011). Toleration in a New Key: Historical and Global Perspectives. *Critical Review of International Social and Political Philosophy, 14*(3), 349–361.

Newcomb, S. T. (2008). *Pagans in the Promised Land: Decoding the Doctrine of Christian Discovery*. Fulcrum.

Nicholls, R. (2002). Voltaire and the Paradoxes of Fanaticism. *Dallhouse Review, 82*, 441–467.

Nongbri, B. (2013). *Before Religion: A History of a Modern Concept*. Yale University Press.

Orsi, R. A. (2016). *History and Presence*. The Belknap Press of Harvard University Press.

Pagden, A. (1998). The Struggle for Legitimacy and the Image of Empire in the Atlantic to c. 1700. In *The Oxford History of the British Empire, Volume 1: The Origins of Empire: British Overseas Enterprise to the Close of the Seventeenth Century* (pp. 42–47). Oxford University Press.

Pelckmans, P. (2020). *Op wereldreis met Voltaire: Filosofen en Frankrijk in de achttiende eeuw*. Doorbraak.

Pettegree, A. (1996). The Politics of Toleration in the Free Netherlands, 1572–1620. In O. P. Grell & B. Scribner (Eds.), *Tolerance and Intolerance in the European Reformation* (pp. 182–198). Cambridge University Press.

Rabin, D. Y. (2006). The Jew Bill of 1753: Masculinity, Virility, and the Nation. *Eighteenth-Century Studies, 39*(2), 157–171.

Renwick, J. (2009). Voltaire and the Politics of Toleration. In N. Cronk (Ed.), *The Cambridge Companion to Voltaire* (pp. 179–192). Cambridge University Press.

Russo, R. (2002). Locke and the Jews: From Toleration to the Destruction of the Temple. *Locke Studies, 2*, 199–223.

Santing, C. (2007). Tirami sù: Pope Benedict XIV and the Beatification of the Flying Saint Giuseppe da Copertino. In O. P. Grell & A. Cunningham (Eds.), *Medicine and Religion in Enlightenment Europe* (pp. 79–99). Ashgate.

Sutcliffe, A. (1998). Myth, Origins, Identity: Voltaire, the Jews and the Enlightenment Notion of Toleration. *The Eighteenth Century, 39*(2), 107–126.

Sutcliffe, A. (2000). Can a Jew Be a *philosophe*? Isaac de Pinto, Voltaire, and Jewish Participation in the European Enlightenment. *Jewish Social Studies, 6*(3), 31–51.

Sutcliffe, A. (2003). *Judaism and Enlightenment*. Cambridge University Press.

Sutcliffe, A. (2017). Toleration, Integration, Regeneration, and Reform: Rethinking the Roots and Routes of 'Jewish Emancipation'. In A. Sutcliffe & J. Karp (Eds.), *The Cambridge History of Judaism, Volume 7: The Early Modern World, 1500-1815* (pp. 1058–1088). Cambridge University Press.

Sutcliffe, A. (2020). *What Are Jews for? A People's Search for Purpose*. Princeton University Press.

Sweetman, W. (2021). Reading Jesuit Readings of Hinduism. In *Jesuit Historiography Online*. Brill. Retrieved from https://referenceworks.brillonline.com:443/entries/jesuit-historiography-online/reading-jesuit-readings-of-hinduism-COM_217891

Toscano, A. (2017). *Fanaticism: On the Uses of an Idea* (New and expanded ed.). Verso.

Van Veen, M. G. K. (2012). *De kunst van het twijfelen: Sebastian Castellio (1515–1563): Humanist, calvinist, vrijdenker*. Meinema.

Van Veen, M., & den Hollander, A. (2019). Introduction. *Journal of Early Modern Christianity, 6*(1), 1–2.

Voltaire. (1721–1730). *Correspondance de Voltaire: années 1721 à 1730*, Œuvres complètes de Voltaire 33. Garnier.

Voltaire. (1736, trans. 1841). *The Important Examination of the Holy Scriptures, Attributed to Lord Bolingbroke, But Written by M. Voltaire, and First Published in 1736. Now first translated from the French*. J. Watson.

Voltaire. (1749). *Sermon des cinquante: on l'attribue à Mr. du Martaine ou du Marsay, d'autres à la Métrie*. [s.n.].

Voltaire. (1763, ed. 2013). *Traité sur la tolérance*. Arvensa Éditions.

Voltaire. (1764–1785, ed. 2020). *Dictionnaire philosophique*. Arvensa Éditions.

Voltaire. (1772). *Lettres de Memmius à Ciceron*. Chez Antoine Pancouke.

Voltaire. (1785, trans. 2006). *Voltaire's Philosophical Dictionary*. Carlton House.

Voltaire. (1785, ed. 2020). *Essai sur les mœurs et l'esprit des nations*. Arvensa Éditions.

Voltaire. (Ed. E. de Pompéry) (1889). *Correspondance de Voltaire avec le roi de Prusse / notice par E. de Pompery*. Librairie de la Bibliothèque nationale.

Voltaire. (Ed. A. Lefèvre) (1985). *L'A.B.C.: dix-sept dialogues politiques traduits de l'anglais de M. Huet*, Bibliothèque de Philosophie politique et juridique. Textes et Documents. Centre de Philosophie politique et juridique de l'Université de Caen.

Voltaire. (Ed. N. Cronk) (Trans. J. Fletcher) (2011). *A Pocket Philosophical Dictionary*. Oxford University Press.

Walsham, A. (2015). Reformation Legacies. In P. Marshall (Ed.), *The Oxford Illustrated History of the Reformation* (pp. 227–268). Oxford University Press.

Yelle, R. A. (2011). Moses' Veil: Secularization as Christian Myth. In W. F. Sullivan, R. A. Yelle, & M. Taussig-Rubbo (Eds.), *After Secular Law* (pp. 23–42). Stanford Law Books.

Yountae, A. (2020, 28 February). A Decolonial Theory of Religion. Retrieved from https://contendingmodernities.nd.edu/decoloniality/a-decolonial-theory-of-religion/

PART 4

The World Religions Paradigm and the Turn to Dialogue

In the final part of this book, I zoom in on the emergence of a new, modern taxonomy of religion, which emerged towards the end of the nineteenth century and was more or less established at the beginning of the twentieth century. Up until the eighteenth century, it remained common to differentiate between Christians, Jews, Muslims, and pagans. However, around the 1850s, this fourfold medieval map of the world lost its 'ruling authority' and began to give way to another taxonomic model, which consists of a list of different world religions, that is sometimes complemented with primitive, tribal, or oral traditions (Masuzawa, 2005). Today, this new taxonomy is called the World Religions Paradigm. This paradigm shift not only changes the light in which the traditions of people all over the world are now interpreted, it is also a new normative organizational system, which has implications for the way societies deal with religion. While until recently, the World Religions Paradigm was understood as descriptive, it is also a normative redescription of the beliefs and practices of 'non'-Christians; it builds on older patterns of religionization and bends these according to its own interests.

1   What Is the World Religions Paradigm?

The World Religions Paradigm assumes the religio-secular divide: it projects religion as a category *sui generis*, namely a stand-alone category (Fitzgerald, 2011, p. 1), clearly differentiated from other secular realms such as economics, science, or politics. These different realms are imagined as essentially having nothing to do with each other (Fitzgerald, 2011, p. 5). Put differently, it is assumed here that those 'beliefs and activities' that are 'bounded by a common notion "religion"', are 'set apart from the "non-religious" or secular domains of human existence'. Religious activities are emphatically not economic or political activities (Harrison, 2015, p. 3). The general thrust, however, is not only that religion essentially is but also that it should be distinguished from these other realms. When mixing occurs – for example when religion and politics become entangled – violence lurks around the corner.

Christian Imaginations of the Religious Other: A History of Religionization, First Edition. Marianne Moyaert.
© 2024 John Wiley & Sons Ltd. Published 2024 by John Wiley & Sons Ltd.

Mixing with other realms is perceived as a pollution or perversion of religion. The religio-secular divide, therefore, restores religion to its original 'purity'.

The World Religions Paradigm, furthermore, plays with the distinction between the singular – *religion* – and plural – *religions* – and projects the idea that there are multiple 'religions' that may be understood as variations or species of a single genus, the category called 'religion'. Religion, generically understood, is 'geared to a transcendental "beyond" that [is] "immaterial"' (Meyer & Houtman, 2012, p. 3). To be religious, therefore, is a matter of the heart, of the interior, spiritual life and it 'transcends the mundane world of language and history' (Nongbri, 2013, p. 18). As Robert Orsi puts it, the common assumption of this paradigm is that 'religion is primarily private and interior, not shamelessly public; mystical, not ritualistic; intellectually consistent and reasonable, not ambivalent and contradictory'. It is 'transcendent not present in things' (Orsi, 1997, p. 6). This *inner* experiential world – often depicted in terms of 'faith' – is distinguished from and takes priority over the outer world of the *external* religious traditions. Faith, namely the personal human response to ultimate reality precedes any doctrinal, ritual, creedal, or communal expression. This reasoning is frequently complemented with the claim that religion is a human universal, an innate impulse, or implicit desire. Deep down, all human beings are fundamentally religious, directed towards a transcendent reality (Fitzgerald, 2000, p. 5).

The counterpart of religion as 'universal' are the 'particular' world religions, namely Christianity, Judaism, Islam, Buddhism, Hinduism, sometimes extended to include Jainism, Sikhism, Daoism, Confucianism, and Shintoism. When presenting the different world religions the emphasis tends to be on their stable and essential characteristics – their founder, key historical moments, central beliefs, sacred texts, core rituals, and ethical prescripts – and less on lived religion, namely on what people do in the messiness of their daily lives and in concrete socio-cultural and political contexts. Often these characteristics are systematized as coherent worldviews, according to which evocative symbolic practices (ritual realm) express core beliefs (creedal realm), which inspire believers to act according (ethical realm) to the example of their founder, whose teachings have been written down in authoritative texts that continue to be commented on (textual realm). These core elements of for example Islam or Judaism may be listed separately and compared to one another.

The central category in the World Religions Paradigm has been that of 'belief/creed', namely confirming or assenting to propositional statements such as: the world is created or the divine is immanent. Such beliefs are the more or less unchanging core of religions and make it possible to clearly demarcate Christians from Jews and Buddhists from Hindus. If one wants to know what religion someone adheres to, we ask, 'What do you believe?' Creed and belief often function as the most plausible substitutes for the term 'religion' (Bell, 2009, p. 192). With the focus on belief comes a focus on questions of truth: how do conflicting truth claims relate and do different religions believe the same thing? Different truth claims may be rationally scrutinized and measured against each other or 'against some intellectualist criterion of truth' as would be the case in the philosophy of religion (Harrison, 1990, p. 2).

2 Old Patterns of Religionization Function as Building Blocks

The World Religions Paradigm made its entrance in the late 1860–1870s (Masuzawa, 2005). Nevertheless, it was 'not the result of a sudden blinding flash of insight on someone's part. Rather its emergence represented the germination of seeds planted and watered over many centuries of Western history. For in a sense, the entire history of the study of religion in the Western world may be seen as an extended prelude to' its emergence (Sharpe, 1986, p. 1). When we zoom in on the World Religions Paradigm we may still encounter traces of that extended prelude. To be more precise, this paradigm assumes what I have called in previous chapters interiorization, confessionalization, and religio-secularization.

Interiorization

During the Renaissance, some humanists projected the idea of *religio* as an innate human impulse.[1] Marsilio Ficino (1433–1499), for example stated that *religio* is a human universal: *Homo est animal rationale religionis capax* [the human being is a rational animal capable of religion] (quoted in Leinkauf, 2014, p. 163). Genuine worship, which is directed towards God, is universal. To his mind, the very existence of different worship rituals (*ritus adorationis*) not only reaffirms that religion is natural to human beings, but also that God condones, even permits, these different rituals or ways of worshipping. Religion is one, stable, and unchangeable, but its expressions may be manifold depending on time and place. While the different traditions may exhibit different degrees of authenticity, the ideal expression of *religio*, however, remains founded in Christ; Christian revelation of God in Christ is the climax of God's plan for humanity.

Such Renaissance ideas went back to those Christian church fathers, who considered *religio* to be a universal gift that God bestowed on all people, even the gentiles. Here we may recall Tertullian's notion of *testimonium animae naturaliter Christianae* [the soul is in its very nature Christian]. To be human is to be religious, and even false worship like idolatry, is a sign that people have a natural desire for God, which needs to be cultivated. Epiphanius, furthermore, considered true *religio* not only as one and universal but also as transhistorical and transcultural. That *religio* is a human universal that can be abstracted from historical-cultural particularities and that even precedes and transcends Christ as God incarnate, is, therefore, an ancient idea, an idea that was developed by Christian apologists arguing in favour of the antiquity of Christian *religio* in a context of contestation.

The Long Reformation set in motion a further trajectory of interiorization, which builds on the above. When it comes to religiosity, what counts as religious are not merely outward, rule-governed actions, but personal dedication and commitment. Lay people too can be *religiosi*, and religious people – people that have taken vows – can be *irreligiosi*. *Religio* is a virtue, an inner quality. This turn inward was intensified by an at the time prevailing suspicion vis-à-vis material and ritual practices, which became associated with empty formalism and submission to clerical authorities that had fallen prey to power and lack devotion. Calvinist reformers especially associated externalities with the risk of idolatry and even magic.

Confessionalization

During the era of confessionalization, the ideal of the *Corpus Christianum*, while losing nothing of its appeal, fragmented: *religio* splintered into different confessions, each claiming finality for its own creed and denying others the right to exist. The reality of multiple Christian religions/confessions went hand in hand with the very denial of that multiplicity. However, the genie was out of the bottle and religious plurality was now a fact of life with which people had to deal. Efforts at clear confessional demarcation and identity construction ('us' versus 'them') increased, until different religions/confessions came to embrace different scriptural hermeneutics, creeds, rituals, symbols, buildings, and so forth. Besides, confessionalization also instilled in people the notion that religion, at least to a certain extent, is territorially bound. The ideal of the *Corpus Christianum* made way for multiple *Corpora Christiana* each following its separate rule and establishing a different norm: Lutheran, Calvinist, Roman Catholic, Anglican, and so on – one people, one territory, one confession, multiple Christian confessions, multiple contesting Christian norms, multiple others of Christianity. Here we see how religion pluralizes and is linked to a people and a territory. It is a defining category for people and thus a matter of identity.

At the same time, this (proto-national) ideal of one people, one religion, one territory became increasingly difficult to maintain, and people and their rulers had to find ways to live together in a context of religious plurality, albeit grudgingly. Councils were organized

252 PART 4 The World Religions Paradigm and the Turn to Dialogue

to come to interconfessional agreement, usually by trying to define shared beliefs across traditions and by projecting certain differences as *adiaphora* (that is irrelevant for salvation).

Religio-secularization

Key advocates of toleration, like Castellio and Locke, argued for a religio-secular divide, and they did so, partly, based on Christian theological arguments. Tolerance went from being a loser's creed to being the Christian thing to do. It is in line with the gospel to tolerate those who believe and practise differently and it is in line with the gospel not to confuse word and sword.

Notice how the projection of the religio-secular divide also assumes a reinvention of Christianity. The self-understanding of proper Christian religion changes, and this change allows Christian *religio* to re-establish itself as normative. Gil Anidjar says the following about this reinvention of Christianity:

> *The only tradition that has found itself secularized, that has reinvented or simply transformed itself as secular, is Western Christianity, so whatever changes Christianity has undergone in the last 300 years, are still changes that* Christianity *has undergone as a cultural unit (however porous and problematic and invested in claiming its own 'purity' that unit might be).*[2]

Religion is cast as a separate realm to politics (and by extension to economics, etc.) and, significantly, this continues to be projected as being in line with the Christian spirit of reformation and restoration: those arguing for toleration are likewise claiming to restore religion to its proper meaning. When we say that religion is a private affair, it means that it may not be coerced; any person may believe as his or her conscience dictates. We have seen this when discussing Locke, who thinks about religion in terms of a group of individuals who freely chose to associate themselves for the purpose of attaining salvation, and who may also freely choose to disassociate themselves from this gathering. The state should refrain from any interference in these matters of salvation. Pushed to the margins of the private sphere, 'Christianity' was reinvented as religion which accepts the dictates of modernity. Reinvented as secularized, Christianity continued to set the norm, a norm which would soon be projected onto other traditions as religion properly understood.

The underlying reasoning is that religion which does not accept this division is untrue to its proper nature: the religio-secular divide is presented as Christian. Intolerance is not a truly religious attitude; to be Christian entails being tolerant. In one move, the argument in favour of toleration is made by projecting problematic religion onto Jews, Mohammedans, and papists. In the writings of philosophers like Locke and later Voltaire, the fragmentation of religion, that was set in motion during the confessionalization era, is carried through and expanded. Locke in his reflections on how one may recognize particular religions does not hesitate to recognize Islam and Judaism as religions (these traditions have a rule of faith and worship, and a Scripture). Enlightened philosopher and self-acclaimed deist, Voltaire, was far more radical in his thinking and associated revealed religion with problematic, intolerant religion. For him, true religion is tolerant religion, peaceful religion, religion devoid of revelatory claims, clerical structures, and ritualized magic. This ideal of docile, pious religion sets the norm to judge and reject both Judaism and Islam, and especially Roman Catholicism, as problematic religions. Voltaire, as Guy Stroumsa puts it, 'exemplifies the vitality of a Judeophobia' and I would add, of an Islamophobia (Stroumsa, 2021, p. 55). The 'dissolution of Christian identity', or the transformation of Christian identity, clearly, does not lead to an abandonment of older patterns of religionization. Binaries follow one after the other: good/bad religion, tolerant (peaceful)/intolerant (violent) religion, deist/revelatory religion, and so forth. Both Jews and Muslims are used to attack Catholics and to project the ideal of tolerant religion.

3 Gathering Data in a Context of Colonization

Gradually, the reach of the term religion is extended. First, the modern devout claim it as a *virtue* that may not be limited to the *religiosi* that have taken monastic vows. All men and women may be *religiosi*, regardless of their status in the church. Next, amidst the conflict between Catholic and Protestant reformers, the idea of the *Spaltung der Religion* [fragmentation of religion] gained a foothold. There are now multiple, competing, and conflicting Christian religions, which all claim to be absolute. Next, the term is increasingly applied not only to different Christian confessions but also to Jews, Muslims, and other people, and to their traditions, rituals, customs, and opinions. The name that Christianity had claimed for itself for so long – religion – was now granted to (some) foreign traditions. Thus, we may 'underscore' how

> one particular religion is the one whose self-identification with, whose understanding and enforced institutionalization of that most Latin of words, shaped the current, hegemonic use and dissemination of that very same word and its ensuing division of the real, what Jacques Derrida has called mondialatinisation *and Peter van der Veer* 'the globalization of Christianity'. This one but complex and, again, divided entity has turned against itself, as it were, emancipating itself as if by fiat, by renaming itself religion rather than preserving the name it had long given itself as vera religio: *Christianity. (Anidjar, 2006, p. 59)*

Just as the factual recognition of Christian religious/confessional plurality could go together with the denial of the religious nature (true worship) of these religions/confessions, other non-Christian traditions could now be called religions (*de facto*/as a matter of fact) without being recognized as true (*de jure*/in principle). In the nineteenth century, some would bracket the question of truth, while others would claim that there might be many religions but only one universal religion (Christianity). But that is for later.

The projection of religion onto other people and their traditions (or the denial of that projection), however, cannot be viewed apart from the effects of colonization and exploration (Vial, 2016, p. 192). As Europeans expanded their reach over the globe, they had to learn more about the people they encountered in Asia, Africa, and the Americas. They had to learn their language (at least to a certain extent) and understand at least some of their habits, customs, and practices. Against this background, intellectual amateurs with a deep and sincere interest dedicated their time and energy to making sense of the diversity of people and their traditions. They observed rituals, learned languages, collected texts, and undertook efforts to translate the sources they gathered. This sincere interest in foreign and exotic people often went hand in hand with 'flagrant political interests' (Kippenberg, 2002, p. 26). The knowledge produced was both important for the missionaries trying to evangelize native people and for the colonizers, whether in their role as administrators (e.g. collecting taxes), traders, or land owners trying to establish a governing system. They had to engage in some kind of ethnography in an effort to make sense of the foreign world in which they found themselves and the knowledge they gathered travelled back to Europe in the form of reports. As a consequence, the sixteenth and the seventeenth centuries saw an explosion of information:

> There was an increasing knowledge of Southern Africans, thanks to the Portuguese and later the Dutch. The English and the Dutch presence in India brought about more awareness of the Indian subcontinent. French Jesuit missionaries of the seventeenth century took Catholic teachings to the Chinese and brought back knowledge of ancient Chinese scripts and gods. The most surprising new people, though, were certainly the Americans about whom nothing was known previously. (Nongbri, 2013, p. 107)

The resulting explosion of information did not spring from a reciprocal intercultural exchange occurring between equals. Rather it was collected, produced, and circulated in the interaction between 'colonial agents' operating 'on the noisy frontlines of intercultural contacts, encounters, and exchanges', 'indigenous people who were caught up in webs of colonial displacement, containment, and exploitation', and 'imperial theorists, surrounded by texts, in the quiet of their studies' (Chidester, 2014, pp. xx and 54). All of them were part of a system of oppression in which they nevertheless played quite different roles. This history affirms that 'religion' is a political category; it is related to things people do to gain or keep power or an advantage within their group.

Initially, the comparative interest in these foreign people and their strange practices was more like a 'prescientific and nonvocational interest of a purely consumptive sort' (Masuzawa, 2005, p. 63) and the fourfold taxonomy of Christians, Jews, Muslims, and pagans did not waver. Indeed, as long as these people could be discarded as mere pagans, savages, and barbarians, this medieval paradigm was not really challenged, and paganism continued to be a 'vast and murky area of the religious beliefs and practices of the world's pre-literate peoples' (Sharpe, 1986, p. 18). Only when Christianity itself began to be fiercely criticized by Enlightened philosophers were the data gathered about other people and their customs used to challenge the age-old Christian framework and to further destabilize and decentralize Christianity (Kippenberg, 2002, p. 25).

Paganism, the fourth category in the traditional taxonomy of religions, was a label assigned to the potpourri of all the other religions of humankind. In early modern times, however, with the new knowledge about the various religions of the world spreading widely, the simplistic designation of 'pagan' was becoming increasingly unsatisfactory. The multiplication of religions demanded a richer, more sophisticated taxonomy. With the great European discoveries, both in the New World and in Asia, and the progressive emergence of knowledge about the religious systems of the Amerindians, the Indians, the Chinese, the Japanese, 'paganism' as an all-embracing concept starts to crumble. (Stroumsa, 2021, pp. 36–37)

The more data about other people were gathered and the more the classical fourfold taxonomy came under pressure, the greater became the need to develop new taxonomies with which to organize and interpret the new information. What belongs together? Where does one draw the lines between traditions? How do these traditions compare with one another and how do they relate to one another? How do you determine what is or is not religious? There is also the question of which criteria you use to group traditions. Shared history? Geography? Beliefs (e.g. in one or more gods), and so on? A lot of knowledge about people who used to be cast aside as pagans (i.e. an 'all the rest' category) was acquired: knowledge about rituals, symbols, texts, and so on. Beliefs and practices that had previously been dismissed as mere idolatry were now seriously studied, and a real effort was made to make sense of all this information.

From the nineteenth century onwards, the study of religion emerges as a new scientific discipline, soon to be institutionalized at the university. This new discipline claimed to be non-theological, even though many who were committed to this field were Christian theologians or Christians, some of them secularized. The method used to make sense of the relations between the different traditions was that of comparison (Stroumsa, 2021, pp. 2–3), and more precisely that of comparative philology. At the time, many scholars were convinced that the study of language (by means of the study of written documents) gave access to the essence of people and their religious traditions – what they are truly about – and would help to trace their history and mutual relations (see Chapter 8). Based on comparative philological research, new ethnoreligious taxonomies were devised until finally, in the second half of the nineteenth century, the so-called World Religions Paradigm emerged as we know it to this day.

4   The World Religions Paradigm: Another Emancipatory Myth?

The World Religions Paradigm is often presented as a modern scholarly paradigm that finally overcomes Christian triumphalism and breaks away from theological normativity. The dominant narrative goes as follows: in the nineteenth century, by using new data, scientific methods, and scholarly reflection, it finally became possible to revise, refine, and differentiate the groups which had previously been called pagans or heathens or idolaters in a way that was far less ideological (read Christian theological). From being quasi anonymously lumped together, Hinduism and Buddhism and, by extension, Daoism, Shintoism, and Confucianism, could now emerge as unique traditions, with their own leader(s), texts, rituals, and moral norms. Put like this, the World Religions Paradigm is an expression of a greater attentiveness to the self-understanding of these other traditions; an attentiveness made possible because scholars of religion, as distinct from Christian theologians, were able to rid themselves of religionized assumptions which discriminate between Christians and others. Thus if we, today, have a list of 10 or 12 world religions, that is 'simply because there really are just so many major religions in the world, together with numerous other minor traditions that may be roundly called "others"' (Masuzawa, 2005, p. xii). When we tell the story of the birth of the World Religions Paradigm like this, it is really yet another version of the modern narrative of progress, emancipation, and enlightenment.

Several scholars of religion argue that things are more complex than this. Knowledge production is never interest-free and this also obtains for the study of religious diversity. The World Religions Paradigm 'cannot be studied in isolation from its broader societal context' and cannot be abstracted from the realities of unequal power relations (Stroumsa, 2021, p. 2). These critical scholars urge us to step away from the idea that the World Religions Paradigm is merely a descriptive framework and to understand it as a new modern expression of religionization (Thatamanil, 2020), which builds on previous patterns of religionization. This paradigm too is implicated in a process of selfing and othering predicated on religious difference.

In the final part of this book, I first explore the emergence of this modern religionized taxonomy that we now know as the World Religions Paradigm. Following scholars like Tomoko Masuzawa (2005), Maurice Olender (1992), Anya Topolski (2018), and Theodore Vial (2016), to name only some, I argue in Chapter 8, *Religio-racialized Taxonomies Based on Comparative Philology*, that the World Religions Paradigm is inextricably related, once again, to fundamental transformations of Christian European identity. Indeed, the construction of new taxonomies of religion(s) has been part of the political effort to (re)affirm the supremacy of Christianity and of European civilization (selfing) (Topolski, 2020), by recrafting and delegitimizing the traditions of others (othering) (Cavanaugh, 2009, p. 59). Far from being the neutral scholarly description it claims to be, the World Religions Paradigm is also implicated in the governance of religious difference (Nye, 2019) and Christianity now becomes one of many religions, while at the same time reinforcing its position as the *default* religion (Daggers, 2010, p. 963). Understood in this way, the World Religions Paradigm builds on a long history of normative Christian constructions of self and other in which some traditions came to be delegitimized, and others legitimized. In brief, it is yet another stage in the history of religionization.

In Chapter 9, *The Dialogical Turn beyond Religionization*, I zoom in on the emergence of the so-called interfaith movement, which aims at promoting friendly relations between people who orient around religion differently (Patel et al., 2018). I do not only trace the emergence of dialogue as a religious and societal ideal, I also seek to examine how this dialogical ideal, which emphasizes the importance of the face-to-face, relates to religionization. Does dialogue break with the past of religionization – a past in which the ‘religious other’ was for the most part named, essentialized, categorized, and inferiorized as a rhetorical figure with the purpose of bolstering a sense of Christianness or does the dialogical ideal itself build on new and transformed patterns of religionization? What is the critical potential of interreligious dialogue? And what is the place of Christianity in all of this?

Notes

[1] For an in-depth discussion of Renaissance humanism and the contribution to the emergence of the World Religions Paradigm, see Cavanaugh (2009) and Nongbri (2013).

[2] The Jew, the Arab. Interview with Gil Anidjar, n.d. https://asiasociety.org/jew-arab-interview-gil-anidjar.

References

Anidjar, G. (2006). Secularism. *Critical Inquiry, 33*(1), 52–77.

Bell, C. (2009). *Ritual Theory, Ritual Practice*. Oxford University Press.

Cavanaugh, W. T. (2009). *The Myth of Religious Violence: Secular Ideology and the Roots of Modern Conflict*. Oxford University Press.

Chidester, D. (2014). *Empire of Religion: Imperialism and Comparative Religion*. University of Chicago Press.

Daggers, J. (2010). Thinking ‘Religion’: The Christian Past and Interreligious Future of Religious Studies and Theology. *Journal of the American Academy of Religion, 78*(4), 961–990.

Fitzgerald, T. (2000). *The Ideology of Religious Studies*. Oxford University Press.

Fitzgerald, T. (2011). *Religion and Politics in International Relations: The Modern Myth*. Continuum.

Harrison, P. (1990). *‘Religion’ and the Religions in the English Enlightenment*. Cambridge University Press.

Harrison, P. (2015). *The Territories of Science and Religion*. University of Chicago Press.

Kippenberg, H. G. (2002). *Discovering Religious History in the Modern Age*. Princeton University Press.

Leinkauf, T. (2014). The Concept of Religion in Early Modern Philosophy – Three Examples: Machiavelli, Cardano and Bruno. *Problemata: International Journal of Philosophy 5*(1), 160–181.

Masuzawa, T. (2005). *The Invention of World Religions, or, How European Universalism Was Preserved in the Language of Pluralism*. University of Chicago Press.

Meyer, B., & Houtman, D. (2012). Introduction: Material Religion – How Things Matter. In D. Houtman & B. Meyer (Eds.), *Things: Religion and the Question of Materiality* (pp. 1–23). Fordham University Press.

Nongbri, B. (2013). *Before Religion: A History of a Modern Concept*. Yale University Press.

Nye, M. (2019). Decolonizing the Study of Religion. *Open Library of Humanities, 5*(1), Article 43. https://doi.org/10.16995/olh.421

Olender, M. (1992). *The Languages of Paradise: Race, Religion, and Philology in the Nineteenth Century*. Harvard University Press.

Orsi, R. (1997). Everyday Miracles: The Study of Lived Religion. In D. Hall (Ed.), *Lived Religion in America: Toward a History of Practice* (pp. 3–21). Princeton University Press.

Patel, E., Peace, J. H., & Silverman, N. J. (2018). *Interreligious-interfaith Studies: Defining a New Field*. Beacon Press.

Sharpe, E. J. (1986). *Comparative Religion: A History* (2nd ed.). Open Court.

Stroumsa, G. G. (2021). *The Idea of Semitic Monotheism: The Rise and Fall of a Scholarly Myth*. Oxford University Press.

Thatamanil, J. J. (2020). *Circling the Elephant: A Comparative Theology of Religious Diversity*, Comparative Theology: Thinking across Traditions 8. Fordham University Press.

Topolski, A. (2018). The Race-Religion Constellation: A European Contribution to the Critical Philosophy of Race. *Critical Philosophy of Race, 6*(1), 58–81.

Topolski, A. (2020). The Dangerous Discourse of the ‘Judaeo-Christian’ Myth: Masking the Race-Religion Constellation in Europe. *Patterns of Prejudice, 54*(1), 71–90.

Vial, T. M. (2016). *Modern Religion, Modern Race*. Oxford University Press.

CHAPTER 8

Religio-racialized Taxonomies Based on Comparative Philology

The nineteenth century was marked by a firm belief in human progress, as well as by unequal power relations. Through colonization, Europeans established their hegemonic position over the rest of the globe. England, France, Germany, Belgium, the Netherlands, and other (emerging) nation states were competing to acquire a firm hold on their overseas colonies, which were to provide them with raw materials for their luxury products while at the same time opening vast new markets for their cheaper products. Large areas of Africa and Asia were divided between competing European powers with little concern for how this would affect the people who lived there. Borders and relations between ethnic groups, kingdoms, and city states were ignored, applied, or changed in the interest of the colonial powers. Oppression and exploitation were everywhere. Straightforward capitalism, militarism, and imperialism were mixed up with a civilization mission. Depending on the context and the colonial power at stake, efforts were made to implement modern European idea(l)s about the division between church and state and this effort went hand in hand with a differential treatment of indigenous people based on 'religious' grounds. At the same time, Roman Catholic as well as Protestant missionaries, convinced that they were called to evangelize the world, sought to reinforce or establish their position in the colonies as the true religion by saving as many souls as possible. Their evangelizing mission was sometimes in sync and sometimes in contention with imperialist and colonial objectives (Gerbner, 2018). In any case, at a time when secularization was growing fast in Europe, mission was also a way for various Christian churches to expand their activities to new frontiers. The religious 'ground' lost in Europe could be compensated by territorial gain elsewhere (Fernández-Armesto & Wilson, 1996).

Emerging scientific disciplines were implicated in Europe's effort at establishing itself as the centre of the world. If the natural sciences were expected to contribute to the economy (chemistry to the pharmaceutical industry; physics to the production of electronic devices), newly established human sciences, like Oriental studies, philology, comparative religion, and anthropology invested in the development of ideological theories to bolster Europe's hegemonic position, authorize its self-perception as the most advanced civilization, and justify its claim over the rest of the world's populations (Laruelle, 2009, p. 108). Theologians as well as religious scholars were also producing knowledge in support of colonial and other systems of oppression; these religious experts forged religionized images of Christianity's others to justify the legal and political subjection of Europe's others to differential and unequal treatment (Hill Fletcher, 2017; Newcomb, 2008).

Christian Imaginations of the Religious Other: A History of Religionization, First Edition. Marianne Moyaert.
© 2024 John Wiley & Sons Ltd. Published 2024 by John Wiley & Sons Ltd.

In Europe itself, however, the Enlightenment criticism of Christianity continued and Voltaire's effort to decentre Christianity in the global history of humankind was picked up by Romantic philosophers. Politically, this was a time in which the Christian churches lost much of their ruling power, but, also at the level of science, the traditional biblical truth claims were out of touch with many modern developments. Ecclesial authorities and Christian theologians had to refigure how they would position Christianity vis-à-vis new scientific methods and the knowledge these methods produced (Text Box 1).

Text Box 1: The Modernist Crisis in the Catholic Church

The Roman Catholic Church took a reactionary stance vis-à-vis the modern world and rejected both new scientific methods (like historical criticism) and political liberalism. This rejection was centred in the antimodernist documents that were produced during the long pontificate of Pope Pius IX (r. 1846–1878). A key example is the *syllabus errorum* consisting of 80 errors, published in 1864. Under the heading of 'Indifferentism', the syllabus refutes the idea of freedom of religion [15] and states that the Catholic Church *is* (!) the only true religion. The syllabus [18] also rejects the so-called branch theory, according to which Protestantism is another form or expression of Christian religion. This theory basically put the Catholic Church on a par with the heresy [*sic*] of Protestantism. In 1869–1870, Pope Pius IX convened the First Vatican Council, which promulgated the doctrine of infallibility (*Pastor Aeternus*, 1870), stating that the Pope cannot err when teaching *ex cathedra* on matters of faith or morals (Mettepenningen & Schelkens, 2010, p. 52). The truth is on the side of the church.

Around the turn of the nineteenth century and during the first decades of the twentieth century, modern voices, whether political, historical, philosophical or other, were increasingly imagined as being part of a heretical movement, called 'modernism'. The heresy of modernism was first officially condemned in the decree *Lamentabilii* (1907). A few months later, the encyclical *Pascendi Domini Gregis* called modernism 'the synthesis of all heresies'. 'Modernist heretics' were imagined as sharing a predetermined plan to intentionally bring harm to the Catholic Church (Denzinger et al., 1996, p. 1907). To root out the problem of modernism, an entire system of control was established, consisting of a book index (abolished in 1966), an international committee tasked with detecting and reporting modernist heresies (*Sodalitium Pianum*, 1862–1934), and an antimodernist oath (1910, abolished in 1967). Those Catholics suspected of *modernism* would be reprimanded, condemned, or excommunicated (Mettepenningen & Schelkens, 2010, p. 81): '[u]ntil the early twentieth century, the Catholic hierarchy was still battling the critical methods in the study of the Scriptures, and Catholic theological faculties mostly resisted the study of religious phenomena and history in a modern, non-traditional way' (Stroumsa, 2021, p. 20). Up until the Second Vatican Council historical criticism was prohibited. The data provided by Catholic missionaries, however, contributed greatly to anthropological studies and the science of religion. The religionized categories of Aryans and Semites, which we will discuss in this chapter, were picked up by Catholic theologians, but were never referenced in official Catholic documents (Schelkens, 2015).

As more and more knowledge about foreign people and their traditions reached Europe, the question as to the place of (secularized) Christianity in Europe became an ever more pressing issue. For quite some time, it seemed as if Christian tradition would finally lose its central place in history to India as Voltaire had already suggested. Once again, however, a refigured sense of Christianness, embodying modern ideals of progress, emancipation, and creativity would emerge, and old and novel patterns of religionization would now be dressed up in scientific discourses. The theological taxonomy of Christians, Jews, Muslims, and pagans was replaced by the religio-scientific World Religions Paradigm and Christianity, or at least a certain understanding of Christianness, would both lose and reinforce its place as the religion in sync with modern Europe and as the absolute religion of the world. This taxonomic paradigm shift went hand in hand with a racialization of religionized categories of self and other. This is the time when Jews and Muslims became Semites, and Christians became Aryans (Topolski, 2018). How this happened is the central question in this penultimate chapter.

1 The Fixation on Creating 'Scientific' Taxonomies of Race

The colonies flooded Europe not only with new and strange specimens of plants and animals, but Europeans also learned more about the vast diversity of humankind than ever before. There was an explosion of information about foreign lands, peoples, and their traditions. Apart from the excitement to learn more about 'foreign' people, and their cultures, this information raised many questions about identity and alterity, unity and plurality. Think of questions about the relationship between these people (do they all stem from one common ancestor?), about the differences between them at the level of physiognomy (How can one explain these differences? Is it still feasible to speak about one humankind in the face of such vast diversity?). Questions also came up about the different languages spoken across the globe (Can linguistic difference be traced back to some kind of pre-Babelish *Ursprache*, and if so, which one?). These questions intersected with questions about origins and descent. As Europeans learned about previously unknown 'cultures completely independent of the Old World, some of which even predated it', they started to ask about the genealogical relations between these people and their traditions (Kippenberg, 2002, p. 25) and how to catalogue human diversity, and they pondered their own (hegemonic) place within it. Questions about genealogy took central place in the 'European mind'. Following the example of the natural sciences, efforts were also made 'to lay the grid of reason over the unwieldy stuff' of human diversity and to find 'new and simple principles that would hold universally' (Schiebinger, 1990, p. 389). This was the era of classification, and more often than not the effort to taxonomize people resulted in their racialization. Indeed, the category of race was ubiquitous in the European effort to understand the diversity of human species.

Biblical Taxonomies

For many Europeans, the biblical theological framework would continue to function as the frame of reference, even though its chronology became increasingly doubtful in the light of paleontological, archaeological, and other findings. The story of the creation (Adam and Eve are the progenitors of all people) emphasized the priority of unity over diversity, and many remained convinced that people originally spoke the same language in the garden of Eden. Furthermore, the story of Babel helped to explain the fragmentation of language, culture, and civilization as a punishment for human *hybris* (Moyaert, 2009) and spurred on the efforts being made by some scholars to retrace the pre-lapsarian *Ursprache* (Was it Hebrew or some other language?). The story of Noah and his three sons – Japhet, Shem, and Ham – was also referenced to explain the cultural, linguistic, and physiognomic diversity of people, as well as their social 'status'. The Japhetic race – identified as Christian – was said to have populated Europe, Shem's descendants (consisting of Jews and Muslims) populated Asia and Africa, while the Hamitic race was fated to be burdened with the curse of blackness and slavery (Goldenberg, 2003; Topolski, 2018). The more scientific findings sunk in; however, the more biblical chronology came under pressure, and theologians worked overtime to figure out how new scientific findings could fit into the biblical frame. In the eyes of many scholars, it was difficult if not impossible to reconcile Christian biblical tradition with the ideals of modern scientific emancipation. The resulting embarrassment about the Christian narrative translated into an eagerness to find 'new ancestors' for Europe, that is, ancestors that do not follow the biblical family tree (Poliakov, 1974, p. 314). The theological maps of the world, including the fourfold map of Christians, Jews, Muslims, and pagans, came under scrutiny and other sciences claimed to be more appropriate for organizing humanity and classifying its wide range of people (Topolski, 2016, p. 271).

Ethnographic Explorations

Scholars pursuing an ethnographic line of research mapped people based on their physiognomic differences, thereby contributing to scientific racism or biological racism. This form of racism was the product of 'the rise of scientific biological taxonomy, which is the formal clustering of animals analytically into groups, along with a parallel dissolution of large groups of animals into their constituent smaller groups' (Marks, 2022). Such taxonomic efforts were also extended to explain human diversity (Text Box 2). While most scholars continued to operate within the framework of monogenesis and subscribed to the idea that differences in climatic conditions explained the diversity of human varieties, some began to embrace theories of polygenesis, thereby questioning the unity of humankind. Polygenetic or not, classifying difference easily slipped into ranking differences and people. Many scholars not only claimed that people's moral and intellectual capacities as well as their physiognomics and aesthetics (e.g. fair people were beautiful and elevated and superior in all respects compared to darker people) would vary because of the environment in which they lived (Fredrickson, 2002, p. 43), but also that they could determine people's nature by reading their bodies – the size of skull, length, facial features, the colour of skin, and so forth. The basis for claims of European superiority now became a pseudo-scientific analysis of natural processes rather than revealed truth (Burris, 2001, p. xxiii). After 1860, social Darwinism, especially, would reinforce the evolutionary juxtaposition of the primitive and the modern, the irrational and the rational, the civilized and the barbarian, science and nature. This pseudo-scientific framework helped to legitimize the hold of industrialists, free traders, and settlers over people deemed inferior: so-called superior people were 'morally' obliged to invest in the colonial project to civilize inferior people by spreading culture, language, and religion and by developing their economy, agriculture, and infrastructure.

Text Box 2: Taxonomies

Botanist Carl Linnaeus (1707–1778), sometimes called the father of taxonomy, was probably the first to explicitly place 'man' in the realm of nature. In his *Systema naturae*, he stated that man is animal and he created the category 'anthropomorpha', consisting of men, apes, and sloths. What made man different from other animals (mammals) was the ability to think for itself. Linnaeus further distinguished between four varieties of humans: *Europaeus albus* (people from Europe), *Americanus rubescens* (people from the Americas), *Asiaticus fuscus* (people from Asia), and *Africanus niger* (people from Africa). These varieties were not stable types. They differed according to skin colour, hair colour, but also behaviour, clothing, political organization. While Linnaeus did not set out to explicitly develop a hierarchical taxonomy, he did rank these various humans, with the *homo Africanus* being clearly inferior. Linnaeus' taxonomy into four peoples was still influenced by biblical assumptions. This division into four 'reflected a tendency within European natural philosophy to divide the world into sets of four: the four rivers in the Garden of Eden; the four (known) continents; the four universal elements (earth, air, fire, and water); and the four humors (blood, yellow bile, black bile, and phlegm) that governed human health' (Kenyon-Flatt, 2021).

This superior self-image of European progress, innovation, power, and success would be disseminated in many different ways, one of them being the organization of world fairs or world exhibitions, which allowed empires, nations, and particular cities to display their European superiority and national pride in a context of globalization, colonization, and pluralization. Christian missionaries, while often critical of the way indigenous people were treated and of the imperial project in general, at the same time shared this stratified view of humankind and assumed the proclamation of the gospel to be a key element in the civilization of these people.

Comparative Philology

In the eighteenth and nineteenth centuries, scholarly efforts to make sense of the vast plurality of peoples and cultures also followed another path, namely that of comparative philology (Masuzawa, 2005; Olender, 1992). Philologists, mostly from France and Germany, considered it their mission to understand the progress of human history in relation to this vast plurality, and they claimed that the knowledge produced by their human science was complementary to, and equally scientific as, the knowledge produced by the natural sciences. The general thrust at the time was that language reflected the nature of people (Todorov, 1998, p. 96). To study language, therefore, was to study people; to trace the history of a language was to study the history of a people, and to grasp the core or essence of a language was to capture the true spirit of a people, what makes them who they are and defines their role and place in the progress of human history. Language thus became the primary criterion with which to categorize people, to determine their nature, and to establish genealogies and kinship relations between them (Harpham, 2009, p. 44). Similarities between languages pointed in the direction of a common lineage, whereas the absence of similarities signified that there was no kinship between the people in question. This philological project also intersected with the project of scientific racism. Reading, analysing, and comparing literary documents from all over the globe, comparative philologists constructed, crafted, created, and essentialized peoples/races as distinct from or akin to other people/races based on linguistic differences and/or similarities. Philological scientists invented new categories, drew and redrew boundaries between people, and rewrote the histories of people. This is why Edward Said once stated that nineteenth-century European processes of mapping and remapping the world were happening in the 'workplace' of the philologist (Said, 2003).

The most important taxonomy that emerged from the philological workplace was based on the normative distinction between Aryan (or Indo-European) and Semitic languages. This pair, Aryan/Semitic, which went on to have such devastating effects in history, was quickly extended into essentializing discourses about Aryan and Semitic people/races and their culture, morality, behaviour, and intellectual capacities (Said, 2003). Aryans (also called Indo-Europeans or Indo-Germans) were associated with political power, scientific creativity, ongoing progress, in brief with superior civilization, while those deviating from this norm, the Semites, simply would never be able to reach the level of development attained by the former (Said, 2003, p. 149). Trailblazing comparative religious scholars, like Ernest Renan (1823–1892) and Max Müller (1823–1900), extrapolated this emblematic philological distinction between Aryan and Semitic languages/people into a new taxonomy of religious traditions, which would replace the fourfold medieval (theological) taxonomy of Christians, Jews, Muslims, and pagans. This new racial-religio-philological taxonomy, which finally resulted in the Semitization of Judaism and Islam and the Aryanization of Christianity, not only formed the basis for the World Religions Paradigm but also endeavoured to re-establish Aryan Christianity as the European norm of civilization (Masuzawa, 2005, p. xii). The 'ineradicable feelings and resentments of the Christian West [vis-à-vis the Jews and Muslims, as well as the depreciation of the 'pagans' would now] be expressed in a new [pseudo-scientific] vocabulary' (Poliakov, 1974, p. 194). Tracing back the emergence of these refigured religionized understandings of self and other is the theme of this chapter. The question is: where does this distinction between Semitic and Aryan languages come from and how does it relate to previous patterns of religionization? To answer this question, we have to turn to the work of the Romantic philosophers, who were seeking to retrace and revitalize Europe, by tracing its 'true origins', and this would direct them towards the Orient, and more precisely to India (Vial, 2016).

262 CHAPTER 8 Religio-racialized Taxonomies

Text Box 3: On the Notion of Race as a Social Construct

Race is a social construct; it is fluid, malleable, and adaptable, and the work of racialization (race-making) is creative and inventive. How boundaries are crafted between people (us/them) varies from time to time and from context to context. Today, there is a tendency to recognize race-making as a nineteenth-century effort and to identify race-making with the modern project of scientific or biological racism, centred around physiognomic differences, with colour as prime signifier (cf. the colour line of Du Bois) (Topolski, 2018, p. 59). There are, however, several reasons why the reduction of racism to its 'biological', nineteenth-century expression, needs to be qualified.

First, staying within the nineteenth century, philology also claimed scientific status and was, by many, recognized as such. The philological distinction between Semites and Aryans at least in a European context, became the key racial distinction between inferior and superior people. Denying or downplaying the philological contribution to emerging scientific racism simply reflects what 'we' today deem to be scientific. Furthermore, the fixation on biological racism steers our attention away from the intersection between religionization and race-making: in the nineteenth century, the effort to categorize, essentialize, and hierarchize people based on religious difference would graft itself on racist taxonomies based on philological distinctions, and these philological distinctions themselves were already a refiguration of older religionized patterns of thinking. In addition, the fixation on bodily differences, symbolizing both religious and racial differences, is not a nineteenth-century invention but goes way back. We encountered this in the late Middle Ages (think of the diseased bodies of Jews and the pure blood laws). However, long before that, the *adversus Iudaeos* tradition already imagined Jews as a group that bore a hereditary mark identifying them as different and as born inferior to Christians. The church father Augustine argued that the Jews were turned into a race protected and cursed by Cain's mark. This mark – the mark of Cain – was also called a blood curse. It is an unremovable, unchangeable mark that passes from one generation to another (Kaplan, 2019). In any case, it is not always clear where religion ends and race begins or if race operates under the guise of religion. I cannot but agree with Geraldine Heng, who states: 'The refusal of race destigmatizes the impacts and consequences of certain laws, acts, practices, and institutions in the medieval period, so that we cannot name them for what they are, and makes it impossible to bear adequate witness to the full meaning of the manifestations and phenomena they install' (Heng, 2018, p. 4).

2 Romantic Musings about Language as the Gateway to the Spirit of People

Confronted with the polluting effects of the industrial revolution, Romantic philosophers became critical of the technological innovations of modernity, which they associated with the destruction of nature. In response, Romantic thinkers approached nature more holistically. As they focused their attention on the beauties of nature, the rich palette of human emotions, the power of intuition, and the primacy of the senses over the intellect, they also contrasted the wisdom of the Orient to Europe. Romantic thinkers, like Novalis (1772–1802), Johann Gottfried von Herder (1744–1803), and Friedrich (1772–1829) and August (1776–1845) Schlegel were fascinated by the Orient, and they dreamed of an Oriental Renaissance: just as the return to Greco-Roman culture and Early Christianity had brought about a cultural revival during the fourteenth to sixteenth centuries, why, so they asked, could not the Orient 'become the source of a renaissance in the modern age' (Kippenberg, 2002, p. 28). If Europe was marked by fragmentation and disarray (cf. the splintering of religion), the Orient embodied the ideal of a holistic society that was attuned to nature. Romantic thinkers welcomed the Orient 'as a salutary *derangement*' of the 'European habits of mind and spirit [and] [...] overvalued its pantheism, its spirituality, its stability, its longevity, its primitivity, and so forth' (Said, 2003, p. 150). They would, however, find more than they initially bargained for: the Orient would not only hold up a mirror to Europe, but eventually also revealed itself as the mother of European civilization, thereby at once turning Indians and Europeans into siblings.

While Romantic philosophers were trying to revitalize Europe's identity, similar questions presented themselves at the level of the various burgeoning nation states. Especially in the aftermath of the Napoleonic wars and the Congress of Vienna (1815), a widespread emancipatory movement emerged made up of people who claimed to belong to one *Volk* and claimed the right to establish 'their own nation', while simultaneously granting or denying it to others (e.g. the Basques and the Spanish). Many people sought to liberate themselves from foreign powers (e.g. Belgium and also the United Kingdom of the Netherlands) and attempted to unite different regions into one nation (e.g. Italy, Germany). So they asked, 'What is a nation?' Romantic philosophers, like Herder, came up with the idea that humankind is divided into separate 'peoples' (*Volkern*), which were distinct from one another because of their shared cultural heritage, their shared history, and also because they spoke the same language and embraced the same values.

> *Every* Volk *has its identity through their language [...]. Whoever has been educated in the same language, whoever has poured their heart into it and learned to express their soul in it, belongs to a* Volk. *(Herder, cited in Fox, 2003, p. 247)*

A *Volk* should be allowed to unite on ancestral territory and organize as a nation. Interestingly, Romantic philosophers also wondered about which 'national culture incarnated the true European civilization' the best, and which nation-state in effect held 'in its hands the "fate" of Europe – and, by Euro-universalist extension, the "fate of humanity"' (Weller, 2021, p. 72). Nationalist pride and Eurocentrism often went hand in hand.

Comparative Philology, Grammar, and Race

In their effort to rejuvenate Europe's identity and bolster nationalist claims, Romantics mobilized a fascination for the study of Oriental languages. 'Ancient languages' were considered to be 'fossils or petrifactions' of a people's history; they gave 'access to past human experience in the same way that rocks displayed in a museum revealed the geological record' (Harpham, 2009, p. 42). Johann David Michaelis (1717–1791) regarded language as the cultural archive of a people: it contained its memories, its experiences, and its values. Étienne Bonnot de Condillac (1715–1780) in turn, imagined language as a mirror of the soul of a people, bearing testimony to its moral character (Olender, 1992, pp. 4–5). This explains why, partly under the impulse of Romanticism, comparative philology would become the queen of science of the eighteenth and nineteenth centuries with the world as its territory (Turner, 2014).

Most philologists agreed that grammar, a language's deeper laws, provided the best starting point to learn more about the nature of the people that spoke this language. Grammar supposedly protected the nature of a people in all its purity and spirit against the fuzzy hybridity and mixing of ever-changing historical circumstances (Engelstein, 2017, p. 161). It is the aspect that is most resistant to historical change and thus functions as a stable core containing the true identity of people. That is why, 'comparative grammar of the language furnishes as certain a key to their genealogy, as the study of the comparative anatomy has done to the loftiest branch of natural science' (Schlegel, trans. Millington, 2014, p. 439). No matter where a people migrated, where it settled down and with whom it mixed, or who it borrowed its vocabulary from, none of this mattered in determining its true nature. Beneath the mixture (which is notable mainly at the level of vocabulary) lies original (grammatical) identity (Text Box 4). Here in Max Müller's words:

> *[I]f strictly defined, the science of language can declare itself completely independent of history [...]. A Celt may become an Englishman, Celtic and English blood may be mixed [...]. But languages are never mixed [...] not a single drop of foreign blood has entered into the organic system of the English speech. The grammar, the blood*

and soul of the language, is as pure and unmixed in English as spoken in the British Isles, as it was when spoken on the shores of the German ocean by the Angles, Saxons, and Juts of the continent. (Müller, 1866, pp. 76–78)

The retrieval of grammatical laws, abstracted from historical contingencies, enabled philologists to retrieve descent, define identity, and classify people (Poliakov, 1974, p. 24).

Text Box 4: Binary Romantic Philological Patterns

To privilege the inner structure of language over those aspects of language, like vocabulary, that change under the influence of historical-cultural encounters, is an ideological decision (Engelstein, 2017, p. 158). It entails the assumption that (i) there is some pure, original core – an essence – that resists change or is even immune to change and that (ii) this essence defines a people's identity. Finding one's pure identity thus means stripping away layers of foreign influence. Identity is the nucleus; it stays the same, remains stable, and resists change (Moyaert, 2014, Chapters 1 and 4). In any case, this ideological decision pits purity over impurity; inner over outer; uniformity over mixture; and identity over alterity. Furthermore, because of the way the relation between language, descent, and immutability is imagined, a path is paved in the direction of the racialization of linguistic and/or religious differences. Zooming in on grammar enabled the scholar to distinguish between language families, and to essentialize, segregate, and trace people's genealogies.

Furthermore, comparative philologists not only promised 'to discover a history' but also pledged 'a characterological analysis of peoples and nations through a [...] study of language' (Harpham, 2009, p. 42). Indeed, many were convinced that the nature of a language reflects the nature of the people who speak it and their contribution to human civilization. While some people would be incapable of formulating original thoughts or making any progress because the grammatical structure of their language was too rigid and limited, other languages, on the contrary, were marked by creativity, thereby explaining the ongoing progress, development, and innovation of the people speaking this language. Distinguishing separate language groups (Stoler, 1989, p. 635) paved the way for a stratified taxonomizing of people who speak different languages (Masuzawa, 2005, p. 209).

Finally, let us have a word on what we may call the biologization of language. Nineteenth-century comparative philology organized languages in a taxonomy that followed the principles of genealogy and the relations of descent and kinship (Adluri & Bagchee, 2013). Since the same blood runs (cf. quote from Müller above) through all the languages which belong to the same language group, so it runs through people. Language groups imply kinship and shared blood. The language used in the field of philology affirms this; we speak about a mother tongue or a parental language, language families, and sister languages which spring from these same ancestors. Genealogy of peoplehood and philology merge together in such a way that a linguistic-racial project came into being (Text Box 5).

Text Box 5: The Linguistic-racial Project

Comparative philology, underpinned by Romantic ideas, suggested that humankind (i) may be organized into different clearly bounded peoples (*Rasse, Volkern, Geschlechten*); (ii) which share certain innate or hereditary characteristics – moral, intellectual, dispositional, and by extension biological – because they belong to a certain social group; and (iii) that some groups feature more developed characteristics than others and are therefore naturally superior to others.

Against the background of imperialism and colonialism, philology provided an ideological discourse that helped to legitimize claims to superiority (superior language – superior people) and to justify hegemonic actions, aimed at patrolling boundaries and protecting identities against a mixture of superior and inferior people. While many philologists would object to the hierarchical accounts of linguistic, religious, or biological differences, philologists *did* provide the groundwork for categorization and essentialization. Furthermore, stratification was carried out on the basis of that groundwork, and many intellectuals *did* draw on comparative philology to support racist, and nationalist discourses. The English historian Edward Freeman, writing in 1879, already understood this much when he stated that the doctrine of race stems from the science of philology (Freeman 1879, ed. 1958, p. 31).

'If races and nations [...] are still real and living things [...] how are we to define our races and nations? How are we to mark them off from one another? [...] I say unhesitatingly that for practical purposes there is one test, and one only, and that that test is language' (Freeman, 1879, ed. 1958, p. 33, quoted in Ashcroft, 2009, p. 13). For all these reasons, we might speak of a linguistic-racial or an ethnolinguistic project (Kouloughli, 2007, p. 104).

3 The Discovery of the Indo-European Language Family

One of the turning points in the Romantics' effort to revitalize Europe's identity was the discovery of the so-called Indo-European language family, consisting of Sanskrit, Greek, and Latin. This finding gave scientific backing to the idea 'of a common history of European languages and – in prolongation – even mythologies, literature, and people'. Those eager to decentre the biblical myth of creation, rallied to embrace this alternative origin myth: Eden was replaced by India, Hebrew by some Indian *Ursprache*, and the Hebrew people by the ancient noble Indians (Mohnike & Grage, 2017, p. 1). Significantly, the sibling relationship between Indian and European languages seemed to imply that Indians and Europeans were in fact 'long-lost brothers' and belonged to the same people: the same blood flowed through the veins of Europeans and Indians.

Oriental Jones and the Indo-European Hypothesis

The hypothesis of the Indo-European language is usually attributed to William Jones (1746–1794), a British judge and a co-founder (with Warren Hastings) of the Royal Asiatic Society (1784). He worked in Calcutta at a time when the British imperial presence in India was being increasingly formalized (Hutton, 2019, p. 120). Jones, who mastered about 12 languages, complemented his language skills and literary interests with knowledge of legal practice. While he believed it was legitimate for the British to rule the Indians, he was equally convinced that British authority had to be established on the basis of the ancient laws of the Indian people. Not trusting what the pandits were telling him about Indian laws, he decided to learn Sanskrit so that he could understand their legal code for himself. All this work would result in the creation of a digest of Hindu and Muslim laws, which he used in his function as chief magistrate of Calcutta.[1]

In 1786, only a few months after he had started to study Sanskrit, Jones discovered similarities between Sanskrit, Greek, and Latin, and several Germanic languages. On 2 February 1786, he gave a lecture to the Asiatic Society of Bengal in which he briefly touched upon his discovery. In tune with the zeitgeist, the overall topic of his lecture was the early relationship between the different 'races/people' of Asia. In a now famous passage, known as the 'philologer passage', he proposed the hypothesis of a lost Indo-European language (mother language) and suggested classifying Greek, Latin, and Sanskrit, along with various Germanic languages, as descendants of this extinct common ancestor. Following genealogical lines, these languages now became sister languages that belong to one family.

> *The Sanscrit language, whatever be its antiquity, is of a wonderful structure; more perfect than the Greek, more copious than the Latin, and more exquisitely refined than either, yet bearing to both of them a stronger affinity, both in the roots of verbs and in the forms of grammar, than could possibly have been produced by accident; so strong indeed, that no philologer could examine them all three, without believing them to have sprung from some common source, which, perhaps, no longer exists.*
> *(Jones, ed. Ghose, 1875, p. 18)*

Jones' discovery was radical: it ranked a language of 'a darker-skinned, colonized people above the revered classical languages of European palefaces', placed the origins of Europe in India and established a civilizational kinship between the people that belonged to this one language family: their shared language points at a shared ancestry, a shared history, shared character, shared soul, and nature (Turner, 2014). The histories of European and Indian people were now joined together at the root and this seemed to radically alter the genealogy of Europeans, their history, and their future (Masuzawa, 2005, p. 151). As Max Müller, put it: 'We [Europeans and Indians] are long-lost kin; we are Aryan brethren'. Not Greece and Rome, and certainly not the biblical lands in the Middle East, but India now became the cradle of human civilization (Figueira, 2002, p. 16).

The Indo-European Myth as Colonial Ideology

Jones' hypothesis of an Indo-European language family (later called Aryan) went hand in hand with a wider hypothesis, which projected the existence of a noble people – an *Urvolk* – that had spoken the now lost Indo-European *Ursprache*. These fictional people were projected as the true forerunners of Greek ancient culture, its philosophy, and pantheon, and by extension of Europe's culture. Jones, however, maintained that over time, this race of noble people became gravely diluted. If we now consider 'how degenerate and abased [...] the Hindus [...] appear', it is almost impossible to imagine 'that in some early age they were splendid in arts and arms, happy in government, wise in legislation, and eminent in various knowledge' (Jones, ed. Ghose, 1875, p. 17). Contemporary Europeans, so he assumed, were closer to that original high civilization than those still living in India.

This discovery of the Indo-European language family, as well as Jones' hypothesis of an original noble people, would be used in the service of the British Empire and its colonial ambitions. Indeed, the British could now trace back their lineage to the people and the land they happened to rule, and they could justify their colonial or imperial rule both in terms of a rediscovery of Europe's past and as a restoration of India's long-forgotten past. The British Empire was now helping India to retrieve its true self. As Thomas Trautmann puts it, the Indo-European myth supported the British colonial project as some kind of happy family reunion, as if coercion had nothing to do with it (Trautmann, 1997, p. 17). This is quite the reverse of the original idea of the Oriental Renaissance: if, at first, India was to revitalize Europe, now Europe would revitalize, restore, and reform India to what it once was. This line of reasoning can already be found in Jones' attitude towards the Indian sages who helped him understand Indian law: he did not trust their knowledge, and preferred to study Sanskrit himself, feeling more confident in his own ability to decipher the sense of these sources than in the knowledge of contemporary Indian sages. With the proper skill set and critical tools, Europeans would be best placed to restore the Orient and its proper relation to Europe. Still later, this legitimization of colonial rule would intersect with a discourse that distinguished and stratified people based on the colour of their skin (Laruelle, 2009, p. 110). When, at the beginning of the twentieth century, the Aryan (Indo-European) myth became one of the main European ideological racist discourses, all recollection of white Europeans being related to the dark-skinned Indians had been removed from this imaginary (Text Box 6).

4 Friedrich Schlegel's Comparative Philology and German Romanticism

German philosophers in particular further developed the Indo-European hypothesis. In the aftermath of the French Revolution and the Napoleonic wars, German intellectuals were struggling to construct a sense of nationhood around shared language, culture, and history. Jones' hypothesis, albeit adapted to their interests, proved to be inspirational in this regard (Tzoref-Ashkenazi, 2006, p. 717).

About the Language and Wisdom of the Indians

One of the most important German Romantic philologists was Friedrich Schlegel (1772–1829), who studied Indology and comparative philology at the Collège de France in Paris, where he gained expertise in Indian history, literature, mythology, and philology. In his book, *Über die Sprache und Weisheit der Indier* [On the Language and Wisdom of the Indians, 1808], Schlegel introduced a wider audience to the idea that there was a deep affinity between Sanskrit and the European languages, Greek, Latin, and German. Not only did he generalize the notion of Aryan as a synonym for Indo-European, he also applied it to the ancestors of the Germans (*arische Völkerfamilie*) (Schlegel, trans. Millington, 2014, p. 442).

Just like most of his contemporaries, Schlegel took an interest in language for the sake of genealogy. In his own words: 'the [...] importance of the comparative study of language', is 'in elucidating the historical origin and progress of nations, and their early migration and wanderings' (Schlegel, trans. Millington, 2014, p. 429). Drawing on 'affinities in language, in mythology, in law, and in architecture', he concluded that 'the greatest empires and most noble nations' of the ancient world had been 'colonies' founded by Indian noblemen. The ancestors of the German people (Northern Europe) descended directly from these noble, warlike, and heroic Aryans. Therefore, he concluded that 'the blood of Sanskrit flowed into the veins of German – more or less literally' (Turner, 2014, p. 130). In clear contrast to the unbroken continuity between Sanskrit and German, Schlegel argued that later migration streams led the originally noble Aryan people via different routes southwards into Europe (in the direction of what is now France, Italy, Spain, etc.). On their way there, Aryan people mixed and mingled with people from Mesopotamia, Phoenicia, and Asia Minor, as well as with barbarian people, and they lost their noble nature.

Schlegel altered Jones' hypothesis in several ways, two of which are significant here. First, he suggests that Sanskrit is itself the *Ursprache*, rather than some lost Indo-European language. Second, he argues that German is more directly related to Sanskrit than French, which is only indirectly related to it via Latin. Thus, he established a hierarchy between the Germanic and Roman languages, and by extension between their cultures. The German language is closer to the Indo-European (Sanskrit) language and German people are closer to the people that once spoke this original language. This also makes Germans morally and culturally superior to those who cannot claim such direct descendance, read: the French. By directly linking German nationalism and Orientalism, Schlegel engaged in a process of selfing and othering predicated on ethnolinguistic difference, and he used India 'as a screen on which to project his own discomforts with modernity and his resentments against the French' (Dusche, 2009, p. 6).

Inflection and Agglutination

Schlegel classified different languages on the basis of a comparative analysis of their grammar. Such a grammatical study was necessary to distinguish between essential similarities, which point to family resemblances and similarities that derive from intermixture (Schlegel, trans. Millington, 2014, p. 439). Key to his classification system, according to Tomoko Masuzawa,

268 CHAPTER 8 Religio-racialized Taxonomies

was a grammatical distinction between languages that make use of inflection and those that are incapable of inflection and that are agglutinative (Masuzawa, 2005, p. 163).

> *Modifications of meaning, or different degrees of signification, may be produced either by inflection or internal variations of the primitive word, or by annexing to it certain peculiar particles, which in themselves indicate the past, the future, or any other circumstance. (Schlegel, trans. Millington, 2014, p. 446)*

This results in two distinctive linguistic branches; they are governed by these two contrasting laws and are completely different. In his own words, these linguistic differences are essential, '[e]very additional difference or variation appears, on closer inspection, to be nothing more than an inferior modification or secondary consequence of the two grand divisions' (Schlegel, trans. Millington, 2014, p. 446).

This fundamental distinction between inflection and agglutination would cluster with a Romantic binary between mechanic and organic development, a distinction which has to be understood against the background of the Romantic critique of the Industrial Revolution and its mechanical developments. Those languages that are inflectional grow organically; they are marked by an innate impulse towards growth and perfection. Here words are formed by internal modification pointing to the intrinsic creativity of these languages. Schlegel compared those roots which produce inflection to plant stems that grow and bloom into flowers or fruits. He writes of the Indian language, 'it must be allowed that its structure is highly organized, formed by inflection [...] not by the merely mechanical process of annexing words or particles to the same lifeless and unproductive root' (Schlegel, trans. Millington, 2014, p. 445). Agglutinating languages, on the other hand, are mechanical languages: they only develop and expand their vocabulary by adding prefixes or suffixes to the 'lifeless and unproductive' roots (445). They need an external impulse to avoid stagnation. Such languages are irredeemably inferior, even to the extent that they are animal-like.

> *In the Indian and Greek languages each root is [...] like a living and productive germ, [...]; freer scope is given to its development, and its rich productiveness is in truth almost illimitable. Still, all words, thus proceeding from the roots bear the stamp of affinity, all being connected in their simultaneous growth and development by community of origin. From this construction a language derives richness and fertility [...] on the one hand, and on the other strength and durability.*
>
> *Those languages, on the contrary, in which the declensions are formed by supplementary particles [...] have no such bond of union: their roots present us with no living productive germ, but seem like an agglomeration of atoms, easily dispersed and scattered by every casual breath [...]. They have no internal connexion beyond the purely mechanical adaptation of particles and affixes. [...] Its apparent richness is in truth utter poverty, and languages belonging to that branch [...] are [...] defective. (Schlegel, trans. Millington, 2014, pp. 449–450)*

Sanskrit is the most perfect language, followed by German, Latin, and Greek. The grammar and internal structure of these languages is similar and this similarity cannot be traced back to mixture [*Einmischung*]. In any case, their transformative power was evidence of the superior cultural capacity of the people who speak them, and of course in particular of the Indo-Germanic race, which was gifted with high spirituality. Those tongues that are mechanical, rather than organic, are simple, rude, and imperfect. Schlegel's favourite examples are the Semitic languages, Hebrew and Arabic. Further down Schlegel's linguistic ladder, one would find many other isolated languages, which do not even form a family but stand on their own. Thus, Schlegel writes, 'we must [...] admit that *every* language formed by inflexion rises from one source; but the incalculable diversity of languages belonging to the other branch makes it impossible to trace *them* back to any point of union even at their source, as is sufficiently proved by examining many languages of Asia and Europe, not to mention the countless dialects of the American continent' (Schlegel, trans. Millington, 2014, p. 450). These languages resemble the cry of an animal; they have no syntax and express no intelligence. The simplicity of these languages reflects the primitivity of the people that speak them. When we study the history of human civilization through the lens of language, they are not to be taken into consideration. From this perspective, philology also reinforced the dichotomy between civilized and primitive.

> ### Text Box 6: German Romanticism, the Jews, and Antisemitism
>
> The reception of the Aryan myth by German Romantic scholars can in part be understood against the struggle for German nationhood. Until the eighteenth century, Germany consisted of different states. In the aftermath of the French Revolution and the Napoleonic wars, German people were strongly opposed to everything French and sought to establish their own identity as not French or anti-French. They rejected the ideals of the Republic and its civic rights and sought to establish their identity in terms of *Volk*. Some started to dream of a unification of the different states into one nation. The idea of *Volk* occupied the collective German mindset in the nineteenth and twentieth centuries. Initially, sentiments of antisemitism were not part of early *Volk* ideologies. However, the Germans' rejection of everything French did impact the fate of the Jews, whose situation had improved under the French emancipation, which was extended to German territories during the Napoleonic wars. In German territories this translated into hostility vis-à-vis the Jews, 'not least because one of the egalitarian reforms forced by Napoleon on defeated or compliant German principalities was Jewish emancipation' (Fredrickson, 2002, p. 69). Germans, influenced by romantic ideas of *völkisch* identity projected the Jews as *Fremdkörper*, namely as other. The 'otherness' of the Jews was 'constantly presented through both physical and psychological stereotypes, and they were seen as personally embodying the concepts which *Volk* culture had formed in opposition to' (Levin, 2021).
>
> Several Romantic philosophers, like the above-mentioned Michaelis, actively advocated against the emancipation of the Jews. The German scholar Fichte (1762–1814), best known for his *Judenfeindschaft* (enmity against the Jews), feared that the Jews would form a state within the state. He wrote the following in his *Beitrag zur Berichtigung der Urteile des Publikums über die Französische Revolution* [Contribution to the Correction of the Public's Judgments on the French Revolution, 1793], which he published anonymously: 'A powerful, hostile state is spreading through almost all European countries, which is constantly at war with all the rest, and which in some is oppressing the citizens terribly; it is Judaism' (*Fast durch alle Länder Europas verbreitet sich ein mächtiger, feindselig gesinnter Staat, der mit allen übrigen im beständigen Kriege steht, und der in manchen fürchterlich schwer auf die Bürger drückt; es ist das Judenthum*) (Fichte, 1793, p. 149). Schlegel, however, advocated in favour of Jewish emancipation. Many of his contemporaries 'reproach[ed] him with a lack of "racial instinct" because he married the daughter of the Jewish philosopher Moses Mendelssohn' (Poliakov, 1974, p. 191). Jewish emancipation only became a reality in Germany after German unification, in 1871. However, that did not end the problem of antisemitism, which would resurge in all vehemency (Newcomb, 2008; Robertson, 1999). To be German, according to *Völkisch* ideology, was never merely a matter of citizenship, so that even when Jews obtained citizenship they were still not German. They were forever foreign. Indeed, long into the twentieth century, the notion of *Volk* would be used to project Jews as non-German, up until the time that Hitler would call for their extermination.

Schlegel could not have foreseen the trajectory that this normative philological divide between inflective and agglutinative languages would take. Nevertheless, he did plant 'a seed [...] for the claim that Indo-European languages and their speakers are in their very essence superior to other languages and their speakers, including the Semitic ones' (Hock, 2021, p. 896). Other philosophers further elaborated on this distinction and took it in new directions. However, the idea that Indo-European people, because of the organic, life-giving nature of their language, were superior to Semitic people would return time and

270 CHAPTER 8 Religio-racialized Taxonomies

again, and would have detrimental consequences for the European Jewish population especially. Wilhelm von Humboldt (1767–1835), for example, argued that the 'Sanscritic family' demonstrated a uniquely generative power, possessing virtually as an organic fact a 'stronger and more variously creative life-principle than the rest' (Humboldt, ed. Losonsky, 1999). By emphasizing that Aryan people were more creative than other people, von Humboldt also affirmed the supremacy of Europe. Christian Lassen (1800–1876), one of Schlegel's students, went even further. He bolstered the idea of Aryan or Indo-German supremacy by claiming that the Aryans were white, and that their original homeland in fact had not been India. He supported his reflections not only by philological reasoning but also by ethnographic and physiognomic observations made by British anthropologists working in India. He concluded, 'without furnishing even a shred of substantiation – that the Indo-Europeans were (and are) of superior moral character compared to the Semites, whom he characterized as egocentric, exclusivist, and intolerant' (Hock, 2021, p. 896). Increasingly, the philological science became dressed in essentializing discourses, which legitimized the superiority of Aryans, even though several respected philologists objected to such a conclusion.

5   Ernest Renan and the Invention of the Semite

We now leave Germany and turn to the French scholar Ernest Renan (1823–1892), who to this day figures in the pantheon and the streets of France (Kouloughli, 2007, p. 91). Renan is particularly interesting because he further developed the binary between Aryan and Semitic languages and people, and applied it to religious traditions. In so doing, he developed a new religionized taxonomy, which intersected with philological-racialized patterns of thinking.

Renan was destined for the priesthood, but he left the seminary of Saint-Sulpice after struggling to reconcile his critical reading of the Bible with the teachings of the Roman Catholic Church. He continued his career in secular academia where he became one of the most important historians, biblical scholars, and philologists of his time. Contemporaries perceived him as a man of science. His works often scandalized the Catholic clergy, in whose eyes he was no longer a Christian. Renan himself always retained a warm sympathy for Christianity and the figure of Jesus. One of the questions that occupied his mind was how one could craft an emancipatory religion in line with modern European society.

Semitic and Aryan People

Like many of his contemporaries, Renan studied languages in order to understand the different people/races and by extension the history of religion (Renan, 1863a, p. vii). For Renan, as for so many of his contemporaries, race is not about biological differences. It is concerned with linguistic differences because language captures the spirit of people. When it comes to understanding the nature of people, language has more explanatory power than biology. Thus, Renan stated,

> *It is in fact in the diversity of races [*dans la diversité des races*] that we must seek the most effective causes of the diversity of idioms [*de la diversité des idiomes*]. The spirit of each people and its language are in the closest connection: the spirit makes the language, and the language in turn serves as formula and limit to the spirit [*L'esprit de chaque peuple et sa langue sont dans la plus étroite connexité*]. (Renan, 1858a, p. 190, my translation)*

In 1863, he published the book *Histoire générale et système comparé des langues sémitiques* [The General History and Comparative System of the Semitic Languages], thanks to which he immediately gained a reputation 'on the European philological scene' (Priest, 2015,

p. 312). This work builds on the Indo-European hypothesis and elaborates on the qualitative, grammatical distinction between Aryan (or Indo-European) languages and Semitic languages (Arabic and Hebrew), and by extension on the difference between Aryan people (races) and Semitic people (races – the Jews and Arabs/Muslims). To his mind, the Aryans on the one hand and Semites on the other formed the 'wellspring' for the entire civilization (Text Box 7).

As for the lower races [races inférieures] of Africa, Oceania, the New World, [...] an abyss separates them [un abîme les sépare] from the great families of which we have just spoken. [...] To imagine a savage race speaking a Semitic or Indo-European language is a contradictory fiction [une fiction contradictoire], to which anyone initiated into the laws of comparative philology [...] will refuse to lend themselves. (Renan, 1863a, p. 495, my translation)

Inferior races have no memories, [and they] cover the ground from a time which one cannot possibly study historically [and] whose determination belongs to [the field of] geology. In general, these races have disappeared in [those] parts of the world where the great civilized races have spread. Everywhere, in fact, the Aryans and the Semites [les Ariens et les Sémites] find on their path, when coming to settle in a country, half-savage races which they exterminate [qu'ils exterminent], and which survive in the myths of more civilized peoples in the form of gigantic or earth-born magicians, often in the form of animals.

The parts of the world where the great races have not gone, Oceania, southern Africa, northern Asia, have remained within [the ambit of] primitive humanity, which gave way to the most profound diversity, from the gentle and naive child of the West Indies, to the wicked populations of Assam and Borneo, to the voluptuous Tahitian, but always [marked by] an absolute incapacity for organization and progress. (Renan, 1863a, p. 501, my translation)

Text Box 7: Laying the Foundation for a New Religionized Map of the World

According to Renan, primitive people belong to the past literally, in the sense that they have been exterminated, or metaphorically because they are unable to progress. Their insignificance in view of the study of human history does not only become clear from the passage just cited but even more so from the complete disregard Renan shows for them in the rest of his research. The hermeneutical figure of the primitive or savage (noble or wild) now occupies a similar place to that which the pagan (illiterate people, associated with infantile ignorance) used to take up in the Christian imagination, with that further specification that the figure of the primitive would be mainly associated with those people who had left no written resources to subject to comparative philological research. Of course, primitive language and primitive societal organization would also translate into primitive (tribal, oral, etc.) religion. It should not surprise us that this line of reasoning will result in a certain pattern of religionization (see Müller below) that contrasts the religions of the book with non-textual traditions. Here we see once again: recategorization, essentialization, and the ranking of people based on religious difference clothed in a new dress.

The racial-philological distinction between Semites and Aryans is central to Renan's work.

The essential result of modern philology has been that of showing in the history of civilization the action of a double current, produced by two races profoundly distinct in customs [produit par deux races profondément distinctes de mœurs], language and spirit: on the one hand, the Indo-European race, consisting of the noble populations of India, Persia, the Caucasus, and all of Europe; on the other hand, the [race] designated by the name [...] of Semitic, comprising the indigenous populations of western and southern Asia from the Euphrates. (Renan, 1855a, p. 751, my translation)

272 CHAPTER 8 Religio-racialized Taxonomies

Renan explicitly states that these two races are perennially opposed to one another and that, in almost everything, the Semites are inferior to the Aryans. Whereas he describes the latter as the noblest of all races, gifted with a rich, creative imagination, a philosophical and scientific mind, and a profound political instinct, he found 'the simplicity' of the Semitic people simply astonishing (Renan, 1858b, p. 156). Renan linked the linguistic characteristics of the Semites, as well as their intellectual, ethnic, and religious characteristics, to the natural environment in which they supposedly lived (Renan, 1890, p. 378). Contrary to the Aryan people, who stemmed from a diverse environment with mountains, forests, and rivers, the Semitic people are desert people, and their mind is as dry and barren as their monotonous natural environment (Renan, 1858a, pp. 95–96). The barrenness of the natural environment of the Semitic Orient translated into a cultural barrenness: they lack creativity and curiosity; they lack nuance and humour. The French philologist even goes as far as asking: 'What have the *Semites* really contributed to human civilization?' When it comes to politics, there can be no doubt; we owe them nothing. Semitic people lack political skills and military discipline, which is why they have never been able to form a nation: 'The true Semitic society is that of the tent and the tribe' (Renan, 1863a, p. 13, my translation). And elsewhere:

> theocracy, anarchy, despotism, that just about sums up Semitic politics; fortunately it is not ours [...]. In politics [...] the duty of the Indo-European peoples is to seek nuance, the reconciliation of opposing positions, [such] complexity, [is] so utterly unknown to the Semitic peoples, whose organization has always been of an appalling and fatal simplicity. (Renan, 1862, p. 16, my translation)

Nor have the Semites contributed anything to culture, art, or architecture. '[Our] art', so Renan claims 'comes entirely from Greece' (Renan, 1862, p. 16, my translation). Considering that the simplicity of the Semitic language reflects the simplicity of Semitic people, it should come as no surprise that they do not have the analytical spirit necessary to philosophize. Therefore, 'we' are Greek (Renan, 1862, p. 16). However, one may contend, have the Arabs not given us access to science and philosophy during the Middle Ages? Yes, but this was 'hand-me-down' science and philosophy: the Arabs conserved knowledge which they had received from the Greeks, but contributed nothing of originality. The same, for that matter, holds true for the Jews, who do not succeed in transcending the role of simple interpreters. Jewish philosophy is Arab philosophy without modification (Renan, 1862, p. 17). Put more forcefully, the spirit of the Semites is anti-philosophical and anti-scientific (Text Box 8).

Text Box 8: The Semite as a Hermeneutical Figure

Renan typically speaks about people and their language in the singular. Despite obvious differences between languages within one language group, deep down he seems to assert that these differences are of secondary importance, that they are superficial. In essence, the Semitic language is one and the same, just as the spirit of the people that speak this language is uniform (Kouloughli, 2007). Thus, the novel category of the Semite falls prey to essentialization, and just as 'the Jew', 'the Saracen', 'the pagan', and 'the heretic' were transhistorical and transcultural rhetorical figures, deprived of complexity, texture, and particularity, so too the figure of the Semite is flat, 'purporting to predict every discrete act of "Semitic" behavior on the basis of some pre-existing "Semitic" essence, and aiming as well to interpret all aspects of human life and activity in terms of some common "Semitic element" ... [The Semite] was a constructed object, it is true, but it was considered logical and inevitable as a protoform, given the scientifically apprehendable and empirically analysable data of specific Semitic languages. Thus, in trying to formulate a prototypical and primitive linguistic type (as well as a cultural, psychological and historical one), there was also an "attempt to define a primary human potential" out of which completely specific instances of behavior uniformly derived' (Said, 2003, p. 232).

Semitic Monotheism and a Religious People

Did the Semites, then, have nothing to offer to human civilization? On the contrary, we do owe to the Semites our alphabet, and more importantly, 'we owe them religion [*Nous leur devons la religion*]', and more precisely we owe them monotheism. The Semitic people are people of God.

> *To the Indo-European race belong almost all the great military, political, and intellectual movements in the history of the world; to the Semitic race, the religious movements. [...] The Semitic race [...] guided by its firm and certain views, first extricated the Divinity from its veils, and without reflection or reasoning [sans réflexion ni raisonnement] attained the purest religious form that humanity has known [...]. (Renan, 1854, p. 85, my translation)*

When it comes to religion, Renan states, the Aryan races had little to offer. Their religion consists of polytheistic mythology, which casts nature as divine. The old myths about the many gods (pantheism) that dominated the Greek and Roman civilizations are amusing at best but have little religious value, and, by the time these civilizations ran into the world of the Jews, they had lost all credibility.

> *Founded on the clear and simple dogma of unity [le dogme clair et simple de l'unité], setting aside naturalism and pantheism with this marvellously clear phrase: 'In the beginning, God created heaven and earth', possessing a law, a book, a depositary of high moral teachings and religious poetry, Judaism had an indisputable superiority, and it was possible to foresee that one day the world would become Jewish [qu'un jour le monde deviendrait juif], that is to say, would leave the old mythology for monotheism [le monothéisme]. (Renan, 1862, p. 24, my translation)*

This idea of a universal God, however, was not a creation of the Semitic people, rather it came to them without any proper merit (Renan, 1854, p. 86). To explain this, Renan refers to the context in which the Semites lived and to the nature of their language. The Semites were a nomadic people, who lived in the desert, a vast and desolate area. The desert is monotone, sublime in its uniformity, and that is why it could reveal to mankind the idea of the infinite (Renan, 1872, VIII, p. 147). The Semites, however, did nothing with the idea of God; they only protected it against everything and everyone that disputed it (Renan, 1854, pp. 85–86). Clearly, the simple mind of the Semites and their rigid fixation on the protection of the idea of God has a dark side, namely that of fanaticism and intolerance.

> *The intolerance of the Semitic peoples is the necessary consequence of their monotheism. [...] The Semites, [...] aspiring to realize a worship independent of provinces and countries, were to declare bad all religions different from their own [...]. The extraordinary phenomenon of the Muslim conquest was only possible within a race like this incapable of grasping diversity, and whose whole symbol is summed up in one word: God is God. (Renan, 1855b, p. 7, my translation)*

The Semites carry within them the seeds of violence: because of who they are, they simply cannot deal with plurality and diversity of (religious) opinion (Renan, 1855a, p. 753). Consistent with their nature, the Semites 'sacrificed complexity, nuance, and multiplicity for unity' (Benes, 2008, p. 227). If Voltaire associated revealed religions with intolerance and fanaticism, Renan associates Semitic people, who have received via an intuition the idea of God, with the problem of intolerance and fanaticism. Similar idea, different frame. Along with Semitism, monotheism is discredited, and polytheism, thriving on plurality and diversity and linked to the East, is associated with tolerance. The problem of religious violence is a problem of monotheism.

Text Box 9: On the Notion of Antisemitism

It is usually assumed that Wilhelm Marr first coined the notion of *Antisemitismus* in his 1873 pamphlet *Der Sieg des Judenthums über das Germanenthum*. Guy Stroumsa, however, found that the notion of antisemitism predates Marr's pamphlet and can be traced back to Moritz Steinschneier, 'a renowned Jewish scholar and bibliographer of Judaism and Islam, precisely in order to describe Renan's approach and in response to his theories'. Steinschneier calls Renan's depreciation of the Semitic people *Antisemitismus*. Here the term refers to both the Jews and the Muslims. Only later, that is since Marr's pamphlet, would this notion refer only to the Jews (Stroumsa, 2021, p. 116). In a European context, antisemitism means hatred against the Jews. It is a notion that is not used for hatred against Muslims. Many have forgotten the shared history of hatred against Jews and Muslims (Hedges, 2021; Renton, 2017) and have forgotten that the figure of the Semite, which brings Jews and Muslims together underlies antisemitism (Jansen & Meer, 2020).

Comparing Religions

On the one hand, Renan argues that Judaism, Christianity, and Islam, three religious traditions, 'are three Semitic facts, three branches of the same trunk, three versions, unequally fine, of the same idea. From Jerusalem to Sinai, from Sinai to Mecca, the distance is but a few leagues' (Renan, trans. Frothingham, 1864, p. 115). On the other hand, there remained for him 'a deep abyss, at once racial, cultural, and religious; between Christianity (i.e. Europe) and Judaism and Islam, the other two faiths birthed in the Levant' (Stroumsa, 2021, p. 119). Part of his scholarly project consists in refiguring the nature of Christianity in relation to its Semitic roots, which presented an embarrassment for modern Europe. Thus, Renan set in motion an Aryanization of Christianity, which also entailed a projection of modern ideals of tolerance and universal brotherhood onto Jesus, who supposedly broke away from Semitic tribalism and fanaticism. True Christianity is not Semitic. The problem of Semitism is not the problem of Christianity.

On Judaism   When it comes to the Jews, Renan states that their only role in history and their sole contribution to human civilization was to conserve the formula 'The Lord is God', without adding any novel digressions. This conservative spirit has many dimensions. First, the nature of the Semitic language, 'devoid of syntax, lacking conjunctions, incapable of inversion' simply did not allow them to think 'multiplicity'. Second, thanks to the preservation of the monotheistic idea, Israel paved the way for the coming of Christ, the pivot of human history (Renan, 1854, p. 130). Third, Jews' conservative attitude, so expressive of the rigidity of their language and so typical of the Semitic spirit that is incapable of renewal, prevented them from recognizing the novelty of the message of Jesus, the simple carpenter from Galilee. Without Judaism no Christianity, but with the coming of Christ the role of the Jewish people had come to an end.

> *Having produced its fruit, Judaism was to continue through the centuries its long and tenacious existence. Only now, the spirit of life had left this people; its history is still beautiful and curious, but it is the history of a sect, it is no longer the history of religion par excellence. [...] Has Israel fulfilled its calling? Has [this people] retained in the great mix of peoples the function originally assigned to them? Yes; we will answer without hesitation. Israel was the trunk on which was grafted the faith of mankind [Israël a été la tige sur laquelle s'est greffé la foi du genre humain]. No people has taken its destiny so seriously as Israel, no one has felt its joys and sorrows as a nation so keenly: no one has lived longer for an idea. (Renan, 1855a, p. 774, my translation)*

Notice how Renan is reiterating a classical religionized understanding of the place and role of the Hebrew people in history as both unique (preparing the way for Christianity) and anachronistic (because they had missed the fulfilment of their own calling). It is in this sense a tragic people: they were so faithful to their calling as conservators that they were unable to see what was before them, blind as ever. Supersessionism takes on a new form.

But what does this mean for Christianity, and especially for its Semitic roots? How can it be that a Semitic religion, which Renan associates with the past, with intolerance and fanaticism, forms one of the building blocks of the European civilization? How is it possible that Europe, which is by language Aryan, is by religion Semitic? Is not Christianity, understood as a Semitic religion, holding Europe back? (Masuzawa, 2005). What may still be the future of Europe as Christian, and of Christianity as European? In response to these questions, Renan would set up a 'rescue operation', aimed at turning Christianity into a religion that is more suitable to modern progressive Europe (Olender, 1992, p. 69). Key to that rescue operation is his claim that Christianity, while Jewish at root, in fact embodied a rupture with – if not the destruction of – Judaism and the Semitic spirit. There is nothing Jewish about Jesus. Just as he is saving Christianity from Judaism, so too he is saving Europe from the stain of Semitism (Heschel, 2008).

On Christianity   In Renan's reading, Jesus liberated the Christian religion from Semitism, and in so doing anticipated the modern 'dream of an apolitical, "religion-less" universal religion based on the "fraternity of Man" and individual free conscience by 1800 years' (Lentz, 2014, p. 19). This emancipatory process, which was set in motion by Jesus, would be continued when Aryan people, Greek and Roman, converted to Christianity, and when Christianity adapted to and took over their Aryan spirit. In his words, 'Christianity, absorbed by Greek and Latin civilization, had become Western' (Renan, 1862, p. 24, my translation). Hence, Christianity is Aryan and Occidental, rather than Semitic and Oriental.

In *Vie de Jésus* [Life of Jesus], Renan depicts Jesus as the son of a Galilean carpenter, unique in the way he tried to bring all humanity closer to God. Jesus, so he argued, was not the Son of God, but a sublime person, whom people understandably called divine, even though there could be no doubt about the fact that he came from the ranks of humans.

> *We are allowed to call this sublime person, who [to this] day presides over the destiny of the world, divine, not in the sense that Jesus absorbed the divine [...], but in the sense that Jesus is the individual who made his species take the greatest step toward the divine. [...] In him was concentrated all that is good and elevated in our nature. (Renan, 1863b, pp. 458–459, my translation)*

Jesus' teaching stood out in all its modesty, proclaiming a message of love, founded on the purity of the heart and universal human brotherhood (Renan, 1863b, p. 443). This spiritual religion stood out as non-dogmatic, non-clerical, non-ritual, and apolitical. Indeed, Jesus' mission was to purify religion from superstition, and from hypocrisy, ritualism, and dogmatic fanaticism, all of which Renan associated with the Semitic mind, and more precisely with pharisaic or rabbinic legalism (which Renan saw reinforced in the Catholic tradition). Jesus' religion was all about interiority and spirituality, rather than about external mediation and clerical authority. It was a cult without priests, without external practices, revolving only around pure sentiments of the heart and a direct relation with God (Renan, 1863b, p. 86). It is not difficult to see his work as reinforcing the imaginary religionized binary of Protestant-Catholic, as well as the older anti-Jewish one of law and spirit. In Renan's words:

> *Jesus founded the eternal religion of humanity [*la religion éternelle de l'humanité*], the religion of the spirit [*la religion de l'esprit*], free from all priesthood, from all worship, from all observance [*dégagée de tout sacerdoce, de tout culte, de toute observance*], accessible to all races, superior to all castes, absolute in a word: 'Woman, the time has come when we will no longer worship on this mountain or*

276 CHAPTER 8 Religio-racialized Taxonomies

in Jerusalem, but when the true worshipers will worship in spirit and in truth'.
(Renan, 1862, p. 34, my translation)

For Jesus to bring this message of a pure creed, he had to break with the constraints of the Semitic mind. Jesus, while being Jewish, owed nothing to Judaism (except the idea of the universal God) and his message of love and universal brotherhood contradicted the rigidity of the Semitic mindset and only came into being by radically rejecting the Jewish tradition as he himself imagined it.

> *Far from Jesus being the continuator of Judaism, he represents the break with the Jewish spirit. [...] The general journey of Christianity has been to move further and further away from Judaism. Its perfection will consist in returning to Jesus, but certainly not in returning to Judaism. (Renan, 1863b, p. 455, my translation)*

And elsewhere,

> *[Jesus] is not [...] a Jewish reformer, he positions himself as a destroyer of Judaism [destructeur du judaïsme]. (Renan, 1863b, p. 221, my translation)*

By purging himself from Judaism, and Christianity from its Semitic constraints, Jesus prepared the way for this religion of universal brotherhood to become truly European (read Aryan): free, tolerant, apolitical (read also secularized). This religion is unique, universal, and final. It is the true religion of humankind, conforming to the demands of the age of science. At this point, Renan makes a bold statement saying, '"Christianity" has thus become almost synonymous with "religion". Anything outside of this great and good Christian tradition will be sterile' (Renan, 1863b, p. 446, my translation). Christianity is religion; it embodies what religion is in essence. To Renan's mind, this religion of universal brotherhood is true religion; it is the shared past and future of Europe; it transcends all fragmentation and restores Europe as one.

Significantly, Renan's rejection of *biological* racism (see above) is framed as a binary pattern contrasting Christianity's universal brotherhood, and Jesus' religion of pure love, with the tribal, monotheistic religion of the Jews, who claimed to be a *race* revolving around the pride of blood rather than a religion! It is precisely this Jewish pride of blood that Christ came to supersede. True religion trumps race as a claim, a claim which is used to inferiorize the Semites *and* depict them as anti-European (Engelstein, 2017). Susannah Heschel sums up:

> *[Renan] provided a vocabulary and a logic, couched in the language of romantic pieties, to transform Jesus as a figure who was said to have criticized the Judaism of his day into one whose religiosity was determined by his Aryan identity, an identity he achieved by ridding himself of Jewish dross. [...] Renan's contribution was an argument of racial purification through mutability: Jesus purged himself of Judaism, as did Christianity, and emerged transformed from Jew to Aryan. Renan's contribution was to convert discomfort over Jesus's Jewishness into a further indication of Aryan genius, which knew how to transform an odious Hebrew monotheism into a glorious Christianity. The cleverness of Renan's argument was that it made room for viewing monotheism as a divine gift and Christianity as the successful human activity of transforming and enriching it on behalf of the Aryan race. (Heschel, 2008, pp. 37–38)*

This line of reasoning is a variation on the universalizing pattern of ethnoreligious thinking, discussed in the first chapter. The effort to project tribalism onto Judaism and claim universal inclusivism for Christianity is a running thread in the religionization of Christianity and its others (Horrell, 2020). It will also play a key role in the religionized taxonomy that underlies the so-called World Religions Paradigm.

Renan's effort to purge Jesus from Judaism takes on many forms. Here, I mention just a few. First, Renan notices that Jesus came from Nazareth, in the province of Galilee (Renan, 1863b, p. 19), and not, so he would always add, from Jerusalem. Galilee was a green and fertile earthly paradise, rather like India, and it stood out because of its mixed population, many of them non-Jews (*Phéniciens, Syriens, Arabes et même Grecs*) (Renan, 1863b, p. 22). This environment in which Jesus moved was a token of the fact that he could not be reduced to the Semitic mind and certainly did not share its barrenness. To further enhance this argument, Renan notes that Jesus would finally be killed in Jerusalem, which he called 'the saddest region in the world' and which symbolized the Semitic mind. Furthermore, Renan projected that Jesus was not killed by the Romans, who, while not happy with Jesus' message, nevertheless tolerated him. Rather, the pharisaic leaders, who simply could not recognize Jesus' prophecy of love, carry the burden of his death; they were the true enemies of Jesus.

On Islam   Renan distinguished between the biblical people, Israel, who had prepared the way for Christianity and thereafter lost all religious significance, and contemporary Jews. The latter, so he believed, had transcended their Semitic condition through the process of civilization. His harsh sayings about the Semites, therefore, do not necessarily apply to the Jews who lived in nineteenth-century Europe, a time marked by the so-called Jewish emancipation. Renan condemned the ongoing persecution Jews suffered in Europe in his time (Stroumsa, 2021, p. 120). Later antisemitic interpreters, however, would find in Renan's work all they needed to discriminate against the Jews that lived among them. The project that Jesus had supposedly started, namely that of destroying Judaism, would be continued by destroying European Jewry.

In Renan's own understanding, the true heir of the Semitic spirit is Islam, which he viewed as a fanatical and intolerant political religion through and through. To his mind, Islam was a sort of resurrection of Judaism, which had come to a dead end after the coming of Christ. It is this religion and this race which presents a real and contemporary threat to the project of Christian Europe. If the Hebrew people could at least be applauded for having conserved the idea of the universal God and for having prepared the way for Christianity, Islam, from the very beginning, was directed towards a dead end. In everything, this religion symbolizes the persistent narrow-mindedness of the Semite, if not also his backwardness. In this sense, Renan placed Islam in the past, and this in contrast to Christianity, which he regarded as the religion of the future. For Renan, all of this is obvious, simply by looking at the current state of Islamic states:

> *Anyone with even a little knowledge of the things of our time clearly sees the inferiority of Muslim countries, the decadence of the States governed by Islam, the intellectual nullity of the races which derive their culture and education solely from this religion. All those who have been in the Orient or in Africa are struck by the inevitably limited nature of the mind of a true believer, [...] which makes him absolutely closed to science, incapable of learning anything or of opening up to any new ideas [...]. The apparent simplicity of [the Muslim's] worship inspires him with an unjustified contempt for other religions. Convinced that God gives wealth and power to whomever he pleases regardless of education or personal merit, the Muslim has the deepest contempt for education, for science [profond mépris pour l'instruction, pour la science], for all that constitutes the European spirit [l'esprit Européen]. (Renan, 1883, p. 120, my translation)*

Renan was convinced that Islam was irreconcilable with Europe. It is a fanatic and intolerant religion, it does not know the distinction between the temporal and the spiritual realm (Renan, 1883, p. 143). The Muslim knows no other 'fatherland' than Islam, and, in line with what Locke and Voltaire had previously suggested, he is incapable of national loyalty. Furthermore, 'The Muslim is [sic] the hatred of science' (Renan, 1883, p. 147, my translation). He continues by saying that the Muslim 'by killing science, he has killed himself, and condemned himself in the world to complete inferiority' (Renan, 1883, p. 148, my translation).

278 CHAPTER 8 Religio-racialized Taxonomies

For all these reasons, Islam was the complete negation of Europe. To save Europe would mean to eradicate the Semitic mind.

> *At the present time, the essential condition for the spread of European civilization is the destruction of the Semitic par excellence, the destruction of the theocratic power of Islamism, [and] consequently the destruction of Islamism; because Islamism can only exist as an official religion: when it is reduced to the state of a free and individual religion, it will perish. The future, Gentlemen, therefore belongs to Europe and to Europe alone. Europe will conquer the world and spread its religion there, which is law, freedom, respect for men, this belief that there is something divine within humanity. (Renan, 1862, p. 26, my translation)*

Renan, in his effort to establish modern religion (which is really liberal Protestantism), projects problematic religion (in other words religion that is holding society back and that inhibits progress) onto Judaism and Islam. These two religions symbolize narrow-minded religion (Nash, 2014, p. 27). Once again Muslims (Arabs) and Jews (Hebrews) shared the fate of being cast as the current others of secularized European Christianity, which 'sought to distinguish itself from Judaism and Islam by reassessing roles and redrawing boundaries' (Olender, 1992, p. 15). The role that was previously projected onto Jews and Saracens because of their deviating beliefs and practices, is now projected onto them as Semites, whose spirit is irreconcilable with the European spirit.

Text Box 10: Algeria, Islam, and Islamophobia

Renan's discussion of the Semitic spirit, and especially of Islam as an anti-European religion, was developed against the background of France's colonization of Algeria. In this context, imaginary religionized constructions were materialized into a legal system that justified a differential treatment of Muslim subjects based on the idea that Muslims were fundamentally other: anti-European and anti-French. In 1865, the French Algerian civil code [*Statut Juridique des indigènes en Algérie*], which determined the legal rights of the indigenous people, projected a stratified society based on religionized differences (Lorcerie, 2005–2006; Silverstein, 2005). Whereas Algerian Jews were naturalized as French citizens in line with the emancipation of the Jews in France, this remained inconceivable for Algerian Muslims, 'even for Algerians who converted to Catholicism. One's identity as Muslim was indeed not viewed solely as a confession' or a creed (modern religion as belief), but as an 'ethnic-political' identity marker – Islam is a political religion – and as a marker of one's nature (Fadil et al., 2019). Even conversion could not undo one's Islamic nature. Muslims were a perpetual enemy of France; when they resorted to violence, to revolt against colonial oppression, their rebellion was viewed by French administrators as a perpetual holy war against European infidels. It is furthermore in this context that 'French ethnologists, working for the colonial administrations in West Africa, coined the term Islamophobia, [...] to describe [this] differential mode of treatment of Muslim subjects based on a view that Islam was fundamentally "other"' (Fadil et al., 2019).

Text Box 11: Adapting Patterns of Religionization in a Context of Secularized Christianity

While orientalist philologists like Renan had endeavoured to break with previous, Christian-theological, frameworks and rejected biblical explanations of origins and descent, and while they considered themselves as modern, liberal, emancipated, progressive, secular, and scientific, they seem to have exchanged one linear and teleological understanding of history and the progress of humanity for another.

The Christian-theological frame of salvation history, which revolved around the promise of redemption given to all, but possible only to Christians, placed Jews and Muslims in a non-salvific past, stuck in time, unable to move forward, fixated on an inauspicious tradition. Their fate was sealed because of how they relate to and deviate from the Christian norm. Jews especially had been given a gift, a blessing, a promise, but were unable to act upon it and recognize its fulfilment in Christ. Muslims were not latecomers, but rather symbolized a return to what they should have recognized as an inanimate tradition.

While Renan rejected this Christian soteriological frame, he nevertheless starts from a progressive understanding of history in which the Aryan civilization forms the pivot and the driving force. Progress is contrasted to regression, development to deterioration, emancipation to imprisonment. The problem now is not the rejection of Christian *religio* (true worship); the problem is the Semitic mind, constrained by the rigidity of language, which locks the Semite into the past, while Aryans move forward.

6 Friedrich Max Müller: 'He Who Knows One Religion, Knows None'

One more figure deserves our attention, namely Friedrich Max Müller (1823–1900). Born in Germany, he settled in Oxford in his early twenties, where he developed his career as a Sanskrit scholar and comparative philologist and as a historian of religion. Müller is especially known for his translation of the Vedas and for his compilation and translation of the sacred books of the various great traditions (Stone, 2002, p. xiii). This Oxford don was well acquainted with the methods of critical biblical scholarship and, considering how many new insights historical criticism had brought to Christianity, he saw no reason why these methods could not be applied to the sacred books of other traditions. '[W]e [Christians]', so he would state, 'are not the only people with a Bible' (Müller, quoted in Molendijk, 2016a, p. 160). While he was of the opinion that all these scriptures were man-made, he also maintained that a scholarly analysis of them could 'have its very important bearing on the questions nearest to our own heart' (Müller, 1884, ed. 2002, p. 263). For him the pluralization of religion – the idea that there are many traditions deserving the name religion – is a given. He wanted to 'widen the study of religion beyond its narrow theological and traditionally Christian province', even though his theological presuppositions continued to impact the way he approached the history of religion and he remained convinced of the absolute truth of Christianity. Thus, in his own words,

> A Science of Religion, based on an impartial and truly scientific comparison [...] of the most important religions of mankind, is now only a question of time. [...] It becomes therefore the duty of those who have devoted their life to the study of the principal religions of the world in their original documents, and who value religion [...] in whatever form it may present itself, to take possession of this new territory in the name of true science. (Müller, 1873a, pp. 34–35)

Because of his contribution to this emerging field, Müller is often called the father of the science of religion (Sharpe, 1986). However, even during his lifetime some of his ideas were contested and today many regard him as a typical armchair scholar of religion, who claimed to speak authoritatively about the Aryan religions while never having set foot in India. This critique notwithstanding, his contribution to the emerging World Religions Paradigm is beyond doubt, and to this day the field of religious studies recognizes him as a pioneering scholar, even though his religionized taxonomy is criticized.

While Müller's questions were very much in line with the zeitgeist (How do the different religions/languages/people relate to one another? How might we distinguish between

280 CHAPTER 8 Religio-racialized Taxonomies

primitive and more developed people and their traditions? To what extent can the study of the Orient revitalize Christianity?), he did not share Renan's (and others') essentialized reading of the language-race-religion nexus. On various occasions, he made his disagreement explicit (Müller, 1860, ed. 2002). Nevertheless, like most of his contemporaries, he was fixated on the project of classifying people, languages, and religions and he considered this to be his primary scholarly task. In his own words, 'All real science rests on classification' (Müller, 1873a, p. 123). In line with this task, his motto was *divide et impera*, which he translated as 'classify and conquer' (Chidester, 2014; Masuzawa, 2005). Theodore Vial has called this motto 'chilling', because it denotes how comparative religion and imperial Europe have been, historically speaking, 'part of the same project' (Vial, 2016, p. 101).

Religion as One and Plural

Müller uses the word religion in two different senses. On the one hand, he was convinced that originally, in some remote prehistory, humankind had been one, but for a variety of reasons, the human race split up into different people speaking various languages. However, the unity of humankind is still reflected in the fact that all people, regardless of their level of progress, had been given an intuition of the Infinite. That is the *Urdatum* of religion. Without this transcultural and transhistorical human intuition for the Infinite, without this divine gift, there is no religion.

> *No doubt there existed in the human mind, from the very beginning, something, whether we call it [...] an innate idea, an intuition, or a sense of the Divine. [That is an] ineradicable feeling of dependence and reliance upon some higher power, a consciousness of bondage, from which the very name of 'religion' was derived. (Müller, 1857, p. 6)*

This original intuition projects religion as a universal human potential. Religion, thus understood, distinguishes man from animal.

> *As there is a faculty of speech, independent of all the historical forms of language, so there is a faculty of faith in man, independent of all historical religions. If we say that it is religion which distinguishes man from the animal, we do not mean the Christian or Jewish religion; we do not mean any special religion; but we mean a mental faculty, [...] which [...] enables man to apprehend the Infinite under different names, and under varying disguises. Without that faculty, no religion, not even the lowest worship of idols and fetishes, would be possible; and if we will but listen attentively, we can hear in all religions [...] a struggle to conceive the inconceivable, to utter the unutterable, a longing after the Infinite, a love of God. (Müller, 1873a, pp. 17–18)*

Thus, Müller gave a theological-anthropological foundation to religion, which renders religion very much akin to what we earlier referred to as natural religion and the *consensus gentium*. Consider in this regard the following passage in which he refers to Augustine:

> *when he says: 'What is now called the Christian religion, has existed among the ancients, and was not absent from the beginning of the human race, until Christ came in the flesh: from which time the true religion, which existed already, began to be called Christian'. (Müller, 1867, ed. 2002, p. ix)*

Religion as a universally applicable category – and also as a category *sui generis* – is known within the Christian tradition as 'natural religion'. To express that original intuition of the Infinite, humans have no other recourse than language, and, more precisely, they resort to the use of metaphors, and ultimately mythology, to put their experiences into words. This is, according to Müller, the drama of religion: humans need metaphorical language to express complex experiences, but metaphors tend to multiply and reify and turn into entire mythological constructs, which in the end obscure the original intuition and steer attention away from it. Especially when people start confusing the metaphors for the real, and when a process of reification sets in, language becomes idolatrous. Müller famously captured this process by saying that people tend to take the *Nomina* (names) for the *Numina* (gods). From this perspective, religion as a linguistic phenomenon is susceptible to corruption. Müller also spoke about the disease of language. We may recognize in his analysis of linguistic corruption the problem of superstition and even idolatry, when people confuse the Infinite and the finite. In Müller's comparative reading, this is an all too human problem, precisely because it is a linguistic problem.

> *Mythology is inevitable, [...] it is an inherent necessity of language, if we recognize in language the outward form and manifestation of thought; it is, in fact, the dark shadow which language throws on thought, and which can never disappear till language becomes altogether commensurate with thought, which it never will.* (Müller, 1873a, pp. 353–354)

No religion, not even Christianity, understood as a linguistic phenomenon, escapes this problem.

Müller, however, emphasizes that the differences that exist between the religions are in form only. In essence, all religions, again including Christianity, go back to this primary intuition of the Infinite. Indeed, the origin of the world's great traditions is the same.

> *[T]hough each religion has its own peculiar growth, the seed from which they spring is everywhere the same. That seed is the perception of the infinite, from which no one can escape, who does not wilfully shut his eyes. (Müller, 1878, p. 50)*

Thus, religion as a category refers to a singular and universal category as well as to the different belief systems and their creeds, texts, rituals, and moral prescripts. The task of the comparative religious scholar is to 'collect all the evidence that can be found on the history of religion all over the world, to sift and classify it' with the purpose of tracing back the deepest source from which all the religions spring and restore religion to its purity (Müller, 1878, p. 219). In this sense, comparative religious scholarship is healing and restorative, because it will enable the detection of this primary apprehension of the infinite in the different traditions and the discovery of a common core shared across the religions, even the most primitive.

> *There are philosophers, no doubt, to whom both Christianity and all other religions are exploded errors, things belonging to the past, and to be replaced by more positive knowledge. To them the study of the religions of the world could only have a pathological interest [...]. But if they would but study positive facts, if they would but read, patiently and thoughtfully, the history of the world, as it is, not as it might have been: they would see that, as in geology, so in the history of human thought, theoretic uniformity does not exist, and that the past is never altogether lost. The oldest formations of thought crop out everywhere, and if we dig but deep enough, we shall find that even the sandy desert in which we are asked to live, rests everywhere on the firm foundation of that primeval, yet indestructible granite of the human soul, – religious faith. (Müller, 1867, ed. 2002, p. xxxi)*

The reforming adage 'back to the sources' is also applicable in this context, and to Christianity as well. In fact, Müller hoped that comparative religion could bring about the rebirth of Christian religion 'out of its basic sources', 'interiorized in the human heart', and 'freed from later incrustations'. If comparative religion can achieve this work of reform, a bright future awaits Christianity (Molendijk, 2016b, p. 155). He even hoped that this renewed Christianity would conquer the world, but this would only be possible if it succeeded in throwing off its ballast: 'We want less of creeds, but more of trust; less of ceremony, but more of works; less of solemnity, but more of genial honesty; less of doctrine, but more of love' (Müller, 1873b, p. 52).

282 CHAPTER 8 Religio-racialized Taxonomies

Müller was convinced, furthermore, that comparative religion would help to overcome religious division and enable humanity to reunite in universal brotherhood. This would require the comparative religious scholar to peel away those metaphorical and mythological layers that distract from the original religious core shared by all humans (Vial, 2016, p. 113).

7 The Task of Classification

The task that lies before the comparative religious scholar is that of classification. The question is, however: on the basis of which criteria does classification of the different religious systems become possible? Which traditions belong together, which need to be set apart? In response to these questions, Müller starts by refuting older criteria, the criteria which have dominated past efforts to map the world, such as the distinction between true and false religion, and between natural and revealed religions.

> If we speak, therefore, of a classification of all historical religions into revealed and natural, what is meant by natural is simply the negation of revealed, and if we tried to carry out the classification practically, we should find the same result as before. We should have on one side Christianity alone, or, according to some theologians, Christianity and Judaism; on the other, all the remaining religions of the world. This classification, therefore, [...] is perfectly useless for scientific purposes [...]. (Müller, 1873a, pp. 127, 131)

Müller also rejects the distinction between monotheistic and polytheistic religions, as well as between national and individual religions. To his mind, and in the spirit of the time, he stated that

> the only scientific and truly genetic classification of religions is the same as the classification of languages, and that, particularly in the early history of the human intellect, there exists the most intimate relationship between language, religion, and nationality – a relationship quite independent of those physical elements, the blood, the skull, or the hair, on which ethnologists have attempted to found their classification of the human race. (Müller, 1873a, p. 143)

In a similar vein to Renan previously, he explicitly distinguishes himself from any endeavour to classify people based on physiognomic features. His classification will be scientific, and therefore it will be based on the study of language. Language trumps biology when it comes to explanatory power.

In contrast to most of his contemporaries, Müller operated with a tripartite division, distinguishing between Semitic, Aryan, and Turanian languages (see Masuzawa, 2005, Chapter 7).

> The Semitic nations appear first on the stage of history. [...] The second family of languages is the Arian, or, as it used to be called, the Indo-European. The latter name indicates the geographical extent of this family from India to Europe, the former recalls its historical recollections, Arya being the most ancient name by which the ancestors of the family called themselves. [...] The third family is the Turanian. It comprises all languages in Asia and Europe not included under the Arian or Semitic families, with the exception of the Chinese and its dialects. (Müller, 1855, pp. 23, 27, 86)

In his understanding, the Chinese language stands on its own 'as monosyllabic, the only remnant of the earliest formation of human speech' (Müller, 1865, ed. 2002, p. 53).

Etymologically, the category 'Turanian' stems from the Persian Turan, meaning Turkestan. This category groups together all the peoples that are simply not included in the former two categories. Müller legitimized his decision to group these languages in this way by stating that they are all nomadic languages; what they hold in common is that they actually have nothing in common. This third category would never really catch on in academic circles and was already disputed in his time.

Zooming in on what he calls the 'two races that have been the principal actors in that great drama which we call the history of the world, the *Aryan* and the *Semitic*' (Müller, 1873a, p. 103), he makes a remarkable move, saying that both the Aryans and the Hebrews have produced in fact only two book religions: Hinduism and Buddhism, and Mosaism and Christianity (see Masuzawa, 2005, Chapter 7 for a more in-depth analysis). He adds immediately that the third religion generated by each of these people, can 'hardly lay claim to an independent origin, but is only a weaker repetition of the first'. This applies, on the one hand, to Zoroastrianism and, on the other hand, to Islam and its sacred book, the Qur'an. Once again, an age-old pattern of religionization, which degrades Islam to being a heresy of true worship, returns, albeit in a new form. In the context of comparative religion, this pattern is also applied to the relation between the three Aryan religions: Hinduism, Buddhism, and Zoroastrianism and he uses the word 'deviation' to explain the relation between the different traditions.

> *While Buddhism is the direct offspring, and, at the same time, the antagonist of Brahmanism, Zoroastrianism is rather a deviation from the straight course of ancient Vedic faith, though it likewise contains a protest against some of the doctrines of the earliest worshippers of the Vedic gods. The same, or nearly the same relationship holds together the three principal religions of the Semitic stock, only that, chronologically, Mohammedanism is later than Christianity, while Zoroastrianism is earlier than Buddhism. (Müller, 1873a, pp. 104–105)*

Comparing religious traditions and their histories, Müller goes on to note yet another parallel, between the trajectory of Buddhism in relation to Brahmanism, and Christianity in relation to Mosaism:

> *Buddhism, which is the offspring of, but at the same time marks a reaction against the ancient Brahmanism of India, withered away after a time on the soil from which it had sprung, and assumed its real importance only after it had been transplanted from India, and struck root among Turanian nations in the very centre of the Asiatic continent. Buddhism, being at its birth an Aryan religion, ended by becoming the principal religion of the Turanian world. The same transference took place in the second stem. Christianity, being the offspring of Mosaism, was rejected by the Jews as Buddhism was by the Brahmans. It failed to fulfil its purpose as a mere reform of the ancient Jewish religion, and not till it had been transferred from Semitic to Aryan ground, from the Jews to the Gentiles, did it develop its real nature and assume its world-wide importance. Having been at its birth a Semitic religion, it became the principal religion of the Aryan world. (Müller, 1873a, pp. 105–106)*

Müller's classificatory project would finally result in the publication of the *Sacred Books of the East*, which consisted of 51 volumes covering the books that were deemed authoritative in the different great religious traditions. Together, they formed the library of the sacred books of the world. This landmark series included English translations of texts from seven traditions: Hinduism, Buddhism, Zoroastrianism, Confucianism, Taoism, Jainism, and Islam. Müller called these major traditions the 'small [...] aristocracy' of canonical book religions (Müller, 1873a, pp. 102–103). Literacy sets these religions apart from 'the vulgar and nondescript crowd of bookless or illiterate religions' (Müller, 1873a, p. 102). Without any doubt, Müller contributed to the idea that texts form the heart of religious traditions and that reading and comparing religious texts across different traditions is the best way to do justice to some of the intricate complexities of strange traditions, and to really delve deeply into their different layers of meaning.

> *Like the Christian Bible these texts had to be read and understood, not just memorized and recited by an educated caste. It is probably not too far-fetched to see at work here the Protestant ideal of the individual reading the whole sacred text(s) and not being satisfied with cherry-pickings [...]. (Molendijk, 2016b, p. 177)*

The Religions of the Book and the Rest

By projecting literate traditions and their sacred books as the material for the study of religion, and by qualifying these traditions in terms of a 'small aristocracy', Müller established a religionized norm, which reaffirmed an existing binary between elite and primitive, civilized and savage (cf. the pagan). This binary became self-evident in the field of comparative religion most likely because it intersected with so many other normative assumptions. Müller, however, did recognize that the textual traditions offered only a limited scope, and to his mind it was important to take account of the non-textual traditions as well. In his words:

> [A] study of the religions of the uncivilised races would help us reach a lower,
> that is, a more ancient and more primitive stratum of religious thought than we
> could reach in the sacred books of the most highly civilised races of the world.
> (Müller, 1892, p. 147)

As David Chidester, who works in the context of South Africa, notes, Müller's binary between textual and non-textual traditions certainly established a powerful pattern of religionization, and it influenced not only the way scholars see and approach non-literate traditions, but also how the wider public appreciates these traditions – the rest – which fall outside the scope of Müller's religious archive. They are primitive, less developed, belonging to a past where time stood still. Chidester notes that to this day 'indigenous religions' are often 'incorporated in introductory textbooks to "world religions" as traces of origins and absences' (Chidester, 2018, p. 46).

The publisher, Oxford University Press, refused Müller's proposal to insert the Bible, namely the Old and New Testaments, in his study because that would put Christianity on a par with the other religions of the book. In this decision the reluctance of many to recognize Christianity as a religion of the book comparable to other religions is made clear. Christianity is religion, 'the' religion and therefore beyond compare; the study of religion is theology, not the science of religion, and the publisher deemed it unacceptable to treat Christian tradition as one would treat the other traditions. Certainly, in ecclesial circles, the paradigm of the great traditions of the world met with resistance because it seemed to pave the way to relativism, which is irreconcilable with the absolute truth claim of Christianity. Müller, however, disagreed. In his understanding, comparative religion posed no threat to the absolute and exalted nature of Christianity; on the contrary, it would once and for all make clear that Christianity embodied the ideal of 'the' universal religion. Jesus, so he claimed, was a messenger of love, and was not to be confused with the Christ of dogma and theology. As a liberal Lutheran, he took a positive stance vis-à-vis scientific and historical-critical readings of the Bible and he was eager to extend that to other religious traditions, just as he was convinced that this critical approach would only reaffirm Christianity as the universal religion:

> The Science of Religion will for the first time assign to Christianity its right place
> among the religions of the world; it will show for the first time fully what was
> meant by the fulness of time; it will restore to the whole history of the world, in
> its unconscious progress towards Christianity, its true and sacred character.
> (Müller, 1867, ed. 2002, p. xx)

Müller believed that the comparative study of religion would reinvigorate Christianity and make it more appealing to non-Christians. Therefore, Müller felt as a Christian he had nothing to fear from science. Christianity would in fact shine even brighter if it were compared to other religions. He was even convinced that comparative religion would support the important work of the missionaries. In his words:

> I make no secret that true Christianity, [...], seems to me to become more and
> more exalted the more we appreciate the treasures of truth hidden in the despised

religions of the world. But no one can honestly arrive at that conviction, unless he uses honestly the same measure for all religions. It would be fatal for any religion to claim an exceptional treatment, most of all for Christianity. Christianity enjoyed no privileges and claimed no immunities when it boldly confronted and confounded the most ancient and the most powerful religions of the world. Even at present it craves no mercy, and it receives no mercy from those whom our missionaries have to meet face to face in every part of the world. Unless our religion has ceased to be what it was, its defenders should not shrink from this new trial of strength, but should encourage rather than depreciate the study of comparative theology. (Müller, 1873a, p. 37)

Elsewhere, he made a similar point, saying that as a Christian one should not fear comparative religion, but on the contrary, one should have faith that it will bring out the truth of Christianity:

If missionaries could show to the Brahmans, the Buddhists, the Zoroastrians, nay, even to the Mohammedans, how much their present faith differs from the faith of their forefathers and founders, if they could [...] read with them in a kindly spirit the original documents in which these various religions profess to be founded, and enable them to distinguish between the doctrines of their own sacred books and the additions of later ages, [...] the choice between Christ and other Masters would be rendered far more easy to many a truth-seeking soul. But for that purpose it is necessary that we [...] should see the beam in our own eyes, and [...] distinguish between the Christianity of the nineteenth century and the religion of Christ. If we find that the Christianity of the nineteenth century does not win as many hearts [...], let us remember that it was the Christianity of the first century in all its dogmatic simplicity, but with its overpowering love of God and man, that conquered the world [...]. If we can teach something to the Brahmans in reading with them their sacred hymns, they too can teach us something when reading with us the Gospel of Christ. (Müller, 1867, ed. 2002, pp. xxiv–xxv)

Where this left Judaism is not clear, however. On the one hand, one could argue that it is placed on a similar level to Christianity, via the authority of the *Old Testament*; on the other hand, we must recognize that this line of reasoning denies the reality that Judaism continued to flourish as a living tradition and continued to produce its own authoritative text traditions after the coming of Christ (Daggers, 2013, p. 25) (Text Box 12).

Text Box 12: The Problem of Recognizing Judaism as a Religion, Separate from Christianity

Not including the authoritative books specific to Jewish tradition is a form of latent anti-Judaism and a continuation of long-established patterns of religionization. This exclusion reduces the authoritative books of the Jewish tradition to the Old Testament (sometimes also called the Hebrew Bible). The implication is that the meaning of Judaism is reduced to its role as prophecy of Christ's coming. After that Christological event, Jewish tradition, so the assumption goes, came to a dead end and no longer developed in any significant way. Consequently, the religious meaning of rabbinic tradition is denied. That the Tenach and the Old Testament do not completely overlap is disregarded, and that for Jewish people the Torah (the five books of Moses) must be read in combination with the Oral tradition (Talmud) is not considered. Excluding Judaism as an afterthought to excluding Christianity from comparative religion studies underscores the fact that the former was seen as no more than the foreshadowing of the latter (Moyaert, 2017). This is a continuation of anti-Jewish religionization.

8 Conclusion

Nineteenth-century Europeans faced profound questions of identity in the context of the industrial revolution, scientific innovation, and colonialism/nationalism. The Christian tradition and its biblical framework had come under severe critique and had lost much of its authority as a hermeneutical framework, and this largely explains why Europeans began to look for new and more scholarly theories; theories that could help to make sense of the history of humankind in all its diversity, while reaffirming Europe's hegemonic position in the world at large. These identity questions were mainly picked up by Romantic philosophers and philologists, who argued that a people's identity, its essence, could be derived from the nature of their language. Indeed, language was considered to reflect the spirit of a people. By comparing languages one could not only compare people, but also gain more insight into how different people relate to one another. Such relations were typically imagined in terms of genealogical relations.

These Romantic musings and philological explorations led to unexpected findings and resulted in a whole new taxonomy of languages, people, and even religions. The fourfold religionized taxonomy of Christians, Jews, Muslims, and pagans gave way to a taxonomy based on an at-first-glance binary pattern contrasting the Semitic and Aryan languages, peoples, and religions. This process of reclassification has many aspects, and here I mention just a few. First, Jews and Muslims were now re-labelled as Semites, while the religions that belong to India – Hinduism and Buddhism – were cast as Aryan. Those things that were previously said about Jews and Muslims because they rejected Jesus and deviated from true *religio*, were now explained through the lens of language. The projection of Judaism and Islam as Europe's problematic others not only remained intact but became even more forceful, since these two traditions were now presented as contrary to the progressive, emancipatory, tolerant Aryan spirit of Europe. Second, this new taxonomy initially placed Christianity in an awkward position, for its Semitic roots seemed to disqualify its claim to being Europe's privileged religion. It was as if Europe was being pulled in two directions, one towards the future, spurred on by modern (Aryan) values of critique, emancipation, creativity, renewal, and progress, the other towards the past, held back by the rigid, fanatic, and conservative Semitic spirit. Once again, however, Christianity displayed its capacity for refiguration and showed its superiority in having liberated religion from the shackles of Semitism. Indeed, Jesus set in motion a process of Aryanization which was later continued when Greek and Roman civilization became Christian. The challenge for the future was to protect Europe against the ongoing threat of the Semitic spirit, now mainly embodied in the figure of the Muslim/Arab and his political religion. As Christianity – understood as secularized, liberal, Protestant religion – reinvented itself as the universal and absolute religion of brotherhood and re-established itself as European, it synchronously cast Muslims and Jews as Europe's others and as belonging to the Orient and to the past. This process of religionized selfing and othering once again takes the form of superiorizing and inferiorizing. The violent language surrounding the destructive anti-European power of the Semites seemed to legitimize colonial oppression, and was aimed at Christianizing, and westernizing, the Semitic Orient. At this point, I wish to highlight once more that this binary pattern of Semites and Aryans actually comes at the exclusion of a whole legion of people who are deemed savage. The nature of their language is such that they were simply unable to contribute anything of significance to the development of human civilization. These are illiterate people marked by primitive ignorance. In my reading, they are the pagan remnant of the previous medieval fourfold taxonomy. The primitive nature of their language places them outside the realm of human civilization and also excludes them from the history of religion. Their traditions are magical, fetishist, or animist, suffering still from the confusion between matter and spirit, nature and God. Often their traditions do not even figure in comparative religion studies, or in its emerging paradigm of world religions: Christianity, Judaism, Islam, Buddhism, and Hinduism. More often than not the study of these traditions would be executed by cultural anthropologists rather than comparative religion scholars. Finally, towards the end of the nineteenth century, this process of re-taxonomization translated into a generally accepted re-imagination of the world, and, ever since, people across the globe have imagined themselves as living in a world that recognizes a range of world religions. The fragmentation of Christianity (we are all Christian but express this differently) was now extended to the idea that religion is one but expressed in many ways. The much earlier effort to define some kind of *pure Christianity*, that was shared across traditions and that could restore some kind of unity beyond difference (and fragmentation) was also projected onto the history of religions. Christianity – and some of the scholars we discussed in this chapter are quite explicit in this regard – now goes under the cover of *religion: Christianity is religion and religion is Christianity*. We are not that far removed from what some earlier church fathers claimed when they were speaking about *prisca theologia*. This understanding of religion – as pure, as belonging to the heart, as interiorized – is universal religion. It is this religion which should be restored to the whole world, and it is this religion that is most suited to the future of Europe, which is the future of the world.

Note

[1] 'The most significant nodes of William Jones' work are (a) the need for translation by the European, since the natives are unreliable interpreters of their own laws and culture; (b) the desire to be a lawgiver, to give the Indians their "own" laws; and (c) the desire to "purify" Indian culture and speak on its behalf. The interconnections between these obsessions are extremely complicated. They can be seen, however, as feeding into a larger discourse of Improvement and Education that interpellates the colonial subject' (Niranjana, 1990, p. 774).

References

Adluri, V., & Bagchee, J. (2013). *Indology: The Origins of Racism in the Humanities. Review of Pascale Rabault-Feuerhahn, Archives of Origins: Sanskrit, Philology, Anthropology in 19th Century Germany.* Harrassowitz, 2013. Retrieved from www.indica.today/long-reads/indology-the-origins-of-racism-in-the-humanities-part-2/

Ashcroft, B. (2009). *Caliban's Voice: The Transformation of English in Post-colonial Literatures.* Routledge.

Benes, T. (2008). *In Babel's Shadow: Language, Philology, and the Nation in Nineteenth-century Germany.* Wayne State University Press.

Burris, J. P. (2001). *Exhibiting Religion: Colonialism and Spectacle at International Expositions, 1851-1893.* University of Virginia Press.

Chidester, D. (2014). *Empire of Religion: Imperialism and Comparative Religion.* University of Chicago Press.

Chidester, D. (2018). World Religions in the World. *Journal for the Study of Religion, 31*(1), 41–53.

Daggers, J. (2013). *Postcolonial Theology of Religions: Particularity and Pluralism in World Christianity.* Routledge.

Denzinger, H., Hünermann, P., & Hoffmann, J. (1996). *Symboles et définitions de la foi catholique = Enchiridion symbolorum, definitionum et declarationum de rebus fidei et morum.* Cerf.

Dusche, M. (2009). German Romantics Imagining India: Discursive Tools against French Hegemony and Roots of Ethnic Nationalism in Europe I. The Case of Friedrich Schlegel. *Postkoloniale Arbeiten / Postcolonial Studies.* Retrieved from www.goethezeitportal.de/fileadmin/PDF/kk/df/postkoloniale_studien/dusche_romantics_imagining_india.pdf

Engelstein, S. (2017). *Sibling Action: The Genealogical Structure of Modernity.* Columbia University Press.

Fadil, N., Ragazzi, F., & de Koning, M. (2019). Radicalization: Tracing the Trajectory of an 'Empty Signifier' in the Low Lands. In N. Fadil, F. Ragazzi, & M. de Koning (Eds.), *Radicalization in Belgium and the Netherlands: Critical Perspectives on Violence and Security.* Tauris.

288 CHAPTER 8 Religio-racialized Taxonomies

Fernández-Armesto, F., & Wilson, D. (1996). *Reformatie: Christendom en de wereld 1500–2000*. Anthos.

Fichte, J. G. ([1845], 1793). Beiträge zur Berichtigung der Urtheile des Publicums über die französische Revolution, 1793. In J. H. Fichte (Ed.), *Johann Gottlieb Fichte's sämmtliche Werke* 6 (pp. 39–288). Veit und Comp.

Figueira, D. M. (2002). *Aryans, Jews, Brahmins: Theorizing Authority through Myths of Identity*. State University of New York Press.

Fox, R. A. (2003). J. G. Herder on Language and the Metaphysics of National Community. *The Review of Politics, 65*(2), 237–262.

Fredrickson, G. M. (2002). *Racism: A Short History*. Princeton University Press.

Freeman, E. A. (1879, ed. 1958). Race and Language (1879). In E. T. Thompson and E. C. Hughes (Eds.), *Race: Individual and Collective Behaviour*. Free Press.

Gerbner, K. (2018). *Christian Slavery: Conversion and Race in the Protestant Atlantic World*. University of Pennsylvania Press.

Goldenberg, D. (2003). *The Curse of Ham: Race and Slavery in Early Judaism, Christianity, and Islam*, Jews, Christians, and Muslims from the Ancient to the Modern World. Princeton University Press.

Harpham, G. G. (2009). Roots, Races, and the Return to Philology. *Representations, 106*(1), 34–62.

Hedges, P. (2021). *Religious Hatred: Prejudice, Islamophobia and Antisemitism in Global Context*. Bloomsbury Academic.

Heng, G. (2018). *The Invention of Race in the European Middle Ages*. Cambridge University Press.

Heschel, S. (2008). *The Aryan Jesus: Christian Theologians and the Bible in Nazi Germany*. Princeton University Press.

Hill Fletcher, J. (2017). *The Sin of White Supremacy: Christianity, Racism, and Religious Diversity in America*. Orbis.

Hock, H. H. (2021). *Principles of Historical Linguistics* (3rd ed. revised and updated). De Gruyter Mouton.

Horrell, D. G. (2020). *Ethnicity and Inclusion: Religion, Race, and Whiteness in Constructions of Jewish and Christian Identities*. Eerdmans.

Humboldt, W. von (Ed. M. Losonsky) (1999). *On Language: On the Diversity of Human Language Construction and Its Influence on the Mental Development of the Human Species*, Cambridge Texts in the History of Philosophy. Cambridge University Press.

Hutton, C. (2019). Orientalism and Race: Aryans and Semites. In G. P. Nash (Ed.), *Orientalism and Literature* (pp. 117–132). Cambridge University Press.

Jansen, Y., & Meer, N. (2020). Genealogies of 'Jews' and 'Muslims': Social Imaginaries in the Race–religion Nexus. *Patterns of Prejudice, 54*(1–2), 1–14.

Jones, W. (Ed. J. Ghose) (1875). *The Collected Works of Sir William Jones, Knight; Eleven Discourses*. Trübner.

Kaplan, M. L. (2019). *Figuring Racism in Medieval Christianity*. Oxford University Press.

Kenyon-Flatt, B. (2021, 19 March). How Scientific Taxonomy Constructed the Myth of Race. *Sapiens*. Retrieved from https://www.sapiens.org/biology/race-scientific-taxonomy/

Kippenberg, H. G. (2002). *Discovering Religious History in the Modern Age*. Princeton University Press.

Kouloughli, D. (2007). Ernest Renan: un anti-sémitisme savant. *Histoire Épistémologie Langage, 29*(2), 91–112.

Laruelle, M. (2009). Le Berceau aryen: mythologie et idéologie au service de la colonisation du Turkestan. *Cahiers d'Asie centrale*, 107–131.

Lentz, R. (2014). The Fascist Jesus: Ernest Renan's *Vie de Jésus* and the Theological Origins of Fascism. Diss. University of Wales Trinity Saint David].

Levin, H. (2021). Anti-Semitism in German 'Volk' Culture: Propaganda through the Pen and Screen. Retrieved from http://earlham.edu/wp-content/uploads/2021/03/anti-semitism-in-german-volk-culture.pdf

Lorcerie, F. (2005–2006). L'Islam comme contre-identification française: trois moments. *L'Année du Maghreb, 2*, 509–536.

Marks, J. (2022). Scientific Racism, History of. In *Encyclopedia of Race and Racism*. Retrieved from www.encyclopedia.com/social-sciences/encyclopedias-almanacs-transcripts-and-maps/scientific-racism-history

Masuzawa, T. (2005). *The Invention of World Religions, or, How European Universalism Was Preserved in the Language of Pluralism*. University of Chicago Press.

Mettepenningen, J., & Schelkens, K. (2010). *Van concilie tot concilie: Hoofdlijnen en fragmenten van de geschiedenis van kerk en theologie van Vaticanum I tot Vaticanum II*. Halewijn.

Mohnike, T., & Grage, J. (2017). *Geographies of Knowledge and Imagination in 19th Century Philological Research on Northern Europe*. Cambridge Scholars Publishing.

Molendijk, A. L. (2016a). Forgotten Bibles: Friedrich Max Müller's Edition of the *Sacred Books of the East*. *Publications of the English Goethe Society, 85*(2–3), 159–169.

Molendijk, A. L. (2016b). *Friedrich Max Müller and the Sacred Books of the East*. Oxford University Press.

Moyaert, M. (2009). A 'Babelish' World (Genesis 11:1–9) and Its Challenge to Cultural-linguistic Theory. *Horizons, 138*(2), 215–234.

Moyaert, M. (2014). *In Response to the Religious Other: Ricoeur and the Fragility of Interreligious Encounters*. Lexington Books.

Moyaert, M. (2017). Comparative Theology after the Shoah: Risks, Pivots, and Opportunities of Comparing Traditions. In F. X. Clooney & K. von Stosch (Eds.), *How to Do Comparative Theology*, Comparative Theology: Thinking across Traditions (pp. 164–187). Fordham University Press.

Müller, F. M. (1855). *The Languages of the Seat of War in the East: With a Survey of the Three Families of Language: Semitic, Arian and Turanian* (2nd ed.). Williams and Norgate.

Müller, F. M. (1857). *Buddhism and Buddhist Pilgrims: A Review of M. Stanislas Julien's 'Voyages des pèlerins boudhistes'*. Williams and Norgate.

Müller, F. M. (1860, ed. 2002). Semitic Monotheism. In J. R. Stone (Ed.), *The Essential Max Müller: On Language, Mythology, and Religion* (pp. 25–42). Palgrave Macmillan.

Müller, F. M. (1865, ed. 2002). Lecture on the Vedas, or the Sacred Books of the Brahmans. In J. R. Stone (Ed.), *The Essential Max Müller: On Language, Mythology, and Religion* (pp. 43–68). Palgrave MacMillan.

Müller, F. M. (1866). *Lectures on the Science of Language Delivered at the Royal Institution of Great Britain in April, May, and June 1861* (5th ed rev). Longmans, Green, & Co.

Müller, F. M. (1867, ed. 2002). Preface to *Chips from a German Workshop*. In J. R. Stone (Ed.), *The Essential Max Müller: On Language, Mythology, and Religion* (pp. 69–80). Palgrave Macmillan.

Müller, F. M. (1873a). *Introduction to the Science of Religion: Four Lectures Delivered at the Royal Institution with Two Essays on False Analogies, and the Philosophy of Mythology*. Longmans, Green, & Co.

Müller, F. M. (1873b). *On Missions: A Lecture Delivered in Westminster Abbey on December 3, 1873. With and Introductory Sermon by Arthur Penrhyn Stanley*. Longmans, Green, & Co.

Müller, F. M. (1878). *Lectures on the Origin and Growth of Religion as Illustrated by the Religions of India: Delivered in the Chapter House, Westminster Abbey, in April, May, and June, 1878* (2nd ed.). Longmans, Green, & Co.

Müller, F. M. (1884, ed. 2002). Forgotten Bibles. In J. R. Stone (Ed.), *The Essential Max Müller: On Language, Mythology, and Religion* (pp. 249–264). Palgrave Macmillan.

Müller, F. M. (1892). *Anthropological Religion: The Gifford Lectures Delivered before the University of Glasgow in 1891*. Longmans, Green, & Co.

Nash, G. (2014). Aryan and Semite in Ernest Renan's and Matthew Arnold's Quest for the Religion of Modernity. *Religion & Literature, 46*(1), 25–50.

Newcomb, S. T. (2008). *Pagans in the Promised Land: Decoding the Doctrine of Christian Discovery*. Fulcrum.

Niranjana, T. (1990). Translation, Colonialism and Rise of English. *Economic and Political Weekly, 25*(15), 773–779.

Olender, M. (1992). *The Languages of Paradise: Race, Religion, and Philology in the Nineteenth Century*. Harvard University Press.

Poliakov, L. (1974). *The Aryan Myth: A History of Racist and Nationalist Ideas in Europe*. Heinemann for Sussex University Press.

Priest, R. D. (2015). Ernest Renan's Race Problem. *The Historical Journal, 58*(1), 309–330.

Renan, E. (1854). *Études d'histoire religieuse*. Michel Lévy.

Renan, E. (1855a). Du peuple d'Israël et de son histoire. *Revue des Deux Mondes (1829-1971), 12*(4), 746–774.

Renan, E. (1855b). *Histoire générale et système comparé des langues sémitiques. Première partie, Histoire générale des langues sémitiques*. Imprimerie impériale.

Renan, E. (1858a). *De l'origine du langage* (2nd ed.). Michel Lévy.

Renan, E. (1858b). *Histoire générale et système comparé des langues sémitiques. Première partie, Histoire générale des langues sémitiques* (2nd ed rev. and augmented). Michel Lévy.

Renan, E. (1862). *De la part des peuples sémitiques dans l'histoire de la civilisation: discours* (6th ed.)

Renan, E. (1863a). *Histoire générale et système comparé des langues sémitiques. Première partie, Histoire générale des langues sémitiques* (3rd ed. rev. and augmented). Imprimerie impériale.

Renan, E. (1863b). *Vie de Jésus*. Lévy.

Renan, E. (Trans. O. B. Frothingham) (1864). *Studies of Religious History and Criticism*. Carleton.

Renan, E. (1872). *Œuvres complètes d'Ernest Renan*. Michel Lévy.

Renan, E. (1883). *L'Islamisme et la science: conférence faite à la Sorbonne, le 29 mars 1883.* Calmann-Lévy.

Renan, E. (1890). *L'avenir de la science: pensées de 1848.* Calmann-Lévy.

Renton, J. (2017). The End of the Semites. In J. Renton & B. Gidley (Eds.), *Antisemitism and Islamophobia in Europe: A Shared Story?* (pp. 99–140). Palgrave Macmillan.

Robertson, R. (1999). *The 'Jewish Question' in German Literature, 1749–1939: Emancipation and Its Discontents.* Oxford University Press.

Said, E. W. (2003). *Orientalism.* Penguin.

Schelkens, K. (2015). 'Le plus aristocratique des goûts': Modernist, Orientalist and Antisemitic Bible Readings in Late Nineteenth-century Belgium. *Ephemerides Theologicae Lovanienses, 91*(2), 311–332.

Schiebinger, L. (1990). The Anatomy of Difference: Race and Sex in Eighteenth-century Science. *Eighteenth-Century Studies, 23*(4), 387–405.

Schlegel, F. von (Trans. E. J. Millington) (2014). *The Aesthetic and Miscellaneous Works of Frederick von Schlegel.* Cambridge University Press.

Sharpe, E. J. (1986). *Comparative Religion: A History* (2nd ed.). Open Court.

Silverstein, P. A. (2005). The New Barbarians: Piracy and Terrorism on the North African Frontier. *CR: The New Centennial Review, 5*(1), 179–212.

Stoler, A. L. (1989). Making Empire Respectable: The Politics of Race and Sexual Morality in 20th-century Colonial Cultures. *American Ethnologist, 16*(4), 634–660.

Stone, J. R. (2002). Preface. In J. R. Stone (Ed.), *The Essential Max Müller: On Language, Mythology and Religion* (pp. xiii–xx). Palgrave Macmillan.

Stroumsa, G. G. (2021). *The Idea of Semitic Monotheism: The Rise and Fall of a Scholarly Myth.* Oxford University Press.

Todorov, T. (1998). *On Human Diversity: Nationalism, Racism, and Exoticism in French Thought.* Harvard University Press.

Topolski, A. (2016). A Genealogy of the 'Judeo-Christian' Signifier: A Tale of Europe's Identity Crisis. In A. Topolski & E. Nathan (Eds.), *Is There a Judeo-Christian Tradition? A European Perspective,* Perspectives on Jewish Texts and Contexts 4 (pp. 267–284). De Gruyter.

Topolski, A. (2018). The Race-Religion Constellation: A European Contribution to the Critical Philosophy of Race. *Critical Philosophy of Race, 6*(1), 58–81.

Trautmann, T. R. (1997). *Aryans and British India.* University of California Press.

Turner, J. C. (2014). *Philology: The Forgotten Origins of the Modern Humanities.* Princeton University Press.

Tzoref-Ashkenazi, C. (2006). India and the Identity of Europe: The Case of Friedrich Schlegel. *Journal of the History of Ideas, 67*(4), 713–734.

Vial, T. M. (2016). *Modern Religion, Modern Race.* Oxford University Press.

Weller, S. (2021). *The Idea of Europa: From Classical Antiquity to the Enlightenment.* Cambridge University Press.

CHAPTER 9

The Dialogical Turn beyond Religionization?

The second half of the twentieth century witnessed a shift in the way Christians relate to 'non-Christians'. As Catherine Cornille explains '[r]ather than competing with one another over territories, converts or claims, [people that belong to different] religions have generally come to adopt a more conciliatory and constructive attitude toward one another, collaborating in social projects and exchanging views on common religious questions' (Cornille, 2013, p. xii). This turn towards dialogue signifies a turn away from polemics and intolerance. In the aftermath of this dialogical turn, Christians too have had to learn to acknowledge 'non-Christians' as conversation partners who talk back. From this perspective 'non-Christians' are no longer rhetorical figures but have now become real others with whom one can collaborate.

Since the turn of the twenty-first century, and especially after 9/11, political bodies have also begun to promote interreligious dialogue (Fahy & Bock, 2020; Halafoff, 2013; Ipgrave, 2019). In just a few decades, dialogue went from being, at best, a marginal episodic phenomenon to being part of the governance regimes of religious diversity in Europe and beyond, and state-run interreligious initiatives have become more common (Griera & Nagel, 2018; Körs & Nagel, 2018; Marshall, 2017). '[N]ew partnerships' between faith-based communities and governmental bodies 'are being created, new mandates for moral and spiritual reform are being drafted, and new centers for interfaith understanding are being built' (Hurd, 2017, p. 28). Good religion is now dialogical religion.

In this chapter, I ask how the dialogical turn relates to religionization. Does dialogue, which promises to shift from talking about imaginary others to engaging real others, succeed in disrupting religionization? Are certain patterns of religionization, which European (secularized) Christians 'inherited' from the past, still operative in this turn to dialogue? How does the institutionalization of dialogue as a norm relate to ideas about good and bad religion? And what is the place of Christianity in this? Does the dialogical turn seal the end of (secularized) Christian normativity or rather endorse its re-establishment?

To answer these questions, I revisit three events which are commonly recognized as key turning points in the history of the interreligious movement: the World Parliament of Religions, held in Chicago in 1893 and generally seen as a Christian Protestant initiative; the promulgation of the Roman Catholic declaration *Nostra Aetate* during the Second Vatican Council, which convened from 1962–1965; and the (post)secular political embrace of dialogue after the dramatic attacks on the World Trade Center in New York on 11 September 2001 (Fahy & Bock, 2020; Halafoff, 2013; Howard, 2021; Moyaert, 2013). Zooming in on these three events enables me to explore whether, and to what extent, religionized patterns of thinking are produced and reproduced in modern pleas for interreligious dialogue, and to what extent dialogical encounters have the power to interrupt imaginary constructs of self and other.

Christian Imaginations of the Religious Other: A History of Religionization, First Edition. Marianne Moyaert.
© 2024 John Wiley & Sons Ltd. Published 2024 by John Wiley & Sons Ltd.

1 The World Parliament of Religions in Chicago

The World Parliament of Religions was held in Chicago from 11–27 September 1893 as part of the Columbian World Fair, celebrating the 400th anniversary of Christopher Columbus' 'discovery' of the Americas. For 17 days, the parliament succeeded in captivating an audience of thousands, who came to listen to representatives of 'what were (then) considered the world's ten great religions: Hinduism, Buddhism, Jainism, Zoroastrianism, Taoism, Confucianism, Shintoism, Judaism, Christianity and Islam' (Seager, 1993, p. 15). These representatives made statements about their traditions and about their beliefs and practices and 'the service [their faith] claimed to have rendered to mankind' (Kitagawa, 1987, p. 5). Scholars of religion too spoke about the importance of the emerging science of religion and how it could contribute to understand the progressive history of human civilization.

Three key actors made this event possible: the presbyterian John Henry Barrows (1847–1902), chairman of the 1893 General Committee on the Congress of Religions, the Swedenborgian Charles Carroll Bonney (1831–1903), president of the World's Congresses, and the Unitarian Jenkin Lloyd Jones (1843–1918), who acted as secretary. Together, they determined ten objectives for the parliament. Here, I limit myself to the following four, which give a good sense of the emerging interfaith discourse:

(1) To bring together in conference [...] the leading representatives of the great Historic Religions of the world; (2) To show men [...] what and how many important truths the various Religions hold and teach in common; (3) To indicate the [...] foundations of Theism [...] and [...] unite [...] the forces which are adverse to a materialistic philosophy of the universe; (4) To bring the nations of the earth in a more friendly fellowship, in the hope of securing permanent international peace. (Barrows, 1893, p. 18)

At the time, the parliament was regarded as 'the most sublime expression of the Columbian spirit' of celebration, optimism, and human ability (Seager, 1989, p. 301). It was the most widely publicized of the various intellectual congresses held in conjunction with the Columbian exhibition and the best attended event of the Columbian World Fair (Barrows, 1893). This enthusiasm affirmed Barrows' conviction that 'Religion is the greatest fact of History' (Barrows, 1893, p. vii).

Richard Seager calls the parliament the 'dawn of religious pluralism' (Seager, 1993) and, in a similar vein, Catherine Albanese and Stephen Stein say that it 'was an ecumenical convocation before there was an ecumenical movement' (Albanese & Stein, 1995, p. ix). The 1893 event, however, was not simply ahead of its time; it was also a child of its time. The Columbian exposition was organized at a moment when belief in the supremacy of Western civilization was at its highest and when Christian missionary activities, political expansion, and overseas colonialism were at their most intense; this first global interfaith gathering was in many ways an expression of this self-confident nineteenth-century zeitgeist (Hill Fletcher, 2017a; Tiemeier, 2013). Rather than creating a platform where oppression was questioned, the vision of interreligious brotherhood [*sic*] so central to the parliament steered attention away from such political realities. To understand this, we have to explore the parliament in the larger socio-political context of the world fair of 1893 and 'position the Chicago Fair writ-large as a stage upon which to observe religion enacted and performed' (Kaell & Walker, forthcoming).

World Fairs

In the nineteenth century, world fairs were a matter of prestige. For organizing cities these expositions provided a new opportunity to display their contribution to the industrial revolution and to showcase the latest technologies (such as X-rays), scientific developments, urban planning trends, and architectural masterpieces (such as the Eiffel tower) (Nussbaum, 2013,

p. 214). Later, in 1901, president McKinley would call these exhibitions 'timekeepers of progress' (McKinley, 1901 in Copeland et al., 2012, p. 341). In addition, works of art, artefacts, and products from far away regions were on show, turning world fairs into the most elaborate presentation of 'cosmopolitanism yet seen on the continent'. Visitors could marvel at the world on display (Ziolkowski, 1993, p. 44). The central message of these fairs was the superiority of Western civilization and of the organizing nation/city in contrast to less developed and even 'primitive' people that were culturally backward (Burris, 2001, p. xviii).

In Europe, several world fairs had already been organized – Paris in 1855, London in 1862, Paris again in 1867, and Vienna in 1873; in the United States Philadelphia organized a centennial exhibition in 1876, before Chicago seized the opportunity of the 400th anniversary of Columbus' discovery of the America to organize a grand exhibition.

The Columbian World Fair and National Pride

On the eve of the exhibition, the United States faced a massive economic depression. The country was, moreover, divided over the question of race: the Jim Crow laws and lynching episodes proliferated in the South while Native Americans, following the Indian Appropriation Act, continued to be dispossessed of their ancestral lands as the Indian reservation system was established. At the same time, anti-Asian prejudice was on the rise (Tiemeier, 2013, p. 427). Against this background, American leaders turned to the world fairs to create a sense of national identity. Indeed, Hillary Kaell and David Walker point out that 'the script [of the Columbian fair] was an explicitly nationalist message that framed the United States as the historical effect and present embodiment of Columbus's enterprising spirit. Its message was also a religious one [with the superiority of White Christianity as a key component], and these interlocking messages were articulated multiple times at the Fair' (Kaell & Walker, forthcoming). Consider in this regard, Senator Chauncey M. Depew's (1834–1928) oration at the fair's opening ceremonies – an oration interspersed with teleological reasoning, American pride, and religious triumphalism.

This day belongs not to America, but to the World. [...] We celebrate the emancipation of man. The preparation was the work of [...] countless centuries; the realization was the revelation of one [Columbus] [...]. The spirit of the equality of all men before God and the law, moved westward from Calvary with its revolutionary influence upon old institutions, to the Atlantic Ocean. Columbus carried it westward across the seas [...]. [This] exhibition of arts and sciences, of industries and inventions, of education and civilization [...] displays the [...] fruitage of this transcendent miracle. (Depew, 1892)

The exhibition consisted of three large parts: the White City, the Midway Plaisance, and the World's Congress Auxiliary. Taken together, this tripartite structure painted 'an *imago mundi*, a picture of the world, that revealed both mainstream America's image of itself and its image of the rest of the world' (Seager, 1995, p. 11). Prior to the development of mass communication, these fairs were key in disseminating a certain world view; by 'doing the fair', visitors could appropriate this stratified framework that supposedly reflected the world they inhabited and their place in it (Rydell, 1987, p. 4). Normative distinctions were all-pervasive – distinctions between the new and the old world; the free and the unfree world; progress and deterioration; civilized and savage people; world religions and primitive religions; Christians and non-Christians.

The 1893 event is particularly interesting in view of our interest in religionization because it was the first global event that 'began to imagine the grand conjuncture of cultures through religious categories far more than at previous events' (Burris, 2001, p. 123). For the first time the new religionized taxonomy revolving around world religions as distinct from more primitive traditions was exhibited and performed as a key frame to make sense of the progress of human civilization. Religionized stratification – based on the World Religions Paradigm – was made visible and could be experienced from close by at the fair. Adherents of the world religions – textualized, confessionalized traditions – were for the first time invited to a global discussion about religion. Primitive people and their traditions, on the contrary, were represented in artefacts, houses, or ethnographic villages, 'made available for visual inspection by millions of strolling and staring Western citizens' (Corbey, 1993, p. 338). All the while, white American Christianity, the absolute religion, was projected as the catalyst of progress and success of American society. Thus, the act of welcoming representatives of the world religions went hand in hand with the orientalist gaze that accompanied the colonial mindset, and the American vision of civilization came at the cost of those social groups deemed un-American and uncivilized, and lacking religion.

The Tripartite Structure of the World Fair

The main exhibition ground was called the White City, because its enormous neoclassical buildings were painted in gleaming white and because it was illuminated at night. For a few months, it was 'the brightest spot on earth', displaying more electric light every night than many had seen in their entire lives' (Valance, 2009, p. 431). Architect Burnham was convinced that 'the true source of civic beauty was the Renaissance and Baroque cityscapes based on the classicism of ancient Greece and Rome'. He maintained that for Chicago (and other cities for that matter) to achieve international grandeur it would have to build on the 'achievements of the neoclassical great monuments of Europe' (Hutter, 2016, p. 111). This neoclassical style configured America as the New Rome or Greece, but in a modern disguise. At the same time, Burnham prefigured the White City as an ideal city because 'its dramatic nighttime electrical lighting stood in stark contrast to the industrial city of the day' (Hutter, 2016, p. 113). Chicago was the New Jerusalem and America was the centre of the divinely blessed world (Peskowitz, 1998, p. 245).

The main fairground at the Columbian exhibition 'consisted of [...] a United States Government Building, a Manufacturing Building, a Woman's Building, and several buildings devoted to various areas of commerce, the arts, and science' (Burris, 2001, p. 25). Here products of technological, industrial, and scientific advancement were put on display. Several pavilions were erected by the foreign nations that were deemed exotic but civilized, like India and Japan. A region was deemed civilized when it 'produced the many commodities that were beginning to drive the international economy'; meanwhile, 'the savages were vaguely affiliated with the regions that supplied the bulk of the raw materials from which the commodities were produced' (Burris, 2001, p. 25). This distinction between civilized and 'primitive' intersected with the religionized taxonomy of the World Religions Paradigm: if representatives of the first – Hindus and Buddhists from Japan and India – were invited to the parliament as speakers, the latter by contrast, were absent at this multifaith event and figured in living villages to be stared at or represented in artefacts on display (Burris, 2001, p. 104).

The ethnological display, located towards the south-eastern corner of the White City, added to this stratification of people. This display was the responsibility of Franz Boas (1858–1943), known as one of the founding fathers of cultural anthropology, and Frederic Ward Putnam (1839–1915), the head of Harvard's Peabody Museum of American Archaeology and Ethnology. Together both men took on the task of displaying the primitive life of the 'Indian' from the past – they showcased objects, artefacts, and mannequins dressed in various examples of tribal attire. There was also a living exhibit of indigenous *Kwakwaka'wakw* people, several *Penobscot* bark tipis, and an *Iroquois* village. Some of the inhabitants performed rituals, like the *Hamat'sa* dance, one of the most important rituals of the *Kwakwaka'wakw* and the *hawinalal* warrior dance, which were outlawed in *real life* (Text Box 3) (Raibmon, 2005, pp. 50–73). These displays showed the anthropologists' desire to preserve 'authentic' indigenous culture before it disappeared. Of course, 'such displays in the middle of a World's Fair in Chicago, thousands of miles from the homes of these people, are as distant from any conception of authentic as can be' (Green, 2017, p. 123).

The anthropology department, furthermore, worked in close collaboration with the Bureau of Indian Affairs, which built a boarding school for indigenous children in the immediate vicinity of the ethnographic display. The bureau intended to contrast the 'primitive Indian' – located in the past – with the 'civilized Indian' in the 'character of the student' – symbolizing the future. At the time, the US Bureau of Indian affairs had begun to force Native American children to attend boarding schools distributed across the country so that they would abandon their indigenous traditions and take on White Christian American culture. Indigenous Americans had to be civilized, read Americanized and Christianized. Richard Henry Pratt (1840–1924), an army officer who established the first Indian boarding school, captured this American policy in the phrase, 'Kill the Indian, save the man' (Churchill, 2005). By erecting a boarding school at the fair, attended by indigenous children and school teachers, who stayed there for the duration of the fair, the Bureau of Indian Affairs broadcast its assimilationist ideology. Non-native Americans who participated in the fair could form an image of the 'primitive Indian', exhibited at the ethnographic site as a vanishing race, but one which could be saved, provided they were segregated from their original context, uprooted from their traditions, and turned into Christian Americans. By showing the benefits of education, the bureau intended to 'garner public support' for its vision (Green, 2017, p. 95). Because of financial limitations, the fair's boarding school, however, did not achieve the ambitions of its promoters and became a public relations disappointment. Most of the audience was more interested in the 'savage' Indian than in the 'civilized' one. Nevertheless, the vision of the bureau did harmonize with that of many Americans, whose experience of 'transforming landscapes and overcoming frontiers' reaffirmed that they belonged to a nation that had been elected by God to fulfil his historical purpose: to bring civilization, progress, and brotherhood to the world. It also helped instil the idea that these primitive people and their traditions were to be studied by anthropologists, in contrast to the representatives of the world religions, present at the parliament as speakers with whom scholars of religion could converse.

Next to the White City there was a strip known as the Midway Plaisance. This was a rather 'chaotic assembly of commercialized cultural exhibits' – the focus was on popular entertainment and the atmosphere was carnivalesque (Burris, 2001, p. 99). As well as being a site of pleasure, the Midway Plaisance also served the overall pedagogical purpose of the exhibition: showing the superiority of America. The living villages of foreign people that were displayed at the Midway Plaisance strongly supported this pedagogical purpose. Here again Putnam and his team played an important role. Inspired by 'the 1889 Paris Universal Exposition, where the French government and prominent anthropologists turned representations of the French colonies into living ethnological villages featuring people from Africa and Asia' (Rydell, 2005), Putnam supervised a range of ethnographic exhibitions, displaying both artefacts and living people. These exhibits were in accordance with the nineteenth-century pseudo-scientific framework of social Darwinism, according to which human history 'began in a remote past as a stage of savagery, and moved inexorably and inevitably through various stages of barbarism to reach civilization'. Only the white race, though, had fully evolved and reached the stage of civilization' (Domosh, 2002, p. 185). The villages at the Midway Plaisance were organized hierarchically, starting with 'the ostensibly lowest forms to the purported zenith of civilized whiteness, the White City'.

> At the far end, furthest from the White City, Africans and Native Americans provided twinned examples of assumed 'savagery'. The Dahomeyan village nestled among Tatanka Tyotanka (Sitting Bull's) cabin (he had been killed just three years earlier by state reservation police), a Sámi village, Chinese village, Brazilian concert hall, and Wild West show. The Islamic and Asian World occupied the central midway. A display for Algeria and Tunisia was adjacent to a Cairo Street and was located opposite a Moorish palace and Turkish village. Further on and closest to the main fairground were a Javanese village, Japanese bazaar, German village, Irish village and Dutch settlement. (Qureshi, 2011, pp. 248–249)

The living villages, which visually synthesized the alleged human evolution of the 'human race' at once provided scientific legitimacy to already existing stereotypical images of the people of the world. They also offered another opportunity for Americans to measure their own achievements and be reassured about the cultural sophistication of American life, and its place on the world stage (Seager, 1993, p. 24). If the White City, which 'loomed large in the background', represented the future, the Midway Plaisance represented the past: knowledge is set against ignorance, light against darkness, purity against dirt, ideas against matter, Christianity against the customs of other people (Kaell & Walker, forthcoming). As far as religion is concerned one could say that it was both everywhere and nowhere, or at least nowhere specifically.

The third component of the Chicago fair was the World's Congress Auxiliary; here leading intellectuals gave lectures and discussed topical issues, like medicine, economics, arts, religion, and so forth. To distinguish the intellectual and spiritual achievements of mankind from the exhibits displaying material, technological, and industrial progress in the White City, 'the World's Congress Auxiliary met some miles away at what is now the Art Institute of Chicago, a building near the lakefront in downtown Chicago' (Braybrooke, 1992, p. 10). The Parliament of Religions was one of the events organized as part of the Congress Auxiliary.

Barrows, who helped organize the parliament, was particularly concerned about the growing association between the United States and materialism. He regarded Chicago as symbolizing the 'home of the crudest materialism' (Barrows, 1893, pp. 8–9), devoid of any reference to God and religion. With the parliament, which welcomed religious scholars and leaders from the world, Barrows wanted to underscore that in everything that men create, a divine Creator is assumed. In his words:

> Since [...] worship has been [...] a life-giving and fructifying potency in man's intellectual and moral development; [...], it did not appear that Religion any more than Education, Art or Electricity should be excluded from the Columbian exposition. (Barrows, 1893, p. 3)

The Parliament of Religions as Performance of the World Religions Paradigm

The parliament created quite a spectacle – the word used most often in media coverage of the event (Fader, 1982) – and it is not hard to imagine why. Consider those religious leaders who travelled from 'distant', 'unknown', and 'exotic' lands, mostly coming from the 'East', wearing colourful garments and lecturing on their strange beliefs and practices. The parliament turned the World Religions Paradigm, as projected by the modern science of religion, into a lived reality for the people attending (Burris, 2001). It made the plurality of religions present as never before and it affirmed that all those present were contributing to the history of religion (Text Box 1). The parliament, in line with the Columbian fair, also exhaled the belief that modernity – in contrast to the past, which was marked by discord – was 'moving toward unity'. The ideal of fellowship between the religions permeated this ten-day event. The organizers expected that the emerging science of religion would not only help understand the progressive history of mankind, but would also contribute to the achievement of more collaboration between the religions. In light of the above, we can understand why the parliament is often projected as the 'symbolic' birthdate of the so-called interreligious movement (Halafoff, 2013; Howard, 2021).

Despite its lofty ideals, the World Religions Paradigm, which underpins this gathering of religions, is also a religionized taxonomy which names, essentializes, classifies, and stratifies social groups based on religious difference. It assumes religio-secularization as well as religio-racialization, both of which were based on theological legacies projecting a sense of Christianness as being the religionized norm for the modern world. We can already notice this in Barrows' conviction, shared by many, that Christian America would lead other nations to brotherhood, peace, and civilization (Barrows, 1893, p. 5).

> *Christendom may proudly hold up this Congress of the Faiths as a torch of truth and of love which may prove the morning star of the twentieth century. There is a true and noble sense in which America is a Christian nation [...]. The world calls us, and we call ourselves, a Christian people. (Barrows, 1893, p. 74)*

Rather than creating a platform where exclusion and oppression are questioned, the vision of interreligious fellowship so central to the parliament not only steered attention away from such political realities, but in fact supported and naturalized them: it affirmed the overall *imago mundi* projected by the fair.

Religion Is One and Many   Articles about the 1893 event report that the Liberty Bell rang ten times, in honour of the ten religions that were represented at the parliament.[1] At the very least, Tomoko Masuzawa argues, this means that someone was counting and that the older religionized map of the world, consisting of Christians, Jews, Muslims, and pagans had lost its authority (Masuzawa, 2005, p. 266). The idea of religious plurality was now part of the *imago mundi* projected by the organizers, and the representatives of the world religions made this *imago mundi* real, visible, and palpable. By attending the parliament, people could experience from close by that the world is populated by people who belong to diverse religious traditions; Buddhism, Hinduism, Islam, and so on. They could walk around in a world populated by people that belonged to different religions and be inspired by their words of wisdom. Visitors learned that religion is the key to understanding different cultures in their particularity; religion contains 'the essence of a given people's cultural orientation' (Burris, 2001, p. 124).

The parliament also projected the idea of religion as a human universal. Across particular differences these representatives share religion: they are all included in the larger history of religion that is also the history of 'mankind'. Several speakers depicted 'man' as a religious being and religion as a vital component of human flourishing (De Harlez, 1993; Read Sunderland, 1993; Réville, 1993). Or as Barrows put it, the study of history shows that 'man' longs for God and God is looking for 'man'. The parliament and the 'faces of the living men of all Faiths' was a reflection of that profound human longing (Barrows, 1893, p. viii). Understanding the history of humankind therefore requires the scientific study of religion.

Text Box 1: The Problem of Religionized Essentialization in the Context of Interreligious Dialogue

The World Parliament invited people to speak on behalf of different world religions. This focus on representation risks reinforcing the problem of 'essentialization' that is already implied in the World Religions Paradigm (Thatamanil, 2015).

First, let me approach this from the perspective of collective traditions. The World Religions Paradigm is the result of a scientific approach to religion which privileged texts. The textual bias in the creation of World Religions marginalized ritual, material, and more localized expressions of lived religion, which are often messier than the bounded wholes suggested in the World Religions Paradigm. This text-centred understanding of religion became the 'norm' and it is this tradition that people are asked to represent as Hindus, Buddhists, and so forth. This reinforces the idea of the world religions as bounded '-isms'. What people believe takes priority over what people do; what the elite says, takes priority over what 'ordinary' people say. The result is that religion as a lived reality remains underrepresented and is deprecated as popular religion. In this sense, dialogue grafted onto the World Religions Paradigm tends to reinforce the problem of essentialization and to suppress the heterogeneity of religious expressions.

When one approaches this essentialization from the perspective of personal identity, the problem worsens. The dominance of this World Religions Paradigm means that anyone who does not fit the categories projected will probably not receive a seat at the dialogue table. This is, for example, a problem for people who call themselves spiritual but not religious, and for multiple belongers (Cornille, 2002; Kwok, 2005; Thatamanil, 2020). This is also a problem for those people whose traditions are not organized within a clear hierarchy.

To represent one's 'religion' in a dialogical setting is a tricky matter: on the one hand, one easily buys into the recrafting and essentialization of tradition and gives the World Religions Paradigm public credibility; on the other hand, dialogue is also a setting where one can challenge the process of mislabelling and resist, advocate, and contest. Even then, the World Religions Paradigm operates as a hegemonic norm, which one can only contest by acknowledging it. However, it is also the case that for a variety of individual and institutional reasons people can choose not to contest the frame because it gives them certain rewards and strategic leverage.[2]

Following the dialogical turn, which gained traction after the Second Vatican Council, interfaith scholars as well as grassroots activists realized the limitations of this understanding of interreligious dialogue. Especially feminist and post-colonial thinkers from various traditions began to question the idea that people have to act as 'representatives' of their tradition (Hill Fletcher, 2005; Kwok, 2005). While so-called diplomatic dialogues will still centre the importance of representation, many dialogical initiatives presuppose the complexity of personal identity, and start from a lived religion approach (Gustafson, 2020).

Interreligious Brotherhood and Religio-secularization The idea of the parliament, so Barrows states, met with resistance. Many associated religion with a legacy of conflict; a legacy which they projected onto the old world (Europe) and its old institutions. The quotation below captures this overall sense, and affirms the secular bias vis-à-vis religion: where religion is involved, discord erupts, and the harmony between nations envisioned by the world fair would be disturbed. Thus Barrows:

> [the idea of the parliament] carried the mind back to an era of persecution
> and of abysmal separations between the Christian and non-Christian people.
> Many felt that Religion was an element of perpetual discord, which should
> not be thrust in amid the magnificent harmonies of a fraternal assembly of
> the nations. It was said that there could be no Congress of Religions without
> engendering the animosities which have embittered much of man's past history.
> (Barrows, 1893, p. 5)

The parliament could show the world that religion, and more specifically religious diversity, does not necessarily stand in the way of peace. On the contrary, religion can be 'a boon for society' and 'religions can have a positive and constructive influence on society' (Griera, 2019, p. 43). The parliament's performance of interfaith fellowship thus functioned as a counter-narrative aimed at reshaping a prevailing, in this case religo-secularized, discourse about religion and conflict. The parliament projects an alternative vision for society, one in which religion is not pushed to the margin but can unleash its positive power, at least under certain conditions. These 'unleashing' conditions were supposed to be exceptionally well realized in the new world. Interfaith fellowship, as an ideal, figures in a supersessionist framework in which the new world fulfils and supersedes the old world and its ideals. Several speakers stated that the ideal of universal fellowship could only be realized in the 'peculiar American establishment' of religious freedom (Numrich, 2019, p. 75).

> *It was the spirit of fraternity in the heart of America which succeeded in bringing together such widely separated exponents of religion. Enemies simply met and discovered that they were brothers who had one Father in Heaven. [...] [I]t is not rhapsody to say that 'the age of isolation has passed, and the age of toleration and scientific comparison has come'. (Barrows, 1893, p. 5)*

Thus, the Columbian Parliament was projected as symbolizing the redemptive American project which 'frees mankind' from the history of religious violence associated with the old world (Europe) and its endless religious wars. The new world, where Europeans fleeing from European violence started anew, symbolizes freedom of religion, and the vision of interfaith fellowship is projected as an example to be followed by the rest of the world.

The quotation from Barrows also suggests that interfaith brotherhood is rooted in a more profound, theological-anthropological connectedness: the fatherhood of God forms the basis for the brotherhood of men. This genealogical idea of God's fatherhood, as well as a theistic concept of God, 'served as a bottom-line theology at the Parliament' (Seager, 1995, p. 66). This, rather than strife and conflict, is what God has meant 'men' to be – 'brothers' – and the parliament restores people's awareness of this profound truth. American exceptionalism is peppered with ethnoreligious reasoning, following the logic of encompassment: all are children of God, the father; all are brothers; all, to use an older Christian term, are gentiles [from *gentes*], meaning people with a common father. This universal perspective, however, is immediately particularized, in the claim that Americans realized this calling of brotherhood par excellence, and they walk in front of other people to show them the way. America holds a torch to the rest of the world.

This ideal of interreligious fellowship is informed by the religio-secular divide and its binary between good and bad religion: dogmatism and ritualism especially need to be renounced before peace and fellowship can become reality. Good religion knows what is essential and ultimate; bad religion turns differences that are *adiaphora* (and of penultimate importance with regard to one's salvation) into ultimate concerns. Good religion distinguishes between what is ultimate and penultimate, whereas bad religion renders one perspective absolute; this leads to the sort of conflict that shattered the old world. To realize brotherhood is to do away with dogmatic sectarianism. This would become a dominant storyline of the interreligious movement (see for example Read Sunderland, 1993, pp. 116–117).

None of the above, however, was seen to contradict the conviction shared by the organizing committee and many of the Christian participants, that religion, true religion, absolute religion, is realized in Christian religion. American exceptionalism and Christian exceptionalism go together. There may be many world religions, but Christianity was '*the* world religion' and it is in Christ that the parliament's ideal of brotherhood is realized. In his preface to the (heavily edited!) two-volume publication collecting the parliamentary papers, Barrows expressed his hope that

> *the Oriental reader will discover in these volumes the source and strength of that simple faith in Divine Fatherhood and Human Brotherhood, which embodied in an Asiatic Peasant [Jesus] who was the Son of God and made divinely potent through Him, is clasping the globe with bands of heavenly light. (Barrows, 1893, p. ix)*

The project of interreligious brotherhood is part of the Christian civilizing mission (Müller, 1894, ed. 2002, p. 351). In this sense, the parliament fits perfectly in the emancipatory, redemptive ambitions of modernity (Text Box 2).

Text Box 2: The Religio-secularized Norm of Modern Religion and Its Implications for Minorities

In the previous chapters, I explained that the religio-secular divide and the concomitant plea for religious toleration implies a refiguration of good and bad religion, true and false religion. I elaborated on how the case for toleration was first made based on a refiguration of Christianness: true Christianness is projected as meek and humble, a-dogmatic, de-ritualized and a-political. In a context of persecution, the plea for toleration, with which the religio-secular divide is entangled, was a subversive and marginal discourse of resistance, constructed by projecting bad religion onto Jews, Catholics, and Muslims.

Eventually, this interiorized and personalized understanding of religion became normative and would go on to impact European Jews, who, when faced with this religious norm, had to plead for their inclusion into civic society. To be recognized as fully civic subjects, they had to argue that they were not a 'nation within a nation', that they owed no loyalty to foreign political powers, and that they fully accepted the religio-secular divide. Furthermore, their attachment to ritualized practices – especially circumcision and Kashrut – was considered suspicious. In response, European Jews tried to make the case for continuing these rituals while at the same time projecting themselves as in tune with modernity (e.g. by saying that circumcision was a medical intervention with hygienic value). Here, speaking about German Jewry, Robin Judd writes, 'Emancipation, much like other state intrusions, gradually changed the character of German-Jewish communities. Not only did some states encourage transformation as a prerequisite for civic rights, but German-speaking Jews also responded to emancipation's erratic nature on their own. Those who desired political integration attempted to meet emancipation's demands' (Judd, 2011, p. 28). A seemingly benign discourse about toleration easily turns into a discourse about assimilation.

Discussions like these were also taking place in the United States during the nineteenth century, when Jews faced similar challenges. While '"liberalism" looked and sounded different in these very different settings [,] [...] the pleas of Jewish and Catholic [...] adoptionists were [...] strikingly similar, both to each other, and to the arguments of Protestant liberalism. Each of the three was saying, in effect: "The essential, timeless core of our faith must be preserved, but we must also discard inessential doctrines and practices that are mere artifacts of some past time". Each insisted, in the face of furious objections from conservatives, that the resulting adaptations [...] were not abject capitulations. On the contrary, these adjustments would make the ancestral faith stronger at its core, and in that sense more worthy of an equal place in society as well as more likely to achieve that status' (Hutchison, 2003, pp. 122–123).

At the World Parliament of Religions, Alexander Kohut, a conservative rabbi from New York, who was in fact, 'challenged by those who wanted to accommodate the values of the time',[3] nevertheless made the claim that Judaism is in fact true religion: 'Israel [...] gave the world a pure religion – a creed undominated by cumbrous tyranny, unembarrassed by dogmatic technicalities, unstrained by heavy self-sacrifice and extravagant ceremonialism – a religion sublime and unique in history, free from gaping superstitions, appalling idolatries, and vicious immoralities – a pure, taintless, lofty, elevating, inspiring, and love-permeating faith, originating in a monotheistic conception – a religion at whose sparkling fountain wells of ethical truths, the world's famed pioneers in art, science, literature, politics, philosophy, and architecture slackened their thirst' (Kohut, 1893, p. 725).

The Religions of the World and the Rest: Religio-racialization Exhibited

The parliament, building on the World Religions Paradigm, projects an imaginary ideal of what it means to be religious, an ideal that is rooted in a logic of encompassment: all are included, because all are brothers. Even when the irenic setting of the parliament disables polemical dichotomization, behind the emergence of this dialogical self looms the spectre of the other. The 'others' of this universal religionized ideal are those who belong to primitive, tribal traditions as well as those who are suspected of rejecting tolerant or peaceful religion, and perhaps also those people who have not yet progressed far enough to accept religious freedom. Deviation from this modern ideal of brotherhood locks 'the other' in the (religious/savage) past, to be studied by ethnographers. The primitive other was associated with fetishism and animism or even heathenism. Undoubtedly the Christian, and more specifically the Protestant, understanding of true religion resonates in the background of this negative appreciation. As with the pagans and the idolaters of the past, these uncivilized primitive souls

> *were confused about the true distinctions among humans, things, and divinity: imputing spirit to dead matter, divine agency to ordinary creatures, and so forth. In effect, when the missionaries attacked animal sacrifice, the worship of carvings, or magical language, they took the side of science – at times unwittingly, at others quite purposefully – in disenchanting some part of the world. (Keane, 2002, p. 67)*

The more attached a people was seen to be to material and ritual practices, the less cultivated it presumably was, and, of course, vice versa. The more completely a tradition had successfully expressed its beliefs in textual form, the greater claim it could lay to being cultured.

In terms of religionization, we are therefore witnessing not an interruption, but rather a continuation of the mechanism of selfing and othering predicated on religious difference. The world fair's tripartite structure makes blatantly clear that the ideal of interreligious fellowship was an exclusive ideal, which could go together with the delegitimization and exclusion of those who were deemed uncivilized.

As with all imaginary constructs, this viewpoint also obscures the messiness of social reality. In this case, the self-acclaimed ideal of religious freedom conceals the realities of religious oppression for those deemed undeserving of freedom, and masks the fact that Christian scholars helped produce the knowledge that justified this oppression (Joshi, 2020). Indeed, all this talk about brotherhood was taking place at the height of the colonial era, the time of the Jim Crow laws, an apartheid regime based on colour-line racism and ghettoized black bodies, and the genocide of Native Americans (see Text Box 3). The discourse of 'friendly fellowship', masked and justified white Christian hegemony in the United States and hid the reality that those of other faiths were not meeting as equals. The setting, the agenda, and the frame were Christian, and the same goes for the categories, the questions, and the issues given centre stage; they too were developed by Christians (Tiemeier, 2022, p. 149). Anyone who sought to change the conversation would be faced with the power of the white Christian norm, which, as is typically the case, seeks to be reproduced. While some representatives of the world religions were at least in the position to raise their voices, many were simply held at a comfortable distance at the Midway Plaisance, where they were subject to the colonial gaze. I agree with Khyati Joshi who states that any discourse which treats 'foundational ideals of freedom of religion and "all men are created equal" as if they are realities rather than aspirations', facilitates the concealment of the 'dominance of Protestant Christianity' and the continuation of religionization (Joshi, 2020, p. 18).

Text Box 3: Religionization at Work: Code of Indian Offences

The World Religions Paradigm, as well as the parliamentary ideal of interreligious brotherhood, steers attention away from the fact that the religio-racialized distinction between on the one hand religions that are recognized as world religions and on the other primitive, tribal, and indigenous traditions had serious repercussions for people and their traditions. We are not simply dealing with *prejudice*, but with a religionized hegemonic frame that was supported by knowledge produced by scientists and scholars (including scholars of religion). This knowledge was translated into laws which shaped a stratified society, thereby consolidating the discursive distinction between civilized and uncivilized people, people who are 'conversation partners' and people who are to be domesticated, segregated, and educated (Hill Fletcher, 2017b, p. 83).

Exactly a decade before the parliament convened in Chicago to celebrate progress, peace, and brotherhood, the Religious Crimes Code or Code of Indian offences of 1883

> criminalized 'heathenish' native dances and ceremonies and the practices of 'medicine men'. This code deprived Native Americans of their right to religious freedom, the right in which America took so much pride. Offences against the code could lead to punishment, varying from withholding of rations, fines, hard labour, or even jail. The enforcement of this law, which remained in the body of legislation until 1970, was one of the factors leading to the massacre of Big Foot's band at Wounded Knee in 1890 (Price, 1883). The code came into being because of concerns (i) that these practices impeded the civilization and Christianization of Native Americans and (ii) that the native dances incited violence (Talbot, 2006).

Talking Back

The reactions to the parliament varied. There were Christians who feared that the parliament would hamper the Christian claim to being the sole world religion. Among others, the Moderator of the Presbyterian Church, to which Barrows also belonged, rejected the whole initiative: '[...] Christian religion', he stated 'is the one religion. I do not understand how that religion can be regarded as a member of a Parliament of Religions without assuming the equality of the other intended members and the parity of their positions and claims' (Barrows, 1893, p. 22). The Vatican, too, which was in the midst of the modernist crisis, sounded its disapproval, though the real censure followed only after the parliamentary event. Pope Leo XIII (r. 1878–1903) sent a letter, dated 15 September 1895, to Archbishop Francesco Satolli (1839–1910), the first apostolic delegate to the United States, stating that even though meetings of Catholics with non-Catholics had been tolerated thus far, it was nevertheless advisable for Catholics to refrain from engaging in any such 'future promiscuous conventions'. At the parliament itself there were also speakers who contested the whole idea of an interfaith gathering, basing their argument on what we would now call an exclusivist understanding of 'true religion'.

Then of course there were those who came from colonized territories and were concerned that it would be nothing but an extension of the Christians' insatiable desire for expansion. Some of them used the parliament to criticize Christianity's implication in colonization, to question the West's claim to civilization, and to challenge Christianity's missionary hopes. Some called out the intolerance of the missionaries (Dharmapala, a lay Buddhist, 1893), their dogmatism, bigotry, and pride (Nagarkar, a Hindu reformer, 1893) and challenged the way the Christian religion undermined social order (Pung Kwang Yu, secretary of the Chinese Legation in Washington, 1893). One of the most outspoken critics of Christian missionary religion at the parliament was Kinza Hirai, a Buddhist from Japan. He explicitly referenced the anti-Asian prejudices in America and stated:

> *If any religion urges the injustice of humanity, I will oppose it [...] with my blood and soul. I will be the bitterest dissenter from Christianity or I will be the warmest admirer of its gospels. [...] We, the forty million souls of Japan, standing firmly and persistently upon the basis of international justice, await still further manifestations as to the morality of Christianity. (Quoted by Molendijk, 2011, pp. 14–15)*

Another famous attendee, the Hindu monk Swami Vivekananda (1862–1902), turned the table by saying that his religion was tolerant in contrast to the Christian religion, and that India was the cradle of civilization. He said that he was 'proud to belong to a religion which has taught the world both tolerance and universal acceptance. We believe not only in universal toleration, but we accept all religions as true. I am proud to belong to a nation which has sheltered the persecuted and the refugees of all religions and all nations of the earth'.[4] The binaries opposing tolerant and intolerant religion, spiritual and material interests, word and sword, meekness and power, were used and reversed by several of the Asiatic speakers, who 'were engaged in a process of "strategic occidentalism" [...] As a result of this dialectical embrace of both East and West, leading Asians at the parliament held a position that gave them strategic leverage; they were of the East, and thus untainted by the West, yet able to utilize modern and western concepts, values and sentiments to serve their own ends' (Seager, 1995, p. 96). Those coming from the East reversed Christian claims to inclusion, tolerance, and universality and claimed that their religion realized these ideals. At the same time, it is clear that the discourse about tolerant religion also resonated with and emerged from certain Hindu traditions. In any case, these speakers, despite the unequal power dynamics of the fair, showed religious agency; they held up a mirror and confronted Christian 'superiority' (Text Box 4).

> **Text Box 4: Dialogical Reciprocity and the Interruption of Religionization?**
>
> Some see in the criticism expressed at the parliament the power of dialogue to interrupt religionization. The assumption is that, in a dialogical setting, the other is real and disrupts imaginary boundaries which are being drawn between good and bad, true and false religion. Dialogue is supposed to have this power because it centres reciprocity.
>
> To a certain extent this is true; interreligious dialogue can be a space where imaginary constructs, processes of mislabelling, essentialization, and stratification are defied, and where mutual transformation can occur. Nevertheless, dialogue, despite its discourse of reciprocity, often occurs in a context of power imbalance and does not address this political reality.
>
> This was certainly the case at the parliament, which was organized by 'the West' at the height of the colonial era with liberal Christianness as the norm, and this steered attention away from the manner in which systemic injustice impacts dialogue and hinders the ideal of reciprocity. However, this tendency continues to this day. Epistemologically speaking, those who speak back in a dialogical setting continue to be fighting an uphill battle (Moyaert, 2019a). Interreligious discourses which centre the benign notion of fellowship can mask this struggle and can place those who embody the norm in the comfortable position of the status quo, while putting others in the difficult position of having to change the issue, the question, the language. Until interreligious initiatives make the legacies of religionization part of the conversation, discourses of fellowship and equality will continue to function as a cover, masking the realities of (secularized) Christian hegemony (Moyaert, 2023).

Interreligious Brotherhood as a Depoliticized Discourse

By performing interfaith brotherhood rooted in God's fatherhood, the parliament showed how religion is a factor contributing to peace. While religion may incite violence, recognizing that all religions are historical-culturally determined expressions of an innate human religious impulse facilitates interfaith brotherhood. The parliament projects a modern religious norm which, following the religio-secular divide, is supposed to be a-political, a-dogmatic, interiorized, and personal. This ideal is supposedly realized in white American liberal Protestantism.

This projected religionized norm is, however, profoundly political. Indeed, the effort itself to sequester '"religion" as a standalone analytic and classificatory comparative category' was not only integral to the religio-secular divide, but also to the religio-racialized 'scaffolding of colonial modernity' (Omer, 2021). That this tends to go unnoticed in interreligious circles is the consequence of a process of depoliticization, which hampers the critical potential of interreligious encounters. Depoliticization

> *involves construing inequality, subordination, marginalization, and social conflict, which all require political analysis and political solutions, as personal and individual, on the one hand, or as natural, religious, or cultural on the other [...]*

304 CHAPTER 9 The Dialogical Turn beyond Religionization?

> *[Depoliticization] involves removing a political phenomenon from comprehension of its historical emergence and from a recognition of the powers that produce and contour it. No matter its particular form and mechanics, depoliticization always eschews power and history in the representation of its subject. (Brown, 2006, p. 15)*

The discourse and practice of interreligious fellowship coins religion as a cross-cultural, transhistorical, and universal category: the idea that religion is an innate human impulse naturalizes religion, thereby facilitating a dissociation from the historical-cultural powers that were implicated in its production (Puett, 2014, p. 99). In addition, the dialogical turn is presented as the result of a modern emancipatory process, according to which overcoming fanaticism is made possible by the religio-secular divide. This religio-secular divide supposedly restores religion to its true nature, to what it is essentially: interiorized, spiritualized, and personalized. This holds true for Christianity, but also by extension for all religions. Hidden from view is how this particular modern understanding of religion in fact builds on and transforms existing patterns of religionization that are used to disempower social groups, justify exclusion, and even criminalize 'deviant' others and their traditions (see Chapter 8, Text Box 3). Projected as emancipation and restoration, the modern understanding of religion which underpins the ideal of interreligious fellowship has on more than one occasion legitimized religious discrimination. In any case, the historical context from which the World Religions Paradigm arose is veiled. Its configuration of power and concomitant play on inclusion and exclusion are masked and the (secularized) Christian norms that underpin it are simply reproduced. In addition, the ideal of interreligious fellowship as performed at the parliament conceals the modern, colonial, and missionary interactions that enabled the emergence of the world religions and their implicit but normative hierarchical distinction between good (interiorized) and bad religion. Finally, by framing dialogue as a means to prevent or overcome conflict, other factors, such as economic inequality, political instability, religio-racialized oppression, and exclusion are not addressed. When the turn to dialogue, 'brackets a consideration of the genealogies of its basic terms: "religion" (and, relatedly, the "secular") and "peace"' (and, relatedly, 'violence') (Omer, 2021), it lacks the objective, critical potential to redress some of the structural wrongs that are part of the context in which universal brotherhood is performed. Rather than interrupting religionization, it continues it.

2   The Second Vatican Council as a Watershed

Despite all the excitement it evoked at the time, the parliament, for a variety of reasons, not in the least the two world wars, soon fell into oblivion (Seager, 1993) and so did the ideal of interreligious brotherhood. This would only begin to change from the late 1960s onwards, when the 1893 event began to draw renewed attention and was promoted, in hindsight, as a 'pioneer event', a visionary meeting ahead of its time. The moment of rediscovery happens to coincide, more or less, with the period in which the Second Vatican Council (1962–1965) embraced the value of 'dialogue' and underscored the importance of promoting fraternal, ecumenical, and interfaith relations (Betts, 1964; Cleary, 1970; Feldman, 1967). These two, albeit very different, events become associated because of their promotion of friendship among those of different faith traditions. If the parliament supposedly was ahead of its time, Vatican II stirred the hope that people were now finally ready to invest in deep dialogical learning across traditions.

Opening the Windows

On 20 October 1958, Angelo Giuseppe Roncalli became Pope John XXIII (r. 1958–1963). Within three months of his accession, the pope announced that he would convene an ecumenical council, which later came to be known as the Second Vatican Council. In a timespan of three years, spread over four sessions, almost 2,500 bishops deliberated on a variety of topics, before finally voting on 16 binding ecclesial documents (Connelly, 2012, p. 239). If the Roman Catholic mood during the first half of the twentieth century was one of suspicion against all things modern, resulting in the church's political and scientific isolation in Europe, the Second Vatican Council was meant to bring about an *aggiornamento* (update) to bring the church up to date in its communication of the gospel to the world, as well as a *ressourcement*, a return to the authoritative sources.

The style of Vatican II was pastoral and invitational. *Gaudet Mater Ecclesia* [The Mother Church rejoices], the conciliar opening speech, which Pope John XXIII gave on 11 October 1962, exemplifies this mood. Thus, we read that the council seeks to 'defend and advance the Truth' and guard '[...] the sacred deposit of Christian doctrine'; and while the church 'has always opposed [...] errors' and 'condemned them with the greatest severity', in this age, 'the spouse of Christ prefers to make use of the medicine of mercy rather than that of severity [...]. That being so, the Catholic Church, raising the torch of truth by means of this ecumenical council, desires to show herself to be the loving mother of all, benign, patient, full of mercy and goodness toward the brethren separated from her [...]' (*Gaudet Mater Ecclesia*).[5]

Larger Context

Vatican II took place in a context of tension and rapid change. The world was still coming to terms with the consequences of the Second World War and the Shoah, which cost the lives of 6 million Jews (Text Box 5). In the aftermath of the war, the state of Israel was established. While a symbol of hope and resilience for many Jews, it came at the cost of hundreds of thousands of Palestinians being dispossessed of their land. In any case, this political reality destabilized the region. In 1945, in the aftermath of the war, the United Nations was established with the aim of maintaining international peace and security, promoting social progress, and protecting human rights. In 1948, it published the Universal Declaration of Human Rights, which listed the rights to which all human beings were entitled, regardless of race, religion, sex, and so forth. The promulgation of this declaration did not change the fact that a third of the world's population still lived under colonial rule. In the decades following the war, however, European nations lost much of their immediate colonial power. First, India gained independence, soon followed by other countries in South Asia, as well as several African colonies (Howard, 2021). In the wake of decolonization, migration flows from previous colonies to the 'West' began to change the demographic face of Europe and especially some of its major cities, which became increasingly diverse. In the meantime, the Iron Curtain (and the Berlin wall 1961–1989) divided Europe ideologically, militarily, and culturally into a liberal democratic 'West' and a Soviet communist 'East'. The world population feared the arms race and prepared for a nuclear disaster. Finally, in Europe, the effects of secularization were profoundly felt, and the church, because of the Modernist crisis and having lost much of its authority, appeal, and status, was unable to mitigate those effects. Also internationally, the Catholic Church was no longer considered a key political player (Howard, 2021).

Dialogue as a Key Aspect of Christian Self-understanding

The pressing question for the church, deeply impacted by these socio-political changes, was how to reposition itself in this changing world and how to refigure its self-understanding. In response to this question, dialogue became a key identity marker of what it means to be church.

Several conciliar documents elaborate on the theological justification for this dialogical turn; the encyclical *Ecclesiam Suam* (1964),[6] published during the council by Pope Paul VI (r. 1963–1978), is one of them.[7] It placed the 'noble origin of this dialogue [...] in the mind of God Himself. [...] Religion of its very nature is a certain relationship between God and man' which 'finds its expression in prayer', that is itself a form of 'dialogue'. What is more, 'Revelation', the 'supernatural link which God has established with man', can also be regarded 'as a dialogue'. The document goes on to say that '[i]n the Incarnation [...] [it is] God's Word that speaks to us. That fatherly, sacred dialogue between God and man', which was interrupted after the fall, 'has since [...] been restored'. Theologically, 'the whole history of man's salvation is one long, varied dialogue, which [...] begins with God and which He prolongs with men in so many different ways' (*Ecclesiam Suam* 70). It follows that the church too must enter into a dialogue of salvation with all men and women (no. 38). Here, we may notice how the church takes the role of mediator of salvation and continues God's work on earth.[8] *Ecclesiam Suam* continues by stating that this dialogue ought to reach out to mankind in its entirety, also when it rejects God, think of atheists or secular-minded people (no. 97), and to worshippers of the one God, first the Jews, and the Muslims, and finally 'the followers of the great Afro-Asiatic religions' (no. 107). While Christian religion is the 'one true religion' (no. 107), this should not mean that we cannot promote 'common ideals in the spheres of religious liberty' (no. 108). Dialogue is also to be pursued with those 'who take their name from Christ' or fellow Christians (no. 109). Finally, the pope sees the importance of dialogue among Catholics. The document which further elaborates on the dialogue with non-Christian religions is *Nostra Aetate* (Moyaert, 2016b).

Text Box 5: The Myth of the Dialogical Turn after the Shoah

A story that is often told in dialogical circles goes as follows. In the aftermath of the Shoah and confronted with the devastating effects of the genocide of 6 million Jews in Europe, leading to the near eradication of European Jewry, the Roman Catholic Church became convinced of the urgency of revisiting its anti-Jewish teachings – now known as the teaching of contempt (Isaac et al., 1964).

This is not what happened; it is a myth told to bolster a sense of Christianness in the aftermath of the war, and one which steers attention away from the ambivalent role the church played during the war.

Even though there were Catholic people, in all the layers of the church, who spoke up, we also know that during the war there were bishops, priests, monastics, and lay people who felt that what was happening to the Jews was deserved because they had killed Jesus. Moreover, in the years after the war, 'historians surveying Catholic opinion [...] register embarrassed silence: [there was a] disappearance of overt hostility but an absence of ideas as to how to relate to Jews. Even in the few pieces reflecting upon the events of World War II and antisemitism, there was virtually no questioning of the role of the Catholic Church' (Connelly, 2012, pp. 181–182). In addition, when Pope John XXIII, in making preparations for the council, consulted the church asking which questions or issues should certainly be discussed, only 'a handful of the hundreds of proposals for agenda items (*vota*) mentioned Christian-Jewish relations. [...] In over 800 pages of notes sent from Dutch, Belgian, French, English, German, and Polish bishops, not a single suggestion was made to consider Christian-Jewish relations at the Council' (Connelly, 2012, p. 182). Auschwitz had little impact on the way Catholics thought about the Jews and the idea that Jews were malevolent and irredeemable remained pervasive (Valbousquet et al., 2018).

It took the determination of John XXIII, who because of his personal dealings with Jews during his lifetime became convinced of the importance of revisiting Christian-Jewish relations to bring about the ecclesial turnabout at the council. It also took the resolve of the Jewish historian Jules Isaac, who explained the pervasiveness of the teaching of contempt during an audience with the above-mentioned pope, as well as the work of Abraham Joshua Heschel and the influence of the American Jewish Committee, which demanded the church to speak up. It also took the perseverance of Cardinal Bea who, despite adversity, did not give up on the idea of a declaration on the Jews. Furthermore, it took the efforts of several Catholic intellectuals who had already been involved in Christian-Jewish dialogue before and after the war, some of whom functioned as advisors at the council. Many of these advisors were Jewish or Protestant converts to Catholic traditions. This is particularly relevant, because they were able to look at Catholic tradition with fresh eyes and help the council in finding new theological language to talk about Christians in relation to the Jews. That was a tremendous challenge, for even when council fathers warmed to the idea of a declaration on the Jews, it proved difficult to think outside the frame of supersessionism. The church simply possessed no language to break the power of supersessionist patterns of religionization. That *Nostra Aetate* was ultimately possible shows the power of reading one's own tradition through the eyes of others – in this case, dialoguers and converts. This piece of history should alert us to the challenge of dismantling the supersessionist logic that pervades Christian tradition.

Nostra Aetate

Nostra Aetate [*Declaratio de ecclesiae habitudine ad religiones non-christianas*],[9] proclaimed on 28 October 1965, is the shortest document of the Second Vatican Council, consisting of only five paragraphs (Lamberigts & Declerck, 2010). Originally, the intention was to issue a *Decretum de Iudaeis* (Decree on the Jews). However, 'a complicated history of both church politics and secular politics made it necessary that the document include the Muslims and by extension adherents of other religions as well' (Valkenberg, 2019, p. 58). There was the precarious situation in Palestine/Israel to take into consideration, and concerns were expressed, mainly by oriental fathers, about how a declaration centred exclusively on the Jews might affect the position of Christian minorities living in countries with a majority of Muslims (Tauran, 2018, p. 18). Some voices stated that they simply had more dealings with adherents of Islam, Buddhism, and/or Hinduism. Eventually, the scope of the document was extended to cover the relationship of the church to all non-Christian religions (Lamberigts & Declerck, 2010). That adjustment took considerable deliberation, as a result of which the document was only approved during the final session of the council (Text Box 6).

Nostra Aetate became a document that intends to promote 'unity and love among men, indeed among nations' (no. 1). Rather than focusing on what non-Christians lack or why they should take up a position of inferiority, *Nostra Aetate*, following a logic of encompassment, concentrates on building common ground. The declaration emphasizes that all people belong to one human community: all are created by God and all share the same 'final goal, God'. God's 'providence, His manifestations of goodness, His saving design extend to all men' (no. 1). Here too, human fellowship is rooted in God's fatherhood and Christians ought to behave accordingly. Much later, Pope Francis would state in his encyclical letter *Fratelli Tutti* that the believers of all religions are at the service of fraternity in the world.[10] Dialogue is not only a Christian concern, but a concern of all.

Text Box 6: Finding New Language

The Second Vatican Council opts out of a binary pattern of religionization, which contrasted true and false religion and which viewed the world as consisting of Christians, Jews, Muslims, and pagans (Schmidt-Leukel, 2013, p. 127). It embraces the idea that there are multiple religions in the world, which all spring from a universal human longing for God. We know from previous chapters that this is not new (cf. natural theology, *consensus gentium,* and *prisca theologia*) and that in this inclusive ethnoreligious reasoning, 'all' are children of the Father God, and therefore we are all brothers (and should act accordingly, and converse). We saw this discourse of interreligious brotherhood at work at the World Parliament of Religions. At the same time, the notion of 'non-Christian' continues to project Christianity (here Catholic religion) as the default position. There is one true religion, the Christian religion. In *Nostra Aetate*, the other religions are still grouped together, with further differentiation but based on what they are not, hence the label 'non-Christian'. This is a negative label, which makes sense only from a Christian perspective. Significantly – and this testifies to the power of interfaith dialogue and being in the proximity of the other – the inadequacy of this label would become increasingly clear, and the label 'non-Christian' is now hardly used.

308 CHAPTER 9 The Dialogical Turn beyond Religionization?

The declaration continues by stating that

The Catholic Church rejects nothing that is true and holy in these religions [quae in his religionibus vera et sancta]. She regards with sincere reverence those ways of conduct and of life, those precepts and teachings which, though differing in many aspects from the ones she holds and sets forth, nonetheless often reflect a ray of that Truth [radium illius Veritatis] which enlightens all men [quae illuminat omnes homines]. (no. 2)

That *Veritas* [truth] is written with a capital 'V' here, and in the singular, indicates that the Truth in other religions is of divine origin and not purely the fruit of a human quest for meaning (O'Collins, 2014, p. 163). Where the text speaks about what is true and holy in the other religions, *vera* [true] is written with a small 'v'. In this way, the document indicates that what is true in other traditions cannot surpass the Truth that alone enlightens the whole of humanity (Moyaert, 2016b, pp. 58–59). This passage harks back to earlier theologies of encompassment revolving around the universal power of the divine *logos*, operative throughout human history and sowing seeds among peoples and their traditions (*logos spermatikoi*). It follows, however, that 'because the Christian *logos* was the original source of all truth, anything true was necessarily Christian' (Chidester, 2000). All that is true is included in the Truth revealed in Christ and preserved in the church. This paragraph ends by saying that

The Church, therefore, exhorts her sons, that through dialogue and collaboration with the followers of other religions, carried out with prudence and love and in witness to the Christian faith and life, they recognize, preserve and promote the good things, spiritual and moral, as well as the socio-cultural values found among these men. (no. 2)

Nostra Aetate continues by stating that in Christ, who is 'the way, the truth, and the life', human beings find the 'fullness of religious life' (no. 2). However, fullness is not contrasted with emptiness: rather, other religions contain partial truths of what was fully revealed by God in Christ, and they foreshadow what is fulfilled in Christ. Thus, non-Christian religions may function as *praeparatio evangelica* (see also *Lumen Gentium* 16). While dialogue is part of the church's mission to testify to the gospel in the world, it does not replace proclamation, the aim of which is to convert non-Christians. The church is called to proclaim the gospel and to invite those of other faiths to accept Christ through baptism (no. 2).

So what does the declaration say about these non-Christian religions? First, there are the 'various peoples [among whom is present] a certain perception of that hidden power which hovers over the course of things and over the events of human history'. Sometimes, these people 'have come to the recognition of a Supreme Being, or even of a Father. This perception and recognition penetrates their lives with a profound religious sense' (no. 2). There is no people that is entirely deprived of a sense of the divine, and to this extent all peoples are religious. Next, *Nostra Aetate* values those traditions that have sought to answer these deep human questions 'by means of more refined concepts and a more developed language' (no. 2). Here, the document seems to rank traditions according to the normative assumptions of the World Religions Paradigm: it has a higher appreciation for those religions with an intellectual tradition of philosophical/theological reflections – the so-called world religions, which via their textual traditions have had a major impact on the progress of culture (Text Box 7). *Nostra Aetate* goes on – and this is a first – to mention Hinduism and Buddhism. In Hinduism, as *Nostra Aetate* puts it, 'men contemplate the divine mystery and express it through an inexhaustible abundance of myths and through searching philosophical inquiry. They seek freedom from the anguish of our human condition either through ascetical practices or profound meditation or a flight to God with love and trust' (no. 2). Third, *Nostra Aetate* says that Buddhism 'in its various forms, realizes the radical insufficiency of this changeable world; it teaches a way by which men, in a devout and confident spirit, may be able either to acquire the state of perfect liberation, or attain, by their own efforts or through higher help, supreme illumination'.

Text Box 7: Religionizing Non-Christians and the Possibility of Dialogical Interruption

The document follows the logic of the World Religions Paradigm and the idea that there are five world religions: Judaism, Christianity, Islam, Buddhism, and Hinduism. As argued before, the World Religions Paradigm mapped onto the Christian idea of natural religion by projecting all human beings as religious. In the conciliar framework, these traditions are now recognized as conversation partners in search of Truth (*Semina Verbi*). Christianity, however, sets the norm: in Christ the fullness of truth is revealed. Other religions are religionized into world religions, but Roman Catholic Christianity is 'the' religion. This also explains the organization of the religions into concentric circles. This organization intersects with modern ideas of civilization and more and less advanced cultures.[11] No explicit reference is made here to traditional African religions, nor to the traditions of Native Americans or Australian Aboriginals, who supposedly have not developed major philosophical or theological systems. The distinction between oral and textual, primitive and advanced, tribal and world traditions still prevails. This is a criticism that was already heard during the council. African bishops on the conciliar commission advocated that the document mentions animism, an umbrella term covering all the indigenous practices. But this request was not heeded (Oesterreicher, 1969, p. 86).

The World Religions Paradigm, which underpins the dialogical turn, thus created a boundary which has proven difficult to overcome in dialogical settings. To this day, most interfaith initiatives privilege representatives of the 'world religions', and have difficulties including voices from other traditions. Interreligious dialogue also struggles with the question of how to relate to adherents of oral traditions, which are more ritually oriented (Moyaert, 2016a). At the same time, *Nostra Aetate* itself did not intend to be exhaustive. It was an invitation to learn more about different traditions, also those that are not mentioned. Already in 1969, the Secretariat for Non-Christians published a brochure entitled *Meeting the African Religions*. Still later, there were letters (1988, 1993) by the Pontifical Council for Interreligious Dialogue that dealt specifically with traditional religions, 'those religions which, unlike the world religions that have spread into many countries and cultures, have remained in their original socio-cultural environment' and that are present in Africa, Oceania, and the Americas (1993). After *Nostra Aetate*, there has been an attempt to find appropriate language that does justice to these traditions. That is also the power of dialogue, which creates a setting (i) in which real others, albeit often from a position of power inequality, can contest these boundaries and challenge the religionized framework into which they are forced, and (ii) whereby, because of the self-understanding of Christianity in terms of the dialogical, the church itself can no longer ignore such contestation without losing epistemic and moral credibility.

The third paragraph expresses esteem for Muslims [*Muslimos*], who 'adore the one God, living and subsisting in Himself; merciful and all-powerful, the Creator of heaven and earth, who has spoken to men; they take pains to submit wholeheartedly to even His inscrutable decrees, just as Abraham, with whom the faith of Islam takes pleasure in linking itself, submitted to God' (see also *Lumen Gentium* 16). The document is ambiguous about the precise relationship between Abraham and the Muslims and does not affirm the Muslim claim to biblical and historical filiation to Abraham. Nothing is said about Ishmael, the son of Abraham and Hagar, who in Islamic tradition is the ancestor of Muslims. In all likelihood, 'the Council did not want to explicitly recognize that Muslims are sons of Ishmael *and*, in turn, implicitly include them in biblical revelation [...]' (Moreland, 2020, Chapter 2). *Nostra Aetate* does not mention Muhammad the prophet either, and remains vague about how God 'has spoken to men'. On the one hand, the council fathers 'did not want to give the impression that they agreed that God had spoken through Muhammad' (Moreland, 2020,

Chapter 2). On the other, in order not to offend the Muslims, they did not want to outright deny Muhammed's claim to prophecy. *Nostra Aetate* appreciates that Muslims (i) acknowledge Jesus as a prophet; (ii) honour Mary; (iii) also await the day of judgment, and (iv) lead a highly moral life in which almsgiving, prayer, and fasting – three of the five pillars – occupy a central place. The other two pillars – witness and pilgrimage – were presumably too closely linked with the prophet. The paragraph ends with a recognition of the particularly troubled history of Christian-Muslim relations and the hope that it will be possible to leave the past behind (Text Box 8).

Text Box 8: Finding New Language to Name Muslims

In *Nostra Aetate*, Muslims are called neither Saracens nor Mohammedans, terms which had been used in previous settings in a derogatory way. Establishing friendly interfaith relations begins by using language which does justice to the self-understanding of the people implicated. Naming was part of the process of religionization, and the label 'Mohammedan' was, for example, taken from Christians projecting the idea that Muslims were heretics following a false prophet. Now, they become our [Christians'] brothers and sisters, created by the same Father God.

Nevertheless, it has remained difficult to make theological sense of Islam in the larger history of salvation and revelation. In the aftermath of *Nostra Aetate*, comparative theologians of religion have picked up the question about the theological meaning of Muhammad and the Qur'an and how to deal with conflicting truth claims related to God, Christ, prophecy, and revelation (Moreland, 2020; Stosch & Khorchide, 2016). What is the meaning of Islam in God's plan of salvation?

Finally, the longest paragraph centres on the attitude of the church towards the Jews. This paragraph breaks with supersessionist theologies which projected the Jewish people as accursed because of 'its' rejection of Christ. *Nostra Aetate* stresses the continuity between Jewish and Christian tradition and undoes the *de-Judaization* of the origins of Christianity. Nevertheless, the document continues to place the relationship between Jews and Christians in a typological frame contrasting old people and new people, old covenant and new covenant, exodus and Christ event. 'Jews remain faithful to God', even though this recognition is immediately modified: 'because of the patriarchs'. 'The Church', according to *Nostra Aetate* 4, 'cannot forget that she received the revelation of the Old Testament through the people with whom God in His inexpressible mercy concluded the Ancient Covenant. Nor can she forget that she draws sustenance from the root of that well-cultivated olive tree onto which have been grafted the wild shoots, the gentiles (Rom 11:17–24)'.

Thinking through the precise nature of the relation between the Jewish people and the church, without lapsing back into ethnoreligious binaries that contrast tribal/exclusivist Jews and universal/inclusive Christians, binaries which reintroduce simplistic contrasts between the law and the spirit, remains challenging to this day (Horrell, 2020). Thinking fulfilment without replacement is difficult (Moyaert & Pollefeyt, 2010): How does one avoid projecting God's covenant with the church as universal, inclusive, open, and spiritual whereas God's covenant with Israel is particular, tribal, ethnic, and legalistic, an image which is not that far removed from what Renan suggested when he likewise claimed that 'Israel was the trunk on which was grafted the faith of mankind'? (see p. 274). Thinking outside the frame of anti-Jewish patterns of religionization is an ongoing project.

The document then turns its attention to the fact that Jesus, Mary, the first apostles, and many of the first disciples sprang from the Jewish people, to whom 'the glory and the covenants and the law and the worship and the promises' belong. That many Jews did not accept Jesus does not take away the fact that the Jews are dear to God in the present and that God 'does not repent of the gifts He makes or of the calls He issues'. Furthermore, 'what happened in His [Christ's] passion cannot be charged against all the Jews, without distinction, then alive, nor against the Jews of today'. Furthermore, the church teaches that 'Christ underwent His passion and death freely, because of the sins of men and out of infinite love, in order that all may reach salvation' (no. 4). This is a rejection of the 'deicide' charge.

Text Box 9: Finding New Language to Name Jews and Muslims

One of the challenges with regard to paragraph 4, was finding the 'right' language to talk about the Jews; language which – contrary to the history of religionization – does justice to the self-understanding of the Jewish people. The commitment to emphasize the religious bond between Christianity and Judaism was clear, but doing so in a way that is appropriate to Jewish self-understanding, while being sensitive to various complexities, proved difficult. On the one hand, any language that is or might be interpreted as implicated in antisemitism was to be avoided. This excluded the words 'the Jewish race' but also the word 'Semites'. On the other hand, it was important to emphasize both the religious and the ethnic dimensions of Jewish identity, so 'Jewish people' (not religious enough) or 'the Jews' or 'Synagogue' (too exclusively religious) would not be appropriate. The evident choice, namely 'Israel', was ruled out for political reasons. In early drafts, trying to balance these complexities, the church spoke of itself in relation to the Jews as 'a continuation of that people with whom of old God, out of his ineffable mercy, was pleased to make his Old Covenant'.[12] This solution is a non-solution, because as John Connelly explains, it 'was as though [...] the Jewish people had been erased from history' (Connelly, 2012, p. 259). In the end, a solution was found by calling the Jews, 'Abraham's stock'. This has both a religious and an ethnic quality, without being political or racist.

Next to the Jews, *Nostra Aetate* also associates the Muslims with the figure of Abraham, albeit in a somewhat ambiguous way – Muslims claim that their faith is Abraham's faith – but this claim is not explicitly endorsed. Ishmaelite genealogy is not mentioned in the discussion of Islam. As Anna Moreland explains, doing so would have included them in God's covenantal history of revelation (Moreland, 2020). While Jews and Christians are children of Abraham, this is not said of Muslims (see below for a nuance). Thus, Muslims are not included in Abraham's genealogy because it has significant theological implications. Even in a context of dialogue and openness, boundaries are created and recreated.

While *Nostra Aetate* (and other conciliar documents) did not want to explicitly include Muslims in Abraham's genealogy, it is not so that Christian tradition has always excluded Muslims from Abraham's genealogy, quite the contrary. John of Damascus and Peter the Venerable (1092–1156), to mention two examples, did not see any problem in calling Muslims 'Ishmaelites'. The notion of 'Saracens', which prevailed for centuries, was coined to state that Muslims falsely claimed to descend from Sarah, while they actually descended from Hagar, with whom Abraham fathered Ishmael. In a polemical context, there was no problem in using such ethnoreligious discourses, but at the time of *Nostra Aetate*, the council fathers deemed such genealogy theologically problematic because it was too inclusive.

Clearly, the dialogical turn has not halted the genealogical struggle about who precisely are the children of Abraham (Hughes, 2012), and boundaries continue to be negotiated. Part of this ongoing negotiation is the changed perception of Jews and Muslims in Christian imaginaries: for a long time Jews and Muslims shared a similar place in Christian supersessionist imagination as children of Hagar (or Semites, even though this category did not find its way into official ecclesial documents), but now Jews occupy a unique place in God's plan of salvation (they are the root of the olive tree onto which the church is grafted), while the position of Muslims remains unclear.

Following *Nostra Aetate* however, the notion of the Abrahamic religions has become more established and today we even find Pope Francis praying for the children of Abraham – Jews, Christians, and Muslims – which implies again a shift in the ethnoreligious reasoning of the church compared to *Nostra Aetate* and *Lumen Gentium*.[13] By embracing the notion of 'Abrahamic', Pope Francis reacts against the exclusion of Muslims from a Judeo-Christian story line. The theological implications of this shift are not entirely clear.

From the perspective of Muslims, too, the notion of Abrahamic religions, is ambivalent. Like all interfaith notions which project an inclusive ideal of brotherhood, it brings people together and coins the idea that we belong to the same family. In a context where, especially after 9/11, Muslims are singled out as Europe's others, this is a way to 'soften' Muslims' otherness. At the same time however, this image can mask the reality of Islamophobia.

The paragraph on the Jews ends with the church rejecting 'every persecution against any man [...]' and deploring 'hatred, persecutions, displays of anti-Semitism, directed against Jews at any time and by anyone'.

In the final paragraph, this point is broadened to reject any form of 'discrimination against men, or harassment of them because of their race, color, condition of life, or religion' [*stirpis vel coloris, condicionis vel religionis causa*] as 'foreign to the mind of Christ' (no. 5).

Already in his encyclical *Pacem in Terris* [Peace on Earth] (1963), Pope John XXIII had provided a framework in which to discuss fundamental human rights, emphasizing the human dignity and equality of all people and acknowledging the Universal Declaration of Human Rights (1948). This encyclical paved the way for the conciliar document *Dignitatis Humanae*, which, starting from an affirmation of the 'dignity of the human person' (no. 1), argues in favour of the free exercise of religion in society.[14] Such freedom is necessary for 'men [*sic*] to fulfil their duty to worship God'. This, furthermore, is in line with the gospel itself and the example set by Christ Jesus, who himself was 'meek', 'humble of heart' and an example of 'patience' (no. 11). Christ sought to arouse faith, not exert coercion (no. 16). Here Roman Catholicism finally accepts the religio-secular divide and becomes a religion in the modern meaning of the word. Where exactly the boundary between the secular and religious might lie is not always clear; it even seems that the affirmation of the religio-secular divide enabled the church to re-establish itself in the world, both among religious and political leaders.

The Institutionalization of Dialogue

The Second Vatican Council, and *Nostra Aetate* in particular, projected a profound reconfiguration of Christian identity, one which immediately impacted the understanding of Christianity's others, who were no longer heretics or pagans, Christ-killers or Saracens, but were made into dialogue partners. For this altered sense of Christianness to become more than hollow phrases, it had to be institutionalized; it had to become an intrinsic part of the church's policy and to that end the church had to practise what it preached.

In May 1964, months before the official approval of *Nostra Aetate*, Pope Paul VI established the Secretariat for Non-Christians, which would later be re-named the Pontifical Council for Interreligious Dialogue, and is now known as the Dicastery for Interreligious Dialogue. Thus, dialogue became an institutionalized ecclesial activity. At the time, in a language which would now no longer be used, the pope stated that it was the task of this Secretariat to focus its attention on those who are 'without the Christian religion'. The pontifical council was meant as an 'outward sign' marking the interest of the church in people who belong to other religious traditions: they matter, they exist, they are seen. To this day, the dicastery supports concrete dialogical initiatives throughout the world, produces guidelines on how to conduct dialogue with non-Christians, publishes a journal *Pro Dialogo*, and seeks to form people who are committed to dialogue and to promoting the study of other religions. It has also published 'several additional specific guideline booklets [...] bearing titles such as *Religions: Fundamental Themes for a Dialogistic Understanding* (1970), *Towards the Meeting with Buddhism* (1970), and *Guidelines for Dialogue between Muslims and Christians* (1969)' (Howard, 2021, Chapter 4). The dicastery also sends delegates to interfaith encounters, organizes both bilateral and multilateral encounters, and invites leaders of other religions to take part. Significantly, it does not work in isolation from other Christian bodies, and collaborates intensively with the World Evangelical Alliance as well as with the World Council of Churches, which since 1970 has also embraced the cause of interreligious dialogue.

The institutionalization of the dialogical turn also had repercussions for Catholic and other faculties of theology, which began to take an increased interest in the field of theologies of religions, interreligious dialogue, and later comparative theology. The knowledge produced about Judaism and more precisely the relation between Judaism and Christianity proliferated. New courses were integrated into the curriculum, dissertations written, articles and books published. Research centres for dialogue were established, conferences organized, and various journals, as well as series, saw the light. At a grassroots level, a large number of interreligious groups came into existence, in which believers from different traditions read each other's sacred writings, prayed together, or joined forces to address shared ethical challenges (poverty, social exclusion, etc.). Indeed, Vatican approval and promotion of interfaith engagement implies that the 600 million Catholics around the globe are directly invited by their church's highest authority to engage in such activities. Protestant churches too shouldered the dialogical turn.

The Ritualization of Dialogue

In the past, following the understanding that the other upheld deviant beliefs and practices that could bring harm to the *Corpus Christianum*, practices of separation and rituals of purgation helped to establish boundaries between us and them. Now, in order for dialogue to become real, a counter liturgical formation had to be initiated, one which would profoundly reshape Christians in their fundamental attitudes and relations to others, the world, and God. The sedimented knowledge that had been inscribed on the habitual body has to be un-written, and new knowledge acquired. To that end, new symbols and symbolic practices, expressing respect, appreciation, hospitality, and fellowship, were developed. More than any ecclesial documents, such ritual actions 'remain as icons speaking to people's mind and heart' (Catalano, 2022). Gradually, a new religionized norm based on a changed Christian self-understanding has emerged, one which not only set the tone for Catholic Christians, but also for followers of other religions, both in Europe and beyond.[15] As always, the institutionalization of a new norm goes together with contestation and conflict.

Changes in the Good Friday Liturgy   For centuries, following the supersessionist logic, the Jews were called 'perfidious'. This was also the case in the prayer for the Jews during the intercessions on Good Friday. In 1959, Pope John XXIII deleted the term *perfidi* from the prayer for the Jews (Lamberigts & Declerck, 2010) and in 1970, following the liturgical renewal that was initiated at the Second Vatican Council, the Good Friday prayer underwent an even more profound change (Moyaert & Pollefeyt, 2010):

Good Friday prayer 1948	Good Friday prayer 1970
Let us pray also for the *perfidious Jews* that Almighty God may remove *the veil from their hearts*; so that they too may acknowledge Jesus Christ our Lord. Almighty and eternal God, who dost not exclude from thy mercy even Jewish faithlessness: hear our prayers, which we offer for the *blindness of that people*; that acknowledging the *light of thy Truth, which is Christ, they may be delivered from their darkness*. Through the same Lord Jesus Christ, who lives and reigns with thee in the unity of the Holy Spirit, God, for ever and ever. Amen.	Let us pray for *the Jewish people, the first to hear the word of God*, that they may continue *to grow in the love of his name and in faithfulness to his covenant*. Almighty and eternal God, long ago you gave your promise to Abraham and his posterity. Listen to your church as we pray *that the people you first made your own may arrive at the fullness of redemption*. We ask this through Christ our Lord. Amen

The 1970 missal speaks of the Jewish people in clearly positive wording and it recognizes the soteriological priority of the Jewish people in God's salvific plan. God approached Israel first. Israel is the chosen people that 'God elevates in love for Gods name'. In this new version of the Good Friday prayer, the church no longer prays for the conversion of the Jews to Christianity. Moreover, the 1970 prayer for the Jews mirrors the prayer of the church for itself. In this way, the church indicates that it has not yet arrived at complete salvation itself and recognizes that it is not the church but only God who determines the how and the when of salvation. The completion of salvation is placed in an explicitly eschatological perspective.

Given that Good Friday was for a long time the most dangerous day of the year for Jews, this was an important symbolic act. It was by no means unknown for this liturgical memorial of Christ's death to spark spontaneous or even orchestrated outbursts of anger against the Jewish population, who were thought to be collectively guilty for the death of Christ. Now, the Jews are liturgically recognized as God's beloved people (Text Box 10).

Text Box 10: The Good Friday Controversy

In 1570, Pope Paul V (r. 1605–1621) established the Tridentine rite as the standard liturgy for the Catholic Mass. Up until the Second Vatican Council this rite remained the norm. This old missal has been replaced by the new missal by Pope Paul VI in 1970. However, a small minority of Catholics stuck to the old Tridentine rite even after the council. In 2007, Pope Benedict XVI (r. 2005–2013) formally rehabilitated the old missal through the *motu proprio Summorum Pontificum* as an extraordinary form of the Latin rite. The 1970 Roman Missal would remain the ordinary form of expression.

Even though, at first sight, the decision involved a mere internal Christian matter, this papal initiative ignited concern and irritation among Jews. Catholics engaged in Jewish-Christian dialogue also experienced this *motu proprio* as a step back (Heinz & Brandt, 2008, p. 160). Some feared that the re-evaluation of this old missal would lead to a re-introduction of the classic Good Friday prayer, including the 1948 missal which prays for the 'perfidious Jews'. In reaction, on 28 January 2008, the pope made it known that he intended to write a new prayer, in which he would take into account the sensitivities on the Jewish side, rather than insert the 1970 version into the old missal. The renewed version of the Good Friday prayer is in fact a reformulation of the 1962 missal's Good Friday prayer: 'Let us pray also for the Jews. That our Lord and God may *enlighten their hearts*, that they may *acknowledge Jesus Christ as the savior of all men*. Almighty [...] who wills that all men would be saved [...] grant that all Israel may be saved when the fullness of the nations enter into Your Church. Through Christ Our Lord. Amen'.

Contrary to the 1970 missal, this revised Good Friday prayer appeals for the conversion of the Jews to Christ. Even though the word 'conversion' is not mentioned in the text, it is implied in the petition for 'enlightenment' of the Jews. The notion of 'enlightenment' gives the impression that the Jewish people still find themselves in 'darkness'. This recalls the 1948 Good Friday prayer and the trope of the veil.

The Good Friday controversy led there being two authorized Good Friday prayers in the Catholic Church, both exuding their distinctive theological spirit. This controversy showed (i) the continuing power of age-old patterns of religionization, (ii) how the dialogical turn sets in motion a process of theological contestation as to the precise relationship between church and Israel in God's plan for salvation and (iii) the power of dialogue: the criticisms expressed by Jews were heard and taken into account, to the extent that a new prayer was written (Moyaert & Pollefeyt, 2010). In July 2021, Pope Francis abrogated the *Summorum Pontificum* issued by Pope Benedict XVI with the *motu proprio Traditionis Custodes*.

Interfaith Blessings

In 1967, for the first time, Vatican radio broadcast a message of good wishes to the Muslims on the occasion of *Eid al-Fitr*, the feast marking the end of Ramadan. Since then, the dicastery has sent an annual greeting on this occasion, and sometimes the pope sends a personal greeting. This practice was later extended to include the major world faiths on their important holidays or periods of fasting. Of course, the content of these messages is important, but the gesture itself is just as important. It is a ritualized expression of recognition and respect: we know this is an important time for you and we wish you well. The dialogical virtue of empathy is expressed here in 'sharing other people's joy at a feast' (Sperber, 2019, p. 235). The binary of us and them – Christians versus Jews, Muslims, and pagans – was transformed into a communion of co-journeyers. Consider, just by way of example, the following blessing sent on the occasion of the Feast of *Vesakh*, which commemorates the birth, enlightenment, and death of the Buddha.

> *Dear friends, your religious tradition inspires the conviction that friendly relations [...] and the [...] exchange of views lead to attitudes of kindness and love which [...] generate [...] fraternal relationships [...]. As Buddhists and Christians, we live in a world all too often torn apart by [...] selfishness, tribalism [...] violence and religious fundamentalism [...] Drawing upon our different religious convictions, we are called [...] to be healers who enable others [...] to be reconcilers who break down the walls of division and foster genuine brotherhood [...]. Let us [...] meet each other in order to establish a culture of dialogue in the world [...]![16]*

Greetings, however trifling they may seem at first glance, are part of a ritualized cultivation of a dialogical identity: to be church means to be related to you; to be related to you means that what matters to you concerns us. To be dialogical is the opposite of being indifferent.

John Paul II Visits the Synagogue of Rome

On 13 April 1986, having visited and prayed at the Auschwitz concentration camp in 1979, where he kneeled in prayer in front of the Death Wall, Pope John Paul II (r. 1978–2005) made the first ever official papal visit to a synagogue, the Great Synagogue in Rome to be precise. He was welcomed in an act of 'hospitality' by the Italian capital's chief rabbi, Elio Toaff (1915–2015). During his visit, the pope explained that '[w]ith Judaism [...] we have a relationship which we do not have with any other religion. You are our dearly beloved brothers, and in a certain way it could be said you are our elder brothers'.[17] He also reiterated the words of *Nostra Aetate*, that the church deplores the 'hatred, persecutions, [and] displays of anti-Semitism directed against the Jews at any time and by anyone', and he repeated 'by anyone'. The pope emphasizes that he seeks 'to overcome old prejudices and to secure a [...] recognition of that "bond" and that "common spiritual patrimony that exists between Jews and Christians"'. He expressed the hope that the relations between the two communities will be 'animated by fraternal love'. John Paul II ended his speech with a prayer said in Hebrew from the Psalmist (118:1–4), which affirms the steadfast love of Israel, thus rejecting anti-Jewish ideas which claimed that Israel was no longer beloved by God.

During the ceremony, the pope and the chief rabbi sat side by side on the same level on identical thrones and read in turns from the Psalms, acknowledging 'co-ownership of the shared scriptural tradition'. Compare this to the idea that the Jewish people was blind to the deeper meaning of its own scriptures or had lost any role of significance in God's plan of salvation. What is being performed here is a co-covenanted relationship of some sort. Rather than *Synagoga* being a superseded storyline in a Christian theological frame which projects *Ecclesia* as God's people, the supersessionist logic is reversed and *Ecclesia* (represented by the pope) acknowledges its place as guests in the story line begun between God and Israel (Jennings, 2010). The 1986 visit represented a 'symbolic ceding of power on the part of the Catholic Church, in which the pope relinquished the ceremonial authority derived from ownership of the space of encounter [...]. [This ritual] gesture [...] opens up a world of significance that verbal discourse cannot entertain' (Vincent, 2019, p. 186). Pope John Paul II,

316 CHAPTER 9 The Dialogical Turn beyond Religionization?

in doing what no pope had done before him, paved the way for the next popes, Pope Benedict XVI and Pope Francis, who likewise visited the Great Synagogue of Rome. When Pope Francis visited the synagogue, the rabbi welcomed him saying, that 'according to rabbinic tradition, an act that is repeated three times – in this case, the papal visits to the Great Synagogue of Popes John Paul II, Benedict XVI, and now Francis – becomes a *chazaqà*, a set habit' (Brandfon, 2023, p. 273).

The Day of Prayer in Assisi Many will recall the pontificate of John Paul II because of the day of prayer, which was held in October 1986, and which, for the first time, brought together religious leaders from various traditions. Today, we have become used to this picture of religious leaders not only meeting one another but also praying side by side; we think of this as 'normal'. At the time, this was a ground-breaking and unique gesture that spoke to the imagination. A church, which not that long before had cautioned against any participation in dialogical activities, now took the initiative and invited the leaders of various religions to Assisi, in Italy. If in the past Christian sanctuaries had to be purged of the contaminating presence of non-Christians, now the latter were hospitably received in the hometown of St Francis, who, since *Nostra Aetate*, has been promoted as the patron saint of dialogue (1182–1226). Furthermore, the pope (as host) also welcomed the prayers of these religious leaders, hoping that they would invoke from God 'the gift of peace', a phrase which John Paul II used many times.

After an opening event, at which the pope set out the goal of the meeting, all participants went their separate ways, to various churches and monasteries in the city of Assisi where they prayed for peace according to their own rites. Afterwards, they walked silently to the lower piazza of the church of St. Francis. There the religious leaders presented their prayers and committed themselves in silent mediation to help bring about peace. Together, they performed what 'proper religious conduct' had become following the dialogical turn: working together, collaborating rather than competing, and embracing the cause of peace. In the pope's words

> *The world religions, despite the fundamental differences that divide them, are*
> *all called to contribute to the birth of a more humane, just, and fraternal world.*
> *Having often been the cause of divisions, they all now wish to play a decisive role in*
> *building world peace. [...] If from all human hearts the desire for peace and universal*
> *brotherhood rises up to the one God, united as in one great prayer, then we can never*
> *lack the confidence that he will hear us [...].[18]*

Given that 1986 was the UN year of peace, these religious leaders sent the message to political, read secular, leaders, that there 'exists another dimension of peace and another way of promoting it, which is not a result of negotiations, political compromises or economic bargaining. It is the result of prayer, which, in the diversity of religions, expresses a relationship with a supreme power that surpasses our human capacities alone'.[19] While not all were happy with this initiative and critics accused the pope of syncretism and indifferentism (relativism), since that time the prayer for peace as performed in Assisi has been repeated on several occasions, and it has become a model for similar initiatives in the secular realm.

The Dialogical Turn and the Renegotiation of the Religio-secular Divide

In the aftermath of *Nostra Aetate*, ecclesial authorities have called other religious leaders as well as political leaders to account for the marginalized position of Christian minorities in their societies. Projecting the ideal of religious freedom, they hold them to this standard to improve the predicament of Christians. Sometimes, religious leaders have joined hands to call secular authorities to account for the marginalization of religion and its visible expressions (e.g. in the public domain) in secularized societies. Significantly, religious actors, like the pope, have also used the human rights frame to hold European and other political authorities accountable for failing to live up to their own standards, for example when it comes to the refugee crisis. Pope Francis' symbolic gesture of washing the feet of refugees – Christians, Muslims, and Hindus – on Maundy Thursday is both an act expressing interfaith brotherhood and a public condemnation of European policies which result in the dehumanization of refugees. He appealed for concrete political action to deal with migration issues in a more human way. Thus, the religio-secular divide is both embraced and contested, and renegotiated in a context of dialogue. In my reading, this is made most explicit in the encyclical, *Fratelli Tutti* (2020), which reads:

> *For these reasons, the Church, while respecting the autonomy of political life, does not restrict her mission to the private sphere. On the contrary, 'she cannot and must not remain on the sidelines' in the building of a better world, or fail to 'reawaken the spiritual energy' that can contribute to the betterment of society. [...] [R]eligious ministers [...] can [not] renounce the political dimension of life itself, which involves a constant attention to the common good and a concern for integral human development. The Church 'has a public role over and above her charitable and educational activities'. She works for the advancement of humanity and of universal fraternity. (Fratelli Tutti, no. 276)*[20]

Depending on the context and the actors involved, the invocation of universal fraternity has the power to challenge the political status quo or to reinforce it.

The refiguration of Christian identity in terms of dialogue enabled the church 'to acquire new public visibility and recognition. To some extent, through fostering interreligious dynamics, the church has also carved out a place for religion in the secular public domain' (Griera & Nagel, 2018, p. 306). Being dialogical in a decolonizing and globalizing world, the church reclaimed its role of being a moral light in the world and a reference point for others. 'We' – Christians – have retrieved our dialogical nature (cf. *Ecclesiam Suam*) and now the world should follow this lead if we are to overcome the history of interreligious violence. 'We' – Christians – have faced our problematic expressions of religion (e.g. anti-Jewish bias, prejudice, ...), and now others should do so too. The church respects other religions, and so should others. Not to participate in dialogue is to place oneself outside the realm of peaceful religion and universal fraternal love and civilization. Not to participate in dialogue is to perform bad, problematic, and perhaps even fanatical religion. Against this background, the real religious other is the non-dialogical other, the fundamentalist, the fanatic, the exclusivist.

While dialogue, like tolerance, is a benign ideal, it is also a depoliticized ideal, which steers attention away from more complex realities (Brown, 2006). By naturalizing true religion in terms of dialogical religion, by sequestering religion as a domain separate from other secular domains, and by centring non-dialogical religion as the cause of religious intolerance and violence, we are not inquiring into other economic, political, historical factors leading up to violence, like colonial legacies, capitalist oppression, legal inequalities, and so forth. The myth of religious violence, which is a key part of the religio-secularization is reproduced (Cavanaugh, 2009). If the church positions itself as a light in the world setting the example of dialogue, does this distract from its role in the history of religionization, which was a profoundly political history? Should we not ask if dialogue (a discursive exchange between religious believers) is the road to peace? Should this model be exported and implemented? Are there alternative forms of interreligious relations that work in other contexts? (Swamy, 2017). Should it not concern us that the dialogical turn shapes and reshapes religion as belief-oriented – something that can be discussed rather than something practiced, ritualized, and materialized? Should the genealogy of dialogical religion and its underpinning patterns of religionization not itself be problematized?

318 CHAPTER 9 The Dialogical Turn beyond Religionization?

> **Text Box 11: The Dialogical Turn as an Interruption of Religionization?**
>
> *Nostra Aetate* profoundly changed the way the church related to followers of other religions. The dialogical turn, however, is not rupture, but rather the symbolic beginning of a long process of learning and unlearning. New language needs to be invented and new ritual practices established but, significantly, this is no longer a one-directional endeavour. The religious others with whom the church is now in dialogue are in a position to speak back. As a consequence, the interreligious field is a field where boundaries are constantly being contested and renegotiated, both within the church and outside it.
>
> Certainly, the dialogical process interrupts some of the established patterns of religionization, but the turn to dialogue does not mean the end of religionization. At least two patterns of religionization are assumed in interfaith dialogue: first, the church still taps into the World Religions Paradigm, and continues to claim Christianity as absolute religion. As explained before, problems of categorization, essentialization, and stratification are not alien to this paradigm, which is permeated by various normative binaries (civilized/primitive; textual/oral; spiritual/ritual; official/lived religion; universal/tribal, ...). While the context of dialogue creates a platform for contestation and critique, we are nevertheless dealing with a hegemonic frame. For those who do not fit in, contestation can be an uphill battle and it may even prove difficult to get a seat at the table.
>
> The dialogical turn also taps into the typically modern pattern of religio-secularization which centres the relation between religion and violence. By distinguishing between good and bad religion, the dialogical turn projects an image of religion as acceptable in a context of the religio-secular divide. While acknowledging the problem of religious strife and division, good religion can contribute to peace. Time and again, in a context of interfaith encounter, the church calls on religious leaders to condemn religious violence. At the same time, it sends out the message that terrorism is not due to religion, but is a manipulation of religion (and its sacred texts) for political reasons. True religion is peaceful and knows no coercion (Francis, 2020, p. 285). Here the modern frame of good and bad religion and the projection of violence onto (bad) religion is both affirmed (there is a problem) and contested (it is political manipulation that is the problem). The church, too, has to reckon with hegemonic frames.

The Dialogical Turn and the Erasure of the Religio-racial Constellation

The dialogical turn is often presented as a response to the Shoah and the genocide of European Jews (see Text Box 5). In *Nostra Aetate*, paragraph 4, the church clearly distanced itself from antisemitism and condemned discrimination based on religion, race, or ethnicity while affirming the fundamental right of religious freedom. Ever since, the church has repeatedly condemned racism as a fundamental denial of human dignity and has spoken up for religious minorities whose rights are violated. While this is important, one can also read and understand the dialogical turn in a different vein. We have seen how the European church, legitimized by theologians and supported by secular authorities, has been deeply implicated in the project of religio-racialization. It can be argued that the Second Vatican Council contributes to the erasure of the religio-racial constellation, the term used to refer to 'the connection or co-constitution of the categories of race and religion' (Topolski, 2020, p. 72). This erasure is symbolized by the post-conciliar distinction between anti-Judaism and antisemitism; a distinction that is anticipated in *Nostra Aetate* and finally crystalized in the document *We Remember: A Reflection on the Shoah*. The latter document was promulgated in 1998 by the Commission for Religious Relations with the Jews, in preparation for the upcoming Jubilee year, a special year of remission of sins and universal pardon in the Catholic Church. It explicitly builds on the dialogical turn that was set in motion by *Nostra*

Aetate, and emphasizes that to enable reconciliation between Jews and Christians after a history of prejudice, the past must be confronted. *We Remember*, therefore, urges Catholics to repent for past errors, while also exploring the distinction between anti-Judaism and anti-Semitism [*sic*].

The distinction between anti-Judaism and antisemitism builds on the assumption that race is not religion and racism is not religious prejudice. Racism – here also antisemitism – is placed in the realm of the secular (race could emerge, because man had left God), while anti-Judaism is a problem of religious bias. This line of reasoning, which builds on several arguments that already occupy a central place in *Nostra Aetate* and other conciliar documents, dismantles the religio-racial constellation, and limits the church's capacity to recognize religionization (and religio-racialization) as a political problem.

The Dismantling of the Religio-racial Constellation

First, Vatican II affirms the religio-secular divide and accepts the idea that people are free to choose their religion. This implies that religion is a personal identity marker that one can change; it belongs to the realm of the voluntary: the act of faith is free and contrary to coercion (*Dignitatis Humanae* 10). In view of the distinction between religion and race the idea is that conversion changes a Jew into a Christian, whereas the notion of race fixates difference onto the body. In addition, the church condemns all forms of discrimination, whether based on race, colour, condition of life, or religion (*Nostra Aetate* 4). This condemnation is theological; it is rooted in the ethnoreligious idea that all human beings, regardless of their particularities, are made in the image of God and are thereby equal. All humans are children of God; all are brothers and sisters, and hence they should treat one another alike (*Nostra Aetate* 5). Creation cancels out racism as a Christian ideology. Racism is the abandonment of Christianity. Further, *Nostra Aetate* develops another, more particular, ethnoreligious line of reasoning emphasizing the continuity between Christians and Jews: Jesus' father (St Joseph) and mother were Jewish; Jesus was Jewish and the first Christians were Jewish. All Christians have Jewish roots. Beyond creation – the unity of humankind – Jewish and Christians share a particular genealogy. Before the parting of the ways, Jews and Christians were one people: the Jews are our 'elder brothers'. By affirming the Jewish roots of Christianity, the church claims to distance itself in principle from antisemitism (Text Box 12). Indeed, the document 'Guidelines and Suggestions for Implementing the Conciliar Declaration *Nostra Aetate* 4' (1974) likewise promulgated by the Commission for Religious Relations with the Jews, states that 'the spiritual bonds and historical links binding the church to Judaism condemn (as opposed to the very spirit of Christianity) all forms of anti-Semitism'. Following this line of reasoning, Pope Francis states 'I stress that for a Christian any form of antisemitism is a rejection of one's own origins, a complete contradiction'.[21]

After *Nostra Aetate* and in an effort to facilitate reconciliation between Jews and Christians, some have argued that if Jesus had lived in Europe under the Nazi-regime, he would have been persecuted. Pope John Paul II even compared Auschwitz and Golgotha: where Jews suffer Jesus suffers with them, and Jewish suffering is in that sense Christian suffering. From this perspective, Pope John Paul II deemed it appropriate to erect a large cross in the immediate vicinity of Auschwitz. The church, so this line of reasoning goes, suffers 'with' the Jesus' people (Moyaert, 2016c). Later Pope Francis called the genocide of the Jews the Golgotha of the modern world.

When turning to the document *We Remember*, we now read that the church too was an enemy of the Nazi-regime, which was in fact an atheistic secular ideology. In ecclesial documents Nazism is coined as an anti-Christian and godless ideology aimed not only at destroying Judaism, but also at destroying Christianity. Indeed, the fate of the Jews, shows what 'man is capable of when he turns against God'. 'The Shoah is called the work of a thoroughly modern neo-pagan regime. Its anti-Semitism had its roots outside of Christianity and, in pursuing its aims, it did not hesitate to oppose the church and persecute her members also' (4).[22] When visiting Auschwitz-Birkenau, Pope Benedict XVI said: 'By destroying Israel, by the Shoah, they ultimately wanted to tear up the taproot of the Christian faith and to replace it with a faith of their own invention: faith in the rule of man, the rule of the powerful'.[23]

320 CHAPTER 9   The Dialogical Turn beyond Religionization?

We Remember, does recognize that while 'ecclesial authorities took a stand and expressed their solidarity with the Jewish people', there were 'sons and daughters of the church [who] erred' and acted against the principles of Christian faith. Such errors, the document suggests, were individual, rather than systemic.

Furthermore, the church has to reckon with '[t]he fact that the Shoah took place in Europe, that is, in countries of long-standing Christian civilization'. This 'raises the question of the relation between the Nazi persecution and attitudes, down the centuries, of Christians towards the Jews'. The document *We Remember* addresses this question and recognizes that the history of the 'relations between Jews and Christians is a tormented one', acknowledging the 'long-standing sentiments [*sic*] of mistrust and hostility' of Christians vis-à-vis Jews (4). These sentiments gave way to an effort to 'de-Judaize' Christianity. Unfortunately, anti-Judaism, as these sentiments are termed, led to 'a generalized discrimination, which ended at times in expulsions or attempts at forced conversions' (3). However, *We Remember* states: 'anti-Judaism' must be distinguished from 'anti-Semitism, [which is] based on theories [that are] contrary to the constant teaching of the church on the unity of the human race and on the equal dignity of all races and peoples'. Finally, the assumption is that the problem of anti-Judaism has been 'totally and definitively rejected by the Second Vatican Council', which has rediscovered the Jewish roots of Christianity and in this sense is committed to re-Judaizing Christianity (my terminology). As for the problem of antisemitism: that is projected as inimical to Christian tradition and its theological vision of the unity of the human race.

To sum up: Christians have been prejudiced vis-à-vis Jews for religious reasons. This prejudice has on occasion translated into discriminatory practices, forced conversions, and even persecution. *Nostra Aetate* expressed the church's commitment to halt the history of anti-Judaism by emphasizing the Jewish roots of Christianity and the deep spiritual bond between these two people. Where prejudice was, dialogue will be. De-Judaization is reversed by re-Judaization. Furthermore, the church explicitly condemns any form of racism, in particular, antisemitism, as a non-Christian, neo-pagan, modern ideology that could only emerge because men had turned away from God.

The Masking of the Religio-racial Constellation

The dialogical turn as initiated by the Second Vatican Council 'after the Shoah' enables the church to imagine race and racism (antisemitism) as an un-Christian ideology and to project it onto secular others that were inspired by an ungodly neo-pagan ideology (some Nazi ideologists indeed sought to revitalize 'pagan' Germanic traditions). This line of reasoning masks the religio-racial constellation (and the church's implication in it) in multiple ways.

First, it conceals that the modern effort to classify people into races was built on religionized patterns of thinking. The racialized categories of the Semites and Aryans could not have been imagined apart from religionized ideas about Jews, Muslims, pagans, and Christians (Topolski, 2018). Vice versa, the new religionized paradigm of the world religions was built on the new racialized taxonomy.

In addition, the assumption, based on the religio-secular divide, that religion belongs to the spiritual realm, does not address the fact that religionized difference, already during the Middle Ages, mapped onto the body. Christian anti-Judaism did not target Jews for their deviating beliefs and practices alone; religious differences have always intersected with bodily differences, and anti-Judaism (if we want to retain this term) has also involved the biologization of the differences between Jews and Christians. Also, the idea that race essentializes while religion is a matter of choice obscures the idea that the Jewish people, because of the deicide charge, bore the burden of Cain's hereditary mark.

What is more, to speak about anti-Judaism in terms of sentiments or religious prejudice and to highlight that some individuals were guilty of antisemitism, downplays the political dimension of anti-Jewish patterns of religionization. Religionization, like racialization, categorizes, essentializes, ranks, and governs people based on imaginary differences. The history of religionization is not simply a history of personal bias or prejudiced sentiments. It is a political history of hegemony, institutionalized in the law and materialized in oppressing regulations. In my view, in distinguishing anti-Judaism and antisemitism the dialogical turn exhibits what Geraldine Heng calls a 'refusal of race'. This refusal, 'destigmatizes the impacts and consequences of certain laws, acts, practices, and institutions in the medieval period, so that we cannot name them for what they are, and makes it impossible to bear adequate witness to the full meaning of the manifestations and phenomena they install' (Heng, 2018, p. 4). This dismantlement of the religio-racial constellation is made possible by the religio-secular divide. Prejudice is a religious problem and racism is a secular problem. While dialogue is a place where the problem of religious illiteracy, prejudice, and intolerance is addressed, religious leaders can hold political leaders accountable for the problem of racism, and they may even call it a problem that emerged because people have forgotten that they are all brothers and sisters created by the one God.

The projected distinction between anti-Judaism (religious prejudice against the Jews because of their beliefs) and antisemitism (racist hatred against the Jews because of their nature) makes clear why a *longue durée* approach to the history of religionization is important. This is also important because the dialogical turn and the refusal of race likewise facilitated the forgetfulness of the shared fate of Jews and Muslims in the Christian imagination.

The Dialogical Turn and the (Non-)Shared Fate of Jews and Muslims in the Christian Imagination

Although *Nostra Aetate* is deeply committed to improving Christian-Muslim relations, it does not consider the shared/non-shared fate of Muslims and Jews in Christian imagination as a problem that is rooted in the Christian history of religionization. The vision of universal brotherhood that it initiates and claims as properly Christian, actually masks how the construction of a sense of true Christianness, in various historical-cultural settings, has led to the production of categories of religious deviation, which at one time aided and justified disciplinary practices, and had a real impact on real people. The notion of religious bias and prejudice does not reckon with the systemic nature of religionization, and how it affected not only Jews, but also Muslims, pagans, and heretics.

While it is true that in a European context, antisemitism targeted the Jews primarily, it is also true that both Jews and Muslims were cast as Semites and were projected as people whose very being was irreconcilable with Aryanized Christianity, the religion proper to Europe. True, this pseudo-scientific racist discourse was never picked up in official ecclesial documents (even though Catholic as well as Protestant theologians did give it theological legitimacy); true, in Europe, antisemitism targeted the Jews as Jews (and not Muslims); nevertheless, the distinction between Aryans and Semites was built on medieval religionized discourses which imagined both Jews and Muslims as enemies of Christianity. This too is part of the church's history to be reckoned with.

Text Box 12: Judeo-Christianity

In the aftermath of Vatican II, the notion of Judeo-Christianity gained momentum as a concept that was meant to include Jews positively in God's plan of salvation. The notion, however, is a social construct and its meaning has changed significantly in the span of one century. Surfacing its changing meanings may make us more sensitive to the work of inclusion and exclusion effected by this notion. Depending on the context, the work it does differs.

In the nineteenth century, the term 'Jewish-Christians' was mainly used to refer to those early followers of Jesus who disagreed with Paul's mission to the gentiles and wished to limit Jesus' message to the Jews and who in any case insisted on maintaining Jewish law and ritual (the term was first coined by F. C. Baur [1792–1860], founder of the German Tübingen school, in 1831). Between 1918 and 1939, various interreligious initiatives were taken to protest against the rise of antisemitism. These interfaith initiatives underscored Judeo-Christian friendship. In the aftermath of *Nostra Aetate*, the term 'Judeo-Christian' symbolized a dramatic change in the relations between the

Roman Catholic Church and the Jewish people. From a Catholic perspective, the hyphen between Judaism and Christianity expresses a retrieval of the Jewish roots of Christian tradition. Simultaneously, 'the Judeo-Christian myth's quick dissemination meant that European Jews' very recent tragic reality, along with centuries of Christian violence against Jews, was subordinated to a fabricated "shared memory" of a long-lasting imaginary past (the so-called Judeo-Christian heritage)' (Hochberg, 2016, p. 197).

Since the 1990s, but even more so after the turn of the twenty-first century, the notion of Judeo-Christianity is invoked, mostly by right-wing voices, to question Islam's place in Europe. It then becomes an exclusionary category. Used in this way, the ideas surrounding the Judeo-Christian roots of Europe not only deny or even erase the history of European Christian antisemitism (Teixidor, 2006, p. 166), they also serve to cast Islam as anti-modern and anti-European. As Anya Topolski specifies, 'while implying an association with humanism and secularism', a term like Judeo-Christian disguises 'Islamophobic racism as a form of cultural critique' (Topolski, 2020, p. 71) or critique of religion (Nathan & Topolski, 2016; Silk, 1984; Topolski, 2020). The Judeo-Christian myth goes hand in hand with a forgetting of the figure of the Semite, which referred both to Jews and Muslims as opposed to Aryan Christians.

3   Dialogue in Post-secular Society

For a long time, interreligious dialogue was mostly of interest to (Christian) religious leaders, theologians, and lay people rooted in different religious communities and committed to different traditions. Since the turn of the twenty-first century, and 9/11 especially, political bodies, struck by the resurgence (Berger, 2014) or persistence of religion at local, national, and international levels, have also begun to promote interreligious dialogue (Fahy & Bock, 2020; Halafoff, 2013; Ipgrave, 2019). What started out as an explicitly non-political *religious endeavour* – grafted on the acceptance of the modern separation of church and state – has become part of the governance regimes of religious diversity in Europe and beyond, and state-run interfaith initiatives are becoming increasingly common (Griera & Nagel, 2018; Körs & Nagel, 2018; Marshall, 2017). In just a few decades, dialogue went from being, at best, a marginal episodic phenomenon to 'gaining discursive status and becoming a widely embraced ideal and practice in the twentieth century of how religious communities ought to comport themselves in relation to one another' (Howard, 2021, p. 6). Put differently, dialogue has become a socially constructed norm supported and promoted by policy makers. As is typically the case with social norms, there will be rewards for those who conform, and reprimands or even sanctions for those who do not abide by the norm.

The Return of Religion

Until recently, 'religion was understood to be absent from affairs of state and the law' (Hurd, 2012, p. 943). On the one hand, there was general agreement that 'the problem of religion' had been 'contained', thanks to the separation of church and state. Those who still considered themselves 'religious' had become modern believers, who regard their convictions a personal affair, and they learned not to mix religion and politics. Their understanding and practice of religion no longer posed a problem, politically speaking. On the other hand, many people thought that modern progress would ultimately lead to the disappearance of religion. The more a society progressed into modernity, the less it would remain attached to religion and vice versa. Thus, religion was either regarded as a kind of leftover from the past or something that concerned people in their private lives, and thus politics did not have to bother with it any more.

Today, policy makers have come to realize that religion has not disappeared. As a consequence, they have to learn to consider the presence of religion rather than its absence

(Hurd, 2012, pp. 943–944). Religion is once again a central issue of governance. To high-light this altered understanding of the place of religion in contemporary society, some soci-ologists, philosophers, and political scientists have begun to use the label 'post-secular' to describe the world we now live in (Wilson, 2014). The concept of the post-secular implies that we have moved beyond the secular and therefore beyond the religio-secular divide. This is affirmed by the 'policy paradigm shift' towards positive co-governance between secular and religious actors, who now collaborate to enhance social cohesion (Griera, 2012, p. 577).

In my understanding, the idea of the post-secular, however, is still largely informed by the religio-secular divide and the binary between good and bad religion. From this perspec-tive co-governance may be understood as a more active approach towards the production of good religion *and* the rooting out of the problem of bad religion. A rhetoric of the 'two faces of faith' underpins the post-secular turn and provides the dialogical turn with new impetus (Hurd, 2017; Smith et al., 2020).

The Two Faces of Religion Policy makers first rediscovered religion's political relevance in the aftermath of the Iranian Revolution of 1979. This turnabout was further triggered around the 1990s, with the Salman Rushdie affair and the Satanic verses con-troversy (1989). In 1996, Samuel Huntington (1927–2008) wrote *The Clash of Civilizations and Remaking of World Order*. He developed the theory that in the post-cold war period, people's cultural and religious traditions would become the main source of global conflict (Huntington, 1996). This theory helped popularize the idea that the revitalization of reli-gion was a problem in need of governance (Griera, 2012, p. 579). Religion and conflicting religious worldviews were centred again as a security issue, and many societal problems – local, national, and international – were now approached through the prism of religion. For example, in Europe, some of the challenges related to migration came to be understood in terms of religion. Significantly, many right-wing parties in Europe shifted their focus from ethnicity being the problem to seeing religion (Islam) as the relevant issue. Also, beyond such right-wing discourse, there was a broader concern that newcomers might not share 'our European values rooted in Judeo-Christian and humanistic traditions' and that 'their' reli-gious beliefs might be difficult to reconcile with our 'European culture'. A European 'us' is imagined in terms of sharing a culture, a heritage, a history, and values – religious freedom, respect for difference, gender equality, tolerance – whereas others might need more active support in order to appropriate these values and become citizens too. There was a growing concern that modern, liberal, and tolerant expressions of religion (following the ideal of secularized Christianity) were challenged by exclusive and conservative forms of religion and identity politics (Halafoff, 2013, p. 10). These concerns were exacerbated by 9/11 and by subsequent terrorist attacks on European soil in Madrid, London, Paris, and Brussels. Once again Europe was confronted rather dramatically with the bad face of religion, which is 'barbarous, violent, irrational, [and] causing conflict' (Fitzgerald, 2011, p. 78). Today, the general argument is that policy makers and analysts suffered from 'secularist biases', which blinded them to the prevailing power of religion. Through a process of trial and error, they have come to realize that they cannot ignore the problem of religion.

The discourse about the return of religion does not only assume the idea of bad religion, it also centres the good face of religion, that is religion as benign, gentle, meek, humble, compas-sionate, moderate, and tolerant. Good religion springs from faith, and faith can never be forced. Good religion is supposed to be spiritual. It prioritizes the inner world and values sacrifice, altruism, dedication, responsibility, hope, and resilience. Good religion puts the weak in society first: the widow, the orphan, and the poor, and perhaps also nature which often has no voice at all. Religion true to its core has nothing to do with violence, coercion, or power; rather, it is non-violent, peaceful, and tolerant. It affirms religious freedom and the religio-secular divide and counters any violence in the name of religion. From this perspective, extremism is a misuse or abuse of 'true' religion. Extremists turn religion into an instrument of power, which diverts religion from its peaceful path. Bad religion is false religion; it is a perversion.

We already encountered the discourse about the two faces of religion in the religio-secular pattern of religionization (see Text Box 13), it also pervades the dialogical turn.

324 CHAPTER 9 The Dialogical Turn beyond Religionization?

Today, this discourse is not only applied by Christian leaders and political leaders in Europe, but is also embraced by other religious leaders who plead for peace between the religions. The rise of religious [*sic*] fundamentalism and terrorism calls upon religious leaders to distance themselves (their traditions and religion as a whole) from such violence. Here in the words of the Dalai Lama:

> *Buddhist terrorist. Muslim terrorist. That wording is wrong. Any person who wants to indulge in violence is no longer a genuine Buddhist or genuine Muslim, because it is a Muslim teaching that once you are involved in bloodshed, actually you are no longer a genuine practitioner of Islam. All major religious traditions carry the same message: a message of love, compassion, forgiveness, tolerance, contentment, self-discipline – all religious traditions. (Dalai Lama, 2016)*

Perhaps one could say that bad religion is a form of heresy – a deviation from true religion, and terrorists like heretics in the past are out to destabilize 'our' society from within by perverting 'our values'. Especially, the homebred Islamic terrorist resonates with the figure of the heretic, who sickens 'our institutions', 'our society' from within, having pretended to be one of us (see Text Box 13).

While secular authorities are concerned about bad religion, there is also a notable appreciation for the social capital of good religion (Putnam, 2000). The notion of social capital refers to those 'relational ties and networks that can foster social norms, provide support, and be leveraged for gain' (Park & Sharma, 2016). Increasingly, policy makers recognize that religious communities and faith-based organizations play 'a key part in the voluntary sector, releasing sources of energy and creativity which contribute to the common good' (Barnes, 2008). Furthermore, they also harbour the kinds of cultural, moral, and social resources that are vital for strengthening the social fabric and for fostering precisely those qualities that are essential for good citizenship. In an effort to address complex societal challenges – the COVID crisis, climate change, hunger, homelessness – secular actors increasingly join hands with the faith-based communities and their extended networks of volunteers and seek to support good religion and its conciliatory power (Omer, 2020). Representatives of good religion are in turn expected to take a clear stand against bad religion as inauthentic and invest in dialogue to mitigate religious tensions, foster a climate of tolerance, and strengthen moderate religion. The hope is that 'good religion' will eventually triumph over 'bad religion' once religious actors, supported by secular authorities, join hands. In sum, operationalizing the distinction between good and bad religion in a postsecular society has led to various policies seeking the 'containment' of 'bad' religion and the promotion of good religion through investment in interfaith programming (Omer, 2020).

Text Box 13: The Binary between Good and Bad Religion: An Imaginary Construct

Recall that the binary between good and bad religion first gained momentum when the Voices for Tolerance were trying to make a case for toleration in a context of persecution. Refiguring true Christianness in terms of meekness and humility, they projected a division between church and state, and claimed (i) that those persecuting heretics were in fact heretical and (ii) that those people who were too attached to dogma and ritual and those who mixed religion and politics were prone to violence. The symbolic carriers of bad, intolerant religion were the Jews, Muslims, and Catholics. Significantly, we are dealing again with an imaginary construct that functions in the process of religionization: enhancing a sense of Christianness over against others who then function as rhetorical figures. Apart from the work this binary does in the process of selfing and othering, it has, in all its simplicity, a mobilizing power. In the nineteenth century it placed both Jews and, depending on the context, Catholics and colonized

Muslims in the position of having to prove that they belonged, and it put them at risk of seeing their traditions and by extension their bodies being disciplined.

As is the case with all binaries, this dichotomy is a form of essentialization which reduces complex problems to a single narrative, and this in fact inhibits us from understanding and effectively addressing the phenomenon of extremism. The added value for those who claim to embody the default position of good religion (or no religion) is that they do not have to consider their own role in the eruption of conflict. For those who are suspected of being on the wrong side of the 'faultline', there are serious consequences: their belonging is questioned, and depending on the security risk they are imagined to pose, they will be confronted with constant scrutiny (Fadil et al., 2019). Today, the security risk no longer comes from heretics, or Catholics or even Jews; today, (radical) Muslims are projected as the problem.

Interfaith Dialogue and the Performance of Good Religion

After 9/11, local interfaith initiatives regained momentum, and more often than previously these now included Muslim participants (Griera & Nagel, 2018; Körs & Nagel, 2018; Körs et al., 2020; Lamine, 2004). At an urban level, one may for example notice an increase in interfaith city councils supporting collaborations between secular actors and faith-based organizations (Beaumont & Baker, 2011; Beaumont & Cloke, 2012). At the European level, political bodies, like the Council of Europe, began to underscore the importance of dialogue to the enhancement of social cohesion. At all these levels – local, national, and international – funding was made available to support policies that encourage faith communities to collaborate and engage one another in dialogue. In an effort to counteract the dominant discourse of the clash of civilizations, many interreligious organizations perform the ideal of interreligious solidarity: religions true to their nature as peaceful can be a positive and indispensable societal force. These interreligious organizations are often also the first in line to formulate public statements condemning terrorist attacks, certainly when they target houses of worship. By launching such statements, religious leaders not only condemn senseless acts of violence but also declare that these are a perversion of the true nature of religion. While the Voices of Tolerance called intolerance un-Christian, the Voices of Dialogue now call terrorism anti-religious. They acknowledge the lack of religious literacy as a problem and state that encounter must be promoted to overcome ignorance. They affirm that, at all costs, freedom of religion must be protected. The rhetoric typically displayed in joint interfaith statements expresses the possibility of peaceful co-existence. Consider in this regard the following statement made by the Faith Communities Forum in the United Kingdon on the occasion of the terrorist attack in the Notre-Dame Basilica in Nice, France

We condemn in the strongest terms terrorism and other acts of violent extremism. Such attacks on places of worship are a reminder to stand together and to continue to work together with ever greater urgency against ignorance, prejudice and hatred. There must be freedom for all communities to worship and practise their faith freely and without fear. Terrorists and other violent extremists usually draw on extreme political ideologies or, in some cases, selectively, on religious writings in ways which can distort [...] their fundamental values. [...] It is vital that there is greater faith literacy within as well as about our different faith traditions and that informed voices within those speak out. [...] We call also for increasing spaces for dialogue – within educational and other civil society institutions as well as within faith communities.[24]

This embrace of dialogue in a post-secular society has also given way to an increase of multireligious rituals in response to some external event or challenge. This may be to address a global challenge (e.g. war prompting a prayer for peace), or to commemorate and mourn the victims of a national calamity (e.g. religious leaders standing shoulder to shoulder to remember the victims of 9/11) or to solemnly inaugurate a new academic year. National and international days against discrimination and racism, national liberation days, and national and international women's days can also become occasions for interreligious ceremonies of some sort. These initiatives gather people together and address the need to create a 'we' in the face of shared challenges (Moyaert, 2015). We are also seeing rituals of mutual hospitality emerge whereby 'others' are invited to participate as guests. One example is that of Muslim communities inviting guests to break the fast with them. Sometimes, especially during the so-called holiday season, traditions of Hanukah, Christmas, and Divali are creatively brought together in an interfaith Festival of Lights. Finally, mention should be made of the recent phenomenon of multifaith spaces of worship at airports, at the workplace, and on campuses, as well as larger projects of this kind being established in various European cities. These multifaith houses of worship, usually supported by secular authorities, give interfaith co-existence a permanent, visible presence in a public space. Here one might think of The House of One, in Berlin, which is currently under construction, where Jews, Muslims, and Christians will worship under the same roof as well as the Coexist House in London. The biggest such project, *Haus der Religionen* based in Bern, houses Alevis, Baha'is, Buddhists, Christians, Hindus, Jews, Muslims, and Sikhs. Each community has its own place of worship and in addition there is space for dialogue and education. Here these religions both practise their tradition and live together in peace and harmony (Schneider, 2017). In all these cases, we are dealing with the performance of interreligious fellowship: sacred ground no longer divides or contaminates; it is shared across traditions. In this way, the idea that religion is conflictual is counter-narrated (Griera, 2019; van Es, 2022).

From the perspective of religious communities, especially for religious minorities, taking part in interfaith platforms, initiatives, and rituals not only provides a way of combating misinformation and rectifying misconceptions, but it is also a way of expressing their community and civic engagement, thereby at once dissociating themselves from radical and problematic forms of religion and reaffirming their commitment to non-violence (Halafoff, 2013, p. 118).

> *Religious minority groups know that in order to be taken into consideration by local authorities, they must adapt to the 'rules of the game' and show that they are part of the 'good religion'. Thus, religious minority groups have adapted their discourses and their strategies to this new context in recent years by engaging in interfaith councils or associations, promoting open days at places of worship, inviting local authorities to religious celebrations, etc. (Griera, 2012, p. 583)*

By so doing, they simultaneously create good will among public authorities, and this may help them to become more visible and to make themselves and their concerns heard.

Conversely, the willingness to contribute to society at large, to collaborate with other faith-based communities, and to participate in interfaith platforms can function as an important yardstick to distinguish between good and bad religion and between good and bad religious leaders. The same goes for a possible unwillingness to participate in multireligious rituals, for example on the occasion of a national disaster. Such refusal is suspect and raises the question as to whether this or that religious community is really committed to the European values of freedom and tolerance. For religious actors who disagree with the frame of good and bad religion, it is difficult to express their disagreement without being discredited.

Education, Citizenship, and the Promotion of Interfaith Competences

Political and educational policy makers, on the European, national, and regional level, are increasingly taking an interest in interreligious education, the goal of which is to promote understanding between people who uphold different religious and non-religious worldviews by engaging them in a dialogical learning process. Jacques Delors, with his initiative *A Soul for Europe*, already stated that in order for Europe to create a sense of community the plans will have to revolve around more than legal and economic interests. Dialogue between the European Parliament and 'churches, faith groups and philosophical non-confessional organisations' is now projected as a key aspect of European identity (cf. Article 17 of the Lisbon Treaty) while at the same time functioning as a way of enhancing the European values of religious freedom, tolerance, and respect for difference and promoting active citizenship.[25]

Both the Organization for Security and Co-operation in Europe (OSCE) and the Council of Europe have looked at the importance of religious education – with a specific focus on enhancing religious literacy and interfaith competences – as crucial to protecting the freedom of religion and belief. Further, the Committee of Ministers of the Council of Europe agrees that religious education, which includes addressing religious diversity, is essential for fostering democratic citizenship. In 2008, a Recommendation on the Dimension of Religions and Non-Religious Convictions within Intercultural Education (CM/Rec 2008-12) was published, according to which all member states were to include the study of religions in their curriculum. Its intention: 'to ensure taking into account the dimension of religions and non-religious convictions within intercultural education as a contribution to strengthen human rights, democratic citizenship and participation, and to the development of competences for intercultural dialogue'.[26] The recommendation clearly states that intolerance cannot be remedied by knowledge alone; how people publicize their own worldview identity and relate to other traditions and their adherents must also be dealt with. This concerns, in particular:

Developing a tolerant attitude and respect for the right to hold a particular belief, attitudes based on the recognition of the inherent dignity and fundamental freedoms of each human being; nurturing a sensitivity to the diversity of religions and non-religious convictions as an element contributing to the richness of Europe. (Jackson, 2014, p. 34)

Here, teaching tolerance intersects with citizenship education. In 2015, this interest in education gained momentum when, following the bomb attacks in Paris, the European ministers of education launched the Paris declaration, focusing on the role of education in promoting citizenship and 'the common values of freedom, tolerance and non-discrimination, strengthening social cohesion, and helping young people become responsible, open-minded and active members of our diverse and inclusive society' (Text Box 14).[27] This interest in education springs from profound concerns about the fact that in Europe today 'misunderstandings, negative stereotypes, and provocative images used to depict others are leading to heightened antagonism and sometimes even violence'.[28] Education has to prepare young people for a pluralistic society, where they will in any case have to work and live together with those of other faiths and worldviews. How this will play out in practical terms varies from country to country and depends on the relation between church and state, the structure of the educational system, its history, and current sociological developments. Key, however, is the idea that dialogical education can help to convey key European values like the freedom of religion, as well as tolerance, respect for difference, and the fundamental equality of all people regardless of their ethnicity, gender, class, or religion. From whatever angle one approaches this, it is clear that the need to invest in dialogical education springs from the realization that not all are familiar with or even share 'our' values. Once again, the problem comes from elsewhere.

Text Box 14: Qualifying the Idea of Equality of Religious Freedom

Recently, scholars working in the field of interreligious studies and critical secular studies have been qualifying the idealist projection of religious freedom. More precisely, they point out that the idea of religious freedom for all as a modern European (and American) achievement functions as an 'optical illusion' (Joshi, 2020, p. 26), which enables us to avert our attention from some of the legacies of religionization, as discussed in this book. First, it taps into the myth of the rise of tolerance. In addition, it ignores the fact that arguments for toleration assumed the projection of problematic religion onto Muslims, Jews, and Catholics. Furthermore, it obscures the continued reality of Christian normativity in most European countries and the injustice that some religious minorities continued to experience. Usually, Christian normativity remains under the radar when the ideal of religious freedom is discussed (Moyaert, 2018). 'At first glance, Western European countries such as France, the Netherlands, and the United Kingdom are characterized by religious equality. Religious discrimination is against the law, and governments claim to uphold political secularism and equal treatment of all religious groups. At the same time, we can hardly speak of full equality between Christians and non-Christians. School curricula teach primarily Christian history, Christian architecture can be recognized in almost every city and village, the Christian calendar is used pervasively, and many Christian holidays are institutionalized as national holidays' (Lauwers, 2023, p. 403). Also, the self-congratulatory narrative about European religious freedom often assumes the construction of 'Muslims' as hating 'our freedoms: our freedom of religion, freedom of speech, freedom to vote...' (Green, 2019, p. 123). Hate crimes against, primarily, Muslims and Jews are significantly higher than those against Christians.

Islam as Europe's Other

Calls for interreligious fellowship and dialogue at schools are made in a context in which specifically one religion, namely Islam, is projected as the symbolic carrier of problematic religion. While Islamic extremism is an 'international problem', in Europe there are serious concerns about homegrown extremism, which is seen as a sign of the collapse of the 'multicultural society' and the failure of integration. Right-wing voices, which in many European countries are on the rise, would even question whether Islam is reconcilable with European values. It is against this background that we can situate European calls for an Islamic Enlightenment and a Muslim Reformation. Here, the distinction between good and bad religion is replicated by the distinction between radical, extremist, or fundamentalist Islam on the one hand and moderate, liberal or, even progressive Islam on the other hand. Radical Muslims are projected as dogmatic and legalistic, and like the 'Jews' in the past, they approach their scripture with a literalist hermeneutic. They are not only intolerant and potentially violent, but they also present a threat to our values system. Moderate Muslims in contrast are loyal to our European liberal values and are good, tolerant citizens (van Es et al., 2021). It is often assumed that moderate Muslims, like secularized Christians or liberal Jews, are not too attached to religious rituals and rules, nor do they simply follow religious authorities or read the Qur'an literally. While, in the dialogical context, such stereotypical images are challenged, the image of Islam as potentially dangerous is nevertheless reproduced, even in the denial. We are dealing here with an all too familiar frame, which repurposes age-old anti-Muslim patterns of religionization.

Islam has long been cast as the enemy of Christianity, an image that was recycled during the late Middle Ages and re-found in the modern period. This ideological discourse, which rendered Islam a danger to Christianity and to Europe, not only circulated during the time of the crusades, but was also revived in colonial settings to justify oppression. Sedimented anti-Muslim images that are part of the European cultural archive, continue to pervade the social and public imaginaries of Christians and Europeans into the present-day and they justify the implementation of various disciplinary measures (Takacs, 2022, p. 200), ranging

from relatively benign encouragement of the integration of immigrant populations and discouragement of 'extremism', to the explicit attempt to impose a state-approved formula for the organization of Islamic communities. Despite widely divergent legacies of church-state relations and seemingly disparate nationalist traditions, European governments appear to be converging on a common solution to their Muslim problem – 'religion-change' and the construction of an 'acceptable' Islam. (Haddad & Golson, 2007)

This frame has put Muslims in a constant state of suspicion. Their belonging to Europe and the country in which they live is rendered uncertain, their acceptance of modern values is questioned. They are, more than other 'religious others', under constant pressure to show that they are peaceful, tolerant, and loyal citizens, to condemn terrorism, and to embrace dialogue (van Es et al., 2021).

> *Although few people would argue that all Muslims are terrorists, the underlying assumption seems to be that all Muslims are susceptible to radicalisation. As a result, everyone and everything that is somehow related to Islam becomes a matter of security, and needs to be evaluated in terms of whether it poses a threat or not. Muslims are increasingly put under surveillance – not only literally, in the sense of being monitored by intelligence services, but also in the sense that they are continually viewed and talked about in terms of how dangerous they are. (van Es, 2018, p. 148)*

Especially when Muslims give visible expression to their religious commitment, for example through dress code or ritual practice, they become suspect. In this regard, I would say, Muslims today are faced with a form of prejudice that, inspired by Yolande Jansen and Marieke van der Steen, I would call inquisitive religionization: they are 'being accused of "hiding" [their] political ideas under a religious "cover"' (Jansen & van der Steen, 2023, forthcoming).

Muslims are not to be trusted, since they pretend to be something they are not. I cannot help but be reminded of the way heretics in the Middle Ages were treated; they too were suspected of hiding their true 'identity' under the cover of being Christians. They pretended to be Christian, but they were actually out to harm and destabilize Christian society. One might also suggest that they are being treated like Moriscos and Marranos in the sixteenth and seventeenth centuries: claiming to have converted to Christianity, they were suspected of having remained committed to their old ways. Even Muslims who participate in dialogue or publicly perform interfaith solidarity may be confronted with suspicion: are they not pretending to have converted to the modern 'European' value of dialogue or pretending to participate in secular academy, while they are in fact renegades, holding on to some form of radical Islam? (Moyaert, 2018).

Because of this situation many European Muslims experience pressure to show that they are peaceful and loyal. Participating in dialogue is one way to perform good Islam. However, the moment they participate in dialogue, they also reinforce the frame of good and bad religion, good and bad Islam. This disables them from centring the issues that are more pressing to them: Islamophobia, discrimination, colonial legacies, violence done in the name of secular ideologies, and modern civilization discourses. The focus on interfaith togetherness and solidarity leaves little room to criticize the main frame. This leads to frustration and dialogue fatigue (Moyaert, 2019b).

4 Conclusion

Interfaith dialogue has the potential to transform imaginary others into real others. In fact, the dialogical process that was set in motion in the twentieth century has brought about a tremendous change in the way people who believe and practise differently relate to one another. The face-to-face encounter has also impacted the categories used to speak about 'religious others' and has centred on the importance of respecting people's self-definition and self-understanding. In the context of dialogue, Christians (staying with the focal point of this book) have had to unlearn religionized habits of thinking and behaving, which were aimed at essentializing, inferiorizing, and disciplining non-Christians. Today, at least to a certain extent, the knowledge produced about religion and religious diversity is co-produced, and for the church to maintain its credibility as being committed to dialogue, it has to listen to and learn from those who believe and practise differently.

At the same time, it cannot be denied that the dialogical project is crafted onto (secularized) Christian normative assumptions about true and false religion, good and bad religion. Nor can it be denied that the World Religions Paradigm, which organized the diversity of religions on the basis of a religio-secularized and a religio-racialized frame, with serious social, legal, and political repercussions for people deemed not-modern or not-civilized, continues to determine who is included and who is excluded from the dialogue table. The vision of interfaith fellowship can be subversive and can challenge structures of oppressions, also when based on religionization. However, calls for dialogue can just as easily be invoked to reinforce a civilizational discourse that legitimizes discriminatory practices or enables those in power to overlook the ways they themselves are enmeshed in violence. When legacies of religionization are not made part of interfaith dialogue, calls for fellowship reinforce the status quo and do not change unequal power relations. Here again, this frame does not go uncontested. In fact the opposite is true; but trying to change the game remains challenging and frustrating, certainly when this burden is put on religionized minorities. Contesting a hegemonic norm is an uphill battle.

The World Parliament of Religions is a case in point. It was a place of disputation and protest, but it was also a site which reinforced white Christian supremacy, and legitimized religio-racialized binaries between civilized and uncivilized people, even while launching a vision of universal brotherhood across traditions. We can also consider the Vatican II embrace of dialogue: The church now recognizes the religio-secular divide while simultaneously using interfaith solidarity to claim back power in order to challenge political leaders and their policies. At the same time, the Catholic dialogical turn has enabled the church to turn attention away from the religio-racial constellation. After *Nostra Aetate*, race was no longer religion and antisemitism was no longer anti-Judaism. Here, dialogical reconciliation goes hand in hand with masking the religio-racial constellation. Judaism is included in the Judeo-Christian storyline and the de-judaization effort is halted; the problem of race is now imagined as a secular rather than a religious problem. Finally, when zooming in on the post-secular model of co-governance, we may again ask questions about the critical potential of dialogue. First, we noted a simplistic reiteration of the binary between good and bad religion; this is an imaginary construct which cannot do justice to more complex socio-political realities like fundamentalism and extremism. When the problem is construed as religious, so is the solution. Enhancing religious literacy, addressing religious prejudice, and promoting European values in the context of dialogue is the way forward. Furthermore, the distinction between good and bad religion, in our post 9/11 setting, often implies the distinction between radical and moderate Islam. This distinction reiterates long established patterns of religionization that project Islam as the symbolic carrier of bad religion and enables the process of selfing. Renan's image of Islam as the other, even as the enemy of Europe, is never far away. In this way, and thanks to the religio-secular divide, Europe and its democratic values of tolerance and religious freedom are brought into focus as modern, emancipatory achievements. While this story line is not untrue, it is also self-congratulatory and limited, and basically masks how an argument in favour of toleration (like that in favour of dialogue) was crafted by projecting problematic religion onto Christianity's others. This perspective forgets how the modern norm of religion as a-political, interiorized, and privatized was used to criminalize the beliefs and practices of colonized others. It also forgets the way Europe's identity as modern, progressive, and liberal was crafted by projecting Muslims and Jews as Semites and Europeans as Aryans. So when the Council of Europe, for example, argues in favour of dialogue in order to teach people about 'our' modern values, does it include those histories of European religio-racialization?

More could be said. Depending on the context, interfaith dialogue can affirm and challenge the *status quo*. It can deconstruct religionized patterns, reinvoke them, and adopt new ones. It can be simultaneously inclusionary and exclusionary. Invoking the notion of interfaith dialogue and fellowship will not suffice to interrupt processes of religionization; rather, interruption requires the willingness to explore the past of the present and the present of the past. Emancipation begins when we accept that we are not free from the past, not even when we are committed to dialogue. Emancipation begins when we take religionized legacies seriously.

Notes

1 As in the political arena of a nation's parliament, here too, people functioned as representatives, speaking on behalf of their 'religious constituency'. At the very least, this perspective, taken from the realm of politics, brings 'order and structure' to the messiness of religion (Matthias Smalbrugge, in his comments on Chapter 9). Might one also say, that by bringing all these representatives into one space, by recognizing them as conversation partners, they become *religiones licitae*, pacified in a new *pax deorum*, recognized in as far as they fit the frame?

2 Several interreligious scholars have been challenging the World Religions Paradigm as a hegemonic norm (Gustafson, 2020; Hedges, 2017; Minister, 2020; Swamy, 2017; Thatamanil, 2015).

3 Rachel Mikva, Review Report, 6 April 2023.

4 https://ramakrishna.org/vivekanandaparliament.html.

5 https://vatican2voice.org/91docs/opening_speech.htm.

6 www.vatican.va/content/paul-vi/en/encyclicals/documents/hf_p-vi_enc_06081964_ecclesiam.html.

7 See also *Dei Verbum*, the dogmatic constitution on Revelation as well as *Lumen Gentium*, the dogmatic constitution on the church, and *Ad Gentes*, Decree on the Missionary Activity of the Church.

8 M. Voss Roberts in her feedback on Chapter 9.

9 www.vatican.va/archive/hist_councils/ii_vatican_council/documents/vat-ii_decl_19651028_nostra-aetate_en.html.

10 www.vatican.va/content/francesco/en/encyclicals/documents/papa-francesco_20201003_enciclica-fratelli-tutti.html.

11 Potter (2022, p. 7).

12 For an overview of the different drafts prepared to be discussed at the council, see: The Drafting of *Nostra Aetate*. www.bc.edu/content/dam/files/research_sites/cjl/texts/cjrelations/resources/education/NA_draft_history.htm.

13 Interreligious Meeting, 6 March 2021. www.vatican.va/content/francesco/en/speeches/2021/march/documents/papa-francesco_20210306_iraq-incontro-interreligioso.html.

14 www.vatican.va/archive/hist_councils/ii_vatican_council/documents/vat-ii_decl_19651207_dignitatis-humanae_en.html.

15 For a more extensive elaboration of the ritualization of the dialogical turn see Moyaert (forthcoming).

16 Pope Francis, To Participants in the International Meeting for Peace, Sponsored by the Community of Sant'Egidio, 30 September 2013. www.vatican.va/content/francesco/en/speeches/2013/september/documents/papa-francesco_20130930_incontro-pace-s-egidio.html.

17 Pope John Paul II, The Roots of Anti-Judaism in the Christian Environment, 13 April 1986. www.vatican.va/jubilee_2000/magazine/documents/ju_mag_01111997_p-42x_en.html.

18 https://www.vatican.va/content/john-paul-ii/it/audiences/1986/documents/hf_jp-ii_aud_19861022.html (Rome, 22 October 1986, my translation).

19 Pope John Paul II, Address to the Representatives of the Christian Churches and Ecclesial Communities, 27 October 1986. www.vatican.va/content/john-paul-ii/en/speeches/1986/october/documents/hf_jp-ii_spe_19861027_prayer-peace-assisi.html.

20 www.vatican.va/content/francesco/en/encyclicals/documents/papa-francesco_20201003_enciclica-fratelli-tutti.html.

21 Pope Francis, Address to Members of the American Jewish Committee, 8 March 2019. www.vatican.va/content/francesco/en/speeches/2019/march/documents/papa-francesco_20190308_american-jewish-committee.html.

22 See www.christianunity.va/content/unitacristiani/en/commissione-per-i-rapporti-religiosi-con-l-ebraismo/commissione-per-i-rapporti-religiosi-con-l-ebraismo-crre/documenti-della-commissione/en1.html.

23 Pope Benedict XVI, Address on the Occasion of the Visit to the Auschwitz Camp, 28 May 2006. www.vatican.va/content/benedict-xvi/en/speeches/2006/may/documents/hf_ben-xvi_spe_20060528_auschwitz-birkenau.html.

24 www.interfaith.org.uk/news/statement-following-recent-terrorist-attacks.

25 Council of Europe Ministers of Foreign Affairs, *White Paper on Intercultural Dialogue: 'Living Together as Equals in Dignity'*. Strasbourg, 7 May 2008; www.coe.int/t/dg4/intercultural/source/white%20paper_final_revised_en.pdf.

26 https://rm.coe.int/09000016805d20e8.

27 https://www.eumonitor.eu/9353000/1/j4nvhdfcs8bljza_j9vvik7m1c3gyxp/vjwz4owo0oxk.

28 Organization for Security and Co-operation in Europe. Toledo Guiding Principles on Teachings on Religions and Beliefs in Public Schools. Retrieved from https://www.osce.org/odihr/29154?download=true, p. 9.

References

Albanese, C., & Stein, S. J. (1995). Foreword. In R. H. Seager (Ed.), *The World's Parliament of Religions: The East/West Encounter, Chicago, 1893* (pp. ix–xii). Indiana University Press.

Barnes, M. S. (2008, 3 September). Dialogue and Social Cohesion. *Thinking Faith*. Retrieved from https://www.thinkingfaith.org/articles/20080903_1.htm

Barrows, J. H. (1893). *The World's Parliament of Religions: An Illustrated and Popular Story of the World's First Parliament of Religions, Held in Chicago in Connection with the Columbian Exposition of 1893*. The Parliament Publishing Company.

Beaumont, J., & Baker, C. R. (2011). *Postsecular Cities: Space, Theory and Practice*. Continuum.

Beaumont, J., & Cloke, P. J. (2012). *Faith-Based Organisations and Exclusion in European Cities*. Policy Press.

Berger, P. L. (2014). *The Many Altars of Modernity: Toward a Paradigm for Religion in a Pluralist Age*. De Gruyter.

Betts, J. R. (1964). The Laity and the Ecumenical Spirit, 1889–1893. *The Review of Politics, 26*(1), 3–19.

Brandfon, F. (2023). *Intimate Strangers: A History of Jews and Catholics in the City of Rome*. The Jewish Publication Society / University of Nebraska Press.

Braybrooke, M. (1992). *Pilgrimage of Hope: One Hundred Years of Global Interfaith Dialogue*. Crossroad.

Brown, W. (2006). *Regulating Aversion: Tolerance in the Age of Identity and Empire*. Princeton University Press.

Burris, J. P. (2001). *Exhibiting Religion: Colonialism and Spectacle at International Expositions, 1851-1893*. University Press of Virginia.

Catalano, R. (2022). Pope Francis' Culture of Dialogue as Pathway to Interfaith Encounter: A Special Focus on Islam. *Religions, 13*(4), Article 279. https://doi.org/10.3390/rel13040279

Cavanaugh, W. T. (2009). *The Myth of Religious Violence: Secular Ideology and the Roots of Modern Conflict*. Oxford University Press.

Chidester, D. (2000). *Christianity: A Global History*. HarperSanFrancisco.

Churchill, W. (2005). *Kill the Indian, Save the Man: The Genocidal Impact of American Indian Residential Schools*. City Lights.

Cleary, J. F. (1970). Catholic Participation in the World's Parliament of Religions, Chicago, 1893. *The Catholic Historical Review, 55*(4), 585–609.

Connelly, J. (2012). *From Enemy to Brother: The Revolution in Catholic Teaching on the Jews, 1933–1965*. Harvard University Press.

Copeland, L., Lamm, L. W., & McKenna, S. J. (2012). *The World's Great Speeches* (4th ed.). Dover Publications.

Corbey, R. (1993). Ethnographic Showcases, 1870–1930. *Cultural Anthropology, 8*(3), 338–369.

Cornille, C. (2002). *Many Mansions? Multiple Religious Belonging and Christian Identity*. Orbis.

Cornille, C. (2013). Introduction. In C. Cornille (Ed.), *The Wiley-Blackwell Companion to Interreligious Dialogue* (pp. xii–xvii). Wiley-Blackwell.

Dalai Lama (2016, 19 September). There Is No Such Thing as a Muslim Terrorist. *The Independent*. Retrieved from www.independent.co.uk/news/people/dalai-lama-muslim-terrorism-islam-no-such-thing-as-video-watch-speech-a7317001.html

De Harlez, C. J. (1993). The Comparative Study of the World's Religions. In E. Ziolkowski (Ed.), *A Museum of Faiths: Histories and Legacies of the 1893 World's Parliament of Religions*, AAR Classics in Religious Studies 9 (pp. 95–110). Scholars Press.

Depew, C. M. (1892). *The Columbian Oration: Delivered at the Dedication Ceremonies of the World's Fair at Chicago, October 21, 1892*. E.C. Lockwood.

Domosh, M. (2002). A 'Civilized' Commerce: Gender, 'Race', and Empire at the 1893 Chicago Exposition. *Cultural Geographies, 9*(2), 181–201.

Fader, L. A. (1982). Zen in the West: Historical and Philosophical Implications of the 1893 Chicago World's Parliament of Religions. *The Eastern Buddhist, 15*(1), 122–145.

Fadil, N., de Koning, M., & Ragazzi, F. (2019). *Radicalization in Belgium and the Netherlands: Critical Perspectives on Violence and Security*. Tauris.

Fahy, J., & Bock, J.-J. (2020). *The Interfaith Movement: Mobilising Religious Diversity in the 21st Century*. Routledge.

Feldman, E. (1967). American Ecumenicism: Chicago's World's Parliament of Religions of 1893. *Journal of Church and State, 9*(2), 180–199.

Fitzgerald, T. (2011). *Religion and Politics in International Relations: The Modern Myth*. Continuum.

Green, C. T. (2017). A Stage Set for Assimilation: The Model Indian School at the World's Columbian Exposition. *Winterthur Portfolio, 51*(2–3), 95–133.

Green, T. H. (2019). *The Fear of Islam: An Introduction to Islamophobia in the West* (2nd ed.). Fortress.

Griera, M. (2012). Public Policies, Interfaith Associations and Religious Minorities: A New Policy Paradigm? Evidence from the Case of Barcelona. *Social Compass, 59*(4), 570–587.

Griera, M. (2019). Interreligious Events in the Public Space: Performing Togetherness in Times of Religious Pluralism. In M. Moyaert (Ed.), *Interreligious Relations and the Negotiation of Ritual Boundaries: Explorations in Interrituality* (pp. 35–55). Palgrave Macmillan.

Griera, M., & Nagel, A.-K. (2018). Interreligious Relations and Governance of Religion in Europe: Introduction. *Social Compass, 65*(3), 301–311.

Gustafson, H. (2020). Vitality of Lived Religion Approaches. In H. Gustafson (Ed.), *Interreligious Studies: Dispatches from an Emerging Field* (pp. 91–97). Baylor University Press.

Haddad, Y. Y., & Golson, T. (2007). Overhauling Islam: Representation, Construction, and Cooption of 'Moderate Islam' in Western Europe. *Journal of Church and State, 49*(3), 487–515.

Halafoff, A. (2013). *The Multifaith Movement: Global Risks and Cosmopolitan Solutions*. Springer.

Hedges, P. (2017). Multiple Religious Belonging after Religion: Theorising Strategic Religious Participation in a Shared Religious Landscape as a Chinese Model. *Open Theology, 3*(1), 48–72.

Heinz, H., & Brandt, H. C. H. G. (2008). A New Burden on Christian-Jewish Relations: Statement of the Discussion Group 'Jews and Christians' of the Central Committee of German Catholics on the Good Friday Prayer 'for the Jews' in the Extraordinary Rite Version of 2008. *European Judaism: A Journal for the New Europe, 41*(1), 159–161.

Heng, G. (2018). *The Invention of Race in the European Middle Ages*. Cambridge University Press.

Hill Fletcher, J. (2005). *Monopoly on Salvation? A Feminist Approach to Religious Pluralism*. Continuum.

Hill Fletcher, J. (2017a). Marginal Notes. In T. Merrigan & J. Friday (Eds.), *The Past, Present, and Future of Theologies of Interreligious Dialogue* (pp. 145–163). Oxford University Press.

Hill Fletcher, J. (2017b). *The Sin of White Supremacy: Christianity, Racism, and Religious Diversity in America*. Orbis.

Hochberg, G. Z. (2016). 'Remembering Semitism' or 'On the Prospect of Re-Membering the Semites'. *ReOrient, 1*(2), 192–223.

Horrell, D. G. (2020). *Ethnicity and Inclusion: Religion, Race, and Whiteness in Constructions of Jewish and Christian Identities*. Eerdmans.

Howard, T. A. (2021). *The Faiths of Others: A History of Interreligious Dialogue*. Yale University Press.

Hughes, A. W. (2012). *Abrahamic Religions: On the Uses and Abuses of History*. Oxford University Press.

Huntington, S. P. (1996). *The Clash of Civilizations and the Remaking of World Order*. Simon & Schuster.

Hurd, E. S. (2012). International Politics after Secularism. *Review of International Studies, 38*(5), 943–961.

Hurd, E. S. (2017). *Beyond Religious Freedom: The New Global Politics of Religion*. Princeton University Press.

Hutchison, W. R. (2003). *Religious Pluralism in America: The Contentious History of a Founding Ideal*. Yale University Press.

Hutter, M. (2016). *Experiencing Cities* (3rd ed.). Pearson Allyn and Bacon.

Ipgrave, J. (2019). *Interreligious Engagement in Urban Spaces: Social, Material and Ideological Dimensions*. Springer.

Isaac, J., Weaver, H., & Bishop, C. H. (1964). *The Teaching of Contempt: Christian Roots of Anti-Semitism*. Holt, Rinehart and Winston.

Jackson, R. (2014). *Signposts – Policy and Practice for Teaching about Religions and Non-religious World Views in Intercultural Education*. Council of Europe.

Jansen, Y., & van der Steen, N. (2023, forthcoming). Inquisitive Racialisation or Race 'after' Secularisation: A Critical Phenomenological and Cultural Analytical Approach. *Identities: Global Studies in Culture and Power.*

Jennings, W. J. (2010). *The Christian Imagination: Theology and the Origins of Race*. Yale University Press.

Joshi, K. Y. (2020). *White Christian Privilege: The Illusion of Religious Equality in America*. New York University Press.

Judd, R. (2011). *Contested Rituals: Circumcision, Kosher Butchering, and Jewish Political Life in Germany, 1843–1933*. Cornell University Press.

Kaell, H., & Walker, D. (forthcoming). Religion Performed: The World's Columbian Exposition of 1893. In T. Dubois (Ed.), *A Cultural History of Religion in the West in the Age of Empire*. Bloomsbury.

Keane, W. (2002). Sincerity, 'Modernity', and the Protestants. *Cultural Anthropology, 17*(1), 65–92.

334 CHAPTER 9 The Dialogical Turn beyond Religionization?

Kitagawa, J. M. (1987). *The History of Religion: Understanding Human Experience*, AAR Studies in Religion 47. Scholars Press.

Körs, A., & Nagel, A.-K. (2018). Local 'Formulas of Peace': Religious Diversity and State-Interfaith Governance in Germany. *Social Compass*, *65*(3), 346–362.

Körs, A., Weisse, W., & Willaime, J.-P. (2020). *Religious Diversity and Interreligious Dialogue*. Springer.

Kohut, A. (1893). What the Hebrew Scriptures Have Wrought for Mankind. In J. H. Barrows (Ed.), *The World's Parliament of Religions: An Illustrated and Popular Story of the World's First Parliament of Religions, Held in Chicago in Connection with the Columbian Exposition of 1893* (pp. 724–731). The Parliament Publishing Company.

Kwok, P. (2005). *Postcolonial Imagination and Feminist Theology*. Westminster John Knox.

Lamberigts, M., & Declerck, L. (2010). Vatican II on the Jews: A Historical Survey. In M. Moyaert & D. Pollefeyt (Eds.), *Never Revoked: Nostra Aetate as Ongoing Challenge for Jewish-Christian Dialogue* (pp. 1–12), Louvain Theological and Pastoral Monographs 40. Peeters.

Lamine, A.-S. (2004). *La cohabitation des dieux: pluralité religieuse et laïcité*. Presses universitaires de France.

Lauwers, A. S. (2023). Religion, Secularity, Culture? Investigating Christian Privilege in Western Europe. *Ethnicities*, *23*(3), 403–425.

Marshall, K. (2017). *Interfaith Journeys: An Exploration of History, Ideas, and Future Directions*. World Faiths Development.

Masuzawa, T. (2005). *The Invention of World Religions, or, How European Universalism Was Preserved in the Language of Pluralism*. University of Chicago Press.

Minister, K. (2020). Decolonizing the Study of Religion. In H. Gustafson (Ed.), *Interreligious Studies: Dispatches from an Emerging Field* (pp. 157–163). Baylor University Press.

Molendijk, A. L. (2011). To Unite Religion against All Irreligion: The 1893 World Parliament of Religions. *Journal for the History of Modern Theology*, *18*(2), 228–250.

Moreland, A. B. (2020). *Muhammad Reconsidered: A Christian Perspective on Islamic Prophecy*. University of Notre Dame Press.

Moyaert, M. (2013). Interreligious Dialogue. In D. Cheetham, D. Pratt, & M. Thomas (Eds.), *Understanding Inter-Religious Relations* (pp. 193–217). Oxford University Press.

Moyaert, M. (2015). Introduction: Exploring the Phenomenon of Interreligious Ritual Participation. In M. Moyaert & J. Geldhof (Eds.), *Ritual Participation and Interreligious Dialogue: Boundaries, Transgressions and Innovations* (pp. 1–16). Bloomsbury Academic.

Moyaert, M. (2016a). Christianity as the Measure of Religion? Materializing the Theology of Religions. In E. Harris, P. Hedges, & S. Hettiarachchi (Eds.), *Twenty-First Century Theologies of Religions: Retrospection and Future Prospects*, Currents of Encounter 54 (pp. 239–266). Brill.

Moyaert, M. (2016b). *Dei Verbum*, *Nostra Aetate* and Interreligious Dialogue. *Louvain Studies*, *39*(1), 42–63.

Moyaert, M. (2016c). Who Is the Suffering Servant? A Comparative Theological Reading of Isaiah 53 after the Shoah. In M. Voss Roberts (Ed.), *Comparing Faithfully: Insights for Systematic Theological Reflection* (pp. 216–237). Fordham University Press.

Moyaert, M. (2018). Inter-Worldview Education and the Re-Production of Good Religion. *Education Sciences*, *8*(4), 1–15.

Moyaert, M. (2019a). Interreligious Hermeneutics, Prejudice, and the Problem of Testimonial Injustice. *Religious Education 114*(5), 609–623.

Moyaert, M. (2019b). Interreligious Learning, Ricoeur, and the Problem of Testimonial and Hermeneutical Injustice. *Journal of Nationalism, Memory and Language Politics*, *13*(2), 205–223.

Moyaert, M. (2023). Critical Religious Education and the Deconstruction of Religion. In D. Pollefeyt (Ed.), *From Interreligious Learning to Interworldview Education*, Bibliotheca Ephemeridum Theologicarum Lovaniensium 332 (pp. 67–85). Peeters.

Moyaert, M. (forthcoming). Liturgy and the Religions of the World. In J. Geldhof (Ed.), Cambridge Companion to Liturgical Theology. Cambridge University Press.

Moyaert, M., & Pollefeyt, D. (2010). Israel and the Church: Fulfillment beyond Supersessionism. In M. Moyaert & D. Pollefeyt (Eds.), *Never Revoked: Nostra Aetate as Ongoing Challenge for Jewish-Christian Dialogue*, Louvain Theological and Pastoral Monographs 40 (pp. 160–183). Peeters.

Müller, F. M. (1894, ed. 2002). The Parliament of Religions in Chicago 1893. In J. R. Stone (Ed.), *The Essential Max Müller: On Language, Mythology and Religion* (pp. 343–352). Palgrave Macmillan.

Nathan, E., & Topolski, A. (Eds.) (2016). *Is There a Judeo-Christian Tradition? A European Perspective*, Perspectives on Jewish Texts and Contexts 4 (pp. 267–284). De Gruyter.

Numrich, P. D. (2019). The Rhetoric of American Exceptionalism in the Interfaith Movement in the United States. *Journal of Ecumenical Studies*, *54*(1), 74–106.

Nussbaum, M. C. (2013). *Political Emotions: Why Love Matters for Justice.* Harvard University Press.

O'Collins, G. (2014). *The Second Vatican Council on Other Religions.* Oxford University Press.

Oesterreicher, J. M. (1969). Declaration on the Relationship of the Church to Non-Christian Religions: Introduction and Commentary. In H. Vorgrimler (Ed.), *Commentary on the Documents of Vatican II* (Vol. 3, pp. 1–136). Herder.

Omer, A. (2020, 25 November). Engaging Religion or Domesticating Religion? An Interview with Atalia Omer [Interview]. Retrieved from https://religionanddiplomacy.org/2020/11/25/engaging-religion-or-domesticating-religion-an-interview-with-atalia-omer/

Omer, A. (2021). Religion and the Study of Peace: Practice without Reflection. *Religions, 12*(12), 1069. https://doi.org/10.3390/rel12121069

Park, J. J., & Sharma, G. (2016). Religion and Social Capital: Examining the Roles of Religious Affiliation and Salience on Parental Network Closure. *Religion & Education, 43*(2), 162–177.

Peskowitz, M. (1998). Religion Posed as a Racial Category: A Reading of Emile Burnouf, Adolph Moses, and Eliza Sunderland. *Studies in the History of Religions* (80), 231–252.

Potter, L. M. (2022, 11 June). All Catholic Theology Is Comparative Theology. Paper Presented at the Annual Convention of the Catholic Theological Society of America, Atlanta, GA.

Price, H. (1883). Rules Governing the Court of Indian Offenses. March 30, 1883. Retrieved from https://commons.und.edu/ indigenous-gov-docs/131/

Puett, T. (2014). The Political Discourse of Religious Pluralism: World Religions Textbooks, Liberalism, and Civic Identities. Diss. University of Waterloo, Ontario.

Putnam, R. D. (2000). *Bowling Alone: The Collapse and Revival of American Community.* Simon & Schuster.

Qureshi, S. (2011). *Peoples on Parade: Exhibitions, Empire, and Anthropology in Nineteenth Century Britain.* University of Chicago Press.

Raibmon, P. S. (2005). *Authentic Indians: Episodes of Encounter from the Late-Nineteenth-Century Northwest Coast.* Duke University Press.

Read Sunderland, E. (1993). Serious Study of All Religions. In E. Ziolkowski (Ed.), *A Museum of Faiths: Histories and Legacies of the 1893 World's Parliament of Religions*, AAR Classics in Religious Studies 9 (pp. 111–126). Scholars Press.

Réville, A. (1993). Conditions and Outlook for a Universal Religion. In E. Ziolkowski (Ed.), *A Museum of Faiths: Histories and Legacies of the 1893 World's Parliament of Religions*, AAR Classics in Religious Studies 9 (pp. 85–89). Scholars Press.

Rydell, R. W. (1987). *All the World's a Fair: Visions of Empire at American International Expositions, 1876–1916.* University of Chicago Press.

Rydell, R. W. (2005). World's Columbian Exposition, May 1, 1893–October 30, 1893. In *Encyclopedia of Chicago.* Retrieved from www.encyclopedia.chicagohistory.org/pages/1386.html#:~:text=World's%20Columbian%20Exposition&text=(May%201%2C%201893%E2%80%93October%2030%2C%201893.)&text=Organized%20to%20commemorate%20the%20400th,United%20States%20as%20a%20whole

Schmidt-Leukel, P. (2013). Christianity and the Religious Other. In D. Cheetham, D. Pratt, & M. Thomas (Eds.), *Understanding Inter-Religious Relations* (pp. 118–147). Oxford University Press.

Schneider, M. (2017). Religious Communities and Interreligious Dialogue: Two Guidelines for Living Together in Multi-religious Societies. *Studies in Interreligious Dialogue, 27*(2), 117–130.

Seager, R. H. (1989). Pluralism and the American Mainstream: The View from the World's Parliament of Religions. *Harvard Theological Review, 82*(3), 301–324.

Seager, R. H. (1993). *The Dawn of Religious Pluralism: Voices from the World's Parliament of Religions, 1893.* Open Court.

Seager, R. H. (1995). *The World's Parliament of Religions: The East/West Encounter, Chicago, 1893.* Indiana University Press.

Silk, M. (1984). Notes on the Judeo-Christian Tradition in America. *American Quarterly, 36*(1), 65–85.

Smith, L. D., Führding, S., & Hermann, A. (2020). *Hijacked: A Critical Treatment of the Public Rhetoric of Good and Bad Religion.* Equinox.

Sperber, J. B. (2019). *Anthropological Aspects in the Christian-Muslim Dialogues of the Vatican,* Judaism, Christianity, and Islam – Tension, Transmission, Transformation 14. De Gruyter.

Stosch, K. von, & Khorchide, M. (2016). *Streit um Jesus: Muslimische und christliche Annäherungen.* Schöningh.

Swamy, M. (2017). *Problem with Interreligious Dialogue: Plurality, Conflict and Elitism in Hindu-Christian-Muslim Relations.* Bloomsbury.

Takacs, A. M. O. (2022). Toward a Praxis of Reconciliation: Catholic Theology, Interreligious Studies, and Anti-Muslim Bigotry. In L. Mosher (Ed.), *The Georgetown Companion to Interreligious Studies* (pp. 197–210). Georgetown University Press.

336 CHAPTER 9 The Dialogical Turn beyond Religionization?

Talbot, S. (2006). Spiritual Genocide: The Denial of American Indian Religious Freedom, from Conquest to 1934. *Wicazo Sa Review, 21*(2), 7–39.

Tauran, J.-L. (2018). Introduction: Vatican II – Remembering the Future. In V. Latinovic, G. Mannion, & J. Welle (Eds.), *Catholicism Engaging Other Faiths: Vatican II and Its Impact* (pp. 15–22). Palgrave Macmillan.

Teixidor, J. (2006). *Le judéo-christianisme*. Folio Histoire 146. Gallimard.

Thatamanil, J. (2015). How Not to Be a Religion: Genealogy, Identity, Wonder. In M. Johnson-DeBaufre, C. Keller, & E. Ortega-Aponte (Eds.), *Common Goods: Economy, Ecology, and Political Theology* (pp. 54–72). Fordham University Press.

Thatamanil, J. J. (2020). *Circling the Elephant: A Comparative Theology of Religious Diversity*, Comparative Theology: Thinking across Traditions 8. Fordham University Press.

Tiemeier, T. S. (2013). Asian Participation in Interreligious Dialogue. In S. Henderson Callahan (Ed.), *Religious Leadership: A Reference Handbook* (Vol. 2, pp. 427–433). Sage Publications.

Tiemeier, T. S. (2022). For Whom, and to What End? Possibilities and Implications of Privileging Intersectionality in Interreligious Studies. In L. Mosher (Ed.), *The Georgetown Companion to Interreligious Studies* (pp. 147–156). Georgetown University Press.

Topolski, A. (2018). The Race-Religion Constellation: A European Contribution to the Critical Philosophy of Race. *Critical Philosophy of Race, 6*(1), 58–81.

Topolski, A. (2020). The Dangerous Discourse of the 'Judaeo-Christian' Myth: Masking the Race-Religion Constellation in Europe. *Patterns of Prejudice, 54*(1), 71–90.

Valance, H. (2009). Dark City, White City: Chicago's World Columbian Exposition, 1893. *Caliban: French Journal of English Studies, 25*, 431–444.

Valbousquet, N., Patriarca, S., & Deplano, V. (2018). Race and Faith: The Catholic Church, Clerical Fascism, and the Shaping of Italian Anti-Semitism and Racism. *Modern Italy, 23*(4), 355–371.

Valkenberg, P. (2019). How Others Bear Witness to Our Faith: Aquinas and *Lumen Gentium*. *European Journal for the Study of Thomas Aquinas, 33*(1), 54–75.

Van Es, M. A. (2018). Muslims Denouncing Violent Extremism Competing Essentialisms of Islam in Dutch Public Debate. *Journal of Muslims in Europe, 7*(2), 146–166.

Van Es, M. A. (2022). A Ring of Peace around the Oslo Synagogue: Muslims and Jews Expressing Interfaith Solidarity in Response to the Paris and Copenhagen Attacks. In L. van Liere & E. Meinema (Eds.), *Material Perspectives on Religion, Conflict, and Violence: Things of Conflict*, Supplements to Method & Theory in the Study of Religion 19 (pp. 187–210). Brill.

Van Es, M. A., ter Laan, N., & Meinema, E. (2021). Beyond 'Radical' versus 'Moderate'? New Perspectives on the Politics of Moderation in Muslim Majority and Muslim Minority Settings. *Religion, 51*(2), 161–168.

Vincent, A. M. (2019). Rituals of Reconciliation? How Consideration of Ritual Can Inform Readings of Catholic-Jewish Dialogue after the Holocaust. In M. Moyaert (Ed.), *Interreligious Relations and the Negotiation of Ritual Boundaries: Explorations in Interrituality* (pp. 179–196). Palgrave Macmillan.

Wilson, E. (2014). Theorizing Religion as Politics in Postsecular International Relations. *Politics, Religion & Ideology, 15*(3), 347–365.

Ziolkowski, E. J. (1993). Waking up from Akbar's Dream: The Literary Prefiguration of Chicago's 1893 World's Parliament of Religions. *The Journal of Religion, 73*(1), 42–60.

Conclusion

In this book I have offered a survey of how Christians at key moments in the history of Western Europe have configured a sense of 'religious normativity' (Christianness) by simultaneously crafting various figures of religious deviation (projected onto non-Christians). Others were turned into rhetorical figures – the heretic, the pagan, the Jew, the Saracen, the papist, the fanatic – existing mainly in the Christian imagination where they served the purpose of bolstering a sense of Christianness that functions as default. Therefore, these imaginary constructs tell us more about Christian European concerns and preoccupations than about these others in question. This is why, with Anidjar, I would say these categories are largely 'self-referential'.[1]

Imaginary religionized constructs create boundaries that are not in fact reflected in the messiness of social reality. Both the norm and its deviant counterparts are social constructs. They are conceived in binary schemes, resulting in an exaggeration of differences which mask more complicated realities. Even within a framework that presents itself as descriptive – showing reality as it is – these categories are in fact re-descriptive: they project an ideal reality from a particular Christian vantage point. This was the case for heresiology, but this also applies to the much later World Religions Paradigm.

When religionized categories are institutionalized and normalized, people who embody the norm tend to forget how these categories were crafted and shaped and whose interests they serve(d); they are taken for granted and are considered to depict reality as it is. At different moments throughout the book, I have problematized the projected boundaries by making explicit how in real life, boundaries were not only crossed, but also simply did not exist. Scholars researching religionization have to attend to the difference between what 'should be' the case (according to some) and what 'is' the case. I have, however, also surfaced how these imaginary constructs became powerful and helped to create a real world. Indeed, the notion of religionization takes us beyond the idea that what we are dealing with is merely a history of religious prejudice. It brings into focus that the way Christians have imagined the world of religious diversity is profoundly political. I have surfaced this by showing how religionized categories were institutionalized in the law and by describing the measures taken to discipline people who deviated from the norm. Often *literati*, theologians, and religious scholars – specialists when it comes to true religion – gave religionized categories legitimacy and authority.

Central to this book is the idea that there is a strong interconnection between the way Christian normativity is constructed and how otherness is imagined. When Christian self-understanding changed (e.g. an increased focus on the body and blood as metaphors for purity or tolerance as a Christian identity marker), this impacted the framing of Christianity's others (e.g. as impure or as objects of tolerance or as incapable of tolerance). Because of this interconnection, religionized constructs are volatile; depending on the context boundaries may be pushed, attenuated, or reinforced. At the same time, religionized constructs also resist change. A play of change and continuation, of volatility and fixation can be noticed: images of self and other shift; new layers of meaning are added, while older qualifications become dormant. It may happen that older layers of meaning are forgotten and pushed into the background until they become useful again in the process of selfing and othering. Depending on the context, some stereotypes serve little purpose and vanish, while others are newly created or resurface. Volatility, from this perspective, does not contradict stereotypical fixation. The resulting cultural archive, that for centuries was made and remade in literature, art, songs, architecture, and law, is vast and multifaceted: it functions as an almost inexhaustible resource from which those who embody the norm can draw to delegitimize deviating social groups.

Christian Imaginations of the Religious Other: A History of Religionization, First Edition. Marianne Moyaert.
© 2024 John Wiley & Sons Ltd. Published 2024 by John Wiley & Sons Ltd.

At a meta-hermeneutical level, I have demonstrated that patterns of religionization also impact the way history is related and imagined. There is a tendency to narrate history such that it takes on mythic proportions, with key moments, turning points, heroes and losers, disaster and redemption, corruption and restoration, and so on. Some of these myths continue to impact our understanding of Western European history and of the role of (secularized) Christians and the others of Christianity in it. I have tried to show how those myths are themselves intertwined with and produced by patterns of religionization. Even scholarly discourses have been permeated by normative binaries that oversimplify complex histories, often to the benefit of some and the detriment of others. The contradistinction, for example, between Reformation and Counter-Reformation, which long operated as the dominant frame to make sense of the conflicts during the sixteenth and seventeenth centuries is a point in case. It is a frame that is pervaded by a Protestant bias. I also deconstructed those emancipatory narratives that project the rise of modern Enlightenment and tolerance as a self-congratulatory story; surfacing how the so-called voices for tolerance built their argument on ancient and new patterns of religionization was part of this deconstruction.

The more I zoomed in on discourses that are part of the way (secularized) Western European Christians imagine the world they live in, the more conscious I became of the fact that I am implicated in the history that I am researching. It is too easy to dismiss the problem of religionization as a problem that belongs to a dark, medieval, and pre-scientific past. To this day, I claim, old and new patterns of religionization continue to do real work in today's world: they impact the way we organize 'our personal experience, our social and political relations, and our academic work' (Vial, 2016). Even, the dialogical turn which centres the importance of learning across traditions and creates a context in which others may talk back assumes particular religionized patterns of thinking and even more problematically masks the history of religio-racialization (Topolski, 2018). For dialogue to reach its emancipatory potential it must be complemented with a prolonged effort to deconstruct the concepts with which Europeans have forged a normative sense of (secularized) Christianness. It is for this reason that I embarked on a genealogical exploration of the history of religionization.

Note

[1] The Jew, the Arab. Interview with Gil Anidjar, n.d. https://asiasociety.org/jew-arab-interview-gil-anidjar.

References

Topolski, A. (2018). The Race-Religion Constellation: A European Contribution to the Critical Philosophy of Race. *Critical Philosophy of Race*, *6*(1), 58–81.

Vial, T. M. (2016). *Modern Religion, Modern Race*. Oxford University Press.

Index

The index lists all historical names and documents, supplemented with key terms that appear throughout the book. More systematically covered topics can be easily found by scrolling through the detailed table of contents.

A

Acosta, José de (1539–1600), 172, 174–175
Ad Abolendam (1184), 100, 105
Ad Extirpanda (1252), 106
Ad Gentes (1965), 331
Adoptionism, 49
Adversus Haereses, 15, 40–41, 183
Adversus Iudaeos, 15, 24, 32–33, 61, 262
Agobard of Lyon (ca. 779–840), 93
Al-Andalus, 114–115
Alexander II (pope, r. 1061–1073), 94
Alexander III (pope, r. 1159–1181), 99–100
Alexander VI (pope, r. 1492–1503), 114, 139
Alexios Komnenos (emperor, r. 1081–1118), 83
Alfonso X of Castille (king, r. 1252–1284), 117–119, 121–122, 142
(Ana)baptism/(Ana)baptists, 145–146, 181, 196, 198, 219
Anglicans, 181, 221, 251
Anomoeans, 49, 54
Apollinarians, 54
Arians/Arianism, 46, 49, 52, 54, 58, 98, 183
Aristotle (384–322 BCE), 172–173
Arnaud Amaury (d. 1225), 104
Athanasius of Alexandria (295–373), 58
Atheism/t, 228, 306, 319, 321
Augsburg Confession/*Confessio Augustana* (1530), 181, 192–195, 197
Augsburg Peace Treaty (1555), 181, 191–195, 205, 207
Augustine of Hippo (354–430), 37, 56, 58, 61, 64–66, 92, 94, 118, 133, 152, 214, 262, 280
Augustinians, 157

B

Badge (Jewish), 108, 111
Baldric of Bourgueil (1050–1130), 85
Baptism, forced, 132
Barrows, John Henry (1847–1902), 292
Baur, F. C. (1792–1860), 321
Bede the Venerable (672/3–735), 69

Benedict XVI (pope, r. 2005–2013), 314, 316, 319, 331
Benedictines, 157
Bernard of Clairvaux (1090–1153), 91, 101–102, 116
Beza, Theodore (1519–1605), 184–185
Black(ness), 86–87, 89–90, 96–97, 109, 111–112, 123, 133, 135, 138, 259–260, 301
Blood purity, 93, 114, 120–123, 128–132, 134, 140–141, 163
Boas, Franz (1858–1943), 294
Bohemian Maiestas Rudolphina (1609), 191
Bonney, Charles Carroll (1831–1903), 293
Book of Concord (1580), 197
Brethren/Sisters of the Common Life, 157, 159
Buddhism, 250, **255, 283,** 285–286, 292, 294, 297, 302, **307–309,** 326

C

Cain's mark/curse, **37,** 65, 91, 130, 133, 262, 320
Calas, Jean (1698–1762), 230–231, 233
Calvin, John (1509–1564), 151–152, 184, 186, 191, 199–200, **213–217**
Calvinists, 145–**146, 181,** 183–184, 188, 194, 196, 198, 200, **218,** 251
Canisius, Peter (1521–1597), 185
Carnal/ity, 25, **32,** 34–36, 38, 55, 65, 86, 88, 91, 95, 103, 127, 155, 183–184, 188, 205, 217–218, 222, 226, 238, 244
Carpocratians, 49
Castellio, Sebastian (1515–1563), 42, 146, 212–219, 222, 224, 230, 243–245, 252
Cathars, 4–5, 86, 99–100, 104, 106, 183
Censorship, 165, 203
Chanson de geste, 87–88, 91
Charles V (emperor, r. 1519–1558), 165, 192
Christ-killers, 5, 36, 63, 91, 95, 97–118, 312
Christoph of Württemberg (1515–1568), 214, 218
Cicero (106–43 BCE), 17–20

Christian Imaginations of the Religious Other: A History of Religionization, First Edition. Marianne Moyaert.
© 2024 John Wiley & Sons Ltd. Published 2024 by John Wiley & Sons Ltd.

340 Index

Clement IV (pope, r. 1265–1268), 123
Clement of Alexandria (150–211/215), 23–24
Colonization, 134, 253, 257, 260,
    278, 302, 305
Columbus, Christopher (1451–1506), 114,
    134–139, 172, 241, 292–293
Comparative religion, 11, 142, 246, 256–257,
    280–287, 290
Condillac, Étienne Bonnot de
    (1715–1780), 263
Confiscation, 120, 187, 224, 230
Confucianism, 250, 255, 283, 292
Confucius, 241
Congress of Vienna (1815), 263
Constantine (emperor, r. 306–337), 15,
    43, 46, 60
Conversion, forced, 56, 67, 92–94,
    125–127, 320
Conversion, of mosque, 115–117, 143–144
Conversos, 118, 125–129, 131–132, 177, 204
Corpus Christi (feast), 96, 174, 200, 204
Corpus Christianum, 77–79, 93, 95, 97, 99,
    103–104, 106, 109, 113, 124, 129, 133,
    140, 145–146, 182–183, 186, 188–190,
    192–194, 205, 212, 214, 216, 226, 232,
    243, 251, 313
Costerus, Franciscus (1532–1619), 185
Council of Clermont (1095), 83
Council of Constance (1414), 145
Council of Lyon II (1274), 153
Council of Nicaea I (325), 46–47, 50,
    58, 100
Council of Pisa (1409), 145
Council of Toledo IV (633), 93
Council of Toledo XII (681), 93
Council of Trent (1545–1563), 192,
    195, 197, 202
Council of Valladolid (1322), 142
Counter-Reformation, 194–196, 208–209, 338
Covarrubias, Sebastián de (1539–1613), 130
Crespin, Jean (1520–1572), 185
Crusading ideology/ies, 82, 94, 108, 114, 120

D

Dalai Lama, 324
Daoism/Taoism, 250, 255, 283, 292
Dei Verbum (1965), 331
Deicide, 35–36, 62, 95, 311, 320
Deism/Theism, 238–243, 292
Delors, Jacques, 326
Depew, Chauncy M. (1834–1928), 293
Destruction of the temple of Jerusalem,
    19, 32, 37–38

Devotio moderna → Modern devotion
Dhimmis, 114–115, 142
Diet of Worms (1521), 165, 188
Dignitatis Humanae (1965), 312, 319
Dispar nimirum est (1063), 94
Docetism, 49
Domingo de Guzmán (saint, 1170–1221), 122
Dominicans, 104, 106, 122, 157
Donatism, 56, 98

E

Ebion/Ebionites, 48–49
Ecclesiam Suam (1964), 305–306, 317
Edict of Grace of Alès (1629), 191
Edict of Milan (313), 46
Edict of Nantes (1598), 53, 191, 220, 230
Edict of Thessaloniki (380), 52–53
Edict of Tolerance (1787), 231
Encratites, 54
Enlightenment, 141, 150, 196, 212, 217, 230,
    232, 234–237, 245–247, 255–256, 258,
    290, 314–315, 328, 338
Epiphanius of Salamis (ca. 310/320–403),
    48–51, 55, 68–69, 100, 133, 251
Erasmus, Desiderius (1466–1536), 146, 149,
    159–167, 172, 198, 215
Essenes, 32, 39
Ethnicization, 1, 2, 15
Eusebius of Caesarea (ca. 260–340), 46
Expulsion, 32, 38, 55, 107, 114, 119, 122–125,
    132, 134–135, 187–189, 191, 209, 320
Expulsion (of heretics), 55, 107, 114,
    187–189, 191
Expulsion (of Jews), 19, 32, 37–38, 107, 114,
    122–125, 132, 134–135, 320
Expulsion (of the Moors), 119
Exsurge Domine (1520), 165
Ezour-Vedam, 241–242

F

Fanaticism, 222, 226, 230–234, 236–242,
    247–248, 273–275, 304
Ferdinand I (emperor, r. 1556–1564),
    192, 194, 207
Ferdinand II of Aragon (king, r. 1479–1516),
    79, 83, 109, 114–115, 121–122, 130–132,
    134, 139, 188
Ferdinand III (king, r. 1217–1252), 121
Fichte, Johann Gottlieb (1762–1814), 269
Ficino, Marsilio (1433–1499), 251
Flavius Josephus (37–100 CE), 39
Francesco di Pietro di Bernadone
    (1181–1226), 104

Francis (pope), 307, 311–312, 314, 316–317, 319, 331
Francis (saint, 1182–1226), 316
Francis I (king of France, r. 1515–1547), 188
Franciscans, 104, 106, 122, 157
Franck, Sebastian (1499–1542), 215
Fratelli Tutti (2020), 307, 317
Frederick I (emperor, r. 1155–1190), 100
Frederick II (king, 1712–1786), 234
Frederick the Wise (1463–1525), 188
Freeman, Edward A. (1823–1892), 265
French Revolution, 108, 267, 269

G

Gaudet Mater Ecclesia (1962), 305
Gender/ing, 1–2, 15, 20–22, 40, 43, 48, 63, 75, 142, 144, 162, 187, 207, 323, 327, 332
Gerson, Jean (1363–1429), 156
Gnosticism, 49
Gregory VII (pope, r. 1073–1085), 81–83
Gregory IX (pope, r. 1227–1241), 102–103, 106
Gregory XIII (pope, r. 1572–1585), 204
Grote, Geert (1340–1385), 146, 149, 156–158

H

Hagar/Hagarenes, 69–71, 309, 311
Hegel, Georg Wilhelm Friedrich (1770–1831), 196
Heidelberg Catechism (1563), 197
Helvetic Confessions (1536, 1566), 197, 200
Heraclius (emperor, r. 610–641), 68
Herder, Johann Gottfried von (1744–1803), 262–263
Heresiology, 11–12, 43, 47–49, 51, 54, 68, 74–75, 98, 100, 181, 337
Hilary of Poitiers (ca. 315–ca. 367), 214
Hindus/Hinduism, 241, 250, 255, 266, 283, 286, 292, 294, 297, 307–309, 317, 326
Host Desecration, 96, 111, 170
Huguenots, 188, 207, 220, 230–231
Humanism, 159, 161, 163, 209, 232, 256
Humboldt, Wilhelm von (1767–1835), 270
Huntington, Samuel (1927–2008), 323

I

Iconoclasm, 166, 189, 206, 231
Ignatius of Loyola (1491–1556), 158
Ille Humani Generis (1231), 102
Imperialism, 8, 11–12, 256–257, 265, 287
Index Librorum Prohibitorum, 160, 203
Indulgences, 83, 150–151, 153–154, 159–160, 165–166, 179

Innocent III (pope, r. 1198–1216), 82, 86, 94, 104–106
Innocent IV (pope, r. 1243–1254), 106
Innocent VIII (pope, r. 1482–1492), 203
Inquisition, 79, 99, 102–104, 109, 111, 114, 122, 131–132, 134, 143, 221, 226, 231
Inter Caetera (1493), 139
Inter Multiplices (1487), 203
Interiorization, 6, 141, 150, 155, 187, 215, 250–251
Interreligious dialogue, 256, 291, 297–298, 303, 309, 312–313, 322, 333–336
Investiture, 81, 121, 131
Irenaeus of Lyon (140–220), 33, 35, 39–42, 50, 55
Isabella I of Castile (queen, r. 1474–1504), 79, 83, 109, 114–115, 121–122, 130–132, 134, 139, 188
Ishmael/Ishmaelites, 69–72, 84, 87, 91, 125, 309, 311
Isidore of Seville (560–636), 121
Islam/Islamic, 67–72, 78, 82, 84, 115–117, 120, 122, 131–132, 140, 142, 146, 183, 228–230, 234, 236–238, 240, 242–243, 250, 252, 261, 274, 277–278, 283, 286, 292, 295, 297, 307, 309–311, 322–324, 328–330
Islamophobia, 10, 278, 312, 322, 329

J

Jacob of Edessa (640–708), 71
Jacob of Vitry (ca. 1160–1240), 97
Jainism, 250, 283, 292
James I of Aragon (king, r. 1231–1276), 122
James II (king, r.1685–1688), 220
Jerome (ca. 347–420), 214
Jew Bill (1753), 223
John Chrysostom (347–407), 61–64, 73, 214
John of Damascus (675/6–749), 68–70, 100, 152, 311
John XXIII (pope, r. 1958–1963), 304–306, 312–313
John Paul II (pope, r. 1978–2005), 315–316, 319, 331
Jones, Jenkin Lloyd (1843–1918), 293
Jones, William (1746–1794), 265–267, 287
Judaize, 33, 44, 58, 62–63, 127, 129, 131, 149, 320
Justin Martyr (100–165), 23–24, 26, 34–35, 40–41, 43
Justinian (emperor, r. 529–565), 59, 92
Justinian Code, 92, 118

342 Index

K
King of Tars, 88–89

L
Lactantius (ca. 240–ca. 320), 214
Lamentabilii (1907), 258
Las Casas, Bartolomé de (1484–1566), 173–175
Las Siete Partidas (Alfonso X), 117–120, 142
Lassen, Christian (1800–1876), 270
Lateran Council II (1139), 95
Lateran Council III (1179), 95, 99–100
Lateran Council IV (1213–1215), 78, 82, 96, 106–107, 118–119, 151, 153
Leo XIII (pope, r. 1878–1903), 302
Lessius, Leonardus (1554–1623), 181
Limpieza de sangre, 128–129, 132
Linnaeus, Carl (1707–1778), 260
Locke, John (1632–1704), 53, 146, 212, 220–228, 230, 238, 243–244, 252, 277
Logic of Dichotomy, 15, 21, 25, 32, 37, 51, 54, 239
Logic of Encompassment, 16, 51, 137, 173–174, 239, 300, 307
Louis XIV (king, r. 1643–1715), 53
Lucas de Tuy (d. 1249), 123
Lucius III (pope, r. 1181–1185), 100, 105
Lumen Gentium (1964), 308–309, 312, 331
Luther, Martin (1483–1546), 146, 149–151, 155, 164–171, 178, 184, 188, 191, 196, 199, 203, 215
Lutherans, 145–146, 181, 183–184, 186–187, 191, 193–202, 219, 251

M
Macedonians, 54
Manicheans/Manicheism, 49, 64, 98, 100
Marcion/Marcionites, 41, 48–49
Marr, Wilhelm (1819–1904), 274
Marranos, 127, 132, 144, 226, 329
Maudave, Fayd'herbe de (1725–1777), 242
Maximus the Confessor (580–662), 68
Melanchton, Philip (1497–1560), 178
Melito of Sardis (d. ca. 180), 35–37, 62, 95
Methodius of Olympus (d. 311/12), 39
Michaelis, Johann David (1717–1791), 263
Minucius Felix (d. ca. 250), 22–23
Modern devotion, 155–158, 166
Modernist crisis, 258, 302, 305
Modernity, 7, 144, 178, 180, 196, 209, 212, 229, 251, 262, 267, 288–289, 296, 300, 303, 322, 332–333

Monotheism, 67, 70, 273, 276
Monstrous/monstrosity, 2, 12, 86–87, 89, 95, 109, 112, 183, 209, 216, 230
Müller, Friedrich Max (1823–1900), 261, 263–264, 266, 271, 279–285, 299
Muslims, converted (= Moriscos), 132, 226, 329

N
Nahmanides (1195–1270), 122
Napoleonic wars, 263, 267, 269
Nestorians/Nestorianism, 183
Nicene creed, 46, 51–53, 55, 62, 72, 205
Nostra Aetate (1965), 291, 306–312, 315–321, 330–331
Novalis (1772–1802), 262

O
Origen (185–253), 38
Othering, 1–3, 5–6, 10, 13, 15, 21–22, 30–32, 37, 40, 43, 79, 90, 141, 145–146, 154, 168, 181, 184, 187, 198, 255, 267, 286, 301, 324, 337

P
Pablo Christiani (d. 1274), 122
Pacem in Terris (1963), 312
Pacification of Ghent (1576), 191
Pantheism, 263, 273
Pascendi Domini Gregis (1907), 258
Pastor Aeternus (1870), 258
Paul V (pope, r. 1605–1621), 314
Paul VI (pope, r. 1963–1978), 305, 312, 314
Pax Deorum, 18, 21–22, 52, 195, 331
Pax Romana, 18, 27, 52, 133, 195
Peace of Amboise, France (1563), 191
Peace of Kappel, Switzerland (1529), 191
Pedro Sarmiento (1375–1464), 128
Persecution, 21–22, 27, 29, 40, 46, 51, 56, 72, 75, 79, 92, 100, 103, 114, 187–188, 191, 196, 212–218, 220–221, 229–231, 242, 277, 298, 300, 312, 315, 320, 324
Peter I of Castille and Leon (r. 1350–1369), 124
Peter the Venerable (1092–1156), 311
Peter Waldo (1140–1218), 100
Pfefferkorn, Johann (1469–1523), 163–164
Pharisees, 32, 39, 169, 216–217, 223
Philology, 112, 161, 254–257, 261–265, 267, 269, 271, 287–290
Pius IX (pope, r. 1846–1878), 258
Pliny the Elder (23/24–79 CE), 21
Pliny the Younger (61–113 CE), 22
Polytheism, 50, 69, 273

Pratt, Richard Henry (1840–1924), 295
Pseudo-Clementine *Recognitions,* 24
Purgation, 79, 116–117, 120, 130, 132, 183, 187–189, 202, 205, 313
Putnam, Frederic Ward (1839–1915), 294

R
Racialization, 1–2, 4, 11, 79, 134, 140–141, 163, 244, 259, 262, 264, 296, 300, 318–320, 330, 338
Recarred (king, r. 586–601), 109
Reconquista, 79, 84, 114–117, 120–121, 134, 140, 142
Relief Act (1778), 223, 244
Religio-racialization, 4, 79, 134, 163, 296, 300, 318–319, 330, 338
Religio-secular divide, 3, 7, 146, 219, 226, 229, 243, 249–250, 252, 299–300, 303–304, 312, 316–321, 323, 330
Religio-secularization, 3, 4, 212, 228, 243, 252, 296, 298, 317–318
Religious Peace (Low Countries, 1578), 191
Renan, Ernest (1823–1892), 261, 270–280, 282, 310, 330
Robert of Rheims (Robert the Monk, 1055–1122), 85
Rodrigo Jiménez de Andrada (1170–1247), 121
(Roman) Catholics, 145–146, 181, 183–184, 198, 200, 219, 251
Romanticism, 263, 267, 269

S
Sadducees, 39
Saracens, 1, 4–5, 7, 69, 72, 77–79, 82–91, 94–95, 98, 104, 108, 123, 133, 136–137, 139, 141, 201, 259, 261, 272, 278, 310–312, 337
Satolli, Francesco (1839–1910), 302
Schlegel, August (1776–1845), 262
Schlegel, Friedrich (1772–1829), 262–263, 267–270
Schmalkaldic League, 192
Segregation, 79, 120, 200
Selfing, 1–3, 6, 10, 13, 15, 30, 37, 39–40, 43, 78, 90, 106, 141, 145–146, 168, 175, 177, 181, 187, 197, 255, 267–268, 286, 301, 324, 330, 337
Seneca the Younger (4 BCE–65 CE), 19
Sepúlveda, Juan Ginés de (1490–1573), 172–173
Servetus, Michael (1511–1553), 214
Sexual slander, 12, 15, 45, 63, 183

Sexualization, 34, 40, 183
Shintoism, 250, 255, 292
Shoah, 289, 305–306, 318–320, 334
Sikhs/Sikhism, 250, 326
Simonians, 41, 49
Sixtus IV (pope, r. 1471–1484), 131
Slave/Slavery, 20, 28, 41, 50, 66, 69, 71, 84, 92, 108, 118, 125, 134, 142–143, 167, 172–173, 175, 233, 235–236, 238, 288–289
Sodalitium Pianum (1862–1934), 258
Sophronius (patriarch, r. 634–638), 68
Staupitz, Johannes von (1460–1524), 164
Steinschneier, Moritz (1816–1907), 274
Stephan, Joachim (1544–1623), 193
Suetonius (69/70–140 CE), 22
Summorum Pontificum (2007), 314
Supersessionism/t, 34–35, 37, 45, 50, 91, 222, 299, 307, 310–311, 313, 315
Supremacy (white), 75, 246, 288, 333
Synod of Dort (1619), 197
Synod of Verona (1184), 105

T
Tacitus (56–117 CE), 21–22
Tertullian (155–220), 23, 26–30, 174, 251
Test Acts (1673), 220–221
Theodosian Code, 46–47, 52–55, 59–62, 66–67, 72–73, 92, 118, 133, 205
Theodosius (emperor, r. 379–395), 51
Theodosius II (emperor, r. 408–450), 54
Thomas Aquinas (1225–1274), 152, 155
Thomas of Monmouth (fl. 1149–1172), 95
Toaff, Elio (1915–2015), 315
Toleration Act (1689), 221
Traditionis Custodes (2021), 314
Treaty of Lisbon (2007), 327

U
Umar (caliph, r. 634–644), 68
Ummayad dynasty, 68, 82, 114–115, 121
Universal Declaration of Human Rights (1948), 305, 312
Urban II (pope, r. 1088–1099), 83
Urban IV (pope, r. 1261–1264), 96
Usury, 94–95, 107, 110, 170

V
Valentinians, 41
Valla, Lorenzo (1407–1457), 159
Vatican I (1869–1870), 258
Vatican II (1962–1965), 53, 142, 258, 291, 298, 304–321, 330
Vincent Ferrer (1350–1419), 125

344 Index

Voltaire, 146, 212, 226, 229–245, 252, 258, 273, 277
Vox in Rama (1233), 103

W

Waldensians, 86, 99–100, 104, 106, 183
We Remember (1998), 318–320
Westphalian Peace Treaty (1648), 191
William of Hesse (1743–1821), 214–215
William of Norwich (1132–1144), 95
World Parliament of Religions (Chicago, 1893), 291–304, 307, 330

World religions, 25, 249–250, 255, 284, 286–287, 293–295, 297, 299, 301–302, 304, 308–309, 316, 320
World Religions Paradigm, 3–4, 10, 249–250, 254–256, 258, 261, 276, 279, 293–294, 296–298, 300, 304, 309, 318, 330–331, 337

Z

Zealots, 39
Zoroastrianism, 283, 292
Zwingli, Huldrych (1484–1531), 151, 186
Zwinglians, 196, 219